THE COMPLETE
CROSSWORD COMPANION

THE COMPLETE

CROSSWORD COMPANION

Fourth Edition

Jeremy Howard-Williams

TED SMART

This edition specially produced in 1997
for The Book People Ltd, Catteshall Manor,
Catteshall Lane, Godalming, SURREY GU7 1UU

HarperCollins*Publishers*
77–85 Fulham Palace Road,
Hammersmith, London W6 8JB

This paperback edition 1997
9 8 7 6 5 4 3 2

Fourth Edition first published by
HarperCollins*Publishers* 1993

First published in Great Britain by
Granada Publishing 1984

ISBN 0-583 33328 1

Set in Times

Printed in Great Britain by
Creative Print and Design (Wales), Ebbw Vale

Contents

PREFACE TO THE FOURTH EDITION

It must always be a source of pleasure and not a little pride for any author to see his or her book go into more than one edition. If nothing else, in this case, it means that other people are presumably finding it of some interest and use – even if only as a form of quick-reference encyclopedia; which it also is.

A dictionary or thesaurus, of course, doesn't just reprint without alteration like a novel or an historical work; each new edition means more work for the author, as fresh material is researched and added. But *The Complete Crossword Companion* to me has always been a labour of love, because playing with words has a fascination of its own – or else why do so many people throughout the land find such relaxation and amusement, not to say therapy, in crossword puzzles? Several recent weekend magazine supplements to our daily newspapers have written about crosswords, the people who set them, and those who solve them.

The study of linguistics (language in general) quickly leads to semantics (the relationship between words and meanings), usually accompanied by a fascinating delve through the labyrinth of both dictionary and thesaurus. Before I started this new Preface, I looked up the word 'homonym' (one of a group of words which are pronounced or spelled the same, but which have different meanings), and this led to 'homograph' (spelled the same, but meanings different, e.g. 'fair' and 'fair', meaning travelling entertainment and just), and 'homophone' (pronounced the same, but meanings different, e.g. 'bear' and 'bare', and 'fair' and 'fare'; 'fair' and 'fair' could also, strictly speaking, be homophones). 'Row' and 'row' could only be homophones when they are both pronounced 'roh' (as in rank and paddle); when one is pronounced 'r-ow' (as in din or noise), they would be homographs because they are still spelled the same. From there I proceeded to 'heteronym' (pronounced differently, but spelled the same; we can now allow 'row' [rank or paddle] and 'row' [din or noise]; 'bow' and 'bow' come under this heading when the words mean obeisance and fancy slipknot respectively). And of course we have 'synonym' (meanings the same, e.g. 'confine' and 'imprison' are synonyms), and 'antonym' (meanings opposite; 'bad' and 'good' are antonyms).

A pretty useless exercise, you may say. But to the verbalist (someone interested in words for words' sake), it represents a pleasant jaunt through linguistics which will help to keep an ageing brain ticking over.

Thus we have homonyms, synonyms and antonyms all mixed up with origins, the *double-entendre*, and even with onomatopoeia (words formed from sounds associated with the object, e.g. 'cuckoo'). A diversion down which the crossword addict might stray in this connection could derive from this last thought. **Said to produce a smile** (6) might give us CHEESE. Useless information can be accumulated to clutter the brain, but it sometimes brings a wry smile as well. Did you know that the word 'orange' derives from the Persian 'narang' via the Arabic 'naranj'? To this day the fruit is called 'naranje' in Spanish and, when it was first introduced into England from that country, it was called, quite properly, a 'norange', which quickly became an 'orange'. The same process happened in the case of the snake called the 'adder'; Old English 'naedre' became 'naddre' in Middle English, and then 'addre' or 'adder' with the passage of time.

This sort of thing may not come into crossword clues too often, but a mind which notes that kind of background to words will not be seriously held up by **Has difficulty achieving a defeat when there's military cover** (5); SHAKO is produced by an anagram of **Has** (it's got **difficulty**), with KO for **defeat**. The whole word means a type of military hat – or **cover**.

A ploy which I have noted becoming more common in recent years is to require a short word, or even part of a word, to be removed in order to arrive at the solution. For instance, **Defect lacking sound strength as a rule** (3) = LAW. This is reached by **Defect** = FLAW, and **sound strength** = F (forte in music); the latter is **lacking**, so take it away from the former, and you are left with (f)LAW = **rule**. Further examples include **Anti-government activity didn't start in printing** (7) = (s)EDITION, which is fairly straightforward; and **Some of the boat's crew in the Navy occupy the top position** (5) = R·EIG(ht)·N (a **boat's crew** is nearly always a rowing eight). Steady on, I hear you cry, we get the message, don't crowd us out with examples of a pretty arcane device. But let me tell you that those three were all included in a single *Sunday Express* skeleton crossword in 1991 – plus two more in that same puzzle: **Lines from a sailor away from home** (3) = (ab)ODE; and **Line around, almost identical with height** (7) = EQUA(l)TOR.

But I'm sure that most of my readers will understand a lot of those stratagems by now – if not, there is some masochistic pleasure to come from them, as brain is pitted against brain. What perhaps is more important here and now is: what's new in the book?

In response to many requests, I have included the full Greek alphabet (and, for good measure, the Hebrew one as well). Clowns and jesters have been divided into separate entries – though where one stops and the other begins must of necessity be a personal assessment (but at least it has meant a thorough overhaul, with listings of the names of nearly 50 of them, both fact and fiction). There are now over 30 fictional or mythical countries, some 250 alternative names for flowers (such as clematis/old man's beard/traveller's joy), 20 sculptors, an entry on various poisons (of interest perhaps to blood-and-thunder writers), and I have done some cleaning up of the entry concerning **Q without U** (most of the rather improbable place names have been removed, and some new actual words added – I wish I could persuade my correspondent the Revd Clifford Warren to take up the search for these elusive little fellows, for he is indefatigable once he gets on a scent). One entry which I have revised and expanded (without prompting by readers) is the one giving the names of **Shakespearean characters;** I have tried to list them all (there are over 600); no doubt an eagle-eyed reader will spot an omission or two. The purist may find fault that I haven't differentiated enough between the various Henries (Bolingbroke, Hotspur, prince, king, king's father, king's son, etc), but they can become quite confusing at times, even in one play, especially where a prince becomes a king on the death of his father; and the same can be said in a lesser way about the various Richards (dukes as well as kings and princes), and some of the more prolific earls. But we have made a start.

As I indicated in previous editions, most of these changes have been as a direct result of suggestions made by readers (I am glad to report that my earlier rearrangement of **RED INDIANS** has succeeded in stopping my sister-in-law Wendy's regular complaints, so I know that this revision will find favour in at least one reader's eye). It is, of course, feedback from the public which points me in the right direction, so keep it coming or I won't know what to do in any fifth edition which may eventually be launched.

As ever, I must acknowledge my major written sources. Apart from crosswords published in the principal daily and weekly newspapers of this country (and in particular the *Daily Telegraph* and the *Sunday Express*), the list previously published has had one or two new references added. Once again, however, I must stress that any errors are mine alone.

Bibliography

The Bible (King James Authorised Version)

Brewer's Dictionary of Phrase and Fable (Evans) Cassell 1986

Chambers English Dictionary (various editors) Chambers and CUP 1988

Cambridge Guide to English Literature (Stapleton) CUP (Newnes) 1985

Classified Quotations (Benham) Cassell 1921

Collins English Dictionary (Hanks) Collins 1985

Collins Thesaurus (ed. McLeod) Collins 1986

Complete Works of William Shakespeare (ed. Alexander) Collins 1966

Concise Oxford Dictionary (Fowler) OUP 1958 and 1979

Crossword Dictionary (Ace/Stoneshire 1984) Dawn Gorrick, Aus 1981

Crossword Puzzle Dictionary (Swanfeldt) Harper & Row, USA 1990

Dictionary of the Bible (Hyamson) George Routledge *c*.1940

Dictionary for Crossword Puzzles (Newman) Doubleday, USA 1967

Dictionary of the English Language (Dr Johnson) Longman 1786

Everyman's Factfinder (Dempsey) Dent 1882

Halliwell's Film Guide (Halliwell) Grafton Books 1989

How to do Crosswords (Abbott) Collins 1984

International Thesaurus of Quotations (Tripp) Penguin 1979

Jack's Reference Book (was Pannell's) TC & EC Jack Ltd 1921

Library of Modern Knowledge (3 vols) Reader's Digest 1979

New Age Encyclopedia (Maine & Foreman) Collins 1958

Oxford Companion to Music (Scholes) OUP 1950

Oxford Companion to Ships and the Sea (Kemp) OUP 1979

Oxford Companion to Sports and Games (Arlott) OUP 1977

Oxford Dictionary of Quotations (Darwin) OUP 1979

Quickway Crossword Dictionary (Hill) Warne & Co 1958

Reverse Dictionary (ed. Kahn) Reader's Digest 1989

Roget's International Thesaurus (Chapman) Harper & Row, USA 1984

Sailing Dictionary (Schult) Adlard Coles Ltd 1992

Smaller Classical Dictionary (Marindin) Murray 1910

Thesaurus of Book Digests (Haydn & Fuller) Avenal, USA 1977

Thesaurus of English Words and Phrases (Roget) Longman 1958

INTRODUCTION

History

I feel that a new Introduction is now due – three editions is quite enough for the same preamble.

We saw in the first editions how the poet Samonicus told of the use of the word *Abracadabra* in a pyramid form as a charm against disease; we also saw how word squares (which read the same down as across, and some of which read the same backwards) have caught the imagination from time immemorial. But it was not until this century that the crossword as we know it was born. An ex-Liverpudlian by the name of Arthur Wayne went to live in the USA, where he became Puzzles Editor of the New York Sunday paper *The World*. It was his idea to run a regular word-cross (as he called it) in the paper, and it slowly took root.

As far as I can find out, the first crossword puzzle to be published in England was in the *Sunday Express* for November 1924. This was followed by one in the *Daily Telegraph* in July 1925. Apart from a somewhat scathing article in December 1924 (about how the little squares were 'a menace . . . making inroads on the working hours of every rank of society'), *The Times* seems to have held aloof from the new craze for five years. Early in 1930, however, a crossword appeared in the weekly edition of the paper, and the editor followed the suggestion from a reader that it be reprinted in one of the daily editions; subsequent demand saw it as a regular feature, falling into line with the other dailies. In *The Times*, it started among the sports features, and did not achieve permanent migration to the back page until after World War I.

The clues of the early puzzles were pretty straightforward, and cannot have taxed the brain too severely.

Sunday Express No 1 (2 Nov, 1924)

Counters of votes (7) = TELLERS
Snake-like fish (3) = EEL
Cosy little room (3) = DEN

Daily Telegraph No 1 (30 Jul, 1925)

Recess in a church (4) = APSE
Greek god of love (4) = EROS
A seat of learning is the key to this (4) = YALE

It will be noted that only the last of these examples had anything cryptic about it; but it was a beginning.

The Clues

Crosswords have gone through quite a sea-change since their early days. At the beginning, the difficult part of compiling a puzzle lay in arranging the words to fit the appropriate grid; the rest was a matter of having a dictionary and a good encyclopedia, because the clues were mostly definitions, or descriptions of gods, goddesses, rivers or place names. These days, the existence of various books giving alphabetical lists of words by number of letters (and even alphabetically by their 2nd, 3rd, 4th letters, and so on), has made filling out the grid easier (computers can now do it themselves), so the clue has become the harder part.

I must say a quick word here about foreign crosswords. They mostly seem not to have symmetrical grids – at least the ones which I have tackled from the USA, France and Germany – and to contain far fewer black squares (many have no blacks at all, preferring to use heavy dividing lines to mark the ends of words which the compiler has failed to link up). Some commentators find this disagreeable, but I cannot agree – it does nothing more than provide extra words for a given-sized grid.

In the UK as elsewhere there are, of course, still straightforward question-and-answer puzzles – what might be termed Quick Crosswords. In fact, far from being quick, these can sometimes be harder to get started than more complicated affairs. Take as an example the clue **Head** (4); you might have any of the following answers: BEAN, BOSS, CAPE, CONK, CROP, FOAM, HAIR, LEAD, MIND, NESS, PATE or POLL, to name but a few. **Conduct** (6) could give: ACTION, ATTEND, BEHAVE, CONVEY, CONVOY, CUSTOM, DEMEAN, DEPORT, DIRECT, DOINGS, ESCORT, GOVERN, MANAGE, PRAXIS or SQUIRE. This kind of puzzle becomes easier once you have made a start, so that a few letters in the solution will narrow the options (if the last letter in either of the two examples above is known to be an S, only two of the various solutions will be possible in either case); but each corner tends to need its own start.

The Art of the Setter

Turning to cryptic crosswords, where the clues are convoluted, punned, turned inside out, falsely punctuated and distorted in any way the setter can devise within the strict etiquette of the game, we have a different problem (a topical clue from a recent *Times* competition eliminator, used as a part-clue: **crosswords initially**; this turned out to be INRI – the initials over Our Lord's cross).

The Crossword Editor of *The Times* is on record (31 December, 1981) as warning would-be solvers to distrust every word in a clue, because the compiler's aim is to say one thing while meaning another. You therefore have to decide what each clue means because, rest assured, they won't always say what they mean (although they should always mean what they say). You have to decide how you are going to tackle them.

Once the ruthless nature of the setter has been established, the solver is halfway towards success. The master-craftsman of the setting world is devious, inventive, clever, impudent and extremely cunning, but always scrupulously fair (well, nearly always). An average cryptic clue will usually have two indications or pointers to its solution, both twisted and often deliberately mingled. If the attention of the solver can be directed onto a false trail, then the setter will consider that he or she has won a partial victory. Many stratagems will be adopted to this end but, in the final analysis, the solver should be able to say: 'Oh, I see. Well done', even if, once the answer is known, he or she adds 'What a nerve!'

The compiler's art is revealed by the way in which the two parts of the clue are linked. It is the essence of a good setter that he or she produces clues which flow smoothly and innocently. A clue which reads oddly is usually both poorly contrived, and too revealing as to how to set about its solution.

Asterisks and Brackets

Before embarking on explanations and examples of different forms of cryptic clue and answer, it should be pointed out that the asterisk is used throughout this *Companion* to indicate where a letter has been omitted or two words joined to form one. Brackets in an answer show where a letter or word has been inserted. This is purely a mechanical aid to understanding how an answer is reached, and the solver should read such words as though the intruders were not there. Thus **It is**

forbidden to have a girl in bed (6) = B(ANN)ED, should be read as
BANNED; in **The boy loses some time** (3) = TIM*, the asterisk should
be ignored.

Quotations

As with any new field of endeavour, development has occurred over
the years, and clues have become more abstruse. This started gently
enough with the use of classical quotations and clearly stated anagrams (**I cut a moat** (anag) = AUTOMATIC). From there, puzzle setters
progressed with the times, and they recognized that the general level
of classical knowledge was reducing, so they reduced their quotation
quota in parallel (in any case, there are too many excellent books of
quotations, which make life far too easy). Some of the early cryptic
clues tended to be too long, and it is now generally recognized that
brevity is one of the hallmarks of a good compiler.

Anagrams
As this development progressed, the custom of signalling anagrams
by crudely putting (anag) was discarded in favour of implication by an
appropriate word slipped into the clue. As I said in the Introduction
to the previous edition, some 10 per cent of all adjectives, verbs and
adverbs (and even some nouns) may be taken to indicate anagram:
tortured, scrambled, twisted, agonized, stew, badly, grim, wry, and
half a hundred others all point that way. Thus, **Taped, but made sure
it could be altered** (8) = MEASURED (the anag here is of **made sure**,
which is signalled by the anagram word **altered**).

A number of the better instances which I shall be giving in this
new Introduction are taken from fairly recent copies of the *Daily
Telegraph* and the *Sunday Express*; these are the two newspapers
which I take regularly, and I don't think that I can do better than
to lean on them for some excellent examples. In any case, they were
pioneer puzzle publishers, so they have been at it longer than most.
I have, of course, also culled a few from other sources, and my wife
and I have made up some ourselves.

In the body of this *Companion* I have included the word *Anag*
where an entry word might imply that there may be an anagram
hidden somewhere in any clue with that entry word. Thus we get
the entry **WILD** (*anag*). ANGRY, BARBAROUS, DESOLATE etc, etc.

The word in a clue which implies that there is an anagram involved
is the better if it sits well with its partners, thus **Turbulent priest died
like a tiger** (7) conjures up the assassination of Thomas à Becket in
Canterbury Cathedral at the behest of King Henry II ('Who will rid

me of this turbulent priest?'). If it diverts attention like that, the clue has achieved what it set out to do, namely to distract the solver's mind from all idea that the answer lies in an anagram of anything (though **turbulent** is the pointer), followed by D for **died;** this gives STRIPE*D **(like a tiger).** How much less challenging would have been **Worried priest died like a tiger,** or even **Distracted priest** . . .

Another good clue, where the anagram word was well camouflaged because it went well with its noun, I spotted in the *Telegraph*: **Spider natural at spinning** (9) = TARANTULA (the words **natural at** are sent **spinning** into an anagram).

Part Anagrams
Further complication is sometimes added by making only part of the solution an anagram (what Philip Howard in *The Times* called the Chimera clue: lion's head, allusion's tail and anagram's body), as in **Poet worried about quotation is a mess** (7) = POT(TAG)E. Solvers should beware that an anagram often means any rearrangement of letters, even if they do not make a new word in themselves. In POTTAGE above, the **poet, worried** into anagram, reads POTE round the answer to **quotation** (TAG).

Brevity
I said just now that brevity is a hallmark of a good compiler. The most succinct example which I can offer is **Dog food** (4). Remembering that we should have two lines of reasoning, we have to find a four-letter word which responds to both **Dog** and **food;** the answer in this case is CHOW. Another short one is **Safe channel** (5), which the *Telegraph* had recently for SOUND.

An example of something which reads awkwardly was used this year in one of the daily papers: **Settle on a piece of wooden dowelling** (5). Some of the words which have been used make them immediately suspect; nobody and nothing settles on wooden dowelling (or even a wooden block, for that matter), so as to be worthy of any note. When you see **a piece of,** you can start looking round for a hidden word right away, almost certainly joined to the out-of-place **dowelling.** It won't take long to find ENDOW (meaning **Settle on**). There has been little to tax even the weakest solver.

Punctuation
It is considered entirely fair to play fast and loose with punctuation. In the earlier editions of this *Companion*, I gave a five-word clue without any punctuation, and then showed how the meaning varied according

to where an imaginary comma was placed: after the first, second, third or fourth word. It was rather a cumbersome illustration, but I think it made the point that clues may read altogether differently, depending on punctuation.

Let me now give one or two examples where commas and full stops are critical. **The German double-pistol** (9) evokes the mental picture of a twin-barrelled gun. But the hyphen is suspect (who really ever heard of a double-pistol?). See what happens if we rewrite it as **The, German; double. Pistol** (9). We now have little difficulty in deciding that German for **the** is DER, and that a **double**, in the six letters which remain, may be a RINGER. Taken together, these make DERRINGER, which is a make of **pistol**.

As a second example of punctuation alteration, I think that one of the ones which I used before is good enough to bear repetition. **Forty-nine out for a duck** (3,5) should be read as **Forty. Nine out for a duck**, which gives us TWO SCORE, meaning both **Forty** and also that only two batsmen of a cricket eleven scored any runs, so we have the remaining **nine out for a duck**.

Classical Allusion
As I said above, quotations have diminished almost to vanishing point. There are, however, still some references to the odd classical work. The older solver will probably be glad to know that the days when he or she was not expected to be familiar with anything more modern than Rider Haggard, Dickens, *Alice in Wonderland*, Gilbert and Sullivan, and possibly A. A. Milne, Somerset Maugham or *Gulliver's Travels*, have not entirely gone. The allusion these days will probably be to a title or well-known characteristic, such as **What Tigger mumbled, bounces by the spa waters** (3,7) = HOT SPRINGS (A. A. Milne's Tigger mumbled 'Hot' as he tried eating Eeyore's thistles); or else **Somerset Maugham's downfall** (4) = RAIN (a title from his works). Solvers with a profound knowledge of any fictional detective more modern than Sherlock Holmes are likely to find their learning useless.

Split Words
A ploy which has appeared moderately recently is to vary the split between two words of a solution – with a separate clue for each split. The answer STANDING ROOM can also be written STAND-IN GROOM; these might therefore be jointly clued as **So crowded, when only the proxy husband can be made out** (8,4); the first two words of the clue refer to the 8,4 split, while the rest will produce the 5-2,5 split.

Try this one: **Design fault shortens the day** (5,2). To help you, this solution may also be split 4,3. Of course, in attempting any crossword, you can hope to establish a few guiding letters from other clues which you have solved. In this case, we eventually get DRAWS IN, which responds to the evenings drawing in during the early winter; we also have DRAW SIN responding to **Design fault**. And how about **Dad's Army weapon gets you by** (8) = PASSWORD (try a 3,5 split of the answer)?

Pronunciation
The compiler will also use pronunciation to misdirect the solver if possible. We have already decided that heteronyms are words which are spelled the same but pronounced differently. The setter will use them to encourage the solver to think of the wrong meaning, through use of associated words which foster this incorrect interpretation. For instance, a **Water tower** could refer to a TUG (which is a **tower** of other boats at sea) rather than a high tank of water; a **Flower of France** to the SEINE (which flows); **Exhibition Row** to a FAIR FIGHT (and see another **row** example under the book entry **PRONUNCIATION**); and the **Sewers of Paris** don't necessarily refer to the underground catacombs beloved of readers of Poe's *Murders in the Rue Morgue*, but to the MIDINETTES, who were seamstresses of that city, having nothing to do with drains.

Homonyms
We have similarly established that homonyms are words which are pronounced (homophones) or spelled (homographs) the same, but which have different meanings. Here again is fertile ground for the devious setter, as he or she writes of **bloomers** meaning FLOWERS rather than ERRORS, of **flowers** meaning RIVERS rather than PLANTS, and **operators** meaning SURGEONS rather than WORKERS (the latter are nearly always ANTS or BEES). Once more I repeat a clue which I have found in the past to be a particularly good example of the genre: **Get rid of the batter and wash the dish** (5,4) = CLEAN BOWL. This, of course, uses **batter** as a homonym in the cricketing rather than the culinary sense (although the latter interpretation is encouraged by use of the words **wash the dish**).

Proper Names
By and large, proper names are usually confined to Quick Cross-words. Their use in cryptic puzzles depends partly on their suitability for punning, and partly on how well they are known (and how durable

they are – people suddenly and briefly in the news, no matter how widespread, will as quickly fade from the public eye). Bush, Thatcher and Major all offer possibilities (**High American woody plant**; **Roofer no longer employed at the top of the house**; **Man of the Army? Not necessarily; of the State**). But names like Kinnock would have to depend on breaking up the word into constituent parts, such as **Fashion in rap leader**, which gives us K(IN)NOCK. It is virtually impossible to set down any comprehensive guidelines, so we will leave them alone.

Hidden Words
These might be considered as among the easier solutions – but how often have I puzzled endlessly over a clue, and finally appealed for help from my wife, only to have her reply, 'It's what so often foxes us'? And then I know that I have been caught again. Much depends on the skill with which the compiler hides the solution (and often on how the clue is spaced – a word which spans two lines is difficult to spot). Find AGNES, for example, in:

   The girl in Maxim's champagne supper (5); and then look for her in:
   The girl in Maxim's champagne supper (5)

or how about **She takes a long time to grasp the point in the champagne supper scene** (**long time** = AGES; **point** = N; if the one grasps the other in **the champagne scene**, AG(N)ES is hidden)? Or again, **The party's a little over-scrupulous – idealistic even** (4) which hides SIDE; and **Discourage the use of some trade terms** (5) = DETER.

Synonyms
I feel that I should repeat the warning which I gave in the earlier editions about the use of the word 'distress' in a clue. The puzzler who has taken aboard my words of wisdom about hidden signals for anagrams may immediately (and reasonably) take **distressed** to be one. Take the example **Pounded, distressed and hair-brained** (7); could there be an anagram of **pounded** which means **hair-brained**? UNDOPED? DEPOUND? No, the word **distressed** calls for a synonym of **tress** to be removed from the clue, and **hair-brained** thereby becomes BRAINED (which can mean **pounded**). Similarly **One in charge of a distressed lock-keeper** (6) = KEEPER, not an anagram of anything at all.

   This device covers any word which starts **dis-**, for instance **Ireland's dismembered Empire** (4) = EIRE (E(mp)IRE, with MP – or **member** of parliament – removed).

Inversion

An inversion is where the solution to be written into the grid is, in fact, the clue; the clue is the solution. This sounds complicated, but is quickly clarified by an example: **Sore perhaps, for not being cultivated** (4,4) = WILD ROSE. This means that ROSE written in a WILD manner (i.e. anag) would produce **sore** as in the clue. Another along the same lines might be **Ulster not the answer?** (5,6) = WRONG RESULT (RESULT being **Ulster** written **wrongly**). This one reminds me of the anagram-rhyme about the evils of drink.

> A *sutler* sat in his *ulster* grey,
> Watching the moonbeams' *lustre* play
> On a keg which low in the rushes lay;
> The pipes of the *luters* started to say:
> 'Thou *rulest* the weak and *lurest* the strong,
> Thou feedeth the urge of the *luster* all wrong,
> And to thee the *result* of battles belong.'
> The leaves with their *rustle* took up the song.

Favourite Clues

A number of people have gone on record as having favourite clues, and I thought that it might be interesting to list a few of them (alphabetically, to avoid any partiality).

Colin Baker, actor. **HIJKLMNO** (5) = WATER; I have also seen it written **Not A to G, nor P to Z** (i.e. H to O or H2O).

Douglas Barnard, Telegraph *compiler*. **Better leave out the teetotaller** (4) = BEER (which is reached via BE(tt)ER).

Adrian Bell, The Times *compiler*. **Die of cold** (3,4) = ICE CUBE; and **Spoils of war** (4) = MARS.

Jane Carton, The Times. **The greater snowdrop** (9) = AVALANCHE; and **Foreign entanglements** (9) = SPAGHETTI.

Allan Cash, Telegraph. **After getting in the beer, he went round preaching** (7) = A(POST)LE.

Peter Chambers, Telegraph. **A cake walk? More than enough!** (9) = A*BUN*DANCE.

Val Gilbert, Telegraph *Crossword Editor*. **!** (4,3,3,1,4) = HAVE NOT GOT A CLUE; and **SOS offences** (13) = NAUGHT*IN*ESSES; or **Burns 'em in boxes** (8) = CR(EM)ATES.

Roger Squires, BBC. **Dead centre** (8) = MORTUARY, or **A stiff examination** (4,6) = POST MORTEM.

Leslie Stokes, Telegraph. **Safety precautions for smokers in bed** (8,6) = ASBESTOS SHEETS.

Ann Tait, Telegraph. **Lots of lucre, but little luck** (5,7) = SMALL FORTUNE.

And my own? There are so many that it is hard to choose, but I did like one which I have seen a couple of times: **Eavesdropper** (6) = ICICLE and, having been in the LDV myself, I quite like the one which I made up as an example of split words: **Dad's Army weapon gets you by** (8) = PAS·SWORD. And how about **Columns assembled by the press gang** (9) = NEWSPAPER?

Single-letter Examples
In the earlier editions, I gave a number of ways of clueing a single letter of the alphabet, giving an alternative clue in brackets (which could be used with or without the first part). These must of necessity be terse and to the point, because they will almost always form part of a clue to a complete word. These clues are different from the ones in the earlier editions, and are offered as examples of how many tunes may be played on the same theme.

A	One (article)
B	Second class (baron)
C	Caught (cold)
D	Daughter (Penny)
E	East (English)
F	French (Fahrenheit)
G	£1,000 (gravity)
H	Hard (hotel)
I	A (second time)
J	Jack (man in a boat)
K	1,000 (kilos)
L	Left (Luxembourg)
M	Male (Frenchman)
N	North (point)
O	Nil (ordered to start)
P	Subdued (President)
Q	Second equal (queen)
R	Right (reverend)
S	Southern (saint)
T	First^2 (Tuesday)
U	Universal (upstart)
V	Victory (volume)
W	Wed (a wife)
X	Mark (with a kiss)

| Y | Penultimate (ordinate) |
| Z | Last letter (from Zanzibar) |

Try Your Hand

Now here are some clues which start by being short and not too difficult, and gradually become longer and more cryptic as we progress. So that you can have a go at them, I have left the answers to a later page, each with a short explanation as to how it is reached.

1. A quiet wood (3).
2. Ban the twisted bra (3).
3. Strike miss's partner (3).
4. Juggle with Italian money in wages (4).
5. Move towards an honour in the church (4).
6. Deprive of French-American city (4).
7. Bound by reverse-angled maths (4).
8. Some backward corner (4).
9. Obliged to mould (4).
10. Dad's car has had it (4).
11. Adamson sounds like he said it (4).
12. Prepare for the ebb-tide (4).
13. Tribe of backward Paraguay, America (4).
14. I'm caught between loud and soft; what an angle (4).
15. Dad's second-hand (4).
16. Fell for the anti-royalist lizard(4).
17. It's wrong to live badly (4).
18. Cry for understanding about the English (4).
19. Cabinet-making superman (4).
20. A goblin according to me (4).
21. Night-flying first man on the moon (4).
22. Fellow round a very quiet fish (5).
23. Boadicea's lot from the frozen province (5).
24. Channel for very acid messages? (5).
25. Endless body of troops (5).
26. Edge up to the team about the start of the League (5).
27. Civic old city prohibition (5).
28. Go the way to a lovers' rendez-vous (5).
29. Heard after the first and last row (5).
30. The way to tear off one's clothes (5).
31. After a short while, Napoleon's general gets the loot (5).

32. Classic porcelain (5).
33. Blackball a couple of points about the First Lady (5).
34. You may eat this under holy writ (down clue) (5).
35. Paved the way for a barbecue (5).
36. Settle the floor mat as a gesture (5).
37. Possibly an obtuse point of view (5).
38. Spiritual leader of a Burmah district (5).
39. Big guns brought under last month's topmost secret (down clue) (5)
40. Result points to legal proceedings (5).
41. Pester from the church like a dimwit (5).
42. Energy through hot spice (6).
43. Nudge in a ship's bars (6).
44. It is said with a foul snub in dark surroundings (6).
45. Destroy the 5-year-old artist (6).
46. Guide to a swindler? (6).
47. Herb becomes a course with the well-bred (6).
48. Hero's misguided lover was no fool (7).
49. Embroider initial on the French glove – how chic! (7).
50. Proceed slowly in the Grand Antechamber (7).
51. Laughed out of the saddle? (7).
52. Break mineral and then mend it (7).
53. To a large extent, some years after the plot (7).
54. Efficient oriental paperwork ensures that I have the bank transfer back before morning (7).
55. Support troops dug their teeth into the cheese for starters (7).
56. Bring back to scratch the Sapper's procession (7).
57. Double top for game (7).
58. Dead-end for dead-beat (7).
59. Interim construction at ends of the line (7).
60. Artist's polite cry shows distress (7).
61. Scientific apparatus mirrored by a governor to sift atoms (7).
62. Cure for lack of rhythm (7).
63. Reinvest after final strike high up in the world (7).
64. A mistake for the traitor to be in such doubt (7).
65. Conceal a note by a wrapper (8).
66. Hesitate in a way, indeed abandoned (8).
67. Upright jerk is sentimental (8).
68. Playing for money sounds fun (8).
69. Ex-union member may possibly assert -isms (8).
70. Twin sets, for instance, locked together (8).
71. Near-miss for the Lancers, perhaps (9).

72. Columns assembled by the pressgang (9).
73. Affords a view of the eyebrows (9).
74. Not prepared to become a highbrow (9).
75. Returns and backs around a very quiet corner (9).
76. Barely daring to emerge (9).
77. A moron takes one in, but loses his head when full up (9).
78. Garnish with ribbon (10).
79. You'll find zebras, pedestrians and a grouch here (10).
80. Quick delivery to the pad was his motto (10).
81. Robber who would soon cut you down to size for litter (10).
82. Just the reason for exhibition base (10).
83. Purposeful study – to bring back to prison? (10).
84. Labour issue (10).
85. Profiteer from extra duty (10).
86. Show the devil the way to scold (11).
87. Leader of the Commons, at Westminster for example (11).
88. Book the proclamation (11).
89. Swift wit (11).
90. Making the acceptable truth into dung (11).
91. A palace of a house or school (11).
92. Prominent position for getting wet in the rain (11).
93. Wrote plays of the Tabard of a von Hohenzollern (11).
94. Head up! What lack of effort! (12).
95. Lustrous South American lineage (12).
96. Good carriage for easier childbearing (12).
97. On the other side of the way it came down and tried too hard (12).
98. State control for rapid transport (7,5).
99. There is no bread after his rounds (7,6).
100. Prepare bird for table and get into the habit of eating (5,3,6).
101. Once said at Waterloo, but now they wave flags (2,6,3,2,2).

Answers to Try Your Hand Clues

1. ASH. **Quiet** is often taken as P or SH; here it is the latter which, with A in front of it, gives the answer.
2. BAR. An anagram of **bra**, signalled by **twisted**.
3. HIT. The **partner** to **miss** in 'Hit or miss' is obviously HIT, which = **strike**.
4. PLAY. **Italian money** is the Lira or L, which is put into a synonym for **wages** = P(L)AY = **juggle with**.

5. COME. **Honour** = OM (this is a favourite honour in crosswords); **the church** = CH or CE (Church of England); OM in CH/CE = C(OM)H or C(OM)E, the latter of which = **move towards**.
6. DENY. **Of** in **French** = DE; **American city** = New York or NY. DE*NY = **Deprive**.
7. GIRT. **Angled maths** is trigonometry, or trig as it is called. If trig is **reversed** = GIRT which means **Bound by**.
8. TRAP. **Some** = part, which reads TRAP **backwards**, which also means to **corner** someone or something.
9. MUST. It means both **obliged** and fungus or **mould**.
10. PAST. **Dad** is Pa and his **car** is a model T Ford (another favourite for a single letter) = Pa's T. If it has '**had it**', it is PAS*T its prime.
11. SETH. One of the sons of Adam (**Adamson**) was SETH, which **sounds like** saith, or **said it**.
12. EDIT. **Ebb-tide** = tide going back = EDIT = **Prepare for**.
13. MAYA. Hidden word **backwards**, meaning **American tribe**.
14. FISH. **I am caught**, or put between, F (for **loud** in music) and SH (for **soft**) = F(I)SH. The whole word is the verb to **angle**.
15. PASS. Once again **Dad** = Pa, so **Dad's** = Pa's; a **second** = sec or s. PAS*S = to **hand** something (e.g. pass the salt).
16. SKIN. A **lizard** = skink; if it is **anti-royalist** it has not got a k for king = sink or SKIN, which = **Fell** (rare usage).
17. EVIL. Responds both to **wrong**, and as an anagram of **live** written **badly**.
18. KEEN. **Understanding** = ken which, written **about** E (for **English**) = KE(E)N = **cry** (Irish).
19. KENT. William KENT was a furniture designer and **cabinet maker**. Clark KENT was the name of **Superman** in his daily life as a reporter.
20. PERI. **According to** = per; **me** = I. PER*I = **A goblin**.
21. MOTH. The **first** letters of **Man On The Moon** = MOTH = **night-flying** creature.
22. GUPPY. A **fellow** is often either F (as in FRCS) or guy/chap; put guy round pp (**very quiet** in music) and you get GU(PP)Y = **fish**.
23. ICENI. **Frozen** = ice, and Northern Ireland (or NI) is often called **the Province**; thus ICE*NI, which was **Boadicea's lot** or tribe.
24. PHONE. The Ph system measures acidity (e.g. in soil); Ph 7 is neutral and Ph 1 (Ph one) is **acid**. PH*ONE is a **channel for messages**.
25. CORPS. A **body** = corpse; **endless**, it = orpse or CORPS, or **troops**.

26. SIDLE. **The team** = eleven or side which latter, placed about **the start of the League** (L) = SID(L)E = **edge up to**.
27. URBAN. An **old city** is very often Ur (of the Chaldees) in crosswords; **prohibition** = ban. UR*BAN = **civic**.
28. TRYST. **Go** = try (give it a go); **the way** in crosswords often means avenue (ave), road (rd) or street (st). Together as TRY*ST = **lovers' rendez-vous**.
29. BLAST. **The first** (letter of the alphabet) = A; **after the first** comes B; **last** = LAST. Together, B*LAST = a **row** which is **heard**.
30. STRIP. **The way** = ave/rd/st; **to tear** = rip. ST*RIP = **tear off one's clothes**.
31. MONEY. **A short while** = moment or mo (half a mo); **after** it comes one of **Napoleon's generals** (Ney in this case). MO*NEY = **loot** (a slang word for money).
32. DERBY. The DERBY is one of the **classic** races; it is also **porcelain**.
33. SEVEN. **A couple of points** can be any two of north, south, east and west (N,S,E,W); S and N in this case. **The First Lady** was Eve. The former placed about the latter = S(EVE)N, which is the value of the **black ball** at snooker.
34. PILAW. **Holy** = pi; **writ** = law. In a down clue, law is placed **under** pi = PI*LAW, a rice dish which **you may eat**.
35. PATIO. A patio is a **paved way**, or open space, for **a barbecue**.
36. SHRUG. **Settle** = calm = Sh! **Floor mat** = rug. SH*RUG = **gesture**.
37. ANGLE. An ANGLE is either acute or **obtuse;** it is also a **point of view**.
38. MAHDI. A hidden word, meaning a **spiritual leader**.
39. ULTRA. **Big guns** belong to the Royal Artillery (RA); in a down clue, if they are **brought under** ult (i.e. **last month** in business letters), you get ULT*RA, which was WW2's **topmost secret** category.
40. ENSUE. As in example No 33, **points** = E and N in this case; **to** (or written next to) **legal proceedings** (sue) = EN*SUE, which means **Result**.
41. DUNCE. **Pester** = dun; **the church** = ch or CE (again). DUN*CE = **a dimwit**.
42. PEPPER. **Energy** = pep; **through** = per. PEP*PER = **hot spice**.
43. SPOKES. **Nudge** = poke; **a ship** = ss (steam ship). S*POKE*S = the **bars** of a steering wheel.
44. DICTUM. **Snub** = cut which, **foul** (anag) = ctu; **dark** = dim which, **surrounding** ctu = DI*CTU*M, something which **is said**.

45. RAVAGE. **Artist** = RA; **5-year-old** = v*age (Roman numeral). RA*V*AGE = **destroy**.
46. BEACON. The solution, split 2,1,3 = BE*A*CON (instruction to be **a swindler**); as one word = **guide**.
47. SAVORY. The **herb** SAVORY, **with the well-bred**, or U, would become savo(u)ry, or **a course** at a meal.
48. LEARNED. The mythical **Hero** had Leander for a **lover;** if he is **misguided** (i.e. anag) = LEARNED or **no fool**.
49. ELEGANT. The **initial** of **embroider** is E; if that is added to **(on) the French glove** (le gant) = E*LE*GANT, which is **chic**.
50. ANDANTE. Hidden word in **Grand Antechamber**, meaning **proceed slowly** (in music).
51. DERIDED. The answer means **laughed;** if someone is de-rided, may they be said to be no longer riding, or **out of the saddle?**
52. RESTORE. **Break** = rest; **mineral** = ore. REST*ORE = **mend**.
53. ACREAGE. **The plot** = acre; **some years** = age. ACRE*AGE = **a large extent**.
54. ORIGAMI. **Bank transfer** = giro; when written towards the **back** = orig; **before morning** = before a.m.; **I have** it = I (at the end). ORIG*AM*I = Japanese or **Efficient oriental paperwork**.
55. RAREBIT. Royal Artillery (RA) and Royal Engineers (RE) are **support troops;** if they have **dug their teeth into** something, they **bit** it. RARE*BIT = a **cheese starter** at a meal.
56. RETRAIN. **The Sapper** = RE; **procession** = train. RE*TRAIN = **bring back to scratch** (or up to the mark).
57. DIABOLO. This **game** uses a form of twin or **double top**.
58. IMPASSE. If I am **dead-beat**, I am past it, or passé. IM*PASSE = **dead-end**.
59. TERMINI. **Interim** is **constructed** of letters which will anag to TERMINI, which are **ends of the** (railway) **line**.
60. TIEPOLO. **Polite** can **show distress** (i.e. be anag) as tiepol; **cry** = o! TIEPOL*O is the name of an **artist**.
61. ISOTRON. Word hidden backwards (**mirrored**) in **governor to sift**, meaning **scientific apparatus** (dealing with **atoms**).
62. NOSTRUM. If something has a **lack of rhythm**, it does not have, or has **no strum** to it; NO*STRUM = a **cure**.
63. EVEREST. **Reinvest** = re in vest = ve(re)st; **final** (letter of) **strike** = e. If the first is after the second, we get E*VE(RE)ST, which is a mountain **high up in the world**.
64. ERRATUM. **Traitor** in crosswords is nearly always rat; to be **in such doubt**, he is between er and um (both words commonly

used by compilers for **doubt** or **hesitation**) = ER(RAT)UM, meaning **a mistake**.

65. ENVELOPE. **Conceal** = envelop; **a note** may be any of doh, ray, me, etc., or A, B, C, D, E, F or G (E in this case). ENVELOP*E = **a wrapper**.
66. DESERTED. **Hesitate** (as we saw above) is er; **a way** = st in this case. If the first is put in the second = s(er)t. All this **indeed** (or in de*ed) = DE*S(ER)T*ED = **abandoned**.
67. ROMANTIC. **Upright** letters in typescript are roman (as opposed to italic); a **jerk** can be a tic. ROMAN*TIC = **sentimental**.
68. GAMBLING. **Playing for money** = GAMBLING, which **sounds** like gambolling or having **fun**.
69. DIVORCEE. **Ex-union member** is someone who is no longer in the union of marriage – a DIVORCEE in this case, who may **assert** that she now **is Ms**, rather than Mrs or Miss.
70. KNITWEAR. **Twin-sets** are instances of KNITWEAR, which are made with **locked** stitches.
71. CHAPERONE. Has to keep **near** a **miss** at a ball, where they may perhaps dance **the Lancers**.
72. NEWSPAPER. Has **columns** of news, **assembled** by a **gang** of people who work the **press**.
73. OVERLOOKS. The **eyebrows** are over a person's looks (or the eyes which do the looking); anything which OVERLOOKS an object, **affords a view** of it.
74. SURPRISED. Anyone **not prepared** is SURPRISED, and raises his or her eyebrows (and has then become **a highbrow**).
75. REAPPEARS. **A very quiet quarter** = A, pp (music), E (one of the 4 quarters of the compass). **Backs** = rears which, going **around** A pp E = RE(A*PP*E)ARS, which means **Returns**.
76. STREAKING. If you **dare to emerge, barely** (without any clothes) you are STREAKING.
77. IMPLETION. **Moron** = simpleton which, if it **takes one in** (i.e. is written round the letter I) = simpletion. If that **loses its head**, the letter s is removed = IMPLETION, which means **full up**.
78. DECORATION. Responds to both **garnish** and **with ribbon** (medal).
79. CROSSPATCH. The answer may cryptically apply to a **pedestrian** or a **zebra** crossing, and is also a **grouch**.
80. HIGHWAYMAN. He was a foot-**pad**, who demanded **quick delivery** of money.
81. PROCRUSTES. Greek mythological **robber**, whose victims were **cut down to size**, to fit his bed or **litter**.

82. FAIRGROUND. **Just** = fair; **reason** = ground (e.g. grounds for divorce). **Exhibition base** = FAIR·GROUND.
83. DELIBERATE. If someone who was liberated from gaol is de-liberated, he or she is **brought back to prison**. DELIBERATE = **purposeful study**.
84. CHILDBIRTH. Involves **labour** and results in **issue** (or children).
85. OVERCHARGE. **Extra** = over; **duty** = charge. OVER·CHARGE = **profiteer**.
86. DEMONSTRATE. **Devil** = demon; **way** = st (again!); **scold** = rate. DEMON·ST·RATE = **Show**.
87. HOUSEMASTER. **Leader** = master; **Commons** = House. HOUSE·MASTER could be at the public school **Westminster, for example**.
88. PUBLICATION. Responds both to a published **book** and to **procla-mation**.
89. PHILOSOPHER. Jonathan **Swift** was a PHILOSOPHER, which also means a **wit**.
90. MANUFACTURE. **Acceptable truth** = u fact; **dung** = manure. Put the former into the latter = MAN(U·FACT)URE = **Making**.
91. WESTMINSTER. Both a **palace** (of the **Houses** of Parliament) and a public **school**.
92. OUTSTANDING. **Prominent** = OUTSTANDING; anyone standing out-side **in the rain**, would be in a **position for getting wet**.
93. SHAKESPEARE. Hidden in **Tabard of a von Hohenzollern** is Bard of Avon, a euphemism for SHAKESPEARE, who **wrote plays**.
94. LISTLESSNESS. A **head**, or ness, which is told to list less (lean over less), must keep more upright or **up**. The solution also means **lack of effort**.
95. INCANDESCENT. Incan = **South American**; lineage = descent. INCAN·DESCENT = **lustrous**.
96. PERAMBULATOR. A **good carriage** does indeed make for **easier childbearing**; it is also a PERAMBULATOR.
97. OVERSTRAINED. **On the other side** = over; **the way** is still st; **it came down** = rained. OVER·ST·RAINED = **tried too hard**.
98. EXPRESS TRAIN. **State** = express; **control** = train (e.g. ivy up trellis). EXPRESS TRAIN is a form of **rapid transport**.
99. AMATEUR GOLFER. Designed to evoke thoughts of the baker, **rounds** here = golf rounds, and **bread** is slang for money. An AMATEUR GOLFER gets no money for playing.
100. DRESS FOR DINNER. Someone who **prepares a bird** dresses it; **for the table** = for a meal (dinner in this case). **Get into the habit** = get into the clothes.

101. UP GUARDS AND AT EM. **Said** by Wellington **at** the battle of **Waterloo**. At the railway station Waterloo, guards **now wave flags**.

How to Use This Companion

The puzzle setter uses devious methods of saying one thing while meaning another, thereby hoping to distract the would-be solver's mind from the correct line of approach to a clue. This *Companion* uses different typefaces to encourage the reader into lateral thinking, and thus to avoid the traps with which most cryptic clues abound. The reader must usually expect to refer to a second entry, suggested either [by square brackets] as an associated idea, or else (*by italics*) as an alternative meaning with its own entry.

CAPITALS
Capitals are used for words which are either entries or answers.
   BOLD CAPITALS. All main entries are in bold capital letters.
   PLAIN CAPITALS. A word suitable as an answer to the entry against which it appears is in plain capital letters.
   ITALIC CAPITALS. A word suitable as an answer, which is also an entry in its own right (having further possible answers with different connotations), is in italic capital letters.
   SMALL CAPITALS. Answers to example clues within an explanation are printed in small capital letters. They are largely used to demonstrate clue construction, and therefore are not direct answers to the entry under which they appear.

ITALICS
Italic letters are used to show that the word concerned forms an entry elsewhere in the *Companion*, either as it stands, or else in allied form (thus *relative* appears as **RELATED** and **RELATION**, and *lovely* as **LOVE** and **LOVER**).
   ITALIC CAPITALS. Since the letters are capitals, they show a possible answer to the entry against which they appear. Since they are italic, they also show that the word has an entry in its own right.
   Italic lower case. Because the word is not in capital letters, it does not form a direct answer to the entry against which it appears. But its italic lettering shows that it has an entry in its own right, which could lead to a different train of thought and a possible answer.

To save space, an entry with several synonyms will only give any list under one synonym; the others will refer to it by using italics as just described or, in important cases, will tell the reader directly where to 'see' any list, or will use 'q.v.'.

BOLD LETTERING
Bold lettering is reserved for clue-words in one form or another.

BOLD CAPITALS. Bold capitals are used for main entries, which are normally words taken directly from the clue being examined.

Bold lower case. Bold lower case letters are used for example clues within an explanation. They are also used for sub-entries within an explanation, thus the entry **VICTORY** has a sub-entry **Goddesses**, giving the names of the Greek and Roman goddesses of victory.

Order and Punctuation
Different meanings of a particular entry obey no hard and fast rule as to the order in which they appear in the explanation. In broad terms, abbreviations tend to come first, and the rest follow in alphabetical order. Commas divide words of similar meaning within an explanation; semi-colons make a bigger difference, perhaps between nouns and verbs of the same meaning. Colons introduce a list of words: breeds of dog, characters from Shakespeare, rivers of the world, etc. An equals sign shows a direct link with the preceding word(s), thus **VICTORY** has **Goddesses: Gk** = NIKE; **Rom** = VICTORIA.

A full stop signifies that the meaning changes completely, thus **BOOT** has SHOE; WELLINGTON. DISMISS, FIRE, SACK. TRUNK (US). AVAIL. Where an entry has textual as well as one-word explanations, these are differentiated by use of 1, 2, 3, etc.

( ) Round brackets enclose words which augment an explanation. When used in an answer to an example clue (which therefore has small capital letters), they reveal where a letter or letters have been inserted in the cryptic make-up of that answer, and they should be mentally dismissed when reading such a word. Thus, **All at sea, I'm in the hill** = T(IM)OR shows that the letters IM have been inserted in TOR, and it should be read as TIMOR.

[ ] Square brackets enclose words which suggest further avenues for possible investigation. The words are not answers in themselves,

but are an encouragement to lateral thinking.

* An asterisk shows where a word has been split, or else letters have been removed, to form a cryptic answer. Asterisks should be mentally ignored when reading the word concerned because, like round brackets, they are purely a mechanical method of showing how an answer has been reached. Thus, **A quiet time for the attendant** = P*AGE, shows that the letter P represents **quiet**, while AGE = **time** but, when read as PAGE, the word means **attendant**.

~ A swung dash signifies repetition of the entry word, or of the word immediately preceding the sign itself; identification will be evident from the sense of the text.

Registered Trade Names
Many proprietary names and trade marks have passed into the language as everyday terms. Where such words have been knowingly included in this *Companion*, they are indicated by the symbol ®. Unwitting inclusion of further unidentified trade marks does not imply that they have necessarily acquired a general significance in the legal sense; their omission is regretted, as is any wrong attribution which may have been made. Corrections will be made in subsequent reprints, if substantiated objections are made with adequate notice.

Cross-reference
If an entry fails to satisfy, don't give up! Any word in italics has its own entry, so the reader should cross-refer. For instance, when wanting to know Red Indian tribes, the reader who looks up any one of those three words will find *AMERICAN INDIAN* (in italics); the entry **AMERICAN INDIAN** lists over 70 tribes. Equally, the entry **SHIP** gives (among others) *BOAT*; the entry **BOAT** gives 80 different types of ship or boat. *Cross-refer to words in italics.*

Abbreviations

The following abbreviations are used in this *Companion*. They are not necessarily such as may appear in clues or solutions, although inevitably some of them might do so.

A	Austria, ~n	Can	Canada, ~ian
abbr	abbreviated	celeb	celebrated
aero	aeronautical	Celt	Celtic
Af	Africa, ~n	cent	century
Afghan	Afghanistan	char	character
A-Hung	Austro-Hungary,	Ch	China, ~ese
	~ian	ch	church
anag	anagram	chem	chemical
anon	anonymous	CI	Channel Islands
Arab	Arab, ~ian, ~y	CIS	Soviet Russia, ~n
arch	archaic	coaln	coalition
archit	architecture	C of E	Church of Eng;
Arg	Argentina, ~ian		Protestant
A-Sax	Anglo-Saxon	coll	collector
ass	assassinated	comm	commercial
Aus	Australia, ~n	comp	companion
av	aviation	Cong	Congo, ~lese
		Cons	Conservative
b	before; born	cook	cookery, ~ing
Bab	Babylon, ~ian	crypt	cryptic
Belg	Belgium, ~ian	Cz	Czechoslovakia, ~n
bibl	biblical		
Bol	Bolivia, ~n	d	daughter; died
bot	botanical	Dem	Democrat
Br	Britain, ~ish	dial	dialect
br	brother	div	divorced
Braz	Brazil, ~ian	dn	down clue only
Bud	Buddha, ~ist		
Bur	Burma, ~ese	E	east
		eccles	ecclesiastic, ~al
C	Cambridge	e.g.	for example
Cam	Cambodia, ~n	Egy	Egypt, ~ian

elect	electrical	It	Italy, ~ian
Eng	England, ~ish		
Eq	Equatorial	Jap	Japan, ~ese
esp	especially	Jew	Jewish
Eur	Europe, ~an	Jor	Jordan, ~ian
ex	dead, extinct, former	jun	junior
f	father	k	killed
fem	female	K	king
fict	fictional	Kt	Knight
fig	figurative, figure		
Finn	Finland, ~nish	Lab	Labour
Fr	France, French	Lat	Latin
		leg	legal
Gab	Gabon	Lib	Liberal
Gam	Gambia	lit	literal, ~ly
G & S	Gilbert & Sullivan		
gent	gentleman	m	mother of
geog	geographical	mar	married; marriage
Ger	German, ~y	masc	masculine; male
Gk	Greece, Greek	math	mathematics
gram	grammatical	mech	mechanical
Guy	Guyana, ~anian	med	medical
		Med	Mediterranean
h	husband	met	meteorological
Heb	Hebrew	Mex	Mexico, ~an
hem	hemisphere	mil	military
herald	heraldry	Mong	Mongolia, ~n
Hind	Hindu, ~i	Mos	Moslem
hist	historical	Moz	Mozambique
HK	Hong Kong	Ms	manuscript
Hung	Hungary, ~ian	mus	music(al)
		myth	mythology, ~ical
i.e.	that is		
incl	include(d), inclusive	N	north
Ind	India, ~n	naut	nautical
int	international	Nig	Nigeria, ~n
IOM	Isle of Man	NL	Netherlands, Dutch
Ire	Ireland, Irish	Nor	Norse, Norway
IS	Isles of Scilly	NT	New Testament
Is	island	NZ	New Zealand
Isr	Israel, ~i		

O	Oxford	Shak	Shakespeare
obs	obsolete	Sh	Shetlands
OE	Old English	sig	signature
ON	Old Norse	Sing	Singapore
opp	opposite	sis	sister
Ork	Orkneys	sl	slang
OT	Old Testament	s/l	sounds like
		Som	Somalia
Pac	Pacific	Sp	Spain, Spanish
Pak	Pakistan, ~i	sui	suicide
Para	Paraguay, ~n	Swe	Sweden, ~ish
para	paratroop	Swi	Switzerland, Swiss
parl	parliament, ~ary		
Pers	Persia, ~n	Tanz	Tanzania, ~n
	Iran, ~ian	tech	technical
Phil	Philistine	theat	theatrical
Phoen	Phoenicia, ~n	trad	traditional
photo	photography, ~ic	trans	translate, ~ion
Pl	plural	Turk	Turkey, ~ish
pois	poisoned, ~ous	TV	television
Pol	Poland, ~ish		
polit	political	UK	United Kingdom
Port	Portugal, ~uese	US	United States of
print	printing		America
pte	private		
		v	very
Q	queen	Venez	Venezuela, ~n
q.v.	which see	Viet	Vietnam, ~ese
Rep	Republic, ~an	W	west
rh sl	rhyming slang	w	wife
rly	railway	Wal	Wales, Welsh
Rom	Roman		
Rum	Romania, ~n	Y	Yugoslavia, ~n
Russ	Russia, ~n		
		Z	Zanzibar
S	south	Zam	Zambia, ~n
s	son	Zod	Zodiac
SA	South Africa, ~n	zool	zoological
Sax	Saxon		
Sc	Scotland, Scottish		
Scand	Scandinavia, ~n		

Mini-biographies

Fact

Aaron
Abraham
Absalom
Alban
Antony
Archimedes
Artemisia
Attila
Belshazzar
Boadicea
Caesar
Caligula
Cato
Chaucer
Claudius
Cleopatra
Daniel
David, King
Eli
Elijah
Elisha
Enoch

Esau
Galahad
Guinevere
Herod
Hippocrates
Homer
Horace
Incitatus
Isaac
Jacob
Jehu
Jeroboam
Jesus
Joab
Joan of Arc
Joseph
Joshua
Judas
King Arthur
Lancelot
Mohammed
Moses

Nebuchadnezzar
Nero
Paul
Peter
Pilate
Plato
Pompey
Ptolemy
Pytheas
Rehoboam
Ruth
Salmanazar
Salome
Samson
Samuel
Saul
Sheba, Queen of
Socrates
Solomon
Terpander
Xanthippe
Xerxes

Fiction

Acheron
Achilles
Actaeon
Adonis
Aeneas
Aeolus
Aesculapius
Agamemnon

Amazons
Amphitrite
Amphitryon
Andromeda
Anubis
Aphrodite
Apollo
Argonauts

Argus
Ariadne
Artemis
Asclepius
Astarte
Atalanta
Athene
Atlas

Augeas
Aurora
Autolycus
Baal
Bacchus
Balder
Bellerophon
Cassandra
Castor
Cercyon
Charon
Chiron
Clytemnestra
Daedalus
Danae
Daphne
Demeter
Deucalion
Diana
Dido
Doris
Echo
Electra
Eris
Eurydice
Frey
Freya
Frigg
Galatea
Ganymede
Grundy, Solomon
Hades
Hebe
Hecate
Hector
Hecuba
Hel
Helen
Helios
Helle

Hera
Hercules
Hermes
Hero
Hiawatha
Hippolyte
Holmes, Sherlock
Hyperion
Icarus
Isis
Janus
Jason
Job
Juno
Jupiter
Kali
Leander
Leda
Loki
Maia
Mars
Medea
Medusa
Menelaus
Mercury
Methuselah
Midas
Minerva
Minos
Minotaur
Narcissus
Neptune
Nereus
Nimrod
Niobe
Noah
Nyx
Oceanus
Odin
Oedipus

Orcus
Orestes
Orion
Orpheus
Osiris
Pallas
Pandora
Paris
Penelope
Periphites
Persephone
Perseus
Phaeton
Pluto
Poseidon
Priam
Procrustes
Prometheus
Psyche
Pygmalion
Python
Remus
Rhea
Romulus
Saturn
Sciron
Selene
Sisyphus
Tantalus
Terpsichore
Theseus
Thor
Typhon
Ulysses
Uranids
Uranus
Woden
Zeus

Authors' works

Andersen, Hans
Austen, Jane
Brontës, the
Chaucer, Geoffrey
Cicero
Conan Doyle, Sir
  Arthur
Dickens, Charles
Gilbert, W. S.
  (G & S)
Grahame, Kenneth
Haggard, Rider
Homer
Hope, Sir Anthony
Horace
Kipling, Rudyard

Lear, Edward
Lofting, Hugh
Milne, A. A.
Orwell, George
Potter, Beatrix
Scott, Sir Walter
Shakespeare,
  William
Shaw, G. B.
Stevenson, R. L.
Sullivan, see Gilbert
Swift, Jonathan
Tacitus
Twain, Mark
Wilde, Oscar
Wodehouse, P. G.

Heading Lists

African tribes
Aircraft
Airlines
Airports
Alice in Wonderland chars
American Indians
Andersen, Hans
Anniversaries
Antelopes
Ants
Apples
Architectural terms
Argonauts
Assembly, nouns of
Austen, Jane, books
Aversions
Awards (theat)
Ballet terms, companies
Ball games
Bath deaths etc.
Bats, breeds
Battles, air, land, sea
Bears
Beetles
Bell-ringing, changes
Bells
Biblical towns
Big game
Birds
Birthstones
Board games
Boat types
Bones of the body
Bottle sizes
Brontës, the, books
Butterflies, see Lepidoptera

Capital cities
Captains (fict)
Card games
Car plates (countries)
Carriages
Cartoonists
Castles in the UK
Cathedrals in the UK
Cats
Cattle
Ceramics
Chairs, see Furniture
Chaucer characters
Cheeses
Chemical elements
Chesspiece
Chinese calendar
Chinese dynasties
Church, parts of
Church dress
Churchmen
Cigarette brands
Circuses
Clerks
Clocks, see Furniture
Clowns, jesters
Clubs, London
Coins
Collectors
Colonels (fict)
Colours
Comics
Commonwealth countries
Composers
Companies, City livery
Companions, celebrated

Constellations
Counties, see Divisions
Country houses (fict)
Cricket grounds
Crustaceans
Currencies
Dances
Deer
Deserts
Desks, see Furniture
Detectives
Dickens chars, books
Dinosaurs
Discoveries
Dive positions
Dive types
Divisions of the UK
Doctors, celebrated
Dog breeds
Drinks
Ducks
Dwarfs
Eagles
Ear parts
Emperors
Empresses
Epicureans
Episcopal signatures
Explorers
Eye parts and disorders
Fairies
Fates
Fishes
Five towns
Flowers
Football teams and grounds
Forests
French Revolutionary calendar
Friars
Fruit
Furniture terms, types
Gaols
Games, indoors
Games, outdoors
Gates of London
Gems
Ghosts
Gilbert & Sullivan, see G & S
Gods
Goddesses
Governesses
Grahame, Kenneth, chars
Grasses
Guards (mil)
Gulfs
Habitations
Haggard, Rider, books
Hats
Heraldic terms
Herbs
Hercules' labours
Holmes, Sherlock, cases
Horses
Hunchbacks
Indian provinces
Insects
Instruments (mus)
International units
Inventions
Islands of the UK
Japanese words
Jesters/clowns
Jews
Kings, biblical
Kings, fict
Kings, early Eur
Kipling, Rudyard, books
Knighthood, orders of
Knots
Lakes, principal
Landladies (fict)
Landlords (fict)
Law practitioners (fict)
Lear, Edward, books
Legislative assemblies
Lemurs

Lepidoptera
Liqueurs
'Little' people (fict)
Lizards
Lovers, celebrated
Lovers of . . . (-ophiles)
Maids (fict)
Majors (fict)
Male and female animals
Many-armed, -eyed,
    -headed, -legged
Markets (London)
Materials
Measures
Metals
Military leaders
Milne, A. A., chars
Minerals
Mister (forms of address)
Models for fict chars
Monarchies of the world
Monarchs of Eng/UK
Monkeys
Monsters
Monuments
Moths, see Lepidoptera
Muses
Musical instruments, see
    Instruments (mus)
Music terms
Nicknames
Nine angelic orders
Nine worthies
Nobles
Numbers, specific
Nurses, celebrated
Obsessions
Offspring
One-armed, -eyed, -legged
Organ parts (mus)
Orwell characters
Outlaws
Owls

Oxen
Painters
Palaces
Palms
Parasites
Parrots
Parsons (fict)
Patron saints
Pears
Philosophers
Pigs
Pirates
Planets
Plants
Poets
Potter, Beatrix, books
Presidents (USA)
Prime Ministers (UK)
Prisoners
Prophets
Provinces of Canada
Public schools
Q without U, words
Rabbits
Racetracks, horses
Racetracks, motor cars
Reactors
Red Indians, see American ~
Reference books
Religion
Rhyming slang
Rivers of the world
Robbers, celebrated
Roman place names, UK
Roman roads in England
Round Table knights
Royal families
Rugby grounds
Sailors
Sails
Salmon
Satirists
Schoolmasters

Schools (fict)
Scott, Sir Walter, books
Seas
Seaweeds
Secret police
Servants (fict)
Seven ages of man
Seven deadly sins
Seven hills
Seven sages
Seven seas
Seven wonders of the world
Shakespeare chars
Shakespeare plays
Sharks
Shaw, G. B., plays
Sheep
Shells (zool)
Shoes
Slaves
Snakes
Soldiers
Songs
Spacecraft
Space travellers
Spices
Spirits (drink)
Sports, indoor, outdoor
Sports, water
Sports, winter
Stately homes
States of the USA
Stevenson, R. L., books
Stoics
Straits of the world
Street markets
Study of . . . (-ology)
Swift, Jonathan, books

Swiss cantons
Tables, see Furniture
Tarot cards
Taverns (fict)
Teeth, see Bones
Tempi (mus)
Ten commandments
Tennis venues
Thames bridges
Theatre awards (see Awards)
Theatres
Titans
Trees
Tribes (Roman Britain)
Tribes (World)
Twins, celebrated
Typefaces
Underworlds
Unions, initials
Universities
Unseen characters (fict)
Vegetables
Violin parts, makes
Waterfalls
Weapons
Weights in boxing
Whales
Wild plants/weeds
Windows
Winds, local, celebrated
Winds, Gk and Rom
Wines
Winter sports
Wodehouse, P. G., books
Woodpeckers
World girdlers
Writers
Zodiac, signs of

This represents over 300 lists with a total number of interpretations
which exceeds 15,000.

The Companion A – Z

A (s/l *eh*). *ABOUT*. ACROSS. ADULTS ONLY, ADVISORY,
PARENTAL GUIDANCE (film *censorship*). ALPHA. AREA.
ARGON (*chem*). AUSTRIA (*car plate*). Austria, ~n. *BEST*.
KEY; *NOTE*.

AA ALCOHOLICS ANONYMOUS. ANTI-AIRCRAFT; FLAK.
AUTOMOBILE ASSOCIATION; CAR CLUB. *MILNE*.
FILM *CENSORSHIP*. *LAVA*. RIVER (Fr; CIS).

AARON 1. Bibl br of *Moses*, his rod (with that of *Moses*) was
transformed into a *serpent* when cast down before *Pharaoh*;
it later sprouted to bear almonds. ~ d on Mt Horeb. 2. Moor
(*Shak* char), loved by Tamora.

AB *SAILOR*. BACKWARD SCHOLAR (crypt). Heb month.

ABACK 1. BACKWARDS, BEHIND. DISCONCERTED,
SURPRISED. MOUNTED, RIDER. 2. Word/answer reversed,
e.g. **Little Trevor's taken aback and green** (4) = VERT.

ABBEY MONASTIC BUILDING; **celeb**: BATTLE, BUCKFAST,
FOUNTAINS, FURNESS, GLASTONBURY, KIRKSTALL,
MELROSE, NETLEY, RIEVAULX, ROMSEY, TINTERN,
TITCHFIELD; [Abbess, Abbot]. NORTHANGER ~
(*Austen*).

ABC ALPHABET [Reading]. RATING. *BROADCASTING* (*Aus*;
US). *REFERENCE WORK* (rly).

ABCDEFGHIJKLM A*TO*M (crypt).

ABEL (s/l *able*). s of *Adam*; *Adamson*, FIRST VICTIM, THIRD
PERSON; [Garden of Eden; murder; *ghost* of ~, Wm Blake].
Comp = *Cain*. Bibl town.

ABERDEEN *UNIVERSITY*. **Episcopal sig** = ABERDON.
[Granite]. THE DONS (*football*).

ABERDON *Episcopal sig* of ABERDEEN.

ABET AID, *ASSIST*, EGG, ENCOURAGE, URGE; (**opp** =
hinder). A*WAGER (crypt).

ABIGAIL 1. MAID (The Scornful Lady, Beaumont and Fletcher).
'FATHER'S DELIGHT'. 2. Brought food to *David* who later
mar her.

ABLE (s/l *abel*). ADROIT, CLEVER, SKILLED (**opp** = inept).

ABOARD ON BOARD, SHIPPED; hence put S*S round,

e.g. **Very French aboard leads to an accent** (6) = s*tres*s.
A*PLANK (crypt).

ABOMINABLE SNOWMAN MONSTER (Himalayan), YETI;
BIGFOOT (Can; US); BUNYIP (Aus); SASQUATCH (US);
YAMINSKAY (S Andes).

ABOUT 1. A, C, CA, RE. ON, NEAR, *ROUND*, TURN. A
*FIGHT (crypt). 2. Reverse word. 3. Put word round another,
e.g. **It's about the backward writer, and incompetent** (5) =
I*NEP*T.

ABRAHAM Bibl founder of the Jewish nation, f of *Isaac* whom
God reprieved from sacrifice. Also known to Mahommedans,
who believe he was cast into fire which turned into a bed
of *roses*.

ABROAD 1. FOREIGN. OUTDOORS; WIDELY. 2. Translate,
e.g. **I'm abroad** = JE or ICH etc.

ABSALOM 1. Bibl s of *David*, who rebelled against his f; fled
from battle of Wood of Ephraim on an ass or mule, but became
entangled in an oak tree by his *hair* and k (against orders)
by *Joab*. 2. Duke of Monmouth in Dryden's satire '~ and
Achitophel' (Lord Shaftesbury).

ABSORB ENGROSS. BLOT, MOP UP (**dn** = POM), SOAK.

ABSTAINER *AA*, *TT*. MUSLIM; RECHABITE; [drink,
pussyfoot, Johnson, *Turner*].

ABSTRACT ABSTRUSE, IDEALISTIC (**comps** = animal,
vegetable, *mineral*). DEDUCT, DISENGAGE, REMOVE,
SEPARATE; DIGEST, SUMMARY; [legal evidence].

AC *ACCOUNT*, (~ANT), BILL, *SETTLEMENT*. ACROSS.
ACTINIUM (chem). AIRMAN. ALTERNATING CURRENT,
hence *CURRENCY* (crypt); **comp** = DC.

ACCENT PRONUNCIATION; STRESS. Such a mark: ACUTE
(´), BREVE (˘), CEDILLA (¸), CIRCUMFLEX (ˆ),
DIAERESIS (¨), GRAVE (`), MACRON (¯), TILDE (˜),
UMLAUT (¨).

ACCEPTABLE U. PLEASING, TOLERABLE, WELCOME.

ACCOMPANIST 1. APPENDAGE, ESCORT, SUPPORTER
(**opp** = loner). 2. Word often going with another, e.g. **Bill's
accompanist** (3) = COO.

ACCOUNT AC. NARRATIVE, *REPORT*, STATEMENT,
STORY. CONSIDER, ESTIMATE; PROFIT, REGARD,
RECKONING. ALLOW, JUSTIFY. [*money*].

ACCOUNTANT CA, FCA. CASHIER. AUTHOR, *REPORTER*,
STORY-TELLER, *WRITER* (q.v. for list); [Scheherazade].

ACCUMULATOR *COLLECTOR*, GATHERER. *BET.*
BATTERY, *CELL* (elect). COMPUTER, *MEMORY*,
RETRIEVAL *BANK*.
ACE 1, MONAD, ONE. BEST, CHAMPION, EXPERT, TOP.
CARD, ONE CARD. SERVICE (*tennis*). FIGHTER PILOT,
TOP GUN.
ACELDAMA BLOODSHED, SLAUGHTER (bibl).
ACHERON Gk myth s of *Ceres*. He was changed into a river
across which (with the *Styx*) *Charon* ferried the souls of
the dead.
ACHIEVEMENT 1. ACCOMPLISHMENT, COMPLETION,
DEED, PERFORMANCE, SUCCESS. 2. ARMOUR,
BEARINGS, ESCUTCHEON, HATCHMENT, *SHIELD* (all
herald).
ACHILLES Gk myth s of Peleus and Thetis. Invulnerable except in
his heel, where he was k in the war of *Troy* by an arrow shot by
Paris. His *horse* was *Xanthus* (*Shak*, T and C).
ACID BITING, SEVERE, SHARP, SOUR; [PH, silica] (**opp** =
alkali). *DRUG*, LSD (sl).
ACOLITE (s/l *acolyte*). BRIDGE PLAYER (crypt).
ACOLYTE (s/l *acolite*). ATTENDANT (eccles), BEGINNER,
CHURCHMAN.
ACT *DEED*, OPERATION; BEHAVE, DO, PERFORM,
PORTRAY. LAW.
ACTAEON Gk myth hunter trained by *Chiron*. He spied on
Artemis (**Rom** = *Diana*) bathing, and was *transformed* into a *stag*
which was killed by his own dogs.
ACTION ACT, *DEED*, EVENT, EXERTION (**opp** = inertia).
ENGAGEMENT, FIGHTING, OPERATIONS (mil).
CASE, LEGAL PROCESS, SUIT. MECHANISM, WORKS.
INACTION, STRIKE.
ACTOR PERFORMER, PLAYER, THESPIAN; AESOPUS
(Rom tragic), ROSCIUS (Rom comic). OLIVIER, IRVING,
TREE etc. [*stage*].
ACUTE CRITICAL. KEEN, POINTED, SHARP (**opp** = blunt).
HIGH, SHRILL. *ACCENT*(´).
AD (s/l *add*). ANNO DOMINI, NOWADAYS, YEAR . . .
ADVERT (~ISEMENT), HOARDING, NOTICE, POSTER.
TO.
ADAM FIRST FALLER, FIRST PERSON, FIRST GARDENER;
comp = *Eve* [Eden]. A *BARRIER; A *MARE (crypt).
ARCHITECT, CABINET MAKER [fireplace]. COMPOSER

(Giselle; *mad*). *ISLAND*. SERVANT (*Shak*).
ADAMSON ABEL, CAIN, SETH (crypt).
ADD (s/l *ad*). SUM, TOT, TOTAL (**opp** = subtract). INCLUDE.
ADDER *SNAKE*, VIPER [*Wyvern*]. CALCULATOR,
 COUNTER, TELLER; *SUMMER* (crypt).
ADDITIONALLY ADDED, SUPPLEMENTARY. Add to word.
ADDRESS HOME. POISE, PRESENCE (**opp** = gaucherie).
 SPEAK TO, SPEECH, AIM AT, APPLY.
ADD UP CALCULATE, COMPUTE, SUM, TOTAL, TOT UP.
 MAKE SENSE. DDA (dn).
ADJUST *Anag*. ADAPT, ARRANGE, *ORDER*.
ADMIT CONCEDE, CONFESS, OWN (**opp** = deny). ALLOW,
 LET IN.
ADMIX ADD, MINGLE, STIR IN. YEAR 1009 (crypt – Lat).
ADONIS 1. PHEASANT'S EYE (*flower*). 2. Gk myth handsome
 youth loved by *Aphrodite* (**Rom** = *Venus*). After he was k by
 a boar, he was allowed by the Gods to spend half of each year
 with her. The *flower* anemone sprang from his blood in the
 earth. [Good looks].
ADORN BEDECK, *DECK*, ORNAMENT.
ADRIFT *Anag* (e.g. **Gone adrift** = NEGO, ONGE etc). ILL-
 INFORMED, OUT OF ORDER, OUT OF TOUCH.
 DRIFTING, UNFASTENED [flotsam, jetsam, lagan].
ADVANCE GO FORWARD, GO ON (**opp** = retreat). FLOAT,
 LEND, LOAN, PAY ON ACCOUNT, RAISE A LOAN.
 PROMOTE, PROGRESS.
ADVERTISEMENT *AD*, PR. ANNOUNCEMENT, *NOTICE*,
 PUBLICITY.
AEGIS 1. COVER, DEFENCE, PROTECTION. 2. The shield of
 Athene and *Zeus*.
AENEAS Rom hero of *Troy*; founder of the Roman state.
 Companion = Achates. (*Shak*, T and C). Loved in vain
 by *Dido*.
AEOLUS Gk myth K of Aeolia, god of the *winds* (q.v. for names),
 which he kept shut up in a *cave* [harp, *instrument* (mus)].
AESCULAPIUS Rom equivalent of *ASCLEPIUS* (Gk), *god* of
 medicine [*Hippocrates*].
AESIR Chief Nor gods, dwelt in Asgard.
Af Africa.
A FRENCH UN, UNE.
AFRESH *Anag*. ANEW.
AFRICAN ASHANTI, BANTU, BERBER, BOER,

HOTTENTOT, IBO, KIKUYU, MASAI, MOOR [Othello],
TAUREG, XHOSA, ZOUAVE, ZULU etc. [*tribe*].
AFRICUS Rom myth SW *WIND* (**Gk** = LIPS).
AFTERTHOUGHT PS. ADDED; CODICIL, *RIDER*. LATER
CHILD.
AG *SILVER* (*chem*). LIMITED COMPANY (Ger).
AGAIN *Anag*. BESIDES, FURTHER, ONCE MORE, RE-. A
*PROFIT (crypt).
AGAINST V, VS, VERSUS. ANTI, *CON* (**opp** = for, *pro*).
AGAMEMNON Gk myth K of Mycenae (and br of *Menelaus*), who
led the Greeks to *Troy*. Quarrelled with *Achilles* over slave-girl
Briseis. On his return to Argos k in his *bath* by his unfaithful
wife *Clytemnestra* and her lover Aegisthus. Father of *Electra*.
(*Shak*, T and C).
AGATE *GEM*, SEMI-PRECIOUS *STONE*, *CHALCEDONY*:
CORNELIAN, ONYX, SCOTCH PEBBLE; *Birthstone* (June).
MARBLE, TAW. *WRITER*. *TYPEFACE* (US). A *BARRIER,
AN *ENTRANCE, AN *OPENING, A *MOUTH (crypt).
AGE GET ON, GROW OLD. [Picture of Dorian Gray
(Wilde)]. PERIOD (in hist order): *STONE*, EOLITHIC,
PALAEOLITHIC, MESOLITHIC, NEOLITHIC, *COPPER*,
BRONZE, *IRON*. **Pl** = *Seven* ~*s* (*Shak*).
AGENT FACTOR. A *GENTLEMAN (crypt). MOLE, SPY;
celebrated (fact): NURSE EDITH CAVELL, ODETTE
CHURCHILL, MATA HARI, VIOLETTE SZABO; (fiction):
DICK BARTON, JAMES BOND, BULLDOG DRUMMOND,
THE SAINT, SMILEY, SIMON TEMPLAR.
A GERMAN EIN, EINE.
AGORAPHOBIA *Aversion* to open places.
AGREE CONCUR, CONFORM, CONSENT, GET ON (**opp** =
dissent). AT *ONE (crypt).
AHAB *SAILOR*, *WHALER* (Moby Dick, Herman Melville; *ship* =
Pequod). Bibl *king* who mar Jezebel.
AHEAD ON. IN FRONT (**opp** = behind). A *HEAD (crypt).
AHEM COUGH, HESITATION. A *BORDER (crypt).
AI BEST, FIRST CLASS [*Lloyds*]. 3-TOED *SLOTH* (S Am).
Bibl town.
AIM DESIGN, END, GOAL, INTENT, OBJECT, TARGET;
DIRECT, POINT.
AIRBORNE FLYING (**opp** = grounded). PARA, RED BERET,
RED DEVIL, SAS. [AWACS; Huma, myth bird which
never lands].

AIRCRAFT FLYING MACHINE: AEROPLANE, AIRPLANE (US), AIRSHIP, BALLOON, GLIDER, HANG-GLIDER, HOVERCRAFT, MICROLIGHT, UFO.

Celeb (fighters) many ®:

BEAUFIGHTER (UK)	MIG (CIS)
BUCCANEER (UK)	*MOSQUITO* (UK)
CAMEL (UK)	MUSTANG (UK/US)
CORSAIR (US)	*PHANTOM* (UK/US)
HARRIER (UK)	*PUP* (UK)
HAWK (UK)	*SABRE* (UK/US)
HELLCAT (US)	SPITFIRE (UK)
HUNTER (UK)	*TEMPEST* (UK)
HURRICANE (UK)	*THUNDERBOLT* (US)
LIGHTNING (UK)	TYPHOON (UK)

Celeb (bombers) many ®:

AVENGER (US)	*LINCOLN* (UK)
BADGER (CIS)	*MOSQUITO* (UK)
BEAR (CIS)	STIRLING (UK)
BOSTON (UK/US)	SUPERFORTRESS (US)
FLYING FORTRESS (US)	TORNADO (UK)
GOTHA (Ger)	VALIANT (UK)
HALIFAX (UK)	VICTOR (UK)
HUSTLER (US)	*VULCAN* (UK)
LANCASTER (UK)	*WELLINGTON* (UK)
LIBERATOR (UK/US)	WHITLEY (UK)

AIRFIELD AERODROME, *AIRPORT* (q.v. for list).
AIRLINE BREATHING TUBE, TRACHEA, WINDPIPE (all crypt). AIR SERVICE, CIVIL AIR-CARRIER; **celeb** (all ®): AEROFLOT (CIS), *BA* (UK), BEA (ex-UK), BOAC (ex-UK), CAC (Ch), EL AL (Isr), IBERIA (Sp), KLM (NL), *LOT* (Pol), PAN-AM (US), QANTAS (Aus), SABENA (Belg), *SAS* (Scand), *TAP* (Port), TWA (US), VIRGIN (UK).
AIRMAN AC, FO, PO. BALLOONIST, FLYER, *PILOT*. *DAEDALUS*, *ICARUS*, PEGASUS (*horse* of *Bellerophon*) (myth). BARITONE, *BASS*, BUGLER, FLAUTIST, OBOIST, ORGANIST, *SINGER*, TENOR, TRUMPETER (crypt). SHOW-OFF, SWANKER.
AIRPORT NOSTRIL, MOUTH (crypt). AERODROME, AIRFIELD; **celeb**:

Aberdeen, DYCE; **Amsterdam**, SCHIP(H)OL; **Ayr**,
PRESTWICK; **Azores**, SANTA MARIA; **Berlin**,
SCHONEFELD, TEGEL, TEMPELHOF; **Birmingham**,
ELMDON; **Blackpool**, SQUIRES GATE; **Boston**, LOGAN;
Bournemouth, HURN; **Buenos Aires**, EZEIZA, JORGE
NEWBERY; **Cardiff**, RHOOSE; **Chicago**, O'HARE;
Copenhagen, KASTRUP; **Corfu**, KERKYRA; **Dallas**, FORT
WORTH; **Fiji**, NADI; **Frankfurt**, RHEIN MAIN; **Geneva**,
COINTRIN; **Hamburg**, FUHLSBÜTTEL; **Hong Kong**, KAI
TAK; **Isle of Man**, RONALDSWAY; **Leeds**, YEADON;
Limerick, SHANNON; **Liverpool**, SPEKE; **London**,
CROYDON (ex), GATWICK, HEATHROW, HESTON (ex),
HOUNSLOW (ex), MAPLIN, NORTHOLT, STANSTED;
Lydd, FERRYFIELD; **Malta**, LUQA, VALETTA; **Manchester**,
RINGWAY; **Marseilles**, MARIGNANE; **Melbourne**,
TULLAMARINE; **Middlesbrough**, TEES-SIDE; **Minneapolis**,
ST PAUL; **Montreal**, DORVAL, MIRABEL; **Moscow**,
BYKOVO, DOMODEDOVO, SHEREMETYEVO,
VNUKOVO; **New York**, IDLEWILD, JFK, KENNEDY,
LA GUARDIA; **Oslo**, FORNEBU; **Paris**, DE GAULLE,
LE BOURGET, ORLY, ROISSY, VILLACOUBLAY;
Peking, BEIJING; **Rio de Janeiro**, SANTOS DUMONT;
Rome, CIAMPINO, FIUMICINO, LEONARDO DA
VINCI; **Rotterdam**, WAALHAVEN; **Saigon**, TAN-SON-
NHUT; **Seattle**, TACOMA; **Southampton**, EASTLEIGH;
Stockholm, ARLANDA, BROMMA; **Sydney**, KINGSFORD
SMITH; **Tel Aviv**, LOD; **Tokyo**, NARITA; **Washington**,
DULLES.
AIRWOMAN STEWARDESS, WAAF, WRAF. Fem pilot;
celeb: JEAN BATTEN, MRS VICTOR BRUCE, AMELIA
EARHART, AMY JOHNSON, SHEILA SCOTT;
YOUWARKEE (fict Poltark).
AL ALUMINIUM (chem). CAPONE, GANGSTER. ALBERT,
ALEC (abbrs). ALABAMA (US *state*). ALBANIA (*car plate*).
ALBERTA (*province*, Can). HALF-HEARTED (crypt).
ALAS PITY! WOE! [Yorick, Hamlet, *Shak*]. ALASKA (US *state*).
ALBAN 1. Roman soldier who was first Christian martyr in Britain,
A.D. 304; canonized. 2. *Episcopal sig* of ST ALBANS.
ALBATROSS *BIRD*, PETREL [ill-omen]. Three under *par* on *golf
course*.
ALECTO One of the *FURIES*.
ALEXANDER 1. ~ the Great; s of Philip II of Macedon and

Olympias; b 356 B.C., br of *Cleopatra* (3). Mar (1) Roxana
(1 s) and (2) Barsine. *Emperor* and general who conquered Gk,
Pers, Egy, Mesopotamia and part of Ind, before he d aged 33.
Founded many cities named after himself. 2. Many tsars, princes
and Ks, incl three of Sc. 3. Eight popes, incl a Borgia. 4. Br
Field Marshal. 5. Beetle (*Milne*). 6. *Shak* char.

ALGOPHILE *Lover* of pain.

ALGOPHOBIA *Aversion* to pain.

ALIAS OTHERWISE. NOM DE PLUME, PEN NAME.

ALIBI ELSEWHERE (**opp** = ibid). EXCUSE [crime].

ALICE 1. Girl's name, especially character by Lewis Carroll (Rev
Charles Lutwidge Dodgson) in '~ in Wonderland'; drawings by
John Tenniel; **other chars**: Dinah the *cat*, the White *Rabbit*, Bill
the *lizard* (curiouser and curiouser); Dodo, *Dory*, *Duck*, Eaglet,
Mouse (Caucus-race); Caterpillar (hookah, mushroom, Father
William); Dormouse, Mad Hatter, March Hare (tea-party);
King, Queen and Knave of *Hearts*, 1–10 of *Hearts* (children),
2, 5 and 7 of *Spades* (*gardeners*), courtiers (*Diamonds*), *soldiers*
(*Clubs*), Duchess, Cheshire *Cat* (vanished but for its smile),
hedgehogs, flamingos and soldiers (respectively, croquet balls,
mallets and hoops; 'off with his head'); Mock Turtle, Gryphon
(arithmetic: ambition, distraction, uglification, derision; mystery
ancient and modern; sea-ography; drawling, stretching and
fainting in coils; laughing and grief; lobster quadrille, porpoise,
snail, whiting). Also 'Through the Looking-Glass (and what
Alice Found There)'; **other chars**: Red and White Kings, Queens
and Knights; Dinah the *cat*; Tiger-Lily; Jabberwock, Tove,
Borogrove, Mome Rath, Jubjub Bird, Bandersnatch, Tumtum
Tree, Vorpal Sword, Tulgey Wood; Tweedledum, Tweedledee,
Humpty Dumpty; Gnat, Goat, *Beetle*, Rocking-horse fly,
Walrus, *Carpenter*, *Oysters*, *Lion*, Unicorn; Haigha, Hatta
(*messengers*). *Model* = Alice Liddell. 2. *Nanny* of Christopher
Robin (*Milne*), *modelled* on Olive Brockwell. 3. *Shak* char.

ALIGNMENT DRESSING, *ROW*.

ALIVE ACTIVE, BRISK, RESPONSIVE; SWITCHED ON,
WORKING, LIVING, QUICK (**opp** = *dead*).

ALKALINITY PH (**opp** = acidity).

ALL 1. (s/l *awl*). WHOLE, WHOLLY (**opp** = none). BOTH
SIDES, EACH, EVERYBODY. *SUM*, TOTAL (**opp** =
part). ENTIRELY, QUITE. *HUNDRED*, C (crypt); A
*FIFTY*FIFTY (crypt, hence A HALF). 2. Start antonym with
O, e.g. **All female sign** (4) = OMEN.

ALLOCATED *Anag.* ALLOTTED, ASSIGNED, DEVOTED, PUT IN PLACE; APPORTIONED.

ALLIGATOR *CROCODILE* (q.v.) [~ pear; avocado]. CLIP, GRIP (mech).

ALLOW ADMIT, CONCEDE (**opp** = deny). *LET*, PERMIT, TOLERATE (**opp** = *refuse*). ASSERT, CONSIDER. ADVANCE, GIVE.

ALLOY *Anag.* DEBASE, MIX, MODERATE.

ALMOND BIRD, PIGEON, TUMBLER. COLOUR (yellow/brown). TREE; KERNEL, NUT. NARROW, OVAL SHAPED [~ eyed (Ch, Jap); *Aaron's* rod; dragee; marchpane, marzipan; ratafia (liqueur); tipsy cake].

ALMOST 1. NEARLY, NIGH. 2. Word less one or two letters, e.g. **Almost dinner on target** (5) = *INNER.

ALONE 1. EXCLUSIVELY, ONLY. APART, NOT WITH OTHERS, SOLO. 2. 'One is one and all alone' in *song*.

ALPH 1. Sacred Gk *river*. 2. First half of alphabet, i.e. A*TO*M.

ALPHA A, FIRST, GOOD. CHIEF STAR.

ALPHABET **Greek**: alpha, beta, gamma, delta, epsilon, zeta, eta, theta, iota, kappa, lambda, mu, nu, xi, omicron, pi, rho, sigma, tau, upsilon, phi, chi, psi, omega. **Hebrew**: aleph, beth, gimel, daleth, he(h), vau/waw, zain/zayin, (c)heth, teth, iod/yod, caph/kaph, lamed, mem, nun, samekh, ain/ayin, pe(h), sadhe/tzaddi/zade, koph/qoph, resh, s(c)hin, tau/taw.

ALSO-RAN FAILURE, UNPLACED (**opp** = *first*, winner).

ALTERNATING *Anag.* CHOICE, OR. DEPUTY, SUBSTITUTE; INTERCHANGING.

~ **CURRENT** AC.

ALTERNATIVE CHOICE, EITHER, OPTION, OR, OTHER; DISJUNCTIVE (gram). UNCONVENTIONAL. ALTERNATE (obs). And see **FLOWER** for ~ names.

ALUMINIUM *AL* (*chem*). LIGHT *ALLOY*, *METAL*.

ALWAYS EER, EVER, REPEATEDLY (**opp** = *never*). NESW or any *anag* (crypt).

AM AMERICUM (*chem*). Amplitude modulation (radio). ANTE MERIDIEM, MORNING. I EXIST. FIRST AID MAN (crypt).

A – M A*TO*M (crypt); hence *ALPH* (crypt).

AMAZON 1. WARRIOR (fem); masculine woman (butch). 2. Legendary female warrior tribe of S Am, said to have removed the right breast to aid drawing their bows. 3. In Gk myth, race of fem warriors, the d of *Ares*, living in Pontus or Scythia; **queens**: Penthesilea (*Troy*); *Hippolyte* (sis to Antiope and *Shak*

MND char). 4. *River* of S Am. PARROT. ANT.

AMERICAN INDIAN BRAVE, REDSKIN, TRIBESMAN (**opp** = paleface); HIAWATHA, MINIHAHA (Longfellow); INJUN JOE (*Twain*); POCAHONTAS [squaw, kloo(t)ch, teepee, wigwam]; **celeb**:

3-letters

FOX (N)	UTE (N)	WEA (N)

4-letters

CREE (N)	HOPI (N)	MAYA (S)
CROW (N)	INCA (S)	TUPI (S)
ERIE (N)	KOGI (S)	ZUNI (N)

5-letters

ADENA (N)	MIAMI (N)	OSAGE (N)
AZTEC (S)	MOATI (Mex)	PONCA (N)
CREEK (N)	NAZCA (S)	SIOUX (N)
HAIDA (N)	OLMEC (Mex)	YAQUI (N)
HURON (N)	OMAHA (N)	

6-letters

APACHE (N)	MICMAC (N)	OTTAWA (N)
APINAI (S)	MOHAVE (N)	PANARE (S)
ATOARA (S)	MOHAWK (N)[6]	PAWNEE (N)
CAYUGA (N)[6]	MOJAVE (N)	SENECA (N)[6]
DAKOTA (N)	MUISCA (S)	SIWASH (N)
KAYOPO (S)	NOOTKA (N)	TOLTEC (N)
LENAPE (N)	ONEIDA (N)[6]	TUPIAN (S)

7-letters

ARAPAHO(E) (N)	FUEGIAN (S)	TAIRONA (S)
ARAUCAN (S)	MOHICAN (N)	TLINGIT (N)
CATAWBA (N)	OJIBWAY (N)	WAIMIRI (S)
CHIBCHA (S)	QUECHUA (S)	WYANDOT (N)
CHOCTAW (N)	SHAWNEE (N)	ZAPOTEC (S)

CHINOOK

8-letters

ARAPAHO(E) (N)	CHIBCHAN (S)	IROQUOIS (N)
ARIKAREE (N)	CHIPPEWA (N)	MESQUITO (S)
CHEROKEE (N)	COMANCHE (N)	NEZ PERCE (N)
CHEYENNE (N)	DELAWARE (N)	ONONDAGA (N)[6]

| PUEBLOAN (N) | SEMINOLE (N) | SIHASAPA (N) |
| QUICHUAN (S) | SHOSHONE (N) | SILKSIKA (N) |

9+ letters

ALACALUFAN (S)	BLACKFOOT (N)	MICCOSUKEE (N)
ALGONQUIAN	CHAMACOCO (S)	PATAGONIAN (S)
(N)	CHICKASAW (N)	PUELCHEAN (S)
ATHABASCAN	GUARANIAN (S)	SAC AND FOX (N)
(N)	HOOCHINOO (N)	TUSCARORA (N)[6]

6 = One of the Confederation of Six Nations.

AMETHYST *GEM*, PRECIOUS STONE; *Birthstone* (February). *COLOUR* (purple).

AMISS *Anag.* INAPPROPRIATE, OFFENCE, WRONG. A *GIRL, A *SPINSTER (crypt).

AMONG AMID, AMIDST. Hidden word.

AMOR = *CUPID*, Rom *god* of *LOVE*; (Gk = EROS).

AMP AMPERE (elect). A member (crypt).

AMPHITRITE Gk myth *Nereid* or Oceanid, goddess of the sea. The d of *Nereus*, mar to *Poseidon*, she was m of Triton.

AMPHITRYON In order to seduce ~'s wife Alcmena, *Zeus* gave a party in ~'s house in his absence. ~ returned home and claimed to be the *host* but, as Molière put it, he who gives the party is reckoned to be the host (the other is presumably the *servant*). In Gk myth, Alcmena subsequently gave birth to *Heracles*.

AN Article. IF (arch).

ANAESTHETIC *DRUG*, DULLER, GAS, NEEDLE; NUMBER (crypt). [hospital, operation].

Anag ANAGRAM. ADJUST, ARRANGE, *ORDER*, RE-ORDER. About ten per cent of all clues are capable of being interpreted as intending an anagram. To give just a few examples from the first letter of the alphabet, of words which can be so interpreted: adrift, afresh, allocated, alloy, altered, alternate, amiss, angled, annoyed, anyway, arranged, awful, awkward. All those can be construed in another way (both 'construed' and 'in another way' are also candidates). In this *Companion*, the word 'anagram' is taken to mean any re-ordering of letters, even if they do not in themselves make a word – they may form only part of the final word. So, if a clue is troublesome, try looking for an anagram somewhere – and the word or words giving the letters may not necessarily be actually in the clue. Thus: **I cut a deep ditch arranged for defensive purposes** (9) gives: **I cut a moat**

(anag) = AUTOMATIC. The anagram indicator may appear in the answer, i.e. **Ham for cat** = ACT BADLY.

ANAPAEST *FOOT*.

ANATOLE *FRANCE* (*writer*).

ANDERSEN Hans Christian ~, Danish writer; **stories**: Emperor's New Clothes (*nude*); Inchelina (Maja); Little Mermaid; *Nightingale* (clockwork); Princess and the Pea (*bed*); Red Shoes (*dancing*); Snowman (stove); Snow Queen; Tinderbox (*dogs*); Tin Soldier (ballerina, steadfast); Ugly Duckling (*swan*); Wild Swans (Elisa).

AND NOT 1. NOR. 2. Add NOT before or after word, e.g. **Cold and not remarked** (7) = NOT·ICED.

ANDREW *PATRON SAINT* (Sc) [Apostle, Fisherman, 30 Nov]. SWORD.

ANDROMEDA 1. Gk myth heroine who was chained to a rock as sacrifice to a *monster* sent by the *Nereids*, who were angry at her beauty. *Perseus* turned the monster to stone by exhibiting the head of *Medusa*, and he then married Andromeda. 2. A *constellation* in N hemisphere.

ANGEL *BACKER* (theat). *CAKE. COIN*. CHERUB, MESSENGER, SAINT, ST. *SPIRIT*. ITHURIEL (Paradise Lost, Milton). [*Nine* angelic orders]. *SHARK. WATERFALL*. **Pl** = HEIGHT (RAF sl).

ANGER DISPLEASURE, DISTEMPER, ENRAGE, HEAT, *INCENSE*, IRE, RILE, *TEMPER*, WRATH (**opp** = pleasure).

ANGLE ARRANGE, CONTRIVE. ASPECT, *BEARING*, POINT OF VIEW. *FISH. TRIBESMAN* (Eur).

ANGLOMANIA *Love* of English ways.

ANGLOPHOBIA *Aversion* to English ways.

ANNA *COIN* (⅙th of A RUPEE, hence any one of those six letters, crypt). *GOVERNESS*.

ANNIVERSARY DATE (yearly return); CELEBRATION.

(1) *PAPER*
(2) *COTTON*
(3) *FEATHER*
(4) *FLOWER*
(5) *WOOD*
(6) *CANDY*
(7) *WOOL* or *COPPER*
(8) *BRONZE*
(9) *POTTERY*
(10) *TIN*
(11) *STEEL*
(12) *SILK*
(13) *LACE*
(14) *IVORY*
(15) *CRYSTAL*
(20) *CHINA*
(25) *SILVER*
(30) *PEARL*
(35) *CORAL*
(40) *RUBY*
(45) *SAPPHIRE*
(50) *GOLD*

(55) *EMERALD*   (70) *PLATINUM*
(60) *DIAMOND*   (75) (*DIAMOND*)
(65) BLUE *SAPPHIRE*

ANNO DOMINI AD, NOWADAYS. TO (if allied to 'shortly' or similar word indicating abbreviation to A.D.; crypt).
ANNOY *Anag.* GALL, HARASS, IRRITATE, MOLEST, RILE (**opp** = *please*).
ANNUAL *FLOWER.* YEARLY. *BOOK*, DIARY.
ANON *SOON*; **comp** = ever. ANONYMOUS, UNKNOWN.
ANT INSECT; EMMET, FORMICA, PISMIRE, PISSANT, TERMITE; **kinds**: AMAZON ~, ARMY ~, BLACK ~, BULLDOG ~, CARPENTER ~, LEGIONARY ~, QUEEN ~, RED ~, SLAVE ~, SOLDIER ~, WHITE ~, WOOD ~, WORKER ~; **assembly**: colony; **pl** = TUC (workers; crypt) [Myrmidons]. ARE NOT, IF IT (arch).
ANTE (s/l *anti*). BEFORE, PRE. *BET*, STAKE, WAGER.
ANTELOPE Ruminant quadruped, like a *deer*; **breeds**:

3-letters

GNU	KOB	NYL
GOA		

4-letters

HART	ORYX	TORA
KUDU	THAR	

5-letters

ADDAX	GUEVI	*ROYAL* ~
AUDAX	IZARD	SAIGA
BEIRA	KAAMA	SASIN
BEISA	KEMAS	SEROW
BONGO	KONZE	TAKIN
BUBAL	NAGOR	WANTO
CHIRU	NYALA	YAKIN
ELAND	OKAPI	
GORAL	ORIBI	

6-letters

DIK-DIK	IMPALA	PALLAH
DUIKER	INDIAN ~	PYGARG (bibl)
DZEREN	NILGAI	QUREBI
DZERON	OTEROP	REEBOK

7-letters

BLESBOK	GAZELLE	TARTARY
BUBALIS	GEMSBOK	UNICORN (myth)
CHAMOIS	GRYSBOK	
CHIKARA	SASSABY	

8+ letters

BLACKBUCK	CHOUSINGHA	REEDBUCK
BONTEBOK	HARTEBEEST	*SPRINGBOK*
BUSHBUCK	KLIPSPRINGER	STEINBOK
CHINKARA	PRONGHORN	WILDEBEEST

ANTE MERIDIEM *AM*, FORENOON, MORNING.
ANTEPENULTIMATE LAST BUT TWO, SECOND FROM
　　LAST, CHI (Gr), X.
ANTHONY (s/l *Antony*). *HOPE* (Sir ~, writer). PATRON OF
　　SWINEHERDS. RUNT.
ANTI (s/l *ante*). AGAINST, VERSUS, V, VS (**opp** = *pro*).
ANTI-AIRCRAFT *AA*, FLAK. V-BOMBER (crypt).
ANTICIPATE 1. EXPECT, FORESTALL. 2. Come before in a
　　word, e.g. **He anticipates the record to be of assistance** (4) = HE*LP.
ANTONY (s/l *Anthony*). 1. MARK ~, lived 83–30 B.C. Ally of
　　Caesar, mar (1) Fulvia, (2) Octavia, (3) Cleopatra (paramour).
　　Triumvirate 43 B.C. Infatuated with Cleopatra, he forsook *Rome*
　　and turned Egyptian. Beaten at sea by Octavian (his br-in-law)
　　at Actium, he committed sui in Alexandria. 2. ~ and Cleopatra
　　(*Shak*).
ANUBIS Gk rendering of Egy *conductor* of souls to *Osiris*; it had a
　　hyena's head (sometimes jackal).
ANVIL BLOCK, SHAPE [*smith*]. BONE (*ear*). *INSTRUMENT*
　　(mus).
ANYWAY *Anag*. IN ANY WAY, IN ANY CASE, AT ANY
　　RATE, REGARDLESS.
AOC AIR OFFICER COMMANDING (mil).
AP ASSOCIATED PRESS; *PRESS, REPORTERS*. SON
　　OF (Wal).
APE COPY, IMITATE, MIMIC, TAKE OFF. TAILLESS
　　MONKEY (hence MONKE, crypt); **breeds**: BARBARY,
　　CHIMPANZEE, GIBBON, GORILLA, MAGOT, ORANG-
　　(O)UTANG.
APELIOTES Gk myth EAST *WIND* (**Rom** = SUBSOLANUS).
APHRODITE Gk *goddess* of LOVE (**Rom** = *VENUS*), d of *Zeus*

and Dione; mar Hephaestus (**Rom** = *Vulcan*), and m of *Eros* by
Ares. [*ASTARTE, FREYA, ISHTAR, ISIS*].

APOCRYPHA 1. PSEUDEPIGRAPHA (RC). 2. Appendix of
13 books to OT (not C of E): Baruch, Bel and the Dragon,
Ecclesiasticus, Epistle of Jeremy, Esdras, Esther, History of
Susanna, Judith, Maccabees, Prayer of Manasses, Song of the
Three Holy Children, Tobit, Wisdom of Solomon.

APOLLO 1. Gk *god* of beauty, music, prophecy, sun etc; s of
Zeus and Leto, *twin* of *Artemis* and f of many gods, including
Asclepius. **Rom** = *PHOEBUS*. 2. SPACECRAFT. THEATRE.

APOSTLE MESSENGER. **12 of Christ**: ANDREW,
BARTHOLOMEW, JAMES, JAMES THE LESS, JOHN,
JUDAS ISCARIOT, MATTHEW, PHILIP, SIMON PETER,
SIMON THE CANAANITE, THADDEUS, THOMAS;
later: BARNABAS, ST PAUL, MATTHIAS: also the 70
disciples. *Song*.

APOSTROPHE 1. Sign of omission of letter(s). An ~ often denotes
the possessive case, as in Shakespeare's writing (an elision of
'Shakespeare, his writing'), meaning the work of the Bard. But
an alternative interpretation can be 'Shakespeare is writing', and
the puzzle setter can adopt this in order to confuse the issue.
It avoids the somewhat clumsy construction shown by the clue
Silver in the church is a lock-up (4); this not only reads better
as **Silver in the church's lock-up** (4), but also distracts some
attention from **lock-up** as the principal synonym; = c(AG)E. The
opposite application is exampled by the clue **Countryman's
against a trap** (4); this looks as though a rustic peasant is against,
or does not hold with, the use of traps. In fact, it should be read
in the possessive sense to imply the form or sound of 'against'
as used by a countryman, which = AGIN (also meaning a trap
when split A'GIN). 2. Dropping the letter H from the start of a
word is indicated by substitution of an apostrophe. This implies
either a Cockney or slang interpretation or, more likely, an
equal omission of H from the answer, e.g. **'E's fit to drink** (3)
= (h)ALE. 3. ~ can be an answer in itself, and a suitable clue
might refer to the omission of the letter I from 'Who is Who' as
follows: **Indicates I am not in Who's Who** (10) = APOSTROPHE.
4. ADDRESS, SPEECH (to an absent or imaginary person).

APPEAL ATTRACT, PLEASE. RETRIAL [judge]. ASK, BEG,
IMPLORE, IMPORTUNE [umpire (cricket)]; HOW'S THAT?
HEY, HOY, O, OH.

APPEAR 1. MANIFEST (**opp** = *vanish*) [ghost]. SEEM. 2. Read as . . . , or include word mentioned, e.g. **It appears to me on reflection** (4) = IT˙EM.

APPLE FRUIT; TREE (genus Malus). NEW YORK (sl). [*Adam, Atalanta, Eris, Heracles, Hesperides, Paris*]; types: BRAMLEY'S SEEDLING, CAPE DELICIOUS, COX'S ORANGE PIPPIN, DISCOVERY, EGREMONT, ELLISON'S ORANGE, EPICURE, GEORGE CAVE, GOLDEN DELICIOUS, GOLDEN NOBLE, GRANNY SMITH, GRENADIER, HOWGATE WONDER, IDARED, JAMES GRIEVE, KIDD'S ORANGE RED, LANE'S PRINCE ALBERT, LAXTON'S FORTUNE, LORD DERBY, LORD LAMBOURNE, MERTON KNAVE, NON PAREIL, ORLEANS REINETTE, RUSSET, SPARTAN, ST EDMUND'S RUSSET, SUNSET, WORCESTER PEARMAIN. **Pl** = *STAIRS* (rh sl). Isle of ~s = Avalon (King Arthur).

APPOINTMENT ASSIGNATION, *DATE*, *ENGAGEMENT*, MEETING, TRYST. *DEGREE*, *OFFICE*, ORDINANCE, POSITION, POSTING. EQUIPMENT, FITTING; FURNISHING, OUTFIT (and pl).

APRIL (4th) MONTH, M, APR (Rom Aprilis, bud-opening); (**birthstone** = *diamond*) [~ fool; ~ showers]. Girl's name.

APT APPROPRIATE, SUITABLE. CLEVER, QUICK-WITTED. *TEND*. ADVANCED PASSENGER TRAIN (rly).

AQUAMARINE *GEM*; *BERYL*. *COLOUR* (blue-green).

AQUILO Rom myth NE *WIND* (**Gk** = KAIKAS).

ARACHNE Gk myth d of Idmon (dyer of purple), who turned into a *spider*.

ARCH *BRIDGE*, SPAN, VAULT. *COY*, *CUNNING*, PERT, PLAYFUL, SAUCY, *SHY*, *TEASING* (**opp** = *modest*). CHIEF, SUPERIOR. ARCHAIC (abbr). ARCHITECTURE (abbr).

ARCHER 1. *BRIDGE*, SPAN, VAULT (crypt). *BOWMAN*, TOXOPHILIST; **celeb**: *CUPID*, DAN (radio), ROBIN *HOOD*, WILLIAM TELL. *PAINTER*. *WRITER*. 2. *Constellation* (Sagittarius); (9th) sign of *Zodiac*.

ARCHIMEDES Gk mathematician (287–212 B.C.) who invented the *screw* for pumping water (cochlea); also discovered the principle of water displacement [eureka!], and the use of the lever.

ARCHITECT THE CREATOR, GOD. ACHIEVER, SCHEMER. BUILDER, DESIGNER, PLANNER; **celeb**: *ADAM*, AHOLIAB (bibl), BEZALEEL (bibl), DAEDALUS (Gk myth), INIGO JONES, WILLIAM *KENT*, LE

CORBUSIER, LUTYENS, SIR GILES GILBERT SCOTT, SIR JOHN SOANE, VANBRUGH, *WREN* [si monumentum requiris, circumspice].

ARCHITECTURE BUILDING ART, ~ CONSTRUCTION, ~ LAYOUT, ~ SCIENCE; **styles:** Arenated, Byzantine, Decorated, Early English, Eastern, Egyptian, Gothic, Grecian, Jacobean, Minoan, Norman, Perpendicular, Pointed, Rectilinear, Renaissance, Romanesque, Sumerian, Superimposed, Trabeated, Transitional; **Five Orders:** Composite, Corinthian, Doric, Ionic, Tuscan. **Terms** (and see *Cathedral parts*; *castle*; *temple*; *window*):

4-letters
ARCH (cinquefoil, elliptical, gothic, horseshoe, ogee, norman, pointed, segmented, semi-circular, trefoil)
DADO (body of a pedestal)
JAMB (side of a chimney, door or window)
OGEE (round and hollow moulding; type of arch)
STOA (portico, roofed colonnade)

5-letters
AMBRY (niche)
ATLAS (column)
GABLE (triangular upper part of wall)
NICHE (recess for statue, vessel or ornament)
OGIVE (gothic arch)
OVOLO (convex moulding)
SHAFT (main part of column)
SOCLE (plinth)
TORUS (semi-circular moulding)

6-letters
ABACUS (upper part of capital)
ALMERY (niche)
ARCADE (series of arches [colonnade])
ASHLAR, -ER (hewn stone)
AUMBRY (niche)
AUMERY (niche)
COLUMN (vertical pillar comprising plinth, foot, base, dado, cornice and capital)
CORBEL (projecting frame support)
CUPOLA (ceiling of a dome)
FINIAL (pinnacle or spire ornament)

FLECHE (spire)
FRIEZE (relief band on entablature)
IMPOST (top of pillar)
LANCET (arch)
LIERNE (cross rib)
LINTEL (top of doorway)
METOPE (recess in frieze [*intaglio*])
PILLAR (vertical support or ornament)
PLINTH (projecting base of column)
SCREEN (partition)
SOFFIT (undersurface of arch or ceiling)
VOLUTE (spiral scroll)

7-letters
CALOTTE (concavity in niche)
CAPITAL (head of column)
CORNICE (top of column)
ECHINUS (egg and anchor ornament)
ENTASIS (swelling column)
PORTICO (range of columns)
TELAMON (column)
TRANSOM (horizontal bar in window)

8-letters
ABUTMENT (pier, wall of arch)
ASTRAGAL (beading)
ATLANTES (male supporting figs [fem = Caryatides])
BUTTRESS (support)
GARGOYLE (grotesque animal forming water spout)
KEYSTONE (topmost voussoir)
PEDESTAL (base of column; specially, a whole Classical column)
PEDIMENT (triangular gable)
PILASTER (square supporting column)
TRIGLYPH (projection on frieze [*cameo*])
VOUSSOIR (tapered archstone)

9+ letters
ARCHITRAVE (ornamental door moulding)
BALUSTRADE (parapet)
COLONNADE (series of columns [arcade])
ENTABLATURE (superstructure across two columns)

CARYATIDES (fem supporting figs [masc = Atlantes])
STANCHION (vertical bar in window)
TRIFORIUM (gallery)

ARENA RING, SPHERE, ZONE.
ARE NOT AINT, ANT, ARENT.
ARES Gk *god* of WAR (**Rom** = *MARS*); s of *Zeus* and *Hera*.
Arg Argentina, ~ian.
ARGENT AG (*chem*); *SILVER* (*herald*). FRENCH MONEY (crypt).
ARGON A (*chem*); GAS (inert).
ARGONAUT CEPHALOPOD, CUTTLE(FISH), (PAPER) NAUTILUS (zool). **Pl** = Gk myth adventurers who sailed in the Argo under *Jason* in search of the *golden fleece*: ADMETUS (mar Alcestis), AMPHIARUS (a *prophet*), CALAIS (s of *Boreas*), *CASTOR*, *DEUCALION* (sense 2), GLAUCUS (builder, but see *Argus*, and *steersman* of the Argo), *HERCULES*, MOPSUS (a *prophet*), NESTOR (a *sage*), *ORPHEUS* (a *singer*), PELEUS (f of *Achilles*), PHILAMON (a *poet*), *POLLUX*, *THESEUS*, TYDEUS (f of Diomedes), ZETES (s of *Boreas*).
ARGUS 1. Gk myth *god* with 100 eyes, set by *Hera* to watch *Io*. Stolen by *Hermes*, his eyes were placed on the peacock's tail. 2. *Ulysses'* dog (also ARGOS). 3. Some say builder of the Argo (but see *Argonaut*); s of Phrixus. 4. PHEASANT.
ARIADNE 1. Gk myth d of *Minos* and Pasiphaë, who mar *Dionysus*. Helped *Theseus* to escape from the *labyrinth* by means of a silken thread, and then went to Naxos. 2. A minor *PLANET*.
ARIEL (s/l aerial). SPRITE, *SPIRIT*. Char in Temp (*Shak*).
ARMOUR MAIL, PROTECTION (chain ~, plate ~); **parts**: ACTON (jacket), BEAVER (jaws), BREASTPLATE (breast), CUIRASS (body), CUISSE (thigh), GORGET (neck), GREAVE (shin), HABERGEON (coat), HAUBERK (coat), HELM (head), PANOPLY (suit), PAULDRON (shoulders), TASSET (hip), VAMBRACE (arm), VISOR (eyes). [*patron saint*].
ARMS (s/l alms). LIMBS, MEMBERS (*bone*). SLEEVES. BRANCHES. *WEAPONS*. *HERALDRY*.
ARMY 1. *SA*. *TA*. CORPS, HOST, *SOLDIERS* [~ and Navy *Club*/Stores; Fred Karno's ~; Salvation ~]. *ANT*. 2. Of the arm, e.g. **army cover** = SLEEVE; **army connections** = SHOULDERS.

Hence *KALI* (crypt).
AROUND 1. ABOUT. A **ROUND* q.v. A **BULLET (crypt).
  2. Reverse the word, e.g. **Idol to follow around** (3) = GOD.
ARRIVAL TIME ETA. BIRTHDAY (crypt).
ARRIVED CAME, HERE. MADE.
ARRIVES ARR. COMES. (**opp** = *leaves*).
ARROW *DART*, FLECHETTE, FLIGHT, QUARREL;
  MISSILE, WEAPON [*Bowman*; St Sebastian]. **Comp** = *bow*;
  pl = *game* (*darts*). *GRASS*. DIRECTION INDICATOR,
  POINTER, SIGNPOST. ~ ROOT (*plant*; starch).
ARSENIC MINERAL; AS (*chem*). POISON, SEMI-METALLIC
  ELEMENT. [Old Lace].
ARSON FIRE-RAISING, INCENDIARISM; LIGHT CRIME
  (Pyro-*mania*).
ARSONIST BLAZER, FIREMAN, PYRO-*MANIAC*.
ART 1. CRAFT, KNACK, SKILL. ARTICLE. ARE (arch).
  ARTHUR (abbr). PAINTING, SCULPTURE. **Pl** = Creative,
  imaginative and non-scientific branches of knowledge, e.g.
  dance, drama, literature, *music* and visual ~s. 2. **Goddess: Gk** =
  ATHENE, **Rom** = MINERVA.
ARTEMIS 1. Gk virgin *goddess* of *nature* and *hunting*; CYNTHIA
  (**Rom** = *DIANA*); d of *Zeus* and Leto, and *twin* of *Apollo*
  (*temple* at Ephesus, one of the *Seven Wonders*), [UPIS,
  HECATE, SELENE]. 2. A minor *PLANET*.
ARTEMISIA 1. Q of Halicarnassus who fought with *Xerxes* at
  Salamis 480 B.C. 2. d of Hecatomnus, who mar her br Mausolus
  350 B.C., and built the *mausoleum* as his tomb. 3. *SPICE* (q.v.
  for list).
ARTHUR *ART*. See also *KING* ~.
ARTICLE A, AN, ART, THE. ITEM, THING. CLAUSE,
  PARTICULAR. LITERARY PIECE, WRITING. **Pl** =
  APPRENTICESHIP.
ARTILLERY *RA*; GUNS, ORDNANCE, *WEAPONS*.
ARTIST (s/l *Artiste*). *RA*; *PAINTER* (q.v. for list).
  CRAFTSMAN, DEVOTEE; THESPIAN.
ARTISTE (s/l *Artist*). DANCER, PERFORMER, SINGER,
  THESPIAN [*stage*].
ARTS MAN BA, MA.
AS *ARSENIC* (*chem*). ROMAN *COIN*. BECAUSE; LIKE.
  WHEN. FRENCH *ACE*.
AS AT QUA.
A-Sax Anglo-Saxon.

ASCENT 1. CLIMB, MOUNTING, RISE. 2. Word reads upwards (dn).

ASCLEPIUS Gk *god* of medicine, s of *Apollo*; mar Epione and f of *Hygieia*; k by *Zeus* with a *thunderbolt*. His attribution is a *staff* with entwined winged serpent (caduceus). *Hippocrates* was one of his supposed descendants (the Asclepidae) [*Oath*]. **Rom** = AESCULAPIUS.

ASP *SNAKE* [A and C, *Shak*]. AS SOON AS POSSIBLE.

ASPIRATION AMBITION, HOPE. Sound the letter H. BREATHING, VENTILATION.

ASS ASSASSINATED, ~ION. BURRO (US), DONKEY, MOKE; NEDDY [mule; *Absalom*; Balaam; *Bottom*; Poppaea; *Silenus*]; **breeds**: CHIGETAI, DZIGGETAI, ONAGER; **male** = *JACK*, **female** = *JENNY*; [hinny]. FOOL ABOUT. BACKSIDE (US).

ASSEMBLY DELIBERATIVE BODY, *LEGISLATIVE* COUNCIL. FITTING TOGETHER, MANUFACTURING, PRODUCTION. *MUSTER* (mil); CONCOURSE, *CROWD*, *GATHERING*, MEETING; COLLECTION OF ANIMALS as:

Ambush	Tigers
Army	Ants, Frogs
Band	Jays
Bank	Swans
Barren	Mules
Bevy	Larks, Quails, Otters, Swans
Bob	Seals
Bouquet	Pheasants
Brood	Hens
Building	Rooks
Bunch	Widgeon
Bury	Rabbits
Business	Ferrets
Cartload	Monkeys
Cast	Falcons, Ferrets, Hawks
Cete	Badgers
Charm	Finches
Chattering	Choughs
Chine	Polecats
Clowder	Cats
Cluster	Cats
Clutch	Hens

Coil	Teal, Widgeon
Colony	Badgers, Frogs, Gulls, Herons, Penguins, Rabbits
Company	Moles, Widgeon
Congregation	Plovers
Convocation	Eagles
Coven	Witches
Covert	Coots
Covey	Grouse, Partridges
Crash	Rhinos, Seals
Deceit/Desert	Lapwings
Den	Snakes
Destruction	Wild cats
Dole	Doves, Turkeys
Down	Hares
Drove	Cattle, Donkeys, Hares, Kine, Pigs, Sheep
Exaltation	Larks
Fall	Woodcock
Farrow	Piglets
Fesnying	Ferrets
Flight	Doves, Ducks
Flock	Chickens, Geese, Goats, Pigeons, Sheep, Turkeys
Flush	Mallard
Gaggle	Geese
Gam	Whales
Game	Swans
Gang	Elk
Gathering	Clans
Glaring	Cats
Harass	Horses
Harem	Seals
Herd	Antelope, Boars, Cattle, Deer, Donkeys, Elephants, Giraffes, Goats, Kangaroos, Pigs, Seals, Sheep, Swans, Swine, Walruses, Whales, Wolves, Zebras
Host	Sparrows
Hover	Crows

Hurtle	Sheep
Husk	Hares
Kennel	Hounds
Kindle	Kittens
Knob	Teal, Widgeon
Labour	Moles
Lead	Foxes
Leap/Lepe	Leopards
Leash	Deer, Hares, Hawks, Plovers
Litter	Cats, Dogs
Mob	Kangaroos
Movement	Moles
Murder	Crows
Murmuration	Starlings
Muster	Peacocks
Mutation	Thrushes
Nest	Ants, Rabbits, Snakes
Nide	Geese, Pheasants
Nye	Pheasants
Pace	Donkeys
Pack	Grouse, Hounds, Hyenas, Wolves
Paddling	Ducks
Parcel	Deer
Parliament	Owls, Rooks
Party	Jays
Pit	Snakes
Pitying	Doves
Plump	Woodcock
Pod	Seals, Walruses, Whales
Pride	Lions, Peacocks
Race/Rag	Colts
Raffle	Turkeys
Raft	Coots, Teals, Turkeys
Rake	Colts, Mules
Rookery	Penguins, Rooks, Seals
School	Cardplayers, Fish, Porpoises, Whales
Sedge	Herons
Shoal	Fish
Shrewdness	Apes
Singular	Boars, Swine
Skein	Geese

Skulk	Foxes
Sleuth/Sloth	Bears
Smuck	Jellyfish
Sord	Mallard
Sounder	Swine
Sowse	Lions
Span	Mules
Spring	Teals
Stare	Owls
Swarm	Bees
Team	Draught animals, Oxen, Young ducks
Tiding	Magpies
Tittering	Magpies
Trace	Hares
Trembling	Finches
Tribe	Goats, Monkeys, Sparrows
Trimming	Finches
Trip	Hares, Seals
Troop	Antelopes, Horses, Kangaroos, Lions, Monkeys
Unkindness	Ravens
Walk	Snipe
Warren	Rabbits
Watch	Nightingales
Wedge	Swans
Whisper/Wisp	Snipe
Whiteness	Swans
Wing	Plovers
Yoke	Oxen

ASSESS ESTIMATE, VALUE. JENNY, SHE-MULE.
ASSIST *ABET*, AID, GUIDE, HELP. BE PRESENT, TAKE
PART. MULETEER (crypt).
ASSOCIATION FRIENDSHIP. CONNECTION. CLUB,
ORGANIZATION. [*Football*].
ASSUME POSIT, POSTULATE. DON, PUT ON. SIMULATE.
ARROGANT. UNDERTAKE.
ASSUMPTION 1. ARROGANCE, SIMULATION, TAKING,
UNDERTAKING. CLOTHING (crypt). 2. Reception of Virgin
Mary in Heaven.

ASTARTE 1. MOLLUSC. 2. Phoen *goddess* of *LOVE*; **Gk** =
APHRODITE; **Rom** = *VENUS*. 3. Heroine of Byron's poem
'Manfred'.
ASTRONOMY STARGAZING, STUDY OF THE HEAVENS.
Gk Muse = *URANIA*.
ATALANTA Gk myth maiden who avoided mar by *refusing*
suitors who could not beat her in a race; she k the unsuccessful.
Eventually Milanion (or Hippomenes) distracted her by dropping
golden *apples* given him by *Aphrodite*, and he won.
ATE 1. (s/l *eight*) CONSUMED. 2. Gk *goddess*, d of *Zeus*;
personification of *RETRIBUTION*. 3. A minor *PLANET*.
ATHENE = PALLAS. Gk *goddess* of *ART*, *WAR*, and *WISDOM*;
d of *Zeus*, her *shield* was called *Aegis*. **Rom** = *MINERVA*.
ATHENIAN ATTIC, GREEK [TIMON (*Shak*)].
ATHLETE *BLUE*; COMPETITOR; RUNNER.
ATHLETIC AGILE, SUPPLE; FIT, MUSCULAR, STRONG. **Pl**
= EXERCISES, *SPORTS* EVENTS, e.g. **field events**: discus,
hammer, high jump, hop-step-jump, javelin, long jump, pole
vault, shot put; **track events**: hurdles, marathon, long distance,
middle distance, sprint, steeplechase. And see *SPORT*.
AT HOME IN, NOT OUT (**opp** = *out*). COMFORTABLE.
ATHOS MUSKETEER (Dumas; Aramis, Porthos [d'Artagnan]).
MOUNTAIN (Gk holy).
ATLAS 1. MOUNTAIN RANGE. *BONE*, FIRST VERTEBRA.
WORLD MAP. CHARLES ~ (*strength*). COLUMN (arch).
2. Gk myth *TITAN*, who bore the universe on his shoulders; he
was turned by *Perseus* into *stone* (and thus became the Atlas
mountains). 3. *SPACECRAFT*.
ATOM 1. PARTICLE. SMALL PORTION/QUANTITY. 2. First
half of alphabet (i.e. A*to*M) hence *ALPH* (crypt).
ATOMIC NUMBER 1 = HYDROGEN. **92** = URANIUM.
~ **WEIGHT 1** = HYDROGEN. **238** = URANIUM.
ATONE 1. ABY(E), EXPIATE, MAKE AMENDS,
RECONCILE. 2. A sound (**a*tone**, mus); agree (**at*one**);
both crypt.
ATTEMPT ENDEAVOUR, ESSAY, *GO*, STAB, *TRY*, *TURN*.
ATTENDANT AIDE DE CAMP, PAGE, *SECOND*, SERVANT;
WAITING. CONCOMITANT.
ATTENTION HARK, HEED, *LIST*, LISTEN. ERECT, READY,
SHUN. CARE, CONSIDERATION.
ATTIC LOFT, TOP ROOM. ATHENIAN, GREEK. *ELEGANT*,
PURE, *SIMPLE*.

ATTILA K of the *Huns*. He sacked eastern Europe and extorted tribute from Emperor Theodorus. Advancing into *Gaul*, he was defeated in A.D. 451 near Châlons-sur-Marne. He d advancing on Rome two years later.

ATTRACT *DRAW*, PULL (**opp** = *repel*).

ATTRACTIVE ARRESTING, GOOD LOOKING, PRETTY, TAKING (**opp** = *ugly*); MAGNETIC.

AU *GOLD* (*chem*). TO THE FRENCH (crypt).

AUC AB URBE CONDITA (foundation of *Rome*).

AUGEAS Gk legendary K of Elis. Owned stables housing 3,000 oxen, which were cleansed by *Hercules* in one day, when he diverted two rivers for the purpose.

AUGUST IMPRESSIVE, MAJESTIC, NOBLE, VENERABLE. (8th) MONTH, M, AUG (Augustus *Caesar*); **birthstone** = *sardonyx*.

AUK SEABIRD; **breeds**: GUILLEMOT, GREAT ~ (ex), LITTLE ~, PUFFIN, RAZORBILL [cormorant, shag].

AUNT SALLY *SHY*. Tom Sawyer's aunt (Mark Twain).

AURAL (s/l *oral*). AUDITORY, BY *EAR*.

AURORA 1. Rom *goddess* of *DAWN* (**Gk** = EOS). She rose in the east at the end of night, and crossed the sky in a chariot drawn by two horses; m by Astraeus of the beneficial *winds*. 2. A minor *PLANET*.

Aus Australia, ~n; and *car plate*.

AUSTEN 1. CHAMBERLAIN (polit). 2. JANE, WRITER; **books**: Emma (Hartfield, Highbury; Emma Woodhouse, Mr Knightley, Frank Churchill); Mansfield Park (Northampton; Lady Bertram, Fanny Price); Northanger Abbey (Wiltshire; Morlands, Thorpes, Tilneys); Persuasion (Kellynch Hall, Somerset; Sir Walter Elliot, Anne Elliot, Capt Wentworth); Pride and Prejudice, ex First Impressions (Longbourn, Netherfield Park, Herts; Elizabeth Bennet, Mr Darcy; Jane Bennet, Mr Bingley; Lydia Bennet, Mr Wickham); Sense and Sensibility (Norland Park, Barton Park, Sussex; Dashwoods, Ferrars, Lucy Steele); The Watsons (unfinished).

AUSTER Rom myth SOUTH *WIND* (**Gk** = NOTOS). AIRCRAFT.

AUSTRIA A; and *car plate*.

AUTHOR *ACCOUNTANT* (crypt). CRIME WRITER, DRAMATIST, NOVELIST, PLAYWRIGHT; ORIGINATOR. See *poets* and also *writers* for lists.

AUTHORITY POWER, SAY-SO, *SEAL*. EXPERT. *BOOK*.

AUTOLYCUS 1. Gk myth s of *Hermes*; a *robber* who could change all he touched, and so avoid detection. Trapped by *Sisyphus* who marked under the hooves of cattle. 2. Gk astronomer of 4th century B.C. 3. A salesman in the Winter's Tale (*Shak*); 'a snapper-up of unconsidered trifles'.

AUTOMATIC MECHANICAL, NECESSARY, SELF-ACTING, UNCONSCIOUS (**opp** = *contrived*). BREN, BROWNING, COLT, LUGER, STEN, *WEAPON*.

AUTOMATICALLY MECHANICALLY, UNCONSCIOUSLY. OF GUNS, ORDNANCE.

AV AUTHORIZED VERSION, BIBLE. AVIATION.

AVAILABLE DISPOSABLE, ON OFFER, UP FOR GRABS. APPROACHABLE.

AVE HAIL, WELCOME. ALOHA, FAREWELL. AVENUE.

AVENGER 1. *AIRCRAFT*. 2. EXACTOR OF RETALIATION/ RETRIBUTION/SATISFACTION. *ELECTRA*; *ORESTES*.

AVER AFFIRM, ASSERT, DECLARE. PART MEANS (AVERage; crypt).

AVERAGE ESTIMATE, *MEAN*, ORDINARY, *PAR*. DAMAGE, LOSS.

AVERSION 1. ANTIPATHY, DISLIKE, FEAR, *HATRED*, PHOBIA (**opp** = *lover*), as:

Beards	POGONOPHOBIA
Dogs	CYNOPHOBIA
Enclosed spaces	CLAUSTROPHOBIA
English customs	ANGLOPHOBIA
Feet	PODOPHOBIA
Fire	PYROPHOBIA
Foreigners	XENOPHOBIA
French customs	GALLOPHOBIA
Heights	ACROPHOBIA
Horses	HIPPOPHOBIA
Marriage	GAMETOPHOBIA
No 13	TRISKAIDEKAPHOBIA
Open places	AGORAPHOBIA
Pain	ALGOPHOBIA
People/races	GENOPHOBIA
Poisons	TOXIPHOBIA
Russian customs	RUSSOPHOBIA
Sleep	HYPNOPHOBIA

Spiders	ARACHNEPHOBIA
Strangers	XENOPHOBIA
Teeth	ODONTOPHOBIA
Travel	(H)ODOPHOBIA
Water	HYDROPHOBIA
Women	GYNOPHOBIA
Work	ERGOPHOBIA

2. AN *ACCOUNT, A *BOOK, A *TRANSLATION; A *TURNING (crypt).
AWARD ASSIGN, GRANT, PAYMENT, PENALTY. JUDICIAL DECISION. *HONOUR, PRIZE,* TROPHY (theat) most ®: BAFTA (Br film, TV), CEZAR (Fr *Oscar*), *EMMY* (US TV), GOLDEN GLOBE (Hollywood Foreign Press Association), GOLDEN PALM (Cannes film), GOLDEN ROOSTER (Ch film), GOLDEN ROSE (Montreux film), GRAMMY (US popular music), IVOR NOVELLO (US music), OLIVIER (ex SWET, UK West End theat), *OSCAR* (US film), STELLA (UK film), TONY (US stage).
AWFUL *Anag.* IMPRESSIVE, NOTABLE. APPALLING. *BAD*; FRIGHTENING.
AWKWARD *Anag.* BUNGLING, CALLOW, CLUMSY; EMBARRASSED, *SHY.*
AWL (s/l *all*). AUGER, *DRILL.*
AZURE *BLUE* (*herald*). CLOUDLESS, SERENE.

B (s/l *bee*). BARON. BEFORE. BELGIUM (*car plate*). BETA. BISHOP. BLACK. BORN. BORON (*chem*). BOWLED. KEY, NOTE. SECOND CLASS. SOFT (pencil). 300 (Rom).
b born.
BA ARTMAN: BACHELOR OF ARTS. BARIUM (*chem*). *AIRLINE* (UK).
BAAL Phoen chief god (& of Sun & of Fertility) *c.*1000 B.C. An object of phallic worship by Isr under *Ahab*, so that *Elijah* was forced into hiding. Any false god.
Bab Babylonia, ~n.
BACCHUS (s/l *back us*). Rom *god* of *WINE* and *FERTILITY*; also IACCHUS, mar *Ariadne* and was worshipped in drunken orgies (**Gk** = DIONYSUS) [*drink*].

BACHELOR BA, MB. UNMARRIED [*Lear*].

~ OF ARTS BA.

~ OF MEDICINE MB.

BACK 1. BET ON, WAGER. SECOND, SUPPORT. GO BACK, REVERSE. RIVER (Can). **Pl** = *GROUNDS* (C). 2. Reads backwards, e.g. **Backward** = DRAW. **Back seat** = DEB (crypt; but beware, it can also = SADDLE!).

BACKED WAGERED. SUPPORTED. REVERSED, WENT ASTERN. MOUNTED, RIDING, SADDLED [*horse*] (crypt). DE (crypt).

BACKER BETTER, PUNTER. SECOND, SUPPORTER; *ANGEL*. LORD CHANCELLOR (ceremonial). RE (crypt). RIDER (crypt).

BACKWARD 1. ASTERN, REARWARD. UNDEVELOPED. *DRAW* (crypt). 2. Word reversed, e.g. **Backward scholar** = AB.

BACKWATER CUL DE SAC, DEAD END, STAGNATION POINT. WAKE, WASH. RETAW, OOH (H_2O backwards, crypt – but *chem* inaccurate).

BACKYARD COURTYARD; GARDEN (US). NEIGHBOURHOOD. DRAY (crypt).

BAD(LY) *Anag.* AWFUL. COUNTERFEIT, DEFICIENT, DUD, FOUL, INFERIOR, NO GOOD, ROTTEN, UNPLEASANT, WORTHLESS (**opp** = *good*, *well*).

BADGER HARRY, WORRY, *TEASE*. ANIMAL [*assembly* (cete); *habitation* (sett)]. SHAVING BRUSH. *AIRCRAFT* (CIS). *ISLAND*.

BAD PRESS CRITICISM, POOR PUBLICITY. *RAG*. SPERS etc (*anag*).

BAFFLED *Anag.* FRUSTRATED, PERPLEXED. DAMPED, SILENCED.

BAG *BOOK*, DEMAND, RESERVE. KILL. CASE; *SACK*; **types:** ATTACHE CASE, BRIEFCASE, CARPET ~, DESPATCH CASE, DIPLOMATIC ~, DITTY ~, ETUI, GLADSTONE ~, KIT ~, PORTFOLIO, POUCH, RETICULE, RUCKSACK, SADDLE ~, SA(T)CHEL, SCRIP, VANITY ~, WALLET. **Comp** = *baggage*. **Pl** = *BAGGAGE*. TROUSERS; PANTS (US).

BAGGAGE BAGS, CASE, EQUIPMENT, GEAR, GRIP, KIT, LUGGAGE, *TRAPS*, TRUNK; **comp** = *bag*. HUSSY, JADE, MINX, SAUCY PIECE.

BAGPIPE INSTRUMENT (mus; Ire, Sc); MUSETTE (Fr); **parts:** bag, bellows, blowpipe, bourdon, chanter, drone.

BAIL (s/l *bale*). SECURITY, SURETY. LIBERATE, RELEASE. CASTLE WALL. WICKET TOP (cricket). HOOP HANDLE. ACCOST, BUTTONHOLE (Aus). PUMP OUT, SCOOP OUT (and *BALE*; naut). [parachute].

BALD BLUNT, PLAIN, SIMPLE. BARE, HAIRLESS, (CLEAN) SHAVEN [Brynner, Charles the ~, coot, ~ eagle, *Elisha*, Kojak, Marquis of Granby]. ~ money = spignel (*plant*).

BALDER 1. LESS HAIR, SMOOTHER [Brynner; coot; *Elisha*; Kojak]. 2. *God* of *SUN* (Nor), s of *Odin* and *Frigg(a)*, mar Nanna; k by his blind br Hod, who unwittingly used a poisoned mistletoe dart supplied by *Loki*.

BALE (s/l *bail*). DESTRUCTION, EVIL, MISERY, PAIN, WOE. PACK, WRAP. *MEASURE* (paper). PUMP OUT, SCOOP OUT (and *BAIL*; naut). [parachute].

BALL (s/l *bawl*). *DANCE*. PILL; BEAMER, BOUNCER, DELIVERY, FULL TOSS, LEG BREAK, LONG HOP, OFF BREAK, YORKER; BOUNDER (crypt). [baseball, billiards, *cricket, football*, hockey, *rugby, snooker, squash, tennis*].

BALLET *DANCE* (classical, mime, Fr, Russ); **terms**: arabesque (position), ballerina, -o (dancer, fem, male), barre (exercise bar), battement (leg movement), batterie (crossing feet), chassé (step), coda (dance section), coryphée (junior ballerina), coupé (step), elevation (jump), entrechat (leap), fouetté (whip turn), glissade (glide), jeté (leap), *leotard* (exercise costume), pas (step; ~ de basque, ~ de chat, ~ de deux, ~ glissé, ~ seule), pirouette (spin), plié (bend), pointe (tip-toe), prima ballerina assoluta (principal star), répétiteur (rehearsal teacher), ronds de jambe (leg movements), tutu (stiff skirt). [Noel Streatfeild]; **celeb companies**: Bolshoi (Moscow), Eng National ~ (was Festival ~), Kirov (Kiev), New York ~,~ Rambert, Royal ~, Birmingham Royal ~ (was Sadler's Wells); **celeb personalities**: Ashton, Diaghilev, Dolin, Dowell, Fokine, Fonteyn, Grey, Markova, Massine, Nijinsky, Nureyev, Pavlova, Rambert, Shearer, Sibley, Soames, de Valois.

BALL GAME Any game played with a ball (usually out of doors); **types**: *BASEBALL* (US), BILLIARDS, *CRICKET*, CROQUET, *FIVES*, *FOOTBALL* (Association, Am, Aus Rules, Gaelic, Rugby, ~ League), *GOLF*, HANDBALL, HOCKEY, HURLING (Ire), LACROSSE, NETBALL, PALL MALL, PELOTA (Basque), POLO, *RACKETS*, ROUNDERS, *RUGBY*, SHINTY (Sc), *SNOOKER*, SOFTBALL, SQUASH, *TENNIS* (lawn, real/royal, table), VOLLEYBALL, WATER

POLO (and see *board game*, *game*, *sport*).

BALTHAZAR 1. *BOTTLE* (wine *measure* = 16 normal ~s).
2. Bibl; one of the *Magi* [Caspar, Melchior (Matthew 2)].
3. *SERVANT* (M of V, Much Ado, R & J, *Shak*). 4. Variant of
Belshazzar.

BAN *BAR*, FORBID, PROSCRIBE. VETO.

BAND (s/l *banned*). BOND, OBI (Jap), SASH, STRIP, TIE.
CARTEL, CLIQUE, COTERIE, GANG. HOOP, LOOP,
STREAK, STRIPE. ORCHESTRA, *PLAYERS*.

BANG DIN, EXPLOSION, NOISE. *FIRE*, *SHOOT*. BUMP,
KNOCK. CURL, FRINGE.

BANGER AUTOMATIC, *GUN*, *REVOLVER*, *ROCKET*,
SHELL. FIRECRACKER, *FIREWORK*; *REPORTER* (crypt).
CAR, OLD CROCK (sl). SAUSAGE (sl).

BANK EDGE, *LEAN*, *TILT*. RIVERSIDE, SLOPE; BUND.
PANEL, *ROW*. RELY ON. MONEY BOX, SAFE DEPOSIT;
LODGE (Barclays, *Lloyds*, Midland, NatWest, Tellson's
[2 Cities, *Dickens*]). MUD ~, SAND ~ (naut). **Pl** = *STRAIT*.

~ **CHARGES** INTEREST, COMMISSION. FERRY TOLL,
RIVER TOLL (crypt).

BANKER CASHIER. ROTHSCHILD. DEALER (cards).
AILERON (aero). *RIVER* (crypt) e.g. **London banker** =
THAMES. [football pools].

BANNED (s/l *band*). FORBIDDEN, TABOO, TABU (**opp** =
allowed).

BAR (s/l baa). BISTRO, *DIVE*, INN, *PUB*, SNUG, *TAVERN*;
COUNTER [*drink*]. REST (mus). ESTOP, OBJECT,
PREVENT, SHUT, *STOP*. BAN, FORBID, VETO. GRILLE,
GRATING. LEVER. EXCEPT, SAVE. SANDBANK. **Pl** =
PRISON.

BARABBAS *Robber* released by Pilate instead of Jesus.

BARGE CHARGE, LURCH, PUSH, SHOVE. *BOAT*: CANAL
BOAT, FREIGHTER, HOY, THAMES, WHERRY;
HOUSEBOAT; STATE CRAFT.

BARIUM BA (chem). *METAL*.

BARK (s/l barque). HOWL, YAP. RIND, SKIN. ABRADE,
GRAZE. *CRY*, *HAWK*, PEDDLE, TOUT. *BOAT*, CLIPPER,
SAILING SHIP.

BARKER CRIER, PEDLAR, TOUT. *DOG*. [Actors' benevolent
fund].

BARMAID 1. SERVING WENCH, HOSTESS. ALTO,
CONTRALTO, SOPRANO (crypt). 2. Gk myth *HEBE*,

cupbearer to the *gods* (**Rom** = JUVENTAS).
BARMAN *HOST*, INNKEEPER, *LANDLORD*, PUBLICAN
[*Ganymede*]. MUSICIAN (crypt).
BARNET Place (UK). HAIR (*rh sl*).
BARON B. LORD, *NOBLE*. [Richthofen; Rothschild].
MERCHANT. *JOINT* (meat).
BARONET BT, BART, KT; KNIGHT; SIR.
BARREL CASK, *MEASURE* (beer). CYLINDER, DRUM
(capstan, winch). GUN PART.
BARRIE J. M., *WRITER* [Peter Pan; **chars**: *Crocodile, Darlings,*
Capt *Hook*, Lost boys, Nana, *Peter, Smee*, Tiger-Lily,
Tinkerbell, *Wendy*; (Never-)Never Land].
BARRIER *FENCE, GATE*, RAILING; BOUNDARY,
OBSTACLE. DAM. *LISTS*, PALISADE (jousting).
DIVIDER; *NET* (*tennis*).
BART BARONET. BARTHOLOMEW. *PIRATE*.
BASE (s/l *bass*). *BOTTOM* (**opp** = *top*); FOUNDATION,
GROUNDWORK, PRINCIPLE [~ on, see *model*].
ARMY CAMP, SUPPORT AREA. ESTABLISH. RELY.
COWARDLY, DESPICABLE, LOW, *MEAN*, MENIAL.
BASEBALL *FOOTBALL GROUND* (Derby County). GAME
(**originator**: Cartwright) [Joe di Maggio, Babe Ruth, rounders,
softball]; **celeb teams** (*US*): Boston Red Sox, Brooklyn Dodgers,
Chicago Cubs, Knickerbockers, New York Giants, New York
Yankees, Phillies; **venue**: Houston Astrodome.
BASHFUL COY, DIFFIDENT, *MODEST*, SHEEPISH, *SHY* (**opp**
= arrogant). *DWARF* (Snow White).
BASIC EDUCATION RRR (crypt).
BASKERVILLE *TYPEFACE*. **Pl** = Hound of ~ (*Holmes*).
BASS (s/l *base*). DEEP-SOUNDING, LOW (**opp** = alto). *FISH,*
PERCH, SEA-DACE, SEA-WOLF. *STRAIT. BEER* ®,
DRINK. FIBRE, LIME-BARK, TIER [*raffia*].
BASTARD 1. ABNORMAL, BOGUS, COUNTERFEIT,
DIFFICULT, INFERIOR, IRREGULAR, SPURIOUS.
2. HYBRID, ILLEGITIMATE, WHORESON (arch); **celeb**:
Philip Falconbridge (*Shak*, John); ~ of Orleans (*Shak*, H.vi);
Don Juan (*Shak*, Much Ado); Margarellan (*Shak*, T & C); ~
son of Gloucester (*Shak*, Lear); Duke William of Normandy
(William I of Eng).
BAT 1. IMPLEMENT; RACKET, RACQUET; **comp** =
ball. STRIKE; BATSMAN. PACE, *RATE*, WINK.
BINGE, SPREE. 2. Nocturnal flying mammal: Barbastelle,

Bechstein's ~, Big-eared ~, Brown ~, Bulldog ~, Corollea
~, Daubenton's ~, Dawn ~, Diadem ~, Flittermouse,
Flying Fox, Free-tail ~, Fruit ~, Fruit-eating, Ghost ~,
Grey ~, Horseshoe ~, Kalong (largest), Leaf-nosed ~,
Long-eared ~, Mastiff ~, Noctule ~, Pipistrelle, Pteropus,
Rear/reremouse, Rosetta ~, Serotine, Tent-making ~, Tomb
~, Vampire, Wrinkle-faced ~. 3. BAGGAGE (arch mil). Pl =
CRAZY, *MAD*.
BATH 1. DECORATION, ORDER. CITY, SPA; AQUAE SULIS
(Rom); ~ and Wells (eccl See). BATHE, LAVE, RINSE,
SOAK, WASH; LAVATORY, TUB, VESSEL, WASH-TUB,
JACUZZI, SAUNA, STEAM ~, TURKISH ~. Pl =
SWIMMING ~; HAMMAM (Turk). 2. **Celeb ~ connections**:
Agamemnon (k in ~ by *Clytemnestra*); *Archimedes* (discovered
displacement in his ~; Eureka!); Diogenes (lived in a tub;
crypt); Marat (k in ~ by Charlotte Corday); Poppaea (~ of
asses' milk for complexion); Anthony Perkins (as Norman Bates
in Hitchcock film Psycho, murdered girl in *shower* ~).
BATTALION BN, MEN, *SOLDIERS*, TROOPS.
BATTER BEAT, BREAK, BRUISE, HAMMER, HIT, *STRIKE*.
COOKING MIX. PLAYER AT BAT (*baseball, cricket*).
BATTERY ASSAULT, BEATING. *GUNS* (crypt).
ACCUMULATOR, PILE (elect). COOP, HENHOUSE.
INNING(S) (*baseball, cricket*; crypt).
BATTING WINKING. AT STRIKE, *IN*, STRIKING (*baseball,
cricket*).
BATTLE STRUGGLE. ARGUMENT. TOWN. *FIGHT, WAR*:
celeb:

Air

ATLANTIC	GULF	MOHNE DAM
BERLIN	LEYTE GULF	PEARL HARBOR
BLITZ	*LONDON*	PLOESTI
BRITAIN	MALTA	RUHR
CORAL SEA	MATAPAN	SCHWEINFURT
GUERNICA	MIDWAY	TARANTO

Sea

ACTIUM	COPENHAGEN
ARMADA	CORAL SEA
ATLANTIC	FALKLANDS
CAPE ST VINCENT	GUADALCANAL

JUTLAND   PEARL HARBOR
LEPANTO   RIVER PLATE
LEYTE GULF   *SALAMIS*
MATAPAN   TARANTO
MIDWAY   TRAFALGAR
NILE

Nelson

BASTIA (siege)   NILE (Aboukir Bay)
CALVI (lost eye)   TENERIFE (lost arm)
COPENHAGEN ('I see no   TOULON
   signal')   TRAFALGAR (death)
CAPE ST VINCENT

Land

ALAMEIN   GALLIPOLI
ANZIO   GETTYSBURG
ARDENNES   HASTINGS
ARNHEM   IWO-JIMA
AUSTERLITZ   JENA
BALACLAVA   KOREA
BORODINO   LITTLE BIG HORN
BULGE   MARNE
BULL RUN   MONS
BURMA   OKINAWA
CASSINO   SHILOH
CORUNNA   SOMME
CRETE   STALINGRAD
DIEN BIEN PHU   TOBRUK
DIEPPE   VERDUN
DUNKIRK   VIMY RIDGE
FALKLANDS   *WATERLOO*
FLANDERS   YPRES

Civil War

ADWALTON MOOR   LANSDOWN
CHALGROVE FIELD   LOSTWITHIEL
CROPREDY BRIDGE   MARSTON MOOR
DUNBAR   NASEBY (last)
EDGEHILL (first)   NEWBURY
GAINSBOROUGH   PRESTON

ROUNDWAY DOWN
SELBY
TURNHAM GREEN

WINNINGTON BRIDGE
WORCESTER (final)

Alfred the Great

ALDERSHOT
ASHDOWN (first)
BENFLEET (last)
CHICHESTER
CHIPPENHAM
EDDINGTON (Ethandun)

EXETER
LONDON
RIVER STOUR
ROCHESTER
WAREHAM

Wars of the Roses

BARNET
BOSWORTH FIELD (last)
EDGECOT
HEDGLEY MOOR
HEXHAM
LOSECOAT FIELD

MORTIMER'S CROSS
ST ALBANS (first)
TEWKESBURY
TOWTON
WAKEFIELD

Classical

Megiddo	1479	B.C.	Deborah & Barak	beat Sisera (Armageddon)
Troy	1250	B.C.	Agamemnon (Gk)	beat Paris (Trojan)
Marathon	491	B.C.	Miltiades (Gk)	beat Datis (Pers)
Thermopylae	480	B.C.	Xerxes (Pers)	beat Leonidas (Sparta)
Salamis	480	B.C.	Themistocles (Gk)	beat Xerxes (Pers)
Plataea	479	B.C.	Themistocles (GK)	beat Mardonius (Pers)
Granicus	334	B.C.	Alexander	beat Memnon (Pers)
Issus	333	B.C.	Alexander	beat Darius (Pers)
Arbela	331	B.C.	Alexander	beat Darius (Pers)
Hydaspes	326	B.C.	Alexander	beat Darius (Pers)
Cannae	216	B.C.	Hannibal	beat Romans
Zama	202	B.C.	Scipio (Rom)	beat Hannibal
Philippi	42	B.C.	Octavian & Antony	beat Brutus & Cassius
Actium	31	B.C.	Octavian	beat Antony & Cleopatra
Masada	73	A.D.	Romans	beat Jews

American War of Independence

Brandywine River
Brooklyn
Bunker Hill
Camden

Charleston
Concord
Cowperis
Germantown

Guilford Court House
Heights of Abraham
Lexington (1st)
Saratoga

Trenton
White Plains
Yorktown (last)

American Civil War

Antietam
Appomatox (last)
Atlanta
Bull Run
Chancellorsville
Chattanooga
Cold Harbor
Fort Hudson

Fredericksburg
Harper's Ferry (1st skirmish)
Fort Sumter (1st)
Gettysburg
Vicksburg
Shilo
Wilderness

BATTLESHIP HMS, USS. DREADNOUGHT. CAPITAL SHIP, IRONCLAD. SHIP OF THE LINE. *WEAPON*.

BATTLE ZONE ARENA, FIELD, FRONT, *THEATRE*, WAR ZONE.

BAWL (s/l *ball*). CRY, HOWL, SHOUT, WAIL. REPRIMAND.

BAY (s/l *Bey*). BARK, HOWL [*dog, hound*]. *LAUREL TREE. HERB. HORSE*. BIGHT, *GULF*, INLET. RECESS, *SIDELINE*. BROWN *COLOUR*.

BB BOYS BRIGADE, CADETS. BARDOT (theat). BIG BROTHER (*Orwell*). VERY SOFT (pencil).

BBC BROADCASTING, RADIO, TV. AUNTIE.

BC BEFORE CHRIST. BRITISH COLUMBIA (*Province*, Can).

BDS DENTIST.

BEACHCOMBER LONGSHOREMAN, SCAVENGER, VAGRANT. *WAVE*. HUMORIST.

BEADLE CANDLE. ATTENDANT (Heb); OFFICIAL, USHER; **celeb**: BUMBLE (*Dickens*, Oliver).

BEAK *BILL*, NEB (Sc), PECKER (mandible). *MASTER*, TEACHER (sl). MAGISTRATE (sl).

BEAKER BRONZE *AGE* FOLK, PRIMITIVE MAN. EWER, JAR, JUG, POT, URN. *BIRD*, HEN, LAYER (crypt).

BEAM LIGHT, RAY, SHAFT, SPOT. SMILE. JOIST, RAFTER, *SUMMER, TIMBER*. BREADTH, WIDTH (naut).

BEAR (s/l *bare*). ANIMAL; URSA, URSUS; BRUIN; ['Exit, pursued by a ~' W Tale, *Shak*; *Elisha*]; **assembly**: sleuth; **breeds**: BLACK, BROWN, BRUANG, GIANT PANDA, GRIZZLY, HIMALAYAN, HONEY, KOALA, KODIAK,

POLAR, *SLOTH*, SPECTACLED, SUN [**offspring** = cub];
celeb: ARCAS (his m changed to a ~ by Zeus), BALOO,
BOOBOO, MARY PLAIN, PADDINGTON, POOH,
RUPERT, THREE BEARS (Goldilocks), YOGI. *AIRCRAFT*
(CIS). CARRY, GIVE BIRTH. ENDURE, SUPPORT.
OVERLOOK, SUBTEND. *ISLAND. CONSTELLATION.*
SPECULATOR (comm; **opp** = *bull*). **Pl** = *Football team* (US).
BEARD *BEAVER*. BRISTLES, GROWTH: goatee, imperial,
Vandyke. AWN, EAR (wheat). DEFY.
BEARER *BED*. CARRIER, *MESSENGER. MOTHER* (crypt).
BEARING 1. E, N, S, W (or NE, SW etc); HEADING. AIR,
APPEARANCE, ASPECT, *CARRIAGE, LOOK*, MIEN;
PORT, PORTAGE. ACCOUCHEMENT, CHILDBIRTH,
LYING-IN (crypt). BALL-RACE, ROLLER. LEANING,
PUSHING, RELATION, REFERENCE. CHARGE,
DEVICE (*herald*). 2. Word attached to or 'bearing' another, e.g.
Harsh south wind bearing east (7) = AUSTER*E.
BEAT BEST, CHASTISE, LATHER, LICK, OVERCOME,
WORST; SLIPPER, *TAN*, THRASH, WHIP (**opp** = *lose*).
WHISK (cook). PULSE, RHYTHM. PERPLEX. DEFORM,
SHAPE (metal). CLOSE-HAUL, WORK TO WINDWARD
(naut).
BEATER (s/l *beta*). CONQUEROR, *VICTOR*. GAME ROUSER
(shooting). CARPET DUSTER. MIXER, WHIPPER,
WHISK; COOK (crypt). HEART, PULSATOR. TANNER.
DRUMMER (crypt).
BEAT UP COSH, MUG [GBH]. TAEB (dn).
BEAUTY 1. PULCHRITUDE, GOOD LOOKS. 2. **Gods: Gk**
and Rom = *APOLLO*; **goddesses: Gk** = *APHRODITE*,
THE GRACES (q.v.); **Rom** = VENUS. [*Adonis*, Antineus,
Aphrodite, Apollo, Ganymede, Helen, Paris, Psyche, Venus (de
Milo)].
BEAUTY SPOT FACE-PATCH. DELL, PANORAMA, VISTA.
BEAVER *BEARD*. FUR. *RODENT* (*habitation*). WORK AT.
FACEGUARD, VISOR [*armour*].
BECAUSE AS, FOR, SINCE.
BECK *BROOK, RIVER*, STREAM. NOD, SIGNAL; **comp** =
CALL.
BECOME TURN INTO. BEFIT, FLATTER, *SUIT*.
BED COUCH, DIVAN, *LITTER*, MATTRESS (and see
furniture for types); **comp** = board, breakfast [*Hans Andersen.*
Procrustes]. BASE, FOUNDATION, *SEAT*, STRATUM.

PLANT. FLOWER~, *PLOT.* SEABOTTOM.
BEDDING BEDCLOTHES, BEDLINEN, BLANKETS, DUVET,
EIDERDOWN, SHEETS; TUCKING UP. GARDENING
(crypt).
BEE (s/l *B, be*). *INSECT*; (BUSY) WORKER (**Pl** = TUC);
COMBER (crypt); **assembly** = hive, swarm. 'DEBORAH'
[*Potter.* Queen ~]. **Comps** = birds, knees.
BEER (s/l *bier*). ALE, BASS ®, BITTER, *DRINK*, LAGER,
MILD, OCTOBER. MUG, PINT (*measure*) [**comp** = skittles].
PIG'S EAR (*rh sl*) [*inventor* = Gambrinus].
BEES AND *MONEY* (*rh sl*).
BEETLE 1. BUG, INSECT (coleopter) [*collector*; *study*]; **breeds**:
BEECHAFER, BISCUIT ~, BLACK ~, BOMBARDIER ~,
BUPRESTID, (COCK)CHAFER, COCKROACH,
DEATH WATCH ~, DOR, DRUGSTORE ~, DUNG ~,
GLOW-WORM, RAM ~, SCARAB, SPIDER ~, TIGER ~,
WILLOW ~: **celeb** (**fict**): Arthur Corkran, M'Turk
and ~ (Stalky & Co, *Kipling*); ALEXANDER ~ (*Milne*);
JABIZRI (*Lofting*); Through the Looking-Glass (*Alice*).
2. ANASTIGMATIC. DICE GAME. OVERHANGING,
PROJECTING; SCOWLING, SHAGGY. RUN, SCURRY.
CAR (VW, VOLKSWAGEN ®). HAMMER, MAUL.
BEFORE ANTE, B, ERE, PRE (**opp** = after).
~ **CHRIST** B.C.
BEGETTER WH (Shakespeare). *FATHER*, SIRE.
BEGGAR MENDICANT [*friar, patron saint*]. BREAK;
EXHAUST.
BEGINNER 1. L; DEB, LEARNER, TYRO. *STARTER.* **Pl** =
opening actors of new scene (theat). 2. Use first letter of word
concerned, e.g. **Circus beginner** = C.
BEHEAD 1. DECAPITATE, EXECUTE, GUILLOTINE, TOP.
2. Omit first letter, e.g. **Behead them on the edge** (3) = (*)HEM.
BEHIND TIME 1. *LATE.* 2. Word after synonym for time, e.g.
Under age or behind time (5) = MIN*OR.
Belg Belgium, ~ian.
BELGIUM B (*car plate*). COCKPIT (of Europe).
BELL (s/l belle). DINGALING, DING-DONG, *RINGER*;
INSTRUMENT (mus) [campanology: ANGELUS, SANCTUS,
Quasimodo (Dumas)]; **celeb**: BIG BEN (Westminster), BOOM
(RAF ch), CENTENNIAL (US 1976), CZAR KOLOKOL
(Moscow), GREAT TOM (Oxford), GT PAUL (St Paul's),
GT PETER (York Minster), LIBERTY (US 1752), LUTINE

(*Lloyd's*), SEBASTOPOL (Windsor). INVENTOR (Alexander
Graham ~, telephone). *PAINTER. Model (Holmes).* WRITER
(*Brontë*). **Pl** = TIME (naut watchkeeping).
BELLEROPHON 1. Gk myth hero who rode *Pegasus* and slew
the *monster Chim(a)era.* 2. Br warship which took Napoleon's
surrender.
BELLOWS MAKER *BULL, COW,* OX; *LOWER* (crypt). *FLUTE*
(*Shak*, MND).
BELL RINGING CAMPANOLOGY; **changes**: Bob Major, Bob
Maximus, Bob Minor, Bob Royal, Bob Triple, Grandsire
Triple, Great Tom, Nine Tailors, Oxford Treble Bob, Treble
Bob, Yorkshire Surprise Major [Quasimodo]. TINNITUS.
TINTINABULATION.
BELONG *FIT,* GO WITH, *SUIT.* OWNED BY.
PROCRASTINATE, TARRY (crypt).
BELSHAZZAR Variant spelling of *BALTHAZAR.* The bibl s of
Nebuchadnezzar; at ~'s feast a moving hand wrote 'Mene mene
tekel upharsin.' *Daniel* interpreted this as 'You are weighed in the
balances and found wanting.' That night ~ was k.
BEM BRITISH EMPIRE MEDAL: *DECORATION, MEDAL.*
BEND *S; U;* CURVE. *BOW,* STOOP, SUBMIT. APPLY (to task).
KNOT (*fisherman's* ~, sheet ~). PERVERT. SPREE. STRIPE
(*herald*) [dexter; sinister (bastardy)]. **Pl** = Decompression
sickness (astronauts, divers).
BENDER BINGE, SPREE. STOOP. PERVERTER. HINGE,
JOINT; ELBOW, KNEE, KNUCKLE (crypt). *S, U* (crypt).
BENT *BOWED,* CRANKED, CURVED, OUT OF TRUE,
TWISTED (**opp** = straight); EMBOWED (*herald*).
DISHONEST.
BERMUDA ISLAND. *TRIANGLE.* **Pl** = *SHORTS.* London
district (arch).
BERRY DOLLAR (US), POUND (sl). *FRUIT* (without stone);
also HIP, HAW, SLOE. [Dornford Yates char].
BERYL *GEM,* PRECIOUS STONE; AQUAMARINE,
EMERALD (blue, green, white, yellow). GREY, REID (theat).
BESIDES *AGAIN,* AS WELL, ELSE, MOREOVER,
OTHERWISE. ALONGSIDE.
BE SORRY APOLOGIZE, CARE, MOPE, REGRET, RUE.
BEST A, AI, *ACE,* NO I; CHOICE, FIRST RATE, TOPS (**opp**
= *worst*). *BEAT*; WORST.
BET ANTE, STAKE. GAMBLE, PUNT, RISK, SPECULATE,
WAGER; **types**: *ACCUMULATOR,* CANADIAN, DOUBLE,

HEINZ, TREBLE, TRI-CAST, YANKEE.

BETA (s/l *beater*). B, *SECOND* (LETTER). ELECTRON.

BETRAY(ER) GIVE AWAY, *GRASS*, INFORM, NARK, PEACH, RAT, *SHOP*, SING, SNEAK, SNOUT, SPLIT, SQUEAL, STOOL PIGEON, TELL-TALE(S).

BETTER IMPROVED, SUPERIOR. GAMBLER, PUNTER, SPECULATOR; LAYER (crypt).

BETTING ODDS, SP. GAMBLING (and see *bet*).

BEVY *ASSEMBLY*, COMPANY (of beauty, ladies, *larks*, *quails*).

BEY (s/l *bay*). GOVERNOR, *NOBLE*, OFFICIAL (*Turk*).

BIBLE AV, RV; NT, OT. BOOK OF BOOKS. LAST WORD, MANUAL. [see *Kings* ~].

BIBLICAL TOWN AERE, *AI*, APHEK, BETHEL, CANA, DAN, *DOR*, ENDOR, GATH, GAZA, GEBA, JAHAZ, JERICHO, NAIN, NEVE, NOB, SIDON, *TYRE*, UR, ZIPH.

BIBLIOMANIA *Obsession* with books.

BIBLIOPHILE *Lover* of books.

BIER (s/l *beer*). FUNERAL LITTER, HEARSE, LAST TRIP/VEHICLE.

BIG OS, LARGE (**opp** = little, small); TIDY (sl). BOASTFUL.

BIG GAME 1. CHAMPIONSHIP, (CUP) FINAL, (TEST) MATCH (all crypt). 2. BEASTS, JUNGLE DWELLERS, WILD ANIMALS, -LIFE, e.g. *ANTELOPE* (q.v.), *BEAR*, *CAT* (q.v.), *CROCODILE*, ELEPHANT, ELK, GIRAFFE, HIPPOPOTAMUS, HYENA, JACKAL, *KANGAROO*, MAMMOTH (ex), *MONKEY* (q.v.), RHINOCEROS, WOLF, *ZEBRA* [*deer*, *dolphin*, *shark*, *whale*].

BIGHT (s/l *bite*, byte). *BAY*, *GULF*, INLET. COIL, LOOP (naut).

BIKE RACE TT [Isle of Man]. TOUR DE FRANCE.

BILL *AC*, *ACCOUNT*, *CHECK*, INVOICE, *NOTE*, RECKONING, *SETTLEMENT*, TAB. BANKNOTE. POSTER; ANNOUNCE. *MEASURE* (parl). HALBERD, *PIKE*, *WEAPON*. WILLIAM, WM [Old ~ (Bairnsfather)]. *BEAK*; PECK; **comp** = coo; Mary (William and ~). *LIZARD* (*Alice*). **Pl** = *Football team* (US).

BILLIARDS *GAME* [*Cleopatra*; ' . . . elliptical ~ balls' (Mikado, *G and S*); cannon; *snooker*, spot].

BILLYCOCK BOWLER *HAT*.

BINGO 1. (BOARD) GAME: HOUSEY-HOUSEY, KENO, LOTTO, TOMBOLA. 2. Exclamation as Eureka! ~ Little (*Wodehouse* char).

BIRD *GIRL*, POPSY, YOUNG WOMAN (sl). RASPBERRY (sl). PRISON SENTENCE, *TIME* (sl). *WRITER*. FEATHERED VERTEBRATE; BEAKER, DICKY, LAYER; and see **flightless** ~s [Audubon, *Male & female, offspring, study*]; **celeb**: EPOPS (Aristophanes); **comp** = bees; **pl** = aves; **breeds**:

2-letters
KA
OO

3-letters

AUK (ex)	ERN	*MOA* (ex)	ROC (myth)
AWL	HEN	*NUN*	ROK (myth)
BEE	JAY	*OWL*	RUC (myth)
COB	KAE	PAU	SUN
COW	KEA	*PEN*	*TIT*
ELK	MAO	*PIE*	TUI
EMU	MAY ~	POE	WRY

4-letters

BAYA	*HAWK*	NYAS	*SMEE*
BELL	HERN (arch)	OVEN ~	SMEW
BLUE	HUMA (myth)	PAUW	*SWAN*
BUBO	IBIS	PAVO	TAHA
CIRL	KAGU	PERN	TEAL
COCK	KAKA	PICA	TERN
COOT	KITE	PIET	TODY
CRAX	KIWI	*POLL*	URIA
CROW	*KNOT*	PUFF ~	WEKA
DODO (ex)	KOEL	*RAIL*	*WREN*
DOVE	*LARK*	RHEA	XEMA
DUCK	LOON	RICE ~	YAUP
ERNE	LORY	*ROOK*	YITE
EYAS	LOVE ~	*RUFF*	YOIT
FOWL	LYRE ~	RYPE	YUNX
GAWK	MINA	SAND ~	ZATI
GOWK	MYNA	SONG ~	
GUAN	NENE	SHAG	
GULL	NIAS	SKUA	

5-letters

AGAMI	ANNET	BIDDY	BOWET
AMSEL	*ARGUS*	BOOBY	BRENT

BUCCO	JAGER	POKER	SKITE
CAPON	JUNCO	POLLY	*SNIPE*
CHICK	*LAYER*	POULT	SPIZA
CLAIK	LOXIA	PURRE	*STILT*
COLIN	LYRIE	*QUAIL*	STINT
CRAKE	MACAW	RALPH	STORK
CRANE	MADGE	RAVEN	STRIX
CURRE	MAVIS	*REEVE*	*SWIFT*
DAKER	MERLE	RIFLE ~	TARIN
DIVER	MOLLY	RISSA	TEREK
DRAKE	MONAL	*ROBIN*	TIDDY
DUNNE	MURRE	RODGE	TOPAU
EAGLE	MYNAH	RUDGE	TOPET
EGRET	NANDU	RYPER	TWITE
EIDER	NELLY	SAKER	URILE
FINCH	NODDY	SALLY	URUBU
FRANK	ORNIS	SCAUP	VEERY
GLEDE	ORTYX	SCOBY	VIREO
GOOSE	OUSEL	SCOPS	WADER
GREBE	OUZEL	*SCOUT*	WHAUP
HERON	PAAUW	*SCULL*	WHILK
HOBBY	PEWIT	SENEX	WONGA
HOMER	PICUS	SERIN	YACOU
IMBER	PIPIT	SITTA	

6-letters

ADELIE	CUSHAT	HOOPOE
AIGLET	CYGNET	HOOPOO
ANANAS	DARTER	JABIRU
ANCONA	DIPPER	JACANA
ARGALA	DRONGO	JERKIN
AVOCET	DUNLIN	KELTIS
BOWESS	EAGLET	KONDOR
BULBUL	FALCON	LANNER
CANARY	FULMAR	LINNET
CHOUGH	GANDER	LORIOT
CONDOR	GANNET	*MAGPIE*
CORBIE	GENTOO	MARROT
CORVUS	GODWIT	MARTIN
CUCKOO	GRAKLE	*MERLIN*
CULVER	*GROUSE*	MERULA
CURLEW	*GUINEA*	MISSEL

MISTLE	PUFFIN	TATLER
MOPOKE	PULLET	TERCEL
MOT-MOT	QUEEST	TEWHIT
MUTTON	QUELEA	THRUSH
NANDOO	QUEZAL	TOM-TIT
NESTOR	RAPTOR	TOUCAN
NICKER	*REDCAP*	TROGON
ORIOLE	ROLLER	TURBIT
OSPREY	RUDDOC	TURKEY
OUZLEM (myth)	SCOTER	*TURNER*
OXBIRD	SEAHEN	TYSTIE
PARROT	SEAMEW	*WEAVER* ~
PARSON	SERULA	WIGEON
PASTOR	SHRIKE	WILLET
PAVONE (arch)	SICSAC	WITWAL
PEAHEN	SIMBIL	XENOPS
PEEWIT	SIMURG	YAFFLE
PETREL	(Persmyth)	YAFFIL
PHENIX (myth)	SISKIN	YUCKER
PHOEBE	SOLAND	ZICSAC
PIGEON	SPARVE	ZOO-ZOO
PLOVER	SULTAN	
POUTER	SURREY	

7-letters

APTERYN	CROMBEC	HAWK-OWL
AWL-BIRD	DIDIDAE	HICKWAY
BEE-BIRD	DOTTREL	HOATZIN
BITTERN	DUNNOCK	JACAMAR
BLUE-CAP	FEN-DUCK	JACKDAW
BLUE-JAY	FERN-OWL	KESTREL
BLUE-TIT	FLUSHER	LAPWING
BUNTING	GADWALL	LAVROCK
BUSHTIT	GOBBLER	*MALLARD*
BUSTARD	GORCOCK	MARABOU
BUTCHER ~	GOSHAWK	MARTLET
BUZZARD	GRAY-LAG	MAY-BIRD
CHICKEN	GRAY-OWL	MINIVET
COAL-TIT	GREY-HEN	MOCKING ~
COLIBRI	GREY-LAG	MOORHEN
COW-BIRD	HALCYON (myth)	ORTOLAN
CREEPER	*HARRIER*	*OSTRICH*

OVEN-TIT	ROOSTER	TARROCK
PEACOCK	ROSELLA	TIERCEL
PELICAN	ROYSTON	TITLARK
PENGUIN	RUDDOCK	TOURACO
PETEREL	SAWBILL	TUMBLER
PHAETON	SAWWHET	VULTURE
PHOENIX (myth)	SCOOPER	WAGTAIL
PINNOCK	SEA-CROW	WARBLER
PINTADO	SEA-DOVE	WAXWING
PINTAIL	SEA-DUCK	WHOOPER
POCHARD	SEAGULL	WIDGEON
POULTRY	SEA-HAWK	WILLOCK
QUABIRD	SKIMMER	WIMBREL
QUETZAL	SKYLARK	WOOD-OWL
RADDOCK	SNOW-OWL	WRYBILL
RATITAE	SPARROW	WRYNECK
REDPOLL	SUNBIRD	WYANDOT
REDTAIL	*SWALLOW*	YELDRIN
REDWING	TANAGER	

8-letters

ACCENTOR	DUN-DIVER	MARSH-HEN
ADJUTANT	EAGLE-OWL	MARSH-TIT
ALCATRAS	ELEPHANT ~	MIRE-CROW
AMADAVAT	FALCONET	MOORCOCK
BARNACLE	FENGOOSE	MOREPORK
BEE-EATER	FIRETAIL	NESTLING
BELL-BIRD	FISH-HAWK	NUTHATCH
BLACKCAP	FLAMINGO	OVEN-BIRD
BLUEBIRD	FORKTAIL	OX-PECKER
BOATBILL	GARGANEY	PARADISE, ~ of
BOBOLINK	HACKBOLT	PARAKEET
CARACARA	HAWFINCH	PARAQUET
CARDINAL	HEATH-HEN	PAROQUET
CARGOOSE	HOACTZIN	*PENELOPE*
CHURN-OWL	HORNBILL	PHEASANT
COQUETTE	LANDRAIL	PHILOMEL
CURASSOW	LANNERET	PICKEREL
DABCHICK	LINGBIRD	PUFF-BIRD
DINORNIS	LOVEBIRD	RAINBIRD
DOTTEREL	LYRE-BIRD	REDSHANK
DUCKLING	MARABOUT	REDSTART

REEDBIRD
REEDLING
RICE-BIRD
RING-BILL
RING-DOVE
RINGTAIL
ROCKDOVE
RUBECULA
SAND-BIRD
SAND-COCK
SAND-LARK
SARCELLE
SARDELLE
SCREAMER

SEA-EAGLE
SEA-QUAIL
SEA-RAVEN
SEDGE-HEN
SHELDUCK
SHOEBILL
SNOWBIRD
SONGBIRD
SONGSTER
STARLING
THRESHER
THROSTLE
TITMOUSE
TITTEREL

WATER-HEN
WHEATEAR
WHIMBREL
WHINCHAT
WILDFOWL
WOODCOCK
WOODLARK
WRANNOCK
XANTHURA
YELDRING
YELDROCK
ZOPILOTE

9-letters

ALBATROSS
BALTIMORE ~
BECCAFICO
BLACKBIRD
BLACKCOCK
BLACK SWAN
BOWERBIRD
BRAMBLING
BULLFINCH
CASSOWARY
CHAFFINCH
CHICKADEE
COCKATIEL
CORMORANT
CORNCRAKE
CROSSBILL
FIELDFARE
FIRECREST
GALLINULE
GERFALCON

GOLDCREST
GOLDENEYE
GOLDFINCH
GOOSANDER
GUILLEMOT
GYRFALCON
HIRUNDINE
KITTIWAKE
LORRIKEET
MERGANSER
NIGHTHAWK
OSSIFRAGE
PARDALOTE
PARTRIDGE
PEREGRINE
PHALAROPE
PHILOMELA
PTARMIGAN
RAZORBILL
REDBREAST

RED GROUSE
RIFLE-BIRD
RING OUSEL
ROSSIGNOL
SANDPIPER
SAPSUCKER
SECRETARY ~
SHELDRAKE
SNOW GOOSE
SOOTY TERN
SPOONBILL
STONECHAT
SWORDBILL
THICKHEAD
TROCHILUS
TRUMPETER
TURNSTONE
WATERFOWL
WIDOWBIRD

10+ letters

ARCHAEOPTERYX (ex)
BALTIMORE BIRD
~ OF PARADISE
BISHOPBIRD

BLACK GROUSE
BLACKTHROAT
BUDGERIGAR
BLUETHROAT

BRENT GOOSE
BUSH CREEPER
BUTCHERBIRD
CANADA GOOSE
CANVAS-BACK
CAPERCAILLIE
CARRION CROW
CHANTICLEER
CHIFFCHAFF
CORNBUNTING
CRESTED GREBE
CRESTED PIGEON
CRESTED TIT
DEMOISELLE
DISHWASHER
EMPEROR PENGUIN
FANTAIL PIGEON
FLYCATCHER
GOLDEN EAGLE
GOLDEN ORIOLE
GOLDEN PHEASANT
GREENFINCH
GUINEAFOWL
HERRING GULL
HOUSEMARTIN
HUMMINGBIRD
KINGFISHER
KING PENGUIN
KOOKABURRA
LAMMERGEIER
MARSH WARBLER
MEADOW PIPIT
MISSELTHRUSH
MOCKINGBIRD

MUTTONBIRD
NIGHTINGALE
NUTCRACKER
OYSTER-CATCHER
REED WARBLER
RIFLE WARBLER
ROADRUNNER
ROCK PIGEON
SANDERLING
SAND GROUSE
SAND MARTIN
SCISSORBILL
SEA SWALLOW
SECRETARY BIRD
SHEARWATER
SNOW BUNTING
SOLAN GOOSE
SONG THRUSH
SPARROWHAWK
STORMY PETREL
TURTLEDOVE
WATERWAGTAIL
WEAVERBIRD
WHIP-POOR-WILL
WHITETHROAT
WILLOW WARBLER
WHOOPER SWAN
WOODPECKER
WOODPIGEON
YAFFINGALE
YELLOW BUNTING
YELLOWHAMMER
ZEBRA FINCH

BIRDIE One under par on a *golf-course*, hence PAR*I or PAR*ONE (dn). [camera].

BIRTHSTONE Jan = *GARNET*; **Feb** = *AMETHYST*; **Mar** = *BLOODSTONE*; **Apr** = *DIAMOND*; **May** = *EMERALD*; **Jun** = *AGATE*; **Jul** = *CORNELIAN*; **Aug** = *SARDONYX*; **Sep** = *CHRYSOLITE*; **Oct** = *OPAL*; **Nov** = *TOPAZ*; **Dec** = *TURQUOISE*.

BISHOP *CHURCHMAN* (q.v. for list), CLERGYMAN, DIOCESAN [*episcopal sig; see*]; BB, RR, Rt Rev; **celeb**: Ely (*Shak*); Winchester (*Shak*: Beaufort, Carlisle, Gardiner); CHESSPIECE, *ROOK*. *Military leader* (air). *POET*.

BIT *BORE*, CUTTING IRON, DRILL, *HEAD*, PIECE. CHEWED, GRIPPED, NIPPED. BRIDLE, HACKAMORE, SNAFFLE (*harness*). MORSEL. SOMEWHAT. CONTRIBUTION. BINARY DIGIT, COMPUTER INFORMATION. **Pl comp** = *pieces*.

BITCH *FEMALE* DOG/FOX/OTTER/WOLF. MALICIOUS WOMAN, TERMAGANT, VIXEN. GRUMBLE, MUDDLE.

BITE (s/l *bight*, byte). CHEW, NIP; FOOD, MEAL. BORROW, EXTORT. STING. GRIP. INFECT.

BL BRITISH LEGION. BRITISH LEYLAND.

BLACK B; *COLOUR*; DARK; SABLE (*herald*); [~ Rod, Garter]. *SEA*. SNOOKER BALL (score 7). **Comp** = *blue; white*.

BLACKBIRD SONGBIRD (turdus merula; thrush family); MERLE (arch, Sc) [24 ~s baked in a pie]. NEGRO SLAVE. SPY-PLANE (US mil).

BLACKFRIARS DOMINICANS, PREACHING *FRIARS*. *THAMES BRIDGE*.

BLACKSMITH FARRIER, FORGER, METAL-WORKER [*Company* (livery)]; **celeb**: JAMES BURTON (Kingsley), JOE GARGERY (Great Ex, *Dickens*), THE VILLAGE ~ (Longfellow). ST DUNSTAN (trad).

BLADE LEAF. CHISEL, KNIFE, SWORD. DASHING FELLOW. Part of bat, oar, paddle wheel, propeller, spade, turbine.

BLAZE BRIGHT FLAME, BURN, *FIRE*. *COLOUR*, EMIT LIGHT. PROCLAIM. MARK ON HORSE; SLASH A TREE.

BLAZER COLOURED JACKET, SCHOOL COAT. ARSONIST; FIREMAN (crypt).

BLEND(ED) *Anag. ADMIX*, AMALGAM, MIX, MIXTURE.

BLEW (s/l *blue*). PANTED, PUFFED, WAFTED. BURST, EXPLODED, FUSED. SPENT. SQUANDERED.

BLIND 1. RASH, RECKLESS, UNSWERVING. CONCEALED, DEAD-END, PLAIN, WALLED-UP. DAZZLE, DECEIVE. ANOPTIC, SIGHTLESS, UNSEEING; **celeb**: Earl of Gloucester (Lear, *Shak*); Edward *Rochester* (Jane Eyre, *Brontë*); Hod (Nor myth [*Balder*]); Homer (Gk); *Isaac* (bibl); Helen Keller (US); King John of Bohemia (hist); Milton (*poet*);

Nydia (Bulwer Lytton); *Oedipus* (Gk myth); ~ Pew (*pirate, Stevenson*); Phineus (Gk myth); *Samson* (bibl); Tiresias (Gk myth); Wandering Willie (*Scott*, Redgauntlet); *bat*, mole, *owl*. And see *one-eyed*. 2. AWNING, CURTAIN, SCREEN, SHUTTER, SUNSHADE. DUMMY, MASK, PRETEXT, SMOKE-SCREEN, STALKING-HORSE, SUBTERFUGE, VEIL. DRUNK (sl).

BLONDEL MINSTREL [*Lionheart*, ransom, Richard].

BLOODSTONE *GEM*, SEMI-PRECIOUS STONE. CHALCEDONY (green/red). *Birthstone* (Mar).

BLOODSUCKER LEECH, *MOSQUITO*, *TICK*, VAMPIRE. GOLD-DIGGER (sl).

BLOOMER BLUNDER, ERROR, MISTAKE. FLOWER (crypt). Pl = *DRAWERS*, KNICKERS, UNDERWEAR.

BLOOMING FLOWERING, *OUT*. DASHED, WRETCHED.

BLOW PANT, PUFF, VENT, *WIND*. EXPLODE, PUNCTURE. BREAK, FUSE, MELT. *BETRAY*. FLY'S EGGS. HIT, KNOCK, ONER, *SMACK*. DISASTER, SHOCK. SPEND, SQUANDER. *COMPOSER*.

BLOWER *WIND*. ENGINE, PUFFER, STEAM-TRAIN. SUPERCHARGER (sl). TELEPHONE (sl).

BLOW-OUT PUNCTURE; FUSED. VOLCANO (crypt). MEAL. *Anag* 'blow'.

BLUE (s/l *blew*). *COLOUR*, AZURE (*herald*), INDIGO (anil, woad); **comp** = *black*. SNOOKER BALL (score 5). COLD, DEPRESSED, DISCONSOLATE, DISPIRITED, DOWN, LOW. BRUISED. FEAR. INDECENT, SALTY. LEARNED. *GRASS*. *OXFORD* or *CAMBRIDGE ATHLETE* or *PLAYER*. SPEND. Pl = DEPRESSION, DUMPS. HORSEGUARDS, HOUSEHOLD CAVALRY. UNIVERSITY TEAM (O and C).

BLUSH *COLOUR*, FLUSH, REDDEN. GLANCE, GLIMPSE.

BM BRITISH MUSEUM.

BMA BRITISH MEDICAL ASSOCIATION.

B MUS MUSICIAN.

BN BATTALION, *SOLDIERS*, TROOPS.

BO BODY ODOUR [perspiration, sweat]. Sacred tree of Buddha.

BOADICEA BOUDICCA. Widow of Prasutagus. Q of the *Iceni*, she withstood the *Romans*, defeating them at Camulodunum (*Colchester*) and London, where she slew 50,000. Was finally defeated by Suetonius Paulinus, and committed sui in A.D. 61.

BOAR (s/l *bore*). *MALE PIG*/GUINEA-PIG. [Labour of *Hercules*].

BOARD (s/l *bored*). *FOOD*, KEEP, MEALS; *TABLE*; **comp** = bed; lodging. PLANK, SLAB. COVER OVER. EMBARK, GET ABOARD/ON. SHIP'S SIDE, TACK. *DIRECTORS*. BULLETIN ~, NOTICE ~, HOARDING. **Pl** = *STAGE, THEATRE.*

BOARD GAME Game played on a board: **types**: L'ATTAQUE ®, BACKGAMMON, BAGATELLE, *BINGO* (Housey Housey, Keno, Lotto, Tombola), CHECKERS (US), CHESS, CLUEDO ®, CROWN & ANCHOR, DRAUGHTS, FOX & GEESE, GO(H) (Jap), HALMA, LUDO ®, LURCH, MAH-JONGG, MONOPOLY ®, PACHISI (Ind), RISK ®, SCRABBLE ®, SEPTEMBER ®, SHOVE HA'PENNY, SNAKES & LADDERS, SOLITAIRE, TIC(K)-TAC(K), TRIVIAL PURSUIT ®; CRIBBAGE, DARTS, DECK HOCKEY/TENNIS (all crypt).

BOARD, ON 1. EMBARKED. 2. Word with S . . . S round it, e.g. **I go on board to find my little sister** (3) = s*i*s. 3. Game played on a board, any *board game* (q.v. for **types**). 4. AT TABLE, DINING.

BOAT ARGO(SY), *CRAFT*, PACKET, SHIP, SS, *VESSEL*, WARSHIP; **types**:

3-letters

ARK	*COB*	GIG	MTB (mil)
CAT	*FLY*	*HOY*	TUG

4-letters

BARK	KOFF	*PUNT*	YAWL
BRIG	*PINK*	SCOW	ZULU
BUSS	PRAM	SHIP	
DORY	PRAU	SKIP	
JUNK	PROA	*SNOW*	

5-letters

BALSA	*FUNNY*	Q-BOAT (mil)	U-BOAT (mil)
BARGE	*KETCH*	SKIFF	XEBEC
CANOE	*LINER*	SLOOP	YACHT
DANDY	PRAAM	*SMACK*	ZABRA
E-BOAT (mil)	PRAHU	TRAMP	ZEBEC

6-letters

ARGOSY	BARQUE	BIREME	CURAGH

Boat-girl

CUTTER	HOWKER	ROWING	VESSEL
DINGHY	LAUNCH	SAMPAN	*WHALER*
DOGGER	LORCHA	SETTEE	WHERRY
DUGOUT	LUGGER	SURFER	
GALLEY	PACKET	TARTAN	
HOOKER	RANDAN	TENDER	

7-letters

BEAN-COD	CURRACH	LYMPHAD (*herald*)
BUGALET	CURRAGH	MONITOR (mil)
CARAVEL	DRIFTER	PATAMAR
CARRACK	FELUCCA	PINNACE
CARRIER (mil)	FRIGATE (mil)	PIROGUE
CHAMPAN	GALLEAS	POLACRE
CLIPPER	GALLEON	SHALLOP
COASTER	GALLIOT	TRIREME
CORACLE	HOUARIO	
CRUISER (mil)	LIGHTER	

8+ letters

BATTLESHIP (mil)	DESTROYER (mil)	SAILBOARD
CARACORE	HERRINGBUSS	*SCHOONER*
CATAMARAN	IRONCLAD	SUBMARINE (mil)
COCKBOAT	OTAHEITE	TRIMARAN
CORACORE	OUTRIGGER	WINDSURFER ®
CRUMSTER	PERIAGUA	

BOAT-GIRL FLORA (MacDonald). STEWARDESS. WAVE (US), WREN, WRNS.

BOB ROBERT. S, SHILLING, VP, XIID. HAIRSTYLE, PAGEBOY, TASSEL. SLED, SLEDGE, SLEIGH. BOUNCE, CURTSEY, *DANCE*, *DUCK*, JERK, WEAVE. PLUMB, WEIGHT. CHANGE (*bell ringing*). ETONIAN (**dry** ~ = cricketer, **wet** ~ = rower).

BOBBY ROBERT. *POLICEMAN* (*Peel*). *CALF*.

BOFFIN 1. BACKROOM BOY, SCIENTIST (sl).
2. NICODEMUS ~ (*Dickens* char, Mutual F; dustman who became rich).

BOGEY BUGBEAR. GOBLIN, *SPIRIT* (q.v. for list). PAR (golf). *Colonel* ~ (Sousa, mus). SWIM (Aus). Unidentified *aircraft* (mil).

BOIL *Anag.* BUBBLE, SEETHE, STEW, UNDULATE (all of

which also mean *anag*). GATHERING, TUMOUR (med).
BOMBER *AIRCRAFT*.
BONDED DUTY-FREE, EX-CUSTOMS, SCOT-FREE, TAX-
FREE. GLUED, SEALED, TIED UP. [Ian Fleming; 007].
BONE *ROB*, *STEAL* (sl). *PAINTER*. FILLET. STIFFEN.
HARD TISSUE, DENTINE, IVORY, WHALEBONE
[scrimshaw, *study*]. ~s of the body: **head**: CRANIUM (skull)
[antrum, sinus], ALVEOLUS, MANDIBLE, MAXILLA
(jaw); BICUSPID, CANINE, EYETOOTH, INCISOR,
MILKTOOTH, MOLAR, PREMOLAR, WISDOM TOOTH
(teeth); **neck**: *ATLAS*, AXIS; **shoulder**: CLAVICLE (collar ~),
CORACOID, SCAPULA (shoulderblade); **spine**: COCCYX,
SACRUM, VERTEBRA [cervical, thoracic, lumbar]; **arm**:
HUMERUS (upper), ELBOW, RADIUS, ULNA (forearm);
hand: CARPUS (wrist), METACARPUS, *PHALANX* (finger),
TRAPEZIUM; **chest**: RIB, STERNUM (breastbone); **hip**:
ILIUM, PELVIS, SACRUM; **leg**: FEMUR (thigh), PATELLA
(kneecap), FIBULA, TIBIA (shin) [Pott's fracture]; **foot**:
TALUS (ankle), CALCANEUM (heel), *PHALANX* (toe),
METATARSUS, TARSUS; [calcium, marrow, necrosis, ossify].
Comp = rag. **Pl** = DICE (sl); SKELETON. ESSENTIALS,
FRAMEWORK. CASTANETS, *INSTRUMENT* (mus).
BOOK ENTER, LIST, LOG. BAG, *ENGAGE, RESERVE*.
BETTING. *ANNUAL*, EDITION, ISSUE, MISSAL,
PUBLICATION, VOL(UME), TOME. BIBLE. [*measure*
(paper size)]. **Comp** = *bell* and candle.
BOOKED ENTERED, LISTED, LOGGED. BAGGED,
ENGAGED, RESERVED. BOUND, ISSUED, PUBLISHED,
WRITTEN ABOUT (crypt); PAGED (crypt).
BOOKLET BK, ED, VO, VOL.
BOOKMAKER AUTHOR, COMPILER, EDITOR, PAGE(S),
PUBLISHER, *WRITER* (all crypt). [*patron saint*]. BETTING
MAN, BOOKIE [*racetrack*, tote].
BOOT *SHOE*; *WELLINGTON*. *DISMISS, FIRE, SACK*.
TRUNK (US). AVAIL.
BORACIC LINT BROKE, SKINT (*rh sl*).
BORE (s/l *boar*). MINE, WELL. AUGER, AWL, DRILL;
MISER. CALIBRE. EAGRE, (TIDAL) *WAVE*. TIRE (**opp** =
enchant). BEGAT.
BOREAS Gk myth NORTH *WIND*.
BORED (s/l *board*). DRILLED. RIFLED. *TIRED*.
BORING DRILLING. ENNUI, TEDIOUS, TIRING; *DRY*, DULL.

BORN (s/l *borne, bourn*). B, NE, NEE. DESTINED. *NATIVE*, ORIGINATED. **Comp** = bred.

BORNE (s/l *born, bourn*). CARRIED. NARROW MINDED.

BORON B (*chem*).

BORROW INCUR DEBT, RAISE (money, the *wind* [IOU]); **opp** = lend; ADOPT, APPROPRIATE. *COPY, IMITATE, PIRATE*, PLAGIARIZE. UPHILL, SLOPE; DEVIATION, SWERVE (golf putting). George ~, Eng *writer*.

BOSIE LORD *ALFRED* DOUGLAS. *CHINAMAN* (Bosanquet, *cricket*).

BOSPHORUS *STRAIT*; *OX-FORD* [*Io*].

BOSS EMPLOYER, FOREMAN, MANAGER, OVERMAN, OVERSEER; M (Bond's ~). KNOB, STUD, UMBO. *SECRET POLICE* (S Af).

BOTHER CONFOUND, DAMN, DRAT. ADO, FUSS, TODO. IRRITATE, *NETTLE*, WORRY.

BOTH SIDES 1. EW, LR (crypt). 2. Word at start and end, e.g. **One on both sides** (5) = ON·I·ON.

BOTTLE RESTRAIN, STOP UP (hence POTS, dn) (**opp** = decant; release). ELAN, NERVE; DUTCH COURAGE (crypt). *JAR. ISLAND*. CONTAINER, *MEASURE*, VIAL [~d = place word in ~ (or synonym), e.g. **Lively bottled car** (5) = VI(T)AL]; **types**: SPLIT (¼bot), HALF-BOTTLE, BOTTLE (80 cl), MAGNUM (2 bots), *JEROBOAM* (4 bots), *REHOBOAM* (6 bots), *METHUSELAH* (8 bots), *SALMANAZAR* (12 bots), *BALTHAZAR* (16 bots), *NEBUCHADNEZZAR* (20 bots); DEMIJOHN. CARAFE, CARBOY, PHIAL [ten green ~s].

BOTTOM 1. *BASE*, BASIC, FUNDAMENTAL, LOWEST, NADIR, NETHERMOST, UNDERNEATH. BACKSIDE, BEHIND, BUTTOCKS, SIT-UPON. RIVERBED, SEABED; RUN AGROUND. *BOAT* (arch; q.v. for list), HULL, SHIP, *VESSEL* (q.v. for **celeb**). HOLLOW, VALLEY. 2. A *weaver* in MND (*Shak*), whose head was *transformed* into that of an *ass*, and with whom Titania was made to fall in love on waking.

BOUDICCA *BOADICEA* (q.v.).

BOUGH (s/l *bow*). BRANCH, STEM.

BOUNCER CHUCKER-OUT, DOORMAN. BUMPER. SHORT BALL (hence *BAL*, crypt, cricket). DUD CHEQUE. *BOUNDER, JUMPER*, LEAPER; **celeb**: Mrs ~ (*landlady*, Box and Cox, Morton); *GORGON*; TIGGER (*Milne*).

BOUND BOUNCE, JUMP, LEAP, RECOIL, SPRING. TIED, LIMIT(ED). *BOOK*, PUBLISHED (crypt). CERTAIN,

DESTINED, SURE.
BOUNDARY BARRIER, EDGE, LIMIT, PALE; MARCH; **Rom god** = TERMINUS. FOUR (*cricket*). TRAMPOLINE (crypt).
BOUNDED DELINEATED, EDGED, LIMITED. JUMPED, LEAPED, SPRANG. TIED UP.
BOUNDER *HOPPER, JUMPER* [*Gorgon*]; *CRICKET*, FROG, GOAT, GRASSHOPPER, *KANGAROO* (all crypt). CAD. *BALL* (crypt).
BOURN (s/l *born, borne*). *BROOK*. GOAL, LIMIT.
BOVINE COWLIKE, OX-LIKE, STUPID.
BOW (s/l *bough*). NOD, OBEISANCE, SALUTE, SUBMIT. FRONT, STEM (naut); ROWER. SLIPKNOT. *ARCH*, CURVE. LONGBOW, *WEAPON* [black ~ of Euryatus (*Ulysses*)]; **comp** = *arrow*. RAINBOW. PLAY *FIDDLE/ VIOLIN* etc.
BOWED *ARCHED*, BENT, CURVED, HUNCHED. NODDED, SALUTED. FIDDLED, PLAYED (crypt). SHOT ARROW (archery, crypt).
BOWER *CELLIST*, FIDDLER, VIOLINIST (crypt). ARCHER, ROBIN *HOOD*, WILLIAM TELL (crypt). ARBOUR. CONSENTER, NODDER, SUBMITTER; COURTIER, LACKEY, USHER. ANCHOR. BIRD. *CARD* (euchre, knave).
BOWERY 1. OBEISANCE (crypt). ARBOUR. 2. District of New York.
BOWL BASIN, DISH. DELIVER, TAKE OVER (*cricket*). TRUNDLE. BIASED BALL, JACK, WOOD [bowls, skittles].
BOWLED B, DELIVERED, SENT DOWN (*cricket*). SALAD (crypt).
BOWLER CRICKETER, DELIVERY MAN, PITCHER. DRAKE (crypt). BILLYCOCK, *HAT*. POTTER (crypt).
BOWMAN ARCHER; CUPID, ROBIN *HOOD*, WILLIAM TELL. *CELLIST, FIDDLER*, VIOLINIST (crypt).
BOX *FIGHT, SPAR* [pugilism]. CARTON, CASE, *CHEST*. TELLY, TV. *TREE. MEASURE* (fish). *PLANT*. **Comp** = Cox (Mrs *Bouncer*).
BOXER *FIGHTER*, PUGILIST; *POLLUX. HORSE* (Animal Farm, *Orwell*). CASE-MAKER, PACKER. CHINAMAN. LETTER-SENDER/POSTER (crypt). SENTRY (crypt).
BOXING 1. FISTICUFFS, PUNCHING; BAREKNUCKLE, THE FIGHT GAME; THAI ~ [Queensberry rules]; **weights:** fly ~, bantam ~, feather ~, junior light ~, light ~, junior

welter ~, welter ~, light heavy ~, heavy ~. 2. ENCASING,
WRAPPING (presents [~ Day]). UNDERTAKING, LAYING
OUT (sl). Planting a hedge, shrub; HEDGING (crypt). Reciting
compass points in order. CUFFING, SLAPPING (ears).
BOY 1. KID, LAD, NIPPER. DICK, ED, JACK, SAM, TOM
etc. 2. Three lily-white ~, in *song*. [~ **and girl** = pigeon pair].
~s BRIGADE BB, CADETS.
BR BRAZIL (*car plate*). *BRIDGE*. BRITISH *RAIL*. BROMINE
(*chem*). *BROTHER*. **Pl** = BRITISH ROAD SERVICES.
Br Britain, ~ish. Brother.
BRAG BOAST, SHOW OFF (**opp** = *modest*). *CARDS*. Nor *god*.
BRAHMA Principal Indian *god*.
BRAKE (s/l *break*). BROKE (OE). BRACKEN, BRUSHWOOD.
SKID, SLIPPER (tech); CHECK, CRUSH, RETARD, SLOW.
CARRIAGE, ESTATE CAR, WAGON.
BRANCH STEM [tree: *Absalom*]. OFFSHOOT, SUB-OFFICE.
JUMP.
BRAND BURN, CHAR. MARK, STIGMA. LABEL,
TRADEMARK; HOT IRON. SWORD. BLIGHT.
BRASS 1. *MONEY*: **comp** = muck. BUGLE, TROMBONE,
TRUMPET, TUBA etc (mus). STAFF OFFICERS.
2. Copper/Zinc alloy, hence CU*ZN.
BRAVE FACE UP TO; BOLD, FEARLESS, *GAME*.
AMERICAN INDIAN (q.v. for tribes); **opp** = paleface.
Braz Brazil, ~ian.
BREAD CRUST, *LOAF*, ROLL; DOUGH [~ into *roses* (St
Elizabeth)]; **comp** = *butter, cheese*. *MONEY* (sl).
BREAK (s/l *brake*). *Anag*. BUST, *CRACK*, FRACTURE,
SEPARATE, SHATTER, SNAP. GAP, INTERVAL.
ESCAPE; *EXHAUST*. SCORE (billiards, snooker). TAME.
Comp = *make*.
BREAKER KEG. *COMBER*, SURF, *WAVE*. CRACKSMAN,
ROBBER. CB ENTHUSIAST (radio, sl). PLAYER
(billiards/pool/snooker, crypt).
BREAKING Word in another, e.g. **We are breaking the collection,
Honey** (5) = s*WE*ET.
BREAKPOINT CRUNCH. PUBERTY (crypt).
BREATHER *REST*. GILL, LUNG, MOUTH, *NOSE*,
WEASAND, WINDPIPE. VENT.
BREED RAISE, REAR. RACE, STOCK, TYPE.
BREEDING GROUND ATOMIC/NUCLEAR *REACTOR* (crypt).
INCUBATOR, NURSERY, STOCK/STUD FARM.

BREVE *NOTE. ACCENT* (˘ = short). AUTHORITY, *LETTER* (papal, royal).

BREW *Anag.* CONCOCT, INFUSE. MAKE BEER/TEA [*Company* (livery)]. FESTER.

BRIBE GREASE, OIL (palm); PALM-OIL (crypt). INDUCE, SQUARE, SUBORN, TEMPT.

BRIDGE BR. ARCH, ARCHER, PONTOON, SPAN(NER) (crypt); RIALTO, *THAMES*. [Bifrost, rainbow ~ of Nor gods from Asgard to earth]. CONNING TOWER/DECK. *CARD GAME*, TRUMPERY (auction, contract) [Acol, Blackwood]. LOAN. REST (snooker). **Pl** = *POET, WRITER*.

~ **GAME** *CARDS*. TRUMPERY (crypt). POOHSTICKS (A. A. *Milne*).

BRIDGEHEAD INROAD, SALIENT. CARD BUFF (Acolite; crypt).

BRIDGE PLAYER E, N, S or W; EAST, NORTH, SOUTH, WEST; BRIDGER, WE, THEY.

BRIDGER *BRIDGE PLAYER* (crypt). CAPTAIN, NAVIGATOR (crypt). HORATIO (crypt).

BRIDGING TEAM ENGINEERS, RE, SAPPERS. BRIDGE PLAYERS, EW, NS, WE/THEY (crypt). APPEASERS, CONCILIATORS, ACAS (crypt).

BRIG BRASSHAT, BRIGADIER, SOLDIER. *BOAT. GAOL* (naut). *BRIDGE* (Sc).

BRISTOL BREAST (*rh sl*). *UNIVERSITY*.

BRITISH LEGION BL.

~ **LEYLAND** BL.

~ **MUSEUM** BM.

~ **RAIL** BR, RLY, RY, LINES.

BROADCAST SCATTER, SOW. AIR(ING), RADIATE, TRANSMIT; BBC, IBA, ITA, ITV (UK); ABC, CBS, NBC (US).

BROKE BANKRUPT, INSOLVENT, PENNILESS, RUINED; BORACIC LINT (*rh sl*); **opp** = *rich*. DID *BREAK*, BUST. [Evans of the ~].

BROKEN *Anag* e.g. **Heartbroken** (5) = HATER. WAS *BROKE*. SNAPPED. TAMED.

BROKEN FUSE BLOWN OUT, FUSED. Anag 'fuse' i.e. FUES.

BRONTË 1. *WRITER;* ANNE ~ = Acton Bell (Agnes Grey; *Tenant* of Wildfell Hall). CHARLOTTE ~ = Mrs Nicholls = Currer Bell (Jane Eyre; The Professor; Shirley; Villette; Land of Angria). EMILY (JANE) ~ = Ellis Bell (Wuthering

Heights; Land of Gondal). PATRICK BRANWELL ~ 2. Lord
Nelson and ~ (*military leader*; Emma Hamilton). 3. Gk myth
THUNDER [blacksmith]. **Pl** = CYCLOP.
BRONZE 1. *AGE*. THIRD PRIZE. *Anniversary* (8th).
2. Copper/Tin alloy, hence CU*SN.
BROOK BECK, *BOURN*, BURN, CREEK, RILL, *RIVER*,
RIVULET, STREAM. TOLERATE.
BROTHER BR, *SIB*. FRIAR, *MONK*. ASSOCIATE, EQUAL.
[~ Jonathan (Uncle Sam)]; **celeb**: Brer Fox, Brer Rabbit
(Harris); Nelson's Band of ~s. **Pl** = TUC.
BROTHERHOOD ASSOCIATION, FRATERNITY. COWL
(crypt).
BROWN ROAST; *TAN*. *COLOUR*. *PAINTER*. *SNOOKER*
BALL (score 4). FATHER ~ (*Chesterton*). JOHN ~
(body). Lancelot 'Capability' ~ (*gardener*). TOM. SHOOT
HAPHAZARDLY (hence HOOTS etc). [Queen Victoria
(ghillie)]. **Pl** = *Football team* (US).
BROWNE *SAM* (belt). *CARTOONIST* (Phiz, *Dickens*).
BROWNIE GOBLIN, *SPIRIT* (q.v.). YOUNG GUIDE.
CAMERA ®.
BROWNING AUTOMATIC, *WEAPON* ®. DYE, TANNING.
FIRING WILDLY. GRAVY. *WRITER*.
BRS BRITISH ROAD SERVICES. Pl of BR.
BRUNNHILDA 1. Nor myth Chief of the *Valkyries*. 2. A minor
PLANET.
BRUTUS *CONSPIRATOR*; *STOIC* [honourable; Caesar's ghost,
(*Shak*)].
BT BARONET.
BTU BRITISH THERMAL UNIT (heat).
BUCCANEER *PIRATE*. *AIRCRAFT*.
BUCEPHALUS ALEXANDER'S *HORSE*.
BUCK *DOLLAR*. JUMP, THROW. DANDY, FOP. CART.
SAW-HORSE. PEARL (films). *WRITER*. *DOG*. *Male* deer,
hare etc.
BUFF ENTHUSIAST. POLISH. NUDE, SKIN. *COLOUR*. **Pl** =
EAST KENT REGIMENT. ['Steady the ~s' (*Kipling*)].
BUFFALO *CATTLE*, WATER ~ (Af); BISON (US) [Ch
calendar]. US port.
BUG *BEETLE*, PARASITE. EAVESDROPPER, LISTENER,
TRANSMITTER. RIVER (Pol).
BUILD *Anag*. CONSTRUCT, COMPOSE, MAKE.
PROPORTIONS, SHAPE.

BULL 1. ROT, RUBBISH. CENTRE, GOLD (archery). DECK
GAME. PAPAL EDICT. DRINK. PRICE RAISER (**opp**
= *bear*). TAURUS; *male* cow, elephant etc; SIRE. [*Europa*,
Mithra(s), *Minos*, Seventh labour of *Hercules*]. APIS (Egy god).
2. *Constellation* (Taurus); sign of *Zodiac* (2nd).
~ **AND COW** *ROW* (*rh sl*).
BULLETHOLE BARREL, CHAMBER, RIFLING (all crypt).
BULLFIGHTING Words: aficionado (enthusiast, *fan*), alguacile
(*constable*), assessor (judge), banderilla (*dart*), banderillero (foot
assistant), barrera (barrier), burladero (short barrier), callejon
(alleyway), capote (*cloak*), corrida de toros (bull running),
cuadrilla (team), estoque (sword), matador (killer), montera
(*hat*), muleta (*cloak* on shaft), paseilo (parade), percale (cloth),
picador (mounted assistant), puntilla (dagger), punterillero
(dagger-man), puya (goad), suerte (*stage*), toreador (mounted
bullfighter), torero (participant), toril (bull-pen), toro (bull),
vara (lance), veronica (a pass), [Bouphonia (*Zeus*); Gilgamesh
(Bab); *Mithras* (pers); *Minotaur* (Gk)].
BULLSEYE CENTRE, *GOLD* [inner, magpie, outer].
LANTERN. *COMIC*. CANDY, GOBSTOPPER, SWEET.
DOG (Bill Sikes, *Dickens*).
BULLY BRAVO! EXCELLENT! FIRST RATE! CORNED
BEEF. START (hockey). OPPRESSOR, THUG, TYRANT;
celeb: CERCYON (myth), FLASHMAN (Tom Brown's
Schooldays), FRONT DE BOEUF (Ivanhoe, Scott), JOSIAH
BOUNDERBY (Hard Times, *Dickens*), SIR JOHN CHESTER
(Rudge, *Dickens*), LEGREE (Uncle Tom's Cabin, Harriet
Beecher *Stowe*).
BUMMEL JOURNEY, STROLL (Three Men on the ~, Jerome
K. Jerome).
BUN HAIRPIECE; UPBRAIDED (crypt). BREAD ROLL:
BATH, CHELSEA, CURRANT, HOT CROSS etc.
BUND *BANK;* QUAY.
BUNTER SCHOOLBOY, OWL OF THE REMOVE (*Greyfriars*
School, Richards). *SERVANT* (to Lord Peter Wimsey, Dorothy
L. Sayers).
BUNTING *BIRD*. *FLAG*, WORSTED (*material*).
BURDEN LOAD, OPPRESS, SADDLE; OBLIGATION,
LIABILITY, PASSENGER. TONNAGE. CHORUS,
REFRAIN, THEME.
BURGLAR *ROBBER*, THIEF, YEGG. FAGIN (*Dickens*), Raffles
(Hornung).

BURLAP CANVAS, JUTE, *MATERIAL*.
BURLINGTON HOUSE RA, (ROYAL) ACADEMY [*painters*].
BURN *BROOK*. BLISTER, SORE; *BLAZE, CHAR*,
  CONSUME, *FIRE*, PARCH, SCORCH, TAN. **Pl** = RABBIE,
  POET (Sc).
BURRO (s/l *burrow*). *DONKEY*.
BURROW (s/l *burro*). MINE. RABBIT WARREN/
  HABITATION. ISLAND (Eng).
BUSH *PLANT* (q.v. for list), SHRUB; FOREST, WOODLAND.
  HAIR. *PIG*. LINING, SLEEVE, WASHER. RIVER (Ire).
  PRESIDENT (US).
BUSINESS *CO*, FIRM, TRADE. AFFAIR, CONCERN, DUTY,
  OCCUPATION, TASK. AGENDA.
BUT (s/l *butt, butte*). EXCEPT, HOWEVER, ONLY. WITHOUT.
  YET. *UTTER*. **Pl comp** = ifs.
BUTCHER MEAT TRADER [*Company* (livery)]. SLAUGHTER.
  CUMBERLAND. *BIRD* (Shrike). **Pl** = *LOOK* (*rh sl*).
BUTT (s/l *but, butte*). CASK, KEG, *MEASURE*. AIM, OBJECT,
  RANGE, STAND (shooting). HANDLE; ABUT(MENT).
  FISH: FLATFISH, PLAICE, SOLE. STUB, TREE TRUNK.
  CUE (snooker). NUDGE (with head). TARGET (for jokes).
BUTTE (s/l *but, butt*). *HILL*.
BUTTER FAT. ADULATE, PRAISE. GUNNEL (*fish*). GOAT
  (crypt, nudge). LANDLORD (crypt, cask). MARKSMAN
  (crypt, range). SNOOKER PLAYER (crypt, cue). SMOKER
  (crypt, stub). COASTER (crypt, Masefield). **Comp** =
  bread; *toast*.
BUTTERFLY *LEPIDOPTERA* (q.v. for breeds); **coll** =
  LEPIDOPTERIST. MADAM ~ (Puccini; Nagasaki; Cho Cho
  San, Lt *Pinkerton*). [*Psyche*]. *Swimming* style (q.v.). ~ *SHARK*.
BUTTER UP FLATTER, PRAISE. RETTUB (dn, crypt).
BUTTRESS PIER, PROP, SUPPORT (*architecture* term, q.v.).
  Part of horse's hoof. Fem goat (crypt), hence *NANNY*.
BUZZ BOMB DOODLEBUG, FLYING BOMB, V1 [revenge].
BY (s/l *bye*). *NEAR*, NEXT, PER, THROUGH. SECONDARY,
  SIDE. SECRET. Fathered/sired by . . . **Comp** = *large*.
BYE (s/l *by*). *PASS*. *EXTRA* (cricket). INCIDENTAL. SIDE.
  SECRET.
BYE-BYE *FAREWELL*. **Pl** = SLEEP.
BYGONE ANTIQUE. PAST.

C (s/l sea, see). CABRIOLET. *CAMBRIDGE.* CARBON (*chem*). *CAUGHT.* CELSIUS, CENTIGRADE. CHAPTER. CIRCA. *CLUB.* COLD. CONSERVATIVE. CUBA (*car plate*). ABOUT. *KEY*; *NOTE.* 100, ONE HUNDRED; MANY. SQ NO (10 × 10 = 100 = C).

C3.3 OSCAR WILDE (prison number).

CA ABOUT, CIRCA. CHARTERED ACCOUNTANT. CALIFORNIA (US *state*). CALCIUM (*chem*).

CABINET MAKER PRIME MINISTER, PM. *ADAM, CHANNON, CHIPPENDALE, HEPPLEWHITE, KENT, SHERATON.*

CABLE WIRE; MESSAGE, TELEGRAM. 200 YARDS, CCYD, *MEASURE* (naut).

CACUS Rom myth s of *Vulcan*, who *robbed Hercules* of some of his cattle and was slain.

CAD *BOUNDER*, BRUTE, LOUT, SCOUNDREL, *SWINE.*

CADETS ATC, *BB*, JTC, OTC; BOYS BRIGADE, SCOUTS. YOUNGER SONS.

CADMIUM *METAL*; CD (*chem*). *COLOUR* (orange).

CAESAR 1. AUTOCRAT, CZAR, DICTATOR, EMPEROR, KAISER, TSAR; **celeb**: AUGUSTUS, CALIGULA, CLAUDIUS, NERO or, specifically, GAIUS JULIUS ~, 102–44 B.C., s of Caesar and Aurelia; mar (1) Cossutia (div, unconsummated), (2) Cornelia, d of Cinna (died; one d: Julia), (3) Pompeia, d of Pompeius Rufus (div for adultery), and (4) Calpurnia, d of Piso. Brilliant general, orator and writer, he was ass Ides (15) Mar 44 B.C. by *conspiracy* of Brutus, Casca, Cassius etc. [Invasion of Britain, Rubicon (crossed to Italy and civil war), veni, vidi, vici (Pharnaces at Zela), leap year (introduced), *July, Cleopatra* (one s: Caesarion), Mark *Antony, Pompey*, et tu Brute! *Conspirators.* Appeared as *ghost* to *Brutus* before the battle of Philippi. *Shak* (A and C; Caesar); *Shaw* (~ and Cleopatra)]. 2. Implies put into Latin, e.g. **Seen (or conquered) by Caesar** (4) = VIDI (or VICI).

CAIN (s/l *cane*). ADAMSON, FIRST BORN, FIRST ISSUE [murderer]. **Comp** = *Abel.*

~ **& ABEL** *TABLE* (*rh sl*).

CAKE SWEETBREAD; **celeb**: *Angel*, banana, beef~, bride's, cherry, chocolate, Christening, *Christmas*, coffee, cream, Dundee, éclair, *fairy*, fish~, fruit~, gâteau, Madeira, marble, Parkin (Guy Fawkes; ginger), plum, rock, *Sally Lunn*, seed, Simnel, soda, sponge, Swiss roll, tea~, tipsy, wedding etc.

OATBREAD (Sc). CONGLOMERATE, WAD. *COAT, COVER*. BENEFITS, NATIONAL OUTPUT, PROFITS.

CALCULATOR ABACUS, *ADDER*, COMPUTER, *SUMMER. GOLD DIGGER.*

CALENDAR (s/l calender). CHRONOLOGICAL LIST, DATING SYSTEM, DIARY (*Chinese* ~; *French Revolution*; Julius *Caesar*). *LIST*, REGISTER, SCHEDULE, *TABLE*.

CALF BACK OF LEG, LEG MUSCLE, STOCKING-FILLER (crypt). SMALL ICEBERG. *ISLAND. Offspring* of *cow, elephant*, walrus, *whale*; BOBBY.

CALIGULA Rom *emperor* and *tyrant*, an illness rendered him *mad* and savagely cruel. He declared himself a god, made his horse Incitatus a consul, caused men and women to be tortured to d at his meals, threw part of the audience to the wild beasts at the *circus*, and gave a banquet on a bridge then threw guests into the water. He was ass in A.D. 41.

CALL 1. PHONE, *RING*, TELEPHONE; *PAGE*, SHOUT: HI, HEY, HO etc. CHRISTEN, NAME, NOMINATE. BECK, SIGNAL. 2. *Pronounce as* . . . sound like. **Comp** = *beck*.

~ **GIRL** TELEPHONIST. PROSTITUTE.

CALLIOPE One of the nine Gk *MUSES* (epic *poetry*).

CALL SYSTEM DIAL, PAGING, PUBLIC ADDRESS, STD, TANNOY ®, TOCSIN.

CAMBRIDGE C, CANTAB; LIGHT BLUES; *UNIVERSITY* (q.v. for colleges) [Cantabrigian]. DUROLIPONS (*Roman*). *Shak* (*conspirator*, H.v).

CAMEL RUMINANT; OONT, SHIP OF THE DESERT [*llama*]; **breeds**: ARABIAN, DOOD, DROMEDARY (one hump), BACTRIAN (two humps). CIGARETTE (US). *COLOUR* (fawn). SPONSON. *AIRCRAFT* (fighter). RIVER (Eng).

CAMELOT Site of *King Arthur*'s court: CADBURY CASTLE, CAMELFORD or TINTAGEL [round table].

CAMEO BROOCH, RELIEF WORK (**opp** = intaglio). THUMBNAIL SKETCH.

CAMP *BASE* (mil), FORT, SETTLEMENT; CASTRA (Rom). TENTS (gipsies, guides, holiday-makers, scouts etc); LODGE. ADHERENTS, FOLLOWERS. ~ DAVID (US). AFFECTED, BIZARRE, DRAG, EFFEMINATE, EPICENE, EXAGGERATED, GAY, HOMOSEXUAL, TRANSVESTITE.

CAMPTOWN *RACETRACK*. ALDERSHOT, CHESTER, LARKHILL, TIDWORTH (mil bases). [*Roman place name*].

CAN *TIN*; PRESERVE. IS ABLE. *GAOL* (sl). RIVER (Eng).
Pl = HEADPHONES (sl).

Can Canada, ~ian.

CANADA CDN (*car plate*). [Canuck. Maple leaves].

CANARD *HOAX*. DUCK (Fr). CONTROL SURFACE (aero).

CANDY SWEETMEAT; CRYSTALLIZE, PRESERVE.
Anniversary (6th). GIRL. Old Man (Steinbeck).

CANE (s/l *Cain*). *BEAT*, CHASTISE, *TAN*, THRASH; BIRCH,
ROD, *SWITCH*, MALACCA, STICK. SUGAR.

CANNED DRUNK (sl). PRESERVED; TINNED, hence word in
'can' or 'tin', e.g. **Skirt canned Egyptian god** (5) = T*RA*IN.

CANNON (s/l *canon*). *GUN, ORDNANCE* (q.v.), PIECE,
WEAPON; RA. COLLIDE, STRIKE; KISS (billiards).

CANON (s/l *cannon*). CHURCH DECREE, PAPAL LAW;
CRITERION, PRINCIPLE. CATHEDRAL OFFICIAL,
CHURCHMAN. TYPEFACE.

CANT CANNOT, UNABLE (**opp** = *may*). CATCHPHRASE,
JARGON; HYPOCRISY. BEVEL, SLOPE, *TILT*; *LEAN*,
SLEW, SWING, *TIP*. CANTICLES.

CANTAB Of C University.

CANTABRIGIAN Member of C or of Harvard University.

CANTERBURY 1. MUSIC HOLDER (*furniture*). *UNIVERSITY*
(NZ). DUROVERNUM (*Rom*). 2. **Episcopal sig** = CANTUAR.
3. ~ Tales (*Chaucer*).

CANTON DIVISION ON SHIELD (*herald*). SUB-DIVISION OF
COUNTRY (see *Swiss* ~ for list). TOWN (Ch).

CAP *HAT*, HEADGEAR; COLOURS (team, int). CAPITAL.
CHAPTER. COMMON AGRICULTURAL POLICY
(European farming). COVER, TOP. **Comp** = gown.

CAPE HEADLAND, NESS, *POINT*, PROMONTORY. CLOAK,
TALMA, TIPPET. APPLE.

CAPER FRISK, LARK, LEAP. *SPICE*. BOER, S AFRICAN
(crypt).

CAPITAL AI, FIRST RATE; VITAL. CORNICE (*architecture*).
CHIEF, HEAD, LEADING, IMPORTANT, PRINCIPAL. UC,
UPPER CASE (**opp** = lower case). First letter, first city, seat of
government e.g.:

Country	Capital
Abyssinia (now Ethiopia)	ADDIS ABABA
Aden (now S Yemen)	ADEN
Afghanistan	KABUL

Capital

Albania	TIRANA
Algeria	EL DJEZAIR (was ALGIERS)
Andorra	LA VIEJA
Angola (was Port W Africa)	LUANDA
Antigua Is	ST JOHN'S
Argentina	BUENOS AIRES
Ascension Is	GEORGETOWN
Australia	CANBERRA
Austria	VIENNA
Bahamas	NASSAU
Bahrain	MANAMAH
Balearic Is	PALMA
Bangladesh	DHAKA (was DACCA)
Barbados	BRIDGETOWN
Basutoland (now Lesotho)	MASERU
Bechuanaland (now Botswana)	MAFEKING
Belgian Congo (now Zaire)	LEOPOLDVILLE
Belgium	BRUSSELS
Belize (was Br Honduras)	BELMOPAN
Benin (was part Fr W Africa, then Dahomey)	PORTO NOVO
Bermuda	HAMILTON
Bhutan	THIMBU
Bolivia	SUCRE
Botswana (was Bechuanaland)	GABORONE
Burkina Faso (was Upper Volta)	OUAGADOUGOU
Brazil	BRASILIA (was RIO DE JANEIRO)
Britain (Rom)	CAMULODUNUM
Br Honduras (now Belize)	BELIZE
Bulgaria	SOFIA
Burma (now Myanmar)	RANGOON
Cambodia (was part Fr Indo-China, was Kampuchea)	PHNOM PENH
Cameroon	YAOUNDE
Canada	OTTAWA
Canary Is	LAS PALMAS
Cape Verde Is	SAO THIAGO

Central African Republic (was part Fr Eq Africa)	BANGUI
Ceylon (now Sri Lanka)	COLOMBO
Chad (was part Fr Eq Africa)	NDJAMENE (was FORT LAMY)
Chile	SANTIAGO
China	PEKING (was XIAN)
CIS (was USSR)	MOSCOW
Colombia	BOGOTA
Corsica	AJACCIO
Costa Rica	SAN JOSE
Crete	CANEA
Cuba	HAVANA
Cyclades Is	HERMOUPOLIS
Cyprus	NICOSIA
Czechlands	PRAGUE
Dahomey (now Benin)	PORTO NOVO
Denmark	COPENHAGEN
Djibouti (was Fr Somaliland)	DJIBOUTI
Dominica Is	ROSEAU
Dominican Republic	SANTO DOMINGO
Dutch East Indies (now Indonesia)	BATAVIA (now JAKARTA)
Dutch Guiana (now Surinam)	PARAMARIBO
Ecuador	QUITO
Egypt	CAIRO (was MEMPHIS)
Eire	DUBLIN
Elba Is	PORTO FERRAIO
El Salvador	SAN SALVADOR
England	LONDON
Eq Guinea (was Sp Guinea)	MALABO (was SANTA ISABEL)
Eritrea (now part Ethiopia)	ASMARA
Est(h)onia	TALLINN
Ethiopia (was Abyssinia)	ADDIS ABABA
Faeroe Is	THORSHAVN
Falkland Is	PORT STANLEY
Fiji Is	SUVA
Finland	HELSINKI
Formosa (now Taiwan)	TAIPEH

France	PARIS
Fr Eq Africa (now Cameroon, Central Af Republic, Chad, Congo and Gabon)	BRAZZAVILLE
Fr Guiana	CAYENNE
Fr Indo-China (now Cambodia, Laos and Vietnam)	SAIGON (now HO CHI MINH CITY)
Fr Somaliland (now Djibouti)	JIBUTI
Fr W Africa (now Benin, Guinea, Ivory Coast, Mauritania and Senegal)	DAKAR
Friendly Is (Tonga)	NUKUALOFA or TONJOTABU
Gabon (was part Fr Eq Africa)	LIBREVILLE
Gambia	BANJUL (was BATHURST)
Germany	BERLIN (Bonn)
Ghana	ACCRA
Granada (ancient kingdom)	GRANADA
Greece	ATHENS
Greenland	GODTHAB
Grenada Is	ST GEORGE'S
Guadeloupe	BASSE-TERRE
Guam	AGANA
Guatemala	GUATEMALA
Guinea (was part Fr W Africa)	CONAKRY
Guinea Bissau (was Port Guinea)	BISSAU
Guyana	GEORGETOWN
Haiti	PORT AU PRINCE
Holland	AMSTERDAM
Honduras	TEGUCIGALPA
Hong Kong	VICTORIA
Hungary	BUDAPEST
Iceland	REYKJAVIK
India	DELHI
Indonesia (was NL E Indies)	JAKARTA (was BATAVIA)
Iran (was Persia)	TEH(E)RAN
Iraq (was Mesopotamia)	BAGHDAD

Ireland, North	BELFAST
Ireland, Rep of	DUBLIN
Israel (disputed)	JERUSALEM
Italy	ROME
Ivory Coast (was part Fr W Africa)	ABIDJAN (OR YAMOUSSOUKRO)
Jamaica	KINGSTON
Japan	TOKYO (was EDO, YEDDO)
Jordan	AMMAN
Kampuchea (now Cambodia)	PHNOM PENH
Kenya	NAIROBI
Kiribati (was Gilbert Is)	JARAWA
Korea, North	PYONGYANG
Korea, South	SEOUL
Kuwait	KUWAIT
Laos (was part Fr Indo-China)	VIENTIANE
Latvia	RIGA
Lebanon	BEIRUT
Leeward Is	ST JOHN
Lesotho (was Basutoland)	MASERU
Liberia	MONROVIA
Libya	TRIPOLI
Liechtenstein	VADUZ
Lithuania	VILNA
Luxembourg	LUXEMBOURG
Macau	MACAU
Madagascar (now Malagasy Rep)	ANTANANARIVO
Malagasy Rep (was Madagascar)	TANANARIVE
Malawi (was Nyasaland)	LILONGWE
Malaysia (was Fed Malay States)	KUALA LUMPUR
Maldives	MALE
Mali (was Fr Sudan, Fr W Af)	BAMAKO
Malta	VAL(L)ETTA
Manoa (myth)	EL DORADO (myth)
Martinique Is	FORT DE FRANCE

Mauritania (was part Fr W Af)	NOUAKCHOTT
Mauritius	PORT LOUIS
Mesopotamia (now Iraq)	BAGHDAD
Mexico	MEXICO CITY
Micronesia	KOLONIA
Moçambique (was Port E Africa)	MAPUTO (was LOURENÇO MARQUES)
Monaco	MONACO
Mongolia	ULAN BATOR (was URGA)
Montenegro	CETINJE
Morocco	RABAT
Muscat & Oman (now Oman)	MUSCAT
Myanmar (was Burma)	RANGOON

Namibia (was S W Africa)	WINDHOEK
Nauru	YOREN
Nepal	KAT(H)MANDU
Netherlands	AMSTERDAM
New Zealand	WELLINGTON
Nicaragua	MANAGUA
Niger (was part Fr W Africa)	NIAMEY
Nigeria	ABOUGA (was LAGOS)
North Vietnam	HANOI
North Yemen	SANA
Norway	OSLO
Nyasaland (now Malawi)	ZOMBA

Oman (was Muscat & Oman)	MUSCAT

Pakistan	ISLAMABAD (was KARACHI)
Palestine (disputed)	JERUSALEM
Panama	PANAMA
Papua New Guinea	PORT MORESBY
Paraguay	ASUNCION
Patagonia (now Argentina & Chile)	PUNTA ARENAS
Persia (now Iran)	TEH(E)RAN
Peru	LIMA
Philippines	QUEZON CITY
Poland	WARSAW (was CRACOW)

Portugal	LISBON
Port E Africa	LOURENÇO MARQUES
(now Moçambique)	
Port Guinea	BISSAU (was BOLAMA)
(now Guinea Bissau)	
Port W Africa (now Angola)	LUANDA
Puerto Rico	SAN JUAN
Qatar	DOHA
Rhodesia (now Zambia	SALISBURY
and Zimbabwe)	
Romania	BUCHAREST
Ruritania (fict)	STRELSAU (fict)
Russia	MOSCOW
Rwanda	KIGALI
Sabah (was N Borneo)	KOTA KINABALU
St Helena Is	JAMESTOWN
St Kitts-Nevis Is	BASSETERRE
St Lucia Is	CASTRIES
St Vincent Is	KINGSTOWN
Samoa	APIA
San Marino	SAN MARINO
Sarawak	KUCHING
Sardinia	CAGLIARI
Saudi Arabia	RIYADH (was MECCA)
Scotland	EDINBURGH
Senegal (was part	DAKAR
Fr W Africa)	
Seychelles	VICTORIA
Siam (now Thailand)	BANGKOK
Sicily	PALERMO
Sierra Leone	FREETOWN
Sikkim (now part India)	GANGTOK
Singapore Is	SINGAPORE
Slovakia	BRATISLAVA
Solomon Is	HONIARA
Somali (Br and It E Africa)	MOGADISHU
Somaliland, Br	HARGEISA
(now part Somali)	
Somaliland, Fr (now Djibouti)	JIBUTI

Somaliland, It (now part Somali)	MOGADISHU
South Africa	PRETORIA
South Yemen (was Aden Protectorate)	MADINAT ASH SHAB
Spain	MADRID
Sp Guinea (now Eq Guinea)	SANTA ISABEL
Sp Sahara (now Saharan Arab Dem Rep)	VILLA CISNEROS
Sri Lanka (was Ceylon)	COLOMBO
Sudan	KHARTOUM
Surinam (was NL Guiana)	PARAMARIBO
Swaziland	MBABANE
Sweden	STOCKHOLM
Switzerland	BERNE
Syria	DAMASCUS
Taiwan (was Formosa)	TAIPEH
Tanganyika (now Tanzania)	DAR ES SALAAM
Tanzania (was Tanganyika)	DODOMA
Thailand (was Siam)	BANGKOK
Tibet	LHASA
Togo	LOME
Tonga (Friendly Is)	NUKUALOFA or TONJOTABU
Transkei	UNTATA
Transylvania (was part Hungary, now part Romania)	CLUJ
Trinidad & Tobago	PORT OF SPAIN
Tristan da Cunha	EDINBURGH
Tunisia	TUNIS
Turkey	ANKARA
Tuvalu (was Ellice Is)	FUNAFUTI
Uganda	KAMPALA
United Arab Emirates	ABU DHABI
Upper Volta	OUAGADOUGOU
Uruguay	MONTEVIDEO
USA	WASHINGTON
Utopia (fict)	AMAUROTE (fict)

Vanuatu (was Espiritu Santo)	VILA
Venezuela	CARACAS
Vietnam (was part Fr Indo-China)	HANOI
Virgin Is, Br	ROADTOWN
Virgin Is, US	CHARLOTTE AMALIE
Wales	CARDIFF
Western Sahara	AAIUN
Wessex (ex)	WINCHESTER (ex)
West Irian (was NL New Guinea/Irian Jaya)	JAYAPURA
Windward Is	ST GEORGE
Yemen, North	SANA
Yemen, South (was Aden Protectorate)	MADINAT ASH SHAB (Aden)
Yugoslavia (former)	BELGRADE
Zaire (was Belgian Congo)	KINSHASA
Zambia (was N Rhodesia)	LUSAKA
Zimbabwe (was S Rhodesia)	HARARE (was Salisbury)

CAPPED (s/l *capt*). CHOSEN, PICKED, SELECTED; awarded cap/colours for club/county/country. COVERED, PROTECTED, SHEATHED. FOLLOWED/IMPROVED (story, yarn).

CAPT (s/l *capped*). CAPTAIN, *OFFICER*. HEAD BOY/GIRL, *LEADER*, MASTER; **celeb**: ABSOLUTE (*Rivals*, Sheridan); *AHAB* (Moby Dick); NOLL BLUFF (Congreve); BOBADIL (*coward*, Jonson); BUOTH (Fielding); *CAT* (Mrs Dale's Diary, radio); CUTTLE (Dombey, *Dickens*); *DOG* (Archers, radio); FLINT (*parrot*, Treasure Island); GADSBY (*Kipling*); GULLIVER (*Swift*); HOOK (*Barrie*); HORNBLOWER (Forester); *JEHU* (bibl); *JOAB* (bibl); KETTLE (Hyne); NAAMAN (bibl); OSBORNE (Thackeray); *SENTRY* (Addison); DISCO TROOP (*Kipling*); EDWARD WAVERLEY (*Scott*); *Shak* char.

CAPTURE *CATCH, COP, TRAPPED*; TAKING.

CAR AUTO. VEHICLE; **types**: beach buggy, cabriolet, coupé, estate, formula 1, 2, etc, GT, hatchback, jeep, limousine, rally, runabout, saloon, sedan, sports [*Toad* of Toad Hall]; **makes**

(all ®): AUSTIN, BENTLEY, *BL*, BUICK, CADILLAC,
CHEVROLET, CITROËN, DARRACQ, *DODGE*, FIAT,
FORD, GENERAL MOTORS, HONDA, LANDROVER,
MAZDA, MERCEDES, *MG*, *MINI*, MODEL T, MORRIS,
NISSAN, PEUGEOT, PORSCHE, RANGE ROVER,
RENAULT, ROLLS, ROVER, SAAB, SUNBEAM, *T*,
TOYOTA, TRIUMPH, VAUXHALL, VOLKSWAGEN,
VOLVO, etc. *CARRIAGE*, CHARIOT, NACELLE,
GONDOLA (aero).
CARBON *MINERAL*; C (*chem*).
CAR CLUB *AA*, RAC.
CARD CAUTION, *CASE*, CHARACTER, WAG. CARDINAL.
TAROT; CLUB, DIAMOND, HEART, SPADE; TRUMP;
ACE, KING, QUEEN etc; (*Alice*); **coll** = cartophilist; **games**:

3-letters
GIN	MAW	*NAP*	PIT
LOO			

4-letters
BRAG	FARO	SKAT	SOLO
CRIB	GRAB	*SNAP*	*STOP*

5-letters
BUNKO	OMBRE	RUMMY	*WHIST*
DEMON	PITCH	SPOOF	
MONTE	POKER	VINT	

6-letters
BOSTON	ECARTE	FAN-TAN	RED DOG
BRIDGE	EUCHRE	PIQUET	*SPIDER*
CASINO			

7-letters
BEZIQUE	CARLTON	PONTOON	THE STAR
CANASTA	CASSINO	PRIMERO	STREETS

8-letters
ALL FOURS	THE CLOCK	KLONDYKE	PINOCHLE
BACCARAT	CRIBBAGE	*NAPOLEON*	
CANFIELD	GIN RUMMY	PATIENCE	

9+ letters

AUNT	HAPPY	THE
AGATHA	FAMILIES	REGIMENT
BEGGAR-MY-	MISS	ROUGE
NEIGHBOUR	MILLIGAN	ET NOIR
BLACKJACK	ONE	TRENTE ET
FOUR SEASONS	FOUNDATION	QUARANTE
GERMAN	RACING	TWENTY-ONE
FLEET	DEMON	VINGT-ET-UN

CARDIGAN *JERSEY*, PULLOVER, SWEATER, WOOLLY. EARL (Balaclava). *CASTLE.*

CARDINAL FUNDAMENTAL, IMPORTANT, *CHURCHMAN*; BOUCHER, WOLSEY (*Shak*); HUME [eminence, HE]. SONGBIRD (US). CLOAK. E, N, S, W (naut). *SPIDER.*

CARE ATTENTION, CAUTION, PAINS, TROUBLE. *CHARGE*, LOOK AFTER, PROTECT(ION), TEND. ANXIETY, WORRY; CONCERN, REGARD, *SORROW*. AFFECTION, LIKING, *LOVE*. [~ of = CO].

CARMELITE MENDICANT *FRIAR*, WHITE *FRIAR* [Berthold].

CARNATION *FLOWER*. BUTTONHOLE. MOTOR-RACE (crypt).

CARP *FISH, ID, ROACH*. CRITICIZE, FIND FAULT [captious].

CARPENTER *CABINET-MAKER*, JOINER, WOODWORKER [*Company* (livery)]; **celeb**: ADAM BEDE (Eliot), *JESUS, JOSEPH*, QUINCE, SNUG (MND, *Shak*), MUDDLE (Marryat); [*Alice; Chaucer*]. *ANT.*

CARPET DRUGGET, PILE, RUG [Axminster, Persian, Wilton, *tapestry*]. REPRIMAND, REPROVE, *ROCKET*, TELL OFF (sl).

CAR PLATE REGISTRATION. **Int identification:**

Country	Letters
Albania	AL
Alderney	GBA
Algeria	DZ
Argentina	RA
Australia	AUS
Austria	A
Bahamas	BS
Belgium	B

Brazil	BR
Bulgaria	BG
Canada	CDN
Colombia	CO
Costa Rica	CR
Cuba	C
Cyprus	CY
Czechoslovakia	CS
Denmark	DK
Egypt	ET
Finland	SF
France	F
Germany, East	DDR (ex)
Germany,	D
Great Britain	GB
Guernsey	GBG
Hong Kong	HK
Hungary	H
Iceland	IS
India	IND
Iran	IR
Ireland	IRL
Isle of Man	GBM
Israel	IL
Italy	I
Jamaica	JA
Japan	J
Jersey	GBJ
Luxembourg	L
Malta	M
Morocco	MA
Monaco	MC
Netherlands	NL
New Zealand	NZ
Norway	N
Panama	PA
Peru	PE
Poland	PL
Portugal	P
Romania	R
South Africa	ZA

Spain	E
Sweden	S
Switzerland	CH
Turkey	TR
UK	GB
USA	USA
USSR (former)	SU
Vatican City	V
Vietnam	VN
Yugoslavia (former)	YU
Zaire	ZR
Zambia	Z

CARRIAGE *DELIVERY*, FREIGHT. *BEARING*, GAIT. PRAM, PUSH-CHAIR. HORSE-DRAWN VEHICLE [Dalmatian]; **types**:

3-letters
CAB	*FLY*	GIG

4-letters
BIGA	EKKA	SHAY	TRAP
DRAY			

5-letters
BRAKE	*COACH*	GARRY	*SULKY*
BUGGY	COUPE	*STAGE*	TONGA

6-letters
BERLIN	HANSOM	*SPIDER*
CALASH	HERDIC (US)	TANDEM
CHAISE	JINGLE	TELAGA
DENNET	LANDAU	TROIKA
FIACRE (Fr)	RANDEM	*WHISKY*
GHARRI, -Y	SURREY	

7-letters
CALÈCHE (Fr)	GROWLER	RATTLER
CAROCHE	HACKERY	*TILBURY*
CHARIOT	HACKNEY	VIS-A-VIS
CRAWLER	KIBITKA (Russ)	
DROSHKY	*PHAETON*	

8-letters

BAROUCHE	CURRICLE	SOCIABLE
BROUGHAM	DEARBORN	STANHOPE
CARRIOLE	QUADRIGA	*VICTORIA*
CLARENCE		

9+ letters

BONESHAKER	FOUR-IN-HAND	POST-CHAISE
CABRIOLET	KITTEREEN	STAGECOACH
CURRICULUM	LANDAULET	TARANTASS
DILIGENCE	OPPENHEIMER	WAGONETTE

CARRY *BEAR*, SUPPORT, TOTE. BE PREGNANT.
~ **ON** CONTINUE. FLIRT. EMBARK, LOAD.

CARTOONIST ARTIST, CARICATURIST, DRAWER; **celeb**:
ARNO, Peter (US); BAIRNSFATHER, Bruce (Old Bill, Eng);
BATEMAN, H. M. (Eng); BIRD, Kenneth (Fougasse, Eng);
BROWNE, H. K. (Phiz, *Dickens*); CRUIKSHANK, George
(*Dickens*); HEATH ROBINSON, William (Eng); KEENE,
Charles Samuel (Punch, Eng); LANCASTER, David (Maudie
Littlehampton, Eng); LANGDON, David (Eng); *LOW*, Sir
David (Col Blimp, NZ); PHIZ (*Browne, Dickens*); SEARLE,
Ronald (St Trinian's, Eng); SHEPARD, Ernest H. (*Milne*,
Eng); *SPY (Ward)*; TENNIEL, Sir John (*Alice*); THELWELL
(ponies, Eng); *WARD*, Sir Leslie (*Spy*, Eng); *WREN*, Chris
(aircraft, Eng).

CASE 1. *BAGGAGE*, BOX, GRIP. COVER, ENCLOSE.
CAUSE, EVENT, SUIT (leg). CIRCUMSTANCE,
INSTANCE, POSITION. CONDITION (med). NOUN
FORM (gram): ABLATIVE, ACCUSATIVE, DATIVE,
NOMINATIVE, POSSESSIVE. UPPER/LOWER
TYPEFACE. *CARD*, CAUTION, *CHARACTER*,
COMEDIAN, *COMIC*, RIGHT ONE, WAG. 2. **In** ~: IF,
LEST. CRATED, ENCASED (crypt). Put designated word
round another as a ~ or enclosure, e.g. **In his case, biscuit
without it is a plant** (8) = HI(BISCU**)S, or else **Refusal in any case
is to give offence** (5) = AN(NO)Y.

CASH *MONEY*, READY; *COIN* (Ch and Ind); CENT,
DOLLAR, PENNY, POUND etc [*currencies*, q.v. for list].
DRAW OUT, PLAY WINNER (cards).

CASHIER ACCOUNTANT, BANK CLERK, TELLER.

DISCHARGE, DISMISS (mil).

CASSANDRA 1. Gk myth d of *Priam* and *Hecuba*. *Apollo* gave her the ability to prophesy, but always unheeded. She was k by *Clytemnestra*. [T and C, *Shak*]. 2. A minor *PLANET*.

CASSOWARY Flightless bird (Aus) [Dinornis (ex, NZ), Emu, Moa, Nandoo, Ostrich].

CAST (s/l *caste*). PITCH, *SHED, SHY*, THROW. *FORM*, FOUND, MOLD (US), MOULD, SHAPE. ACTORS, DRAMATIS PERSONAE, PLAYERS, THESPIANS. WORM MOUND. TWIST; SQUINT. SHADE, TINGE. QUALITY, TYPE. *Assembly* of hawks.

CASTE (s/l *cast*). CLASS (Hind).

CASTLE *CHESSPIECE, ROOK*. WICKET (cricket sl). CITADEL, FORT(RESS), STRONGHOLD [**arch**: bailey (courtyard), ballistraria (arrow slot), barbican (outwork), bartizan (overhanging turret), bastion (rampart), battlement (indented parapet), crenel (embrasure), donjon (keep), drawbridge (lifting access), embrasure (battlement niche), keep (inner fort), merlon (battlement upright), moat (ditch), motte (fortified mound), oilette (missile slot), parapet (low projecting wall), portcullis (drop gate), postern (private entrance), rampart (defensive wall), turret (tower)]. **Examples in UK:**

3-letters

HAY (Wal)	MEY (Sc)	ODO (Wal)	*RED* (Sc)
MAY (Sc)	MOY (Sc)	OER (Sc)	

4-letters

ACRE (Eng)	DOTE (Eng)	MAOL (Sc)	*RING* (Eng)
AVON (Eng)	DRUM (Sc)	MAUD (Sc)	ROCH (Wal)
BERE (Wal)	DUNS (Sc)	PIEL (Eng)	*STAR* (Wal)
DEAL (Eng)	*FAST* (Eng)	POOL (Wal)	UDNY (Sc)
DOON (Sc)	HOLT (Wal)	RABY (Eng)	*YORK* (Eng)
DORE (Eng)	LEOD (Sc)	RAIT (Sc)	

5-letters

BLAIR (Sc)	CLARE (Eng)	CROFT (Eng)
BORVE (Sc)	COITY (Eng)	CUTRA (Ire)
BOYNE (Sc)	COMBE (Eng)	DONNE (Sc)
BURGH (Eng)	COOLE (Ire)	DOVER (Eng)
CAREW (Wal)	CORFE (Eng)	DROGO (Eng)
CHIRK (Wal)	COWES (Eng)	DUART (Sc)

ELCHO (Sc)
EWLOE (Wal)
FLINT (Wal)
FYVIE (Sc)
GYLEN (Sc)
HAWEN (Ire)
HEVER (Eng)
HURST (Eng)

KEISS (Sc)
KELDY (Eng)
KNOCK (Sc)
LEEDS (Eng)
LEWES (Eng)
LYMNE (Eng)
MYLOR (Eng)
POWIS (Wal)

RIBER (Eng)
SLANE (Ire)
SCONE (Sc)
SKIBO (Sc)
STOBO (Sc)
SWEEN (Sc)
TENBY (Wal)
ZENDA (fict, *Hope*)

6-letters

ABOYNE (Sc)
AIRLIE (Sc)
AUCHEN (Sc)
BODIAM (Eng)
BOLTON (Eng)
BRODIE (Sc)
BROUGH (Eng)
BUILTH (Wal)
CAMBER (Eng)
CAWDOR (Sc)
CAWOOD (Eng)
CONWAY (Wal)
CORNET (CI)
DUDLEY (Eng)
DUFFUS (Eng)
DUNDEE (Sc)
DUNURE (Sc)
DURHAM (Eng)

EDZELL (Sc)
FLOORS (Sc)
FORTER (Sc)
FRASER (Sc)
GLAMIS (Sc)
GORDON (Sc)
GWRYCH (Wal)
GWYDIR (Wal)
HAILES (Sc)
HODDOM (Sc)
HOWARD (Eng)
HUNTLY (Sc)
KENDAL (Eng)
LATHOM (Eng)
LUDLOW (Eng)
LUMLEY (Eng)
MAIDEN (Eng)
MIDMAR (Sc)

MILLOM (Eng)
MORTON (Sc)
NEWARK (Eng)
NUNNEY (Eng)
OGMORE (Wal)
OXFORD (Eng)
PICTON (Wal)
RAGLAN (Eng)
RAHEEN (Ire)
RIPLEY (Eng)
ROWTON (Eng)
SPYNIE (Sc)
STRAME (Sc)
TARBET (Sc)
WALMER (Eng)
WALTON (Eng)
YESTER (Sc)

7-letters

ADAMANT (*G and S*)
AFFLECK (Sc)
ALNWICK (Eng)
APPLEBY (Eng)
ARDROSS (Sc)
ARUNDEL (Eng)
BALLOCH (Sc)
BARBURY (Eng)
BARHOLM (Sc)
BEESTON (Eng)
BELVOIR (Eng)

BLARNEY (Ire)
BRAEMAR (Sc)
BRAMBER (Eng)
BRATTON (Eng)
BRODICK (Sc)
CADBURY (Eng)
CAISTER (Eng)
CALSHOT (Eng)
CARDIFF (Wal)
CHESTER (Eng)
COMPTON (Eng)

COOLING (Eng)
COWDRAY (Eng)
CRATHES (Sc)
CULZEAN (Sc)
DENBIGH (Wal)
DITCHES (Eng)
DOUGLAS (Sc)
DUNLUCE (Ire)
DUNSKEY (Sc)
DUNSTER (Eng)
DUNTULM (Sc)
DYNEVOR (Wal)
FINAVON (Sc)
GILLING (Eng)
GUTHRIE (Sc)
HARLECH (Wal)
HUNTLEY (Sc)
KANTURK (Ire)
KENNEDY (Sc)
KIELDER (Eng)
KILMORY (Sc)
KINKELL (Sc)
LANGLEY (Eng)
LOCHNAW (Sc)
LOWTHER (Sc)
MINGARY (Sc)
NAWORTH (Eng)
NEWPORT (Wal)

NORWICH (Eng)
OLDBURY (Eng)
PENRHYN (Wal)
PENRICE (Wal)
PENRITH (Eng)
PRUDHOE (Eng)
RATTRAY (Sc)
RUTHVEN (Sc)
SADDELL (Sc)
ST DENIS (Wal)
ST MAWES (Eng)
SEAGATE (Sc)
SIZERGH (Eng)
SKIPTON (Eng)
STALKER (Sc)
SUDELEY (Eng)
SWANSEA (Wal)
TAUNTON (Eng)
THREAVE (Sc)
TILBURY (Eng)
TUTBURY (Eng)
UISDEIN (Sc)
WARDOUR (Eng)
WARWICK (Eng)
WIGMORE (Eng)
WINDSOR (Eng)
WRESSLE (Eng)

8-letters

ABERDOUR (Sc)
AMBERLEY (Eng)
ARDMADDY (Sc)
BALMORAL (Sc)
BALVENIE (Sc)
BAMBURGH (Eng)
BERKELEY (Eng)
BROUGHAM (Eng)
BRUCKLEY (Sc)
BURLEIGH (Sc)
CAMPBELL (Sc)
CARDIGAN (Wal)

CARLISLE (Eng)
CARSLUTH (Sc)
CHEPSTOW (Wal)
CIGERRAN (Wal)
CORGARFF (Sc)
CRAWFORD (Sc)
CRICHTON (Sc)
DARNAWAY (Sc)
DEGANWY (Wal)
DELGATIE (Sc)
DIRLETON (Sc)
DOUBTING (Pilgrim's Progress)

DRUMMOND (Sc)
DRYSLWYN (Wal)
DUNOTTAR (Sc)
DUNTRUNE (Sc)
DUNVEGAN (Sc)
FINLARIG (Eng)
GOODRICH (Eng)
HELMSLEY (Eng)
HERTFORD (Eng)
KIDWELLY (Wal)
KILCHURN (Sc)
LANGWELL (Sc)
LONGFORD (Eng)
LUSCOMBE (Eng)
MAXSTOKE (Eng)
MOUNTJOY (Ire)
MUCHALLS (Sc)
NEIDPATH (Sc)
NOTTLAND (Sc)
PEMBROKE (Wal)
PEVENSEY (Eng)

PITCAPLE (Sc)
PITSLIGO (Sc)
PITTULIE (Sc)
PLYMOUTH (Eng)
RHUDDLAN (Wal)
RICHMOND (Eng)
ROTHESAY (Sc)
ST DONAT'S (Wal)
SANDWICH (Eng)
SOUTHSEA (Eng)
STIRLING (Sc)
STOKESAY (Eng)
STORMONT (Ire)
SYCHARTH (Wal)
TAMWORTH (Eng)
THETFORD (Eng)
TINTAGEL (Eng)
URQUHART (Sc)
WALWORTH (Eng)
YARNBURY (Eng)

9-letters

ALLINGTON (Eng)
BEAUMARIS (Wal)
BLACKNESS (Sc)
BORTHWICK (Sc)
CARDONESS (Sc)
CARLSWITH (Sc)
CAULFIELD (Ire)
CILGERRAN (Wal)
CLAYPOTTS (Sc)
CLITHEROE (Eng)
COMLONGON (Sc)
CRAIGNISH (Sc)
CRICCIETH (Wal)
CROOKSTON (Sc)
DALHOUSIE (Sc)
DALNAGLAR (Sc)
DINAS BRAN (Wal)
DONNAMORE (Ire)
DRUMMINOR (Sc)

DUMBARTON (Sc)
DUNDONALD (Sc)
EARLSHALL (Sc)
EAST COWES (Eng)
EDINBURGH (Sc)
FINDLATER (Sc)
FINDOCHTEY (Sc)
GLASCLUNE (Sc)
GREYSTOKE (Eng)
HAVERFORD (Wal)
HEDINGHAM (Eng)
HERMITAGE (Sc)
INVERARY (Sc)
KIESSIMUL (Sc)
KILDRUMMY (Sc)
KILKERRAN (Sc)
KILLOCHAN (Sc)
KILRACOCK (Sc)
KIMBOLTON (Eng)

LANCASTER (Eng)
MANORBIER (Wal)
MELBOURNE (Eng)
MIDDLEHAM (Eng)
MUNCASTER (Eng)
NEWCASTLE (Eng)
OLD SLAINS (Sc)
PEMBRIDGE (Eng)
PENDENNIS (Eng)
PICKERING (Eng)
POWDERHAM (Eng)
RESTORMEL (Eng)

ROCHESTER (Eng)
ST ANDREWS (Sc)
SAN SIMEON (US)
SCALLOWAY (Sc)
SHERBORNE (Eng)
SKENFRITH (Wal)
TANTALLON (Sc)
THORNBURY (Eng)
TREGENNIS (Eng)
ULZIESIDE (Sc)
WARKWORTH (Eng)

10+ letters

ABERYSTWYTH (Wal)
ARMATHWAITE (Eng)
ASHBY DE LA ZOUCH
  (Eng)
AUCHINDOWN (Sc)
AUGHENTAINE (Ire)
BERRY POMEROY (Eng)
BODELWYDDAN (Wal)
CAERLAVEROCK (Sc)
CAERNARFON (Wal)
CAERPHILLY (Wal)
CARISBROOKE (Eng)
CARMARTHEN (Wal)
CARNASSERIE (Sc)
CARREG CENNEN (Wal)
CASTELL Y BERE (Wal)
CASTLECRAIG (Sc)
CHILLINGHAM (Eng)
CHRISTCHURCH (Eng)
COCKERMOUTH (Eng)
COLCHESTER (Eng)
CONISBROUGH (Eng)
CRAIGIEVAR (Sc)
CRAIGNETHAN (Sc)
DOLWYDDELAN (Wal)
DONNINGTON (Eng)
DUNSTANBURGH (Eng)
EILEAN DONNAN (Sc)

FORT GEORGE (Sc)
FORT WILLIAM (Sc)
FOTHERINGHAY (Eng)
FRAMLINGHAM (Eng)
FRAOCH EILEAN (Sc)
HARRY AVERY'S (Ire)
HERSTMONCEUX (Eng)
INVERALLOCHY (Sc)
INVERLOCHY (Sc)
KAIM OF MATHERS (Sc)
KENILWORTH (Eng)
KINLOCHALINE (Sc)
KIRKCUDBRIGHT (Sc)
LAUNCESTON (Eng)
LINDISFARNE (Eng)
LINLITHGOW (Sc)
LLANSTEPHAN (Wal)
LOCHINDORE (Sc)
LOUGH CUTRA (Ire)
OKEHAMPTON (Eng)
PAINSCASTLE (Wal)
PONTEFRACT (Eng)
POR(T)CHESTER (Eng)
PORTSMOUTH (Eng)
RAVENSBURGH (Eng)
RAVENSCRAIG (Sc)
ROCKINGHAM (Eng)
ST BRIAVEL'S (Eng)

SCARBOROUGH (Eng)   TOWER OF LONDON
SMAITHAM TOWER (Sc)   (Eng)
SUTHERLAND (Eng)   WHITE SHEET (Eng)
TATTERSHALL (Eng)   *WINCHESTER* (Eng)

[~s **in the Downs** = DEAL, *SANDWICH*, WALMER].
Comp = *Elephant*.
CASTOR (s/l caster). 1. (SWIVEL) WHEEL. BEAVER
EXTRACT. OIL. *HAT* (sl). 2. Gk myth *twin* of *Pollux*. A horse
tamer and patron of seamen. One of the *ARGONAUTS*. With
Pollux, two stars: Dioscuri.
CAT 1. RAISE/WEIGH ANCHOR (naut). BURGLAR,
ROBBER. JAZZ ENTHUSIAST. LASH, SCOURGE,
WHIP [~ o' nine tails]. *FAMILIAR*, GRIMALKIN [*witch*].
MALICIOUS WOMAN. VOMIT (sl). 2. Feline animal.
KITTY, MOGGIE, PUSS(Y), TOM; MARMALADE,
TABBY, TORTOISESHELL [T. S. Eliot; Bast (Egy *god*);
Freya; Lear; 9 lives]; **breeds**: ABYSSINIAN (swims),
AFGHAN, BLOTCHED, BLUE RUSSIAN, BURMESE,
CHARTREUSE, KILKENNY (fighting), MALTESE, MANX
(tailless), PERSIAN, SIAMESE; **male** = TOM, GIB (Sc);
fem = QUEEN, DOE (Sc); **offspring** = KITTEN; **assembly**
= cluster (but kindle of kittens); **comp** = mouse; ~ **family**:
BOBCAT, CARACAL, CHEETAH, CIVET, COUGAR,
EYRA, GENET, JAGUAR, (SNOW) LEOPARD, *LION*,
LYNX, MARGAY, NANDINE, OCELOT, *OUNCE*,
PUMA, RASSE, SERVAL, *TIGER*, TIGON, WILD~
(Geoffroy's ~, Kodkod, Oncilla, Pampas ~) [feral; *weasel*];
celeb: BAGHEERA (*Kipling*), CAPTAIN (Mrs Dale, radio),
CHESHIRE (*Alice*), DINAH (*Alice*), FELIX (Sullivan
cartoon), HODGE (Dr Johnson), MITTENS, MOPPET
(*Potter*), ORLANDO (Marmalade ~), SHERE KHAN
(*Kipling*), SILVESTER (Tweetie Pie cartoon), SIMPKIN
(*Potter*), TABITHA TWITCHIT (Beatrix *Potter*), ~ that
walked by himself (Just So Stories, *Kipling*), TOM (~ and
Jerry cartoon), TOM KITTEN (Beatrix *Potter*) and, all
from T. S. Eliot: BUSTOPHER JONES (~ about Town,
club), OLD DEUTERONOMY (*long life*), GROWLTIGER
(bargee, GRIDDLEBONE), GUS (theatre), JELLICLE
~s (*dancing*), JENNYANYDOTS (Gumbie), MACAVITY
(*Napoleon* of crime, *unseen*), MR MISTOFFELEES (conjuror),

MORGAN (*pirate*, commissionaire), MUNGOJERRIE and
RUMPLETEAZER (*robbers*), RUMPUSCAT (fierce), RUM
TUM TUGGER (curious), SKIMBLESHANKS (*railway*). [Dick
Whittington; Puss in Boots].

CATCH ARREST, CAPTURE, LAND, NET, SNARE, *TRAP*.
INCUR, RECEIVE. AIR, DITTY, *SONG*. HIT. BAG (fishing,
shooting). DISMISS (*cricket*). COUP, GOOD MATCH.

CATHAY CHINA (arch).

CATHEDRAL CHURCH (diocesan) [*bishop; episcopal sig;
see*]. ~ **parts**: adytum, aisle, altar, apse, aumbry, baldachin,
blindstor(e)y, chancel, chapterhouse, choir school, chrismal,
ciborium, clerestory, cloisters, confessional, crypt, faldstool,
font, jube, Lady chapel, lectern, lich/lych (corpse) gate,
muniment room, nave, organ loft, pew, porch, presbytery,
pulpit, reredos, rood screen, sacristy, sanctuary, side chapel,
tabernacle, transept, triforium, vestry (and see *Architecture;
Window*). **Celeb** ~s: Aberdeen, Bath, Bristol, Canterbury,
Chester, Chichester, Coventry, Durham, Edinburgh, Ely, Exeter,
Glasgow, Gloucester, Guildford, Lichfield, Lincoln, Liverpool,
Manchester, Norwich, Oxford, Peterborough, Ripon, Rochester,
St Albans, St Paul's, Salisbury, Tewkesbury, Truro, Wells,
Winchester, Worcester, York Minster. ~ **vessels:** see *church*.

CATO 1. Rom statesman/general (234–149 B.C.). Consul and
censor, he disliked Carthage. 2. Descendant of (1), *Stoic
philosopher* who lived 95-46 B.C., and was enemy of *Caesar*.
3. ~ Street, the site of an unsuccessful plot to murder Castlereagh
in 1820.

CATTLE *BISON, BUFFALO,* COW(S), KINE, LIVESTOCK,
NEAT, *OX(EN)*, STOCK; LOWER (crypt); **assembly**
= drove, herd, **male** = BULL, **fem** = *COW*, **offspring**
= *CALF*; **breeds**: ABERDEEN ANGUS, AYRSHIRE,
CAT(T)ALO, CHAROL(L)AIS, CREOLE, *DEXTER*,
FRIESIAN, *GUERNSEY*, HEREFORD, HIGHLAND,
HOLSTEIN, *JERSEY*, KERRY, KYLOE, REDPOLL,
SHORTHORN, SOUTH DEVON, WELSH BLACK.

CAUCASIAN *WHITE*.

CAUGHT (s/l *court*). C, CT, DISMISSED (*cricket*). SNAGGED,
SNARED, TRAPPED.

CAURUS Rom myth NW *WIND* (Gk = SKIRON).

CAUTION PRUDENCE; WARNING. *CASE*, CHARACTER,
WAG.

CAVE CELLAR, ROCK DWELLING, POTHOLE [*Aeolus;*

study]. *FORE*, LOOK-OUT (Lat), WARNING. COLLAPSE, SUBSIDE.

CAVEMAN *HERMIT*, TROGLODYTE; CELLIST (crypt). LOOK-OUT, SENTRY (crypt). POTHOLER.

CB COMPANION (Order of the Bath), *ORDER*. RADIO.

CBE COMPANION (Order of the Br Empire), *MEDAL*.

CBI BOSSES, EMPLOYERS (Confederation of Br Industry).

CBS *BROADCASTING* (US).

CC CUBIC CENTIMETRES. TWO HUNDRED.

CD CADMIUM (*chem*). CIVIL DEFENCE. CORPS DIPLOMATIQUE.

CDR COMMANDER, OFFICER.

CE CERIUM (*chem*). CHURCH (OF ENGLAND). CIVIL ENGINEER.

CEASEFIRE Stop shooting, hence CUT (film, crypt).

CEDILLA *ACCENT* (ç = sibilant).

CELEBRATED EXTOLLED, FAMOUS, PRAISED, WELL-KNOWN, HONOURED, OBSERVED, OFFICIATED, PERFORMED, SUNG.

CELEBRITY BIG-WIG, *LION*, N, NAME, *STAR*, VIP.

CELLIST *BOWMAN* (crypt); FIDDLER. CAVEMAN, *HERMIT*, *PRISONER*, RECLUSE (crypt). *GAOLER*, JAILER, WARDER (crypt).

CELSIUS C (Centigrade; temperature).

CENSORSHIP CUTTING, FAULT-FINDING, PRUNING, SCREENING [*Cato*]; **film categories**: A (adults only; advisory), AA (over 15, was over 14), G (general audience – US), H (horrific; over 16), PG (parental guidance), R (clubs; and restricted – US), U (universal), X (sexy – over 18).

CENT (s/l *scent*, sent). CENTURY. *COIN*.

CENTAUR 1. Myth horse with human head (thus with man's head, M*ORSE); *CHIRON*, NESSUS (*Hercules*), PHOLUS. 2. *CONSTELLATION*.

CENTIGRADE C [Celsius; temperature].

CENTRE MIDDLE. Centre of word or phrase, e.g. **Civic centre** = v, or **Town centre** = ow (crypt).

CERAMICS *CHINA*, EARTHENWARE, PORCELAIN, *POTTERY*; **types**:

BOW	CHELSEA	DAVENPORT
BRISTOL	COALPORT ®	DELFT (NL)
CAUGHLEY ®	COPELAND ®	*DERBY*

DOULTON ®	MEISSEN (Ger)	SEVRES (Fr)
DRESDEN (Ger)	MING (Ch)	SPODE ®
DUX	MINTON ®	STAFFORDSHIRE
LOWESTOFT	NEW HALL	TANG (Ch)
MASON	ROCKINGHAM	*WORCESTER*

CERBERUS Gk myth three-headed dog, guarding *Hades* on the banks of the *Styx*. UNDERDOG (crypt).

CERCYON Gk myth *bully*, who wrestled strangers to death; k by *Theseus*.

CERES (s/l *series*). 1. Rom goddess of *NATURE*; EARTH MOTHER; m of *Acheron*. **Gk** = *DEMETER*. 2. Largest of the minor *PLANETS*, with orbit between *Mars* and *Jupiter*. 3. *Shak* char (Temp).

CERTAIN *BOUND*, SPECIFIC, SURE.

CESTR *Episcopal sig* of *CHESTER*.

CETACEA AQUATIC MAMMAL: *DOLPHIN, PORPOISE, WHALE*.

CEZAR ® *AWARD* (films, Fr).

CF COMPARE. CONFER. CARRY FORWARD (comm).

CH CHAPTER. CHILD. CHINA. CHURCH. (*COMPANION* OF) HONOUR. SWITZERLAND (*car plate*).

Ch China. ~ese.

CHAFF BADINAGE, BANTER, *TEASING*. HUSKS. ANTI-RADAR FOIL; WINDOW (mil code name).

CHAIR FASTENING, RAILHOLDER, SOCKET (rly). PROFESSORSHIP. ~MAN, PRESIDENT; CONTROL, PRESIDE. THE ELECTRIC ~. SEAT, STOOL; and see *FURNITURE* for list.

CHAIRED CONTROLLED, TOOK THE CHAIR. CARRIED SHOULDER-HIGH. SEATED, UPHOLSTERED (crypt). Railway lines (crypt).

CHAIRMAN *MC*, PRESIDENT, SEDAN-BEARER (arch). Cabinet/furniture maker, upholsterer (crypt) e.g. ADAM, CHIPPENDALE, HEPPLEWHITE, SHERATON.

CHALCEDONY *GEM*, SEMI-PRECIOUS STONE; *AGATE, BLOODSTONE*, CHRYSOPRASE, *CORNELIAN, ONYX, SARD*, SARDONYX.

CHAMPION ACE, RECORD HOLDER. *COMIC*. WONDER *HORSE*.

CHANGE *Anag*. 1. ALTER, EXCHANGE, SUBSTITUTE, SWITCH, VARIETY. REDRESS (crypt). LOOSE COINS,

MONEY: CENTS, PENCE etc. 2. Appearing as part of the answer, *anags* its fellow word, e.g. **Rove, for instance, the switch** (10) = CHANGEOVER.

CHANGE SIDES 1. CROSS THE FLOOR, DEFECT, SWITCH ALLEGIANCE, TURNCOAT. 2. *Anag* of 'sides', e.g. SISED, DISES etc (crypt).

CHAOS 1. CONFUSION, PANDEMONIUM, UPROAR (**opp** = *order*). FORMLESS SPACE, PRIMORDIAL DEEP, VOID. 2. Gk *goddess* of vacant space which existed before the Creation, m of Erebus and *Nyx*, and the oldest of the gods. **Egy** = *Nun*.

CHAPERONE DUENNA; GUARD OF HONOUR, NEAR MISS (crypt).

CHAPMAN COMMERCIAL TRAVELLER, DRUMMER, PEDLAR, *REP. WRITER*. COWBOY (crypt).

CHAPTER C, CH. ACT, STATUTE. ORDER. SECTION.

CHAR BURN, SCORCH. CHARACTER (abbr). CLEAN(ER), DAILY, DO, DOMESTIC, MRS MOPP, TREASURE, WASHERWOMAN. TEA (sl); **comp** = wad. *FISH*, TROUT.

CHARACTER IDENTITY, PERSON(ALITY), TRAIT; TYPE (*study*). **Pl** = CAST, DRAMATIS PERSONAE (theat). ATTRIBUTE, PROPERTY, QUALITY. LETTERS. *CASE*, COMEDIAN.

CHARGE CARE; *MINOR, WARD*. ASSAULT, ATTACK, HURTLE, ONSLAUGHT, RUSH. BOOST, ENERGIZE, REVITALIZE. LEVY, PAYMENT, PRICE. ACHIEVEMENT, ARMS, BADGE, BEARINGS, DEVICE, SHIELD (herald).

CHARIOT HORSE-DRAWN *CARRIAGE*, CURRICULUM (race ~), *JUGGERNAUT*, QUADRIGA (mil) [*Aurora, Boadicea, Elijah, Freya, Jehu, Medea, Phaeton*; *constellation*] (tarot).

CHARM ATTRACTION, BEWITCH, DELIGHT, ENCHANT, ENTICE, *ENTRANCE*, FASCINATE, TEMPT, WINSOME, *GRACE*, IT, SA. AMULET, FETISH, MASCOT, TALISMAN; CANTRIP, INCANTATION, SPELL. *Assembly* of FINCHES.

CHARON Gk myth s of Erebus and *Nyx*. FERRYMAN of the dead over the rivers *Acheron* and *Styx* [*Cocytus, Lethe, Periphlegethon*], past the dog *Cerberus*; his fee was the Obolus.

CHART DIRECT, *PLOT*, RECORD. MAP, PLAN, SEA-MAP. **Pl** = RATING [top ten etc].

CHARTER *DEED*, GRANT. HIRE. *RIGHTS*. NAVIGATOR (crypt).

CHARY *SHY*, WARY.

CHARYBDIS A whirlpool which, with the rock *Scylla*, formed a hazard to seafarers in the Straits of Messina; now called Galofaro.

CHAUCER GEOFFREY (*c.*1340–1400); s of Agnes and John ~, vintner, mar Philippa and f of Lewis. *Page* to wife of Edward III's son and a court diplomat. Father of English poetry. **His works include**: Consolations of Philosophy (trans of treatise on the astrolabe), Romance of the Rose (trans), The Book of the Duchess, The House of Fame, The Legend of Good Women, The Parliament of Fowls, Troilus and Cressida, and The Canterbury Tales with its Prologue, whose **chars** assembled at the Tabard Inn, Southwark, **include**: the Canon's Yeoman, the *Cook*, the *Doctor* of Medicine (Physician), the Franklin, the *Friar* (a Limiter), *Host* (Harry Bailey), the *Knight*, the Lady Prioress (Madam Eglantine), the Manciple, Milibeus, the Merchant, the Miller (a *wrestler*), the *Monk*, the *Nun*'s Priest, the Pardoner, the *Parson* and his br the Ploughman, the *Reeve*, the *Scholar* (Clerk), the Sea Captain, *Sailor* or Shipman (his boat, the Magdalen), the Second *Nun*, the *Sergeant-at-Law* (Man of Law), Sir *Topaz*, the Squire (s of the Knight), the Summoner, and the Wife of Bath (gap-toothed); also travelling, but without a recorded tale, were the *Carpenter*, the Dyer, the Haberdasher, the Ploughman, the Tapestry Maker, the *Weaver* and the Yeoman.

CHCH CHRISTCHURCH.

CHE GUEVARA, REVOLUTIONARY.

CHEAT CON, COZEN, DECEIVE(R), FIDDLE, FRAUD, SWINDLE(R), TRICK(STER).

CHECK DAM, HOLD IN, IMPEDE, PAUSE, SLOW, *STEM*. CONTROL, MAKE SURE, *MARK, TICK*. REBUFF, REBUKE, RESTRAIN(T). THREATEN (chess). *BILL*, CHEQUE, DRAFT, LETTER OF CREDIT (US). HATCH, PLAID, SQUARED, *TARTAN*.

CHEESE MALLOW FRUIT. SKITTLES DISC. VIP (sl). Decorative coil of rope (naut). [camera, smile]. PRESSED CURDS; **comp** = *bread*; **types (many ®)**:

under 8-letters

BLUE	CREAM	GOAT	STILTON
BOURSIN	CURD	GOUDA	SWISS
BRIE	DANISH	GRUYERE	
CHEDDAR	*DUTCH*	MYCELLA	
COTTAGE	EDAM	*SAGE*	

8+ letters

BRICKBAT	PARMESAN
CAMEMBERT	PECORINO
CHESHIRE	PORT SALUT
COTSWOLD	PROVOLONE
GAMBOZOLA	ROQUEFORT
GLOUCESTER	TILSITER
GORGONZOLA	WENSLEYDALE
JARLSBERG	WESTMINSTER BLUE
LYMESWOLD	

CHEM Chemistry.
CHEMICAL ELEMENT BASIC SUBSTANCE,
IRRESOLVABLE; e.g.:

Actinium	$= AC$
Aluminium	$= AL$
Argon	$= A$
Arsenic	$= AS$
Barium	$= BA$
Boron	$= B$
Cadmium	$= CD$
Carbon	$= C$
Chromium	$= CR$
Cobalt	$= CO$
Copper	$= CU$
Fluoride	$= F$
Gold	$= AU$
Helium	$= HE$
Hydrogen	$= H$
Iodine	$= I$
Iridium	$= IR$
Iron	$= FE$
Krypton	$= KR$
Lead	$= PB$
Magnesium	$= MG$
Mercury	$= HG$
Neon	$= NE$
Nickel	$= NI$
Nitrogen	$= N$
Oxygen	$= O$
Palladium	$= PD$

Phosphorus	= *P*
Platinum	= *PT*
Potassium	= *K*
Silicon	= *SI*
Silver	= *AG*
Sodium	= *NA*
Sulphur	= *S*
Tin	= SN
Titanium	= TI
Uranium	= *U*
Wolfram	= *W*
Xenon	= XE
Zinc	= ZN
A	= ARGON
AC	= ACTINIUM
AG	= *SILVER*
AL	= ALUMINIUM
AS	= ARSENIC
AU	= *GOLD*
B	= BORON
BA	= BARIUM
C	= CARBON
CD	= CADMIUM
CO	= COBALT
CR	= CHROMIUM
CU	= *COPPER*
F	= FLUORINE
FE	= *IRON*
H	= HYDROGEN
HE	= HELIUM
HG	= *MERCURY*
I	= IODINE
IR	= IRIDIUM
K	= POTASSIUM
KR	= KRYPTON
MG	= MAGNESIUM
N	= NITROGEN
NA	= *SODIUM*
NE	= NEON
NI	= *NICKEL*
O	= OXYGEN

P	= PHOSPHORUS
PB	= *LEAD*
PD	= PALLADIUM
PT	= *PLATINUM*
S	= SULPHUR
SI	= SILICON
SN	= *TIN*
TI	= TITANIUM
U	= URANIUM
W	= WOLFRAM
XE	= XENON
ZN	= ZINC

CHEMIST DISPENSER. MPS.

CHESSPIECE BISHOP, *CASTLE*, *KING*, *KNIGHT*, PAWN, *QUEEN*, *ROOK*. BOARDMAN (crypt).

CHEST BREAST, BUST, FRONT TORSO, THORAX [pectoral]. FUND. COLLECTOR, CONTAINER, RESERVOIR (tech). *BOX*, STORAGE CONTAINER; and see *FURNITURE* for list.

CHESTER 1. DEVA (*Rom*). *CASTLE*. *RACETRACK* (horses). 2. **Episcopal sig** = CESTR. 3. *Herald*.

CHESTERTON 1. Gilbert Keith, *poet* and *writer*; **books**: The *Club* of *Queer* Trades, Father Brown *detective stories*, The Man who was *Thursday*, The *Napoleon* of Notting Hill. 2. DURNOVARIA (Rom).

CHIC À LA MODE, ELEGANT, FASHIONABLE, IN, SMART.

CHICHESTER 1. *WORLD-GIRDLER*. NOVIOMAGUS (*Rom*). 2. **Episcopal sig** = CICESTR.

CHICKEN AFRAID. YOUNG WOMAN. BIDDY, HEN, POULTRY (*male and female*). **Breeds**: Ancona, Bantam, black/blue/buff Orpington, Cochin, Faverolle, Leghorn, Minorca, Plymouth Rock, Rhode Island red/white, Wyandotte.

CHIEF GOD Gk = *ZEUS*, **Rom** = JOVE, *JUPITER*, **A Sax** = *WODEN*, **Bab** = ANU, BEL/BELUS, **Ch** = XANGTI, **Egy** = *OSIRIS*, TEMU, **Ind** = BRAHMA, SHIVA, **Nor** = *ODIN*, **Phoen** = *BAAL*.

CHIEF GODDESS Gk = *HERA*, **Rom** = *JUNO*, **Egy** = *ISIS*, **Ind** = *DEVI*, **Bab** = BELIT/BELTIS.

CHILD 1. CH, ISSUE. TOT. Human *offspring*. [*Dickens; Moloch; patron saint*]. 2. Monday's ~ is fair of *face*; Tuesday's ~ is full of *grace*; Wednesday's ~ is full of

woe; Thursday's ~ has far to go; Friday's ~ is *loving* and
giving; Saturday's ~ works hard for its *living*; but the ~
that is born on a Sabbath day is bonny and blithe, and *good*
and gay.

CHILDBIRTH 1. BEARING, DELIVERY, LABOUR.
2. **Goddess: Gk** = *HERA*, **Rom** = *JUNO*.

CHIM(A)ERA Gk myth firebreathing *MONSTER* (front lion,
middle goat, back dragon), k by *Bellerophon*. VOLCANO.
[*Typhon*].

CHINA Ch. CATHAY, MANGI [mandarins, *study*]. *CERAMICS*;
DISHES, PLATES, SERVICE. 20th *anniversary*. MATE
(rh sl).

CHINAMAN *BOXER*, CHINK, MANDARIN. *BOSIE*,
GOOGLY (*cricket*).

CHINESE CALENDAR In order to get to know the animals better,
Buddha called them to him, and promised to reward all who
came. Only twelve turned up, so he dedicated a year to each in
order of arrival.

Goat	1943	'55	'67	'79	'91	03 15
Monkey	1944	'56	'68	'80	'92	04 16
Cock	1945	'57	'69	'81	'93	05 17
Dog	1946	'58	'70	'82	'94	06
Pig	1947	'59	'71	'83	'95	07
Rat	1948	'60	'72	'84	'96	08
Buffalo	1949	'61	'73	'85	'97	09
Tiger	1950	'62	'74	'86	'98	10
Rabbit	1951	'63	'75	'87	'99	11
Dragon	1952	'64	'76	'88	'00	12
Snake	1953	'65	'77	'89	'01	13
Horse	1954	'66	'78	'90	'02	14

(The Year of the Monkey always exactly divides by 12)

CHINESE DYNASTY *Noble* house (or *royal family*) of Ch; in
order: HSIA *c.*2205–1750 B.C.; SHANG *c.*1750–1127 B.C.;
CHOU *c.*1127 – 225 B.C. (Confucius); QING 225–206 B.C.
(Great Wall); HAN 206 B.C.–A.D. 220; Three Kingdoms A.D.
220–265; Six Dynasties A.D. 265–588; SUI A.D. 589–618 (*Huns,*
Attila, Hsiung-Nu); TANG A.D. 618–906; Five Dynasties
A.D. 906–959; SUNG 960–1260; YUAN 1260–1368 (Mongols,
Genghis Khan, Kublai Khan, Marco Polo); MING 1368–1644;
MANCHU or CHIN 1644–1911.

CHIRON 1. Gk myth wise CENTAUR, teacher of *Achilles*, Diomedes and *Jason* in gymnastics, hunting, medicine, music and prophecy. 2. A minor *PLANET* orbiting the *Sun* between *Saturn* and *Venus*.

CHLORIS Gk *goddess* of *FLOWERS*. **Rom** = *FLORA*.

CHOICE OPTION, PREFERENCE, SELECTION. APPROPRIATE, ELITE, EXQUISITE, *FLOWER*, SELECT. ALTERNATIVE [Devil and deep blue sea; Hobson's ~; Scylla and *Charybdis*].

CHOPSTICKS CLEAVE/SPLIT FIREWOOD. PIANO TUNE. EATING TOOLS, KHAI-ZI (Ch).

CHORIAMB *FOOT*.

CHRISTCHURCH CHCH. (*University*) COLLEGE. *CASTLE*.

CHRISTMAS NATIVITY. PRESENT DAY (crypt) [Santa Claus]. ~ box, ~ cake, ~ card ~ present, ~ stocking, ~ tree, ~ *song*:

(12) *Lords* a-leaping	(6) *Geese* a-laying
(11) Ladies *dancing*	(5) Golden *rings*
(10) *Pipers* piping	(4) Calling (Colly) *birds*
(9) *Drummers* drumming	(3) French *hens*
(8) *Maids* a-milking	(2) Turtle *doves*
(7) *Swans* a-swimming	A *partridge* in a pear-tree.

CHRISTOPHER *KIT*, TRAVELLER. *PATRON SAINT* (wayfarers).

CHROMATIC INTERVAL, SCALE (mus). BRIGHT-COLOURED.

CHROMIUM CR (*chem*).

CHRYSOBERYL *GEM* (green/yellow).

CHRYSOLITE *GEM*, PRECIOUS STONE; OLIVINE, PERIDOT. *Birthstone* (September).

CHRYSOPRASE *GEM*, SEMI-PRECIOUS STONE; CHALCEDONY (green).

CHURCH CH. CE, RC. HOUSE OF WORSHIP. ESTABLISHMENT. ~ **parts**: see *cathedral*. ~ **vessels**: chalice, chrismal, ciborium, cruet, monstrance, ostensory, plate, purse.

CHURCH DRESS Headgear: BIRETTA (RC), CALOT(T)E (RC), HOOD (friar), MITRE (abbot, bishop), SHOVEL HAT (clergy), TIARA (pope). **Vestments**: ALB (clergy), AMICE (shoulders), APRON (bishop), CANONICALS (clergy), CASSOCK (clergy), CHASUBLE (clergy), CHIMERE (bishop), COPE (processional cloak), CORPORAL (cloth), DALMATIC (bishop, deacon), DOMINO (cloak), EPHOD (Jewish), FANON (Pope's collar), GREMIAL (bishop's apron), MANIPLE (eucharistic napkin), MORSE (cope fastening), ORPHREY (embroidered scarf), ROCHET (surplice), SCAPULAR, ~Y (monk), SOUTANE (RC), STOLE (scarf), SURPLICE (clergy), TIPPET (cloth band), TUNICLE (bishop), VEXILLUM (crosier cloth).

CHURCHMAN WREN (crypt). CLERGY, DD, *FATHER*, PRELATE, PRIEST, REVEREND, RR, THEOLOGIAN, VEN; ORDERED (crypt). **Pl** = CLOTH. **Kinds:**

4-letters

ABBÉ (RC)	GURU (Ind)	*MONK*
CURÉ (RC)	IMAM (Mos)	POPE (Gk; RC)
DEAN	LAMA (Bud)	YOGI (Ind)

5-letters

ABBOT	*FRIAR*	PRIOR
CANON	HADJI (Mos)	VICAR
DRUID (Wal)	MUFTI (Mos)	
FAKIR (Mos)	PADRE	

6-letters

BEADLE	DEACON	RECTOR
BISHOP	MULLAH (Mos)	SCRIBE (Heb)
CLERIC	*PARSON*	SEXTON
CURATE	PASTOR	VERGER

7-letters

ACOLYTE	MUEZZIN (Mos)	PRELATE
BRAHMIN (Ind)	PONTIFF (RC)	PRIMATE
BROTHER		

8+ letters

ARCHBISHOP	ECCLESIASTIC
ARCHDEACON	GODBOTHERER (sl)
AYATOLLAH (Mos)	*METROPOLITAN* (Gk)
CARDINAL (RC)	MINISTER
CHAPLAIN	MISSIONARY
CHURCHWARDEN	PATRIARCH (Gk)

PREBENDARY   PRESBYTER
PRECENTOR   SKYPILOT (*sl*)

CHURCHWOMAN ABBESS, CANONESS, MOTHER
SUPERIOR, NOVICE, NUN, POSTULANT, PRIORESS,
SISTER.
CI CHANNEL ISLANDS. CIRRUS. (Order of the) CROWN OF
INDIA.
CIA CENTRAL INTELLIGENCE AGENCY.
CICERO 1. DRUM *HORSE*. *TYPEFACE*. 2. TULLY, Rom
ORATOR, 104–43 B.C.; mar (1) Terentia (one d Tullia, one s
Marcus), (2) Publiia. Ass by Mark *Antony* 43 B.C. Writings
include: De Oratore, De Republica, De Legibus, De Officiis,
De Finibus etc.
CICESTR *Episcopal sig* of CHICHESTER.
CIGARETTE CANCER STICK, CIG(GY), COFFIN NAIL,
DOG END, FAG END, GASPER, JOINT, *REEFER*
(drugged), SMOKE, SNOUT, WEED (all sl); **brands** (most
®): ARDATH, B & H, *CAMEL* (US), DE RESKE, DU
MAURIER, GAULOIS (Fr), KENSITAS, KENT, LUCKY
STRIKE (US), MARLBORO, PALL MALL, PASSING
CLOUD (Turk), *PLAYERS* (Please), STATE EXPRESS,
STUYVESANT, V, *VICTORY, WEIGHTS, WILLS*,
WOODBINE.
CINQUE PORTS DOVER, HASTINGS, HYTHE, ROMNEY,
SANDWICH (+ *RYE* and WINCHELSEA) [Lord Warden.
Walmer *Castle*]. Vessel (*Crusoe*).
CIPANGU *JAPAN*.
CIRCA *ABOUT, C, CA*.
CIRCE A *sorceress*, d of *Helios* and Perse (*Oceanid*), she lived on
the island of Aeaea, where Odysseus (*Ulysses*) tarried for a year.
CIRCLE O, *RING*, ROUNDEL, *ZERO* [*Pi*].
CIRCUMFLEX BENDING, CURVED. *ACCENT* (ˆ).
CIRCUMNAVIGATORS EXPLORERS, *WORLD-GIRDLERS*.
CIRCUS 1. Convergence of streets, e.g. Oxford ~, Piccadilly ~.
2. AMPHITHEATRE, STADIUM; ARENA (~ Maximus,
Rom) [*Caligula*]. 3. Travelling company of barnstormers (flying
~) or acrobats, animals, *clowns*, jugglers and trapeze artistes,
working in a tent or big top; **celeb**: ASTLEY'S, BARNUM &
BAILEY, BERTRAM MILLS, CHIPPERFIELD, HENGLER,
Rolf KNIE (Swi), PINDER (Fr), RINGLING (US), SANGER.
CIRRUS *CI, CLOUD*, MACKEREL SKY.
CIS Commonwealth of Independent States (ex *USSR*)

CISTERCIAN *MONK*; BENEDICTINE, *TRAPPIST*.

CITY 1. Large municipality, normally with a *bishop*; style granted in the UK by the *monarch*; **comp** = town. 2. Financial centre of *London*; EC, SQUARE MILE [*company*]. 3. Abbr for certain *football* teams, e.g. Bristol ~, Leicester ~, Manchester ~.

CIVIL SERVICE CS, CURIA (RC) (**Unions** = NALGO, NUPE) [Bumble (Oliver, *Dickens*); Dogberry (Much Ado, *Shak*); mandarin]. REGISTRY OFFICE WEDDING (crypt). POLITE WAITER (crypt).

CLASS *FORM*, *REMOVE*, SCHOOL. TYPE, RANK. STYLE, TONE, *U* (and crypt, e.g. **Quietly classy** = U*P).

CLASSED DESIGNATED, RANKED, REGISTERED. AT SCHOOL, IN FORM, LEARNING (crypt).

CLASSIC 1. A1, FIRST CLASS, STANDARD. 2. Five specific horse races (One Thousand Guineas, Two ~, Derby, Oaks, St Leger). 3. A word or phrase based on Lat or Gk, hence implies put into Lat or Gk, e.g. **Classically where** . . . = UBI . . .

CLAUDIUS Rom s of Drusus and Antonia (the d of Mark *Antony*), he was made *emperor* by the soldiers in A.D. 41. Weak, with a stammer, ~ mar four times, incl (3) Valeria Messalina (1 s Britannicus) and (4) Agrippina (~'s niece), who had *Nero*, her s by a previous mar, declared successor instead of Britannicus; Agrippina then had ~ k A.D. 54. [Ostia (harbour)].

CLAUSTROPHOBIA *Aversion* to enclosed spaces.

CLEAN SHEET FRESH START. UNWRITTEN, VIRGIN PAPER. NEW *BEDDING*.

CLEAVE DIVIDE, PIERCE, SEPARATE, *SPLIT*. ADHERE, *STICK*, UNITE.

CLEF BASS, TREBLE; *KEY*.

CLEOPATRA 1. Gk myth d of *Boreas* and Orithia; mar Phineas. 2. Gk myth d of Idas and Marpessa; mar Meleager. 3. d of Philip II of Macedonia and Olympias (sis of *Alexander* the Great); mar Alexander, K of Epirus (on their wedding, Philip II was k because of his bigamy with ~ (4) following). 4. d of Attalus; mar Philip II of Macedon as his 2nd w, while 1st w Olympias was still mar to him. Olympias had Philip II k at wedding of ~ (3) above. 5. Successive Q's of Egy (see *Ptolemy*), in particular.

CLERGY *CHURCHMEN*.

CLERK CLERGYMAN, LAY OFFICER (~ of Oxenford, *Chaucer*). HOTEL/SHOP ASSISTANT (US). AGENT, COURT OFFICIAL, RECORDER. OVERSEER.

BANK/OFFICE WORKER; **celeb** (all *Dickens*): BOB
CRATCHIT (Scrooge's in Xmas Carol); URIAH HEEP
('umble to Wickfield in Copperfield); TIM LINKINWATER
(Cheerybles' in Nich Nick); NEWMAN NOGGS (Ralph
Nickleby's in Nich Nick); JOHN WEMMICK (Jaggers' in
Great Ex).

CLIFFHANGER TENSE SITUATION, THRILLER. NEST
(crypt). ROCKY PLANT e.g. IVY, MESA VERDE,
SAMPHIRE (crypt).

CLIMBER ALPINIST, MOUNTAINEER. IVY, *PLANT*,
LIANA, MESA VERDE, SAMPHIRE, STEPHANOTIS.
SOCIAL SNOB, PUSHER.

CLIMBING 1. MOUNTAINEERING, MOUNTING, SCALING.
PUSHING. 2. Word reads upwards (dn) e.g. **Climbing weed** =
DEEW (crypt, dn).

CLIMBING FRAME STILE; LADDER (crypt). EMARF
(dn, crypt).

CLINK *GAOL* (sl). CLANK, *RING*.

CLIO One of the nine Gk *MUSES* (myth).

CLIPJOINT DIVE, NIGHTCLUB, SPEAKEASY. STAPLE,
PAPER-CLIP (crypt). BARBERSHOP, HAIRDRESSER
(crypt).

CLIPPER *BOAT*, SAILING SHIP, SCHOONER (Cutty Sark,
China tea ~). SCISSORS, SHEARS, SNIPPERS; HEDGE-
TRIMMER. BARBER (crypt).

CLOAK CONCEAL. DISGUISE, MASK. GARMENT;
CAPE, CLOKE (arch); **types:** BURNOUS (Arab), CAPOTE
(bullfighting), DOLMAN (Turk), KIRTLE (arch), MULETA
(bullfighting), PALETOT (19th cent), PALLIUM (Gk),
SULHAM (N Afr), *TABARD* (herald, knight), TOGA (Rom).
[*Penelope*; Raleigh]; **comp** = dagger.

CLOCK TIME-KEEPER, TIME-PIECE, *WATCH*; CLEPSYDRA
(water ~); TICKER; GRANDFATHER [*Company* (livery);
Knibb, Tompion]. FACE (sl). And see *furniture* for types.

CLOSE *NEAR*, NIGH. MEAN, MISERLY, NIGGARDLY,
STINGY, TIGHT. *END*, FINISH; *SEAL*, SHUT. PRIVATE,
QUIET [oyster]. MUGGY, OPPRESSIVE, *SULTRY*, WARM
(**opp** = *cold*). COURTYARD, QUAD.

CLOTH FABRIC, *MATERIAL* (q.v. for list of **types**), RAG
[*Company* (livery); *measure*]. DUSTER. *CLERGY*.

CLOTHES CLOBBER, *DRESS(ES)*, DUDS, GEAR, GLAD
RAGS, RIG. BEDECKS. [Hans *Andersen*].

CLOUD BEFOG, OBFUSCATE. WATER-VAPOUR e.g. *CI, CIRRUS, CU*, CUMULUS, NIMBUS, STRATUS.
CLOVE 1. Past tense of *cleave* (q.v.). *MEASURE* (weight of cheese or wool). *SPICE*, CLOW (Sc). 2. Part or segment of bulb (bot); hence BU, BUL, ULB etc (crypt).
CLOWN 1. BUFFOON, introduced into circus, play or story to amuse, either as a comic or the butt for another's humour. Compare *JESTER* (q.v. for further lists), who was a court or household retainer. BERGOMASK, BUFFOON, FOOL, *JESTER*, JOKER, PANTALOON, PRANKSTER, TRICKSTER [circus]. **Celeb fact**: ROBERT ARMIN (*Shak*'s players); AUGUSTE (Fr); COCO (circus); GRIMALDI (Joseph, 18th C); GROCK (Adrien Wettach, Swi); WILL KEMP (Shak's players); JOHN RICH (Harlequin, 18th C). **Celeb, fict**: COSTARD (*Shak*, LLL); HARLEQUIN (trad); JUPE (*Dickens*, Hard Times); LAUNCE (*Shak*, 2 G of V); *MUCH* (Morris dancing); PAGLIACCIO (Leon cavallo); PANTAGRUEL (Rabelais); PANTALONE (It); POMPEY (*Shak*, M for M); SCARAMOUCHE (It); *SPEED* (*Shak*, 2 G of V); TOUCHSTONE (*Shak*, AYLI); TRINCULO (*Shak*, Tempest); two gravediggers (*Shak*, Hamlet); and (all *Shak*, MND): *BOTTOM* (*weaver*), *FLUTE* (*bellows mender*), *QUINCE* (*carpenter*), SNOUT (tinker), SNUG (joiner), STARVELING (*tailor*). 2. BOOR, COUNTRYMAN, RUSTIC (arch).
CLUB 1. COSH, CUDGEL, NIGHTSTICK, TRUNCHEON, *WEAPON* [*Periphites*]. GOLF STICK; **types**: BLASTER, BRASSIE, CLEEK, *DRIVER, IRON*, MASHIE, NIBLICK, *PUTTER*, SANDWEDGE, *SPOON, WEDGE, WOOD*. **Pl** = *CARDS, SUIT*; SOLDIERS (*Alice*). 2. C; ASSOCIATION, SOCIETY [*Cat; Chesterton*]; **celeb London** ~s:

Alpine	Carlton
Army & Navy (the Rag)	Cavalry
Athenaeum	Cavendish
Bachelors	Conservative
Badminton	Constitutional
Bath	Diogenes (*Holmes*)
Bellona (Sayers)	Drones (*Wodehouse*)
Boodle's	Eccentric
Brooks's	Garrick
Buck's	Guards

Junior Carlton
Junior Naval & Military
Kit-Cat
Lyceum
Marlborough
National Sporting
Naval & Military (In
   and Out)
Oxford and Cambridge
Pickwick (*Dickens*)
Portland
Pratt's
Public Schools
Reform
Royal Air Force
Royal Automobile
Royal Thames Yacht
St James's
Savage
Savile
Travellers'
United Services
United Universities
White's

CLUBLAND ST JAMES. GOLF COURSE (crypt).
CLUBMAN ROTARIAN. GOLFER (crypt). COSHER, THUG
   [*Periphites*].
CLYTEMNESTRA 1. Gk myth sis of Castor, *Pollux* and *twin*
   of *Helen*; mar *Agamemnon* (one s *Orestes*, three d *Electra*,
   Chrysothermis and Iphigenia), whom she k in his *bath*; k by her
   s Orestes for adultery with Aegisthus while Agamemnon was
   fighting at *Troy*. 2. A minor *PLANET*.
CO CARE OF. COBALT (*chem*). (COMMANDING)
   OFFICER. COLORADO (US *state*). COLOMBIA (*car plate*).
   COMPANY, FIRM.
COACH BUS, *CARRIAGE*, CHARABANC, TRANSPORT.
   CRAMMER, INSTRUCT(OR), TEACH(ER), TRAIN(ER),
   TUTOR. **Comp** = *horses*.
COATED 1. CAKED. PAINTED. DRESSED (crypt). 2. Word
   outside another, e.g. **Beaten egg is sent back coated with mud** (6)
   = MU*GGE*D.
COATING COVERAGE, LAYER. JACKET, OVERCOAT,
   REEFER.
COB *BOAT*. BREAD, LOAF. CLAY BRICK. COAL. GULL
   (dial). *HORSE*. NUT, PIPE. *SPIDER*. SWAN (*male*).
COBALT *METAL*; CO (*chem*).
COBBLER CORDWAINER, SHOEMAKER, SNOB [*last*,
   Manette (*Dickens*)]. *DRINK*. **Pl** = BALLS (*rh sl*).
   NORTHAMPTON (*football* team).
COCAINE *DRUG*, SNOW; NUMBER (crypt). [*Holmes*].
COCK Male *BIRD*, FOWL, *LOBSTER, SALMON*. ON/OFF,
   SPOUT, *TAP. HAMMER* (gun). NONSENSE, RUBBISH.
   FELLOW, FRIEND, MATE, PAL.

COCKTAIL *Anag. DRINK*: JOHN COLLINS, HIGHBALL, MARTINI ®, SCREWDRIVER, SIDECAR etc. AMALGAM, MIX(TURE). FEATHER (crypt). K (crypt).

COCYTUS Gk myth tributary of the river *Acheron* [*Underworld*].

COD *FISH.* CASH ON DELIVERY.

CODE LAWS, RULES, STATUTES. ETHIC, STANDARD. CRYPTOGRAM, CYPHER, ENIGMA (mil). *MORSE*, SEMAPHORE, W/T. STD.

COIGN (s/l *coin*). CORNER, VANTAGE POINT.

COIN (s/l *coign*). 1. INVENT, MAKE; UTTER. Put CO* in word (crypt), e.g. **Coin sop ladle** (5) = s*co*op; **vague inherent coin** (5) = IN*co*HERENT. 2. *CURRENCY* (q.v.), MONEY, SPECIE, SMALL CHANGE (hence MALLS; crypt); C, D, P, S. **Types (OE gold)**: JOANNES (36s), MOIDORE (27s), JACOBUS or UNITE (25s), CAROLUS (23s), *GUINEA* (21s), *MARK* (13s 4d), *ANGEL* (10s), NOBLE (6s 8d), *DOLLAR* (4s 6d); **(OE silver)**: *TESTER* (6d), GROAT (4d). **Old Scots**: BODLE (2d), PLACK or GROAT (4d), BAWBEE (6d), SHILLING (12d), *POUND* (20s), MERK (13s 4d). **Others**:

2-letters

AS (Rom)

3-letters

BOB (Br sl)
ECU (Fr)
SOU (Fr)

4-letters

ANNA (Ind)	*MARK* (Eng, Fin, Ger)
ASH (Ch, Ind)	MITE (bibl)
CENT (US etc)	PEAG (Ind)
DIME (US)	REAL (Sp)

5-letters

CROWN (Eng, Scand)	OBANG (Jap)
DARIC (Pers)	*PENNY* (UK)
DUCAT (Eur)	POUND (UK)
FRANC (Fr)	*ROYAL* (Eng)
FRANK (Eur)	

6-letters

AUREUS (Rom)
BEZANT/BYZANT
  (Turk)
DOLLAR (US et al)
GUINEA (UK)
NICKEL (US)
OBOLUS (Gk)
PESETA (Sp)

ROUBLE (CIS)
SHEKEL (Hebr)
STATER (Gk)
STIVER (sl)
TALENT (bibl)
TANNER (UK)
TESTER (Eng)
ZECHIN (Hebr)

7+ letters

CAROLIN (Ger)
DANDIPRAT (OE)
DENARIUS (Rom)
DOUBLOON (Sp)
FARTHING (UK)
KRUGERRAND (SA)
MARAVEDI (Sp)

MARIA THERESA
  DOLLAR (A)
PIECE OF EIGHT (Sp)
PRINDLE (Sc)
QUARTER (US)
SOLIDUS (Rom)
SOVEREIGN (UK)

~ **Coll** = numismatist. And see *currency*.
COL *COLONEL, SOLDIER. COLUMN. DEPRESSION, LOW.*
  DEFILE, PASS, SADDLE.
COLCHESTER 1. *CASTLE.* NATIVE, *OYSTER* [Whitstable].
  2. Scene of battle by *Boadicea.* CAMULODUNUM (Rom).
COLD C, CHILLY, NIPPY, FRIGID, ICY (**opp** = *close, heat*).
  CORYZA, SNIFFLES [catarrh]. **Comp** = *hot.*
COLLECTION ACCUMULATION, *ASSEMBLY*,
  GATHERING, GROUP. CALLING FOR, FETCHING;
  REMOVAL (postal) [*COD*]. OFFERING [eccles].
  CONCENTRATION, RECOVERING (senses).
COLLECTOR ADMINISTRATOR (Ind). ACCUMULATOR,
  ASSEMBLER, GATHERER, HOBBYIST, *MAGPIE* (sl),
  SETTER (crypt), SQUIRREL (sl). In the list which follows,
  some words have been coined by enthusiasts to describe their
  own hobby; a few of these creations have been accepted into the
  dictionaries (deltiologist, phillumenist); some have encountered
  opposition (arcturologist, tegestologist); some are admittedly
  rather far-fetched, but have been included in this first-ever
  collection of collectors because they are used by aficionados
  of the subject concerned (buttonier, programmaniac). Other
  hobbyists have adopted existing words which have had their
  original meaning extended to cover collection, as well as

a love or knowledge of the subject (bibliophile, horologist, gemmologist – but see my remarks below, regarding the difference between the Greek word 'logos' and the Latin 'legere'). Somewhat surprisingly, however, the most popular kind of collector has no generic noun known to this lexicographer, who has been unable to resist the temptation to suggest a word for a collector of autographs. The first candidate was sigillarist, deriving from sigillary (in most dictionaries as the adjectival form of sigil, a seal or signet). This was discarded in favour of signaturist, largely because Dr Johnson includes it as 'One who holds the doctrine of signatures; a word rarely used.' It would have been nice to revive a word already going out of use in 1757, but it has a suspect pedigree for our usage, so the impeccable Latin ancestry of signalegist was finally preferred (signum, a sign + legere, to collect), much as florilegist comes from florilegium (which finds a place in the Collins English Dictionary).

Amateur lexicologists should note that -logy derives from the Greek 'logos' meaning a word or reasoning, and implies the study of a subject, and that the Latin verb 'legere' means to collect; thus the suffix -logist = expert, while -legist = collector (not always the same thing). There are therefore grounds for using gemmolegist, horolegist and even ichthyolegist when meaning collectors (rather than devotees) of gems, clocks or fishes. **Examples**:

antiques	ANTIQUARY
archaic words	ARCHAIST
autographs	SIGNALEGIST
bank notes	NOTAPHILIST
beer mats	TEGESTOLOGIST
beetles	COLEOPTERIST
birds' eggs	OOLOGIST
bookplates	EX-LIBRIST
books	BIBLIOPHILE
butterflies	LEPIDOPTERIST
buttonhooks	BUTTONIER
certificates	SCRIPOPHILIST
cheese labels	FROMOLOGIST
cigarette cards	CARTOPHILIST
clocks	HOROLOGIST
coins	NUMISMATIST

ephemeral trivia	EPHEMERIST
exotica	EXOTICIST
fishes	ICHTHYOLOGIST
flowers	FLORILEGIST
gramophone records	DISCOPHILE
Greek philosophy	DOXOGRAPHER
herbs (med)	HERBALIST
husbands	POLYANDRIST
insects	ENTOMOLOGIST
languages	GLOSSOLOGIST
literary excerpts	CHRESTOMATHIST
matchboxes	PHILLUMENIST
medals	NUMISMATIST
moths	LEPIDOPTERIST
poems, writings	ANTHOLOGIST
postcards	DELTIOLOGIST
precious stones	GEM(M)OLOGIST
programmes	PROGRAMMANIAC
proper names	ONOMASIOLOGIST
quotations	COLLECTANEIST
shells	CONCHOLOGIST
stamps	PHILATELIST
teddy bears	ARCTUROLOGIST
telephone cards	FUSILATELIST
walking sticks	RABDOPHILIST
wives	POLYGAMIST

COLLEGE *ETON*, *LANCING*, MARLBOROUGH, *WINCHESTER* [and see *universities*].

COLONEL (s/l *kernel*). CO, COL, OFFICER; REGIMENTED (crypt); **celeb**: BLIMP (Low, *cartoonist*); BOGEY (Sousa, *composer*); BLOOD (*Scott*); BRAMBLE (Fr, Les Silences du Colonel ~; Maurois); DIRKOVITCH (*Kipling*); NEWCOMBE ('Adsum', Thackeray).

COLOUR INFLUENCE; INTEREST. BLUSH, FLUSH, REDDEN. PAINT; HUE e.g.:

Blacks (q.v.)

COAL	*JET(TY)*	SOOT
DUSKY	*PITCH*	SWART
EBON(Y)	SABLE (*herald*)	

Blues (q.v.)

ANIL	CYAN	*SAPPHIRE*
AQUAMARINE	*ELECTRIC*	*SEA*
AZURE (*herald*)	INDIGO	SKY
BERYL	LAPIS LAZULI	SMALT
BICE	*NAVY*	*TURQUOISE*
CAMBRIDGE	OXFORD	ULTRAMARINE
CERULEAN	PERSE	WATCHET
COBALT	*ROYAL*	WOAD

Browns (q.v.)

AUBURN	HENNA	*TAN*
BAY	KHAKI	TAUPE
BISTRE	OCHRE	TAWNY
CAMEL	PUCE	TENNY (*herald*)
DUN	RUSSET	UMBER
ECRU	SARD	VANDYKE
FAWN	SEPIA	
HAZEL	SORREL	

Greens (q.v.)

BERYL	OLIVE	VERDIGRIS
BICE	RESEDA	VERT (*herald*)
EMERALD	*SAGE*	
JADE	*TURQUOISE*	

Oranges (q.v.)

BRASS	*COPPER*	OCHRE
CADMIUM	FLAME	SARD

Purples (q.v.)

AMETHYST	LILAC	PUCE
INDIGO	MAUVE	PURPURE (*herald*)
LAVENDER	*PLUM*	VIOLET

Reds (q.v.)

BURGUNDY	GULES (*herald*)	*RUBY*
CARMINE	MAGENTA	RUST
CERISE	MAROON	SARD
CINNABAR	MINIUM	SCARLET
COQUELICOT	MODENA	VERMILION
CRIMSON	PILLAR-BOX	

Whites (q.v.)

BLANCH	CREAMY	*MILK*
BLEACH	GRAY/GREY	OYSTER
BLOND(E)	*IVORY*	*PEARL*
CHALKY	*LILY*	SILVER

Yellows (q.v.)

AMBER	GAMBOGE	PRIMROSE
AUREATE	GILDED	SAFFRON
BUFF	GILT	SULPHUR
CREAM	*GOLD*	TOPAZ
FALLOW	*LEMON*	XANTHIC

Heraldic colours: black = *SABLE*, **blue** = *AZURE*, **brown** = TENNE/TENNY, **green** = VERT, **gold** = OR, **purple** = PURPURE, **red** = GULES, **silver** = ARGENT. **Primary colours:** *GREEN*, *RED*, VIOLET. **Primary colours (painting):** *BLUE*, *RED*, *YELLOW*. **Rainbow colours** (from outside to in): *RED*, *ORANGE*, *YELLOW*, *GREEN*, *BLUE*, INDIGO, VIOLET. **Pl** = CAP (sport).

COLT 1. GREENHORN, TYRO. AUTOMATIC, WEAPON ®. 2. *Offspring* of camel or horse. **Pl** = JUNIOR TEAM. *Football team* (US).

COLUMN COL. FILE, TROOPS. VERTICAL CYLINDER/DIVISION/JET, PILLAR (and see *architecture*). ARTICLE, REPORTING.

COMBER BREAKER, FOAM, SURF, WAVE. HAIRDRESSER (crypt) [curry ~]. *BEE* (crypt). FISH.

COMEBACK 1. ENCORE, RETURN, REVIVAL. EMOC (crypt). 2. Word written backwards, e.g. **Elba's comeback looks gloomy** (5) = SABLE.

COMEDOWN ANTICLIMAX. ALIGHT, *LAND* (crypt).

COMET 1. TAILED STAR, SUN SATELLITE (Biela, Ericke, Halley). AIRCRAFT. *REINDEER*. 2. First Br passenger (paddle) steamer.

COMFORTER DUMMY. SCARF. HOLY SPIRIT. One who eases pain or affliction; **opp** = *Job's* ~.

COMIC AMUSING, BURLESQUE, FACETIOUS, *FUNNY*, HUMOROUS, LAUGHABLE, RIDICULOUS, RISIBLE, WITTY; *CASE*, COMEDIAN. Children's periodical, **names** (all ®): BEANO, BEEZER, BOP, BOY'S OWN PAPER, *BULLSEYE, CHAMPION, DANDY, EAGLE*, HOTSPUR,

MAGNET, ROVER, TIGER TIM, *WIZARD*.

COMING TO One word precedes another, e.g. **Commie coming to see** . . . (3,4) = RED SPOT.

COMMANDER AOC, CINC, FOC, GOC (mil), [SEAC]. *TARTAN* (bibl). WOODEN MALLET.

COMMANDING DIGNIFIED, IMPRESSIVE. OVERLOOKING. CO, *COMMANDER*, IC, IN CHARGE.

COMMANDMENT DIVINE COMMAND, *TEN* ~s (q.v.) [Moses, Mt Sinai]. Ten in *song*.

COMMON(LY) 1. PUBLIC, SHARED. VILLAGE GREEN. ORDINARY, REGULAR, USUAL; **comp** = *garden*. NOUS, SENSE (sl). **Pl** = FOOD, RATIONS. *HOUSE, LEGISLATIVE ASSEMBLY.* 2. INFERIOR, PLEBEIAN, *SLANG* (q.v.), VULGAR (**opp** = *noble, U*); NON-U (sl), hence (crypt) remove letter U from clue-word, e.g. **An example of common cause** (4) = CA*SE; or else **Commonly laud the boy** (3) = LA*D. 3. Employ slang in the answer, e.g. **Son is not commonly a good man** (5) = S*AINT.

COMMONSENSE NOUS.

COMMONWEALTH GOVERNMENT (Cromwell). STATE. **British members**: Australia, Bahamas, Bangladesh, Barbados, Bermuda (colony), Botswana, Brunei, Canada, Cyprus, East Caribbean States, Fiji, Gambia, Ghana, Grenada, Guyana, India, Jamaica, Kenya, Lesotho, Malawi, Malaysia, Malta, Mauritius, Nauru, New Zealand, Nigeria, Papua New Guinea, Sierra Leone, Singapore, Sri Lanka, Swaziland, Tanzania, Tonga, Trinidad and Tobago, Uganda, United Kingdom, Western Samoa, Zambia.

COMMUNIST COMMIE, RED, *TROT*; IVAN.

COMMUNITY BODY, FELLOWSHIP. EEC (Treaty of Rome).

Comp Abbr for *COMPANION*; esp in this book means any word commonly associated with the entry word, e.g. bill/coo, coach/horses.

COMPANION 1. DECKHOUSE, HATCHWAY, hence ACCESS STEPS (naut). ASSOCIATE, BROTHER IN ARMS, FELLOW, FRIEND, *MATE*, OPPO (sl), PAL. AU PAIR, HOUSEKEEPER, LIVER-IN. *REFERENCE WORK. CH* (crypt). 2. Word commonly associated with another (crypt), e.g. **Bill's** ~ = COO; **Cop's** ~ = PROP; **Jeff's** ~ = MUTT; **celeb** ~s: AENEAS/ACHATES, BIRDS/BEES, BOSWELL/JOHNSON, CASTOR/POLLUX, DAMON/PHINTIAS (not Pythias), DANTE/BEATRICE,

DARBY/JOAN, DAVID/JONATHAN, EURALUS/NISUS,
FORTNUM/MASON, GIN/TONIC, MASON/DIXON,
MOHAMMED/MOUNTAIN, ORESTES/PYLADES,
PETRARCH/LAURA, PUNCH/JUDY, ROLAND/OLIVER,
ROMEO/JULIET, SOHRAB/RUSTAM (-EM, -UM),
SNAKES/LADDERS, SWAN/EDGAR, WHISKY/SODA or
SPLASH, WILL/WAY (see also *inspiration, model* and *lovers*).
COMPANY *ASSEMBLY*, *COMPANIONS*, GUESTS, *PARTY*,
VISITORS. ACTORS, CAST [touring ~]. CREW (naut).
BODY OF MEN, *SOLDIERS*, TROOPS. BUSINESS, *CO*,
CONCERN, CORPORATION, *COY, FIRM*, GUILD, PLC;
City livery ~s:

APOTHECARIES
BAKERS
BARBERS
BASKET MAKERS
BLACKSMITHS
BREWERS
BUTCHERS
CARPENTERS
CLOCKMAKERS
CLOTHWORKERS
COACH & COACH HARNESS MAKERS
COOPERS
CORDWAINERS
CURRIERS
CUTLERS
DISTILLERS
DRAPERS
DYERS
FANMAKERS
FARRIERS
FELTMAKERS
FISHMONGERS
FLETCHERS
FOUNDERS or COPPERSMITHS
FRAMEWORK KNITTERS or STOCKING WEAVERS
FRUITERERS
GIRDLERS
GLASS SELLERS
GLAZIERS

GOLD & SILVER WYRE DRAWERS
GOLDSMITHS
GROCERS
HABERDASHERS
INNHOLDERS
IRONMONGERS
LEATHER SELLERS
MASONS
MERCERS
MERCHANT TAYLORS
PAINTERS or PAINTER STAINERS
PATTEN MAKERS
PEWTERERS
PLAISTERERS or PARGETTORS
PLAYING CARD MAKERS
PLUMBERS
POULTERS
SADDLERS
SALTERS
SCRIVENERS
SHIPWRIGHTS
SKINNERS
SPECTACLE MAKERS
STATIONERS
TALLOW CHANDLERS
TIN PLATE WORKERS
TURNERS
TYLERS & BRICKLAYERS
VINTNERS
WAX CHANDLERS
WEAVERS
WHEELWRIGHTS

COMPARE (s/l compère). *CF*, LIKEN. *MEASURE.*
COMPASS *BOUNDARY*, CIRCUMFERENCE, LIMIT
 [*Joshua* (Jericho)]; EXTENT, RANGE, SCOPE. GYRO,
 LODESTONE, PELORUS (naut). INSTRUMENT, SCRIBER
 [dividers].
COMPLAINT AILMENT: CHICKENPOX, DIPHTHERIA,
 FEVER, MALARIA, MEASLES, MUMPS, POX, TYPHOID
 etc. ACCUSATION, CASE, GRIEVANCE.
COMPOSED OF *Anag.* COMPRISING, MADE OF.

COMPOSER CONSTRUCTOR. PEACE-MAKER, *SETTLER*. ARRANGER, MUSICAL AUTHOR; **celeb**:

3-letters

BAX, Sir Arnold Edward Trevor (Eng)
CUI, César (Fr/Russ)

IVE, Simon (Eng)
MAW, Nicholas (Eng)

4-letters

ARNE, Thomas Augustine (Eng)
BACH, Johann Sebastian (Ger)
BERG, Alban (A)
BLOW, John (Eng)
BYRD, William (Eng)
HART, Lorenz (US)
IVES, Charles (US)

KERN, Jerome (US)
LOWE, Frederick (US)
LOWE, Karl (Ger)
NERI, St Philip (It)
ORFF, Carl (Ger)
PERI, Jacopo (It)
RICE, Tim (Eng)
WOLF, Hugo (A)

5-letters

BALFE, Michael William (Ire)
BIZET, Georges (Fr)
BLISS, Sir Arthur (Eng)
BLOCH, Ernest (US)
CESTI, Marcantonio (It)
ELGAR, Sir Edward (Eng)
FAURÉ, Gabriel Urbain (Fr)
GLUCK, Christoph von (Ger)
GRIEG, Edvard Hagerup (Nor)
GROFE, Ferdie (US)
HANDY, William Christopher (US)

HAYDN, Franz Joseph (A)
HOLST, Gustav (Eng)
LISZT, Franz (Hung)
LOEWE (see *LOWE*)
POWER, Lionel (Eng)
RAVEL, Maurice (Fr)
SOUSA, John Philip (US)
SUPPE, Franz von (A)
VERDI, Giuseppe (It)
WEBER, Carl Maria von (Ger)
WEILL, Kurt (Ger/US)

6-letters

ARNOLD, Matthew (Eng)
BARTOK, Bela (Hung)
BERLIN, Irving (Israel Baline) (USSR/US)
BOULEZ, Pierre (Fr)

BRAHMS, Johannes (Ger)
CHOPIN, Frederic François (Pol)
COWARD, Sir Noel (Eng)
DELIUS, Frederick (Eng)

DVORAK, Antonin (Cz)
FLOTOW, Friedrich
von (Ger)
FOSTER, Stephen (US)
FRANCK, César Auguste
(Belg)
GLINKA, Mikhail (Russ)
GOUNOD, Charles (Fr)
HANDEL, George Fredk
(Ger/Eng)
HARRIS, Roy (US)
LANNER, Joseph Franz
Karl (A)

LEFANU, Nicola (Eng, fem)
LENNON, John (Eng)
LERNER, Alan Jay (US)
MAHLER, Gustav (A)
MOZART, Wolfgang
Amadeus (A)
PORTER, Cole (US)
RIDLEY, Arnold (Eng)
SEARLE, Humphrey (Eng)
STRAUS, Oscar (A)
WAGNER, Richard (Ger)
WALTON, Sir Wm
Turner (Eng)

7-letters

ARENSKY, Anton (CIS)
BELLINI, Vicenzo (It)
BENNETT, Sir William
Sterndale (Eng)
BERLIOZ, Hector (Fr)
BORODIN, Alexander
(CIS)
BRITTEN, Edward
Benjamin (Eng)
COPLAND, Aaron (US)
DEBUSSY, Claude
Achille (Fr)
GIBBONS, Orlando (Eng)
HERBERT, Victor (US)
IRELAND, John (Eng)
JANACEK, Leos (A/Cz)
LAMBERT, Constant
(Eng)
LUTYENS, Elizabeth
(Eng)

NOVELLO, Ivor (Eng)
POULENC, Francis (Fr)
PUCCINI, Giacomo (It)
PURCELL, Henry (Eng)
RODGERS, Richard (US)
ROMBERG, Sigmund
(Hung)
ROSSINI, Gioacchino
Antonio (It)
SMETANA, Bedrich (Cz)
STAINER, John (Eng)
STRAUSS, Eduard (A)
STRAUSS, Johann I, II &
III (A)
STRAUSS, Joseph (A)
STRAUSS, Richard (Ger)
TIPPETT, Sir Michael
(Eng)
VIVALDI, Antonio (It)

8-letters

ALBINONI, Tomaso (It)
BENEDICT, Julius (Ger)
BRUCKNER, Anton (A)
CLEMENTI, Muzio (It)
COUPERIN, François (Fr)

GERSHWIN, George (US)
GLAZUNOV, Aleksandr
(Russ)
KREISLER, Fritz (A)

MACONCHY, Elizabeth
(Eng/Ire, fem)
MASSENET, Jules
Emile (Fr)
PAGANINI, Nicolo (It)
SCHUBERT, Franz
Peter (A)
SCHUMANN, Robert
Alexander (Ger)
SIBELIUS, Jean (Fin)

SKRYABIN (SCRIABIN),
Alexander (CIS)
SONDHEIM, Stephen
Joshua (US)
SPONTINI, Gasparo
Luigi (It)
SULLIVAN, Sir Arthur
Seymour (Eng)
WHITEMAN, Paul (US)
ZARENSKI (Pol)

9+ letters

BEETHOVEN, Ludwig
van (Ger)
DONIZETTI, Gaetano (It)
DUNSTABLE, John (Eng)
GRUENBERG, Louis
(CIS/US)
HAMMERSTEIN,
Oscar (US)
HUMPERDINCK,
Engelbert (Ger)
LLOYD WEBBER,
Andrew (Eng)
McCARTNEY, Paul (Eng)
MENDELSSOHN,
Felix (Ger)
MEYERBEER, Giacomo
(Ger)
MONTEVERDI, Claudio
(It)
MUSSORGSKY, Modeste
(CIS)
OFFENBACH, Jacques
(Ger/Fr)
PROKOFIEV, Sergei (CIS)

RACHMANINOV, Sergei
(CIS/US)
RIMSKY-KORSAKOV,
Nikolai (CIS)
SAINT-SAENS, Charles
Camille (Fr)
SCARLATTI, Alessandro
(It)
SCARLATTI, Domenico
(It)
SCHO(E)NBERG,
Arnold (A)
SHOSTAKOVICH, Dmitri
(CIS)
STOCKHAUSEN,
Karlheinz (Ger)
STRAVINSKY, Igor
(CIS)
TCHAIKOVSKY, Peter
Ilyich (CIS)
VAUGHAN WILLIAMS,
Ralph (Eng)
XANARCHIS (Gk)

COMPUTER CALCULATOR, MICRO-PROCESSOR [bits,
bytes, ERNIE, memory, mouse, retrieval bank, VDU].
COMUS Rom god of pleasure and rivalry, s of *Bacchus* and *Circe*;
often shown masked.
CON CHEAT, DIDDLE, *DO. AGAINST* (**opp** = *pro*). *LOOK,*

STUDY. NAVIGATE, PILOT, *SAIL, STEER*. **Comp** = *pro*.
CONCEAL Hidden word. *HIDE, SCREEN*, SECRETE.
CONCERN WORRY. *FIRM, COMPANY*. AFFECT.
CONCERNING *ABOUT*, ANENT, *OVER*, RE.
CONCERTINA ACCORDION; PRESS-BOX (crypt).
COLLAPSE, COMPRESS, *FOLD*, PLEAT.
CONCLUSION 1. DECISION, REALIZATION. *END*. [*Theseus*].
2. Last letter of word concerned, e.g. **Bob's conclusion is
encored** (3) = B*IS.
CONDITION *STATE. TERM*.
CONDUCTOR 1. GUARD, TICKET COLLECTOR.
DRAGOMAN, GUIDE; *SHOWMAN* (crypt). *EARTH*
(elect). **Myth**: *ANUBIS, CHARON*. 2. BAND-LEADER,
MAESTRO, MD (mus); **celeb**: BARBIROLLI, Sir John
(Brit); BEECHAM, Sir Thomas (Eng); BERNSTEIN,
Leonard (US); *BLACK*, Stanley (Eng); BOULEZ, Pierre
(Fr); BOULT, Sir Adrian (Eng); BROWN, Iona (Eng, fem);
COMET, Catherine (US, fem); COSTA, Sir Michael (It/Brit);
DAVIES, Andrew (Eng); DAVIS, Sir Colin (Eng); DEL
MAR, Norman (Eng); DORATI, Antal (Hung); ELDER,
Mark (Eng); FURTWÄNGLER, Wilhelm (Ger); GIBSON,
Sir Alexander (Sc); GLOVER, Jane (UK, fem); GROVE,
Sir Charles (Eng); HAITINK, Bernard (NL); HALLE, Sir
Charles (Ger/UK); HARTY, Hamilton (Ire); INGLIS, Anthony
(Eng); KEMPE, Rudolf (Ger); KLEMPERER, Otto (Ger);
LAMBERT, Constant (Eng); MACKERRAS, Sir Charles
(Aus); MAHLER, Gustav (A); MARRINER, Sir Neville (Eng);
MEHTA, Zubin (Isr); *POTTER*, Cipriani (Eng); PREVIN,
André (Ger/US); PRITCHARD, Sir John (Eng); RATTLE,
Simon (Eng); RICHTER, Hans (Ger); SAFONOV, Vasily
(Russ; 1st); SARGENT, Sir Malcolm (Eng); SINNOPOLI,
Giuseppi (It); SOLTI, Sir Georg (Hung/Brit); STOKOWSKI,
Leopold (Eng/US); STRAUSS, Richard (Ger); TAUSKY,
Vilem (A); TOSCANINI, Arturo (It); VON BULOW, Hans
(Ger); WALTER, Bruno (Ger); WEINGARTNER, Felix (Y);
WOOD, Sir Henry (Eng); YANSONS, Mariss (CIS).
CONFINING 1. BORDERING, ENCLOSING, LIMITING,
RESTRICTING; *GAOLING*. BEDDING, LABOURING
[childbirth]. 2. Word round another, e.g. **He's confining
publicity, and it's Hell** (5) = H*AD*ES. (If it were **tops** as opposed
to **Hell**, it would be HE*AD*S.)
CONFUSED *Anag*. BEWILDERED, MUDDLED.

CONJUROR *MAGICIAN* (q.v.), PRESTIDIGITATOR, *SORCERER* (q.v.). **Celeb**: Roger Bolingbroke (*Shak*, H.vi); *Pinch* (*Shak*, C of E). And see *MAGICIAN, SORCERER*.

CONNECTION 1. AFFILIATION, ASSOCIATION; DEALINGS. JOINERY, UNITY (crypt). TRANSFER (rly). EARTH, ON MAINS (elect). 2. Join two words, e.g. **See the connection bubble up** (4) = SEE*THE = BOIL.

CONQUEROR *VICTOR*, VIC, WINNER, WILLIAM.

Cons Conservative.

CONSCIENTIOUS PUNCTILIOUS, SCRUPULOUS, THOROUGH. HAMLET (crypt).

CONSPIRATOR PLOTTER; **celeb**: MARCUS BRUTUS, DECIUS BRUTUS, CASCA, CASSIUS, METELLUS CIMBER, CINNA, LIGARIUS, TREBONIUS (*Shak*, Caesar); EARL of CAMBRIDGE, LORD SCROOP, SIR THOMAS GREY (all *Shak*, H.v); CLIFFORD, ASHLEY, BUCKINGHAM, ARLINGTON, LAUDERDALE (Cabal). GUY FAWKES (ROBERT CATESBY, THOMAS PERCY).

CONSTABLE ARTIST, *PAINTER*, RA. *POLICEMAN* (q.v.). HEAD OF HOUSEHOLD (hence H, crypt). ALGUACILE (bullfighting), MAJOR DOMO; SENESCHAL; **celeb** (all *Shak*): DULL (LLL), ELBOW (Meas for Meas), MALVOLIO (12th Night), VERGES and DOGBERRY (Much Ado).

CONSTELLATION *STAR* CLUSTER/GROUP/OUTLINE; **celeb**:

3-letters

ARA (altar)

LEO (Zod) (lion)

4-letters

CRUX (southern cross)
GRUS (crane)

LYRA (lyre)

5-letters

ARIES (Zod) (ram)
CETUS (sea monster)
DRACO (dragon)
HYDRA (water-snake)
INDUS
LEPUS (hare)

LIBRA (Zod) (scales)
LUPUS (wolf)
MUSCA (fly)
ORION (hunter)
VIRGO (Zod) (virgin)

6-letters

AQUILA (eagle)
AURIGA (charioteer)
BOOTES (herdsman)
CANCER (Zod) (crab)
CARINA (keel)
CORVUS (crow)
CRATER
CYGNUS (swan)

DORADO (gilded)
FORNAX (kiln)
GEMINI (Zod) (twins)
HYDRUS (water serpent)
PISCES (Zod) (fishes)
PUPPIS (ship)
TAURUS (Zod) (bull)
TUCANA (toucan)

7-letters

CEPHEUS (myth king)
COLUMBA (dove)
PEGASUS (winged horse)
PERSEUS

PHOENIX
SCORPIO (Zod) (scorpion)
SERPENS (serpent)

8+ letters

ANDROMEDA
AQUARIUS (Zod) (water carrier)
CANES VENATICI (hunting dogs)
CANIS MAJOR (great dog)
CANIS MINOR (little dog)
CAPRICORNUS (Zod) (sea-goat)
CASSIOPOEIA (myth queen)
CENTAURUS (centaur)
CORONA BOREALIS (northern crown)

DELPHINUS (dolphin)
ERIDANUS (River Po)
HERCULES
OPHIUCHUS (serpent bearer)
PISCIS AUSTRINUS (southern fish)
SAGITTARIUS (Zod) (archer)
TRIANGULUM (triangle)
TRIANGULUM AUSTRALE
URSA MAJOR (great bear)
URSA MINOR (little bear)

CONSUMER DRINKER, EATER; PURCHASER, USER. SPENDER, WASTER. MOUTH (crypt).
CONTAINS 1. HOLDS, KEEPS IN. 2. Hidden word; one word in another.
CONTEND CLAIM, MAINTAIN. VIE, WAR.
CONTINENT LAND MASS: PANGAEA (pre-hist supercontinent); GONDWANA, LAURASIA (first split); AFRICA, AMERICA, ANTARCTICA, ASIA,

AUSTRALASIA, EUROPE. CHASTE, CONTROLLED, TEMPERATE.

CONTINUOUS 1. ENDLESS, UNBROKEN, UNENDING, UNINTERRUPTED. 2. Join two or more words in clue, e.g. **Heat her continuously for another girl** (5) = HEAT*HER = ERICA.

CONTRACT AGREEMENT. JOB. SHORTEN, SHRINK, TIGHTEN. *BRIDGE* (cards).

CONTRIVED *Anag.* FABRICATED, INVENTED. MANAGED (**opp** = *automatic*).

CONTROL (GEAR) LEVER, THROTTLE, JOY-STICK, RUDDER; *REIN*. DIRECT, MONITOR, ORGANIZE. DISCIPLINE. [AWACS (av)].

CONVERSE 1. CHAT, SPEAK WITH, TALK. OPPOSITE. 2. Word reversed: **Rat's converse shines brightly** (4) = STAR.

CONVICT ADJUDGE, DECLARE GUILTY [belief, convince, persuade]. CRIMINAL, *GAOL*-BIRD, LAG, *PRISONER*; [Botany Bay]. **Celeb**: see *PRISONER*.

COOK *Anag.* CHEF, GALLEY SLAVE; MRS BEETON, BETTY CROCKER, FANNY FARMER (books); KITCHENER (crypt). CONCOCT, PREPARE FOOD. BAKE, BOIL, FRY, GRILL, ROAST, SEETHE, SIMMER, STEW. *FIDDLE*, FIX. *STRAIT. EXPLORER. Chaucer* character.

COOKED *Anag.* DONE (**opp** = *raw*). *FIDDLED*, FIXED, FORGED.

COOKER BURNER, GRILL, HOB, OVEN, STOVE. VOLCANO (crypt). FORGER (crypt). And see *cook*.

COOLER *GAOL* (sl). AIR CONDITIONER, *BREEZE*, DRAFT, DRAUGHT, *FAN*, JALOUSIE, SHADE; LESS HOT, NOT SO HOT (**opp** = *warmer*). DEEP FREEZE, FRIDGE.

COP *POLICEMAN*. ATTRACT, CAPTURE. HA'PENNY (crypt: half cop*per). SPOOL [prop and ~].

COPPER *METAL*; CU (*chem*). *POLICEMAN* (q.v.). PENNY, D. WASH-BOILER. *COLOUR* (orange). *AGE. Anniversary* (7th). **Pl** = CHANGE; POLICE; MPs.

COPY CARBON, CRIB (sl), DOUBLE, DUPLICATE, IMITATION, REPRODUCTION, RINGER; FACSIMILE (any craftsman), REPLICA (original craftsman); TRANSCRIBE. ADVERTISING TEXT; PRINTER'S TEXT. *BORROW*.

CORA *PERSEPHONE*.

CORAL Calcareous secretion of marine polyps; REEF. *COLOUR* (pink). LOBSTER ROE. ~*SEA* [*battle*]. *SNAKE. Anniversary* (35th).

CORALLINE *SEAWEED.* CORAL-RED.

CORDIAL FRIENDLY. *DRINK.*

CORE (s/l caw). 1. CENTRE, KERNEL, MIDDLE. 2. Use middle letter(s), e.g. **Apple core** = P.

CORNELIAN *GEM*, SEMI-PRECIOUS STONE, CHALCEDONY: AGATE (red). *Birthstone* (July).

CORNWALL SW. *WRITER* (Le Carré).

CORPORAL CPL, NCO; **celeb**: HITLER, ~ JOHN (Marlborough), NAPOLEON, NYM (*Shak*), TRIM (Tristram Shandy, Sterne). BODILY. CLOTH, *MATERIAL* (eccles).

CORPORATION TOWN COUNCIL. FATNESS, OBESITY.

CORSAIR *AIRCRAFT. PIRATE.*

CORYBANTES PRIESTS of *Cybele*, frenzied and noisy dancers.

COS BECAUSE (sl). COSINE. *ISLAND.* LETTUCE.

COSH MUG; CUDGEL, CLUB, *WEAPON*; NIGHTCLUB (crypt).

COTTON CLOTH, *MATERIAL*, THREAD. ADMIRE, LIKE, TAKE TO, UNDERSTAND. 2nd *anniversary.*

COUGH *HAWK, HEM.* CONFESS (sl). PAY-UP (sl).

COULD BE *Anag.* MAYBE.

COUNT (E)NUMERATE, *NUMBER*, RECKON, *TELL, TOT.* EARL, *NOBLE; DRACULA.*

COUNTER AGAINST, OPPOSITE; CONTRADICT, OPPOSE, RIPOSTE. DUPLICATE. CHIP, TALLY, TOKEN. ADDER, CALCULATOR, CASHIER, COMPUTER, *SUMMER* (crypt), TELLER. BAR, TABLE; BOARD OF TRADE (crypt). HORSE'S NECK. SHIP'S STERN. SHOE'S HEEL. SKATING FIGURE.

COUNTRY FATHERLAND, LAND, MOTHERLAND, NATION, REGION, TERRITORY. RURAL AREA. And see *capital cities.* **Celeb, fict**: ASGARD (of Aesir, Nor myth gods); ATLANTIS (legend); AVALON (Arthurian legend); BALNIBARBI (*Swift*); BEULAH (Bunyan); BROBDINGNAG (*Swift*); BROCELIANDE (Arthurian legend); CAMELOT (Arthurian legend); COCKAIGNE/ COCKAYNE (Fr legend); DYSTOPIA (19th C); ELYSIUM (Gk myth); EREWHON (Butler); GLUBDUBRIB (*Swift*); HADES (Gk myth); KRYPTON (*Superman*); LAPUTA (*Swift*); LEMURIA (Scott Elliott); LILLIPUT (*Swift*); LIMBO (Christianity); MU (continent); MUSPELHEIM (Nor myth); NARNIA (C.S. Lewis); NEVER LAND (*Barrie*); NIFLHEIM (Nor myth); OLYMPIA (Gk myth); OZ (Frank Baum);

RURITANIA (*Hope*); SHANGRI-LA (Lost Horizon, Hilton); TREASURE IS (*Stevenson*); UTOPIA (More); WONDERLAND (*Alice*); YS (Breton).

COUNTRY HOUSE MANSION, PLACE, SEAT, *STATELY HOME* (q.v. for **celeb, fact**). CHESHIRE HOME, SWISS COTTAGE (crypt); **celeb, fiction**:

BARCHESTER TOWERS (~, Trollope)
BARTON PARK (Sense and Sensibility, *Austen*)
BLANDINGS CASTLE (Lord Emsworth, *Wodehouse*)
BLEAK HOUSE (~, *Dickens*)
BRIDESHEAD (CASTLE) (~ Revisited, *Waugh*)
CASTLEWOOD (The Virginians, Thackeray)
DONNELL ABBEY (Emma, *Austen*)
DORINCOURT (Little Lord Fauntleroy, Burnett)
DORLCOTE MILL (Mill on the Floss, Eliot)
ELSINORE CASTLE (Hamlet, *Shak*)
ENSCOMBE (Emma, *Austen*)
HARTFIELD (Emma, *Austen*)
HEARTBREAK HOUSE (~, *Shaw*)
KELLYNCH HALL (Persuasion, *Austen*)
LOCKSLEY HALL (~, Tennyson)
LONGBOURNE (Pride and Prejudice, *Austen*)
MANDERLEY (Rebecca, du Maurier)
MANSFIELD PARK (~, *Austen*)
NAVRON HOUSE (Frenchman's Creek, du Maurier)
NETHERFIELD PARK (Pride and Prejudice, *Austen*)
NORLAND PARK (Sense and Sensibility, *Austen*)
NORTHANGER ABBEY (~, *Austen*)
OVERCOMBE MILL (Trumpet Major, Hardy)
SATIS HOUSE (Great Ex, *Dickens*)
TARA (Gone with the Wind, Mitchell)
THORNFIELD HALL (Jane Eyre, C. *Brontë*)
USHER (The House of ~, E. A. Poe)
WHITE LADIES (Berry & Co, Dornford Yates)
WILDFELL HALL (Tenant of ~, A. *Brontë*)
WUTHERING HEIGHTS (~, E. *Brontë*)

COUNTY 1. ARISTOCRATIC, LAH-DI-DAH, *U*, WELL-BRED. CO. 2. ~ of the UK, see *DIVISION*.
COURSE E, N, S, W, NE, SE etc. DIRECTION, LINE. *RACETRACK; LINKS*. CURRENT, RIVERBED. PURSUE,

RUN. *SAIL.* LECTURE SERIES. CAREER. *LAYER*,
STRATUM. *MEAL*: AFTERS, DESSERT, ENTREE,
ENTREMETS, HORS D'OEUVRE, MEAT, PUDDING,
SAVOURY, SOUP, *STARTER*, SWEET.
COURT (s/l *caught*). WOO. HALL OF JUSTICE, TRIBUNAL.
PLAYING AREA (squash, *tennis* etc). ROYAL
ENTOURAGE. CT, QUAD(RANGLE), YARD. *Shak*
char (H.v).
COURTED WOOED. JUDGED, SUED (crypt). WIMBLEDON,
TENNIS VENUE (crypt).
COURTESAN ADVENTURESS, CONCUBINE, DOXY. DEMI-
MONDAINE, *ENCHANTRESS*, FAVOURITE, FEMME
FATALE, HETAERA (Gk), MISTRESS, PARAMOUR,
SEDUCTRESS, *SIREN*. **Celeb**: ASPASIA (Gk); BIANCO
(*Shak*, Othello); BARRY, Comtesse du (Jeanne Bécu; Louis
XV); CAMPASPE (*Alexander*); LADY CHATTERLEY
(Connie Reid/Mellors; D. H. Lawrence); DELILAH (*Samson*);
FITZHERBERT, Maria Anne (George IV); MATA HARI
(*spy*); FANNY HILL (John Cleland); JEZEBEL (*Ahab*); LAIS
(Gk); LILY LANGTRY (theat, Edward VII); MAINTENON,
Marquise de (Françoise d'Aubigné; Louis XIV); NELL
GWYNN (Charles II); PHRYNE (Gk); POMPADOUR,
Marquise de (Jeanne Poisson; Louis XV); RACAMIER
(*Napoleon*); THAIS (Gk); VIOLETTA (La Traviata, Verdi).
COURT EXPERT BARRISTER, JUDGE, *LAW*
PRACTITIONER, LAWYER. SEED (tennis, crypt).
COURTING WOOING. ACTION, DEFENDING, PLEADING,
PROSECUTING, SUITING (crypt). SERVING, *TENNIS*
(crypt). ROYAL HOUSEHOLD (crypt).
COVEN *Assembly* of *witches*.
COVER 1. ALTER EGO, DISGUISE, NOM DE PLUME,
PSEUDONYM. ASSURANCE, INSURANCE. CAP,
COWL, *HAT*, HOOD, LID. *CLOAK*, DRESS, SHROUD.
ENVELOPE, WRAP(PING). FRONT PAGE, JACKET.
CRICKETER, FIELDER. 2. Enclose word in another, e.g. **He**
covers the order to get a house (4) = H*OM*E.
COVERING LID, CAP, *HAT. DRESSING.*
COVER STORY BLUFF, FALSE BACKGROUND, LIE.
LEADER, LEADING ARTICLE (crypt).
COVER UP DRESS. CONCEAL(MENT). REVOC (dn).
COVEY *Assembly* of partridges [*Christmas song*].
COW DOMINATE. *CASTLE* (arch). *CATTLE*, KINE, NEAT,

STEER; LOWER (crypt); *female* cattle, walrus etc (**offspring** = calf, **yak/cow** = dzho, dzo). [*Io*].

COWARDLY 1. AFRAID, CHICKEN, FRIGHTENED, SCARED, YELLOW; [Bob Acres (The Rivals, Sheridan); Bardolph, Nym, Pistol (H.v., Merry Wives); Capt Bobadil (Ben Jonson); Braggadochio (Faerie Queene, Spenser); Lion (Wizard of Oz); Parolles (All's Well, *Shak*); Conscience (Hamlet, *Shak*)]. 2. Written by Noël Coward (crypt) hence MASTERLY (from nickname).

COWBOY GAUCHO, HERDSMAN, VAQUERO; STEERSMAN (crypt); **celeb**: GENE AUTRY (singing), HOPALONG CASSIDY, WILLIAM S. HART, TOM MIX, AUDIE MURPHY, ROY ROGERS (horse Trigger), JOHN WAYNE. [Wells Fargo; *outlaw*]. CHAPMAN (crypt). **Pl** = *football* team (US).

COWGIRL Fem *cowboy*; DAIRYMAID, MILKMAID; **celeb**: ANNIE OAKLEY (US); CALAMITY JANE (US); *IO* (myth, crypt); PATIENCE (*G & S*); MAIDEN (all forlorn); My pretty maid (trad) [and see *shepherdess*].

COY *ARCH*, BASHFUL, DIFFIDENT, *SHY*. COMPANY.

CPL *CORPORAL*.

CR CHROMIUM (*chem*). COSTA RICA (*car plate*). CREDIT.

CRAB 1. CRITICIZE, SPOIL. *APPLE*. SOUR PERSON. HOIST, LIFT (mech). GO/WALK SIDEWAYS, SIDLE. CRUSTACEAN (Brachyura). 2. *Constellation* (Cancer); (4th) sign of *Zodiac*.

CRACKED *Anag*. BROKEN, CHIPPED, *SPLIT*, BEATEN, OVERCOME. *CRAZY*.

CRAFT ABILITY, *ART*, SKILL, TRADE. FREEMASONRY. CUNNING, DECEIT, GUILE. *BOAT(S)* (q.v. for **types**), SHIP(S), *VESSEL(S)* (q.v. for **celeb**). AEROPLANE(S), *AIRCRAFT* (q.v. for **types**), *SPACECRAFT* (q.v. for **celeb**).

CRAFTSMAN ARTISAN, SKILLED WORKER. TRICKSTER (crypt). CREWMAN, *SAILOR* (crypt).

CRANE DERRICK, HOIST, JIB. CAMERA PLATFORM, DOLLY. *BIRD*. PEER, STRETCH.

CRAZY *Anag*. CRACKED, DERANGED, LUNATIC, *MAD*. RANDOM, SCATTERED (paving).

CREATOR 1. FABRICATOR, MAKER, MANUFACTURER, ORIGINATOR, PRODUCER. FUSSPOT, GRUMBLER. 2. **Gods: Gk** = ZEUS, **Rom** = JOVE, *JUPITER*, **A-Sax** = *WODEN*, **Bab** = BEL/BELUS, **Egy** = *OSIRIS*, TEMU,

Ind = BRAHMA, SHIVA, **Nor** = *ODIN*, **Phoen** = *BAAL*.
CREDIT CR. BALANCE. *TICK*. ASCRIBE, BELIEF,
BELIEVE, TRUST; ACKNOWLEDGEMENT; MERIT,
REPUTATION.
CREEK *RIVER*. *AMERICAN INDIAN*.
CREEP CRAWL, *INCH*; INSINUATE, SNEAK. TOADY. LOW
ARCH. MOVEMENT. **Pl** = SHIVERS (fear).
CREEPER *BIRD*. IVY, CLIMBING PLANT. *INSECT*.
CRESTA RACE, *RUN* [toboggan].
CREW EIGHT, EQUIPE, FOUR, *TEAM*. DECKHAND, *MAN*,
SAILOR. BOASTED, EXULTED.
CRIB *CHEAT*, COPY, EMULATE. COT, CRADLE. *CARD
GAME*.
CRICKET BAT AND BALL, *GAME*; TEST [Thomas *Lord*].
INSECT. [~ on the Hearth (*Dickens*)].
CRICKETER PLAYER (FLANNELLED FOOL), DRY-*BOB*;
TESTER (crypt). *BATSMAN*: BAT, OPENER, INNER
(crypt), INSIDER (crypt); *FIELDER: BOWLER*, CATCHER,
COVER, FINE-LEG, GULLY, KEEPER, LONG-OFF,
LONG-ON, LONG-STOP, MID-OFF, MID-ON, MID-
WICKET, OUTSIDER (crypt), *POINT*, SHORT-LEG,
SILLY-POINT, SLIP, THIRD-MAN; **celeb**: GRACE, W. G.;
RAFFLES, A. J.
CRICKET GROUND PLAYING FIELD, TEST ZONE, TESTING
GROUND; **celeb**: EDGBASTON (Birmingham), FENNERS
(C), GRACE ROAD (Leicester), THE HILL (Sydney),
HEADINGLEY (Leeds), LORD'S (MCC), OLD TRAFFORD
(Manchester), THE *OUTER* (Melbourne), THE OVAL
(Adelaide, Kennington), THE PARKS (O), TRENT BRIDGE
(Nottingham), WACA (Perth), (WOOLLOON)GABBA
(Brisbane).
CRIPPLED *Anag*. DEFORMED, *GAME*, HALT, *LAME*.
[*patron saint*].
CROCODILE REPTILE (saurian): ALLIGATOR (Amer, Ch),
CAYMAN (S Amer), GHARIAL (Ind), MUGGER (Ind)
[~ tears; Capt Hook (*Barrie*); Punch & Judy show; Sebek
(Egy god)]. Schoolchildren in line.
CROESUS K OF LYDIA, RICH MAN [Dives, *Midas*].
CROMWELL 1. Oliver (1599–1658); MP Hunts then Cambs;
statesman and general. Led New Model Army (Ironsides,
Roundheads) to victory over Royalists (Cavaliers) in Civil
War (see *battle* for list of engagements). Dismissed Long

Parliament and became dictator as Lord Protector; refused
the Crown (the wart on his nose is notorious). Mar Elizabeth
Bourchier, 4 s and one d (Bridget, who mar Gen Henry Ireton).
2. Thomas, secretary to Cardinal Wolsey and adviser to H.viii;
executed 1540.

CRONOS Gk *god* of AGRICULTURE (**Rom** = *SATURN*). s of
Uranus and *Ge*; f by *Rhea* of *Demeter, Hades, Hera, Poseidon*
and *Zeus*.

CROONER BING; *SINGER*.

CROSS 1. X; CRUCIFIX, MARK, ROOD, SALTIRE; VOTE.
ANGRY, ANNOYED, *MAD*. FRUSTRATE, THWART.
HALF-CASTE, HYBRID. 2. *Constellation* (Crux).

CROSSBOW-MAN *CELLIST*, FIDDLER, VIOLINIST (crypt).
ARCHER [*weapon*].

CROSS DECISION ELECTION, VOTE (crypt).

CROSSING *BRIDGE*, FERRY, *FORD*, TRAVERSING.
BELISHA, PELICAN, ZEBRA. KISS (crypt). VOTING,
POLL (crypt).

CROSSPATCH GROUCH, GRUMPY PERSON, SCOLD.
PEDESTRIAN *CROSSING* (crypt).

CROSSWORD PUZZLE. ~ **solver** = cruciverbalist; **lover of** ~ =
cruciverbophile; **aversion to** ~ = cruciverbophobia (myth). **Pl** =
ARGUMENT. *ROW* (crypt).

CROW *BIRD* (corvidae); CARRION ~, CHOUGH, DRONGO,
GREY, HOODED ~, JACKDAW, JAY, MAGPIE, RAVEN,
ROOK, ROYSTON ~ (*assembly, constellation*). BUTTERFLY
(*lepidoptera*). *CRY*, EXULT, TRIUMPH (past tense = *crew*).
AMERICAN INDIAN.

CROWD ATTENDANCE, AUDIENCE, *GATE*, SPECTATORS;
celeb: BLEACHERS (US cheap seats), THE HILL (Sydney
cricket), THE KOP (Liverpool football), THE *OUTER*
(Melbourne cricket), THE SHED (Chelsea football), THE
TAVERN (Lord's cricket).

CROWN 1. CORONET, DIADEM; **comp** = anchor; *rose*.
'STEPHEN'. *WREATH. COIN*. TOP (of anchor/arch/head/
hill). CAP, PROTECTION. 2. *Constellation* (Corona Borealis).

CRUSE (s/l *crews*, cruise). BOWL, VESSEL [widow (*Elijah*)].

CRUSOE Robinson ~. Book by Defoe *modelled* on adventures
of Alexander Selkirk, stranded from the galley *Cinque Ports* on
Juan Fernandez island, 1704–9.

CRUSTACEAN ANTHROPOD, ISOPOD (aquatic, with
carapace); BARNACLE, COPEPOD (plankton), CRAB,

CRAWFISH, CRAYFISH, KRILL, LOBSTER, PILL
BUG, PRAWN, SHRIMP, SQUILLA, WATER FLEA,
WOODLOUSE [mollusc].

CRY *CALL*, EXCLAIM, SHOUT, YELL, YELP: HI, OUCH,
OW [~ Wolf]. APPEAL, ENTREATY. RUMOUR. BEWAIL,
BLUB, *GREET, KEEN*, LAMENT, SHED TEARS, WAIL,
WEEP [*Niobe, Ruth*]. *BARK, HAWK*, PEDDLE, TOUT.

CRYSTAL MINERAL. GLASS. *PALACE. BALL* [forecasting,
prophecy; clarity]. *Anniversary* (15th).

CS CAESIUM (*chem*). *CIVIL SERVICE*.

CT *CAUGHT. COURT.*

CU *COPPER* (*chem*). CUBE, -IC. CUMULUS.

CUB YOUNG SCOUT. YOUNG REPORTER. *OFFSPRING*
(bear, etc).

CUBE CU. BOX. EIGHT (crypt).

CUBIST PAINTER. DICE PLAYER (crypt).

CUDGEL CLUB, STICK, *WEAPON*. RACK, WORRY (brains).

CUER (s/l *queuer*). BILLIARD/POOL/SNOOKER PLAYER.

CULTURE CIVILIZATION [*study*]. FARMING, TILLING
(crypt).

CUMBERLAND A *division* of England. *BUTCHER* (mil).

CUMBRIA NW.

CUPHOLDER 1. CHAMPION, TROPHY WINNER.
BRA (crypt). 2. WINE-SERVER; NEHEMIAH (to King
Artaxerxes); SAKI (Rubaiyat, Omar Khayyam). **Gk god** =
GANYMEDE; **Gk goddess** = *HEBE*, **Rom** = *JUVENTAS*.

CUPID Rom *god* of *LOVE*; also AMOR (**Gk** = EROS). Son of
Venus and *Jupiter* (some say *Mars* or *Mercury*); an *archer*; fell in
love with *Psyche* (q.v.). *Shak* char (Timon). 2. *REINDEER*.

CURE HEAL, MEND; REMEDY, RESTORATIVE
TREATMENT [*spa*]. *DRY*, HARDEN, MATURE,
PRESERVE, SMOKE. *CHURCHMAN*, PRIEST (Fr).

CURRANT (s/l *current*). RIBES; DRIED GRAPE. FRUIT
(black~, red~, white~).

CURRENCY FLUENCY, REPUTATION. RIVER,
WATERFLOW (crypt). AC, DC, ELECTRICITY (crypt).
COINAGE, **celeb** (worldwide):

Country	Currency	Sub-division
Albania	lek	qintars
Algeria	dinar	centimes
American Ind	wampum	peage

Argentina	austral	centavos
Australia	dollar	cents
Austria	schilling	groschen
Bangladesh	taka	paisa
Belgium	franc	centimes
Bolivia	boliviano	centavos
Brazil	cruçado	centavos
Bulgaria	lev	stotinki
Burma	kyat	pyas
Cambodia	riel	sen
Canada	dollar	cents
Chile	peso	centesimos
China	yen/yuan	chiao/fen
CIS	rouble	kopecks
Columbia	peso	centavos
Costa Rica	colon	centimos
Cuba	peso	centavos
Cyprus	pound	mils
Czechoslovakia	koruna	halers
Denmark	krone	øre
Ecuador	sucre	centavos
Egypt	pound	piastres
El Salvador	colon	centavos
Ethiopia	dollar	cents
Finland	markka	pennia
France	franc	centimes
Germany	mark	pfennigs
Greece	drachma	lepton
Guatemala	quetzal	centavos
Guinea	sily	gauris
Haiti	gourde	centimes
Honduras	lempira	centavos
Hungary	forint	fillers
Iceland	krona	aurar
India	rupee	paisis
Indonesia	rupiah	sen
Iran	rial	dinars
Iraq	dinar	fils
Ireland	punt	pennies
Israel	shekel	agorots
Italy	lira	centesimi
Japan	yen	sen

Jordan	dinar	fils
Kenya	shillings	cents
Korea	whan	jun
Laos	kip	at
Lebanon	pound	piastres
Liberia	dollar	cents
Libya	dinar	dirhams
Luxembourg	franc	centimes
Malawi	kwacha	tambala
Malta	pound	cents
Mexico	peso	centavos
Morocco	dirham	francs
Netherlands	guilder	cents
New Zealand	dollar	cents
Nicaragua	cordoba	centavos
Nigeria	naira	kobos
Norway	krone	øre
Pakistan	rupee	paisas
Panama	balboa	centismos
Paraguay	guarani	centismos
Peru	sol	centavos
Philippines	peso	centavos
Poland	zloty	groszy
Portugal	escudo	centavos
Romania	leu	bani
Saudi Arabia	rial	qursh
Spain	peseta	centimos
Sri Lanka	rupee	cents
Sweden	krona	øre
Switzerland	franc	centimes
Syria	pound	piastres
Thailand	baht	satangs
Tunisia	dinar	millimes
Turkey	lira	kurus
UK	pound	pennies
USA	dollar	cents
Uruguay	peso	centesimos
Venezuela	bolivar	centimos
Vietnam	dong	xu
Yemen	riyal	bugshas
Yugoslavia	dinar	paras
Zaire	zaire	makutas

Zambia   kwacha   ngwee

CURRENT (s/l currant). EXISTING, IMMEDIATE,
IN PROGRESS, PRESENT, UP-TO-DATE, VALID.
ACCEPTED, CUSTOMARY, KNOWN, PUBLIC, USUAL,
WIDESPREAD. **Flow (air)**: *WIND* (q.v. for names). **Flow
(elect)**: AC, DC, ELECTRICITY [amps, ohms, volts, watts].
Flow (water): COURSE, DIRECTION, DRIFT, EBB, FLOOD,
(TIDAL) FLOW/MOVEMENT, FLUID, STREAM, TIDE,
UNDERTOW, TREND. *RIVER* (crypt). **World's principal ~s**:
ALASKA ~, ANTILLES ~, AUSTRALIAN ~ (E/W), BEN
GUELA ~, BRAZILIAN ~, CALIFORNIA ~, CANARIES
~, CARIBBEAN ~, EL NINO, EQUATORIAL ~,
FLORIDA ~, GUINEA ~, GULF STREAM, HUMBOLDT
~, IRMINGER ~, JAPAN ~, KURI SHIO, LABRADOR
~, NORWEGIAN ~, OYA SHIO, PERU ~.
CURTAIL 1. DOCK, SHORTEN. 2. Omit last letter, e.g. **Some
curtailed party** (4) = PART.
CURTAIN BARRIER, DRAPE, SCREEN. **Pl** = TABS (theat).
DEATH, FINISH, THE END.
CUSTOM *HABIT*, PRACTICE, PRAXIS, TRADITION,
USAGE, USE, WONT. **Pl** = DUTY, PREVENTIVE MEN,
LEVY [*smuggle, tax*]. MORES [O tempora, O mores!
(Cicero)].
CUT 1. LANCE, PARE, SEVER, SLICE. STOP FILMING.
EDIT(ED); CENSORED. IGNORE, *OMIT*, SEND TO
COVENTRY, SHUN, SNUB. STROKE (*cricket*). 2. Shortened
form of . . . e.g. **Defence cut** (3) = DEF. **Comp** = thrust.
~ DOWN CHOP(PED), FELL(ED). REDUCE(D).
~ UP *Anag.* CHOP(PED), DICE(D), FELL(ED), SLICE(D).
DISTRESSED, HURT, PAINED. TUC (dn).
CWT HUNDREDWEIGHT, *MEASURE*.
CYBELE 1. RHEA. Gk *goddess* of *FERTILITY*, whose priests
were the *Corybantes* (**Rom** = *CERES*). 2. A minor *PLANET*.
CYCLOPES Gk myth one-eyed *monsters*: ACAMAS, ARGES,
BRONTES, POLYPHEMUS (chief of ~; in love with Galatea),
PYRACMON, STEROPES. [*Ulysses*].
CYNIC 1. One who is contemptuous of honest morality.
PESSIMIST; SARCASTIC. 2. Gk sect which scorned worldly
goods and advocated self-control (see also *Stoic*). **Celeb**:
ANISTHENES, CHRYSIPPUS, *DIOGENES* [Spartans].
CYNOPHILE *Lover of dogs.*

CYNOPHOBIA *Aversion to dogs*.
Cz Czechoslovakia.

D DAUGHTER. DAY. DELTA. DENARIUS. DEUTERIUM
(*chem*). *DIED*. *DIRECTOR*, ~ED. *DOWN*. GERMANY (*car
plate*). *KEY*; *NOTE*. PENNY. 500.
d daughter. died.
DACTYL 1. FOOT (⁻ᵛᵛ). FINGER. 2. **Pl** = GIANTS [discovered
iron; served *Rhea*].
DAD *FATHER*. FIRST IN DIVINITY (crypt: D*A*D).
DAEDALUS Gk myth *sculptor*, *inventor* and architect, who k his
nephew Talus and fled to Crete, where he built the *labyrinth*
to house the *Minotaur* at Cnossos in Crete for King *Minos*.
Imprisoned, he made wings for himself and Icarus (his s) and
flew to Sicily; the wax securing Icarus' wings melted, and he fell
into the sea and was drowned.
DAILY *CHAR*. EACH DAY. JOURNAL, *NEWSPAPER*,
PAPER, QUOTIDIAN; EXPRESS, MAIL, MIRROR,
OBSERVER, SUN, TELEGRAPH, TIMES etc (all ®).
~ **LEADER** D (crypt). ED, EDITOR. COVER STORY.
~ **WORKER** (NEWS)PAPER. HAND. *CHAR*. [~ Planet,
reporter Clark *Kent*, Superman].
DAMAGE(D) *Anag*. RUIN(ED), SPOIL(ED). **Pl** =
COMPENSATION.
DANAE 1. Gk myth *goddess* of *FERTILITY*. m of *Perseus* by
Zeus, who came to her in a *shower* of gold. **Rom** = *CERES*,
DIANA. 2. A minor *PLANET*.
DANCE *BALL*, *BALLET* (q.v.), *BOB*, CAPER, *FOOT*,
HOP, JIVE, JUKE, *MEASURE*, ORCHESIS, PAS, *SET*,
STEP, TOE. [*cat*; Hans *Andersen*, *Salome*]. **Gk goddess** =
TERPSICHORE (*Muse*) [*Corybantes*]. **Celeb**:

3-letters			
HAY	JIG	SUN ~	WAR ~
HEY	PAS		

4-letters			
BARN ~	GO-GO	JOTA	SHAG
CLOG~	HAKA	JUBE	
FOLK ~	HORA	*REEL*	
GIGA	HULA	ROCK	

5-letters

BELLY ~	GIGUE	PAVAN	TANGO
BOREE	GO-PAK	POLKA	*TWIST*
CONGA	LIMBO	RUMBA	VOLTA
FLING	*MAMBA*	SAMBA	WALTZ
GALOP	NAUCH	SWORD ~	

6-letters

BALLET	MINUET	PAVANE	*SQUARE* ~
BOLERO	MORRIS	POW-WOW	
CHA-CHA	NAUTCH	RHUMBA	
FLORAL ~	NEWALA	SHIMMY	

7-letters

CZARDAS	HOE-DOWN	MUSETTE	TWO-STEP
FOXTROT	LANCERS	ONE-STEP	
GAVOTTE	MAZURKA	TORDION	

8-letters

BIG APPLE	FANDANGO	HULA-HULA
BUNNY-HUG	FOURSOME	RIGADOON
CAKEWALK	GALLIARD	SARABAND
COTILLON	HORNPIPE	

9+ letters

ALLEMANDE	ECOSSAISE	QUICKSTEP
BLACK BOTTOM	EIGHTSOME	ROCK 'N' ROLL
BUMPS-A-DAISY	FARANDOLE	SCHOTTISCHE
CHA-CHA-CHA	GAY GORDONS	STRATHSPEY
CHARLESTON	LAMBETH WALK	STRIP THE WILLOW
CORROBOREE	PASO DOBLE	TARANTELLA
DASHING WHITE SERGEANT	PAUL JONES	TURKEY-TROT
	PETRONELLA	
	POLONAISE	
	QUADRILLE	

DANCE CENTRE BALLET SCHOOL. MAYPOLE (crypt). N (crypt).

DANDY BLOOD, FOP, *RIP. GOOD*, EXCELLENT, FINE. *COMIC*.

DANIEL Noble bibl youth, with reputation for *wisdom*. Served first

Belshazzar then Darius, who was tricked into casting ~ into a den of *lions*, but ~ was miraculously preserved; d 536 B.C.

DAPHNE 1. Gk myth d of a river god, she was changed into a laurel tree to escape the pursuit of *Apollo*, and it became his favourite tree. 2. A minor *PLANET*. 3. Flowering shrub.

DARBY (s/l *Derby*). Husband of *Joan*. Pl = HANDCUFFS.

DARDANELLES HELLESPONT [*Helle.* Gallipoli].

DARKNESS SWARTHINESS; GLOOM, NIGHT, OBSCURITY, STARLESSNESS; WICKEDNESS. **Egy god** = *SET*; **Gk goddess** = *HECATE*.

DARLING ACUSHLA (Ire), DEAREST, FAVOURITE, *PET*, SWEETHEART. *GRACE* ~ (lighthouse-keeper's d; rescuer). *WENDY* (Peter Pan). RIVER (Aus).

DART *DASH. ARROW*, BANDERILLA (*bullfighting*), FLECHETTE. GUSSET (seam). *RIVER.* Pl = ARROWS, *GAME*.

DASH *DART*, FALL. ADVANCE, MOVE, ONSET, RUSH, SPEED; *WHIP*. BOTTLE (sl), DRIVE, ELAN; *DOG* (Queen Victoria's). CONFOUND, DAUNT, DISCOURAGE, FRUSTRATE, SHATTER. *CAST*, FLING, HURL, KNOCK, THROW, THRUST. DILUTE, DROP, INFUSION, SPLASH, *SPOT*. DAMN, DARN (swear). SCRIBBLE. PARENTHESIS; MACRON, TILDE (accent ~). LONG SIGN (morse; **opp** = *dot*).

DATA GEN, INFORMATION, PARAMETERS, QUANTITIES (math), TABLE [problem].

DATE ESTABLISHED PERIOD; *TIME*; IDES, NONES (Rom). *APPOINTMENT*, MEETING, TRYST; ESCORT, TAKE OUT. *PALM*-BERRY, *PHOENIX*, ~ FRUIT; *TREE*.

DATED AG(E)ING, OLD-FASHIONED, *SQUARE. FRANKED*, *STAMPED*. ESCORTED, SQUIRED, TAKEN OUT, TOOK OUT.

DAUGHTER D; *OFFSPRING*, PROGENY (fem); GIRL.

DAVID 1. *Patron saint* (Wal; 1st Mar), s of Non, uncle of *King Arthur*. 2. K of Sc, s of Robert Bruce. 3. Bibl youngest s of Jesse, mar Michal and f of *Absalom*, Adonijah and Amnon (*c*.1045–975 B.C.). With his sling, ~ the *shepherd* boy k the giant Philistine Goliath, and his rise to favour was rapid. ~ was a *poet*, harpist and psalmist, and was made court musician, soon becoming armour-bearer to *Saul*, k of Judea, with whose s Jonathan ~ formed one of the great friendships of history, and whose d Michal he mar. On Saul becoming too despotic, ~ was

chosen by *Samuel* as successor, but had to flee; his w Michal was
taken from him and he mar *Abigail*, and then had these children
by the following wives and concubines: Amnon (s) by Ahinoam,
Chileab (s) by *Abigail* (w), *Absalom* (s) and Tamar (d) by
Maacah, Adonijah (s; see *Solomon*) by Haggith, Shepatiah
(s) by Abital, and Ithream (s) by Eglah (w). When Saul was
defeated at Gilboa, ~ returned to become an all-conquering
king. He coveted Bathsheba, w of Uriah the Hittite, and caused
Joab, his nephew and mil captain, to contrive Uriah's d in battle,
and Bathsheba later bore him a s *Solomon*. *Absalom* (q.v.) led a
revolt but was k, and ~ was succeeded by Solomon. In his old
age ~ mar Abishag. 4. Jacques Louis ~, Fr court *PAINTER* to
Napoleon.

DAVIDSON ABSALOM, SOLOMON..

DAWN 1. AUBADE, MORNING, SUNRISE. COME TO,
  REALIZE. 2. **Goddess: Gk** = EOS, **Rom** = AURORA, **It** =
  MATUTA.

DAY D. *SUNDAY*, *MONDAY*, *TUES* etc; S, M, T etc (**opp** =
  night). DAYLIGHT. DATE, PERIOD; **comp** = ever; night.
  VICTORY. [Policeman ~ (*Kipling*)].

DB DECIBEL (noise).

DC DIRECT CURRENT; *CURRENCY* (crypt, elect); **comp**
  = AC. DISTRICT COMMISSIONER. DISTRICT OF
  COLUMBIA.

DD DIVINE, DOCTOR OF DIVINITY; *CHURCHMAN*.
  DAUGHTERS.

DDR Was EAST GERMANY (and *car plate*).

DEAD D, DEFUNCT, EX, EXPIRED, LATE, PASSED
  ON/OVER (**opp** = live). FINISHED, OVER. UNCHARGED.
  SEA.

DEAR (s/l *deer*). *DARLING*, DUCK, HONEY, LIEF, *LOVE*,
  LUV, SWEETIE. A LOT, COSTLY, EXPENSIVE, PRICEY.

DEATH 1. EXPIRATION, FATHER TIME, FINIS, REAPER,
  THE END; [*Charon*; 'this fell sergeant ~' (Hamlet, *Shak*)].
  13 (*tarot*). 2. **God: Gk** = THANATOS, **Rom** = MORS, **Egy**
  = ANUBIS/OSIRIS, **Ind** = SHIVA.

DEB L, BEGINNER, DEBUTANTE, TYRO [come out]. BACK
  SEAT (crypt).

DEBT IN THE RED, IOU, MARKER [bankruptcy]. See
  IN ~ (2).

DEBTOR BANKRUPT, *DR*, OWER.

DEC DECLARED, INNINGS CLOSED. DECEASED.

DECEMBER.

DECEMBER (12th) MONTH, M, DEC (Rom 10th month, until
Julius *Caesar* reorganized the calendar). **Birthstone** = Turquoise.

DECIBEL DB, NOISE-LEVEL.

DECK ADORN, BEDECK, DRESS, GARLAND, ORNAMENT.
BRIDGE, LEVEL (naut). GROUND (sl). PACK (*cards*).

DECLARE AFFIRM, ASSERT, *AVER*, SAY, STATE. CLOSE
INNINGS, DEC (*cricket*).

DECLINE *REFUSE*, REJECT. DESCENT, DOWNWARD
PATH/SLOPE, SETTING, STEP DOWN. DECAY, DROOP,
FALL (OFF). INFLECT (gram).

DECORATION *MEDAL*: VC, GC, DSO, GM, CGM, DSC, MC,
DFC, DCM, MM, DFM; RIBBON, *STAR*, GONG (sl); IRON
CROSS etc. ADORNMENT, APPEARANCE, PAINTWORK;
FILIGREE.

DECREASE DIMINISH, LESSEN. *IRON*, PRESS (crypt).

DEED ACT, FACT, PERFORMANCE. CHARTER,
DISPOSITION, INSTRUMENT, PROOF OF TITLE.

DEER (s/l *dear*). RUMINANT QUADRUPED (Cervidae); **breeds**:
AXIS, BARKING, CARIBOU, CHITAL, ELK, FALLOW,
HIND, IZARD, MOOSE, MUNTJAK, MUSK, NUR, *RED*,
REINDEER, ROE, RUSA, SAMBUR, SIKA, *SKIPPER*,
WAPITI. **Assembly** = herd; **male** = *buck*, hart, *stag*; **fem** = doe,
hind; **offspring** = *fawn* [*antelope*, Bambi, *goat*, venison].

DEERSTALKER GHILLIE, KEEPER. *HAT* [*Holmes*].

DEFEAT BEAT, OVERCOME, WORST.

DEFECT FAULT, FLAW. ABANDON, CHANGE SIDES,
CROSS THE FLOOR, RENEGE, SWITCH ALLEGIANCE,
TURNCOAT.

DEFILE GORGE, PASS. MARCH IN FILE. BEFOUL,
CORRUPT, DESECRATE, PROFANE, RUIN, SPOIL.

DEFORMED *Anag. CRIPPLED*. MISSHAPEN, TWISTED.

DEGREE GRADE, LEVEL, SCALE, STANDARD, STEP [hot,
cold]. ANGLE, MEASUREMENT (naut; math) [latitude,
longitude]. CLASS, CONDITION, PROFICIENCY, RANK,
STATUS; BA, MA [*university*].

DEL DELINEAVIT, DREW. LED BACK (crypt).

DELETED 1. ERASED, REMOVED. 2. Delete letter 'd' from
clue, e.g. **Drink deleted is iced** (4) = *RINK.

DELIBERATE EXPRESS, ON PURPOSE, PURPOSEFUL,
STUDIED. CONSIDER, DISCUSS. IMPRISON (crypt).

DELIVERY *BALL. CARRIAGE*, FREIGHT. *CHILDBIRTH*.

POST. TRANSFER. RESCUE, SALVATION. *SPEECH*.

~ **MAN** *BOWLER*, *PITCHER*. ROUNDSMAN. TRADESMAN. DOCTOR, MALE NURSE (crypt).

DELPHI Town in Phocis on Parnassus, with *Oracle*; now Kastri.

DELTA D; 4th Gk letter. RIVER MOUTH.

Dem Democrat [elephant].

DEMAND ASK, REQUEST. MARKET; **comp** = supply.

DEMETER Gk *goddess* of NATURE, d of *Cronos* and *Rhea*. Her d *Persephone* (Proserpine) by *Zeus* was seized by *Pluto*, and *Hermes* brought her back. **Rom** = *CERES*.

DEMIJOHN LARGE *BOTTLE*. JO or HN (crypt).

DEMOCRAT PARTY (polit; anti-Rep) [elephant].

DEMON CRUEL BEING, GHOUL. AFREET, AFRIT (Mos), *DEVIL* (q.v.), EVIL *SPIRIT* (q.v.). *CARD GAME*.

DEMONSTRATE PROVE, SHOW. PARADE, RALLY.

DEN STUDY, WORKROOM. *HABITATION*, LAIR. DENIER (cloth count).

DENARIUS D, COIN (penny). [L, S, D].

DENMARK DK (*car plate*). *STRAIT*. [*Hamlet*].

DENTIST BDS, *DRAWER*, EXTRACTOR, ORTHODONTIST, PULLER; FANG-PRANGER (sl). PANEL-BEATER (crypt).

DEPARTED GONE, *LEFT*, WENT. *DEAD*, EX, LATE.

DEPLOYED 1. *Anag*. ARRANGED, SET OUT. 2. Remove letters PLOY from word(s).

DEPOSIT BANK, *LODGE*. ASH, SILT.

DEPRESSION *BLUES*, DUMPS. DENT, DIP, HOLLOW; GLEN, VALE, VALLEY. *COL*, CYCLONE, *LOW* (met).

DERANGED *Anag*. *CRAZY*. DISTURBED.

DERBY (s/l *Darby*). BOWLER, *HAT*. *CLASSIC*. LORD. *CERAMICS* ®. CITY (baseball ground, *football*).

DESCRIBE 1. ABOUT, ANENT, RE. *DRAW*, ENCIRCLE, MARK OUT. EXPLAIN, QUALIFY, RECITE DETAILS OF. 2. Word round another, e.g. **On foot, she describes a circle** (4) = SH*O*E.

DESERT (s/l *dessert*). 1. *LEAVE*, *RAT*, RUNAWAY [turncoat]. ASSEMBLY OF LAPWINGS. (SANDY) WASTELAND; **celeb**: ARABIAN (Af), ANATOLIAN (Turk), AN NAFUD (Arab), ATACAMA (Chile), AUSTRALIAN (Aus), BARREN (Pers), BLACK SAND (CIS), COLORADO (US), DAHNA (Arab), DASHT-E-LUT (Iran), DEATH VALLEY (US), EASTERN (Af), GIBSON (Aus), GILA (US), GOBI (Ch), GREAT SALT (Pers; US), GREAT SANDY (Arab; Aus),

GREAT VICTORIAN (Aus), KALAHARI (Af), KARA
(CIS), KAVIR (Pers), KYZYL (CIS), LIBYAN (Af), LUT
(Pers), MARGO (Afghan), MOHAVE (US), MONGOLIAN
(Ch), NAFUD (Arab), NAMIB (Af), NAZCA (Peru),
NEGEV (Israel), NUBIAN (Af), PATAGONIAN ~ (S. Am),
QARA QUM (CIS), SAHARA (Af), SECHURA (Peru),
SHAMIYA (Arab), SHAMO (Ch), SINAI (Egy), SOMALI
(Som), SONORAN (Mex/US), SYRIAN (Arab), TAKLA
MAKAN (Ch), THAR (Ind), TURKESTAN (Asia), ZIRREH
(Afghan). **Pl** = *FATE*, MERITS, REWARDS. 2. Remove
letter(s) indicated, e.g. **Trust gunners to desert rarely** (4)
= **RELY.

DESIGN AIM, END, INTENT. DRAWING, PLAN, PATTERN
[archit].

DESIRE LONGING, WISH, *MANIA*.

DESK COUNTER, SERVERY. BOOK REST, LECTERN,
SUPPORT: MUSIC STAND. EDITORIAL DEPARTMENT.
BUREAU, WRITING TABLE; and see *furniture* for types.

DESSERT (s/l *desert*). AFTERS, PUDDING, SWEET: *COURSE*
(FRUIT, NUTS).

DESTROY *Anag*. ANNIHILATE, *BREAK*, CRUSH, FINISH.

DETAIL 1. ITEMIZE, ORDER, TELL OFF, LIST. MINOR
PARTICULAR. DETACHMENT (mil). DOCK (crypt).
2. Remove last letter(s), e.g. **Fine detail at the end** (3)
= FIN*.

DETECTIVE *POLICEMAN*; DICK, FBI, G-MAN, GUMSHOE
(sl), INVESTIGATOR, PRIVATE EYE, TEC [*AGENT*]. **Pl**
= CID, FBI, *Pinkerton* Agency, Scotland Yard; YARDMEN
(crypt). **Comp** = Emil (and the ~s). **Celeb** (fiction):

BERGERAC	(TV)
FATHER BROWN	(*Chesterton*)
BUCKET	(*Dickens*)
FRANK CANNON	(TV)
NICK CARTER	(Hammett)
LEMMY CAUTION	(Films)
CHARLIE CHAN	(Films; Biggers)
COLUMBO	(TV)
AUGUSTE, DUPIN	(Rue Morgue, Poe; 1st fict)
INSP FRENCH	(Allingham)
GREGSON	(*Holmes*)
HARRY O	(TV)

HART & HART	(TV)
SHERLOCK *HOLMES*	(Conan Doyle)
KOJAK	(TV; Mann)
LESTRADE	(*Holmes*)
MAIGRET	(Simenon)
PHILIP MARLOWE	(Chandler)
MISS MARPLE	(Christie)
PERRY MASON	(Gardner)
McCLOUD	(TV)
McMILLAN & WIFE	(TV)
MORSE	(TV)
HERCULE POIROT	(Christie)
TOM SAWYER	(Mark *Twain*)
EDDIE SHOESTRING	(TV)
SAM SPADE	(Hammett)
TENAFLY	(TV)
LORD PETER WIMSEY	(Sayers)

DETOUR *Anag.* 1. DEVIATION, DIGRESSION. 2. Remove letters TOUR (or synonym) from clue, e.g. **Detour along the coast is a fiddle** (3) = CON****.

DEUCALION 1. Gk myth, s of *Prometheus* and Clymene, and progenitor of Gk race. With his w Pyrrha, ~ built a boat to escape the flood sent by Zeus; it came to rest on Mt Parnassus (c.f. *Noah*). They then threw stones over their shoulders to repopulate the earth [*Python*]. 2. Gk myth s of *Minos* and Pasiphae; an *Argonaut* and one of the Calydonian boar hunters.

DEUTERIUM D (*chem*); HYDROGEN ISOTOPE.

DEVELOP *Anag.* PROCESS, TREAT (photo). REVEAL, UNFOLD; ELABORATE. CONVERT LAND. PROGRESS.

DEVI Chief Ind *goddess*, w of Shiva. Depicted with *many arms*; personification of destruction.

DEVIL DEMON, EVIL *SPIRIT* (q.v.), IMP, TEMPTER; ABADDON (Hebr), APOLLYON (bibl), BELIAL (Hebr), DEUCE, *DICKENS*, *DIS*, *HADES* (Gk), LUCIFER (Lat), MEPHISTOPHELES (Ger), (OLD) NICK, OLD *SCRATCH*, PLUTO, SATAN (bibl, lit = accuser). 15 (*tarot*). ERRAND BOY (printer's); JUNIOR (leg); RESEARCH, SORT.

DEVISE 1. CONTRIVE, INVENT, PLAN, PLOT, SCHEME. ASSIGN, BEQUEATH, WILL [testament, testify]. 2. Remove letters 'vise' from word or sentence, e.g. **Derv is eating devised for removal of household tariffs** (8) = DER****ATING.

DEVOUT PI, PIOUS, RELIGIOUS, REVERENTIAL.

EARNEST, GENUINE, HEARTY.

DEXTER RIGHT (*herald*). *CATTLE* (Ire).

DEXTERITY ADROITNESS. ON THE RIGHT, RIGHT-HANDEDNESS.

DEXTEROUS ADROIT, HANDY, SKILFUL. RIGHT-HANDED.

DG DEI GRATIE, BY GOD'S GRACE, DV. DIRECTOR GENERAL.

DI *DIANA*. DOUBLE . . . **Pl** = *PLUTO*.

DIA DIAMETER. ACROSS . . . , APART . . . , THROUGH . . .

DIAERESIS *ACCENT* (ë pronounced separately), UMLAUT.

DIAL FACE (sl). CALL, RING [STD]. INSTRUMENT.

DIAMOND *GEM*, PRECIOUS STONE; RHINESTONE; CARBON, ICE (sl), *ROCKS* (sl) [girl's best friend]; **celeb**: CULLINAN, FLORENTINE, GREAT MOGUL, HOPE, KOH-I-NOOR, SHAH, STAR OF INDIA, GRAND DUKE OF TUSCANY. *DOG* (Newton). LOZENGE, RHOMB. BASEBALL FIELD (US). *Anniversary* (60th or 75th). *Birthstone* (April). *TYPEFACE*. **Pl** = SUIT (*cards*). COURTIERS (*Alice*).

DIANA 1. DELIA, DI; HORSEWOMAN, HUNTRESS. 2. Rom *goddess* of HUNTING, MOON and FERTILITY; d of *Jupiter*; her temple at Ephesus was one of the *Seven Wonders of the World*. **Gk** = *ARTEMIS/HECATE*. [*Actaeon*; *Shak*].

DIARIST LOGGER, RECORDER; **celeb**: FANNY BURNEY, THOMAS CREEVEY (politics), SIR SIMON D'EWES, JOHN EVELYN, ANNE FRANK (NL), CHARLES GREVILLE, REV FRANCIS KILVERT, ADRIAN *MOLE* (fict, Sue Townsend), SAMUEL PEPYS, CHARLIE POOTLE (A Nobody, fict, Grossmith), HENRY CRABB ROBINSON, SAMUEL SEWALL (US), MAJOR THOMPSON (Fr fict, Daninos), JOHN WESLEY (eccles).

DICE Pl of DIE: BONES, CRAPS, LIAR ~, POKER ~. CHECKER (US), CHEQUER, CHOP INTO CUBES, CUT UP.

DICER CRAPS PLAYER/SHOOTER [sharpshooter]. CHOPPER, CUBIST (crypt).

DICKENS 1. *DEVIL*, DEUCE. 2. Monica ~, fem Eng writer. 3. Charles (John Huffam), writer 1812–70; mar Catherine Hogarth 1836, separated 1858. BOZ, QUIZ. **Illustrators**: Hablot Knight Browne (Phiz), George Cruikshank, Richard

Doyle, John Leech, Daniel Maclise, Clarkson Stanfield, Frank Stone, Sir John Tenniel. **Novels: Barnaby Rudge** (abbr: Rudge). Against a background of the Gordon Riots, family enmity is transcended by the love of Edwin Chester for Emma Haredale. Barnaby Rudge and his pet raven *Grip* carry messages; **Bleak House** (abbr: Bleak Ho). Richard Carstone secretly weds his cousin Ada Clare while they are wards of John Jarndyce. Esther Summerson is shown to be the love child of Lady Dedlock. The *lawyers* devour the fortune in the endless case in Chancery of Jarndyce v Jarndyce; **The Christmas Books** (abbr: Xmas books). A series dealing with Christmas: The Battle of Life, The Chimes, A Christmas Carol (Scrooge, Marley's *ghost*), The *Cricket* on the Hearth, and The Haunted Man; **David Copperfield** (abbr: Copperfield). Raised by his wicked step-f Murdstone, ~ finds friendship from the Peggottys, incl his *nurse* Clara (whom 'Barkis is willin'' to mar), and their niece Little Em'ly. After unhappy schooling at Mr Creakle's Salem House, ~ is lodged with the Micawbers and works in Murdstone's warehouse; he runs away to his aunt Betsy Trotwood, who adopts him, and he lodges with her lawyer Wickfield and his charming d Agnes; Uriah Heep is the 'umble clerk. ~ is articled to Spenlow and Jorkins and mar the d Dora as a child bride, who d after a few years. Steerforth, an old school friend, seduces Little Em'ly but is drowned. Uriah Heep's plans to control Wickfield are foiled by Micawber and ~, who finally mar Agnes and finds success as a writer. Largely autobiographical, it also *models* Micawber on the author's f John; **Dombey & Son, Dealings With the Firm of** (abbr: Dombey). Paul ~ is a cold egoist who puts his business standing before all else. His s Paul dies and d Florence is estranged. She eventually mar Walter Gray and forgives her f; **Great Expectations** (abbr: Great Ex). *Recluse* Miss Havisham, who was jilted on her wedding day, lets Pip – Philip Pirrip – believe that he owes his fortune to her, but it comes from the *convict* Abel Magwitch, whom he helped at one time. Estella, whom he loves vainly, is shown to be Magwitch's d, brought up by Miss Havisham to spurn men; **Hard Times, For these Times** (abbr: Hard Times). Josiah Bounderby, a self-made oafish banker, mar young Louisa Gradgrind who, with her br Tom, has been raised by her f in Coketown to acknowledge hard facts. Strife and strikes occur among the workers, and Tom is shown to be a thief; Louisa runs back to her f; **Little Dorrit** (abbr: Dorrit). Amy Dorrit, d of William ~, spends her childhood

unsullied by the corrosive atmosphere of the Marshalsea
debtors' *prison*. Father and daughter inherit money and are
released, while their friend Arthur Clenham is sentenced in
his turn. Intrigue and theft form a damning social comment on
complacent bureaucracy; **Martin Chuzzlewit** (abbr: Chuzzle).
Young Martin ~ is sacked at his grandfather's behest by
Pecksniff, and seeks his fortune in America. He returns to make
peace with the old man; his uncle Jonas ~ commits murder
and suicide. Sarah Gamp, coarse midwife and *nurse* 'dispoged'
to gin, converses with her non-existent and *unseen* friend Mrs
Harris; **The Mystery of Edwin Drood** (abbr: Drood). Edwin
~ breaks off betrothal to Rosa Bud, ward of Mr Grewgious
and music pupil of John Jasper, who lusts after her. Neville
Landless has to flee when Edwin disappears, and the odious
Jasper fosters the suspicion which falls on him. The novel is
unfinished; **Nicholas Nickleby** (abbr: Nich Nick). Ralph ~ places
his nephew Nicholas with Wackford Squeers, *schoolmaster* of
Dotheboys Hall; and his niece Kate with Madame Mantalini, a
dressmaker. Squeers ill-treats all his boys, especially Smike, who
dies and turns out to have been Ralph ~'s s. All is eventually
put right by the *twin* brs Cheeryble; **The Old Curiosity
Shop** (abbr: OC Shop). Nell Trant's grandfather is proprietor
of the shop, and he gets into debt to Daniel Quilp, an evil
dwarf with designs on Little Nell. They have to flee when the
grandfather cannot pay. Quilp victimizes several people who
try to help, and eventually all three die; **Oliver Twist, or The
Parish Boy's Progress** (abbr: Oliver). Oliver ~ grows up in the
workhouse. He runs away and is picked up by Jack Dawkins
(twice) who is one of Fagin's young thieves and known as
the Artful Dodger. Bill Sikes murders Nancy when she tries
to help Oliver, whose genteel background is finally revealed
by Mr Brownlow; **Our Mutual Friend** (abbr: Mutual F).
The body of John Harmon is found in the Thames, and
papers show that his fortune should go to Nicodemus *Boffin*,
a dustman. Mistaken identity, blackmail and greed abound
along the river, as Bella Wilfer rejects intrigue and is united
with the real John Harmon. The deformed Jenny Wren has
to work as a doll's dressmaker to keep her drunken f; **The
Pickwick Papers, or The Posthumous Papers of the Pickwick
Club** (abbr: Pickwick). Adventures of the four members of the
Corresponding Society of the Pickwick Club: Samuel Pickwick,
Augustus Snodgrass, Tracy Tupman and Nathaniel Winkle.

Mr Pickwick, supported by his manservant Samuel Weller, also has to fight a breach of promise case brought by Mrs Bardell; **A Tale of Two Cities** (abbr: 2 Cities). Dr Manette is released from the Bastille after 18 years as a *prisoner* in Cell 105, North Tower, the Bastille, and eventually becomes *mad*; his d Lucie mar Charles Darnay, nephew of the Marquis de St Evremonde. Sidney Carton adores Lucie and eventually substitutes himself for her jailed husband, and goes to the guillotine in his stead: 'It is a far, far better thing . . . than I have ever done'. **Characters**: Artful Dodger (*robber*; Oliver); Bagstock, Major (JB, Josh, Old Joe; Dombey); Bardell, Mrs (Pickwick); Barkis (a carrier; '~ is willin''; Copperfield); *Boffin*, Nicodemus (Mutual F); Brass, Sampson & Sally (solicitors; OC Shop); Brownlow, Mr (Oliver); Bucket (*detective*; Bleak Ho); Bumble (petty official; Oliver); Buzfuz, Serjeant (advocate, Pickwick); Carker, James (office manager; Dombey); Carton, Sidney (2 Cities); Cheeryble brs (*twins*; Nich Nick); Codlin & Short (travelling showmen; OC Shop); Copperfield, David (Trot, ~); Corney, Mrs (workhouse matron; Oliver); Cratchit (*clerk*; Xmas Carol); Crummels, Vincent (theat manager; Nich Nick), and his d 'the infant phenomenon'; Cuttle, Capt (*sailor*; Dombey); Darnay, Charles (2 Cities); Defarge, Mme (knits; 2 Cities); Dodson and Fogg (*lawyers*; Pickwick); Fagin (*robber*; Oliver); Fang (*magistrate*; Oliver); Fips (legal agent; Chuzzle); Flite, Miss (pesters Chancery; Bleak Ho); Gamp, Sarah (*nurse*; Chuzzle); Gargery, Joe (*blacksmith*; Great Ex); Gradgrind (*schoolmaster*, 'facts'; Hard Times); Grimwig ('eat my head'; Oliver); Guster (*maid*; Bleak Ho); Havisham, Miss (*recluse*; Great Ex); Heep, Uriah ('umble lawyer's *clerk*; Copperfield); Jaggers (advocate; Great Ex); Jingle, Alfred (swindling actor; Pickwick); Jo (poor outcast; Bleak Ho); Jorkins (*lawyer*; Copperfield); Jupe (*jester*; Hard Times); Krook (rag-and-bone man; Bleak Ho); La Creevy, Miss (talkative *painter*; Nich Nick); Little Dorrit (*child* of Marshalsea debtors' prison; Dorrit); Little Em'ly (vain; Copperfield); Little Nell (tragic death; OC Shop); Lorry (banker; 2 Cities); Magwitch, Abel (*convict*, Great Ex); Manette, Dr and Lucie (2 Cities); Mantalini (milliner; Nich Nick); Marchioness, the (*nursed* and mar Dick Swiveller; OC Shop); Micawber ('something will turn up'; Copperfield); Miggs, Miss (*maid*; Rudge); Mould (*undertaker*; Chuzzle); Moucher, Miss (*hairdresser*; Copperfield); Nancy (murdered by Sikes; Oliver); Newcome, Clemency (*nurse*, forerunner of Peggotty: the Battle

of Life); Nipper, Susan (Dombey); Noggs, Newman (*clerk*;
Nich Nick); Omer (*undertaker*; Copperfield); Pecksniff, Seth
(hypocrite; Chuzzle); Peggotty, Clara (*maid* who mar Barkis;
Copperfield); Pickwick, Samuel (benevolence; Pickwick);
Pinch, Tom (drudge; Chuzzle); Pip (sis mar Gargery; Great
Ex); Pipchin, Mrs (*landlady*; Dombey); Plummer, Caleb
(*toymaker*; Cricket on the Hearth); Prig, Betsy (*nurse*;
Chuzzle); Pross, Miss (*governess*; 2 Cities); Quilp (*dwarf*; OC
Shop); Sawyer, Bob (surgeon; Pickwick); Scrooge, Ebenezer
(converted miserly killjoy; Xmas Carol); Sikes, Bill (murdering
robber; Oliver); Sleary (circus owner; Hard Times); Slowboy,
Tilly (*nurse*; Cricket); Smike (s of Ralph Nickleby; Nich
Nick); Snagsby (Peffer and ~, law stationers; Bleak Ho);
Snodgrass, Augustus (Pickwick); Spenlow, Dora (child wife
of D Copperfield); Spenlow & Jorkins (*lawyers*; Copperfield);
Squeers (*schoolmaster*, Dotheboys Hall; Nich Nick); St
Evremonde, Marquis de (2 Cities); Steerforth, James (rake;
Copperfield); Swiveller, Dick (debtor; OC Shop); Tackleton
(*toymaker*; Cricket); Tapley, Mark (cheerful *servant*; Chuzzle);
Tiny Tim (lame boy; Xmas Carol); Toots, Mr P ('It's of no
consequence'; Dombey); Traddles, Thomas (sad boy at Salem
House; Copperfield); Trotter, Job (Jingle's servant; Pickwick);
Trotwood, Betsy ('Janet! Donkey!'; Copperfield); Tulkinghorn,
Mr (*lawyer*; Bleak Ho); Tupman, Mr Tracy (lady's man;
Pickwick); Twist, Oliver ('more please'; Oliver); Varden,
Dolly (locksmith's daughter; Rudge); Veck, Trotty (porter's
d; Chimes); Verisopht, Lord (spineless sycophant; Nich Nick);
Weller, Sam (Pickwick's *servant*; Pickwick); Wemmick, John
(*clerk* to Jaggers; Great Ex); Wickfield, Agnes (*lawyer*'s d, mar
D Copperfield); Wilfer (*clerk*; Mutual F); Winkle (Pickwick);
Wren, Jenny (deformed child; Mutual F).

DICKY *Anag.* RICHARD, BOY. ILL, SHAKY, UNSOUND,
UNWELL. BIRD. DONKEY. SHIRTFRONT. BACKSEAT.
RUMBLE-SEAT.

DICTIONARY LEXICON, WORD-BOOK; CHAMBERS ®,
COLLINS ®, OED ®, WEBSTER ®; DR JOHNSON;
[encyclop(a)edia, thesaurus].

DIDO 1. ANTIC, CAPER, PRANK. DID NOTHING (crypt).
2. Princess of Tyre, sis of *Pygmalion*. Real name ELISSA (not
Astarte). Founded Carthage. Stabbed herself on a funeral pyre
rather than marry Iarbas [*Aeneas*]. 3. A minor *PLANET*.

DIED (s/l *dyed*). D, EXPIRED, OBIIT, *OSP* (without issue),

PEGGED OUT.

DIET BANT, SLIM; REGIME. *LEGISLATIVE ASSEMBLY.*

DIFFERENTLY *Anag.* DISSIMILARLY, DISTINCTLY.

DIFFIDENT MODEST, RETIRING, SHY, UNCONFIDENT.

DIG EXCAVATE, FORK OVER, UNEARTH. APPROVE, UNDERSTAND (sl). **Pl** = LODGINGS.

DIGEST ASSIMILATE. ABSTRACT, PRECIS, RESUME, SUMMARY, SYNOPSIS. HEAT (*chem*). ENDURE.

DIGGER MINER, PITMAN. EXCAVATOR. AUSTRALIAN.

DILIGENCE INDUSTRY, PERSISTENCE. *CARRIAGE.*

DIN *ROW.* DRUM (into), REPEAT. German standard (photo).

DINNER LUNCH, MEAL, SUPPER. NOISE-MAKER. PERCUSSIONIST (crypt).

DINOSAUR *REPTILE* (ex); **herbivores**: ATLANTOSAURUS, BRONTOSAURUS, CETIOSAURUS, DIPLODOCUS, GUANODON, STEGOSAURUS, TRICERATOPS; **carnivores**: MEGALOSAURUS, TYRANNOSAURUS.

DIOGENES 1. Gk cynic *PHILOSOPHER* who lived in a *tub*. 2. London club of Mycroft *Holmes*.

DIONYSUS Gk equivalent of *BACCHUS.*

DIPLOMATIC CORPS CD [Court of St James].

DIRAE *FURIES.*

DIRECT *CONTROL*, INSTRUCT, ORGANIZE. ROUTE, STEER. STRAIGHT.

DIRECTION E, N, S, W, NE, SE etc; ROUTE, WAY. *CONTROL*, INSTRUCTION.

DIRECTOR ARROW, SIGN, SIGNBOARD. RUDDER, STEERING. CONTROLLER, MANAGER; **Pl** = BOARD.

DIS = *ORCUS*, *PLUTO.* Rom *god* of the *Underworld* (**Gk** = *HADES*).

DISARMING DEFUSING. DISBANDING, DEPRIVING OF WEAPONS. PACIFYING. AMPUTATING [Venus de Milo].

DISCHARGE BOOT, CASHIER, CANCEL, DISMISS, FIRE, RELEASE, SACK. CARRY OUT, PERFORM. LIQUIDATE, *PAY. SHOOT.* ASSOIL, UNLOAD.

DISCIPLE FOLLOWER (especially the 12 *apostles*).

DISCOVERER *EXPLORER*; *INVENTOR.* DISCLOSER, EXHIBITOR, FINDER. BETRAYER (arch). *SPACECRAFT.*

DISCOVERY 1. DISCLOSURE, REVEALING; *INVENTION*; **celebrated**: DISPLACEMENT, LEVER (3rd cent B.C. *Archimedes*); BLOOD CIRCULATION (1628 Harvey); GRAVITY (1689 Newton); VACCINATION (1798 Jenner);

ELECTRICAL INDUCTION (1830 Faraday); ANTISEPSIS
(1864 Lister); INOCULATION (1886 Pasteur); ELECTRON
(1897 Thomson); RADIUM (1903 Curies); RELATIVITY (1905
Einstein); NUCLEAR PHYSICS (1913 Rutherford and Bohr);
PENICILLIN (1928 Fleming); NEUTRON (1932 Chadwick).
2. SHIP (Baffin, Cook, Scott; *explorers*).

DISPLEASURE *ANGER*, DISAPPROVE, DISSATISFACTION.
HUNTING (crypt).

DISTEMPER *ANGER*, DERANGE, UPSET; DISORDER.
DISEASE (dogs). WALL PAINT.

DISTRESS *Anag.* 1. ANGUISH, PAIN, SORROW, STRAITS,
VEX. MAYDAY, SOS. BREATHLESSNESS,
EXHAUST(ION). CUT HAIR, SHEAR, SCALP (crypt).
2. Remove synonym for hair from clue, e.g. **Distressed warlock
in a fight** (3) = WAR****.

DISTRIBUTION *Anag.* APPORTIONMENT, ARRANGEMENT,
CLASSIFICATION, DISPERSAL, SCATTER, SHARING.

DISTRICT AREA, COUNTY, CANTON, *DIVISION*, REGION,
SHIRE, STATE, TERRITORY, TRACT, *WARD*.

DITTO *DO*, DUPLICATE, SAME [*copy*].

div divorced.

DIVERSION *Anag.* DETOUR, DEVIATION. DISTRACTION,
FEINT. *GAME*, PASTIME.

DIVE 1. DELVE, PENETRATE, SEARCH. HEADER,
PLUNGE, PLUMMET, SUBMERGE, SWIM
UNDERWATER; **positions**: *pike*, straight, tuck; **types**:
armstand, back ~, forward ~, inward ~, reverse ~,
somersault, swallow ~, twist (bellyflop) [aqualung, snorkel,
skindiving, subaqua]; and see *swimming*. 2. *BAR*, HIDING
PLACE, *NIGHTCLUB*, SPEAKEASY (US). **Pl** = RICH
MAN (St Luke) [Croesus, *Midas*].

DIVIDER SEPARATOR, SCREEN; NET (tennis, crypt). **Pl** =
COMPASSES.

DIVINE DD, *CHURCHMAN*, PRIEST. GODLIKE;
BEAUTIFUL, DELIGHTFUL, EXCELLENT, GIFTED.
CONJECTURE, FORESEE, GUESS, PREDICT. DOWSE
(hazel rod).

DIVISION DISTRIBUTION, SHARING. DISAGREEMENT,
DISCORD, SEVERANCE. CLASSIFICATION, GRADE.
FUNCTION, PROCESS (math). NET (tennis). VOTE (polit).
BOUNDARY, *DISTRICT*, PARISH, PART, SECTION,

SEE, ZONE; **specifically** COUNTY, REGION, SHIRE; ~ **of England**:

AVON	
BEDFORDSHIRE	*BEDS*
BERKSHIRE	BERKS
BUCKINGHAMSHIRE	*BUCKS*
CAMBRIDGESHIRE	CAMBS
CHESHIRE	CHES
CLEVELAND	CLEV
CORNWALL	(SW)
CUMBERLAND (ex)	CUMB
CUMBRIA	CUMB
DERBYSHIRE	DERBYS
DEVONSHIRE	DEVON
DORSET	DORSET
DURHAM	DUR
ESSEX	ESX
GLOUCESTERSHIRE	GLOS
GREATER LONDON	
GREATER MANCHESTER	
HAMPSHIRE	HANTS
HEREFORDSHIRE (ex)	
HEREFORD & WORCESTER	H & W
HERTFORDSHIRE	HERTS
HUMBERSIDE	
HUNTINGDONSHIRE (ex)	HUNTS
ISLE OF WIGHT	IOW
KENT	(SE)
LANCASHIRE	LANCS
LEICESTERSHIRE	LEICS
LINCOLNSHIRE	LINCS
LONDON (ex)	
MERSEYSIDE	MERS
MIDDLESEX (ex)	MIDDX
NORFOLK	
NORTHAMPTONSHIRE	NORTHANTS
NORTHUMBERLAND	
NOTTINGHAMSHIRE	NOTTS
OXFORDSHIRE	*OXON*
RUTLAND (ex)	

SHROPSHIRE	SALOP
SOMERSET	SOM
STAFFORDSHIRE	STAFFS
SUFFOLK	
SURREY	
SUSSEX (E & W)	E/W SSX
TYNE & WEAR	T & W (NE)
WARWICKSHIRE	WARKS
WEST MIDLANDS	W MIDS
WESTMORLAND (ex)	
WILTSHIRE	WILTS
WORCESTERSHIRE (ex)	WORCS
YORKSHIRE (N, S & W)	N/S/W YORKS

Subdivisions: hundreds (all counties pre-Conquest), lathes (Kent), rapes (Sussex), ridings (Yorks), wapentakes (Lincs, Notts, Yorks), wards (Cumb, Dur, Northumberland, Westmorland).

~ of Northern Ireland

(Counties)

ANTRIM	FERMANAGH
ARMAGH	LONDONDERRY
BELFAST	TYRONE
DOWN	

~ of Eire

(Counties)

CARLOW	LAOIS (LEIX) (ex QUEEN'S COUNTY)
CAVAN	
CLARE	LEINSTER
CONNAUGHT	LEITRIM
CORK	LIMERICK
DONEGAL (Tirconnel) ex ULSTER	LONGFORD
	LOUTH
DUBLIN	MAYO
GALWAY	MEATH
KERRY	MONAGHAN
KILDARE	MUNSTER
KILKENNY	OFFALY (ex KING'S COUNTY)
KING'S COUNTY (now OFFALY)	

QUEEN'S COUNTY (now   WATERFORD
  LAOIS)   WESTMEATH
ROSCOMMON   WEXFORD
SLIGO   WICKLOW
TIPPERARY

~ of Scotland

(Regions & Island Areas)   LOTHIAN
BORDER   ORKNEY
CENTRAL   SHETLAND
DUMFRIES &   STRATHCLYDE
  GALLOWAY   TAYSIDE
FIFE   WESTERN ISLES
GRAMPIAN
HIGHLAND

(ex Counties of Scotland)

ABERDEENSHIRE   LANARKSHIRE
ANGUS   MIDLOTHIAN
ARGYLLSHIRE   MORAYSHIRE
BANFFSHIRE   NAIRN
BERWICKSHIRE   PEEBLES-SHIRE
CAITHNESS   PERTH
CLACKMANNANSHIRE   RENFREWSHIRE
DUNBARTONSHIRE   ROSS & CROMARTY
DUMFRIESSHIRE   ROXBURGHSHIRE
EAST LOTHIAN   SELKIRKSHIRE
FIFE   STIRLINGSHIRE
INVERNESS-SHIRE   SUTHERLAND
KINCARDINESHIRE   WEST LOTHIAN
KINROSS-SHIRE   WIGTOWNSHIRE
KIRKCUDBRIGHTSHIRE

~ of Wales

(Counties)   GWENT
CLWYD   GWYNEDD
DYFED   POWYS
GLAMORGAN,
  MID/SOUTH/WEST

(ex Counties of Wales)

ANGLESEY   BRECKNOCKSHIRE

CAERNARVONSHIRE
CARDIGANSHIRE
CARMARTHENSHIRE
DENBIGHSHIRE
FLINTSHIRE
GLAMORGAN

MERIONETH
MONMOUTHSHIRE
MONTGOMERYSHIRE
PEMBROKESHIRE
RADNORSHIRE

DIY HOME HELP, SELF-HELP [handyman].

dn Down clues only.

DNA GENES. AND BACK (crypt).

DO ACCOMPLISH, ACHIEVE, ACT, CARRY OUT, EXECUTE, PERFORM, REALIZE, *SHIFT*. *PLAY* (theat). CELEBRATION, FESTIVITY, FIESTA, JOLLIFICATION, PARTY, RECEPTION, TREAT. DITTO. *CHAR*, CLEAN. KILL. CHEAT, CON, COZEN, DEFRAUD, DIDDLE, SWINDLE, TRICK. NOTE (mus; also DOH). **Pl** = *DEER*, HARES (*fem*).

DOC (s/l *dock*). DOCTOR. *DWARF* (Snow White).

DOCH AN DORIS STIRRUP CUP (drink at the door).

DOCK (s/l *doc*). CURTAIL, CUT, LESSEN, LOP. BASIN, JETTY, QUAY, TERMINAL, WHARF. WEED. CRUPPER. ENCLOSURE (leg).

DOCTOR ADULTERATE, FIDDLE, FIX. *WIND* (cricket). DD (eccles); DR, GP, MB, MD, MO (med) [*patron saint*, vet]; B MUS (mus); **celeb**: AMBROSE, AUGUSTINE, GREGORY and JEROME (4 bibl ~s); BUTTS (*Shak*, H.viii); CAIUS (*Shak*); COL BLOOD (crown jewels); CRIPPEN (Edwardian murderer); DOLITTLE (*Lofting*); FAUST/US (*magician*; Goethe, Marlowe); *GRACE* (*cricketer*); GULLIVER (*Swift*); HAKIM (Saladin disguised, Talisman, Scott); HIPPOCRATES (s of HERACLIDES, f of DRACON and THESSALUS, and f-in-law of POLYBUS, all ~s); JEKYLL (*Hyde*); JOHNSON (dict); LIVESEY (Treasure Island, Defoe); LIVINGSTONE (explorer); LUKE (bibl); MANETTE (*Dickens*); MELAMPOS (*prophet* Gk myth, 1st ~); NO (Bond); SCHWEIZER (missionary, *philosopher*); SLOP (Tristram Shandy, Sterne); STRANGELOVE (film); SYN (Russell Thorndike); SYNTAX (William Combe); WATSON (*Holmes*); WHO (TV); ZHIVAGO (Pasternak); *Chaucer* character [*Asclepius*].

DODGE AVOID, *DUCK*, ELUDE, SHUFFLE. ARTIFICE, EXPEDIENT, *SHIFT*, TRICK. RACKET. CAR ®. CITY (US).

DOE JOHN (average man). *CAT* (fem, Sc), DEER (*fem*), HARE
(*fem*). **Pl** = ACTS, PERFORMS (see *DO*).
DOG 1. FOLLOW, PURSUE, TAIL, TRACK. LOCK; BAR,
GRIP, PAWL. **Pl** = *ISLAND*. 2. *Male* canine (**fem** = bitch;
offspring = puppy); **breeds**:

Guard Dogs

AINU	DOGO ARGENTINO
AKITA	GERMAN SHEPHERD
ALSATIAN	GREAT DANE
BANDOG	HOVAWART
BEAUCE	MASTIFF
BOXER	PIT BULL
BULLDOG	ROTTWEILER
CANAAN	TOSA
DOBERMAN	

Gundogs

CLUMBER SPANIEL	SETTER
COCKER SPANIEL	SPANIEL
LABRADOR	*SPRINGER SPANIEL*
POINTER	VIZSLA
RETRIEVER	WEIMARANER

Hounds

AFGHAN	FOXHOUND
BASSET	GREYHOUND
BEAGLE	*HARRIER*
BLOODHOUND	IRISH WOLFHOUND
BORZOI	OTTERHOUND
DACHSHUND	SALUKI
DEERHOUND	WHIPPET
ELKHOUND	

Non-sporting

ALSATIAN	CORGI
BOSTON	DALMATIAN
BOXER	DOBERMAN PINSCHER
BULLDOG	GREAT DANE
BULL MASTIFF	MASTIFF
CHOW	NEWFOUNDLAND
COLLIE	POODLE

PYRENEAN MOUNTAIN
  DOG
ROTTWEILER
ST BERNARD
SAMOYED
SCHNAUZER
SHEEPDOG

Terriers

AIREDALE
BEDLINGTON
BULL TERRIER
CAIRN
DANDIE DINMONT
FOX TERRIER
IRISH TERRIER
KERRY BLUE

NORFOLK
NORWICH
SCOTTISH TERRIER
SEALYHAM
SKYE TERRIER
STAFFORDSHIRE
  TERRIER
WELSH TERRIER

Toy

CHIHUAHUA
GRIFFON
KING CHARLES
  SPANIEL
PAPILLON
PEKIN(G)ESE

POMERANIAN
PUG
SPITZ
TOY POODLE
YORKSHIRE TERRIER

Wild

COYOTE (Am)
DHOLE (Ind)
DINGO (Aus)
HYENA (Af, Asia)
JACKAL (Af, Asia)

PARIAH (Asia)
PI(E)/PYE (Asia)
PRAIRIE WOLF (Am)
WOLF (N Hem)

Celeb: ARGUS (*Ulysses*); ASTA (Thin Man); BALFOUR'S POODLE (House of Lords), BLUEBELL, JESSIE, PITCHER (Animal Farm, *Orwell*), BOATSWAIN (Byron), BOXER (*Dickens*, Cricket), *BUCK* (Call of the Wild, London), *BULLSEYE* (Oliver, *Dickens*), *CAPTAIN* (Archers, radio), CAVALL (King Arthur), *CERBERUS* (*Charon*), *DASH* (Queen Victoria), DIAMOND (Sir Isaac Newton), DIGBY (Biggest in world), DOG OF FO (Ch lion dog), *FIDO* (acronym), FLUSH (Barretts of Wimpole Street), FURY (*Alice*), GYPSY and ROGUE (Charles I), HOUND OF THE BASKERVILLES (Sherlock *Holmes*), JIP (Copperfield, *Dickens*; and Dr Dolittle, *Lofting*), KEP (*Potter*), KRATIM

(Seven Sleepers), LAIKA (first *space traveller*), LASSIE
(films), MICK THE MILLER (greyhound), MONTMORENCY
(*Three* Men in a Boat, Jerome), NANA (Peter Pan), NIPPER
(HMV/RCA/Victor), ORTHRUS (Gk myth, *many-headed*),
OWD BOB (Edinburgh), PILOT (Jane Eyre, C.

Brontë),
PLUTO (acronym and Disney), RIN-TIN-TIN (films),
SIRIUS (Dogstar), SNOOPY (Peanuts), TIMMY (Famous
Five), TOBY (Punch & Judy), TOTO (Wizard of Oz), TRAY
(Struwwelpeter), TRUMP (Hogarth), WISH HOUNDS
(spectral), and (all John Peel) BELLMAN, RANTER,
RINGMAN, RUBY, *TRUE*. Constellations. [*Ch calendar*; Hans
Andersen]; Herne the *Hunter*.

DOLE GRIEF, MISERY, DISTRIBUTION, UNEMPLOYMENT
BENEFIT/PAY, JAM ROLL (*rh sl*) [job centre].

DOLLAR (s/l *dolour*). *BUCK*, *COIN*, *CURRENCY*,
GREENBACK, MONEY, S.

DOLOUR (s/l *dollar*). GRIEF (**opp** = *joy*).

DOLPHIN *CETACEAN* MAMMAL, GRAMPUS; BOTTLE-
NOSE, WHITE-BACKED, WHITE-SIDED; KILLER
WHALE [Pelorus Jack]; *Constellation*. BEACON, STAKE
(naut). **Pl** = *FOOTBALL* TEAM (US).

DOMESTIC *CHAR*. HOMELOVING. HOME MADE, *NATIVE*;
TAME.

DOMINICANS BLACKFRIARS, PREACHING *FRIARS*.

DON FELLOW, TUTOR. NOBLEMAN (Sp). ASSUME, PUT
ON. BRADMAN (*cricket*). RIVER (Eng; Sc; CIS). GOD
(Celt). **Pl** = ABERDEEN; WIMBLEDON (both *football*
teams).

DONE (s/l dun). *Anag*. ACCEPTABLE, MANNERS, U.
COMPLETED, *ENDED*, FINISHED. TIRED. COOKED (**opp**
= *raw*). **Comp** = *said*.

DONKEY *ASS*, BURRO (US), MOKE; NEDDY. [Republican,
Silenus, hinny, *mule*]; **breed**: ONAGER; [*male/female*]. **Celeb:**
Benjamin (*Orwell*); EEYORE (*Milne*). ~ Boy (*Williamson*).
DULLARD, FOOL. **Pl** = [Trotwood, *Dickens*].

DOODLEBUG BUZZBOMB, DIVER (code name), FLYING
BOMB, VI; *MISSILE*.

DOOLITTLE 1. *DUSTMAN*, Eliza's f in Pygmalion, My Fair
Lady (*Shaw*). 2. Hilda ~, US poetess (known as HD). 3. Gen,
USAAF. 4. See *Lofting* for Dr Dolittle.

DOORWAY 1. ENTRANCE, OPENING. 2. **God: Gk** = HORUS,
Rom = JANUS, **Egy** = HOR, SET. 3. Five *symbols* at ~

in *song*.

DOPE *DRUG. INFORMATION.*

DOPEY DRUGGED, SLEEPY. *DWARF* (Snow White).

DOR (s/l door). *BEETLE.* TOWN (*bibl*).

DORADO FISH. EL ~ (*lost city* of gold). *Constellation.*

DORIS 1. GIRL. [*Doch an* ~]. 2. Gk myth d of Oceanus and Tethys; mar her br *Nereus* and m of the Nereides, hence the SEA. Also an area in Greece. [Order (Gk archit)].

DORY *BOAT. FISH. Alice* character.

DOT *MARK*, SPECK, SPOT. DECIMAL POINT. DOWRY. HIT, STRIKE (sl). SHORT SIGN (*morse*; **opp** = *dash*). Girl's name.

DOUBLE 1. DEAD SPIT, DOPPELGANGER, LOOKALIKE, IMAGE, *TWIN* [*Hope* (2); Prince & Pauper (*Twain*)]. STUNTMAN, UNDERSTUDY (theat). TWOFOLD, TWICE. RUN. ROUND, TURN; FOLD, LOOP. 2. Repeat any following letter(s), e.g. **Doubles** = ss.

DOUBLE ENTENDRE AMBIGUITY. *ECHO* (crypt). PORTMANTEAU WORD (crypt).

DOUBLET BODYGARMENT, LEOTARD. TT (crypt).

DOUBLETON TWO *CARDS.* 200; CC (crypt).

DOVE *BIRD*, PIGEON (*Constellation*) [*Noah*]. PEACELOVER (**opp** = *hawk*). HOLY SPIRIT. DIVED. 'JEMIMA'. RIVER (Eng).

DOWN *D*, DN. FROM ABOVE; ALIGHTED. FEATHERS, FLUFF, PLUMAGE. *BLUE*, DEPRESSED, DISPIRITED, LOW. HILLS, OPEN LAND. *DRINK*, SWALLOW. *Division* of N Ire. **Comp** = *out. Assembly* of hares. **Pl** = SEA (N Dover Straits) [**castles in the** ~**s** = Deal, *Sandwich*, Walmer].

DP DISPLACED PERSONS; hence PRONES, SPERON etc (anag).

DR *DEBTOR. DOCTOR.* DRACHM (*measure*). DESPATCH RIDER (mil). TOM (crypt: dr = $^1/_2$ drum = $^1/_2$ tom-tom).

DRACULA Blood-sucking *monster* from Bram Stoker's novel, *modelled* on Prince Vlad of Wallachia in Romania; ~ was a *count*.

DRAGOMAN *CONDUCTOR*, GUIDE, INTERPRETER.

DRAGON BAT, CRONE, SCOLD, *SHREW*, TERMAGANT. *MONSTER*, WYVERN (*Constellation*; *herald*; *Medea*). KOMODO ~ (*lizard*). BEN-ALI (*pirate, Lofting*). CONTINUE, DRAW OUT, PROLONG (all crypt). [*Ch calendar*; ~fly; *insect*; *Python*].

DRAIN 1. DRAW OFF, *EBB, EMPTY*; TRICKLE. *DRINK.*

CONDUIT, PIPE, TUBE (med); *SEWER*. DEMAND,
EXPENDITURE, WITHDRAWAL; SAP. 2. Waterloo & City
Line (sl; rly). 3. Put letters DRA in word(s), e.g. **Drain UN ft for
rehash** (7) = UN*DRA*FT.
DRAKE *DUCK* (*male*) [*Potter*]. *MILITARY LEADER*, PIRATE;
BOWLER (crypt) [Armada (*battle*)]. MAYFLY. **Pl** = ISLAND.
DRAMA PLAY; *THEATRE*. [Aeschylus, Euripides, Sophocles;
Shakespeare].
DRAW DESIGN, DEPICT, PEN, SKETCH [artist].
ATTRACT(ION), EXTRACT, MOVE, PULL, TOW, TUG.
SHARE, TIE. ELONGATE. LOTTERY. SMOKE (crypt).
DRAWBACK CON, DISADVANTAGE (**opp** = *pro*).
DEDUCTION, REMITTED TAX. WARD (crypt).
DRAWER ARTIST, RA. DENTIST (crypt). PUBLICAN,
TAPSTER. *TOWER*, TUG. SLIDING RECEPTACLE
(*furniture*). *SMOKER* (crypt). **Pl** = BLOOMERS, KNICKERS,
PANTIES.
DRAY *CARRIAGE*, CART. *Habitation* (squirrels). BACKYARD
(crypt).
DREAM 1. BROWN STUDY, FANCY, REVERIE, VISION
(oneiric); BEAUTY. 2. **God**: **Rom** = MORPHEUS, **Egy** =
SERAPIS, **Gk** = HERMES.
DRESS *Anag*. BANDAGE. BEDECK, BEFLAG, *COVER*,
DECK; GARNISH, PIPE. CLOTHE (**opp** = *strip*); ATTIRE,
FROCK, *HABIT*, OUTFIT, RIG, ROBE [*suit*]. ALIGN,
RANGE, SIZE. PREPARE (cook).
DRESSING CLOTHING, COVERING, DONNING
(CLOTHES), ROBING. ALIGNMENT, *ROW* (mil).
MAYONNAISE. BANDAGE, PLASTER.
DREW DEL, DELINEAVIT, SKETCHED. ATTRACTED,
PULLED. SHARED, TIED.
DRIER AIRER, SPINNER, TOWEL; LESS WET. OAST
HOUSE.
DRILL COACH, PARADE; *TRAIN*. AUGER, AWL, *BORE*,
GIMLET. BABOON, *MONKEY*. CLOTH, *MATERIAL*.
FURROW, ROW.
DRINK DITCH, OGGIN, SEA (all sl). ABSORB, DRAIN,
LAP, PLEDGE, QUAFF, SIP, SWALLOW, TOAST, TOPE;
(BOTTLE/CUP/GLASS OF) LIQUID, LIQUOR; and see
spirit. BRACER, CHASER, GLASS, JAR, JUG, ONE-FOR-
THE-ROAD, OTHER HALF, PEG, PICK-ME-UP, *POISON*,
QUICKIE, SLURP, SNIFTER, SNORT. **Types** (many ®):

3-letters

ALE	POP	RYE	*TEA*
GIN	RUM		

4-letters

ARAK	FINE	MILD	SAKE, -I
BEER	FLIP	*MILK*	SODA
CHAR	MARC	OUZO	TENT (arch)
COLA	MEAD	PORT	*WINE*

5-letters

BUMBO	JULEP	PIMMS ®	TONIC
COCOA	KVASS	SHRUB	VODKA
GLOGG	LAGER	SIROP	WATER
HOOCH	NEGUS	*SLING*	

6-letters

BITTER	EGG-NOG	KUMMEL ®	SHERRY
BRANDY	GENEVA	*PORTER*	*SPIRIT*
COFFEE	GRAPPA	RED-EYE	*SQUASH*
COGNAC	KIRSCH	*SCOTCH*	WHISKY (Sc)

7-letters

AQUAVIT	COLLINS	MADEIRA	SIDECAR
BOURBON	*CORDIAL*	MARTINI ®	STENGAH
CAMPARI ®	CURAÇAO	MINERAL	STINGER
CINZANO ®	KOUMISS	OENOMEL	WHISKEY
COBBLER	*LIQUEUR*	SHERBET	(Ire)

8+ letters

ABSINTHE	GLUHWEIN	ORANGEADE
ANISETTE	GRAND	SCHIEDAM
APPLEJACK	MARNIER ®	SCHNAPPS
BALDERDASH	HIGHBALL	SCREWDRIVER
BENEDICTINE ®	HOLLANDS	SUNDOWNER
CHOCOLATE	HORSE'S NECK	TIA MARIA ®
COCKTAIL	JOHN COLLINS	TOM COLLINS
COINTREAU ®	LEMONADE	VERMOUTH
DRAMBUIE ®	LIME JUICE	WHITE LADY
DUBONNET ®	MANHATTAN	
GINGER ALE/BEER	OLD-FASHIONED	

Measures

BEVVY	JAR	QUICKIE
CUP	NIGHTCAP	QUICK ONE
DOCH AN	NIP	SHOT
DORIS	NOGGIN	SLUG
DRAM	ONE FOR THE	SNORT
FIFTH	ROAD	SPLASH
FINGER	OTHER HALF	STIRRUP-CUP
GLASS	PINT	TIPPLE

DRIVE ENTHUSIASM, GO, IMPULSE. CONDUCT, STEER;
OUTING. HIT, TEE OFF; STROKE (*cricket, golf*). FORCE,
IMPEL. ENTRANCE, PRIVATE ROAD.
DRIVER 1. *CLUB*, WOOD (**opp** = iron); GOLFER. L,
CHAUFFEUR, CAR-MAN. MARTINET. RAILWAYMAN.
COWBOY, HERDSMAN (drover). 2. **Celeb:** *FREYA*,
PHAETON (myth), TOAD (*Grahame*), *JEHU* (bibl).
DROP 1. LET FALL, RELEASE. FALL, LOWER. OMIT,
SHED. EARRING, PENDANT. CASCADE, SPLASH,
WATERFALL. LOZENGE, SWEET. PARACHUTE. 2. Leave
off letter/word, e.g. **Alfred drops the gangster and is a different
man** (4) = **FRED.
DROP-OUT 1. HIPPIE, LAYABOUT, HERMIT, MONK,
RECLUSE. PARACHUTIST (crypt). 2. Leave out letter
concerned, e.g. **Alice, a drop-out, evinces parasites** (4) = *LICE.
DRUG ANAESTHETIC. MEDICAMENT. HALLUCINOGEN,
NARCOTIC, OPIATE, STIMULANT; **types:** BHANG,
CANNABIS, COCAINE, DOPE, GRASS, HASHISH,
HEMP, HERB, HEROIN, LSD, MARIJUANA, POT, SNOW,
SPEED, WEED [gone, high, mainline, spaced-out, trip].
UNSALEABLE.
DRUM TUB, VAT, BARREL, CYLINDER, SHAFT. BEAT,
RESONATE, SUMMON, TAP, THRUM, THUMP. DRIVE,
INJECT, PLAY. *INSTRUMENT* (mus), BIG~, KETTLE~,
TOM-TOM, TRAP. MOUND. VOID.
DRUMMER 1. BANDSMAN; BEATER, SKINNER, TAPPER.
CHAPMAN, COMMERCIAL TRAVELLER, PEDLAR, REP.
BIRD, BITTERN, SNIPE. *FISH*. TEAPARTY. *EAR* (crypt).
2. Ninth day of *Christmas* in *song*.
DRUNK CONSUMED, DOWNED, SWALLOWED. HIGH,
INEBRIATED, LIT, SMASHED, SOUSED, TIDDLY,
TIGHT (**opp** = sober; *abstainer*). LUSH, SOT.
DRY ARID, PARCHED, THIRSTY. MILKLESS, TT,

WATERLESS. ALCOHOL-FREE. BARE, BITTER, COLD,
IMPASSIVE, MEAGRE, SOLID, STERILE. NOT SWEET,
SEC (Fr). CURE, SMOKE. SUNNY. DRAIN, SPIN, TOWEL,
WIPE; **comp** = *home*.

DUCK O, LOVE, NIL, NOUGHT, NO SCORE, ZERO. *BOB*,
CURTSEY. (NOSE)*DIVE*, PLUNGE. *DODGE. DEAR*,
LUV. CANVAS. **Pl** = PANTS, SHORTS, TROUSERS. [~s
and drakes; ricochet, skim. Bombay ~ (fish)]. *BIRD* of genus
Anatidae; **breeds**:

AYLESBURY	PINTADO
CANVAS BACKED	PINTAIL
EIDER	POCHARD
GADWALL	SCAUP
GOLDENEYE	SCOTER
HARLEQUIN	SHELDRAKE
MALLARD	SHOVELLER
MANDARIN	*SMEE*
MERGANSER	SMEW
MUSCOVY	TEAL
PEKIN	WI(D)GEON

[**assembly** = flight, flock; **male** = *drake*; **fem** = duck; **offspring** =
duckling]. **Celeb**: DAB-DAB (*Lofting*), DAFFY, DONALD
(cartoon film), JEMIMA PUDDLEDUCK (Beatrix *Potter*),
Alice character. [Hans *Andersen; Lear*].

DUD BAD, DEFECTIVE. BAD CHEQUE. **Pl** = *CLOTHES*.

DUN (s/l *done*). IMPORTUNE, PESTER. GREY-BROWN
(*colour*).

DUNELM *Episcopal sig* of DURHAM.

DURHAM 1. *CASTLE. GAOL. UNIVERSITY*. 2. **Episcopal sig** =
DUNELM.

DUSTMAN REFUSE COLLECTOR: NICODEMUS *BOFFIN*
(Mutual F, *Dickens*), ALFRED DOOLITTLE (Pygmalion, G.
B. *Shaw*). SANDMAN.

DUTCH SHARING PAYMENT. *WIFE. CHEESE. HOLLAND*,
NETHERLANDS. [courage = *bottle* (crypt)].

DV DEO VOLENTE, DG, GOD WILLING.

DWARF OVERAWE, TOWER OVER. MINI(ATURE), PUNY,
STUNTED; DANDIPRAT, ELF, GNOME, MIDGET,
PYGMY, RUNT, TROLL (**opp** = *giant*); **celeb**: ALBERICH,
MIME (Wagner's Ring [Nibelheim]); BASHFUL, DOC,
DOPEY, GRUMPY, HAPPY, SLEEPY, SNEEZY (Snow

White); CERCOPES (Gk myth); SIR GEOFFREY HUDSON (Scott); LILLIPUTIANS (*Swift*); MISS MOWCHER (Copperfield, *Dickens*); MUNCHKINS (Wizard of Oz, Frank Baum); QUILP (OC Shop, *Dickens*); RUMPELSTILTSKIN (Grimm); TOM THUMB (US and Perrault); VAMANA (Hindu incarnation). ~ **god** = Bes (Egy).
DYED (s/l *died*). COLOURED, TINTED (blue rinse, highlights, peroxide). [Idmon].
DYNASTY SOAP OPERA (TV). And see *Chinese* ~ and also *Royal Family*.

E 1. *EAST. ENERGY.* ENGLISH. *BRIDGE PLAYER. KEY; NOTE.* POINT. SPAIN (*car plate*). 2. Second class at *Lloyd's*.
EA EACH. EAST AFRICA. EAST ANGLIA. RIVER. Bab Jew god (wisdom).
EAGLE 1. *BIRD* (**habitation** = eyrie; **offspring** = eaglet); **breeds:** bald ~, booted ~, crowned ~, erne, golden ~, hawk ~, sea ~, white-tailed ~ [~ owl; *Ganymede*]. ENSIGN, *STANDARD. ISLAND. COMIC.* $10. LINEAGE (crypt: L*IN*EAG()E). **Pl** = *Football team* (US). 2. Two under par on *golf course*. 3. *Constellation*.
EAR HEAD, SPIKE (corn). HANDLE, LUG. ATTENTION, LISTENING; APPRECIATION. AUDITOR (crypt), HEARING ORGAN; **parts, inner:** cochlea, labyrinth; **middle:** anvil, eustachian tube, incus, malleus (hammer), ossicle; syrinx, tympanum (eardrum, membrane), vestibule; **outer:** concha, helix, pinna, scapha; **disorders:** barotrauma, deafness, mastoiditis, Ménière's, otitis media [cauliflower ~].
EARLY 1. BEFORE TIME, PREMATURE (**opp** = *late*), PREHISTORIC, PRIMITIVE; FORWARD. ARISTOCRATIC, *NOBLE* (crypt). 2. Use first letter(s), e.g. **Early afternoon** = A or AF; or, more cryptically, **Early speech** = DIAL(ect).
EARTH 1. LAND, MOULD, SOIL (Fuller's). WORLD, *PLANET* [*study*]. HABITATION (*badger, fox*). CONDUCTOR, CONNECTION, GROUND (elect). 2. **Goddess:** Gk = *CERES*, GAEA/GE; **Rom** = LUA, MAIA, TELLUS, TERRA.
EARTHQUAKE *QUAKER*, TREMBLER [epicentre; Richter; seismograph]; GROUNDRENT (crypt). HARTE, HEART, RATHE etc. (anag; crypt).

EASE (s/l eee). FACILITY. RELIEVE, LOOSEN, SLACKEN.
REST.

EAST E, LEVANT, ORIENT(AL); CARDINAL (POINT).
ASIA, COMMUNIST, RED. PARTNER (*bridge*).

EASTERN OFFICIAL BEY, CADI, DEWAN, NABOB, NAWAB,
SAHIB, SATRAP, SULTAN, TUAN [*Turkish official*].

EAST KENT SE. **Pl** = BUFFS (mil).

EASY FACILE, RELAXED, SIMPLE; **comp** = *free*. SITTER.
[Midshipman ~].

EAT OUT BARBECUE, PICNIC [al fresco]. ATE, TEA
(anag; crypt).

EAVESDROPPER BUG, LISTENER. ICICLE (crypt).

EBB DRAIN. DECLINE, DECAY. FLOW BACK, hence WOLF
(crypt). RECEDE; **comp** = *flow*.

EBBTIDE *DRAIN*. DECLINE, DECAY. OUTFLOW (hence
WOLF: crypt); EDIT (crypt).

EBOR *Episcopal sig* of *YORK*. RETIRING GOWN (crypt).

EC EAST CENTRAL, EAST END; *CITY*.

ECCENTRIC *Anag*. IRREGULAR, *ODD*, OFF-BEAT,
WHIMSICAL. OFF-CENTRE, CAM. *CARD*.

Eccles Ecclesiastic. *Church*.

ECHO 1. *COPY*, IMITATION, REPEAT, REPETITION,
RESOUND. *SPACECRAFT*. 2. Gk myth mountain *nymph*,
made speechless by *Hera*, so that she could only repeat the last
word of others. Loved *Narcissus* vainly, and pined away. 3. A
minor *PLANET*.

ECONOMIZE BE FRUGAL, DO WITHOUT (hence D . . . . . O;
crypt, e.g. **Do without one race, all the same** (5) = D*ITT*O).
SAVE, SPARE. USELESS (crypt).

EDDY 1. ROTARY MOTION, DUST DEVIL, SWIRL,
VORTEX, WHIRLPOOL, WHIRLWIND; *CHARYBDIS*
(myth, Sicily [*Scylla*]); MAELSTROM (Lofoten Is, Nor).
COUNTER CURRENT. DEVIATION, DISTURBANCE (life,
thought). 2. EDWARD (abbr). 3. Mary Baker ~, founder of
Christian Science.

EDENBURG *Episcopal sig* of EDINBURGH.

EDINBURGH *Capital* of Scotland. *CASTLE*. **Episcopal sig** =
EDENBURG. *RACETRACK* (horses). *UNIVERSITY*.

EDIT *Anag*. ARRANGE, CUT; COOK, GARBLE. PREPARE
(MS). BACKWATER, EBBTIDE (crypt).

EDITION VERSION. BOOK, TOME, VOLUME.

EDMUND IRONSIDE. ED.

EDWARD ED, NED, TED. BEAR (*Milne*). LEAR. R. POTATO. HYDE [Henry Jekyll; R. L. Stevenson].

EEC (COMMON) MARKET, COMMUNITY, EUROPE (Treaty of Rome).

EEL FISH [**offspring** = elver; slippery].

EFGHIJKLMN *ETON* (crypt).

EG EXEMPLA GRATIA, FOR EXAMPLE/INSTANCE.

EGERIA Rom *nymph* or goddess of *fountains*; adviser and patroness [Camerae, Numa]; inspiration to man's work.

EGG ENCOURAGE, EXHORT, SPUR, STIMULATE, *URGE*. OVUM; O. BOMB. PERSON (sl). *ZERO*. **Pl** = OO, OVA, ROE, SPAWN. **Pl comp** = bacon; *ham*.

EGGER *MOTH*. SPUR, STIMULATOR. HEN (crypt).

EGYPTIAN GOD *ANUBIS*, HOR, MAAT, *OSIRIS*, *RA*, SEB, SERAPIS, *SET, TEMU*. See also *god*.

EIGHT (s/l *ate*). 1. See *number*. OCTAD, VIII. BLUE, ROWING CREW; **Reserve** ~s: GOLDIE (C), *ISIS* (O). 2. Bold *rangers* (*song*). Maids a-milking (*Christmas* song). [Pieces of ~ (parrot, Treasure Island, *Stevenson*)].

ELBOW HINGE (crypt); JOINT. NUDGE, PUSH. *Shak* char (M for M).

EL DORADO *Lost city* of gold. **Capital** = Manoa.

ELECTRA 1. Gk myth d of *Agamemnon*, sis of Iphigenia and *Orestes*, with whom she avenged the murder of her f by her m. 2. A minor *PLANET*. *TYPEFACE*. 3. Complex of d on f (**opp** = *Oedipus*).

ELECTRICITY AC, AMPS, DC, VOLTS; CURRENCY (crypt) [BEAB].

ELEGANT CHIC, *FASHIONABLE*, IN, MODISH, STYLISH.

ELEMENT 1. AIR, *EARTH, FIRE, WATER*. COMPONENT, FACTOR, RUDIMENT. RESISTANCE WIRE. 2. Hidden word, e.g. **An element of beach air is relaxing** = CH·AIR.

ELEPHANT ELP, MAMMOTH (ex), PACHYDERM [Democrat; roc]; **celebrated**: BABAR, CELESTE, DUMBO, HEFFALUMP, JUMBO, KALAWAG, NELLIE [**assembly** = herd, **fem** = *cow*, **male** = *bull*, **offspring** = *calf*]. *MEASURE* (paper). **Comp** = *castle*.

ELEVEN 1. See *number*. HENDECA, II, IX; SIDE, SQUAD, TEAM. IMPAIRED (crypt). **Pl** = SNACK. 2. Went to *Heaven* (*song*). Ladies *dancing* (*Christmas* song).

ELI Bibl high priest and *judge* of Israel. *Samuel* was a boy in his house. Hophni and Phineas were the two s of ~, and news of their d caused ~ to fall down d (*c*.1000 B.C.).

ELIA ESSAYIST; LAMB; *WRITER*. **Pl** = *ELIJAH*, PROPHET.

ELIJAH The Tishbite (Elias). 9th cent B.C. bibl prophet who was a
hermit until emerging to rail against *Baal*-worship. Outlawed for
denouncing *Ahab* and Jezebel, ~ spent most of his life on the
run (he was fed by *ravens* and the widow's inexhaustible barrel
of meat and *cruse* of oil). Only ~ was able to call down to Mt
Carmel fire from Heaven. He finally ascended to Heaven in a
fiery *chariot*.

ELIMINATE 1. DEFEAT. REMOVE, GET RID OF. 2. Remove
word(s)/letter(s) indicated, e.g. **A to-do to eliminate to-do** (3)
= A*DO.

ELISHA 9th cent bibl disciple of *Elijah*. Said to have been *bald*,
~ once made an axe-head float; he also sent *bears* to destroy
children who had been teasing him.

ELISSA *DIDO*.

ELIZABETH 1. ASTRAEA, BELPHOEBE, GLORIANA,
MERCILLA (Faerie Queene, Spenser). ER; QUEEN. 2. St ~
of Hungary (bread *transformed* into *roses*). *Shak* char (R.iii).
[German *Garden*].

ELL LENGTH, *MEASURE* (cloth).

ELYSIUM 1. ELYSIAN FIELDS, *HEAVEN*. 2. Gk myth place
where souls of the good dwelt after death [Ambrosia (food),
asphodel (flower), nectar (drink), *Valhalla* (Nor myth)].

EM THEM (abbr). GAUGE (model rly). *MEASURE* (printing).
Pl = RIVER (Ger). EUROPEAN MONETARY SYSTEM
(SNAKE). MINES (crypt, M*in*ES).

EMBARRASSED *Anag*. ASHAMED, AWKWARD;
PERPLEXED. COMPLICATED. ENCUMBERED,
IMPEDED.

EMBRACE 1. CLASP, COMPRISE, ENCLOSE, HUG,
INCLUDE. ACCEPT, TAKE IN. 2. Hidden word; word
contains another, e.g. **He embraces a foreign engineer and swings
for it** (5) = H*ING*E.

EMERALD 1. GEM: BERYL. GREEN. [~ City (Wizard of Oz;
Baum]. 2. *Anniversary* (55th). *Birthstone* (May).

EMINENCE *HILL*, MOUND, MOUNT, TOR. *CARDINAL*, HE.
~ **GRISE** RICHELIEU'S SECRETARY (PERE JOSEPH).
MANIPULATOR, *UNSEEN* INFLUENCE; ROYAL
ENGINEER (crypt).

EMIT GIVE OUT, ISSUE, SEND FORTH, TRANSMIT. TIME
OUT, TIME-WARP, WRONG ITEM (anags; crypt).

EMMY *AWARD* (TV).
EMPEROR 1. BUTTERFLY (purple ~); MOTH (*lepidoptera*).
MEASURE (paper). PENGUIN. *TAROT* (4). 2. SOVEREIGN
of empire [*Andersen* (writer); *Caesar; Ch dynasty;* czar, kaiser,
khan; mikado; *monarch;* O'Neill (writer); *Ptolemy;* shah; tsar];
abbr = IMP (Lat); **fem** = *empress.* **Celeb:**

ALEXANDER (Macedon; Russ)
AUGUSTUS (*Caesar;* 1st Rom)
BOKASSA (Cent Af)
CALIGULA (Rom)
CHARLEMAGNE (H Rom)
CHARLES V (H Rom)
CHI'EN LUNG (Ch)
CLAUDIUS (Rom)
CONSTANTINE (E Rom)
DARIUS (Pers)
DIOCLETIAN (Rom)
FRANZ JOSEF (A)
FREDERICK (Ger)
~ BARBAROSSA (H Rom)
GENGHIS KHAN (Mongol)
HADRIAN (Rom)
HAILE SELASSIE (Ethiopia)
HIROHITO (Jap)
IVAN (Russ)
JOSEF (H Rom)
KUBLAI KHAN (Mongol)
MONTEZUMA (Aztec)
NAPOLEON (Fr)
NERO (Rom)
NICHOLAS (Russ)
OTTO (H Rom)
PAUL (Russ)
PETER (Russ)
PHARAOH (Egy)
PTOLEMY (Egy)
SIGISMUND (H Rom)
TAISHO (Jap)
TIBERIUS (Rom)
TRAJAN (Rom)
WILLIAM (Ger)
XERXES (Pers)

EMPLOY 1. USE. OCCUPY. HIRE. 2. Hidden word, e.g. **Mad
American employs a gardener** (4) = AD*AM.
EMPRESS Fem *emperor* [czarina; *monarch;* tsarina]. *TAROT* (3).
Celeb:

CATHERINE (Russ)
CLEOPATRA (Egy)
EUGENIE (Fr)
IRENE (E Rom)
MARIA THERESA (A)
MARIE LOUISE (Fr)
TZU HSI (Ch)
VICTORIA (Brit)

EMPTY 1. HOLLOW, VACANT, VACATE. 2. Remove middle
letter(s) from word, e.g. **Empty threat** (4) = TH**AT. 3. Insert O
in word, e.g. **Empty cup** (4) = C*O*UP.

EMU FLIGHTLESS *BIRD* (Aus) [cassowary, dinornis (ex, NZ), moa, nandoo, ostrich].

EN 1. Put word in another, e.g. **Enlist Z** (5) = LIS*Z*T.

2. *MEASURE* (printing).

ENCHANT BE WINSOME. *CHARM*, DELIGHT, *ENTRANCE*, SPELLBIND, TRANSPORT (**opp** = *bore*).

ENCOMPASS CONTAIN, SURROUND. NORTH ORIENTATE; relate to magnetic compass, e.g. **Tidings encompassed** (4) = NEWS.

ENCOURAGE ABET, AID, EGG, *URGE*. GO.

END 1. *AIM*, DESIGN, GOAL, OBJECT, PURPOSE. *CLOSE*, CONCLUSION, FINISH (**opp** = *start*). SESSION (bowls).

2. Last letter of word: **Southend** = H. **Pl** = letters at each end of word(s), e.g. **Dead ends** = D**D; **Ends of the earth** = E***H.

ENDANGER JEOPARDIZE, PUT AT RISK. MAKE PEACE, MAKE UP (crypt).

ENDING 1. CLOSURE. 2. Last letter (see *END* above).

ENDLESS 1. CEASELESS, PERPETUAL, UNCEASING. CIRCLE, RING, O. AIMLESS, POINTLESS; TIP OFF (crypt).

2. No first (or last) letter, e.g. **Endless hate** (3) = HAT.

ENERGY FORCE, POTENTIAL, POWER, VIGOUR. E, ERG, ERGON.

ENG ENGLISH [*patron saint*].

Eng England, English. Engineer.

ENGAGED AFFIANCED, BETROTHED, MATCHED, PROMISED, RINGED (crypt) [fiancée, intended]. *BOOKED*, BUSY, OCCUPIED, RESERVED, TIED UP (**opp** = *free*). HIRED, TOOK ON.

ENGAGEMENT AFFRAY, *BATTLE*, COMBAT, SKIRMISH. BETROTHAL, MATCH, INTENTION, RINGING (crypt). OCCUPATION. APPOINTMENT, DATE.

ENGINE MACHINERY, POWER SOURCE; INSTRUMENT, MEANS. WAR MACHINE; CATAPULTA, TESTUDO (Rom).

ENGINEER ARRANGE, CONTRIVE, FIX, MANAGE, ORGANIZE. CE, DESIGNER (mech), ENG. WORKER (elect, mech [**union** = AUEW], rly [**unions** = ASLEF, NUR]). BRIDGEBUILDER. RE, SAPPER.

ENGLISH E, ENG. SIDE, SPIN (ballgames–US). *TYPEFACE*.

ENGRAVE CARVE, ETCH, INSCRIBE, PRINT; FIX, IMPRINT. BURY, *INTER* (crypt).

ENGROSS ABSORB, ENRAPTURE, OCCUPY. DRAW UP,

EXPRESS, PREPARE (leg). CORNER, MONOPOLIZE (arch).

ENIGMATIC *Anag.* BEWILDERING, PERPLEXING, PUZZLING.

ENLARGE EXPAND, EXPATIATE. DILATE, MAGNIFY. FREE, LIBERATE (arch).

ENLIST 1. ENGAGE, ENROL(L), JOIN COLOURS. 2. Word contained in another, especially in 'list' or 'roster', e.g. **Enlist one to revel** (7) = RO•I•STER.

ENOCH 1. Eldest s of *Cain*; founded the first city. 2. Seventh in descent from *Adam*; s of Jared and f of *Methuselah*; a prophet who did not d, but 'walked with God'. 3. Grand-s of *Abraham*. 4. A s of Reuben, and thus a grand-s of *Jacob*.

ENOUGH AMPLE, ENOW, SUFFICIENT.

ENTANGLEMENT *Anag.* 1. AFFAIR, INVOLVEMENT, LIAISON. 2. Caught in barbed wire, brambles, net, etc; **celeb**: *Absalom* (oak tree); fly (spider's web or 'parlour'); *Merlin* (rose bush); Peter Rabbit (Mr MacGregor's gooseberry net, *Potter*); Pooh (Rabbit's front door, *Milne*).

ENTER GO IN (**opp** = *leave*). LOG, *RECORD*, WRITE. BIND (contract, treaty). JOIN (church, forces; **opp** = *desert*).

ENTHUSIAST AFICIONADO, *FAN*, SUPPORTER.

ENTITLED 1. CALLED. ALLOWED, PERMITTED, RIGHTFUL. 2. With a title, e.g. Count, Dame, Sir etc.

ENTRANCE *DOOR(WAY)*, GATE, PASSAGE. ARRIVAL, ENTRY. ADMISSION FEE. *CHARM, ENCHANT*, WIN.

ENVIRONMENT 1. MILIEU, SURROUNDINGS. 2. Word round another, e.g. **Or the environment** = O•THE•R (or TH•OR•E).

EOLITHIC *AGE*.

EOS 1. Gk *goddess* of DAWN (**Rom** = *AURORA*). 2. A minor *PLANET*.

EPICUREAN HEDONISTIC. Follower of Epicurus (Gk), and devoted to sensual pleasure; the garden set (hence *gardeners*); **celeb**: LUCULLUS (Rom), PHAEDRUS (Gk); **opp** = *Stoic*.

EPISCOPAL SIGNATURE Initials or name of bishop, followed by archaic name for his see, e.g.

ABERDON	(Aberdeen)
ALBAN	(St Albans)
CANTUAR	(Canterbury)
CESTR	(Chester)
CICESTR	(Chichester)

DUNELM	(Durham)
EBOR	(York)
EDENBURG	(Edinburgh)
EXON	(Exeter)
NORVIC	(Norwich)
OXON	(Oxford)
PETRIBURG	(Peterborough)
ROFFEN	(Rochester)
SARUM	(Salisbury)
TRURON	(Truro)
VIGORN	(Worcester)
WINTON	(Winchester)

Eq Equatorial. Equals.

EQUAL EVEN, LEVEL, LIKE, PAR, SAME; MATCH. PEER; BROTHER.

~ **WINNER** *TIER;* DEAD-HEATER; DRAWER (crypt).

ERASED 1. DELETED, ERADICATED, REMOVED, RUBBED OUT. 2. Delete D from clue, e.g. **Draft erased is logged** (4) = *RAFT.

ERATO 1. Gk myth; one of the nine *Muses* (love songs and erotic *poetry*). 2. A minor *PLANET.*

ERG ENERGY UNIT [dyne]. SAHARA DUNES [*desert*].

ERIC LITTLE BY LITTLE (Farrar). (THE) RED.

ERICA *HEATH(ER).* GIRL.

ERIE (s/l eyrie). *AMERICAN INDIAN. LAKE.*

ERINYES *FURIES* (q.v.; Gk).

ERIS Gk *goddess* of DISCORD, sis of *Ares* (**Rom** = DISCORDIA). Angry at not being invited to the wedding of Peleus and Thetis, she threw among the guests a golden *apple* inscribed 'To the fairest'. *Aphrodite, Athene* and *Hera* all claimed it, and the judgement of *Paris* was that it be awarded to Aphrodite; this indirectly caused the Siege of *Troy.*

ERMINE STOAT [weasel]. FUR [judges, peers, *herald*].

ERNE BIRD, SEA-EAGLE. RIVER (Ire [Boycott]).

ERNIE *COMPUTER* (Premium Bonds).

EROS Gk *god* of *LOVE* (**Rom** = AMOR, CUPID), depicted as an *archer;* s of *Aphrodite* by *Zeus* (some say by *Ares* or Hermes); see also *Psyche* [Piccadilly Circus]; *Shak* char. **Opp** = Anteros.

ERRATIC *Anag.* WAYWARD, WILD. *ODD.* IRREGULAR, UNCERTAIN.

ERROR *BLOOMER*, BISH, DEVIATION, FAULT,

INFRINGEMENT, MISTAKE, SIN, WRONG.

ERUPTION *Anag.* BREAK-OUT, BURST, OUTBREAK; RASH.

ESAU Bibl s of *Isaac* and Rebecca, elder twin br of *Jacob* and
known as EDOM (the Red) or the HAIRY ONE. A cunning
HUNTER, ~ was tricked by Jacob to exchange his inheritance
or birthright for 'a mess of pottage' (lentils), when ~ was hungry
from the chase; ~ was similarly tricked by his br from the
blessing of Isaac due by custom to the first-born.

ESCAPOLOGIST HOUDINI. JACK SHEPHERD. ESCAPER.

ESSAY (s/l s,a). ATTEMPT, EFFORT, TEST, TRY. ARTICLE.
COMPOSITION [*Elia*: Lamb].

ESSAYIST TRIER. *WRITER*: ELIA, LAMB.

ESTABLISHMENT AUTHORITY, ORGANIZATION,
THEY [Civil Service (**union** = NALGO)]. GROUP, SET,
SETTLEMENT, STAFF, VERIFICATION; AUTHORIZED
HOLDING/MANNING. THE CHURCH.

ESTATE CLASS, ORDER. CONDITION. LAND, PROPERTY.
VEHICLE (hatchback, shooting brake). [*three* ~s; *fourth* ~].

ETA ARRIVAL TIME, EXPECTED TIME OF ARRIVAL (**opp**
= ETD).

ET AL AND OTHERS.

ETC ETCETERA, AND SO ON.

ETERNAL FLOWER ASPHODEL. ARTESIAN WELL,
SPRING (crypt).

ETHIOPIAN KING RA.

ETON 1. COLLEGE, *PUBLIC SCHOOL* [*Pop*]. E–N (crypt).
2. Returned note (crypt).

EUMINIDES *FURIES* (q.v.; Gk).

EUROPA Gk myth d of Agenor and m of *Minos* by *Zeus* (who
took the form of a bull). 2. A satellite of the *planet* Jupiter.

EUROPE EEC [Common Market. Treaty of Rome].
CONTINENT.

EUROS Gk myth SE *WIND* (**Rom** = VOLTURNUS).

EURYDICE 1. Gk myth d of *Nereus* and *Doris*, who mar *Orpheus*.
When she died of a snake bite, Orpheus brought her back from
Hades by magic, but lost her again by *looking back* for her.
2. A minor *PLANET*.

EUTERPE 1. Gk myth; one of the nine *Muses* (lyric *poetry*).
2. A minor *PLANET*.

EVA EXTRA-VEHICULAR ACTIVITY, SPACE-WALK.
GIRL, SPACE-GIRL. PERON. 'LIFE'.

EVE (s/l eave). 1. EVENING, VIGIL. *ISLAND*. 'LIFE'.

2. Mother of Cain, Abel, Seth; wife of Adam. FIRST LADY.
SECOND PERSON [apple; Eden; rib]. **Comp** = *Adam.*
EVELYN *DIARIST.* JOHN; *WRITER* [Pepys].
EVEN LEVEL, *SMOOTH*, UNIFORM. NOT ODD. *JUST,*
QUITE, SIMPLY, STILL. EVENING. EQUABLE,
UNRUFFLED. BALANCED, EQUAL. **Pl** = EQUAL
STAKES [odds]. *IRONS*, SMOOTHS (crypt).
EVENING *PM.* IRONING, SMOOTHING (crypt).
EVENING STAR *VENUS/HESPERUS* (Gk/Rom); **opp** = *Lucifer*
(Venus)/*Phosphorus.*
EVER ALWAYS, EER. STILL. **Comp** = *anon; a day.*
EVERGREEN BAY, CEDAR, FIR, LAUREL etc.
EVERLASTING ENDLESS, ETERNAL, NEVER-ENDING.
EVERMORE ALWAYS. NEVERTHELESS (crypt).
EWE (s/l you, *U*). *SHEEP* (*fem*). *ISLAND.*
EWER CROCK, FLAGON, JUG, PITCHER, POT, URN,
VESSEL. SHEPHERD (crypt).
EX (s/l X). *DEAD*, LATE, FORMER. OUT OF, *OUTSIDE,*
WITHOUT.
Ex No longer extant.
EXALTATION 1. ELATION, *ENCHANTMENT*, RAPTURE,
REJOICING. 2. *Assembly* (larks).
EXAM GREATS (O), LITTLE-GO (C); ORAL, VIVA VOCE,
WRITTEN TEST [sit]. REGARD.
EXCELLENT A1, FIRST CLASS, *NOBLE*, PRE-EMINENT,
VERY GOOD.
EXCEPT *BUT*, NOT INCLUDING; UNLESS. EXCLUDE,
LEAVE OUT.
EXCERPT 1. EXTRACT, QUOTE. 2. Hidden word, e.g. **An
excerpt from Milton's 'Il Penseroso' is throaty stuff** (6) =
TONS*IL.
EXCHANGE *Anag.* CHANGE, INTERCHANGE, SWAP,
SWOP, SWITCH. CURRENCY, MONEY CHANGING.
BOURSE (Fr), COUNTING HOUSE; COMMERCIAL
TRANSACTIONS [Dow Jones; Footsie; Hang Seng; Nikkei].
PBX, SWITCHBOARD, TELEPHONE CENTRE.
EXCLUSIVENESS 1. HIGH-CLASS. SELECTIVITY. 2. Delete
'ness' from clue, e.g. **Exclusiveness makes the prince's address
exalted** (4) = HIGH(ness).
EXECUTE CARRY OUT, *DO*, PERFORM. VALIDATE.
ASSASSINATE, BEHEAD, DECAPITATE, DISPATCH,
EXTERMINATE, FINISH, GAS, GUILLOTINE,

HANG, KILL, MURDER, PUT TO DEATH, SHOOT,
SLAUGHTER, SLAY, WASTE, *TOP*.

EXERCISE PE, PT; DRILL, EXERTION, TRAINING (gym).
PERPLEX, WORRY. DISCHARGE (duty). EMPLOYMENT,
PRACTICE. TASK. COMPOSITION. MANOEUVRE (mil).

EXETER 1. ISCA DUMNUNIORUM (*Roman town*).
UNIVERSITY; UNIVERSITY COLLEGE. 2. **Episcopal sig** =
EXON.

EXHAUST FATIGUE, TIRE; BEGGAR, FINISH. OUTLET,
PORT (tech).

EXHORT *URGE*.

EXIST AM, ARE, BE.

EXIT 1. DEPARTURE, DEATH. WAY OUT. 2. Stage direction
to leave the scene; '~, pursued by a bear' (W Tale, *Shak*).

EXON *Episcopal sig* of EXETER.

EXPEL 1. CAST AWAY/OUT, EJECT, TURN OUT. 2. Remove
letter(s) indicated, e.g. **I am expelled from Sofia for a rest** (4)
= SOF*A.

EXPERIENCED ACQUAINTED; FELT, UNDERWENT.
SKILLED, TRIED (**opp** = *green*, tyro).

EXPERT *ACE*, DAB (HAND), PRO(FESSIONAL) (**opp** =
learner). ABLE, ADEPT, ADROIT, CAPABLE, DEFT (**opp**
= *fool*).

EXPLORER EXAMINER, INVESTIGATOR. *SPACECRAFT,
SPACE TRAVELLER. DISCOVERER*, TRAVELLER; **celeb**:
AMUNDSEN ('Gjoa', 'Maud'), BYRD (North Pole), CABOT
('Mathew'), COLUMBUS ('Nina', 'Pinta', 'Santa Maria'),
COOK ('Discovery', 'Endeavour', 'Resolution'), DARWIN
('Beagle'), DRAKE ('Pelican', 'Golden Hind'), FROBISHER
('Gabriel'), HILARY (Everest), HUNT (Everest, South
Pole), *MAGELLAN* ('Trinidad', 'Vittoria'), NANSEN
('Fram'), SCOTT ('Discovery', 'Terra Nova'), SHACKLETON
('Endurance'), VASCO DA GAMA (Cathay), ZHENG
HE (Ch).

EXPLOSION *Anag*. BURST, OUTBREAK. BANG, LOUD
NOISE.

EXPRESS FORMULATE, SAY, STATE. EXPEDITE, FAST,
SPEEDY. NEWSPAPER ®. TRAIN (rly).

EXTRA ODD, ORRA (Sc), OVER, SPARE,
SUPERNUMERARY; EXCESS; FURTHER. GRACE NOTE
(mus). BIT PLAYER, CROWD (film). PS. BYE, LEG BYE,
NO BALL, RUN, WIDE (cricket).

EXTRACTOR DRAWER, PULLER, FAN, VENTILATOR.
COPIER (crypt). DENTIST (crypt).
EXTRA LARGE OS, OUTSIZE, X.
EXTREME 1. FARTHEST, FURTHEST, OUTERMOST,
UTTERMOST. SEVERE, STRINGENT. 2. **Pl** = use
letters/words at each end, e.g. **Extremes of valour** = VR.
EXTREMELY 1. HIGHLY; SEVERELY, VERY, UNCO (Sc).
2. Use letters/words at each end, e.g. **Extremely kind** = KD.
EYE (s/l Aye, I). EXAMINE, INSPECT, LOOK, REGARD.
SIGHT. OPTIC; **parts**: *ball*, cornea, *iris*, lens, orbit, *pupil*,
retina, rods, sclerotic, white; **disorders**: astigmatism, blindness,
cast, cataract, conjunctivitis, glaucoma, iritis, myopia, myosin,
myosis, myotic, nystagmus, squint, stye, trachoma, tunnel vision.
EYESORE FRIGHT, HIDEOSITY, UGLY, OBJECT. *EYE
DISORDER* (crypt).

F FAHRENHEIT. *FELLOW. FEMININE.* FLUORINE (*chem*).
FOLIO, PAGE. FORTE. FRANCE (*car plate*). FRENCH.
FRIDAY. FINE. *KEY; NOTE. LOUD.*
FA NOTE (mus; also FAH). FANNY ADAMS, NOTHING (sl).
FOOTBALL ASSOCIATION.
FABRIC *MATERIAL* (felt, knit or weave). TEXTURE, TISSUE.
BUILDING, EDIFICE, FRAME, STRUCTURE.
FACE CLOCK, DIAL, *MUG, PAN*, VISAGE [Monday's *child*].
CONFRONT, OPPOSE; LOOK TOWARDS. *OBVERSE* (**opp**
= *reverse*). *TYPEFACE*.
FACTOR AGENT. ELEMENT.
FACTORY MILL, *PLANT*, WORKS.
FACULTY APTITUDE, COMPETENCE, e.g. HEARING,
MEMORY, REASONING, SIGHT and esp the Four ~s:
ARTS, LAW, SCIENCE, THEOLOGY. AUTHORIZATION,
LICENCE. SCHOLASTIC DEPARTMENT; TEACHING
STAFF.
FAHRENHEIT F.
FAIL BREAK. FLUNK, PIP, PLOUGH, PLOW (US).
FAIR (s/l *fare*). EVEN HANDED, EQUAL, IMPARTIAL,
JUST, LEGITIMATE, UNBIASED. QUITE GOOD,
REASONABLE. FAVOURABLE, OPEN,
UNOBSTRUCTED. FINE, SUNNY. CLEAR, LEGIBLE.
REAL, THOROUGH. COURTEOUS, PLEASANT.

BLOND(E), LIGHT. *ISLAND*, ISLE [knitting].
(TRAVELLING) ENTERTAINMENT, EXHIBITION,
(SIDE)SHOW; **celeb**: GOOSE ~, STRAWBERRY ~,
WIDDICOMBE ~. BEAUTIFUL, LOVELY, HANDSOME
[Monday's *child*].

FAIRY HOMO, QUEER; CAMP, GAY. (HOB)GOBLIN,
IMP, SPRITE; **celeb**: TITANIA (queen), OBERON (king),
COBWEB, MOTH, MUSTARDSEED, PEASBLOSSOM,
and PUCK/ROBIN GOODFELLOW (all MND), ARIEL
(Tempest), TINKERBELL (Peter Pan), TRIPSITINKA
(Queen, *Lofting*). [*Barrie*, Grimm; Iolanthe (*G & S*). MND
(*Shak*)].

FALL CROPPER, *DECLINE*, DESCEND, DROP, SLIP.
AVALANCHE, LANDSLIP/-SLIDE. *WATERFALL* (q.v.).
RAIN. ROPE (naut). AUTUMN, *SEASON* (US). *Assembly*
(woodcock).

~ **OUT** HAPPEN. DISAGREE. NUCLEAR DEBRIS/DUST;
SIDE-EFFECTS. DISMISS, LEAVE RANKS (mil).

FALSE *Anag*. ARTIFICIAL, COUNTERFEIT, DECEITFUL,
DUMMY, FICTITIOUS, FRAUDULENT, ILLEGAL,
PHON(E)Y, SHAM, SPURIOUS, WRONG (**opp** = correct).
UNFAITHFUL (**opp** = *true*).

~ **REPORT** CANARD, HOAX, LIE. PORTER, PERROT etc
(anag, crypt).

FAMILIAR COMMON, CURRENT, FRIENDLY, INTIMATE,
USUAL, WELL-KNOWN. CASUAL, INFORMAL,
UNCEREMONIOUS. *CAT*, DEMON, *SPIRIT* (*witch*).
SECRETARY, SERVANT (of pope, RC *bishop*).

FAMILY CHILDREN, DESCENDANTS, HOUSE, KIN, KITH,
LINEAGE. COMMON STOCK, GENUS, RACE. And see
Royal ~ for list.

FAMOUS FIVE ANNE, DICK, GEORGE, JULIAN, TIMMY
(dog) [Enid Blyton]. JOHNNIE BULL, BOB CHERRY,
FRANK NUGENT, HUREE JAMSET RAM SINGH,
HARRY WHARTON [*Bunter*, Greyfriars] (Frank Richards).

FAN WAFT, WINNOW; *COOLER*; (Lady Windermere's ~,
Wilde). PROPELLER (av), SCREW (naut). *SAIL* (windmill).
SPREAD OUT. ADMIRER, AFICIONADO, ENTHUSIAST,
FOLLOWER, SUPPORTER.

FANG 1. *TOOTH* (dog, snake, wolf). PRONG. 2. Char in *Dickens*
and *Shak*.

FANNY ADAMS FA, NOTHING (murder victim). CANNED

MEAT (naut).

FARE (s/l *fair*). *FOOD. PASSAGE* MONEY. *GO*, JOURNEY, TRAVEL. HAPPEN, TURN OUT.

FAREWELL ALOHA, AVE, BYE BYE, GOODBYE, TA-TA, VALE (**opp** = *greeting, hail*).

FARM HOLDING, RANCH; CULTIVATE, TILL [*husbandry*]. HIRE OUT, SPREAD.

FARO (s/l *pharaoh*). *CARD GAME.*

FAR SIDE 1. BEYOND. 2. Second part of word, e.g. **Far side of the Moon** = ON.

FASHION MODE, TON, HAUTE COUTURE. CONSTRUCT, MAKE, *SHAPE.*

FASHIONABLE A LA MODE, CHIC, *IN*, IN THE SWIM, MODISH, NEAT, SMART, UNSQUARE. MALLEABLE, WORKABLE.

FAT CORPULENT, -ENCE, OBESE, -ITY, PLUMP(NESS). BUTTER, GREASE, -Y, LARD, MARGARINE, OILY. BEST, FERTILE, PRODUCTIVE, RICHEST; LUCRATIVE, PROFITABLE. BROAD, EXTENDED, THICK. EMPTY, LITTLE, STUPID.

FAST *FLEET*, QUICK, SPEEDY [*Atalanta*]; **comp** = furious; loose. ABSTAIN, *LENT*; RAMADAN (Mos). *FIRM, SET. CASTLE.*

FATE 1. DESERTS, DESTINY, LOT; KISMET. PREORDAIN. 2. **Pl** = *GODS*, WEIRD SISTERS. Three *goddesses* of DESTINY: **Gk** = MOIRAI: CLOTHO (thread of life), LACHESIS (quality and length), ATROPOS (severance); **Rom** = PARCAE: DECIMA (birth), MORTA (death), NONA (birth); **Nor** = NORN.

FATHEAD CLOT, DUNCE, FOOL. F (crypt).

FATHER (s/l *farther*). ABBOT, *CHURCHMAN*, FR, *FRIAR*. DAD, GENERATOR, GOVERNOR, GUVNOR, OLD MAN, PA, PATER (FAMILIAS), POP; PROCREATE, SIRE, SPAWN (~**'s delight** = *Abigail*). [~ Brown, *Chesterton*; Old ~ William (*Alice*); Old ~ Thames; ~ Time]. And see *Male and Female.*

FATHERLAND *COUNTRY. GERMANY.*

FATHERLESS 1. ORPHAN. *Nyx* (q.v.) had several children without benefit of husband. 2. Remove DAD, PA, POP from clue-word (crypt), e.g. ~ **patron saint shows success as a bridger** (5) = (pa)TRICK.

FAUN (s/l *fawn*). Rom eq of Gk *SATYR.*

FAUNUS Rom *god* of *herds*; s of Picus, f of Acis [see *Galatea*].
Also INUUS, LUPERCUS. **Gk** = *PAN*.

FAVONIUS Rom myth WEST *WIND* (**Gk** = ZEPHYRUS).

FAVOUR BOON, *GRACE*, KINDNESS; **comp** = *fear; grace*.
PREFER. BUTTONHOLE, ROSETTE.

FAVOURITE PET, PREFERRED (**opp** = bête noire).
COURTESAN, MISTRESS.

FAWN (s/l *faun*). CRINGE, GROVEL; LICK-SPITTLE,
TOADY, SYCOPHANT. *COLOUR* (PALE BROWN).
OFFSPRING (DEER).

FBI *DETECTIVES*, FEDS, G-MEN.

FDR ROOSEVELT. Was WEST GERMANY.

FE *IRON* (*chem*). *SMITH* (Lord Birkenhead).

FEAR ALARM, APPREHENSION, *AVERSION*, DREAD,
FRIGHT, PANIC, PHOBIA, SHRINK, TERROR.
COWARDICE, FRIGHT, FUNK [yellow]. **Comp** = *favour*.

FEATHER 1. DOWN, PLUME, QUILL. 2. *Anniversary* (3rd).

FEATURE PORTRAY, *STAR*. LANDMARK. CHIN, EAR,
EYE, MOUTH, NOSE etc.

FEBRUARY (2nd) MONTH, M, FEB (Lat februar = purification
feast). **Birthstone** = *Amethyst*.

FED UP GORGED, SATED. BORED, BROWNED OFF,
TIRED (**opp** = *enchanted*). DEF (dn; crypt).

FEET 1. Pl of *FOOT; MEASURE*. 2. Metric rhythm or scanning of
verse; see *FOOT*.

FELL COLLAPSED, TRIPPED. AXE, CUT DOWN. HIDE,
SKIN. *HILL*, MOUNTAIN. FIERCE, RUTHLESS ['this ~
sergeant, *death*' (Hamlet)].

FELLOW F. CHAP, COVE, DON, GENT, GUY, HE, MAN.
CO-~, PEER.

~ TRAVELLER COMMIE, RED. BACK-SEAT DRIVER,
CREW MEMBER, OBSERVER (av), NAVIGATOR (av),
PILLION PASSENGER.

FEMALE fem; FEMININE, DISTAFF, (CHILD)BEARER,
MOTHER; **opp** = *male*, spear. GIRL, WOMAN. For animal
genders, see *male and female*.

FEMININE F. FEMALE, WOMANLY.

FENCE BANK, BULWARK, ENCLOSE, FORTIFY, HEDGE,
PALISADE, PROTECT, RAILING, SCREEN, SHIELD,
WALL. GAUGE, GUARD, GUIDE (mech). RECEIVER
[*robber*]. PARRY, WORD PLAY. SWORDPLAY [lunge, parry,
riposte; prime, seconde, tierce, quart, quinte, sixte, septime,

Figure 197

octave].

FENCER DUELLIST, SWORDSMAN. STEEPLECHASER
(crypt). BOUNDARY LAYER, FRONTIERSMAN (crypt).

FERRET SCOUT-CAR (mil). HUNT, SEARCH (hence
DETECTIVE). *WEASEL* (**fem** = gill).

FERRY CONVEY, CROSS, TRANSPORT. TENDER,
WORKBOAT. [*Acheron, Anubis, Charon, Lethe, Styx*].

FERTILITY 1. ABUNDANCE, FECUNDITY, FRUITFULNESS.
2. **Gods: Gk** = *DIONYSUS*, HYMEN; **Rom** = *BACCHUS*,
GENIUS, LIBER; **Egy** = OSIRIS; **Ind** = KRISHNA; **Nor** =
FREY. **Goddesses: Gk** = CYBELE, *DANAE*, RHEA; **Rom**
= *CERES, DIANA*, OPS; Other = FRIGG (**Nor**); BELIT,
INNIN, ISHTAR (**Bab**); ATERGATIS (**Syrian**); EOSTRE
(**A-Sax**; Easter).

FF FOLIOS, PAGES. FORTISSIMO, VERY LOUD.

FIBRE FILAMENT, THREAD [~ glass, ~ optics]. CLOTH,
MATERIAL, TEXTURE, TISSUE. CHARACTER, NERVE,
STAMINA, SUBSTANCE. ROUGHAGE, VITAMINS.

FICTIONAL For ~ countries, kings, unseen chars etc, see *country,
king, unseen character* etc.

FIDDLE BOW, PLAY, SCRAPE, VIOLIN. FIDGET.
ARRANGE, *CHEAT*, COOK, FIX, MANIPULATE.

FIDO *DOG*. Acronym (Fog Investigation Dispersal Operation, av).

FIELDING CAMPAIGNING. GRAZING, PLOUGHING
(crypt). *WRITER*. AREA, PANORAMA, SPHERE.
BOWLING, NOT IN (*cricket*). [Bow Street *policeman*].

FIELDSMAN CATCHER, *CRICKETER*; OUTSIDER (crypt)
[MCC]. FARMER, *SHEPHERD* (crypt). GATHERER.
SCARECROW (crypt).

FIFTEEN See *number*. XV, SIDE, TEAM [rugby].

FIFTH 1. AMENDMENT. *DRINK, MEASURE*. VTH. G (mus).
2. Beethoven's ~ = H (crypt).

~ **MAN** GUY FAWKES (crypt) [Robert Catesby, Thomas Percy,
Gunpowder Plot].

FIFTY See *number*. L. HALF TON.

FIGHT *BATTLE*, COMBAT, DING DONG, QUARREL,
SCRAP, SCRIMMAGE, SET-TO, WAR.

FIGHTER COMBATANT, WARRIOR. *AIRCRAFT*; *WEAPON*.
BOXER, PUGILIST.

FIGURE RECKON, THINK, WORK OUT. INTEGER. CONE,
TRIANGLE etc (math). APPEAR, FEATURE. *FORM*,
LINE, *SHAPE* [vital statistics]. CHARACTER, PERSON.

DIAGRAM, DRAWING, ILLUSTRATION; IMAGE, LIKENESS, REPRESENTATION. EMBLEM, SIMILE, TYPE. AMOUNT, PRICE, VALUE. DANCE STEP, SKATING PATTERN.

FILLING REPLENISHMENT, TOP-UP. APPLE, FRUIT, JAM, MINCE, PUREE etc (cook). STOPPING (dental). SATISFYING. OCCUPYING.

FILM COATING, *LAYER*, MEMBRANE, PLATE, SKIN. MOVIE; *SHOOT*; **types**: BIOPIC, B-MOVIE, COMEDY, DOCUMENTARY, FARCE, HORROR, MYSTERY ~ NATURE ~, SCI-FI ~, THRILLER, WEEPIE, WESTERN. CASSETTE, REEL (photo). **Pl** = CINEMA, FLICKS.

~ **CATEGORY** A, AA, G (US), H, PG, R, U, X [*censorship*].

~ **PART** REEL. ROLE, STAR. FI, FIL, ILM etc (crypt).

~ **STUDIO** Room or premises of film company; by association, name of such a company; **celeb**: Allied Artists, Br Lion, Cannon, Columbia, Ealing, Epic (Ind), Fox, Gainsborough, Gaumont, Mancunian, Merton Park, MGM, Monogram, Nettlefold, Paramount, Pathé, PRC, Rank, Republic, RKO, Twentieth Century, United Artists, Universal, Walt Disney, Warner.

FINAL 1. *LAST*, ULTIMATE, Z, OMEGA. CONCLUSIVE, DEFINITE. LATEST EDITION/NEWS. **Pl** = LAST EXAMS, DECIDER (games). 2. Use last letter of word indicated, e.g. **Final destination** = N; **Your final ...** = R. 3. AFL (crypt: F*in*AL).

FINALE 1. CONCLUSION, *END*, ENDING. 2. Add letter E at end of word indicated, e.g. **Artist finale** (7) = ARTISTE. 3. AFLE/ALFE (crypt: F*in*ALE).

FINCH BIRD (**assembly** = *charm*).

FINISH (s/l Finnish). 1. CEASE, COMPLETE, *END* (**opp** = *start*). ANNIHILATE, DESTROY, DISPATCH, KILL, OVERCOME. PERFECT; POLISH, SHEEN. 2. Last letter(s) of word, e.g. **Quick finish** = K.

FINN FINLAND. ~ MacCool (f of Ossian, Ire legend); Huckleberry ~ (*Twain*).

FIRE 1. BLAZE, BRAND, FLAME, INFERNO, SPARK. *LIGHT* [*St Elmo's* ~]; **comp** = brimstone, *water*. BOOT, *DISCHARGE*, DISMISS, SACK. SHOOT. BAKE, GLAZE. 2. **Gods**: **Gk** = HEPHAESTUS; **Rom** = VULCAN; **Nor** = *LOKI*; **Jew** = *MOLOCH*.

FIREMAN ARSONIST, BLAZER. EXTINGUISHER.

GUNNER, MARKSMAN, RA, SNIPER [*patron saint*].
FOOTPLATE-MAN (**Union** = ASLEF, NUR).
FIRE-RAISER ARSONIST; MATCH. ERIF (dn; crypt).
FIREWORK *BANGER*, ROCKET, SQUIB, WHIZZBANG;
 Pl = *ROW*, RUCTION. CHARCOAL BURNING (crypt).
 GUNNERY (crypt).
FIRM COMPACT, FIXED, RIGID, *SET*, SOLID, *SOUND,*
 STABLE, STAUNCH, STEADY. BUSINESS, CO, LTD, PLC,
 WORKS. SIGNATURE, STYLE. CONSTANT, RESOLUTE,
 STEADFAST, UNFLINCHING. 'CONSTANTINE'.
FIRST 1. A1, 1ST, NO 1. ALPHA, BEFORE(HAND).
 EARLIEST, FOREMOST, FORMER (of two), LEADING,
 PRIME, PRIMUS, TOP, WINNER. GOLD MEDALLIST.
 2. Use first letters of word(s) indicated, e.g. **First-aid man** =
 AM; **First of all prehensiles everywhere** (3) = APE. 3. Put letter or
 word in front, e.g. **Try at first to give evidence** (6) = AT*TEST.
~ **BORN** B. CAIN. ELDEST [Herod].
~ **CLASS** C. A1. KINDERGARTEN, NURSERY SCHOOL
 (crypt).
~ **FALLER** F. *ADAM*.
~ **ISSUE** 1. CAIN. ELDEST.
~ **LADY** L. EVE. PRESIDENT'S WIFE (US). *PANDORA*.
~ **OFFENDER** EVE.
~ **OF MONTH** M. J, JAN, JANI; F, FEB, FEBI etc.
~ **PERSON** P. *ADAM*. I, WE.
FISH 1. LOOK FOR (compliment). JOIN/MEND A SPAR
 (naut). 2. *Constellation* (Pisces); (12th) sign of *Zodiac*.
 3. ANGLE, CATCH; TRAWL, TROLL. COLD-BLOODED
 MARINE ANIMAL [hauriant, naiant (herald)]; BOMBAY
 DUCK; **assembly** = school, shoal; **offspring** = fry; **types:**

2-letters

AI	*ID*

3-letters

AYU	DAR	GAR	*RAY*
BIB	*DOG*	GED	TAI
COD	EEL	IDE	
DAB	EFY	(ORC)	

4-letters

AMIA	*BASS*	BIRT	BLAY

BLEY	DACE	LING	RUDD
BRET	DORY	LIPP	*RUFF*
BRIT	ESOX	LOMP	SCAT
BURT	FAAP	LUCE	SCUP
BUTT	GEDD	LUMP	*SEER*
CARP	GOBY	OPAH	SHAD
CHAD	HAKE	(ORCA)	SILD
CHAR	HIND	ORFE	*SOLE*
CHUB	HUSS	PARR	TOPE
CLAM	KELT	*PIKE*	TUNA
CUSK	KETA	*POUT*	TUSK

5-letters

ABLEN	DANIO	MYXON	SNOEK
ABLET	DOREE	*PERCH*	SNOOK
ALLIS	DORSE	POGGE	SOLEN
ALOSE	ELOPS	PORGY	SPRAG
ANGEL	ELVER	PRAWN	SPRAT
ASKER	FLECK	PRILL	SPROD
BANNY	GIBEL	QUARL	SQUID
BASSE	GUPPY	ROACH	SUDAK
BERYX	JULIS	ROKER	SWORD
BINNY	KNOUD	SARDA	TENCH
BLEAK	KRILL	SAURY	TOGUE
BLECK	LOACH	SCROD	TORSK
BONGO	LOCHE	SEPIA	TROUT
(BOOPS)	LOGGE	SEWEN	TUNNY
BREAM	LYTHE	SEWIN	TWAIT
BRILL	MANTA	*SHARK* (q.v.)	UMBRE
CAPON	MARAY	*SKATE*	(*WHALE*)
CHARR	MORAY	SKEET	WITCH
CISCO	MUGIL	*SMELT*	
CNIDA	MURAY	SMOLT	
COLEY	MURRY	SMOUT	

6-letters

ACEDIA	BELONE	BRAIZE	CARVEL
ALEVIN	BELUGA	BRASSE	CEPOLA
ALLICE	BLENNY	BUCKIE	CLIONE
ANABAS	BONITO	BURBOT	CLUPEA
BAGGIT	BOUNCE	CAPLIN	COCKLE
BARBEL	BOWFIN	CARANX	CONGER

CUTTLE	LOLIGO	ROBALO	SEA-RAT
CYPRIS	LOUVAR	ROCCUS	SEPHEN
DENTEX	MAHSIR	ROCHET	SHANNY
DERBIO	MARGOT	ROMERO	SHIPOV
DIODON	MATIES	RUFFIN	SHRIMP
DIPNOI	MEAKER	SABALO	SILURE
DOCTOR	*MEDUSA*	SADINA	SNACOT
DORADO	MENNAD	SAITHE	SOOSOO
(DUGONG)	MILTER	*SALMON*	*SUCKER*
ELLECK	MINNOW	SALTIE	TAMBOR
FINNAN	MORGAY	SAMLET	TARPON
FINNER	MULLET	SARDEL	TARPUM
FINNOC	MUSSEL	SARGUS	TAUTOG
FLYING ~	MYXINE	SARSIA	TINKER
GARDON	(NARWAL)	SAUGER	TITLER
GERVIE	NERITE	SAUREL	TOMCOD
GILPIN	OSTREA	SAURUS	TOMPOT
GORAMY	*OYSTER*	SAYSAY	TRITON
GRILSE	PARTAN	SCARUS	TRYGON
GROPER	PECTEN	SEA-BAT	TURBOT
GUNNEL	PETREL	SEA-BUN	(TURTLE)
GURNET	PHINOC	SEA-CAT	TWAITE
HALION	PHOLAS	SEA-COW	URCHIN
HAUTIN	PLAICE	SEA-DOG	(WALRUS)
HILSAH	PLAISE	SEA-EEL	WAPPER
INKBAG	POLLAN	SEA-EGG	WEEVER
INKSAC	PORGIE	SEA-FOX	WINKLE
IVIGAR	POULPE	SEA-HOG	WRASSE
KIPPER	PUFFER	SEA-ORB	ZANDER
LAITHE	RED-EYE	SEA-OWL	ZINGLE
LAUNCE	REMORA	SEA-PAD	
LIMPET	RIGGLE	SEA-PIG	

7-letters

ACALEPH	BARNAGH	CALAMAR	CROAKER
ACTINIA	BERGYLT	CAPELIN	CROWGER
ALE-WIFE	BIVALVE	CATFISH	CRUCIAN
ANCHOVY	BLOATER	(CETACEA)	CRUSIAN
ANEMONE	BOCKING	CICHLID	(DOLPHIN)
ANODONT	BONETTA	CIDARIS	ECHINUS
ASCIDIA	BRASSIE	CODFISH	ESCOLAR
ASTERID	BRIABOT	CODLING	ETHERIA

FINBACK	MAHSEER	RED-DRUM	SEA-WOLF
FINFISH	(MANATEE)	RED-FISH	SELACHE
FINNACK	MERLING	RHYTINA	SERIOLA
FINNOCK	MOLLUSC	RIPSACK	SEVRUGA
GALUCUS	MONODON	RONCHIL	SHADINE
GARFISH	MOONEYE	RONQUIL	SHALLOW
GARPIKE	MORRHUA	(RORQUAL)	SILLAGO
GARVOCK	MUDFISH	ROTCHET	SILURUS
GIRROCK	(NARWHAL)	SAND-DAB	*SKIPPER*
GLADIUS	NAUTILI	SAND-EEL	SKULPIN
GOSNICK	OARFISH	SARDINE	SNAPPER
GOURAMI	OCTOPUS	SARGINA	SNEDDEN
GOURNET	OPHIURA	SAWFISH	SOCKEYE
(GRAMPUS)	PATELLA	SCALLOP	SPUR-DOG
GROUPER	*PEGASUS*	SCHELLY	STERLET
GRUNDEL	PELAMID	SCOLLOP	SUNFISH
GRUNTER	PENFISH	SCOMBER	TORPEDO
GUDGEON	PETEREL	SEA-BASS	TREPANG
GURNARD	PIDDOCK	SEA-COCK	TRIGGER ~
GWINIAD	PILTOCK	SEA-DACE	TUBFISH
HADDOCK	PINCHER	SEA-FISH	VENDACE
HAGFISH	PIN-FISH	SEA-LILY	VESTLET
HALIBUT	POLLACK	SEA-LUCE	WHIP-RAY
HERLING	POLLOCK	SEA-MINK	WHITING
HERRING	POLYPUS	SEA-PERT	XIPHIAS
ICE FISH	POLYZOA	SEA-PIKE	ZIPHIAS
KEELING	POMFRET	SEA-ROSE	ZYGAENA
LAMPERN	QUAHAUG	SEA-RUFF	
LAMPREY	QUINNAT	SEA-SLUG	
LOBSTER	RED-BASS	SEA-WIFE	

8-letters

ACALEPHA	COALFISH	GILT-HEAD
ACEPHALA	CRAYFISH	GOLDFISH
ALBACORE	DRAGONET	GRAYLING
BILLFISH	EAR-SHELL	(HUMPBACK)
BLUEFISH	ESCALLOP	LUMPFISH
BOARFISH	(FIN-WHALE)	LUNGFISH
BRISLING	FLATFISH	MACKEREL
BUMMALOE	*FLOUNDER*	MONKFISH
(CACHALOT)	FORKTAIL	NAUTILUS
(CETACEAN)	FROGFISH	PICKEREL

PILCHARD   SEA-DEVIL   SOLASTER
(PORPOISE) SEA-PERCH   SPARLING
ROCKFISH   SEA-ROBIN   STARFISH
SAIL-FISH   SEA-SHARK   STINGRAY
SALMONET   SEA-SNAIL   STURGEON
SANDFISH   SEA-SQUID   THRASHER
SEA-ADDER   SEA-TENCH   UNIVALVE
SEA-BREAM   SEA-TROUT   ZOANTHUS

9+ letters

AMBERJACK   GUITAR FISH
ANGELFISH   HAMMERHEAD
ANGELSHARK   HIPPOCAMPUS
ANGLERFISH   JELLYFISH
ARCHERFISH   NEEDLEFISH
BALLOON FISH   PADDLEFISH
BARRACUDA   PARROTFISH
BARRAMUNDI   PERIWINKLE
BASKING SHARK   PILOT FISH
BLACKFISH   PORBEAGLE
BLUE SHARK   *RAINBOW* TROUT
BROWN TROUT   SANDHOPPER
BULLTROUT   SPEARFISH
BUTTERFISH   SPOONBILL
CANDLEFISH   STARGAZER
CARPSUCKER   STICKLEBACK
COELACANTH   STOCKFISH
CONGER EEL   STONEFISH
CUTTLEFISH   SUCKERFISH
DEMOISELLE   SWORDFISH
DEVILFISH   THRESHER *SHARK*
DOLLY VARDEN   TIGER *SHARK*
DRAGONFISH   TRIGGER FISH
FINGERLING   WHITEFISH
FLUTEMOUTH   WOBBEGONG
FLYING-FISH   *ZEBRA* SHARK
GLOBE FISH

FISHERMAN ANCHOR. BEND, *KNOT*. *BOAT*. EVANGELIST (fig, Matt iv, 19). ANGLER, CATCHER, TRAWLER(MAN), TROLLER; BANKER (crypt); **celeb**: ANDREW; PETER, Simon; JAMES (s of Zebedee); JOHN; all *apostles* of

Jesus; Isaak WALTON (The Compleat Angler). GANNET,
KINGFISHER (birds).

FIT HALE, IN FORM, *SOUND*, *WELL*. SEIZURE, SPASM.
CORRESPOND, FILL UP, MATCH, RIGHT SIZE. ADAPT,
COMPETENT, PROPER, RIGHT, SUITED. EQUIP,
MEASURE, TRY ON (clothes).

FIVE 1. See *number*. PENTAD, V. BLUE BALL (snooker).
FAMOUS ~. [*Holmes case*]. 2. *Symbols* at your door *(song)*;
gold *rings* (*Christmas* song). **Pl** = GAME.

~ **CLASSIC ORDERS** COMPOSITE, CORINTHIAN, DORIC,
IONIC, TUSCAN.

500 See *number*. D.

£500 DL, LD, MONKEY.

FIVE TOWNS BURSLEM, FENTON, HANLEY (Etruria;
Wedgwood), LONGTON, STOKE, TUNSTALL (Arnold
Bennett's *potteries*).

FIX DILEMMA, QUANDARY. ARRANGE, *FIDDLE*,
JOIN. BOLT, FASTEN, *NAIL, SCREW*, SECURE. *DRUG*,
INJECTION, SHOT. ESTABLISH POSITION (naut);
DETERMINE, SPECIFY.

FLAG BUNTING, ENSIGN, FLIER, PENNANT, STANDARD.
PIN. *IRIS*, PLANT. DROOP, FADE, FAIL, FALTER.
(PAVING) STONE. QUILL FEATHER.

FLAK AA. AAA, TRIPLE A. CRITICISM.

FLAPPER YOUNG THING. FIN, FLIPPER. BIRD.
PANICKER.

FLAT APARTMENT, BASEMENT, PENTHOUSE,
TENEMENT. EVEN, LEVEL, SMOOTH. RUN DOWN,
UNCHARGED (elect). PUNCTURE (US).

FLATTER BUTTER UP, FAWN, PRAISE. BECOME, SUIT.
MORE EVEN, SMOOTHER, IRONER, LAUNDRYMAID
(crypt).

FLEET *FAST*, QUICK, RAPID. RN, SHIPS, USN, TASK
FORCE. *GAOL*. *ISLAND, RIVER*. [~ Street].

FLIER *FLAG*. AVIATOR, PILOT. *BIRD*. *DAEDALUS,
ICARUS*.

FLIGHT 1. STAIRS, *STEPS*. ARROW. ESCAPE, EVASION.
FLYING, TRAJECTORY. FLOCK. VOLLEY. 2. *Assembly*
(ducks).

FLIGHTLESS BIRDS AEPYORNIS (ex), ALDABRAN *RAIL*,
ASTERYN, CASSOWARY, *CHICKEN*, DINORNIS (ex),
DODO (ex), ELEPHANT BIRD, EMU, GALAPAGOS

CORMORANT, GALLITO, GREAT AUK (ex), KAGU,
KAKAPO, KIWI, MOA (ex), MOORUK, NANDOO,
OSTRICH, PENGUIN, PITTA, RHEA, ROADRUNNER,
SOLITAIRE PIGEON, STEAMER DUCK, STEPHEN
ISLAND WREN, TAKAHE, TINAMON, TUKAPEH,
TURKEY.

FLOCK 1. WOOL, TUFT. CONGREGATION, *FOLD*. TROOP.
2. *Assembly* (*geese, sheep*).

FLORA 1. *FLOWERS, PLANTS* [fauna]. ~ MACDONALD
[Bonnie Prince Charlie]. 2. Rom *goddess* of *FLOWERS* (**Gk** =
CHLORIS). 3. A minor *PLANET*.

FLORENCE *NIGHTINGALE*. FIRENZE (old *capital* city of Italy
in Tuscany).

FLOUNDERING *Anag.* WALLOWING. FISHING (crypt).

FLOW CIRCULATE, GLIDE, MOVE(MENT) [fluent,
smoothly]. GUSH, *RUN*, SPRING, WELL UP. STREAM.
RISE (tide); **comp** = *ebb*. UNDULATE (dress, figure).
BELLY, CAMBER, DRAFT (sails).

FLOWER 1. CHOICE, CREAM, ESSENCE, PICK. CURRENT,
RIVER (q.v.), SPRING, TIDE, WELL (all crypt). BLOOD
(crypt). ICHOR (crypt). 2. ANNUAL, *BLOOMER*,
PERENNIAL. **Pl** = BOUQUET, BUNCH, GARLAND,
LEI, NOSEGAY, SPRAY; **goddess: Gk** = CHLORIS, **Rom** =
FLORA; *anniversary* (4th). [Ikebana (*Jap*)]. **Types:**

3-letters

LIS (herald)   MAY

4-letters

ARUM	*FLAG*	*LILY*	*ROSE*
DISA	FLAX	MUSK	
FAAM	*IRIS*	*PINK*	

5-letters

ASPIC	DILLY	OXLIP	TULIP
ASTER	GOWAN	PANSY	VINCA
BRIAR	LILAC	PEONY	YUCCA
BROOM	LOTUS	PHLOX	YULAN
CALLA	LUPIN	POPPY	
DAISY	OX-EYE	*STOCK*	

6-letters

ADONIS	CROCUS	MOUTAN	SQUILL
AZALEA	CYPHEL	MUGGET	TAGETE
BELLIS	DAHLIA	NERINE	THRIFT
BIZARD	FUNKIA	NERIUM	VIOLET
BOODLE	JASMIN	NUPHAR	YARROW
CALTHA	KERRIA	ORCHID	ZINNIA
CAMASS	KOWHAI	ROSULA	
CISTUS	MARIET	SCILLA	
CLOVER	MIMOSA	SHASTA	

7-letters

ACONITE	FREESIA	NELUMBO	SYRINGA
ALTHAEA	FUCHSIA	NIGELLA	TEA-ROSE
ANEMONE	GLADWYN	PETUNIA	TRIPOLY
BANKSIA	GODETIA	PICOTEE	TRITOMA
BEGONIA	HONESTY	PRIMULA	VANILLA
CAMPION	JASMINE	RAMBLER	VERBENA
COWSLIP	JONQUIL	RAMPION	
CUP-ROSE	KINGCUP	SERINGA	
DOG-ROSE	LOBELIA	SHIRLEY	

8-letters

AGRIMONY	GERANIUM	MAGNOLIA
AMARANTH	GILLENIA	MARIGOLD
ASPHODEL	GIRASOLE	MYOSOTIS
AURICULA	GLOXINIA	NOISETTE
BLUEBELL	GOLD-LILY	OLEANDER
BUDDLEIA	HAREBELL	PLUMBAGO
CAMELLIA	HAWTHORN	PRIMROSE
CLEMATIS	HIBISCUS	SNOWDROP
CYCLAMEN	HOTTONIA	SWEET-PEA
DAFFODIL	HYACINTH	TUBEROSE
DIANTHUS	JAPONICA	TURNSOLE
DOG-BRIER	LARKSPUR	WISTARIA
FOXGLOVE	LAVENDER	WOODBINE
GARDENIA	LENT-LILY	

9-letters

BUSY LIZZY	CANDYTUFT	COLUMBINE
BUTTERCUP	CARNATION	DANDELION
CAMPANULA	CINERARIA	EDELWEISS

EGLANTINE   GOLDENROD   SPEEDWELL
FORSYTHIA   HYDRANGEA   SUNFLOWER
GLADIOLUS   *NARCISSUS*

10+ letters

ANTIRRHINUM   LOVE IN A MIST
BUSY LIZZIE   MARGUERITE
CANTERBURY   MORNING GLORY
  BELL   NASTURTIUM
CHRYSANTHEMUM   PERIWINKLE
CORNFLOWER   POINSETTIA
DELPHINIUM   RED HOT POKER
FORGET-ME-NOT   RHODODENDRON
FRANGIPANI   SNAPDRAGON
GUERNSEY LILY   STEPHANOTIS
GYPSOPHILA   SWEET WILLIAM
HONEYSUCKLE   WALLFLOWER
LADY'S MANTLE

3. Alternative names:

Aaron's Rod   Great Mullein
Acanthus   Bear's Breeches,
Adam's Needle   Spanish Bayonet
Adder's Tongue   Trout Lily (US)
Aesculus   Horse Chestnut
Alkanet   Bugloss
Alpine Auricula   Primula
Amaryllis   Belladonna Lily
Anemone   Paschal Flower, Windflower
Antirrhinum   Snapdragon
Apple Blossom   Hoo (azalea)
Autumn Crocus   Meadow Saffron
Autumn Gentian   Felwort
Avrons   Cloudberry

Bacon and Eggs   Bird's-Foot Trefoil, Lotus
Bald Money   Spignel (parsley)
Balloon Flower   Chinese Bellflower
Balm of Gilead   Ontario Poplar
Bear's Breeches   Acanthus
Bear's Foot   Green Hellebore (buttercup)

Belladonna	Deadly Nightshade, Dwale
Belladonna Lily	Amaryllis
Bells of Ireland	Shell Flower
Bergamot	Oswego Tea
Bilberry	Whortleberry (heather)
Bird's-Foot Trefoil	Bacon and Eggs, Lotus
Bishopweed	Goutweed, Herb Gerard (parsley)
Bistort	Knotweed, Snakeweed
Biting Stonecrop	Wall-Pepper (sedum)
Black Alder	Winterberry (holly)
Black Medick	Nonsuch
Bleeding Heart	Dutchman's Breeches
Bluebottle	Cornflower (daisy)
Bog Myrtle	Sweet Gale
Brandy Bottle	Yellow Waterlily
Brooklime	Hebe, Speedwell, Veronica
Bugloss	Alkanet
Burning Bush	Dittany
Busy Lizzie	Impatiens, Touch-Me-Not, Yellow Balsam
Buttercup	Crowfoot (kingcup)
Cannoch	Cotton Grass (sedge)
Cape Gooseberry	Chinese Lantern
Cat's-Foot	Mountain Everlasting
Cat's-Tail	Timothy
Cherry Pie	Heliotrope
Chinese Bellflower	Balloon Flower
Chinese Kidney Bean	Wisteria
Chinese Lantern	Cape Gooseberry
Clary	Wild Sage
Cleavers	Goosegrass
Clematis	Old Man's Beard, Traveller's Joy
Cloudberry	Avrons
Codlins-and-Cream	Hairy Willow Herb
Cornflower	Bluebottle (daisy)
Corn Salad	Lamb's-Lettuce
Cotton Grass	Cannoch (sedge)
Couch Grass	Twitch (and see *GRASS*)
Cowberry	Mountain Cranberry, Red Whortleberry

Cow Parsley	Wild Chervil
Cow Parsnip	Hogweed (parsley)
Cowslip	Paigle
Crowfoot	Buttercup
Cuckoo Flower	Lady's Smock
Cuckoo Pint	Jack-in-the-Pulpit, Lords-and-Ladies
Daffodil	Lent Lily, Narcissus
Danewort	Dwarf Elder (honeysuckle)
Deadly Nightshade	Belladonna, Dwale
Delphinium	Larkspur
Digitalis	Foxglove
Dittany	Burning Bush
Dutchman's Breeches	Bleeding Heart
Dwale	Deadly Nightshade, Belladonna
Dwarf Elder	Danewort (honeysuckle)
Earthnut	Pignut (parsley)
Erica	Heather, Ling
Eucalyptus	Gum Tree, Ironbark Tree
Fat Hen	White Goosefoot
Felwort	Autumn Gentian
Feverwort	Thorough-wort
Fireweed	French Willow, Oleander, Rosebay
Flamingo Plant	Painter's Palette
Forget-Me-Not	Myosotis
Foxglove	Digitalis
French Willow	Fireweed, Oleander, Rosebay
Garlic Mustard	Jack-by-the-Hedge, Sauce-Alone
Gean	Mazzard
Gillyflower	Stock, Wallflower
Glasswort	Marsh Samphire
Globe Tulip	Mariposa Lily
Goat's Beard	Jack-Go-To-Bed-at-Noon (daisy)
Goat Willow	Sallow
Goosegrass	Cleavers
Goutweed	Bishopweed, Herb Gerard (parsley)

Granny's Bonnet	True Columbine
Great Mullein	Bear's-Foot (buttercup)
Great Plantain	Waybread
Green Hellebore	Bear's-Foot (buttercup)
Guelder Rose	Water Elder
Guimauve	Marshmallow
Guinea Flower	Snake's-Head Fritillary
Gum Tree	Eucalyptus, Ironbark Tree
Hairy Willow Herb	Codlins-and-Cream
Hardheads	Knapweed (daisy)
Hare's-Ear	Thorow Wax (parsley)
Hawthorn	May, Whitethorn
Heartsease	Wild Pansy
Heather	Erica, Ling (and see Bilberry)
Hebe	Brooklime, Speedwell, Veronica
Hedera	Helix, Ivy
Heliotrope	Cherry Pie
Helix	Hedera, Ivy
Herb Bennet	Wood Avens
Herb Gerard	Bishopweed, Goutweed (parsley)
Hogweed	Cow Parsnip (parsley)
Honesty	Lunaria
Honeysuckle	Woodbine
Hoo	Apple Blossom (azalea)
Horse Chestnut	Aesculus
Impatiens	Busy Lizzie, Touch-Me-Not, Yellow Balsam
Incense	Red Cedar
Ironbark Tree	Eucalyptus, Gum Tree
Ivy	Hedera, Helix
Jack-by-the-Hedge	Garlic Mustard, Sauce Alone
Jack-Go-to-Bed-at-Noon	Goat's Beard
Jack-in-the-Pulpit	Cuckoo Pint, Lords-and-Ladies (arum)
Jew's Mallow	Kerria
Kerria	Jew's Mallow
Kidney Vetch	Lady's Fingers
Kingcup	Marsh Marigold (buttercup)

Knapweed	Hardheads (daisy)
Knotweed	Bistort, Snakeweed
Lady's Fingers	Kidney Vetch
Lady's Smock	Cuckoo Flower
Lamb's Lettuce	Cornflower
Larkspur	Delphinium
Lent Lily	Daffodil, Narcissus
Lesser Celandine	Pilewort (buttercup)
Lily Tree	Yulan
Ling	Erica, Heather
Livelong	Orpine (sedum)
Lobster Claw	Parrot's Bill
Lodden Lily	Summer Snowflake
London Pride	Nancy Pretty, St Patrick's Cabbage
Lords-and-Ladies	Cuckoo Pint, Jack-in-the-Pulpit (arum)
Love-in-a-Mist	Nigella
Love-Lies-Bleeding	Tassel Flower
Lunaria	Honesty
Mariposa Lily	Globe Tulip
Marsh Lousewort	Red Rattle
Marshmallow	Guimauve
Marsh Marigold	King-Cup (buttercup)
Marsh Samphire	Glasswort
Martagon	Turk's Cap Lily
May	Hawthorn, Whitethorn
Mazzard	Gean
Meadow Saffron	Autumn Crocus
Milfoil	Yarrow (daisy)
Mithridate Mustard	Pennycress
Monkey Puzzle	Chilean Pine
Mountain Ash	Rowan
Mountain Cranberry	Cowberry, Red Whortleberry
Mountain Everlasting	Cat's-Foot
Myosotis	Forget-Me-Not
Nancy Pretty	London Pride, St Patrick's Cabbage
Narcissus	Daffodil, Lent Lily
Navelwort	Pennywort

Nicotiana	Tobacco Plant
Nigella	Love-in-a-Mist
Nonsuch	Black Medick
Old Man's Beard	Traveller's Joy (clematis)
Old Poet	Pheasant Eye (narcissus)
Oleander	Fireweed, French Willow, Rosebay
Ontario Poplar	Balm of Gilead
Orpine	Livelong (sedum)
Oswego Tea	Bergamot
Oyster Plant	Sea Lungwort
Paigle	Cowslip
Painter's Palette	Flamingo Plant
Parrot's Bill	Lobster Claw
Paschal Flower	Anemone, Windflower
Pennycress	Mithridate Mustard
Pennywort	Navelwort
Pepperwort	Smith's Cress
Pignut	Earthnut (parsley)
Pilewort	Lesser Celandine (buttercup)
Pincushion Flower	Sweet Scabious
Poor-Man's-Weather-Glass	Scarlet Pimpernel
Ramsons	Wild Garlic
Red Cedar	Incense
Red Rattle	Marsh Lousewort
Red Whortleberry	Cowberry, Mountain Cranberry
Rosebay	Fireweed, French Willow, Oleander
Rose Moss	Sun Plant
Rowan	Mountain Ash
St Patrick's Cabbage	London Pride, Nancy Pretty
Sallow	Goat Willow
Sauce Alone	Garlic Mustard, Jack-by-the-Hedge
Scarlet Pimpernel	Poor-Man's-Weather-Glass
Sea Daisy	Thrift
Sea Lungwort	Oyster Plant

Shell Flower	Bells of Ireland
Smith's Cress	Pepperwort
Snake's-Head Fritillary	Guinea Flower
Snakeweed	Bistort, Knotweed
Snapdragon	Antirrhinum
Spanish Bayonet	Adam's Needle
Speedwell	Brooklime, Hebe, Veronica
Spignel	Bald Money (parsley)
Stinkweed	Wall Mustard
Stock	Gillyflower
Stonecrop	Wall Pepper (sedum)
Summer Snowflake	Lodden Lily
Sun Plant	Rose Moss
Sweet Gale	Bog Myrtle
Sweet Scabious	Pincushion Flower
Tassel Flower	Love-Lies-Bleeding
Thorough-Wort	Feverwort
Thorow-Wax	Hare's-Ear (parsley)
Thrift	Sea Daisy
Timothy	Cat's-Tail
Tobacco Plant	Nicotiana
Touch-Me-Not	Busy Lizzie, Impatiens, Yellow Balsam
Traveller's Joy	Old Man's Beard (clematis)
Trout Lily (US)	Adder's Tongue
True Columbine	Granny's Bonnet
Turk's Cap Lily	Martagon
Twitch	Couch Grass (see *GRASS*)
Veronica	Brooklime, Hebe, Speedwell
Wall Barley	Waybent
Wallflower	Gillyflower
Wall Mustard	Stinkweed
Wall Pepper	Biting Stonecrop (sedum)
Water Elder	Guelder Rose
Waybent	Wall Barley
Waybread	Great Plantain
White Goosefoot	Fat Hen
Whitethorn	Hawthorn, May

Whortleberry	Bilberry (heather)
Wild Chervil	Cow Parsley
Wild Garlic	Ramsons
Wild Pansy	Heartsease
Wild Sage	Clary
Windflower	Anemone, Paschal Flower
Winter Cress	Yellow Rocket
Wistaria	Chinese Kidney Bean
Wood Avens	Herb Bennet
Woodbine	Honeysuckle
Yarrow	Milfoil (daisy)
Yellow Balsam	Busy Lizzie, Impatiens, Touch-Me-Not
Yellow Rocket	Winter Cress
Yellow Waterlily	Brandy Bottle
Yulan	Lily Tree

FLUORINE F (*chem*) [halogen].

FLUSH BLUSH, *COLOUR*, REDDEN. POKER HAND; SUITED (crypt). RICH, WELL OFF. PUT UP (game bird). *Assembly* (mallards). *DOG* (celeb).

FLUTE 1. GLASS. FLAGEOLET, *INSTRUMENT* (mus). GROOVE. 2. *Shak* char (*bellows maker*, MND).

FLUTER PHIL; INSTRUMENTALIST, WHISTLER. REBATE PLANE.

FLY DESERT, FLEE, RUN AWAY, TURN TAIL. AVIATE, *PILOT*; SCRAMBLE (code word). *INSECT*. AWARE, KNOWING. *BOAT*. BUTTON. *CARRIAGE*. *RIVER*.

FLYING BOMB BUZZBOMB, DOODLEBUG, DIVER (code name), *ROCKET*, VI.

FLYING FORTRESS *AIRCRAFT* (bomber), B17, BXVII, BOEING: CASTLE IN THE AIR (crypt).

FO FOLIO. FOREIGN OFFICE. BACK OF (crypt, e.g. **Back of Whitehall** = FO).

FOC ADMIRAL, FLAG OFFICER COMMANDING.

FOG BRUME, FRET, HAZE, MIST [FIDO]. CLOUD (photo). BEWILDER, OBFUSCATE, PERPLEX. AFTERMATH, LONG WINTER *GRASS*.

FOLD (s/l foaled). ENCLOSE, *PEN*, POUND. CHURCH, CONGREGATION, *FLOCK*. BEND, *CONCERTINA*, *DOUBLE*. CLASP, EMBRACE, ENVELOP, *WIND*.

FOLLOWER 1. *DISCIPLE*, FAN, SUPPORTER; ADHERENT. DOGGER, PURSUER, TAIL(ER), TRACKER; SHADOW. 2. Next letter in alphabet, e.g. **A follower** = B; **Paul's last follower** = M.

FOOD BOARD, COMMONS, EDIBLES, FARE, GRUB, KEEP, MEALS, MESS, NOURISHMENT, NUTRIMENT, PROVISIONS, RATIONS, SCOFF, *TABLE*, VICTUALS. **Comp** = *drink*.

FOOL ASS, BUFFOON, CLOT, DUPE, GOOSE, IDIOT, JUGGINS, TWERP, TWIT (**opp** = *expert*). *CLOWN* (q.v. for **celeb**), *JESTER* (q.v. for **celeb**). 0 (*tarot*). DECEIVE. PLAY, TINKER. FRUIT CRUSH, PUDDING, SWEET. TRINCULO (Tempest, *Shak*).

FOOT 1. DISTANCE, *MEASURE*, 12 INCHES. *DANCE*, PACE, *STEP*, TREAD. BASE, BOTTOM, PEDESTAL, ROOT. LIMB, MEMBER (*bone*). LEGEND (crypt). SUPPORT, UNDERSTANDING (crypt). 2. Stress on syllable in metre of a verse: AMPHIBRACH (·—·), ANAPEST (··—), CHORIAMB (—··—), DACTYL (—··), IAMBUS (·—), MOLUSSUS (— — —), PYRRHIC (··), SPONDEE (— —), TRIBRACH (···), TROCHEE (—·).

FOOTBALL BALL GAME; AMERICAN ~, ASSOCIATION ~, AUS RULES ~, RUGBY ~, RUGGER, SOCCER [FA, FIFA, UEFA, World Cup (Rimet Trophy); League, Rugby ~]. **Celeb teams (US):**

Home	Name
Atlanta	FALCONS
Baltimore	*COLTS*
Buffalo	*BILLS*
Chicago	*BEARS*
Cincinnati	BENGALS
Cleveland	*BROWNS*
Dallas	*COWBOYS*
Denver	BRONCOS
Detroit	*LIONS*
Green Bay	PACKERS
Houston	*OILERS*
Kansas City	CHIEFS
Los Angeles	RAIDERS
Los Angeles	*RAMS*
Miami	DOLPHINS

Minnesota	VIKINGS
New England	PATRIOTS
New Orleans	*SAINTS*
New York	GIANTS
New York	JETS
Philadelphia	*EAGLES*
Pittsburgh	STEELERS
St Louis	CARDINALS
San Diego	CHARGERS
San Francisco	49-ERS
Seattle	SEAHAWKS
Washington	*REDSKINS*

competition: Superbowl; **venue**: Rose Bowl

Celebrated teams (UK):

Team	Nickname	Ground
Aberdeen	*Dons*	Pittodrie Park
Arsenal	*Gunners*	Highbury
Bournemouth	Cherries	Dean Court
Brighton	Seagulls	Goldstone
Bristol City	*Robins*	Ashton Gate
Cardiff City	Bluebirds	Ninian Park
Chelsea	*Pensioners*	Stamford Bridge
Coventry City	Sky Blues	Highfield Park
Crystal Palace	Glaziers	Selhurst Park
Derby County	*Rams*	Baseball Ground
England		Wembley
Everton	Toffees	Goodison Park
Glasgow Rangers	Light Blues	Ibrox Park
Huddersfield	*Terriers*	Leeds Road
Hull City	*Tigers*	Boothferry Park
Ireland		Lansdowne Road
Liverpool	*Reds*	Anfield
Manchester United	Red Devils	Old Trafford
Mansfield Town	*Stags*	Field Mill
Middlesbrough	Boro'	Ayresome Park
Northampton	*Cobblers*	County Ground
Norwich	Canaries	Carrow Road
Notts County	*Magpies*	Meadow Lane
Portsmouth	Pompey	Fratton Park

Scotland		Hampden Park
Sheffield Wednesday	*Owls*	Hillsborough
Southampton	*Saints*	The Dell
Torquay	*Gulls*	Plainmoor
Tottenham Hotspur	*Spurs*	White Hart Lane
Wales		Cardiff Arms Park
West Ham United	*Hammers*	Upton Park
Wolverhampton Wanderers	*Wolves*	Molineux

FOOTBALLER PLAYER; BACK, CENTRE-BACK, FORWARD, FULL-BACK, GOALIE, GOALKEEPER, HALF-BACK, INSIDE, KEEPER, OUTSIDE, STRIKER, SWEEPER, WINGER.
FOOTMAN BUTLER, *WAITER*. GI, INFANTRY, PBI (crypt). HIKER, PACER, RAMBLER, RUNNER, WALKER. TRIVET. *BUTTERFLY*. CHIROPODIST (crypt).
FOOTWEAR BOOT, CLOG, GUMBOOT, GYMSHOE, MOCCASIN, MULE, PUMP, SABOT, SANDAL, *SHOE*, SLIPPER, SOCK, STOCKING, WELLINGTON BOOT.
FOR (s/l *fore, four*). FAVOURING, IN FAVOUR, PRO (**opp** = *con*). BECAUSE.
FORBIDDEN BANNED, BARRED, EXCLUDED, PREVENTED, TABOO, TABU.
FORCE COERCE, CRAM, DRIVE, LEVER, PRISE, PROPEL, PUSH, SHOVE. IMPOSE, *PRESS*. *POLICE*; TROOPS. EFFORT, IMPETUS, POWER, STRENGTH, VIOLENCE; DYNE, ERG (eng). COMPEL, RAVISH; CAPTURE, OVERPOWER. PRISON (*Dickens*, 2 Cities; Fr).
FORCED SEED HOTHOUSE PLANT. RAPE (crypt).
FORD WADE; CROSSING. CAR®, T. *GAOL*. *PRESIDENT* (US). Mistress ~ (Merry Wives, *Shak*).
FORE (s/l *for, four*). *BOW* (naut). FRONT. *CAVE* (golf).
FOREGROUND FRONT, NEAR PLAN. *GOLF COURSE* (crypt).
FOREIGN 1. ABROAD. STRANGE, UNCO (Sc). 2. Translate, e.g. **He's foreign** = IL (Fr), ER (Ger) etc.
~ **OFFICE** FO. BUREAU (crypt, Fr), AMT (crypt, Ger).
FOREST [football team]. TREES, WOODLAND; TAIGA (CIS) [**opp** = Savannah (tropics), Steppe (CIS), Tundra (Arctic), *desert, plain*]; **celeb (UK)**:

2-letters

AE (Sc)

3-letters

BIN (Sc)   MOY (Sc)   *NEW* (Eng)

4-letters

AMAT (Sc)   DEAN (Eng)   TOWY (Wal)   WYRE (Eng)
BERE (Eng)   PLYM (Eng)   WARK (Eng)

5-letters

ARDEN (Eng)   GAICK (Sc)   STRUY (Sc)
CRAIK (Sc)   ORKEL (Sc)
DREVA (Sc)   SALEN (Sc)

6-letters

ACHRAY (Sc)   EPPING (Eng)   OGMORE (Wal)
ATHOLL (Sc)   FINDON (Sc)   *QUEENS* (Sc)
ATTRIC (Sc)   LAGGAN (Sc)   RADNOR (Wal)
BORGIE (Sc)   LENNOX (Sc)   RHEOLA (Wal)
CLUNES (Sc)   LOSSIE (Sc)   SALCEY (Eng)
COULIN (Sc)   MIDMAR (Sc)
CULBIN (Sc)   MINARD (Sc)

7-letters

ARDROSS (Sc)   DEVILLA (Sc)   LYMINGE (Eng)
ASHDOWN (Eng)   EREDINE (Sc)   MAMLORN (Sc)
BENMORE (Sc)   FIUNARY (Sc)   MILBURN (Eng)
BOWLAND (Sc)   GLENGAP (Sc)   NEWTYLE (Sc)
BOWMONT (Sc)   GLEN LOY (Sc)   ROSARIE (Sc)
CARRICK (Sc)   HARWOOD (Eng)   SKIDDAW (Eng)
CHANGUE (Sc)   KIELDER (Eng)   TRAWDEN (Eng)
CRYCHAN (Wal)   LOCH ARD (Sc)   WAREHAM (Eng)
CULACHY (Sc)   LOCH ECK (Sc)   WINDSOR (Eng)

8-letters

ATTADALE (Sc)   CULLODEN (Sc)
BALMORAL (Sc)   CARDRONA (Sc)
BEINNEUN (Sc)   DELAMERE (Eng)
BEN DAMPH (Sc)   DUNDEUGH (Sc)
BOBLAINY (Sc)   DUNLOINN (Sc)
BORROBOL (Sc)   ERCHLESS (Sc)
BRAEMORE (Sc)   FEARNOCH (Sc)

GLENISLA (Sc)
HAREWOOD (Eng)
KERSHOPE (Eng)
KINFAUNS (Sc)
KNAPDALE (Sc)
LEITHOPE (Sc)
MORANGIE (Sc)
NEEDWOOD (Eng)
QUANTOCK (Eng)
RINGWOOD (Eng)

ROTHBURY (Eng)
ST GWYNNO (Wal)
SHERWOOD (Eng)
SHOTOVER (Eng)
TORRIDON (Sc)
TUNSTALL (Eng)
WAUCHOPE (Sc)
WYCHWOOD (Eng)
YAIR HILL (Sc)

9-letters

ABERNETHY (Sc)
ALICE HOLT (Eng)
BEDGEBURY (Eng)
BLAIRADAM (Sc)
CHARNWOOD (Eng)
CLOCAENOG (Wal)
CORLARACH (Sc)
EAST MONAR (Sc)
FASNAKYLE (Sc)
GLENCOICH (Sc)
GLENDEVON (Sc)
GLENDUROR (Sc)
GLENGARRY (Sc)
GLENLIVET (Sc)
GLENTRESS (Sc)
GLENTROOL (Sc)
GRISEDALE (Eng)
GUISACHAN (Sc)

INVERINEN (Sc)
INVERTAEL (Sc)
INVERWICK (Sc)
LAURISTON (Sc)
LEANACHAN (Sc)
LETTEREWE (Sc)
MONAUGHTY (Sc)
PARKHURST (IOW)
PITFICHIE (Sc)
PORTCLAIR (Sc)
REDESDALE (Eng)
SAVERNAKE (Eng)
SCOOTMORE (Sc)
SPEYMOUTH (Sc)
STRATHYRE (Sc)
TEINDLAND (Sc)
TENTSMUIR (Sc)

10+ letters

ACHAGLACHGACH
  (Sc)
APPLECROSS (Sc)
BALLOCHBUIE (Sc)
BARCALDINE (Sc)
BRIGHTSTONE (IOW)
CAIRN EDWARD (Sc)
CARRON VALLEY (Sc)
CAENNACROC (Sc)

CLASHINDARROCH (Sc)
COIGNAFEARN (Sc)
COIRRIEYAIRACK (Sc)
CORRIEHALLIE (Sc)
DAILNAMAIN (Sc)
DALBEATTIE (Sc)
DRUMTOCHTY (Sc)
DUNDREGGAN (Sc)
FETTERESSO (Sc)

FISHERFIELD (Sc)	PENNINGHAME (Sc)
GLAS FYNYDD (Wal)	RENDLESHAM (Eng)
GLENARTNEY (Sc)	RHIDORROCH (Sc)
GLENBRANTER (Sc)	ROCKINGHAM (Eng)
GLENCARRON (Sc)	ROSSENDALE (Eng)
GLENFESHIE (Sc)	ROWARDENNAN (Sc)
HAMSTERLEY (Eng)	ST LEONARDS (Eng)
INVERMONSTON (Sc)	STRATHCONON (Sc)
KILDERMOIRE (Sc)	STRATHDEARN (Sc)
KILMICHAEL (Sc)	STRATHLACHLAN (Sc)
MACCLESFIELD (Eng)	STRATHNAIRN (Sc)
MICHELDEVER (Eng)	TOLLOMUICK (Sc)
MONTREATHMONT (Sc)	WHITEHAUGH (Sc)

FOR EXAMPLE 1. EG, (FOR) INSTANCE, SAY. 2. Shows
word starting IM (I am), e.g. **Bristol for example** (6) = IM*PORT.
3. Answer describes word indicated, e.g. **I, for example,
accumulated wealth** (7) = CAPITAL.

FORFEND AVERT, KEEP OFF. F (crypt).

FORGER COPIER, COUNTERFEITER, FABRICATOR,
INVENTOR; COMPEYSON (Great Ex, *Dickens*), ERIC
HEBBORN, TOM KEATING, VAN MEEGEREN.
BLACKSMITH, *SMITH* (crypt). ADVANCER,
PROGRESSER (crypt).

FORGET 1. NEGLECT, OMIT: DISREGARD, SLIGHT. 2.
Omit letter(s) indicated, e.g. **Don't forget the duck** = D*NT.

FOR INSTANCE 1. EG, FOR EXAMPLE, SAY. 2. Shows word
starting IM (I am), e.g. **Rose, for instance** (7) = IM*PLANT.

FORM BENCH. CONDITION, *FIGURE*, SCHEDULE, *CLASS*.
CAST, MOULD, *PATTERN, SHAPE*. TRACK RECORD.
Habitation (hare).

FORMER 1. ERSTWHILE, *EX, LATE*, OLD. FIRST (of
two). CASTER, MOULDER, POTTER (crypt). PUPIL,
SCHOOLBOY/GIRL (crypt). 2. Indicates use of old-fashioned
word(s), e.g. **The former** (2) = YE; **was formerly** (4) = WERT.

FORM OF *Anag*.

FORTE (s/l *forty*). F, LOUD. SWORD BLADE, STRONG
POINT. RESTAURANT ®, SERVICE STATION ®.

FORTH (s/l *fourth*). INTO VIEW, OUT; FORWARD. *RIVER*
(Sc). *BRIDGE*.

FORTISSIMO FF, VERY LOUD; NOISY (**opp** = pianissimo,
piano).

FORTUNE 1. CHANCE, DESTINY, LUCK [*tarot*]. *THEATRE*.
PROSPERITY, RICHES, WEALTH; **comp** = fame. HAP,
HAPPEN, OCCUR. 2. **Goddesses: Gk** = TYCHE, **Rom** =
FORTUNA.
FORTY (s/l *forte*). See *number*. XL. *TOPS* (darts). L (crypt; life
begins at ~).
FORWARD ADVANCED, AHEAD, ON. PERT,
PRECOCIOUS. PROMOTE. CENTRE, INSIDE, OUTSIDE,
STRIKER (*football*, hockey). **Pl** = SCRUM (rugby).
FOUL (s/l *fowl*). CONTRAVENTION, ERROR, FAULT,
INFRINGEMENT. BAD, EVIL, LOATHSOME, STINKING.
FOUND DISCLOSED, DISCOVERED, REVEALED; **comp**
= lost. ESTABLISH, ORIGINATE, SET UP. *CAST*, FUSE,
MELT, MOULD.
FOUNDATION *AUC*, ESTABLISHMENT. BASE, GROUND,
PRINCIPLE. [corset]. **Pl** = BASE, UNDERPINNING (archit).
FOUNTAIN CASCADE, JET, SPRAY; **celeb**: AGANIPPE,
ALPHEUS, ARETHUSA, BIMINI, HIPPOCRENE (all Gk
myth); Mimir's ~ (Nor myth) [*nymph*]. **Pl** = *ABBEY*.
FOUR (s/l *for*, fore). 1. See *number*. IV, QUARTET, TETRAD.
BOUNDARY (*cricket*). BROWN BALL (snooker). TEAM
(horses, card players). POMPEY (*rh sl*). **Pl** = RACE (rowing).
GLOVES, SHOES (size). 2. *Gospel*-makers (*song*); calling birds
(*Christmas* song). [*Holmes* case].
~ **POINT** IVE, IVS etc (crypt). NEWS (crypt). SQUARE.
FOURTH (s/l *forth*). QUARTER, QUARTUS. TOP (mech gear).
F, HARMONIC, INTERVAL (mus). INDEPENDENCE
DAY (US).
~ **ESTATE** THE PRESS.
~ **MAN** SETH.
FOX DISSEMBLE, FOOL, OUTWIT. BROADSWORD. FUR.
AMERICAN INDIAN. QUADRUPED; FENNEC, *PUG*,
REYNARD, RUSSEL, VOLPONE (Ben Jonson), ZERDA;
comp = *hounds*; **assembly** = skulk; **habitation** = *earth*; **male** =
dog; **fem** = vixen; **offspring** = cub [cunning; uneatable (Wilde)].
Celeb: BASIL BRUSH (TV), BRER ~ (Uncle Remus,
Tar-baby; Harris), CHARLES JAMES ~ (polit), GEORGE ~
(*Quakers*).
FR FATHER. FRANCE, FRENCH [*patron saint*]. FRANCIUM
(*chem*). **Pl** = Fellow of the Royal Society; SAVANT.
FRANCISCAN *GREYFRIAR*; MENDICANT FRIAR;
BUNGIEBIRD. CAPUCHIN.

FRANK (s/l franc). 1. CANDID, *FREE*, OPEN, OVERT. CANCEL, STAMP. *BIRD. COIN. DIARIST.* 2. **Pl** = Free men of lower Rhine, who warred with the Romans and settled in Gaul under Clovis in A.D. 496.

FRATERNITY BROTHERHOOD, ASSOCIATION; **celeb**: BUFFALOES (RAOB), FREEMASONS, FRIENDS, ODDFELLOWS, PROBUS, QUAKERS, ROTARY, ROUND TABLE.

FREE FOR NOTHING, GRATIS, UNCHARGED. ENLARGE, LIBERATE, RID; LIBERAL, LOOSE (**opp** = *limited*); **comp** = *easy. FRANK*, OPEN. UNOCCUPIED, VACANT (**opp** = *engaged*). 'FRANCIS'.

FRENCH 1. F, FR. DRINK, VERMOUTH; **comp** = *gin.*
2. Translate, e.g. **A (or the) French ...** = UN/UNE or LA/LE/LES.

~ **MAN** M, MONS.

~ **ONE** UN, UNE.

~ **REVOLUTIONARY CALENDAR** Revised calendar of France, 1789. Months (with starting dates) were:

VENDEMIAIRE (22 Sept)
BRUMAIRE (22 Oct)
FRIMAIRE (21 Nov)
NIVOSE (21 Dec)
PLUVIOSE (20 Jan)
VENTOSE (19 Feb)
GERMINAL (21 Mar)
FLOREAL (20 Apr)
PRAIRIAL (20 May)
MESSIDOR (19 June)
THERMIDOR (19 Jul)
FRUCTIDOR (18 Aug)

FRESH *Anag. NEW; GREEN*, YOUNG (**opp** = old, stale). CHEEKY, FORWARD, IMPERTINENT.

FRESHER NEWER, MORE FORWARD. COLLEGE STUDENT (1st year), UNDERGRADUATE.

FRESH START CARTE BLANCHE, CLEAN SHEET. TARTS, RATTS (crypt, *anag*). F(crypt).

FRET ADORN, CHEQUER, PATTERN (saw). CHAFE, CONSUME, CORRODE, GNAW, RUST. ANNOY, DISTRESS, IMPATIENCE, IRRITATE, RUFFLE, WORRY. SEA-MIST. BAR, RIDGE (mus).

FREY(R) Nor *god* of fertility and sunshine; s of Njord, and br of *Freya*; k when he gave away his magic sword to win the love of Gerda.

FREYA Nor *goddess* of love. Second w of *Odin*, d of Njord and sis of *Frey*; travelled in *chariot* drawn by two cats. Received the souls of those k in battle. Her prized possession was the necklace Brisingamen, guarded by Heimdal, *watchman* of the gods.

FRIAR (s/l fryer). *FATHER*, RC MENDICANT, *Chaucer* character. AUGUSTINIAN (Austin Friar, *hermit*), CARMELITE (White Friar), DOMINICAN (Blackfriar, Friars Major), FRANCISCAN (Bungiebird, Capuchin, *Greyfriar*, Friars Minor, Minorite) [Trinity/Red Friar and Crutched/Crossed Friar = Canons Regular. Monks are not friars]. ~ LAWRENCE (mar R & J), ~ *PETER*, ~ THOMAS (all *Shak*).

FRIDAY 1. F. MAN ~ (Robinson Crusoe). 2. Day of *Frigg*. ~'s **child** = loving & giving. [Solomon *Grundy*].

FRIEND ALLY, *COMPANION*, MATE, OPPO (sl), PAL (**opp** = foe). *QUAKER*.

FRIEZE (s/l frees, freeze). RELIEF WORK (sculpture). CLOTH.

FRIGG(A) 1. Nor *goddess* of fertility; mar *Odin*, m of *Balder* [*Friday*]. 2. A minor *PLANET*.

FRINGE BORDER, EDGE, HEM, SURROUND. *BAND*, HAIRSTYLE.

FROG 1. BUTTONING, SWORD STRAP. DENT, DEPRESSION (brick). FASTENING (rly). HEEL (violin bow). FRENCHMAN, PARISIAN (sl). HORN (horse's foot). SWELLING (in throat). 2. Tailless amphibian of genus Ano(u)ra, Hyla, Rana, Salientia etc: ANGLER ~, ASCOPUS, BULL ~, FLYING ~, GOLIATH ~, MARSUPIAL ~, MEGAPHRYS, PADDOCK/PUDDOCK, SPRING PEEPER, TREE ~, XENOPUS. **Offspring** = pollywog, tadpole. JUMPER (crypt). **Celeb**: DAN'L WEBSTER (Mark *Twain*); JEREMY FISHER (Beatrix *Potter*); KERMIT (TV); MOWGLI (*Kipling*); TOAD (*Grahame*). And see *TOAD*.

FROM 1. EX, OUT OF. ORIGIN, STARTING POINT. 2. Hidden word, e.g. **Two from a group Air Show** (4) = P⋅AIR. 3. Indicates *anag*, e.g. **Queen is from army** (4) = MARY.

FROWN DISAPPROVE, FURROW, KNIT BROWS. HEADLINES (crypt).

FRUIT 1. PRODUCT, REVENUE. *OFFSPRING* (bibl). **Pl** = CONSEQUENCE, ISSUE, RESULT. 2. Edible seed; **types**:

3-letters

FIG	HAW	HIP	*NUT*

4-letters

CRAB	EJOO	LIME	SLOE
DATE	GEAN	*PEAR*	TUNA
DIKA	KAKI	*PLUM*	UGLI
DOUM	KIWI	SKEG	

5-letters

ABHAL	GRAPE	MELON	RHEIC
ACORN	GUAVA	MOREL	RHEUM
ANANA	JUMBO	MORUS	RIBES
APPLE	*LEMON*	OLIVE	WHORT
BERRY	LOGAN	PAPAW	
GOBBO	MANGO	*PEACH*	

6-letters

BANANA	DURION	*ORANGE*	RAMOON
BURREL	EGROIT	PAPAYA	RENNET
CHERRY	GROSER	PAW-PAW	RUDDOC
CITRON	LITCHI	PIPPIN	RUSSET
CITRUL	LOQUAT	PISANG	SHARON
CODLIN	LUCAMA	POMELO	TAMPOE
COLMAR	LYCHEE	PUMELO	TOMATO
DAMSON	MAMMEE	PUNICA	WAMPEE
DRUPEL	MEDLAR	*QUINCE*	
DURIAN	MUSCAT	RAISIN	

7-letters

ACHAENE	CURRANT	PASSION	SAFFRON
APRICOT	DEUTZIA	POMELOE	SATSUMA
AVOCADO	ETAERIO	POMEROY	SHALLON
BOUCHET	GENIPAP	POMPION	SOROSIS
BULLACE	GOLDING	POMPIRE	SOURSOP
BURLACE	KARATAS	PUMPKIN	SULTANA
CANDOCK	KUMQUAT	(RHUBARB)	SYRINGA
CODLING	LEECHEE	RIBSTON	TANGELO
COSTARD	MORELLA	ROSE-HIP	WINESAP
CUMQUAT	MORELLO	RUDDOCK	

8-letters

ABDALAVI	FAEBERRY	PEARMAIN
BERGAMOT	FENBERRY	PLANTAIN
BILBERRY	JAPONICA	PRUNELLO
BLENHEIM	MANDARIN	SHADDOCK
BROMELIA	MARIGOLD	SWEETSOP
BURGAMOT	MULBERRY	XYLOCARP
CADILLAC	MUSCATEL	
CLEMATIS	MYOSOTIS	

9+ letters

BLACKBERRY	PERSIMMON
BLACKCURRANT	PINEAPPLE
CUSTARD APPLE	RASPBERRY
GOOSEBERRY	REDCURRANT
LOGANBERRY	STRAWBERRY
MANGOSTEEN	SUGAR APPLE
NECTARINE	TANGERINE
ORTANIQUE	WHITECURRANT

FRY 1. QUAKER (*Fox*). *COOK. PAINTER. WRITER.*
2. *Offspring* of *FISH*.
FUEL ALCOHOL, AVGAS, BUTANE, CALOR ®,
CHARCOAL, COAL, COKE, DERV, DIESEL, GAS(OLINE),
KEROSENE, METHANE, METHS, OIL, PARAFFIN,
PETROL, PROPANE, WOOD; [*Pluto*]. FEED FIRE, STOKE.
FULLER EARTH; CLOTH CLEANER. MORE REPLETE.
GROOVED TOOL. *POET*.
FUNGUS MILDEW, MOULD, MUSHROOM, RUST,
TOADSTOOL, YEAST. **Types**: Beefsteak ~, Blewit, Blue
Legs, Bracket ~, Cep, Cup ~, Chantarelle, Death Cap
(pois), Devil's Boletus (pois), Earthy Inocybe (pois), Egg
Mushroom, Field Mushroom, Fly Agaric (pois), Morel, Oyster
Mushroom, Panther Cap (pois), Parasol, Puffball, Shaggy
Inkcap, Sickener (pois), Stinkhorn (pois), Truffle, Tuckahoe
(US), Wood Hedgehog, Woolly Milkcap (pois), Yellow Staining
Mushroom (pois).
FUNNY COMICAL, HUMOROUS [peculiar/ha-ha]. *BOAT*.
FURIAE The Furies, Rom myth goddesses of revenge (see *FURY*
for Gk and Rom names).
FURNITURE *HARNESS*, TRAPPINGS. STUMPS, WICKET
(cricket sl). CONTENTS, thus ~ of pocket = money, ~ of

mind = knowledge, ~ of shelves = books, and esp the ~ of house = chairs, tables, etc. [*Adam*, Chippendale, Hepplewhite, Sheraton], e.g.

beds: angel ~, bunk ~, camp ~, couch, divan, four-poster ~, hospital ~, litter (and see *bed*).

chairs: arm ~, backstool, Bath ~, balloon-back ~, bentwood ~, berbice ~, bergère, cabriole, campaign ~, cane ~, carver, chaise-longue, cockfighting ~, comb ~, conversation ~, court-cupboard ~, easy ~, faldstool, farthingale, fiddle-back, hall ~, hoop-back ~, joint-stool, kitchen ~, ladder-backed ~, library ~, Morris ~, prie-dieu, ribband-backed ~, rocking ~, Sedan ~, shield-back ~, smoker's ~, spindle-back ~, spoon-back ~, stool, tabouret, tub ~, wheel-back ~, Windsor ~, wing ~ (and see *chair*).

chests: Armada ~, bible box, camphor-wood ~, coffer, Hope ~, nonsuch, ~ of drawers (and see *chest*).

clocks: bracket ~, carriage ~, coaching inn ~, grandfather ~, grandmother ~, (half) hunter, lantern, long case ~, turnip, wristwatch (and see *clock*) [Knibb, Tompion].

desks: ambo, bureau, Davenport, escritoire, fall-front ~, knee-hole ~, office ~, reed-top ~, roll-top ~, school ~, secretaire, tambour ~ (and see *desk*).

tables: architect's ~, butterfly ~, card ~, coach ~, coffee ~, console, dining ~, draw ~, dressing ~, dumb-waiter, games ~, gate ~, gate-leg ~, Kent ~, loo ~, nest of ~s, omnium, opium ~, Pembroke ~, pie-crust ~, pier ~, quartetto ~, refectory ~, Rudd's ~, secretaire, shovel-board ~, side ~, sofa ~, spider ~, Sutherland ~, tea ~, teapoy, trestle ~, tripod ~, what-not, writing ~ (and see *table*).

other: almirah, *canterbury*, cellaret, chesterfield, cheval mirror, commode, cupboard, dresser, jardinière, pier-glass, settee, settle, sociable, sofa, spinning-wheel, tall-boy, tea-caddy, wardrobe, wine-cooler.

terms: acanthus, apron, astragal, banding, bead, boule, cabriole, cartouche, claw and ball, console, cornice, dentil, diaper, endive, escutcheon, finial, gadroon, intaglio, marquetry, ogee, ormolu, patina, pie-crust, plinth, serpentine, spandrel, spindle, splat, swag.

FURY 1. ANGER, PASSION, RAGE. VIOLENCE (met). *DOG* (*Alice*). 2. VIRAGO, *SHREW*. **Pl** = avenging minor *goddesses* with snakes for hair, sent from Tartarus to punish crimes of perjury, murder etc; hence any avenging spirit.

Gk = ERINYES/EUMENIDES (ALECTO, MEGAERA, TISIPHONE); **Rom** = DIRAE/FURIAE.

FUSE AMALGAMATE, BLEND, MELD. DETONATE, IGNITER (impact ~, magnetic ~, proximity ~, time ~, vibratory ~). BLOW-OUT, SAFETY LINK; MELT, SHORT-CIRCUIT; UNEARTH (crypt).

FUSTIAN *MATERIAL*. BOMBAST, TURGID SPEECH.

G GENERAL AUDIENCE (film *censorship*, US). *GERMAN(Y)*. GIGA (*int unit*). GRAMS. *GRAND*. GRAVITY. GREAT. GREEK. *KEY*; *NOTE*. ~-STRING. THOUSAND (sl).

GAEA *GE*.

GALAHAD Kt of the *Round Table*, s of *Lancelot* and Elaine; his strength was 'as of ten' [*Camelot*. Holy Grail. Purity, virtue].

GALATEA 1. Gk myth ivory statue, who came to life and was mar by *Pygmalion*; 1 s, Paphus. [Hermione, W. Tale (*Shak*)]. 2. Gk myth sea *nymph*, d of *Nereus* and *Doris*; she loved Acis (s of *Faunus*, who was k by his rival, the chief *Cyclope* Polyphemus). 3. A minor *PLANET*.

GALL (s/l *Gaul*). ANNOY; NERVE. CLUBROOT, HYPERTROPHY. *FLY*. LIVERBILE. HORSE-SORE.

GALLERY BALCONY, *GODS*. COLONNADE, PORTICO. PLATFORM. CORRIDOR, PASSAGE. EXHIBITION; TATE.

GALLEY SLAVE *PRISONER, ROWER*. CHEF, *COOK*, PANTRY BOY, PROOFREADER, SCULLERY MAID (all crypt).

GALLOPHILE *Lover* of French ways.

GALLOPHOBIA *Aversion* to French ways.

GALOFARO *CHARYBDIS*.

GAMBLE (s/l *gambol*). BET, SPEC(ULATE), WAGER.

GAMBOL (s/l *gamble*). FROLIC, PLAY [*lamb*].

GAME 1. *BRAVE*, COURAGEOUS, PREPARED, WILLING; **opp** = reluctant, *shy*. CRIPPLED, HALT, LAME. 2. WILD LIFE e.g. *ANTELOPE, DEER*, GROUSE, HARE, PARTRIDGE, PHEASANT, WOODCOCK (see also *big game* for bush and jungle dwellers). 3. *MATCH*, PARTIE, PASTIME, RECREATION, *SPORT* (q.v.); **types (indoors)**: *BOARD* ~ (q.v.), *CARD* ~ (q.v.), BADMINTON, *BILLIARDS, BINGO* (HOUSEY-HOUSEY, KENO,

LOTTO, TOMBOLA), BOWLING, CHARADES,
CONSEQUENCES, CRAMBO, CRAPS (US), *DARTS*,
DIABOLO, *DICE*, DOMINOES, DUMB CRAMBO,
FAN-TAN (Ch), FINGERS UP, *FIVES*, GRANDMOTHER'S
FOOTSTEPS, HANDBALL, HIDE AND SEEK, I SPY,
JACKSTRAWS (US), LURCH, MAH-JONGG, *MARBLES*,
MERILS/MER(R)ELS, MOR(R)A, MURDER, NETBALL,
NIM, NINEPINS, NOUGHTS & CROSSES, NOVUM (dice,
Shak), NULLO, PACHISI (Ind), PING-PONG, POOL (US),
POSTMAN'S KNOCK, *RACKETS*, ROULETTE, RUBIK
CUBE, *SARDINES*, SHOVE HA'PENNY, SKITTLES,
SNOOKER, SOFTBALL, SPILLIKINS, SQUASH, *TENNIS*,
TEN-PIN BOWLING, TICK-TACK, TIC-TAC-TOE, TIDDLY-
WINKS, TWO-UP (Aus), UP JENKINS, VOLLEY-BALL;
types (outdoors): BADMINTON, *BASEBALL*, BOULE,
BOWLS, *CRICKET*, CROQUET, CURLING, *FOOTBALL*
(Association ~, Am ~, Aus Rules ~, *Rugby* ~, Rugby
League ~), FRENCH & ENGLISH, *GOLF*, HIDE AND
SEEK, HOCKEY, HOP-SCOTCH, HURLING, KICK THE
CAN, LACROSSE, PALL-MALL, PALLONE (It), PELOTA,
PETANQUE, POLO, QUOITS, ROUNDERS, RUGGER,
SAILING, SHINTY, SOFTBALL, *SWIMMING*, *TENNIS*
(deck ~, lawn ~, padder ~, real/royal ~, table ~), TIPCAT,
WATER POLO, WINTER *SPORTS* (q.v.); and see *SPORT*. **Pl**
= Asian ~, *Commonwealth* ~, *Olympic* ~, Pan-American ~,
Pythian ~.

G & S Gilbert and Sullivan. **Operas:**

Title	Alternative	Detail
The Gondoliers	The King of Barataria	Venice. Duke of Plaza Toro
The Grand Duke	The Statutory Duel	Grand Duchy of Pfennig Halbpfennig, Rudolph, Ernest Dummkopf, Ludwig
Iolanthe	The *Peer* and the *Peri*	*Parliament, Fairies,* Lord Chancellor
Mikado	The Town of Titipu	*Japan.* Nanki-Poo, Yum-Yum, Ko-Ko, Pooh-Bah, Pitti-Sing, Wandering *Minstrel,* Lord High Executioner

Patience	Bunthorne's Bride	Dragoons, Raffle, Capt Reece, Mantelpiece
HMS Pinafore (abbr: Pinafore)	The Lass that Loved a *Sailor*	Dick Deadeye, Buttercup
Pirates of Penzance (abbr: Pirates)	The Slave of Duty	Cornwall. Frederic (*pirate*), *Ruth* (*maid*, *nurse*)
Princess Ida (abbr: Ida)	Castle Adamant	King Hildebrand, Gama (*monster*), Hilarion, *women warriors*
Ruddigore	The Witch's Curse	*Cornwall. Ghosts*, Mad Margaret, Sir Ruthven Murgatroyd
Sorcerer	—	Country house. John Wellington Wells
Trial by Jury (abbr: Trial)	—	Law courts. Angelina, Edwin
Utopia Limited (abbr: Utopia)	—	King Paramount I, Scaphio, Phantis, Tarara, Princess Zara
Yeomen of the Guard (abbr: Yeoman)	The Merryman and his *Maid*	Tower of London. Wilfred Shadbolt (*gaoler*), Col Fairfax, Meryll, Jack Point (*jester*)

GANG GO (Sc), PASSAGE. ROCK (ore-bearing). BAND, CLIQUE, CROWD, LOT, MOB, SET; **celeb**: Baker St Irregulars (*Holmes*); *Famous Five* (q.v.); Gorbals Diehards (Buchan); ~ of Four (polit, esp Ch) [Just *William*].

GANGSTER GODFATHER, GUNMAN, HOOD(LUM), MAFIA BOSS, MOBSTER, VILLAIN; **notorious**: AL CAPONE, BONNIE & CLYDE, PRETTY BOY FLOYD, LUCKY LUCIANO, BUGSY MALONE, DUTCH SCHULTZ, BUGSY SIEGEL.

GANYMEDE 1. Gk myth youth, celeb for his beauty, abducted by *Zeus* (who *transformed* himself into an *eagle*) as his *cupbearer* on Mount *Olympus*. 2. A satellite of the *planet Jupiter*.

GAOL (s/l Jael). BAGNIO (Turk), *BRIG* (naut), CAGE, CAN, CELL, CHOKEY, CLINK, COOLER, GLASSHOUSE (mil), HOOSEGOW (US sl), INSIDE, JAIL (US), JUG, *NICK*, PETER, PRISON, QUOD, SLAM(MER), STIR [porridge. Fry, Howard; M for M (*Shak*); Yeomen (*G & S*)]; **celeb**:

ALBANY	(Eng)
ALCATRAZ	(US, ex)
ARMLEY	(Eng)
BARLINNIE	(Sc)
BASTILLE	(Fr)
BORSTAL	(Eng, jun)
BOTANY BAY	(Aus, hist)
BRIDEWELL	(Eng, ex)
BRIXTON	(Eng)
BROADMOOR	(Eng, med)
CAMP HILL	(Eng)
COOKHAM WOOD	(Eng)
DARTMOOR	(Eng)
DEVIL'S ISLAND	(Fr, ex)
DURHAM	(Eng)
FLEET	(Eng, ex)
LA FORCE	(*Dickens*, 2 Cities)
FORD	(Eng)
FRESNES	(Fr)
HOLLOWAY	(Eng, fem)
HULL	(Eng)
KINGSTON	(Eng)
LONG MARTIN	(Eng)
LEEDS	(Eng)
MARSHALSEA	(Eng, ex)
THE MAZE	(Ire)
MILLBANK	(Eng, ex)
THE *MOOR*	(Eng)
NEWGATE	(Eng, ex)
NORFOLK IS	(Aus, ex)
NORTHEYE	(Eng)
OSSINING	(US)
PARKHURST	(Eng)
PENTONVILLE	(Eng)
PORTLAND	(Eng)
RAMPTON	(Eng, med)
RISLEY	(Eng)
THE SCRUBS	(Eng)
SHOTT'S	(Sc)
SING SING	(US, ex)
STRANGEWAYS	(Eng)
STYAL	(Eng)

VERNE   (Eng)
WAKEFIELD   (Eng)
WALTON   (Eng)
WINSOM GREEN   (Eng)
WINCHESTER   (Eng)
WORMWOOD SCRUBS   (Eng)
Fictional: Château d'If (Dumas), Zenda (*Hope*).

GAOLER JAILER (US), KEY-HOLDER (crypt), KEY MAN
(crypt), PRISON OFFICER, SCREW (sl), TURNKEY (arch),
WARDER. WILLIAM SHADBOLT (*G & S*).
GARBLED *Anag.* MUDDLED, *SCRAMBLED.*
GARDEN CULTIVATION, *PLOT*, YARD (US); **comp**
= *common.* BABYLON (*Seven Wonders*), EDEN, KEW
[Elizabeth and her Ger Garden (Beau champ)].
GARDENER CULTIVATOR. *ADAM* (crypt). 'CAPABILITY'
BROWN; WILLIAM *KENT*; ANDRÉ LENOTRE
(Fr); ANDREW FAIRSERVICE (Rob Roy, Scott).
ELIZABETH, INIGO JONES, MR MCGREGOR (*Potter*).
Pl = EPICUREANS (Gk); SPADES (*Alice*).
GARLAND ADORN, BEDECK, *DECK*, LEI; FLOWERS. JUDY
(films).
GARNET *MINERAL*; GEM (red). *Birthstone* (January).
GARTER *HERALD* [Black Rod]. KNIGHTHOOD [Honi soit qui
mal y pense; stocking]. BAND, STRAP.
GAS BELCH, BOAST, CHATTER, NONSENSE. FUEL (US),
PETROL, VAPOUR; **types**: Acetylene, Ammonia, Argon,
Butane, Carbon Dioxide, ~ Monoxide, CFC, Chlorine, Coal
~, Ethane, Ether, Helium, Hydrogen, *Krypton*, Laughing ~,
Lewisite, Marsh ~, Methane, Mustard ~, Natural ~, *Neon*,
Nerve ~, Nitrogen, North Sea ~, *Oxygen*, Phosgene, Poison
~, Propane, *Sewer* ~, *Tear* ~, Xenon.
GATE (s/l gait). 1. ACCESS, BARRIER, CLOSURE,
ENTRANCE, EXIT, *OPENING*, POSTERN, WICKET.
SHUTTER (mech). ATTENDANCE, CROWD,
SPECTATORS; TAKE, TAKINGS. MOUTH (sl). 2. ~s **of**
London: ALDERSGATE, ALDGATE, BISHOPSGATE,
BRIDESGATE, CRIPPLEGATE, DOWGATE, LUDGATE,
MOORGATE, NEWGATE, POSTERN, PRAETORIAN
WAY.
GATHERING *ASSEMBLY*, MEETING. COLLECTING,
CULLING. BOIL, SWELLING, TUMOUR.

GAUGE *EM*, *TT*, *Z*. CAPACITY, EXTENT, *MEASURE*, SCOPE, STANDARD, WIDTH, *TRACK*. INSTRUMENT. ASSESS, CALCULATE, ESTIMATE.

GAUL (s/l *gall*). GALLIA, ROMAN FRANCE (cisalpine, transalpine).

GB GREAT BRITAIN (*car plate*).

GBA ALDERNEY (*car plate*).

GBG GUERNSEY (*car plate*).

GBJ JERSEY (*car plate*).

GBM ISLE OF MAN (*car plate*).

GE = GAEA. Gk *goddess* of the EARTH. Mother (by Uranus) of the *Titans* (**Rom** = TELLUS, TERRA). GERMANIUM (*chem*).

GEAR *CLOTHES*, GOODS, KIT, RIG. APPARATUS, EQUIPMENT, FITTINGS, *HARNESS*, KIT, TACKLE. MESHING COGS (mech).

GEESE Pl of *goose*.

GEHENNA *HELL* (bibl), PLACE OF BURNING.

GEM BEST/CHOICEST PART. *TYPEFACE*. JEWEL, PRECIOUS STONE, ENGRAVED SEMI-PRECIOUS STONE: *AGATE*, *AMETHYST*, *AQUAMARINE*, *BERYL*, *BLOODSTONE*, *CHALCEDONY*, *CHRYSOBERYL*, *CHRYSOLITE*, *CHRYSOPRASE*, *CORAL*, *CORNELIAN*, *DIAMOND*, *EMERALD*, FIRE OPAL, *GARNET*, HYALITE, *JADE*, *LAPIS LAZULI*, *ONYX*, *OPAL*, *PEARL*, PERIDOT, PYROPE, *RUBY*, *SAPPHIRE*, *SARD*, SARDIUS (bibl), *SARDONYX*, *TURQUOISE*, *ZIRCON* [*anniversary*, *birthstone*].

GEMINI 1. *TWINS*; DIOSCURI (Castor and Pollux). 2. *Constellation*; (3rd) sign of *Zodiac*. 3. *SPACECRAFT*.

GEN *GENERAL* (mil). *INFORMATION*.

GENERAL G (film *censorship*, US). GEN, *TARTAN* (bibl); OFFICER: LEE, SMUTS, SLIM (and see *military leaders*). IMPARTIAL, MAIN, UNIVERSAL (**opp** = particular).

GENES (s/l jeans). CHROMOSOMES, *DNA* (heredity).

GENIE GOBLIN, IMP, *SPIRIT* [Aladdin's lamp].

GENIUS 1. ABILITY, BRILLIANCE. 2. Rom myth *god* of fertility and marriage (**Gk** = *HYMEN*).

GENOPHILE *Lover* of people.

GENOPHOBIA *Aversion* to people.

GEORGE PATRON SAINT (Eng; Port; armourers) [dragon, Order of Garter, 23 April]; 'A RUSTIC'. *WRITER*. [*Three* Men

in a Boat]. KING (Eng/Hanover; *mad*). Autopilot (av sl).
GERMAN 1. G. HEINIE, HEINZ, JERRY, FRITZ, KRAUT,
HUN. D, DDR (*car plate*). 2. Translate, e.g. **The German** =
DAS, DER, DIE; **German song** = LIED.
GERMANY DDR, *FDR*, REICH, FATHERLAND, WEIMAR.
GET ON *AGREE*. *BOARD*, EMBARK. *AGE*.
GET OUT EMERGE, FLEE, *LEAVE*. BOWL, CATCH, RUN
OUT, STUMP (*cricket*).
GET UP STYLE (clothes). *DRESS*, MAKE TOILET, RISE.
MOUNT (horse). Write upwards (dn). BECOME VIOLENT,
WORK UP (sea, temper). ORGANIZE. TEG (dn; crypt).
GHOST ~ *BAT* (Aus). DOUBLE IMAGE, OUTLINE,
SEMBLANCE. (HACK) *WRITER*. APPARITION,
MANES, PHANTOM, *SHADE*, SOUL, SPECTRE, *SPIRIT*,
POLTERGEIST; HAUNT, PROWL; **celeb**: ~ of *ABEL* (Wm
Blake), BANQUO (Macbeth), CAESAR (to *Brutus*, before
Battle of Philippi), CANTERVILLE (Wilde), CLAUDIUS
(Hamlet's father), ELVIRA (Blithe Spirit, Coward), HERNE
(the *Hunter*), MISS JESSEL and QUINT (*governess* and valet;
The Turn of the Screw, James), JACOB MARLEY (Xmas
Carol, *Dickens*), PHANTOM (of the Opera, Leroux; ~s
(Henrik Ibsen) [Ruddigore (*G & S*); *lemur*].
GI SOLDIER, PFC, PRIVATE (US).
GIANT 1. LARGE, MONSTROUS, SUPERHUMAN, TITANIC
(**opp** = *dwarf*). **Pl** = New York baseball team. 2. Myth
MONSTER: *DACTYLS*, *GIGANTES*, GOG, MAGOG,
ORGOGLIO (Faerie Queene, Spenser), GARGANTUA &
PANTAGRUEL (Rabelais), GOLIATH (bibl), NEPHILIM
(bibl), *PERIPHITES* (Gk myth) [Brobdingnag (*Swift*)].
GIBRALTAR ROCK. *STRAIT*. [pillars of *Hercules*].
GIGANTES Gk myth *monsters* (not to be confused with the
Titans); ALCYONEUS, ENCELADUS, EPHIALTES,
MIMAS, PALLAS, PHRYTOS, PORPHYRION, RHOETUS.
They had wings, and snakes for feet.
GILBERT 1. Sir William Schwenck ~, Eng *writer* and librettist;
with *Sullivan* wrote operettas (for details, see *G & S*). 2. Sir
Humphrey ~, navigator. *PAINTER*. Unit of force (elect).
GILL (s/l Jill). GIRL. *MEASURE*, 1/4 PINT, hence P, I, N or T.
DEWLAP, WATTLE (poultry). *BREATHER* (*fish*). RAVINE.
SAIL IDLY. YOUNG WOMAN. FERRET, POLECAT (fem).
GIN (s/l djinn, ginn). *DRINK*, GENEVA, HOLLANDS,
SCHIEDAM; **comp** = *Fr*; *It*; *tonic*. *NET*, SNARE, TRAP.

CRANE, WINDLASS. COTTON MAKER. *CARD GAME.*
GIRDLE BELT, CORD, CORSET. RING, SURROUND.
　GRILL. [labour of *Hercules*].
GIRL HER, SHE. DAMOSEL, DAMSEL, GAL, LASS, MISS,
　WENCH. ANN, DORA, ENID, SUE etc [~ **and boy** =
　pigeon pair].
GIVE AWAY DONATE. *BETRAY*, SHOP.
Gk Greece, Greek.
GLASS 1. BAROMETER. MIRROR. MAGNIFIER.
　MICROSCOPE. GLAZING, QUARREL, WINDOW,
　TRANSPARENCY. DRINKING VESSEL: BUMPER,
　COPITA, POKAL, PONY, SCHOONER, TANKARD,
　TUMBLER; BRANDY ~, LIQUEUR ~, PORT ~,
　RUMMER, SHERRY ~, WINE ~. LORGNETTE,
　MONOCLE, QUIZZING ~. **Pl** = BINOCULARS, BIN(N)S
　(sl), SPECTACLES. 2. Mixture of sand and potash (*chem*),
　hence by *anag* (crypt) A SHOP STAND, or PASS TO
　HAND etc.
GLEE PART-SONG. DELIGHT, MERRIMENT, MIRTH.
GO ANIMATION, DRIVE, *PEP*, *SPIRIT*, VIGOUR, ZIP.
　DEPART, FARE, OFF, PART, *REPAIR*, START. ATTEMPT,
　SHOT, TRY, TURN. BOARD-GAME (Jap). [Little ~
　(exam C)].
GOAT 1. SILLY FOOL. ATTACK, SHOT*AT, TRY*AT (crypt).
　ISLAND. 2. Ruminant, genus CAPRA; BUTTER (crypt).
　MURIEL (*Orwell*). **Breeds**: BAGOT, CHAMOIS, IBEX,
　IZARD (Sp), MARKHOR, TAHR (see also *antelope*, *deer*).
　Assembly = *flock*, herd; **offspring** = *kid*; **male** = BILLY; **fem**
　= NANNY [*Ch calendar*; Vidar (Nor god)]. 3. *Constellation*
　(Capricorn); (10th) sign of *Zodiac*.
GOBLIN BROWNIE, ELF, GENIE, IMP, *SPIRIT*, SPRITE.
GOBY *FISH.* PASS (crypt). TRAVEL*BY/IN (crypt).
GOC GENERAL OFFICER COMMANDING, OFFICER (mil).
GOD 1. ADORED/INFLUENTIAL MAN. DEITY, ADONAI
　(Heb), ALLAH (Arab), ELOHIM (Heb), JAHBULON
　(*Masonic*), JEHOVAH, YAHVEH (Heb), OBJECT OF
　WORSHIP: IDEA, IDOL, IMAGE, SUPERHUMAN
　(MALE) BEING; [ambrosia, nectar, *Elysium*, trinity].
　EXCLAMATION: GOLLY, GOSH. **Pl** = GALLERY (theat);
　opp = parterre, stalls. 2. Gods and *goddesses* figured largely in
　the lives of the ancient world. Most of the seasons, ideas and
　natural events such as love, war, hunting and the harvest (with

earth, sun and moon) which influenced life were personified by
early peoples such as the Egyptians, Phoenicians, Indians and
Norsemen; those of Greece and Rome were particularly literate,
so their deities are well documented. In the lists which follow,
the alert reader will note that interesting qualities such as love
and fertility rate no less than fourteen Greek and Roman gods
and goddesses (not to mention another dozen or so Nordic
and Eastern equivalents), while dull old virginity has only one
deity from among all the nations (and even that one is also the
goddess of Nature, so there is hope for her yet). Greece was
responsible for much of the lore and mythology which grew
up, and much of this was handed on to the Romans; in general
terms, there were six principal Greek gods and six principal
goddesses, who all lived on Mount *Olympus*: *APOLLO,
ARES, HEPHAESTUS, HERMES, POSEIDON* and *ZEUS*;
Aphrodite, Artemis, Athene, Demeter, Hera and *Hestia*. **Celeb**
gods and minor gods include **Greek**:

ABRAXAS	divine emanations
AEOLUS	*winds*
AGATHODAEMON	prosperity
ALASTOR	fate
ALPHEUS	river
APELIOTES	east *wind*
APOLLO	beauty, healing, music, oracles, plagues, prophecy, sun
ARES	war
ASCLEPIUS	medicine
BOREAS	north *wind*
CRONOS	harvest
DIONYSUS	fertility, wine
ERIS	discord
EROS	love
EUROS	SE *wind*
GANYMEDE	cup-bearer
HADES	*underworld*
HELIOS	sun
HEPHAESTUS	fire
HERMES	dreams, messenger, *robbers*
HORUS	doorway
HYMEN	fertility, marriage
HYPNOS	sleep

INACHUS	river
KAIKAS	NE *wind*
LIPS	SW *wind*
MOMOS	ridicule
NEREUS	sea
NOTOS	south *wind*
OCEANUS	river
PAN	herds, hunting, shepherds
PLUTO	*underworld*
PLUTUS	wealth
POSEIDON	sea, *horses*
SKIRON	NW *wind*
THANATOS	*death*
TRITON	sea
URANUS	heaven
ZEPHYRUS	west *wind*
ZEUS	chief ~, king

Roman:

AESCULAPIUS	medicine
AFRICUS	SW *wind*
AMOR	love
APOLLO	beauty, healing, music, oracles, plagues, prophecy, sun
AQUILO	NE *wind*
ATLAS	world
AUSTER	south *wind*
BACCHUS	fertility, wine
CAURUS	NW *wind*
COMUS	revelry
CUPID	love
DIS	*underworld*
DISCORDIA	discord
FAUNUS	herds
FAVONIUS	west *wind*
FULGURATOR	storms
FULMINATOR	lightning
GENIUS	fertility, marriage, prosperity
IACCHUS	= *BACCHUS*
INUUS	= *FAUNUS*
JANUS	doorway

JOVE	chief ~, king, thunder
JUPITER	chief ~, thunder
LAR(ES)	household
LIBER	= *BACCHUS*
LUPERCUS	= *FAUNUS*
MARS	husbandry, war
MERCURY	messenger
MORPHEUS	dreams
MORS	*death*
NEPTUNE	sea, *horses*
ORCUS	*underworld*
PENATES	household
PHOEBUS	sun
PLUTO	*underworld*
PLUVIUS	rain
SATURNUS	harvest
SEPTENTRIO	north *wind*
SILVANUS	*trees*
SOL	sun
SUBSOLANUS	east *wind*
TERMINUS	boundaries
TONANS	thunder
VOLTURNUS	SE *wind*
VULCAN	fire

~s (not Gk or Rom):

AAH (Egy)	moon
AEGIR (Nor)	chief
AGNI (Ind)	fire
AMEN-RA (Egy)	chief, harvest
ANU (Bab)	chief
ANUBIS (Egy)	death
APIS (Egy)	sun
ASMODEUS (Heb)	revelry
BAAL (Phoen)	chief, sun
BALDER (Nor)	sun
BEL(US) (Bab)	chief
BES (Egy)	music, revelry
BRAG (Nor)	poetry
BRAHMA (Ind)	chief
CHAC (Mex)	rain
DAGAN (Bab)	earth

DAGON (Phil)	chief
DON (Celt)	heavens
DONAR (Ger)	thunder
EA (Bab)	wisdom
FREY (Nor)	fertility, sun
GEB (Egy)	earth
HAPI (Egy)	fertility, the Nile (& fem)
HEIMDAL (Nor)	watchman
HOR (Egy)	doorway
HORUS (Egy)	sun
INDRA (Ind)	rain
INTI (Inca)	sun
KAMA (Ind)	love
KHONS (Egy)	moon
KON-TIKI (Inca)	sun
KRISHNA (Ind)	fertility
LOKI (Nor)	fire
MAIT (Egy)	truth
MARDUK (Bab)	healing
MITHRAS (Pers)	sun
MOLOCH (Jew)	fire
MORRIGAN (Ire)	war
NABU/NEBO (Bab)	wisdom
NJORD (Nor)	sea
NJORDHR (Nor)	sea
NK (Egy)	winds
NQA, NQING, NQONG (Aus)	chief (*Kipling*)
NUN (Egy)	chaos
ODIN (Nor)	chief
OG (Celt)	chief, death, fertility
OSIRIS (Egy)	fertility, rain, underworld
PTAH (Egy)	arts, magic, death
RA/RE (Egy)	sun
RAIDEN (Jap)	thunder
SEB (Egy)	agriculture
SEITSEY (Nor)	fire
SERAPIS (Egy)	dreams, underworld
SET(H) (Egy)	night
SHAMASH (Bab)	sun
S(H)IVA (Ind)	chief, death
SHU (Egy)	air

TAMMUZ (Syrian)	sun
TEMU (Egy)	chief
THOR (Nor)	thunder
THOTH (Egy)	wisdom
TIW (Ger)	war
VIDAR (Nor)	silence
VISHNU (Ind)	healing
WODEN (A-Sax)	chief
WOTAN (Ger)	chief
XANGTI (Ch)	chief
YAMA (Ind)	death

Equivalent gods include:

Agriculture: Gk *CRONOS*; **Roman** *SATURNUS*; **Other** SEB (Egy) [*fertility, harvest*]

Beauty: Gk *APOLLO*; **Roman** *APOLLO*

Boundaries: **Roman** TERMINUS

Chief: Gk *ZEUS*; **Roman** *JOVE, JUPITER*; **Other** WODEN (A-Sax), ANU, BEL/BELUS (Bab), OG (Celt), XANGTI (Ch), AMEN-RA, OSIRIS, TEMU (Egy), WOTAN (Ger), BRAHMA, SHIVA, VISHNU (Ind), ODIN (Nor), DAGON (Phil), *BAAL* (Phoen), NQA, NQING, NQONG (Aus, *Kipling*)

Death: Gk *THANATOS*; **Roman** MORS; **Other** ANUBIS/ *OSIRIS*, PTAH (Egy), SHIVA, YAMA (Ind)

Discord: Gk *ERIS*; **Roman** DISCORDIA

Doorway: Gk *HORUS*; **Roman** *JANUS*; **Other** HOR (Egy)

Dreams: Gk *HERMES*; **Roman** *MORPHEUS*; **Other** SERAPIS (Egy)

Fate: Gk ALASTOR

Fertility: Gk *DIONYSUS, HYMEN*; **Roman** *BACCHUS, GENIUS*; **Other** OG (Celt), HAPI, *OSIRIS* (Egy), KRISHNA (Ind), *FREY* (Nor) [*agriculture, harvest*]

God

Fire: **Gk** *HEPHAESTUS*; **Roman** *VULCAN*; **Other** *LOKI* (Nor), AGNI (Ind); SEITSEY (Nor)

Harvest: **Gk** CRONOS; **Roman** SATURNUS; **Other** AMEN-RA, SEB (Egy) [*agriculture, fertility*]

Healing: **Gk** *APOLLO*; **Roman** *APOLLO*; **Other** MARDUK (Bab), VISHNU (Ind) [*medicine*]

Heaven: **Gk** *URANUS*; **Other** ANU (Bab), VALHALLA (Nor)

Herds: **Gk** *PAN*; **Roman** *FAUNUS*, INUUS, LUPERCUS

Household: **Roman** *LAR(ES)*, PENATES

Hunting: **Gk** *PAN*

Husbandry: **Roman** *MARS*; **Other** DAGAN (Bab)

Lightning: **Gk** *ZEUS*; **Roman** FULMINATOR

Love: **Gk** *EROS*; **Roman** *AMOR, CUPID*; **Other** KAMA (Ind)

Marriage: **Gk** *HYMEN*; **Roman** *GENIUS*

Medicine: **Gk** *ASCLEPIUS*; **Roman** AESCULAPIUS [*healing*]

Messenger: **Gk** *HERMES*; **Roman** *MERCURY*

Moon: **Other** AAH, KHONS (Egy)

Night: **Other** *SET(H)* (Egy)

Oracles: **Gk** *APOLLO*; **Roman** *APOLLO*

Plagues: **Gk** *APOLLO*; **Roman** *APOLLO*

Prophecy: **Gk** *APOLLO*; **Roman** *APOLLO*

Prosperity: **Gk** AGATHODAEMON; **Roman** *GENIUS*

Rain: Gk *ZEUS*; **Roman** *JUPITER*, *PLUVIUS*; **Other** *OSIRIS* (Egy), INDRA (Ind), CHAC (Maya)

Revelry: **Roman** *COMUS*; **Other** BES (Egy); ASMODEUS (Heb)

Ridicule: Gk MOMOS

River: Gk ALPHEUS, INACHUS, OCEANUS

Robbery: Gk *HERMES*

Sea: Gk *NEREUS*, *POSEIDON*, TRITON; **Roman** *NEPTUNE*; **Other** AEGIR, NJORDHR, NJORD (Nor)

Shepherds: Gk *PAN*

Storms: Gk *ZEUS*; **Roman** FULGURATOR

Sun: Gk *APOLLO*, *HELIOS*; **Roman** *PHOEBUS*, *SOL*; **Other** APIS, *HORUS*, PTAH, RA/RE (Egy), INTI, KON-TIKI (Inca), *BALDER*, *FREY* (Nor), *MITHRAS* (Pers), *BAAL* (Phoen), TAMMUZ (Syrian)

Thunder: Gk *ZEUS*; **Roman** *JOVE*, *JUPITER*, *TONANS*; **Other** DONAR (Ger), RAIDEN (Jap), *THOR* (Nor)

Truth: **Other** MAAT (Egy)

Underworld: Gk *HADES*; **Roman** *DIS*, *ORCUS*, *PLUTO*; **Other** *OSIRIS*, SERAPIS (Egy)

War: Gk *ARES*; **Roman** *MARS*; **Other** TIW (Ger), MORRIGAN (Ire)

Watchman: **Other** HEIMDAL (Nor)

Wealth: Gk *PLUTUS*

Winds: Gk *AEOLUS* (see *winds*); **Rom** (see *winds*); **Other** VAYU (Pers), NK (Egy)

Wine: Gk *DIONYSUS*; **Roman** BACCHUS, LIBER
[revelry]

Wisdom: Other EA, ENKI, NABU/NEBO (Bab), THOTH
(Egy)

World: Roman *ATLAS*

GODDESS 1. ADORED/INFLUENTIAL WOMAN. DEITY,
OBJECT OF WORSHIP: IDEA, IDOL, IMAGE, (FEMALE)
SUPERHUMAN BEING [ambrosia, nectar]. LOVED ONE.
2. See *gods* for brief description of the deity ethos of ancient
peoples. The Greeks had six principal *gods* and goddesses, who
all lived on Mount *Olympus: Apollo, Ares, Hephaestus, Hermes,
Poseidon* and *Zeus; APHRODITE, ARTEMIS, ATHENE,
DEMETER, HERA* and *HESTIA.* **Celeb** goddesses and minor
goddesses include, **Greek**:

AMPHITRITE	sea
APHRODITE	beauty, love
ARTEMIS	hunting, messenger, nature,
	virginity
ASTRAEA	justice
ATE	infatuation, retribution
ATHENE	arts, war, wisdom
CHAOS	primordial space
CHLORIS	flowers
CYBELE	fertility
DANAE	fertility
DEMETER	nature
ENYO	war
EOS	dawn
ERINYES	*furies*
EUMENIDES	*furies*
GAEA/GE	earth
GRACES	beauty (3 ~s or Charities)
HEBE	cup-bearer, youth
HECATE	night, underworld, witchcraft
HERA	childbirth, queen ~
HESTIA	hearth
HYGIEA	health
IRENE	peace

IRIS	rainbow
MAIA	eldest of the *Pleiades*
MOIRAI	*fates*
NEMESIS	retribution
NIKE	victory
NYX	night
PERSEPHONE	underworld
PLEIADES	rain
RHEA	fertility
SELENE	moon
TERPSICHORE	dance, song
TYCHE	fortune
UPIS	childbirth

Roman:

AURORA	dawn
BELLONA	*war*
CERES	earth, fertility, nature
DIANA	fertility, nature, hunting, moon
FAUNA	earth
FLORA	flowers
FORTUNA	fortune
FURIAE	*furies*
GRATIAE	beauty (3 *Graces*/Charities)
JUNO	queen ~, childbirth, moon
JUVENTAS	youth
LIBERA	= *PROSERPINE*
LUNA	moon
MAIA	oracles
MINERVA	arts, invention, war, wisdom
NOX	night
OPS	earth, nature, fertility
PARCAE	*fates*
PAX	peace
PROSERPINE	underworld
SALUS	health
TELLUS/TERRA	earth
VENUS	beauty, love
VESTA	hearth
VICTORIA	victory

~s (not Gk or Rom):

AMATERASU (Jap)	sun

ASTARTE (Phoen)	love
ATERGATIS (Syrian)	fertility
BAST (Egy)	pleasure
BELIT/BELTIS (Bab)	chief, fertility
BENDIS (Thrace)	hunting, moon
BRUNHILDA (Nor)	war
DEVI (Ind)	destruction
EOSTRE (A-Sax)	fertility (Easter)
FREYA (Nor)	love
FRIGG(A) (Nor)	fertility
GULI (Bab)	healing
HATHOR (Egy)	love
HEL (Nor)	destruction, night
HOLDA (Ger)	nature
INNIN (Bab)	fertility
ISHTAR (Bab)	fertility, love
ISIS (Egy)	chief, love, nature
KALI (Ind)	destruction
LUA (It)	earth
MA/MAAT (Egy)	truth
MATUTA (It)	dawn
MENI (Bab)	retribution
NEPHTHYS (Egy)	funerals
NERIO (Sabine)	war
NUT (Egy)	mother earth
SULIS (Celt)	wisdom
TEFNUT (Egy)	sea
TIAMIT (Bab)	chaos
UPIS (Egy)	chief, nature
UZUME (Jap)	mirth

Equivalent goddesses include:
Arts: Gk *ATHENE*; **Roman** *MINERVA*

Beauty: Gk *APHRODITE, ARTEMIS, GRACES*; **Roman**
    DIANA, GRATIAE, *VENUS*

Chaos: Gk *CHAOS*; **Other** TIAMIT (Bab)

Chief: Gk *HERA*; **Roman** *JUNO*; **Other** *ISIS, UPIS* (Egy),
    DEVI (Ind), BELIT/BELTIS (Bab)

Childbirth: Gk *HERA*; **Roman** *JUNO*; **Other** BESET (Egy)

Cup-bearer: Gk *HEBE*; **Roman** *JUVENTAS*

Dance: Gk *TERPSICHORE*

Dawn: Gk *EOS*; **Roman** *AURORA*; **Other** MATUTA (It)

Destruction: **Other** DEVI, *KALI* (Ind), *HEL* (Nor)

Earth: Gk *GAEA/GE*; **Roman** *CERES, FAUNA, MAIA, TELLUS/TERRA*; **Other** LUA (It) [*fertility, nature*]

Fates: Gk *MOIRAI*; **Roman** *PARCAE*

Fertility: Gk *CYBELE, DANAE, RHEA*; **Roman** *CERES, DIANA, OPS*; **Other** *FRIGG* (Nor), BELIT, INNIN, ISHTAR (Bab), ATERGATIS (Syrian), EOSTRE (A-Sax [Easter]), ISIS, HAPI (Egy; and male) [*earth, nature*]

Fire: **Other** PELE (Hawaiian)

Flowers: Gk *CHLORIS*; **Roman** *FLORA*

Fortune: Gk TYCHE; **Roman** FORTUNA

Furies: Gk *ERINYES*, EUMENIDES; **Roman** *FURIAE*

Health: Gk *HYGIEA*; **Roman** SALUS

Hearth: Gk *HESTIA*; **Roman** *VESTA*

Hunting: Gk *ARTEMIS*; **Roman** *DIANA*; **Other** BENDIS (Thrace)

Infatuation: Gk *ATE*

Invention: **Roman** *MINERVA*

Justice: Gk ASTRAEA

Lightning: Roman *MINERVA*

Love: Gk *APHRODITE;* **Roman** *VENUS;* **Other** *ISHTAR* (Bab), HATHOR, *ISIS* (Egy), *FREYA* (Nor), *ASTARTE* (Phoen)

Messenger: Gk *ARTEMIS*

Moon: Gk *ARTEMIS, SELENE;* **Roman** *DIANA, JUNO, LUNA;* **Other** BENDIS (Thrace)

Nature: Gk *ARTEMIS, DEMETER;* **Roman** *CERES, DIANA, OPS;* **Other** *ISIS, UPIS* (Egy), HOLDA (Ger)

Night: Gk *HECATE, NYX;* **Rom** Nox; **Other** *HEL* (Nor)

Oracles: Roman *MAIA*

Peace: Gk *IRENE;* **Roman** *PAX*

Pleasure: Other BAST (Egy), UZUME (Jap)

Rainbow: Gk *IRIS*

Retribution: Gk *ATE, NEMESIS;* **Other** MENI (Bab)

Sea: Gk *AMPHITRITE;* **Other** TEFNUT (Egy)

Song: Gk *TERPSICHORE*

Space: Gk CHAOS

Sun: Other AMATERASU (Jap)

Truth: Other MA, MAAT (Egy)

Underworld: Gk *HECATE, PERSEPHONE;* **Roman** *LIBERA, PROSERPINE;* **Other** *HEL* (Nor)

Victory: Gk *NIKE;* **Roman** *VICTORIA*

Virginity: Gk *ARTEMIS*

War: Gk *ATHENE*, ENYO; **Roman** BELLONA, *MINERVA*;
Other *BRUNHILDA* (Nor), NERIO (Sabine)

Wisdom: Gk *ATHENE*; **Roman** *MINERVA*; **Other** SULIS
(Celt)

Witchcraft: Gk *HECATE*

Youth: Gk *HEBE*; **Roman** *JUVENTAS*

GOD'S BLOOD ICHOR.
GOD WILLING *DG*, *DV*.
GO IN(TO/SIDE) 1. ENTER, PENETRATE. 2. Hidden word,
e.g. **Miss Theresa Wayman goes in with a will** (6,1,3) = THERE'S
A WAY. 3. Word or letter goes into another, e.g. **To serve, I have
to go into the water** (6) = WA*I*TER.
GOLD *METAL*; AU (*chem*). OR (*herald*). BULLSEYE (archery).
OLYMPIC WINNER. YELLOW *COLOUR*. *Anniversary*
(50th). [**fool's gold** = pinchbeck, pyrites. *Company* (livery);
Danae].
~ **DIGGER** FORTY-NINER, PANNER, PROSPECTOR.
LEECH, TRAMP, VAMPIRE.
GOLDEN FLEECE Skin of fabled golden ram which rescued *Helle*
and her br Phrixus. It was hung in the temple of Ares until
brought back by *Jason* and the *Argonauts*.
GOLF CLUB BLASTER, BRASSIE, CLEEK, *DRIVER*, *IRON*,
MASHIE, NIBLICK, *PUTTER*, SAND-WEDGE, *SPOON*,
WEDGE, *WOOD*, PGA, R AND A, USGA. HOYLAKE,
PORTLAND, ST ANDREWS.
GOLF COURSE LINKS; FOREGROUND (crypt). BIRKDALE,
HOYLAKE, MUIRFIELD, PORTLAND, ST ANDREWS,
SANDWICH, SUNNINGDALE, TROON. [par, bogey (evens),
birdie (1 under), *eagle* (2 under), *albatross* (3 under)].
GOLLY DOLL. GOSH, MY.
GOOD ADEQUATE, EFFICIENT, GENUINE, RIGHT,
SATISFACTORY, SOUND, VALID. AGREEABLE,
BENEVOLENT, COMMENDABLE, EXCELLENT,
FAVOURABLE, KIND, UNTAINTED, VIRTUOUS,
WHOLESOME [Sabbath/Sunday's *child*]; (**opp** = evil).
OBEDIENT, PROPER, WELL-BEHAVED/MANNERED
(**opp** = *bad*). **Pl** = FREIGHT, LINE, MERCHANDIZE,
WARES. THE REAL THING.

GOODFELLOW SOCIABLE PERSON. ROBIN; *FAIRY*. SAINT,
ST (crypt).

GOODMAN FATHER, HUSBAND. SAINT, ST (crypt).

GOON DOLT, FOOL. GUARD (mil sl). HEAVY, THUG.
CONTINUE, PROCEED (crypt go*on).

GOOSE 1. SILLY CREATURE, SIMPLETON. IRON (tailor's).
POKE. 2. *BIRD* of genus ANSER: BARNACLE, BEAN,
BRENT, CANADA, GREYLAG, PINKFOOTED, SOLAN
(gannet), WHITEFRONTED. **Assembly** = flock, gaggle, skein;
male = GANDER; **fem** = GOOSE; **offspring** = gosling. Sixth
day of *Christmas* song.

GORDON 1. Charles George ~, General ('Chinese ~'). Governor
of Sudan; b 1833, k at Khartoum 1885. 2. Lord George ~ of ~
Riots fame (c.f. Barnaby Rudge, *Dickens*). 3. George Hamilton
~, 4th Earl of Aberdeen, Prime Minister during Crimean War.
4. *Dog* (setter). *Soldier* (Highlander). 5. ~ Bennet = God (sl).

GORGON Gk myth winged fem *monsters*, with snakes for hair:
EURYALE (the Leaper), *MEDUSA* (the Ruler), STHENO (the
Strong).

GOSPEL DOCTRINE, GLAD TIDINGS; CHRIST'S
BIOGRAPHY [Matthew, Mark, Luke, John]. Four
gospelmakers in *song*. BASIC TEACHING/TRUTH.

GOVERNESS Privately employed fem teacher, NANNY; **celeb**:
Alice (*Milne*); Anna Leon-Owens (Anna & the King of Siam,
Margaret Landon); Becky Sharp (Thackeray, Vanity Fair);
Henriette Desportes (All This and Heaven Too, Rachel Field);
Jane Eyre (~, C. Brontë; Miss Jessel (*ghost*, The Turn of
the Screw, Henry James); Miss Madrigal (The Chalk Garden,
Enid Bagnold); Maria (von Trapp, The Sound of Music); Mary
Morstan (Sign of Four, *Holmes*; mar Dr Watson); Nana (*dog* in
Peter Pan, J. M. *Barrie*); Mary Poppins (~, P. L. Travers); Miss
Prism (The Importance of Being Earnest, Wilde); Miss Pross
(2 Cities, *Dickens*); The Storyteller (~ to Flora and Miles; The
Turn of the Screw, Henry James).

GOVERNOR 1. ACCELERATOR, CONTROL(LER), REIN,
THROTTLE (mech). *FATHER*. 2. RULER, usually mil
and often on behalf of some other person or authority;
COMMISSIONER, TETRARCH, VICEROY, HE; BEY
(Turk), MUDIR (Eastern); **celeb**: CLIVE (Ind); FELIX (Rom);
LEONATO (*Shak*); WARREN HASTINGS (Brit); PONTIUS
PILATE (Rom).

GO WRONG *Anag*. ERR, SIN. GET LOST. OG (crypt).

GP *DOCTOR. GROUP.*

GR GRAND, GREAT. GREECE. GRAIN. GRAM(ME).

GRACE 1. ADORN, *HONOUR, SET OFF. CHARM*, ELEGANCE, REFINEMENT [Tuesday's *child*]. FAVOUR, LIKING, BOON, CONCESSION, PRIVILEGE. CLEMENCY, MERCY. PRAYERS, THANKSGIVING. ADDRESS (form of, for Archbishop, Duchess, Duke). EXTRA NOTE (mus). BATSMAN, CRICKETER (EM, GF, WG). *DARLING.* 'HANNAH'. 2. Gk *goddess* daughters of Zeus, bestowers of *beauty*, charm and mirth: AGLAIA, EUPHROYSNE and THALIA. CHARITES (Gk); GRATIAE (Rom).

~ **ROAD** TEST GROUND (*cricket*).

GRADUATION MARKING, *MEASUREMENT*, SCALE; VERNIER. ACADEMIC DEGREE, PASS, QUALIFICATION.

GRAEAE The PHORCYDES, Gk myth old women, sis to *Gorgons*: DINO, ENYO and PEPHREDRO. Had the bodies of *swans*, only one tooth and one eye between them; consulted by *Perseus* in his quest for *Medusa.*

GRAHAME KENNETH, *WRITER* (Wind in the Willows; Toad of Toad Hall; *Badger, Mole*, Ratty, *Toad* [cars]).

GRAND G, GR. CHIEF, HIGHEST RANK. DISTINGUISHED, FINE, GRANDIOSE, GREAT, MAGNIFICENT, *NOBLE*, SPLENDID. PIANO. RIVER (Can). WATERFALL. $1,000; £1,000; THOUSAND, hence M or K. *THEATRE.*

GRASS 1. *BETRAY*, NARK, SNEAK. *SNAKE. DRUG*, HERB, POT. FELL, KNOCK DOWN (sl). 2. *PLANT*. GRAZING, HERBAGE, LAWN, PASTURE, *PLAIN*, SWARD, TURF; FODDER. ASPARAGUS (sl) [aftermath; hay, ted]. And see *PLAIN* for geog grasslands. **Types:**

3-letters

ERS	*FOG*	*RYE*

4-letters

AIRA	COIX	KANS	TARE
ALFA	DISS	LYME	TEFF
BENT	DOUB	REED	TORE
BLUE	DURA	RUSA	

5-letters

ARROW	BRIZA	BUNCH	COUCH

CUTCH	HAULM	*PANIC*	VETCH
DURRA	MEDIC	*QUAKE*	
GRAMA	MELIC	SEDGE	
HALFA	ORYZA	*SPEAR*	

6-letters

BAJREE	FESCUE	MEDICK	REDTOP
BARCOO	FIORIN	NARDUS	RUPPIA
CACTUS	LOLIUM	PAMPAS	TWITCH
CLOVER	LUCERN	PHLEUM	UNIOLA
DARNEL	MARRAM	QUITCH	

7-letters

ALFALFA	FESTUCA	SACATON	VETIVER
CLIVERS	FOGGAGE	SORGHUM	WAGWANT
ESPARTO	FOXTAIL	SQUITCH	WHANGEE
EULALIA	LUCERNE	TIMOTHY	ZIZANIA

8+ letters

CITRONELLA	DOG-WHEAT
CLEAVERS	ELEUSINE
COCKSFOOT	GYNERIUM
CREEPING MEDIC	JOB'S TEARS
DOG-GRASS	PURPLE MEDIC
DOGSTAIL	PUSS-TAIL

GRASSHOPPER CICADA, *CRICKET*, GRIG, KATYDID, TETTIX; *INSECT*; JUMPER (crypt).

GRATE (s/l *great*). FIREPLACE [Adam]. GRIND, IRRITATE, RASP, RUB. GRATING, GRILLE. GRATITUDE (arch).

GRAVE TOMB, TRENCH. CARVE, ENGRAVE, ETCH, SCULPT. IMPORTANT, SERIOUS, WEIGHTY; DIGNIFIED, PLAIN, SOLEMN, SOMBRE. CLEAN, SCRAPE, SCRUB (naut). ACCENT (`). 'TRISTRAM'. **Pl** = *POET*.

GRAVITY G. MASS, WEIGHT. SERIOUSNESS.

GRAYS INN LAW SOCIETY [benchers, call to the bar, griffin].

GREAT (s/l *grate*). ABLE, IMPORTANT, PRE-EMINENT; G, BIG, LARGE. **Pl** = Final exam in classics/philosophy (O). [Alexander the ~ (Gk), Alfred the ~ (Eng), Catherine the ~ (Russ), Frederick the ~ (Prussia), Peter the ~ (Russ)].

GREAT LAKES Group of *lakes* in Canada and US: **in both**: ERIE,

HURON, ONTARIO, SUPERIOR (biggest); **in US only**: MICHIGAN.

GREED(Y) AVARICIOUS, CUPIDITY, GLUTTONY, PIGGY (sl), VORACIOUS [*Bunter*, Fat Boy (Pickwick), Phaeax, Mammon, *Seven Deadly Sins*].

GREEK G, Gk; for Gk alphabet, see *alphabet*. CUNNING PERSON, SHARPER. DOUBLE DUTCH, INCOMPREHENSIBLE.

~ **GOD** See *GOD*.

~ **GODDESS** See *GODDESS*.

GREEN *COLOUR*, *SAGE*, VERT (*herald*). IN LEAF, VERDANT, VITAL. FRESH, UNRIPE. ISLAND. DEB, GULLIBLE, IMMATURE, INEXPERIENCED, MILD, *RAW*, TYRO, YOUNG, *VIRGIN* (**opp** = *experienced*). COMMON LAND. PUTTING AREA (golf). RIVER (US). *Shak* char (R.ii). **Pl** = VEGETABLES.

GREENBACK BUCK, DOLLAR (sl). NEERG (crypt).

GREEN RUSHES See *song*.

GREET ACCOST, HAIL, *SALUTE*; AVE, HI, WELCOME. CRY, WEEP (Sc).

GREETING AVE, HEY, HI, HO; *SALUTE*. HALLO, HELLO, HILLO, HOLLO, HULLO (**opp** = farewell). CRYING, WEEPING (Sc).

GREGORY APERIENT, POWDER. PECK (film). POPE.

GREY *COLOUR*. WHIG. DEPRESSING, DISMAL. RIVER (NZ). ANONYMOUS, INDETERMINATE, UNIDENTIFIABLE. ANCIENT, EXPERIENCED, IMMEMORIAL. BERYL ~ (theat). LADY JANE ~. *Shak* char (R.iii, H.v). **Pl** = 2nd DRAGOONS (mil).

GREYFRIAR FRANCISCAN, *FRIAR*. **Pl** = *SCHOOL* [*Bunter*, *Famous Five*].

GRIEF DOLE, DOLOUR, MISERY, REGRET, SORROW, TROUBLE. DISASTER.

GRILSE *FISH*. *Offspring* of *salmon*.

GRIP *BITE*, CLASP, NIP, *PINCH*, SQUEEZE. *BAGGAGE*. RAVEN (Barnaby Rudge, *Dickens*).

GROOM FIANCE, HUSBAND, MATE. OSTLER; BRUSH, CURRYCOMB, TIDY.

GROUND EARTH (elect). EDUCATE, TEACH, TRAIN. Prevent flying, keep out of the air. HONED, POLISHED, POWDERED. BOTTOM, SEABED; SOLID. BASE, FOUNDATION, SUBSTRATUM; SURFACE. AREA,

EARTH, LAND, TERRITORY; STREET-LEVEL. PLAYING
FIELD (*cricket* ~, *football* ~, *golf course, racetrack, rugby* ~,
tennis court). **Pl** = BELIEF, PRINCIPLE, REASONS.
GRANULES, POWDER. PREMISES, PROPERTY.

GROUND RENT HIRE CHARGE, LEASE. CANYON,
CREVASSE, FISSURE, RAVINE (crypt); EARTHQUAKE
(crypt).

GROUNDS FOR 1. AUTHORITY, FOUNDATION, REASON
TO BELIEVE. 2. See *cricket, football, golf, racetrack,
rugby, tennis.*

GROUP GP. CLIQUE, CLUSTER, KNOT. *SET.* CLASSIFY.

GROUSE *BIRD*, GAMEBIRD, CAPERCAILLIE, MOOR
FOWL, PTARMIGAN, RED ~ (**assembly** = pack; **male red** ~
= GORLOCK). COMPLAIN, GRUMBLE, *TICK.*

GRUB STREET THE *PRESS.* HACK WRITERS (now Milton
Street).

GRUMPY BEARISH, ILL-TEMPERED, SURLY. *DWARF*
(Snow White).

GRUNDY 1. Solomon ~ (b on Monday, christened on Tuesday,
mar on Wednesday, took ill on Thursday, got worse on
Friday, d on Saturday and was buried on Sunday). 2. Mrs ~;
personification of prudery (*unseen* neighbour of Mrs Ashfield in
Tom Morton's Speed the Plough).

GUARD PROTECT, SENTRY, *WATCH*, VIGIL; CAVEMAN
(crypt). [~ **of honour** = *chaperone*]. *CONDUCTOR*
(rly), RAILWAYMAN. **Pl** = COLDSTREAM, FOOT,
GRENADIER, HORSE, IRISH, LIFE, SCOTS, WELSH;
BLUES, ROYALS [*household* ~]. OLD ~, PRAETORIAN
~, PRUSSIAN ~, YEOMAN, YOUNG ~.

GUERNSEY SWEATER, WOOLLY (jersey). *CATTLE. ISLAND*
(CI). GBG (*car plate*). *LILY.*

GUEVARA CHE.

GUIDE ASSIST, LEAD, SHOW; ADVISER, CICERONE,
SCOUT. *CONDUCTOR*, DRAGOMAN, INTERPRETER,
PILOT. INSTINCT. MANUAL. STANDARD. CHANNEL.
GUARD, *RAIL*, ROD (mech).

GUIDED MISSILE ARROW, DART. *WEAPON* (and see
MISSILE).

GUINEA *COUNTRY* (ex Fr W Af). GOLD *COIN*, 21
SHILLINGS. (professional) FEE.

~ **BISSAU** *COUNTRY* (ex Port Guinea).

~ **FOWL** *BIRD*.

~ **PIG** CAVY, PET, *RODENT*. TEST CASE. PI (crypt – no tail).
GUINEVERE Q of *King Arthur*, her infidelity with *Lancelot* led to
the break-up of the *Round Table*. [*Camelot*, Mordred].
GULES RED (*herald*).
GULF ABYSS, CHASM, DEPTH, GAP. LARGE INLET/BAY
(geog); **celebrated**:

ADEN (Af/Arab)
ALASKA (US)
ANTALYA (Turk)
AQABA (Isr)
BOTHNIA (Fin/Swe)
CALIFORNIA (Mex)
CAMBAY (Ind)
CARPENTARIA (Aus)
CHIHLI (Ch)
CORINTH (Gk)
FINLAND (~)
GAETA (It)
GASCONY (Fr)
GENOA (It)
GIZHIGA (CIS)
GUINEA (NW Af)
HONDURAS (~)
ISKENDERUN (Turk)
IZMIR (Turk)
KUTCH (Ind)
LAKONIA (Gk)
LIONS (Fr)
MARTABAN (Bur)
MESSINA (Gk)
MEXICO (~/US)

MOSQUITOS (Panama)
OB (CIS)
OMAN (Arab/Pers)
ORISTANO (It)
PANAMA (~)
PAPUA (New Guinea)
PATRAS (Gk)
PERSIAN (Arab/~)
RIGA (CIS)
ST LAWRENCE (Can)
ST MALO (Fr)
SALERNO (It)
SAN JORGE (Arg; Sp)
SAN MATIAS (Arg)
SIAM (~ etc)
SIDRA/SIRTE (Libya)
SPENCER (Aus)
SUEZ (Egy)
TARANTO (It)
TARTARY (CIS)
TONA (CIS)
TONKING (Ch)
VALENCIA (Sp)
VENICE (It)

GULL DUPE, FOOL. SEABIRD; **breeds**: BLACK-BACKED
~, *COB*, COMMON ~, FULMAR, HERRING ~,
KITTIWAKE, MEW ~, TERN. **Pl** = TORQUAY (*football*
team).
GUN ARM, FIREARM, GAT, *PISTOL*, *REVOLVER*, RIFLE,
ROD, ORDNANCE, *WEAPON* (q.v. for list). SHOOT. **Celeb**:
BIG BERTHA, THE KING'S DAUGHTER (H.v), THE
LONDON (H.v), THE MESSENGER (H.v), MONS MEG,
ZAM-ZAMMAH (Kim, *Kipling*). **Pl** = RA (battery).

GUNMAN GANGSTER, MOBSTER. RA (crypt). STARTER.
GUNNEL *BUTTERFISH.* GUNWALE (boat's side).
GUNNER *GUNMAN* (q.v.). RIFLEMAN. [*patron saint*]. RA. **Pl**
= ARSENAL (*football*).
GUTTER PRESS NEWSPAPER, RAG.
GUY CHAP, FELLOW. FAWKES [Robert Catesby, Thomas
Percy, Parkin Cake]. ROPE, STAY.
GYGES Gk myth *MONSTER* (Uranid), s of *Uranus* and *Ge*, with
100 arms and 50 heads.
GYM LESSONS PE, PT; EXERCISES.
GYNOPHOBIA *Aversion* to women.

H 1. HARD. HORRIFIC (film *censorship*). HOSPITAL. HOT.
HOTEL. HOUR. HUNGARY (*car plate*). HYDROGEN
(*chem*). 2. Dropping the letter H is indicated by an apostrophe
in the clue, e.g. **Little brother makes money with 'is loaf** (5) =
BR⋅EAD (**loaf** = head; **money** = bread).
h Husband of.
HA HAHNIUM (*chem*). HORSE ARTILLERY. HALF-LAUGH
(crypt).
HABIT *CUSTOM*, WONT. *DRESS.*
HABITATION ABODE, *HOME*, *HOUSE*, LIVING
QUARTERS; **specifically:**

Animal	**Habitation**
Badger	*EARTH*, SET(T)
Beaver	*LODGE*
Bee	HIVE
Bird	NEST
Cattle	MANGER, MIDDEN
Eagle	EYRIE
Fox	BURROW, *EARTH*
Hare	*FORM*
Heron	COLONY
Horse	*STABLE*
Insect eggs	NIDUS
Otter	*HOLT, LODGE*
Penguin	*ROOKERY*
Pig	*STY*
Rabbit	*BURROW*, WARREN

Rook	*ROOKERY*
Seal	*ROOKERY*
Sparrow	COLONY
Squirrel	*DRAY*, DREY
Swan	COLONY
Wild beast	*DEN*, LAIR

Habitation	**Animal**
Burrow	*FOX, RABBIT*
Colony	HERON, SPARROW, *SWAN*
Den	WILD ANIMAL
Dray, Drey	SQUIRREL
Earth	*BADGER, FOX*
Eyrie	*EAGLE*
Form	HARE
Hive	*BEE*
Holt	OTTER
Lair	WILD ANIMAL
Lodge	*BEAVER*, OTTER
Manger	*CATTLE*
Midden	*CATTLE*
Nest	*BIRD*
Nidus	INSECT EGGS
Rookery	PENGUIN, *ROOK*, SEAL
Set(*t*)	*BADGER*
Stable	*HORSE*
Sty	*PIG*
Warren	*RABBIT*

HADES Gk *god* of the *UNDERWORLD*, s of *Cronos* and *Rhea*, br of *Poseidon* and *Zeus*, mar to *Persephone* (**Rom** = *DIS*, ORCUS, *PLUTO*). By association, *HELL* itself; ABADDON (Heb), EREBUS (Gk), GEHENNA (bibl), INFERNO (Dante), SHEOL (Heb), TARTARUS (Gk myth), VALHALLA (Nor); [*Cerberus, Charon, Hecate, Styx*].

HAGGARD 1. DRAWN, WILD LOOKING. UNTAMED HAWK. 2. (Sir Henry) RIDER ~ (writer; **books**: Ayesha, Dawn, King Solomon's Mines, Jess, She; Allan Quatermain).

HAIL (s/l *hale*). ALOHA, AVE; SALUTE (**opp** = **farewell**). FROZEN RAIN.

HAIR FILAMENT. CURL, LOCK, TRESS [*Absalom*; *Esau*, Nisus, *Samson*; hirsute]; BARNET (*rh sl*).

HAIRDRESSER BARBER, COIFFEUR, WAVER; **celeb**: MISS
MOUCHER (Copperfield, *Dickens*); MR PARTRIDGE (Tom
Jones, Fielding); PAUL SWEEDLEPIPE (Chuzzle, *Dickens*);
FIGARO (Barber of Seville, Rossini); SWEENEY TODD.
BRUSH, COMB, CURLER, *GRIP*, SLIDE (crypt).

HAL HENRY.

HALE (s/l *hail*). FIT, WELL. ORIGINATE. HAUL.

HALF 1. DEMI, SEMI; SPLIT. 2. Half of preceding or next word,
e.g. **Half bottle** = BOT or TLE. 3. As, **Not ~**, remove half of
word, e.g. **Mrs Mopp's charming, not half**! (4) = CHAR(ming).

~ BACK *FOOTBALLER*. IMED, IMES (crypt). BA or CK
(crypt).

~ DAY EARLY CLOSING. AM, PM (crypt).

~ HEARTED 1. LUKEWARM, UNENTHUSIASTIC. 2. Remove
one of two identical letters in middle of word indicated, e.g. **Half
hearted rabble** = RABLE. 3. *AL* (crypt).

~ HUNTER WATCH. HUN or TER (crypt).

~ SOVEREIGN TEN SHILLINGS, XS. WILLIAM or MARY
(crypt).

HALT STOP (**opp** = *go on*). CRIPPLED, LAME, LIMP.

HAM Bibl s of *Noah*. BUTTOCK, THIGH. SALT PIG; **comp**
= *eggs*. AMATEUR RADIO OPERATOR, BREAKER
(sl), CB ENTHUSIAST. ACT BADLY (hence CAT – crypt),
CABOTIN, POOR PERFORMER.

HAMBLEDON *CRICKET* GROUND.

HAMLET VILLAGE. GREAT DANE, PRINCE OF
DENMARK (*Shak*). PIGLET, PORKER (crypt).

HAMMER BALL ~, CLAW ~, PEIN ~, TACK ~; NAILER,
TOOL; BIRMINGHAM SPANNER (sl); CLOUT, HIT,
KNOCK, SLAM, STRIKE, TACK, WALLOP, WHACK.
EDWARD [Wallace (hist)]. PIGFARMER (crypt). **Pl** = WEST
HAM (*football team*).

~ THROWER THOR (Nor myth).

HAMPDEN PARK *FOOTBALL* GROUND (Sc).

HAMPER BASKET [Fortnums; picnic]. HINDER, LET (**opp**
= *help*).

HAND MITT, PALM, PAW (*bone*; *Belshazzar*; *Jeroboam*). HELP;
PASS. HOLDING (cards). CREWMAN, SEAMAN (naut).
BUNCH (bananas). JOINT (pork). POINTER (clock). 4 INS
(horse).

HANDLE FEEL, TOUCH. *GRIP*, HOLDER. MANAGE,
TREAT. DEAL IN. ADDRESS, TITLE (sl).

HANGMAN EXECUTIONER; TOPPER (crypt) [*tarot*]; **celeb**:
ABHORSON (*Shak*), PETIT ANDRÉ (Quentin Durward,
Scott), DENNIS (Rudge, *Dickens*), DERRICK, KETCH,
PIERREPOINT. GALLERY DIRECTOR (crypt).

HAPPY CONTENTED. *DWARF* (Snow White).

HARD H; DURABLE, TOUGH. RELENTLESS.

~ **LINES** TOUGH LUCK. BR, *RAILWAY* TRACK, RLY
(crypt).

HARNESS EQUIP(MENT), FASTEN(ING), LIGAMENT,
STRAP. HORSE TRAPPINGS: BIT, BRIDLE, BRIDOON,
CURB, HACKAMORE, HEADSTALL, MARTINGALE,
PELHAM, REINS, RESTRAINT, SNAFFLE, TRACE
[loriner]. HOOK UP, UTILIZE. DEFENSIVE ARMOUR.

HARP NAG. PLUCK; *INSTRUMENT* (mus), LYRE [*Aeolus*].

HARPY 1. HARRIDAN, *SHREW*, TERMAGANT. LYRICAL
(crypt). 2. Malignant monsters with woman's head and vulture's
body, capable of defiling all they touched: AELLO, CELAENO,
OCYPETE, PODARGE. **Pl** = storm *winds* in the form of the
dd of *Electra* and Thaumas. 3. *Ship* (Mr Midshipman Easy,
Marryat).

HARRIER *BIRD*, HAWK. HUNTING *DOG*. COUNTRY
RUNNER (hare and hounds). *AIRCRAFT* ⓡ: FIGHTER,
JUMP JET, VTO. HARASSER, MOLESTER.

HARRIS 1. *MATERIAL*, TWEED. [*Three* Men in a Boat; *unseen*
in Chuzzle (*Dickens*)]. 2. Joel Chandler ~, creator of Uncle
Remus, Brer Fox, Brer Rabbit, Tar-baby etc.

HARROW BREAKER, DRAG (farm). LACERATE, WOUND.
HARRY, ROB. WRACK. *PUBLIC SCHOOL*.

HARRY HAL, HENRY; 'HOME RULER'. TATE. HARASS,
MOLEST, WORRY. (Old ~ = devil).

HARVARD UNIVERSITY (US) [Cantabrigian]. AIRCRAFT
(trainer).

HARVEST 1. CROP, GATHER. PRODUCE, YIELD. REAP.
HUSBAND, LAY UP. 2. **God: Gk** = CRONOS, **Rom** =
SATURNUS.

HAT HEAD COVERING: BEARSKIN, BERET, BILLYCOCK,
BOATER (straw), BONNET, BOWLER, BUSBY, CAP,
CLOCHE ~, COVER, DERBY (US), EASTER BONNET,
FEDORA (US), FEZ, FLAT ~, GIBUS, HOMBERG,
JULIET (woman's ~), KEPI, LEGHORN (It), LID, MITRE,
MONTERA (*bullfighting*), MORTARBOARD, OPERA ~,
PANAMA (straw), PEAKED ~, PETASUS (Gk),

PILLBOX, PORKPIE, SHAKO, SLOUCH ~, SOMBRERO, SOU-WESTER, STETSON, STOVEPIPE ~, TAMMY/TAM O'SHANTER (Sc), TEN-GALLON ~, TILE, TITFER (*rh sl*), TOP ~, TOPEE, TOP GEAR (crypt), TOPI, TOPPER, TOQUE, TRICORN, TRILBY, TURBAN, WIDEAWAKE. And see *church dress*.

HATRED 1. *AVERSION*, DISLIKE, ABHORRENCE (**opp** = *love*). MILITARY POLICE, MP (crypt). STAFF OFFICER (crypt). 2. Prefix miso- as misogamy (marriage), misogyny (women), misology (reason), misoneism (novelty).

HAVISHAM *RECLUSE* (Gt Ex, *Dickens*). *LAWYER* (Little Lord Fauntleroy, Burnett).

HAWK BIRD OF PREY, RAPTOR; **breeds:** BUZZARD, CARACARA, *EAGLE*, FALCON, GOSHAWK, GYRFALCON, HOBBY ~, KESTREL, LANNER, *MERLIN*, MUSKET, OSPREY, PEREGRINE, SAKER, SPARROW ~, VULTURE; **assembly** = *cast*, **offspring** = bowet [falconer; ostringer]. AIRCRAFT. COUGH, SPIT. PEDDLE. PLASTERER'S BOARD. WARMONGER (**opp** = dove).

HAWKER *AIRCRAFT*. FALCONER [hood, jess, lure]. CHEAPJACK, PEDLAR, TINKER.

HAY DRIED GRASS [*measure*; ted]. *CASTLE*. DANCE FIGURE. *RIVER* (Aus, Can).

HE HELIUM (*chem*). HIS EMINENCE. HIS EXCELLENCY; *GOVERNOR*. HIGH EXPLOSIVE. MAN, MALE.

HEAD 1. BEAN, LOAF (*rh sl*), NAPPER, NOD, NODDLE, *NOGGIN*, NOODLE, ONION, PATE, POLL, SWEDE; **comp** = shoulders [*bone*]. CHIEF, MASTER, TOP. CAPE, NESS (geog). FACE, OBVERSE (coin; **opp** = reverse, tail). 2. Use first letter, e.g. **Spithead** = s.

HEADGEAR *HAT* [*church dress*]. PIT WINDING.

HEADINGLEY TEST(ING) GROUND (*cricket*).

HEADLINE BANNER, LEADER, STREAMER. PROFILE, SILHOUETTE. **Pl** = FROWN (crypt).

HEAD OFF 1. *EXECUTE*, GUILLOTINE. INTERCEPT. 2. Drop first letter, e.g. **Head off Jack's partner, and she's not very well (3)** = (J)ILL.

HEAD OF MI5 M; Q.

HEADQUARTERS CENTRAL OFFICE, HQ. H, E, A or D (crypt). Q (crypt). N, E, S, W (crypt).

HEAL (s/l *heel*). GET BETTER, MEND (**opp** = wound).

HEALING 1. MENDING, RECOVERING. 2. **God: Gk and Rom**

= APOLLO; **Ind** = VISHNU.

HEALTH 1. FITNESS, SOUNDNESS, WELFARE,
WELLBEING (**Unions** = COHSE, NUPE). TOAST (drink).
2. **Goddesses: Gk** = HYGIEA, **Rom** = SALUS.

HEAR (s/l *here*). 1. HARK, LIST(EN), PERCEIVE. 2. *Sounds
like*, often given as 'we hear', e.g. **We hear you when the cuppa's
downed** (5, 3) = AFTER TEA (after T in the alphabet, comes U).

HEARD (s/l *herd*). 1. HARKENED, LISTENED, PERCEIVED.
2. *Sounds like*, e.g. **Elk are heard in loving talk** = DEAR.

HEARER AUDITOR, LISTENER. EAR (crypt).

HEART (s/l *hart*). 1. CENTRE, CORE, MIDDLE. COURAGE,
WILL; BREAST, LOVE, MIND, SOUL, INTELLECT.
ORGAN (med, *study*), PUMP (sl); **comp** = soul. BRAVE
FELLOW. **Pl** = CARDS, SUIT (*Alice*). 2. Middle of word, e.g.
heartbreak = E; **lighthearted** = G. 3. Put word in another, e.g.
A man little by little at heart in the New World (8) = A*M*ERIC*AN.

HEARTH 1. FIREPLACE. 2. **Goddesses: Gk** = *HESTIA*, **Rom** =
VESTA.

HEARTLESS 1. CRUEL, PITILESS, MERCILESS. 2. Omit
middle letters, e.g. **Heartless maple** = MALE.

HEAT ANGER, INFLAME. HOT WEATHER, WARMTH (**opp**
= cold). ELIMINATOR, SINGLE RACE.

HEATHER BILBERRY, BLAEBERRY, CALLUNA,
DABOECIA, ERICA, HUCKLEBERRY, LING, MANOAO,
WHORTLEBERRY. WARM HER (crypt).

HEAVEN 1. FIRMAMENT, SKY, VAULT. EMPYREAN,
GOD'S ABODE, PROMISED LAND; ASGARD,
VALHALLA (Nor); ASSAMA (Islam); ELYSIAN FIELDS,
ELYSIUM, *OLYMPUS* (Gk myth); NIRVANA (Ind); ZION
(Christ). 2. **Gk god** = *URANUS, ZEUS*; **opp** = *underworld*.

HEAVENLY 1. ATTRACTIVE, DIVINE, EXCELLENT. 2. Of
or in the sky, thus **Heavenly pub** (6) = SK*INN*Y.

~ **BODY** MOON, ORB, *PLANET*, STAR, SUN. BATHING
BEAUTY, MISS WORLD ®.

HEBE 1. Gk *goddess* of YOUTH; cup-bearer to the gods; d of
Zeus and *Hera*; mar *Hercules*. DIA. **Rom** = JUVENTAS. 2. A
minor *PLANET*. 3. PLANT (evergreen).

HEBREW ISRAELITE, JEW; also their language (abbr Heb). For
~ alphabet, see *alphabet*.

HECATE 1. Gk *goddess* of night, witchcraft and the *underworld*
[*Nyx, Persephone*, Proserpine]. 2. A minor *PLANET*.

HECTOR *BULLY, HARROW*, HARRY, INTIMIDATE. 2. Gk

myth s of *Priam* and *Hecuba*; mar Andromache; k by *Achilles* at *Troy*. One of the *Nine Worthies*. [T and C (*Shak*)].

HECUBA 1. Gk myth w of *Priam* (king of *Troy*), m of *Cassandra*, *Hector* and *Paris*. 2. A minor *PLANET*.

HEEL (s/l *heal*). BASE OF MAST. PART OF FOOT [*Achilles*; *bone*]. CAD, SCAMP. LEAN, LIST, TILT.

HEL (s/l *hell*). Nor *goddess* who received those who died of misery and darkness; d of *Loki* and Angurboda.

HELD 1. DETAINED, GRASPED, GRIPPED, KEPT, RESTRICTED. OCCUPIED, OWNED, POSSESSED. SUPPORTED. CELEBRATED, OBSERVED (*custom*). CONTINUED. 2. Hidden word, or word in another, e.g. **Wolfishly upheld by a thread** (6) = L*UP*INE.

~ BACK 1. RESTRAINED. HESITATED, IMPEDED, REFRAINED. 2. Hidden word backwards, e.g. **Held back by Sir, approaching the Capital** (5) = PA*RIS. 3. Word reversed in another, e.g. **It's held back by row over a joint** (7) = BA*STI*NG.

HELEN 1. GIRL. 'FIREBRAND'. 2. Gk myth d of *Leda* and *Zeus*, the *twin* of *Clytemnestra*; mar Menelaus, k of Sparta, whence *Paris* carried her off, thus starting the war at *Troy*. Renowned for her *beauty* [T and C (*Shak*)]. 3. A minor *PLANET*.

HELENUS Gk myth s of *Priam*.

HELIOS Gk *god* of the SUN. Son of Hyperion and The(i)a; br of *Eos* (**Rom** = Aurora) and *Selene* (**Rom** = Luna). **Rom** = SOL.

HELIUM HE (*chem*).

HELL (s/l *Hel*). *HADES*, HECK, INFERNO, PIT, *UNDERWORLD* (q.v.); **opp** = *heaven*. HE WILL (crypt).

HELLE Gk myth d of Athamas and Nephele. She and her br Phrixus were rescued by Nephele from sacrifice by Ino; they flew away on a golden ram (origin of the *golden fleece*), but Helle was drowned when she fell into the sea, which was thereafter called the *Hellespont*.

HELLESPONT DARDANELLES. Strait between Asias Major and Minor, named after *Helle*. [*Hero, Leander*].

HELP AID, ASSIST, HAND (**opp** = *hamper*); REMEDY. AVOID, ESCAPE. *CHAR*.

HELPLESS 1. LACKING ASSISTANCE. 2. Remove letters AID or HELP from word indicated, e.g. **Helpless maid** = M or, more cryptically, **Helpless first aid man** (4) = first*man = ADAM.

HEM BORDER, EDGE, RIM, TURN-UP. HESITATION. *COUGH*, HAWK.

HEN-HOUSE BATTERY, COOP.

HENRY HAL, HARRY. MEASURE (elect). DR JEKYLL
[Edward *Hyde*]. *Shak* chars.

~ **VIII's WIVES in order**: CATHERINE OF SPAIN (div),
ANNE BOLEYN or BULLEN (beheaded), JANE SEYMOUR
(d), ANNE OF CLEVES (div), CATHERINE HOWARD
(beheaded), CATHERINE PARR (survived). *Shak* chars.

HEPHAESTUS Gk *god* of *FIRE*, s of *Zeus* and *Hera*. **Rom** =
VULCAN.

HERA Q of Gk *goddesses* (and of childbirth); d of *Cronos* and
Rhea; sis of and mar to *Zeus*; m of Ares (**Rom** = *Mars*), *Hebe*
(**Rom** = Juventas) and Hephaestus (**Rom** = *Vulcan*). **Rom** =
JUNO.

HERACLES Gk myth s of Zeus and Alcmene; mar to Megara;
an *Argonaut*. Maddened by *Hera*, he k his children, and the
Delphic *oracle* made him perform twelve labours; see Rom
equivalent *HERCULES* for details.

HERALD FORESHADOW, FORETELL, *PROPHESY*.
MESSENGER, TRUMPETER, USHER (~ **of the
gods** = *HERMES*). COURT OFFICIAL, OFFICER OF
STATE (armorial bearings, pedigree, precedence): BATH,
CLARENC(I)EUX, *GARTER*, LORD LYON, NORROY,
ULSTER (all kings of arms); and *CHESTER*, LANCASTER,
RICHMOND, SOMERSET, WINDSOR, *YORK*. *MONTJOY*
(*Shak*); STENTOR (*Troy*). **Heraldic colours**: **black** = sable,
blue = azure, **brown** = tenne or tenny, **green** = vert, **gold** =
or, **orange** = tenny, **purple** = purpure, **red** = gules, **silver** =
argent. **Heraldic terms**: accosted (side by side), *achievement*
(shield), addorsed (back to back), cabossed (head cut at the
neck), *canton* (a corner), couchant (beast lying with head up),
crined (bearing a mane), dexter (right-hand side), disclosed,
displayed (wings spread), dormant (beast lying with head down),
embowed (bent), estoile (*star*), fess (horizontal band), gardant
(beast looking outward), gorged (beast with crown round the
neck), hauriant (*fish* with head up), in *pride* (peacock with tail
spread), jessed (with thongs), lion(c)el(le) (small lion), lymphad
(ship with oars), naiant (*fish* swimming), passant (beast walking),
rampant (beast upright on hind legs), regardant (beast looking
over its shoulder), *sinister* (left-hand side), *wyvern* (winged
serpent).

HERB HERBERT (abbr). ANNUAL PLANT, BANE, WORT.
SIMPLE. And see *plant*. [flavour; *spice*]; **types of ~s and spices**

(includes carrots, parsnips, turnips etc):

3-letters
BAY RUE

4-letters
ALOE	GEUM	*MINT*	*SAGE*
BALM	LEEK	MOLY (myth)	WORT
DILL	MACE	*RACE*	

5-letters
AGAVE	CHILI	CURRY	ORVAL
AMENT	CHIVE	INULA	SPIKE
AVENS	CLARY	MOULI	SWEDE
BASIL	CLOVE	MUDAR	TANSY
CAPER	CUMIN	ONION	THYME

6-letters
BENNET	ENDIVE	HERBAR	*RATTLE*
BORAGE	FENNEL	HYSSOP	SAVORY
CARROT	FERULA	LOVAGE	SESAME
CATNIP	GARLIC	NUTMEG	TURNIP
CHILLI	GINGER	ORIGAN	YARROW
CUMMIN	HARMEL	PEPPER	

7-letters
ACONITE	GINSENG	PAPRIKA	RUE-WORT
CARAWAY	HARMALA	PARSLEY	SAFFRON
CAYENNE	KEDLACK	PARSNIP	SHALLOT
CHERVIL	MUSTARD	PIMENTA	SINAPIS
CHICORY	OREGANO	PIMENTO	WITLOOF

8-letters
ALLSPICE	COSTMARY	TRUE-LOVE
BRASSOCK	MARJORAM	TURMERIC
CAPSICUM	ROSEMARY	WOODRUFF
CHARLOCK	SAMPHIRE	
CINNAMON	TARRAGON	

9+ letters
| ARTEMISIA | GILLYFLOWER | MONKSHOOD |
| CORIANDER | HOREHOUND | WOLFSBANE |

HERCULES 1. *Constellation. HORSE.* 2. Latinized name of
HERACLES, also known as ALCIDES. The s of *Zeus* and
Alcmene, and half-br of Iphicles, ~ mar (1) Megara, (2)
Deianira and (3) *Hebe* (after he had been made immortal).
Sentenced by the Delphic *oracle* to perform 12 labours for
Eurystheus as follows:

(1) Fight with Nemean *lion.*
(2) Killing the *hydra* at Lerna.
(3) Capture of the Arcadian *stag.*
(4) Destruction of the Erymanthian *boar.*
(5) Cleansing of the stable of *Augeas.*
(6) Destruction of the cannibal birds of Lake Stymphalis.
(7) Capture of the Cretan *bull.*
(8) Capture of the *mares* of Diomedes.
(9) Seizure of the *girdle* of Queen *Hippolyte.*
(10) Capture of the *monster* Geryon's *oxen* in Erythia.
(11) Fetching the golden *apples* of the *Hesperides.*
(12) Bringing *Cerberus* from *Hades.*

~ d when wife (2) steeped his cloak in the blood of the *centaur*
Nessus (who had been k by ~ with a poisoned arrow) so that
the poison transferred to ~ and k him. [*pillars of* ~].
HERD (s/l *heard*). 1. Noun of *assembly* (buffalo, cattle, elephants
etc); [*shepherd*]. **God: Gk** = *PAN,* **Rom** = *FAUNUS,* INUUS,
LUPERCUS. 2. *Constellation.*
HERE (s/l *hear*). 1. HAS ARRIVED. IN THIS PLACE. 2. Means
'in this answer', e.g. **Here I have a shot at Shakespeare's villain**
(4) = I*A*GO.
HEREWARD THE WAKE. HITHER (crypt).
HERMES 1. Gk myth s of *Zeus,* HERALD and MESSENGER of
the *gods*; he is said to have invented the *lyre* by putting strings
across the shell of a tortoise. (**Rom** = MERCURY) [caduceus;
robbers]. 2. A minor *PLANET.*
HERMIT ANCHORITE, ASCETIC, *CAVEMAN,* CELLIST,
C(O)ENOBITE, EREMITE, LONER, MONK, *RECLUSE*
(q.v.), STYLITE; 9 (*tarot*); **celeb:** *ELIJAH* (bibl); PETER the
~ (Fr monk); SIMON STYLITES; TIMON (of Athens); patron
St Alexis. CRAB.
HERO 1. Gk myth priestess of *Aphrodite* at Seston on the
Hellespont. Her lover Leander used to swim across from
Abydos to see her, and was drowned when the lighthouse failed

one night. 2. IDOL. CHIEF CHARACTER, MALE LEAD (theat). BRAVE SOLDIER, SUPERMAN (**opp** = *coward*); **celeb (male)**: *ACHILLES, ACTAEON, ADONIS, AENEAS, AGAMEMNON, AUTOLYCUS, BELLEROPHON, CASTOR, DAEDALUS, GANYMEDE, HECTOR, HERACLES, HERCULES, ICARUS, JASON, LAERTES, LEANDER,* LYSANDER, *ODYSSEUS, OEDIPUS, ORESTES, ORION, ORPHEUS, PARIS, PERSEUS,* POLLUX, *PRIAM, PYGMALION, NARCISSUS, SISYPHUS, TANTALUS, THESEUS, ULYSSES*; **celeb (fem)**: *ANDROMEDA, ARACHNE, ATALANTA, CASSANDRA, CLYTEMNESTRA, DAPHNE, DIDO, DORIS, ELECTRA, ELISSA, EUROPA,* EURYDICE, *GALATEA, IPHIGENIA,* HELEN, *HELLE, HIPPOLYTE, JOCASTA, NIOBE, PANDORA, PENELOPE.* And *Shak* char (Much Ado).

HEROD 1. ~ the Great (b 73 B.C.); bibl K who mar Mariamne and was grand-f of Herodias [*Salome*]. His massacre of the innocents to avoid the rivalry of *Jesus* is now questioned. 2. ~ Antipas, s of (1), he mar Herodias (his own niece and w of his br) who was m of *Salome* by his br. ~ ordered the d of John the Baptist, when Herodias persuaded Salome to ask for it as payment for dancing (the seven veils) before him. 3. ~ Agrippa, two bibl kings, one of whom (grand-s of (1) and br-in-law of (2)) k James br of John, and the other (s of (3)) tried St Paul.

HERRING *FISH*: ALLICE, BLOATER (dried), KIPPER (smoked), SHAD, TWAIT. [~ bone, ~ gull, ~ pond].

HESITATION DELAY, ER, UM. STAMMERING, STUTTERING.

HESPERIDES Gk myth maidens (AEGLE, ERYTHEIA and HESPERUS), who guarded the golden apples given by *Ge* to *Hera* when she mar *Zeus*. [*Hercules*].

HESPERUS 1. One of the *Hesperides*; Gk and Rom name for *VENUS* as the EVENING STAR; **opp** = *Lucifer* (Rom). *Phosphorus* (Gk). 2. SCHOONER (Longfellow).

HESTIA 1. Gk myth *goddess* of the *HEARTH*; d of Cronos and Rhea (**Rom** = VESTA). 2. A minor *PLANET*.

HE WILL *HELL*.

HE WOULD HED.

HG MERCURY (*chem*).

HIAWATHA *Modelled* on HAIOHRATHA, a Mohawk chief, Longfellow's poetic hero is an Ojibway grand-s of Nokomis (d of the Moon), raised on the shores of Gitche-Gumee,

Big-Sea-Water (Lake Superior); he had magical moccasins (mile-long strides) and mittens (to crush rocks). He fought his f (West Wind) over wrongs done to his m (Wenonah); he defeated the Corn Spirit; he mar Minnehaha (Laughing Water), and thus made peace with the Dakota tribe. His friends were Chibiabos (*musician*) and Kwasind (*strength*); when they d, ~ k Pau-Puk-Keewis over an insult. ~ foresaw the coming of the White Man, which was heralded by a swarm of golden bees.

HIDDEN CACHED, CONCEALED, DOGGO, ESOTERIC, *SECRET*.

Hidden word There are not as many ways of conveying that the answer is hidden somewhere in the clue, as there are of implying that an anagram is intended. Nevertheless, words such as 'found in . . . ', ' . . . we see', 'from', 'part of . . . ', 'reads', 'reveals', 'some of . . . ' and 'taken from . . . ', all suggest that the word lies somewhere written before your eyes (see HELD/*HOLD BACK* for a hidden word reading backwards). The answer may also be revealed if you take note and respond sensibly to undue awkwardness in phraseology (this sentence has been included not only to warn the puzzler to be on the look-out for stilted sentence construction, which may betray the fact that the puzzle setter has been trying to work the answer into the clue, but also as an example itself. It starts by telling us that 'the answer may be revealed'; it goes on to instruct that a note – A, B, C, D, E, F, G or H – should be taken away somewhere from what follows. Thus, if we remove the letter D from 'respond sensibly' we find that we are left with RESPON•SE(nsibly) – which is another word for 'answer'.) So the clue may have to be added to or shortened, or even read in reverse, to find the hidden word; but the instruction will be there somewhere, together with an indication of the meaning of the answer itself – in the example above, it was the phrase 'the answer may also be revealed'.

HIDE (s/l hied, *hyde*). *FELL*, PELT, *SKIN*; CHAMOIS, GOATSKIN, KID, LEATHER, RUSSIA. CONCEAL(MENT). HARBOUR, *SCREEN* (**opp** = reveal, *unearth*).

HIDING CANING, THRASHING, WHIPPING. CONCEALMENT.

HIGHBALL DRINK. LOB (crypt).

HIGH CLASS A1. U. FLYING SCHOOL (crypt).

HIGHLY 1. EXTREMELY, VERY. 2. High in the body, building etc, e.g. **Highly painful** (8) = HEADACHE, MIGRAINE.

HIGH POST TOP JOB. AIR MAIL (crypt).
HIGH STANDING TALL; ON STILTS, hence STILTED (crypt).
HIGHWAYMAN ROAD MENDER (crypt). BANDOLERO,
  FOOTPAD, ROBBER OF THE ROAD; **celeb**: PAUL
  CLIFFORD (Bulwer-Lytton), CLAUDE DUVAL, TOM
  FAGGUS (Lorna Doone, Blackmore), CAPT MACHEATH
  and JEREMY TWITCHER (Beggar's Opera, Gay), DICK
  TURPIN.
HIJKLMNO WATER (H to O, hence H_2O – crypt).
HILL *BANK*, BUTTE, *DOWN*, DUN, EMINENCE, HEAP,
  INCLINE, MOUND, MOUNT, SLOPE, TOR (**opp** = *vale*).
  SYDNEY *CRICKET* GROUND. *POET*. [Roland ~; postage,
  stamp]. And see *Seven ~s of Rome*.
HIND 1. AFTER, BACK, REAR. 2. (RED) DEER. FISH,
  GROUPER. 3. FARMWORKER, PEASANT, RUSTIC,
  STEWARD. 4. HINDI, -U, -USTAN(I), INDIA(N).
HINDER DETER, HAMPER, IMPEDE, *LET*, MAR,
  OBSTRUCT, PREVENT, *STOP* (**opp** = *abet*). REARMOST.
  DEERSTALKER (crypt).
HINGE JOINT, SWING. ANKLE, ELBOW, KNEE, KNUCKLE,
  SHOULDER. GHE (crypt: H*in*GE).
HINNY STALLION/ASS *offspring*. NHY (crypt: H*in*NY).
HINT INDICATION, *TIP*, WRINKLE.
HIPPOCRATES Celebrated Gk *doctor*, b Cos *c*.460 B.C, d Thessaly
  357 B.C. [doctor's oath].
HIPPOLYTE Gk myth d of *Ares*; Q of the Amazons. She wore a
  girdle, the object of one of *Hercules'* 12 labours.
HIPPOPHILE *Lover* of horses.
HIPPOPHOBIA *Aversion* to horses.
HISTORY 1. ANNALS, CAREER, RECORD, SAGA.
  AUTOBIOGRAPHY (crypt). [Herodotus; Pliny; *Tacitus*].
  2. **Gk muse** = *CLIO*.
HIT *Anag.* CUFF, PUNCH, SLAP, STRIKE; **comp** = run.
  SUCCESS (**opp** = *miss*).
HM ER, HER/HIS MAJESTY, KING, QUEEN.
  HARBOURMASTER.
HO HOLMIUM (*chem*). HOME OFFICE. HOUSE. HALLO,
  HELLO, HILLO, HOLLO, HULLO.
HOAX CANARD, FALSE REPORT; JAPE, PRACTICAL
  JOKE. HOCUS.
HOD 1. Shoulder CARRIER, TRAY (bricks, mortar). SCUTTLE
  (coal). HACK (literary). 2. Br of *Balder* (Nor myth).

HOIST JACK (UP). RAISE(D) (**opp** = *lower*). ELEVATOR, LIFT (mech). FLAG SIGNAL (naut). PULLEY, *WHIP* (naut).

HOLD CATCH, CLASP, GET, GRAB, GRASP, *GRIP*, KEEP. DETAIN, RESIST. CONTAIN, RESTRICT. OWN, POSSESS. THREAT. BELIEVE, CONSIDER, THINK. CARGO COMPARTMENT. **Pl** = Hidden word (see *HELD*), or word round another, e.g. **He holds order in the house** (4) = H*OM*E.

~ **BACK** 1. IMPEDE, RESTRICT, RESTRAIN. 2. Hidden word backwards, e.g. **The Royal Aero Club holds back the money – quite right, it's Spanish** = REA*L.

HOLDING FARM, TENURE. PORTFOLIO. FISTFUL, HANDFUL.

HOLD UP 1. DETAIN. PROP, SUPPORT. RAID, STICK UP. 2. Word backwards in another (dn) clue, e.g. **The subject is: he holds me up after the car goes over us both** (5) = T*H*EM*E.

HOLLAND NL, NETHERLANDS. LINEN, *MATERIAL*. **Pl** = DUTCH, GIN.

HOLMES (s/l *homes*). *DETECTIVE*, SHERLOCK. Created by Sir Arthur Conan Doyle and *modelled* on Dr Joseph *Bell*; lived first in Montague Street and then at 221B Baker Street, London. Stamford introduced him to Dr John H. Watson, ex-Indian Army, wounded Afghanistan in the leg/shoulder (some confusion) and saved by Murray his orderly; Watson later mar Mary Morstan, a *governess* from The Sign of Four. Holmes played the *violin*, took *cocaine*, kept his tobacco in a Persian slipper, had a gasogene for soda water, used the door as a target for revolver practice, and wore a *deerstalker* hat; his br Mycroft was a Civil Servant and a member of the *Diogenes* Club; his housekeeper was Mrs Hudson, his pageboy Billy, his young helpers the Baker Street Irregulars (leader: Wiggins); Scotland Yard detectives were Gregson and Lestrade; principal adversaries were Irene Adler ('the' Woman), Col Sebastian Moran, and Professor James Moriarty ('the Napoleon of Crime') who was k – supposedly with Holmes – at the Reichenbach Falls in Switzerland. **Celeb cases**:

A Study in Scarlet	The Five Orange Pips
The Sign of Four	The Man with the Twisted Lip
A Scandal in Bohemia	The 'Gloria Scott'
The Red-headed League	The Musgrave Ritual
A Case of Identity	The Reigate Puzzle
The Boscombe Valley Mystery	The Crooked Man

The Resident Patient	~ the Three Students
The Greek Interpreter	~ the Golden Pince-Nez
The Naval Treaty	~ the Missing Three-Quarter
The Final Problem	~ the Abbey Grange
The Hound of the Baskervilles	~ the Second Stain
The Valley of Fear	~ Wisteria Lodge
His Last Bow	~ the Cardboard Box
The Adventure of:	~ the Red Circle
~ the Blue Carbuncle	~ the Bruce-Partington Plans
~ the Speckled Band	~ the Dying Detective
~ the Engineer's Thumb	~ the Devil's Foot
~ the Noble Bachelor	~ the Illustrious Client
~ the Beryl Coronet	~ the Blanched Soldier
~ the Copper Beeches	~ the Mazarin Stone
~ the Empty House	~ the Three Gables
~ the Norwood Builder	~ the Sussex Vampire
~ the Dancing Men	~ the Three Garridebs
~ the Solitary Cyclist	~ the Creeping Man
~ the Priory School	~ the Lion's Mane
~ Black Peter	~ the Veiled Lodger
~ Charles Augustus Milverton	~ Shoscombe Old Place
~ the Six Napoleons	~ the Retired Colourman

HOLT COPSE, WOOD. *HABITATION*, LAIR (otter). *CASTLE*.
HOLY (s/l wholly). SAINTLY; GOOD. *ISLAND*. HOLED (crypt).
~ **GRAIL** CHRIST'S CUP [*Galahad; Round Table*].
HOME COUNTRY, DWELLING, LAND, REFUGE, VILLA; **comp** = *dry*. FIND, LOCATE (radio). OWN GROUND (*cricket, football, rugby*); **opp** = away. *PRIME MINISTER*.
~ **COUNTIES** SE (geog, crypt).
~ **HELP** *CHAR*. DIY.
~ **OFFICE** HO.
HOMER 1. Gk *poet* b *c*.1000 B.C. **Works** (not all authenticated): Iliad (War of *Troy*); Odyssey (based on legends of Odysseus/ Ulysses after Troy); Homeric Hymns (to *Aphrodite, Demeter, Hermes*, Delian and Pythian *Apollo*). 2. RUN (baseball). *PIGEON* (crypt).
HONEY DARLING, DEAR, PET, SWEETHEART. NECTAR, SWEETNESS [mead].
HONOUR 1. CBE, CH, KBE, MBE, OBE, OM etc. AWARD, GONG, *MEDAL*, KNIGHTHOOD. GRACE, RECOGNIZE.

VIRTUE [**guard of** ~ = *chaperone*]. ACE, KING, QUEEN, JACK/KNAVE (cards). 2. TITLE which goes with some high honours, e.g. **Man of honour** (3) or (6) = SIR or KNIGHT.

HONOURED 1. ACCEPTED, PAID. CBE, CH, KBE etc (see *HONOUR*). DIGNIFIED, ENRICHED. ENTITLED. 2. TITLE which often goes with an honour or ennoblement, e.g. **Honoured lady** (4) = DAME.

HOOCH *DRINK. AMERICAN INDIAN.*

HOOD BONNET, COWL; CANOPY, COVER. GANGSTER, GUNMAN, HOODLUM, THUG; MAFIA. ROBIN, RICHARD LOCKSLEY *modelled* on Robert FitzOoth of Locksley [Friar Tuck, Little *John, Maid* Marion, *Much*, Allen-a-Dale, George-a-Green, Nottingham Sheriff, Sherwood Forest, Will Scarlet]. RED RIDING ~. *POET.* ADMIRAL.

HOOK CATCH, SNARE, TRAP. ANGLED WIRE, ATTACHMENT, CROOK. CURVED BLADE. BEND. *HEEL* (rugby). PULL, STROKE (*cricket*, golf). BLOW, HIT, PUNCH (boxing). *PIRATE.*

HOOKER FORWARD (rugby). PROSTITUTE (US sl). *BOAT,* SHIP (sl). ANGLER, FISHERMAN (crypt).

HOOKY TRUANCY (US). ANGULAR; ANGLING, FISHING (crypt).

HOPE 1. ASPIRATION, DESIRE, EXPECT, WISH. ~ *CHEST.* PROBABILITY, PROMISE. BOB ~ (theat). 2. Sir Anthony ~ (Hawkins), b 1863, d 1933. Barrister and *writer*, his most famous books being The Prisoner of Zenda, and its sequel Rupert of Hentzau. They relate how a *double* secured the Ruritanian *royal family* of Strelsau Palace against a would-be usurper from Castle Zenda. **Characters: (the good guys)** Rudolf Rassendyll (red-headed), King Rudolf Elphberg (his double), Princess Flavia (Elphberg), Col Sapt, Fritz von Tarlenheim; and **(the baddies)** Duke Michael (Elphberg) of Strelsau, Rupert of Hentzau, Bauer and Antoinette de Mauban.

HOPPER *BOUNDER*; CRICKET, FLEA, FROG, *KANGAROO.* CONTAINER. HOP-PICKER; OAST HOUSE.

HORACE Flaccus; Rom *poet* (65–8 B.C.) b Apulia. His patron (with *Virgil*) was Maecenas. Was on losing side at Battle of Philippi. **Works:** Book of Satires; Epistles; Epodes; Odes; and, principally, Ars Poetica.

HORAE (s/l hoary). Gk goddesses of the seasons (especially *rain*) and order (especially *justice* and *peace*). Known in Athens as AUXO, CARPO and THALLO, but named by Hesiod as

DIKE (justice), EUNOMIA (good order) and *IRENE* (peace),
the three dd of Themis and *Zeus*.

HORRIFIC H (film *censorship*). FRIGHTFUL, SCANDALOUS,
SHOCKING.

HORSE (s/l hoarse). CLOTHES DRIER, TRESTLE. *DRUG*,
HEROIN. *ISLAND. LARK, PLAY.* MAINSHEET SPAN
(naut). OBSTRUCTION (mining). BUCK, VAULTING
BLOCK. QUADRUPED of genus equus; DOBBIN, GG, NAG
(all sl); COURSER, MOUNT, MUSTANG, ROCKING; BAY,
CHESTNUT, DAPPLED, GREY, PIEBALD/PINTO, ROAN,
SKEWBALD; PONY, STEED; KELPIE (Sc myth); **types:**
CARTHORSE, CHARGER, CIRCUS ~, *COB*, DESTRIER
(warhorse), HOBBY ~, *RACEHORSE, SCREW*, SHOW ~,
(STEEPLE)CHASER, *THOROUGHBRED*, TROTTER;
breeds: ARABIAN, BARB, CASPIAN, CLYDESDALE,
CONNEMARA, DARTMOOR, HANOVERIAN,
LIPPIZANER, NEW FOREST, PALOMINO, PERCHERON,
PRZEWALSKI'S ~ (wild), QUARTER ~, SHETLAND,
SHIRE, SUFFOLK PUNCH, TARPAN, WELSH. **Assembly**
= *herd;* **habitation** = stable; **male** = stallion (colt), stud ~;
fem = mare (filly); **offspring** = foal (colt, filly). **Celeb:** ARION
(talking ~, offspring of *Poseidon* and *Demeter*), ARKLE
(steeplechaser), BLACK BEAUTY (Anna Sewell), BLACK
BESS (Dick Turpin), BLACK NELL (Wild Bill Hickok),
BOXER (*Orwell*), BORAK (*Mohammed*), BUCEPHALUS
(*Alexander* the Great), CHAMPION (Wonder ~), CICERO
(drum ~, mil), CLOVER (*Orwell*), COPENHAGEN
(*Wellington*), DESERT ORCHID (steeplechaser), GOLDEN
MILLER (steeplechaser), GRANE (Brunhilda, Wagner's
Ring), *HERCULES* (Jorrocks, Soapey Sponge. Steptoe
& Son), INCITATUS (Caligula's consul), LAMRI (King
Arthur), MARENGO (*Napoleon*), MARSALA (Garibaldi),
MARSHLAND SHALES (19th cent; one-eyed), MOLLIE
(*Orwell*), *PEGASUS* (winged ~ of *Bellerophon; constellation*),
RED RUM ® (Grand National), REKSH (Rustam),
RONALD (Lord Cardington's, Charge of the Light Brigade),
ROSINANTE (Don Quixote), SCOUT (Tonto [Lone Ranger]),
SHERGAR (abducted racehorse), *SILVER* (Lone Ranger
[Tonto]), SLEIPNER (eight-legged of *Odin*), SORREL (William
III), TRIGGER (Roy Rogers), TUC ~ (*Low*), VELVET
(Enid Bagnold), VOLONEL (Field Marshal Earl Roberts
VC), WHITE SURREY (Richard III), Wooden ~ of *Troy*;

XANTHUS and BALIUS (*Achilles*; offspring of Zephyrus and
the *Harpy* Podarge) [*centaur; Ch calendar*; ~ power, Munnings
(*painter*); Prince Monolulu ('I got a ~'); *racetrack*; stalking ~;
Thelwell (*cartoonist*); unicorn]. **Pl** = HOUYHNHMS (*Swift*).
Gods: **Gk** = *Poseidon;* **Rom** = *Neptune* [white ~s; wild ~s];
Comp = *coach, hounds*.
HORSEGUARDS BLUES, *ROYALS*. PARADE GROUND.
HORSEPOWER HP (550 ft/lb/sec).
HORUS Gk form of Egy *god* of the SUN; s of *Isis*. God of
doorways.
HOSPITAL H. *NURSERY* (crypt), SANATORIUM,
SICKROOM.
HOST ARMY, COMPANY (arch). GREAT NUMBER, LOTS.
INNKEEPER, *LANDLORD*, *Chaucer* character (Harry
Bailey). ENTERTAINER, PARTY-GIVER, WELCOMER;
AMPHITRYON (Molière). RECEIVER, RECEPTACLE (of
commensal, parasite, transplant). CONSECRATED BREAD
(eccles). **Pl** = ANGELS, STARS.
HOT H; CLOSE, NEAR, OPPRESSIVE, SULTRY,
SWELTERING, TORRID, WARM (**opp** = *cold*). STOLEN
(sl).
~ **SPOT** TROPICS; SAHARA. OVEN. VOLCANO. IN
DEMAND, KEEN.
HOUND HARRY, PURSUE, WORRY. BOUNDER, CAD. *DOG*
(**assembly** = kennel, pack, **male** = dog, **fem** = bitch, **offspring**
= puppy) [Baskervilles (*Holmes*); hunting; Herne the Hunter;
Wish ~s]. **Pl comp** = *fox; horse*.
HOUR (s/l our). H, HR. **Pl** = *HORAE*, the Gk seasons (q.v.).
HOUSE HO. MPs, COMMONS, *LEGISLATIVE ASSEMBLY*,
LORDS, WESTMINSTER. BINGO ®, FULL CARD, LOTTO
®. BUNGALOW, COTTAGE, *HOME*, *LODGE*, PREMISES,
SEMI, VILLA; and see *COUNTRY* ~ for **celeb fict**, and
STATELY HOME for **celeb fact**. *CHINESE DYNASTY*,
ROYAL FAMILY (q.v. for lists). AUDIENCE (theat).
BUSINESS, *COMPANY*, FIRM; TELLSON'S BANK (2 Cities,
Dickens).
HOUSEHOLD CAVALRY BLUES, ROYALS.
HOUSEHOLDER OWNER-OCCUPIER, HEAD OF HOUSE
(hence H). FRANCHISEE (arch). *LAR* (crypt). POKER
PLAYER (crypt). SNAIL, WHELK (crypt). **Pl** = *GUARDS*;
BLUES, ROYALS (crypt). *LARES*, PENATES (Rom, crypt).
HOUSEHOLD GODS *LARES*, PENATES (Rom).

HOUSE OF COMMONS DEBATING CHAMBER,
LEGISLATIVE ASSEMBLY, MPs.
~ **LORDS** UPPER HOUSE, OTHER PLACE. BALFOUR'S
POODLE (fig). *STATELY HOME*. TAVERN (crypt, cricket).
HOUSEPARTY BINGO ®, LOTTO ®.
HOY CALL, HAIL. *BOAT. ISLAND.*
HP HOUSE OF PARLIAMENT, MPs, WESTMINSTER.
HORSEPOWER. SAUCE ®.
HQ HEADQUARTERS, hence H, E, A or D (crypt).
HR HOUR.
HST HIGH SPEED TRAIN.
HUMANIST ERASMUS (NL).
HUN ATTILA (*Ch dynasty*). GERMAN, NOMAD, PRUSSIAN.
HALF-HUNTER (crypt).
HUNCHBACK CROOKBACK, HUMPBACK [*camel, whale*];
cele (fact): Alexander Pope, Richard III; **celeb (fiction)**: ~
of Notre Dame, Quasimodo (Hugo), Punch, Rigoletto (*jester*,
Verdi), Rumpelstiltskin (Grimm).
HUNDRED See *number*. C, CENTURY, TON. 100 [~ days
(*Napoleon*); ~ years war]. LAND AREA.
HUNDREDWEIGHT CWT, *MEASURE*.
Hung Hungary, ~ian.
HUNGRY (s/l Hungary). 1. AVID, KEEN, STARVING. 2. Word
with O added in it, e.g. **Jan is hungry, and is a different girl** (4)
= J(O)AN, or conversely **Joan is no longer hungry, and is quite a
different girl** (3) = J*AN.
HUNTER 1. *HORSE*, HUNTSMAN: JOHN PEEL, JORROCKS
(HERCULES), UNSPEAKABLE (Wilde). CHASER,
SEEKER, ESAU (bibl), *NIMROD* (bibl) [*patron saint*].
AIRCRAFT. (COVERED) WATCH. 2. **Myth**: *ACTAEON,
ARTEMIS, DIANA*, HECATE, HERNE (*ghost*),
MELEAGER, *ORION*, UPIS. 3. *Constellation* (Orion).
HUNTING 1. CHASING, SEEKING (fox); SHOOTING (big
game). OSCILLATING, PULSATING, WAVERING. 2. **God:**
Gk = *PAN*; **goddess: Gk** = *ARTEMIS*, **Rom** = *DIANA*.
HURRIED UP HASTENED. DECAR, NAR (dn; crypt).
HUSBAND CONSORT, MAN, MATE, OLD MAN, PARTNER,
POT AND PAN (*rh sl*) [Darby and Joan]. CONSERVE,
GUARD.
HUSBANDRY 1. *FARMING*. ACCOUNTING, MANAGEMENT.
MARRIAGE (crypt). 2. **Rom god** = MARS.
HUSSY *BAGGAGE*, HUZZY, JADE, MINX.

HYADES Gk myth maidens guarding *Dionysus*, now a group of *seven stars* (in Taurus, near *Pleiades*; rain).

HYBRID CROSSBRE(E)D. *MULE*. HINNY.

HYDE (s/l *hide*, hied). HEATH, PARK. EDWARD ~ [Dr Henry Jekyll; R. L. *Stevenson*].

HYDRA 1. Gk myth nine-headed *monster*, destroyed by *Hercules* at Lerna. 2. *Constellation*. 3. POLYP. WATERSNAKE.

HYDROGEN H (*chem*).

HYDROPHOBIA *Aversion* to water [rabies].

HYENA TASMANIAN WOLF. QUADRUPED (order Hyaenidae) [laughing; *Anubis*; jackal].

HYGEIA 1. Gk myth *goddess* of HEALTH, d of *Asclepius*. 2. A minor *PLANET*.

HYMEN 1. MEMBRANE, VIRGINITY. 2. Gk myth *god* of fruitfulness and marriage; s of *Dionysus* (**Rom** = *Bacchus*) and *Aphrodite* (**Rom** = *Venus*). Also marriage song.

HYMN 1. SONG OF PRAISE. 2. **Gk myth muse** = POLYHYMNIA/POLYMNIA.

HYPERION A *Titan*, s of *Uranus* and *Ge*, f of *Eos*, *Helios* and *Selene*.

HYPNOS Gk myth *goddess* of SLEEP, d of *Nyx* without benefit of father [*Morpheus*].

I (s/l aye, eye). ACE. IODINE (*chem*). ISLAND. ITALY (*car plate*). ME, NUMBER ONE, PERSONAL PRONOUN.

IACCHUS = *BACCHUS*.

IAMBUS *FOOT*.

IAPETUS 1. Gk myth *TITAN*. All men are reputed to be descended from him. 2. A satellite of the *planet* Saturn.

IB(ID) IN THE SAME PLACE (**opp** = *alibi*).

IBA INDEPENDENT *BROADCASTING* AUTHORITY, LOCAL RADIO, TV.

IC IN CHARGE.

ICARUS 1. Gk myth s of *Daedalus*, who flew too near the sun and fell, when the wax securing his wings was melted [mausoleum]. 2. A minor *PLANET*.

ICE HARD WATER. DIAMONDS. CHOC ~, CORNET, DAIRY CREAM ~, KNICKERBOCKER GLORY, SORBET, VANILLA, WHIP. GROWLER, ~BERG, PACK ~ [~ fish].

ICED CHILLED, FROZEN. RINK (crypt).

ICENI Tribe of Ancient Britons in East Anglia [*Boadicea*].
ID I WOULD. THE SAME. *CARP, FISH*. INSTINCT.
IDLE INEFFECTIVE, VAIN, WORTHLESS. TICK OVER.
INDOLENT, LAZY, UNOCCUPIED, USELESS.
IE ID EST, THAT IS.
IF PROVIDED, ~ING, SUPPOSING, AN (arch).
WHENEVER. INTERMEDIATE FREQUENCY. POEM
(*Kipling*). *GAOL* (Dumas). **Pl comp** = *buts*.
IGNIS FATUUS FIRE DAMP, FRIAR'S LANTERN, JACK
O' LANTERN, WILL O' THE WISP; MARSH GAS [c.f. St
Elmo's Fire (which is chem different); methane; *mirage*].
II ELEVEN; TWO. SIDE, TEAM.
IL THE ITALIAN. ISRAEL (*car plate*). ILLINOIS (US *state*).
ILL NOT WELL, SICK. I WILL (crypt). ILLUSTRATED.
ILLINOIS (US *state*).
IM 1. INTRA MUSCULAR. I AM. HALF-TIME (crypt).
2. Used in a clue at the start of a word to describe the solution,
e.g. **'Imperfect' he could have said** (7) = GALAHAD; or may
be included in the answer with the same effect, e.g. **Said by
reporter to cut a figure** (7) = IM·PRESS. As 'im in the clue, implies
omission of H from clue or answer, e.g. **Speech from 'im who
held the bridge to the north** (7) = (H)ORATIO·N; may also in
the answer be written as 'him commonly', e.g. **Years to him
commonly give appearance** (5) = (h)IM·AGE.
IMAGINARY COUNTRY See *COUNTRY* **Celeb fict** for list.
IMITATE *APE*, COPY, MIMIC. *BORROW*.
IMP AFREET, AFRIT, *DEVIL*, *PERI*, EVIL *SPIRIT*.
EMPEROR, IMPERATOR; IMPERIAL. IMPORTANT.
IMPAIRED DAMAGED, WEAKENED. II (crypt); AYE-AYE
(crypt). TWINNED (crypt).
IMPOSING 1. *GRAND, NOBLE*. PRESUMING. LAYING
ON (hands, eccl). LAYING OUT (print). 2. Read as: 'I am
acting/modelling/pretending . . . ' (crypt).
IMPRESS CONSCRIBE, CONSCRIPT, ENFORCE, *PRESS
GANG*, SEIZE, SHANGHAI. DENT, EMBOSS, SEAL,
STAMP, STRIKE. CUT A FIGURE, INFLUENCE. [*im*].
IMPRESSIONIST 1. IMITATOR, MIMIC. *PRESS GANG* (crypt).
CARVER, ETCHER (crypt). INFLUENTIAL (crypt).
2. School of modern painting; **celeb**: BOUDIN, CEZANNE,
DEGAS, MANET, MONET, PISSARO, RENOIR.
IN 1. AT HOME, INSIDE, NOT OUT. *BATTING*. ESOTERIC.
FASHIONABLE. INDIANA (US *state*). INDIUM (*chem*).

2. One word in another, e.g. **An intent to be a leaseholder** (6) = TEN*AN*T, or **Four indulge to reveal** (7) = D*IV*ULGE.

INCENSE *ANGER*, ENRAGE. HOLY SMOKE, SPICE. PRAISE.

INCH IN. *MEASURE*, PART OF FOOT. *CREEP. ISLAND.*

IN CHARGE 1. IC, OVER. 2. By inference, word in synonym for charge, e.g. **The cadets and I are in charge – nonsense** (7) = RU*BB*I*SH.

INCITATUS *Horse* which belonged to the mad Rom emperor *Caligula* (A.D. 12–41), whose reign was characterized by orgies of cruelty and debauchery; he made ~ a Consul.

INCLINED ANGLED, BIASED, LEANING [Pisa], SLOPED, SLOPING, TILTED; BENT. HALF A MIND (hence MI or ND – crypt). READY, TENDED, TENDING.

INCLUDE 1. COMPREHEND, COMPRISE, CONTAIN, EMBRACE, ENCLOSE. 2. The clue contains a *hidden word* as answer, e.g. **The king is included in his will, I am quite sure** (7) = WILL*I*AM.

INCOMPLETE 1. EMBRYO, IMMATURE, PART MADE, UNFINISHED. 2. Part of sentence, as a hidden word, e.g. **Spread an incomplete topic, nicely prepared** (6) = PIC*NIC.

IN DEBT 1. IN THE RED, OVERDRAWN, OWING. 2. Place word indicated into DEBT, e.g. **First appearance of society in debt** (5) = DEB*U*T. 3. Similarly place word in RED, e.g. **Fish in debt was pulled in** (6) = R*EEL*ED. 4. May also have IOUS added, e.g. **Officer in debt takes exception** (8) = CAPT*IOUS.

INDEED 1. CERTAINLY, REALLY, YEA, YES. 2. Word placed in DEED, e.g. **Bit indeed would go against one** (7) = DE*BIT*ED.

INDIA Subcontinent in Asia; Indo (hence inaction, crypt). IND (*car plate*). *ANTELOPE.* HINDU (and see *Religion*). **Provinces**: Andhra Pradesh, Arunnchal Pradesh, Assam, Bengal, Bihar, Gujarat, Haryana, Hyderabad, Mimachal Pradesh, Jamm, Kashmir, Karnatak, Kerala, Madhya Pradesh, Maharashtra, Manipur, Meghalaya, Mysore, Nagaland, Orissa, Punjab, Rajasthan, Sikkim, Tamil Nadu, Tripura, Uttar Pradesh (UP), West Bengal [*American* ~n (Red ~n); ~n ink; ~ paper; ~ rubber; ~ tea].

INDIAN 1. Native product of ~. 2. *American* ~ (q.v. for tribes).

INDIVIDUAL EGO, I, ONE, SELF. CHARACTERISTIC, PARTICULAR, *SINGLE*, SPECIAL.

INDRA Ind *god* of *RAIN*.

INDUCED 1. BROUGHT ABOUT/ON, CAUSED. INFERRED,

PERSUADED, PREVAILED ON. 2. Letter or word put into
another, e.g. **Politician, nothing induced to clean** (3) = M*O*P.
3. Word placed into letters DUCED: **King induced a wetting** (6)
= DUC*K*ED.
INDUS *RIVER. CONSTELLATION.*
INDUSTRY BUSINESS, FACTORY, MANUFACTURING,
WORKS; CBI. APPLICATION, HARD WORK.
IN ERROR *Anag.* 1. OUT, WRONG, MISTAKENLY (**opp** =
right). 2. Word placed in synonym for error, e.g. **Draw off wine
in error; it is salty** = B*RACK*ISH.
INEXPERIENCED DEB, *GREEN*, IMMATURE, TYRO,
VIRGIN, *YOUNG* (**opp** = *expert*).
INFATUATION 1. CRUSH, LOVESICKNESS. 2. **Goddess** =
ATE (Gk).
INFERIOR LESSER, LOWER, SUBORDINATE, UNDER.
NON-U.
INFORMATION DATE, *DOPE*, *GEN*, GRIFF, INFO,
INTELLIGENCE, KNOW-HOW, LOW-DOWN. BETRAYAL
(q.v.). TABLES, TIDINGS. [COI]. FLIGHT, SQUADRON,
VEE (all crypt).
INIGO 1. JONES; *ARCHITECT*. 2. Place letter I in word
indicated, e.g. **Inigo cons money from it** (5) = CO*I*NS.
INITIALLY 1. AT FIRST, STARTING. 2. Use the first letters of
words indicated, e.g. **He is trying initially to make a success** (3)
= H*I*T.
INLAY 1. EMBED, FILLING, INSERT; ORNAMENT;
types: BOULE, BUHL, FILIGREE, MARQUETRY,
OYSTER VENEER, PARQUETRY, PIQUE, POSE D'OR,
TUNBRIDGE WARE. 2. Letter(s) or word(s) placed in letters
LAY, e.g. **Final inlay is idle** (4) = LA*Z*Y.
INN *BAR*, PH (abbr), PUB, REFUGE, *TAVERN*.
INNER INTERIOR, INTERNAL. (Second) TARGET RING,
ON TARGET [*bullseye, magpie, outer*]. BATSMAN (crypt).
PUBCRAWLER, *LANDLORD*, PUBLICAN (crypt).
INNER TEMPLE LAW SOCIETY, *INN OF COURT*.
INNS OF COURT GRAY'S INN, INNER TEMPLE, LINCOLN'S
INN, MIDDLE TEMPLE [benchers; call to the bar].
IN ORDER 1. ALL RIGHT, ALLOWED, OK, PERMITTED.
BY ROTA, ON ROSTER, SERIATIM. SERVICEABLE,
WORKING. **Pl** = *CHURCHMAN*, ORDAINED. 2. Word
placed in *decoration* or order, e.g. **Latin in order like earth** (6) =
OB*LAT*E.

IN RUINS *Anag.* 1. BROKEN, COLLAPSED. 2. Word in ʀᴜɪɴs,
   e.g. **Briefly equal in ruins for French sharks** (7) = ʀ*ᴇǫ*ᴜɪɴs.
INSECT 1. CREATURE, INVERTEBRATE (genus insecta),
   LEPIDOPTERA; SIX-FOOTER (crypt) [arachnid: mite,
   scorpion, *spider*, tick]. **Celeb**: *ALEXANDER* (*Milne*). **Types**:

3-letters

ANT	*BEE*	*DOR*	*FLY*

4-letters

FLEA	MITE	*MOTH*	WASP
GNAT			

5-letters

APHID	EMMET	LOUSE	MIDGE
APHIS			

6-letters

BEETLE	EARWIG	MANTIS	SCARAB
CADDIS	HORNET	MAYFLY	
CICADA	LOCUST	SAWFLY	

7-letters

BLOWFLY	*CRICKET*	CREEPER	DAMOSEL

8+ letters

ALDERFLY	HOUSEFLY
BLUEBOTTLE	*LEPIDOPTERA*
BUTTERFLY	POND SKATER
CADDIS FLY	ROVE BEETLE
COCKROACH	WATER BOATMAN
DRAGONFLY	WATER SCORPION
GRASSHOPPER	WHIRLIGIG
HORSEFLY	BEETLE

   2. Put letter(s) or word(s) into sᴇᴄᴛ, e.g. **Reticent about insect** (6) =
   sᴇᴄ*ʀᴇ*ᴛ, or **The Spanish insect is choice** (6) = s*ᴇʟ*ᴇᴄᴛ.
INSIDE 1. CONTAINED. *GAOL*. FOOTBALLER: FORWARD,
   STRIKER. 2. Word in another, hidden word, e.g. **It's all go,
   inside any pain** (5) = ᴀ*ɢᴏ*ɴʏ.
INSPIRATION ANIMATION, INTUITION, *MUSE* (q.v.),
   PROMPTING, THOUGHT; **celeb**: BEATRICE (Dante);

DARK LADY (sonnets, *Shak*); EGERIA (Rom); FIDRA (Treasure Is); LAURA (Petrarch); WH (Onlie Begetter, sonnets, *Shak*) [Enigma Variations (Elgar); see also *companions, lovers; model* (q.v. for fict characters modelled on real life)]. BREATHING, INHALATION (crypt).

INSTALL(ED) 1. PUT IN, FITTED; STABLED (crypt). 2. Word placed in another, e.g. **Bed with girl installed is forbidden** (6) = B*ANN*ED.

INSTEAD 1. ALTERNATIVE, IN LIEU, SUBSTITUTE. 2. Word placed in letters STEAD, e.g. **Cooked me instead** (7) = STEA*ME*D.

INSTITUTE ORIGINATE, START, *FOUND. ORGANIZATION*, SOCIETY (tech); MIT.

INSTRUMENT 1. IMPLEMENT, TOOL. DIAL, MEASURING DEVICE, POSITION FINDER (aero, naut). ARRANGER, CHANNEL, PERFORMER. FORMAL/LEGAL DOCUMENT. 2. MUSICAL DEVICE, SOUND PRODUCER; **types**:

(**strings, blown**): *AEOLIAN* HARP; (**strings, bowed**): ARPEGGIONE, CELLO, CHIKARA, CRWTH (no *vowel*), DOUBLE BASS, GAMBA, HURDY-GURDY, JAPANESE FIDDLE, REBEC, TROMBA MARINA, VIOL, VIOLA, *VIOLIN*; (**strings, hammered**): CLAVICHORD, CLAVIER/KLAVIER, DULCIMER, PANTALEON, *PIANO*(FORTE), SCHLAGZITHER, ZIMBALON; (**strings, plucked**): BALALAIKA, BANJO, BARREL ORGAN, BELL HARP, CEMBALO, CITHERA, CITHER(N), CITTERN, CLARSACH, DITAL HARP, GITTERN, GUITAR, *HARP*, HARPSICHORD, HURDY GURDY, KITHERA, LUTE, *LYRE*, MANDOLA, MANDOLIN, MANDORA, PSALTERY, SITAR, SPINET(TE), UD (Arab), UKULELE, VICTALELE, VIHUELA, VINA (Ind), VIRGINAL, ZEZE, ZITHER; (**wind, brass**): BUCCINA (Rom), BUGELHORN (Ger), BUGLE, CORNET, FLUGELHORN (Ger), FRENCH HORN, OLIPHANT, POSTHORN, SAXHORN, *SERPENT*, TROMBONE, TRUMPET, TUBA, VAMPHORN; (**wind, reed**): ACCORDION, *BAGPIPES*, BASSOON, BOMBARD, CHENG (Ch), CLARINET, COR ANGLAIS, FLUTINA, HARMONICA, HORNPIPE, *MOUTH ORGAN*, OBOE, PIBCORN, PIBROCH (Sc), *QUAIL*, REGAL, SAXOPHONE, SHAWM, STOCK HORN; (**wind, tube**): ALPHORN, BARREL ORGAN, BIGOPHONE,

BIN (Ind), FIFE, FLAGEOLET, *FLUTE*, GALOUBET, HURDY GURDY, KAZOO, LUR(E), MIRLITON, *NIGHTINGALE*, OCARINA, *ORGAN*, PANPIPES, PENNY WHISTLE, PIPE, *RECORDER*, TIN WHISTLE, WHIFFLE, ZUF(F)OLO; (**percussion**): *ANVIL*, *BELL*, *BONES*, CASTANET, CELESTA, CHANG (Ch), CRESCENT, CYMBALS, DEAGAN, *DRUM*, DULCIMER, DULCITONE, GLOCKENSPIEL, GONG, JEWS HARP, KETTLEDRUM, MARIMBA, MARROWBONES, RATTLE, SALT BOX, SANTIR (Pers), SISTRUM (Egy), SNARE DRUM, TABLA (Ind), TABOR, TAMBOURINE, TARBOUKA, TIMBREL, TIMPANI, *TRAPS*, *TRIANGLE*, WOOD BLOCKS, XYLOPHONE.

INTELLIGENCE BRAINS, NOUS, IQ (**opp** = *stupidity*). *GEN*, CIA, MIV, SOE [espionage; *agent*].

INTENT 1. BENT. MEANING. 2. Word in the letters TENT, e.g. **An intent leases** = TEN*AN*T.

INTER AMONG, BETWEEN, BURY, ENTOMB.

INTERMINABLE 1. ENDLESS, PERPETUAL [eternity]. 2. Omit last letter(s), e.g. **Interminable hate on one's head** (3) = HAT*.

INTERNATIONAL UNITS PEACEKEEPING FORCE, UN PATROLS. MEASUREMENT SYSTEM, SI; **prefixes (multiples)**:

Factor	Prefix	Symbol
10^{12}	tera-	T
10^9	giga-	G
10^6	mega-	M
10^3	kilo-	k
10^2	hecto-	h
10	deca-	da
10^{-1}	deci-	d
10^{-2}	centi-	c
10^{-3}	milli-	m
10^{-6}	micro-	μ
10^{-9}	nano-	n
10^{-12}	pico-	p
10^{-15}	femto-	f
10^{-18}	atto-	a

INTERVAL INTERMISSION, HALF-TIME (hence TI or ME), PAUSE. OCTAVE; SECOND, SEVENTH etc (mus).

INTRIGUE FASCINATE. CABAL, *PLOT.*
INUUS Rom god of *herds.* **Gk** = *PAN.*
INVENTION 1. BRAINCHILD, *DISCOVERY,* IDEA [patent];
   celeb:

CARPENTRY TOOLS	(Gk myth *Daedalus*)
WRITING	(Bab myth Nabu/Nebu)
GUNPOWDER	(1320 Schwarz)
TELESCOPE	(1607 Galileo)
PIANOFORTE	(1710 Cristofalli)
MERCURY	
THERMOMETER	(1721 Fahrenheit)
SPINNING JENNY	(1763 Hargreaves)
STEAM ENGINE	(1764 Watt)
HOT AIR BALLOON	(1783 Montgolfier)
MINER'S SAFETY LAMP	(1815 Davy)
SEWING MACHINE	(1841 Howe)
STEEL	(1856 Bessemer)
DYNAMITE	(1868 Nobel)
TORPEDO	(1868 Whitehead)
TELEPHONE	(1876 Bell)
PHONOGRAPH	(1877 Edison)
WIRELESS	(1898 Marconi)
TANK	(1899 Simms)
AEROPLANE	(1903 Wright)
RADAR	(1935 Watson-Watt)
JET ENGINE	(1939 Heinkel)
POLYESTER	(1941 Whinfield & Dixon)
ROCKET WEAPON	(1944 von Braun)
ATOMIC BOMB	(1945 USA team)

   2. **Goddess** = *MINERVA* (Rom).
INVERSE CAPSIZE, INVERT, UPEND. OPPOSITE.
   POETIC, RHYMING (crypt).
INVEST 1. BESTOW, CLOTHE, ENDOW. BESIEGE. PLOY,
   PUT MONEY IN, SPEND. 2. Place synonym for money
   in word or letters indicated, e.g. **Invested in bed, and lost
   everything?** (4) = B*L*ED. 3. Any word placed round another,
   e.g. **Medical man investing in a foreign currency** (5) =
   D*INA*R.
INVOLVED *Anag.* COMPLICATED, CONVOLUTED,

ENTANGLED, INTRICATE (**opp** = *simple*). ENTAILED, IMPLICATED. CONCERNED, IN QUESTION.

IN WRITING 1. IN LONGHAND, WRITTEN [libel]. 2. Put MS round word or letters indicated, e.g. **Put a small amount of money in writing atlases** (4) = M*AP*S.

IO 1. Gk minor *goddess*, d of King Inachus of Argos. Turned by *Zeus* into a heifer (hence *COWGIRL*, crypt); guarded by *Argus*. Escaped, and swam to Asia Minor (whence Bosphorus = Ox-ford), before reaching Egypt and human form again. 2. A satellite of the *planet* Jupiter.

IODINE I *(chem)* [antiseptic].

ION (s/l *iron*). 1. PARTICLE [atom]. 2. Gk myth s of *Apollo*, who founded the Ionian race.

IOU *DEBT*, MARKER (US), PROOF OF DEBT, OWING.

IQ INTELLIGENCE QUOTIENT.

IR IRAN (*car plate*). IRIDIUM (*chem*).

IRE *ANGER*. IRELAND (*car plate* = IRL).

IRELAND ire. IRL (*car plate*). EIRE, ERIN; EMERALD ISLE; HIBERNIA; THE PROVINCE; for counties of ~, see *divisions* [*patron saint*]. COMPOSER. (*Shak* forger).

IRENE Gk *goddess* of PEACE, d of Themis and *Zeus*; one of the *Horae*. **Rom** = PAX.

IRIDIUM IR (*chem*).

IRIS 1. *EYE*. *FLAG*, *FLOWER*, *LILY*, ORRIS. 2. Gk *goddess* of rainbow, d of *Electra* by Thaumas [*Harpies*], mar to *Zephyrus*. 3. A minor *PLANET*. 4. *Shak* (Temp).

IRISH MICK, PADDY, PAT etc [*RM*]. *SEA*. CONTRADICTORY. ERSE, HIBERNIAN (for ~ counties, see *divisions*).

IRON (s/l *ion*). *METAL*, FE (*chem*). FERROUS [blacksmith; *Dactyls*]. AGE. CLUB; **opp** = *driver* (*golf*). PRESS, SMOOTH(ER); DECREASE, EVENING (crypt). Pl = CUTLERY (mil sl); CHAINS, HANDCUFFS.

IRRITATE *Anag.* ANNOY, BOTHER, IRK, VEX. EXCITE. DEFEAT, NULLIFY.

IS EXISTS. *ISLAND*. ISLES OF SCILLY. ICELAND (*car plate*).

~ DOUBLE *ISIS* (crypt).

ISAAC Bibl s of *Abraham* and *Sarah;* mar his cousin Rebecca and f of twins *Esau* and *Jacob*. When ~ became blind, he was tricked into giving to Jacob the inheritance and blessing which were Esau's right as the first-born; ~ felt the former's hands and neck which had been covered with goatskins to imitate the hairiness of Esau, and said 'The voice is Jacob's voice, but the hands are the hands of Esau.'

ISHTAR *Goddess* of *LOVE* (Bab).

ISIS 1. THAMES (at Oxford). Reserve *eight* (O). IS DOUBLE (crypt). 2. Egy *goddess* of *LOVE,* motherhood and Nature, m of *Horus*. 3. A minor *PLANET*.

ISLAM PREACHER IMAM, MUEZZIN, MULLAH.

ISLAND REFUGE. I, IS, AIT, AYOT, EYOT, *INCH,* ISLE, ISLET. **Celeb (fict):** BARATARIA (Gondoliers, *G & S*), BENSALEM (Bacon), GLUBBDUBRIB (Sorcerers, *Swift*), LAPUTA (flying ~, *Swift*), LILLIPUT (*dwarfs, Swift*), SPIDERMONKEY (Lofting), TREASURE ~ (Defoe), UTOPIA (More). ~s **of Britain and Ireland** (* = non-island):

3-letters

ELY*	(Eng)	NEB	(Eng, IOM)
EVE	(Ire)	RAT	(Eng, Wal)
EWE	(Sc)	*RED*	(Ire)
HOY	(Ork)	ROA	(Eng)
MAN	(Eng)	*RUM*	(Sc)
MEW	(Ire)		

4-letters

ADAM	(Ire)	MUCK	(Ire, Sc)
ARAN	(Ire)	*MULL*	(Sc)
BEAR	(Ire)	NOSS	(Sc)
BIRD	(Ire)	OMEY	(Ire)
BUTE	(Sc)	OSEA	(Eng)
CALF	(IOM, Ire)	PIEL	(Eng)
COLL	(Sc)	RHUM	(Sc)
*DOGS**	(Eng)	RONA	(Sc)
EDAY	(Ork)	*SALT*	(Wal)
EIGG	(Sc)	*SARK*	(CI)
FAIR	(Sc)	SKYE	(Sc)
GOAT	(Ire)	SUNK	(Eng)
GUGH	(IS)	*SWAN*	(Ire)
HERM	(CI)	*TORY*	(Eng)
HOLY	(Eng, Sc, Wal)	UIST	(Sc)
		ULVA	(Sc)
JURA	(Sc)	UNST	(Sh)
LONG	(Eng, Ire)	YELL	(Sh)

5-letters

ANNET	(IS)	HANDA	(Sc)
ARRAN	(Sc)	*HORSE*	(Ire)
BARRA	(Sc)	ISLAY	(Sc)
BARRY	(Wal)	KEDGE	(Ire)
BURGH	(Eng)	*LAMBS*	(Wal)
BURNT	(Sc)	LEWIS	(Sc, Wal)
CALDY	(Wal)	LUING	(Sc)
CAPEL	(Ire)	LUNDY	(Eng)
CARNA	(Sc)	MAGEE	(Ire)
CLARE	(Ire)	*SHEEP*	(Eng, Wal)
CLEAR	(Ire)	SHELL	(Wal)
CONEY	(Ire)	SHUNA	(Sc)
DANNA	(Sc)	SPIKE	(Ire)
EAGLE	(Ire)	STERT	(Eng)
EORSA	(Sc)	SULLY	(Wal)
FARNE	(Eng)	TIREE	(Sc)
FLEET	(Sc)	*WHALE**	(Eng)
FOULA	(Sh)	*WHITE*	(IS)
GRAIN*	(Eng)	WIGHT	(Eng)
GREEN	(Ire)		

6-letters

ACHILL	(Ire)	POTTON	(Eng)
BADGER	(Ire)	*PRIEST*	(Sc)
BOTTLE	(Sc)	PUFFIN	(Wal)
BURROW	(Eng)	RAASAY	(Sc)
CANVEY	(Eng)	*RABBIT*	(Ire)
COQUET	(Eng)	RAMSEY	(Wal)
DRAKES	(Eng)	ROUSAY	(Ork)
DURSEY	(Ire)	SAMSON	(IS)
FETLAR	(Sh)	SANDAY	(Ork)
FLOTTA	(Ork)	SCARBA	(Sc)
JERSEY	(CI)	SKIDDY	(Ire)
JETHOU	(CI)	SKOMER	(Sc, Wal)
HARRIS	(Sc)	STAFFA	(Sc)
HESTAN	(Sc)	STROMA	(Ork)
HILBRE	(Eng)	THANET	(Eng)
HORSEA	(Eng)	TRESCO	(IS)
LAMBAY	(Ire)	UTOPIA	(fict)
MAIDEN	(Ire)	WALNEY	(Eng)
MERSEA	(Eng)	WHIDDY	(Ire)
OLDANY	(Sc)		

7-letters

BARDSEY	(Wal)	PORTSEA	(Eng)
BRESSAY	(Sc)	PURBECK*	(Eng)
CORKBEG	(Ire)	RATHLIN	(Ire)
CUMBRAE	(Sc)	ROCKALL	(Sc)
FOULNEY	(Eng)	ST AGNES	(IS)
GOMETRA	(Sc)	ST MARYS	(IS, Sc)
GORUMNA	(Ire)	SCARIFF	(Ire)
HAYLING	(Eng)	SHEPPEY*	(Eng)
ISLEHAM	(Eng)	SHERKIN	(Ire)
KEERAGH	(Ire)	THORNEY*	(Eng)
KERRERA	(Sc)	WESTRAY	(Ork)
LISMORE	(Sc)	WHALSAY	(Sh)
OWENBOY	(Sc)		

8-letters

ALDERMAN	(Ire)	GRUINARD	(Sc)
ALDERNEY	(CI)	*GUERNSEY*	(CI)
ANGLESEY	(Wal)	MAINLAND	(Ork, Sh)
BIRNBECK	(Eng)	MINGULAY	(Sc)
BROWNSEA	(Eng)	PORTLAND*	(Eng)
CARDIGAN	(Wal)	ST HELENS	(IS)
COLONSAY	(Sc)	ST TUDWAL	(Wal)
COPELAND	(Ire)	SHETLAND	(Sh)
FLAT HOLM	(Wal)	SKOKHOLM	(Wal)
FOULNESS	(Eng)	STRONSAY	(Ork)
GATEHOLM	(Wal)	VALENCIA	(Ire)
GRAEMSAY	(Ork)	VATERSAY	(Sc)

9+ letters

BALLYCOTTON	(Ire)	ISLEWORTH*	(Eng)
BENBECULA	(Sc)	LITTLE CUMBRAE	(Sc)
BURNTISLAND	(Sc)	LITTLE ROSS	(Sc)
CALF OF MAN	(IOM)	LLANDDWYN	(Wal)
EAST MOUSE	(Wal)	MIDDLE MOUSE	(Wal)
GREAT CUMBRAE	(Sc)	MUCKLE ROE	(Sh)
ISLEABBOTTS	(Eng)	N RONALDSAY	(Ork)
ISLE OF BREWERS	(Eng)	NORTH UIST	(Sc)
ISLE OF LEWIS	(Sc)	PAPA STOUR	(Sh)
ISLE OF MAN	(Eng)	PAPA WESTRAY	(Ork)
ISLE OF WIGHT	(Eng)	RONALDSAY	(Ork)
ISLEORNSAY	(Sc)	ST MICHAELS	(IOM)

SHAPINSAY	(Ork)	STEEP HOLM	(Wal)
S RONALDSAY	(Ork)	WEST MOUSE	(Wal)
SOUTH UIST	(Sc)	WHITEHORN	(Sc)

ISLAND AREAS See *Divisions*.

~ **GIRL** MIRANDA (Tempest, *Shak*). *FLORA*.

~ **RACE** BRITONS, IRISH. (MANX) TT.

ISLE OF MAN IOM; GBM (*car plate*). MONAVIA INSULA (Rom). MONA (also Anglesey). MANX.

ISLE OF WIGHT IOW. VECTIS INSULA (Rom).

ISRAEL *JACOB*. JEWISH STATE; **12 tribes:** ASHER, BENJAMIN, DAN, EPHRAIM, GAD, ISSACHAR, JUDAH, MANASSEH, NAPHTALI, REUBEN, SIMEON, ZEBULON.

IS SORRY APOLOGIZES, CARES, REGRETS, RUES.

ISSUE CHILD, *OFFSPRING*, LITTER, PROGENY [*assembly*]. DISCHARGE, *EMIT*, OUTFLOW, OUTLET. COME OUT, EMERGE. OUTCOME, PROCEED, RESULT. POINT, TOPIC. PUBLISH; *BOOK*, EDITION, NUMBER, *VOLUME*.

IT ITEM, THING. SA, CHARM, SEX APPEAL. ITALIAN, VERMOUTH. **Comp** = *gin*.

It Italy, ~ian.

ITA *BROADCASTING*, COMMERCIAL TV.

ITALIAN 1. IT, VERMOUTH. 2. Trans, e.g. **With Italian** = CON.

ITALY I (*car plate*).

ITEM ARTICLE, ENTRY, THING, UNIT. ALSO, LIKEWISE. TIME-OUT, TIME-WARP (crypt).

ITV *BROADCASTING*, COMMERCIAL TV.

IVORY *COLOUR* (white). TOOTH, TUSK; *anniversary* (14th). **Pl** = KEYBOARD (piano).

~ **GATE** Myth gate of sleep, transmission of false hopes from the lower world.

IVY 1. CREEPER, HEDERA, HELIX; (sacred to *Bacchus*); **types:** American ~, Boston ~, ground ~, Jap ~, poison ~, Virginia Creeper, Woodbine. *COLOUR* (green). GIRL.

2. ~ **League.** Top US colleges (as O and C): Brown, Cornell, Columbia, Dartmouth, Harvard, Pennsylvania, Princeton, Yale (US college *football*).

I WILL ILL.

I WOULD ID.

IXION Gk myth king, tied by *Zeus* to an evermoving *wheel*.

J (s/l jay). *JACK*. JAPAN (*car plate*). JOULE. *JUDGE*. [*Three* Men in a Boat].

JACK 1. AB, *SAILOR*, TAR. (COURT) *CARD*, KNAVE. LIFT, HOIST (car). TURNSPIT (cook; hence TIPS, crypt). JOHN; **comp** = Jill (*Gill*). TARGET BALL (bowls). *FISH*, PIKE. *MONEY* (sl). *FLAG* (naut). TUNIC. INDIAN FRUIT. [~ CADE. ~ FROST. ~ O'LANTERN (*ignis fatuus*). ~ SPRAT]. 2. Male animal, e.g. ass.

JACOB Bibl s of *Isaac* and Rebecca; younger twin br of *Esau*. Went to his uncle Laban in Egy and there mar his cousins Leah and Rachel (the former was covertly substituted for the more beautiful latter); f by Leah of Reuben, Simeon, Levi (grand-f of *Moses*), Judah, Issachar, Zebulon and Dinah, and by Rachel of *Joseph* and Benjamin. Had dreams, among them of a ladder to heaven; was renamed *Israel* by an angel. With his m's help, he cheated Esau out of his birthright (for a 'mess of pottage', i.e. lentils) and of the blessing due from *Isaac* to Esau as the first-born. Was renamed Israel by an angel.

JADE *MINX*. *GEM*; BOWENITE, JADEITE, NEPHRITE, YU. *COLOUR* (green). NAG, SCREW (*horse*).

JAILER US for *GAOLER*.

JANUARY (1st) MONTH, M, JAN (**Rom** = *Janus*). **Birthstone** = garnet.

JANUS Rom *god* of the doorway; facing front and rear. **Gk** = HORUS, **Egy** = HOR.

JAPAN 1. LACQUER, PAINT, VARNISH. SEA. 2. J (*car plate*). CIPANGU, NIPPON (country), Jap (abbr); **islands**: Honshu (biggest), Hokkaido, Kyushu, Shikoku. **Words**: aikido (self-defence), bugeikan (karate), bushido (mil honour code), daimyo (noble), dan (judo), *Go* (*board-game*), hara-kiri (ritual suicide), ikebana (flower arrangement), jujitsu (unarmed self-defence), kami (divine spirit), kami-kaze ('divine wind', mil suicide), karate (martial art), kendo (cross-staff fencing), kung-fu (Ch karate), netsuke (pouch toggle), *No* (classic drama), obang (gold coin), obi (sash), origami (paper folding), samurai (mil caste), seppuku (mil suicide), shinto (religion), shogun (hereditary mil ruler), te (karate), Tora-Tora (Pearl Harbor *battlecry*: tiger-tiger) [Mikado, *G & S*].

JAR JERK, JOG, NUDGE. *EWER*; GREYBEARD (*bottle*). GRATING SOUND, SHOCK. DISAGREEMENT, QUARREL.

JASON Gk myth hero, mar to *Medea*. Sent (to get him out of the

way) by his half br Pelias at the head of the *Argonauts* to get the
golden fleece, where he was sure to be k. He returned with it
and k Pelias.

JEANS (s/l genes). DENIM TROUSERS.

JEHU Bibl s of Nimshi, who brought about the death of Jehoram
and Jezebel, and was cruel towards their relations. Renowned
for furious chariot driving. Successor to *Ahab* [*Phaeton*].

JEKYLL Dr in *Stevenson's* book, who *transformed* himself by chem
experiment into the evil Mr *Hyde*.

JENNY 1. LOCOMOTIVE CRANE. JANET; GIRL; LEE;
LIND. SPINNER. 2. *Female* donkey or mule; assess (crypt).

JEROBOAM 1. LARGE *BOTTLE* (4 times normal). 2. Son of
Nabat, K of Israel; set up golden calves at Dan and Bethel.

JERSEY PULLOVER, SWEATER [*cardigan*, Guernsey];
KNITWEAR. *CATTLE*. *ISLAND* (CI). GBJ (*car plate*).

JESTER Court or household retainer, whose job was to amuse
the company by his wit and repartee (and who was allowed a
degree of licence for the purpose). Compare *clown* (q.v. for
further list), who is more of a buffoon. COURT COMEDIAN,
FOOL, JOKER, PRANKSTER, POLTROON, TRICKSTER.
Celeb fact: L'ANGELY (Fr, Louis xiii & xiv); BONNY (Earl
of Morton); HAINCELIN COQ (Fr, Chas vi); ROBERT
GRENE (Eliz i); MUCKLE JOHN (Chas i); PATCH (H.vii);
PIERCE (Earl of Suffolk); RAHERE (H.i); JOHN SCOGAN
(Ed.iv); WILL SOMERS (H.viii). **Celeb fict**: 'SIR' DAGONET
(Arthurian legend); FESTE (*Shak*, 12th N); GOBBO (*Shak*, M
of V); LAVACHE (*Shak*, All's Well); JACK POINT (*G & S*,
Yeomen); RIGOLETTO (*hunchback*, Verdi); WAMBA (*Scott*,
Ivanhoe); YORICK (*Shak*, Hamlet).

JESUS 1. Author of Book of Ecclesiasticus, *c*.180 B.C. 2. A
Christian who was with St Paul in Rome *c*.A.D. 67. 3. CHRIST,
SON OF GOD, SAVIOUR; b at Nazareth or at Bethlehem (*c*.4
B.C.), s of *Joseph* and Mary, and br of James, Joses, Simon and
Judas (Matthew 13). Escaped the massacre of the innocents
(*Herod*), and was raised at Nazareth as a *carpenter*, like his f.
His Ministry lasted from age 30–33, and **His life incl**: genealogy
and birth (Matthew 1–2; Luke 2–3); massacre of the innocents
(Matthew 2); baptism (Matthew 3; Mark 1; Luke 3); temptation
in the wilderness (Matthew 4; Mark 1–3); first miracle (water
into wine; John 2); cleansing the temple (Mark 11); selection
of the 12 *apostles* (Matthew 10; Mark 1); sermon on the mount
(Matthew 4); feeding the 5,000 (Matthew 14; Mark 6; John 6);

walking on water (Mark 6; John 6); transfiguration (Matthew 17; Mark 9; Luke 9); raising of Lazarus (John 11); the last supper, betrayal by *Judas* and denial by Peter (Matthew 26; Mark 14; Luke 22; John 18; Acts 1); Gethsemane (Matthew 26–7; Mark 14); trial before *Pilate* and crucifixion between 2 *robbers* (Matthew 27; Mark 15; Luke 23; John 18–19); resurrection and ascension (Matthew 28; Mark 16; Luke 24; John 20; Acts 1).

JETTY KEY, QUAY, MOLE, PIER, WHARF. BLACK.

JEW HEBREW, ISRAELI, SEMITE; MISER, USURER; **celeb**: ESTHER (bibl); FAGIN (*Dickens*); ISAAC (of York, *Scott*); *JACOB* (bibl); *JESUS* (bibl); ~ of Malta (Marlowe); *JOSEPH* (bibl); *JUDAS* (bibl); MORDECAI (bibl); NATHAN DE WEISE (Lessing); REBECCA (bibl, and Ivanhoe, *Scott*); SHYLOCK, TUBAL (*Shak*); SVENGALI (du Maurier); WANDERING ~ (trad).

JEWEL THIEF *MAGPIE*. CAPT BLOOD (crown jewels, Tower of London).

JM BARRIE (Admirable Crichton. Peter Pan).

JOAB Bibl s of Zerniah and nephew of *David*, c.650 B.C. A great mil capt of David, ~ defeated *Absalom* at Gilboa, and caused the d of Abner, Amasa and Uriah the Hittite (see *David*). When David d, ~ fled to sanctuary where he was found and k on *Solomon's* orders.

JOAN 1. ~ OF ARC, LA PUCELLE, THE *MAID* (of Orleans); *Shak* character (H.vi). Book by Mark *Twain*. 2. Wife of John Darby (Darby and ~).

JOB 1. DUTY, OCCUPATION, RESPONSIBILITY, TASK, WORK. BURGLARY, CRIME, ROBBERY (sl). BUY/SELL (as middleman). 2. Patient Jewish bibl patriarch, who maintained his faith under test, despite so-called ~'s comforters who merely added to his distress [~'s Tears, *grass*].

JOCASTA Mother and w of *Oedipus*.

JOG *TROT*. REMIND. *JAR*, NUDGE.

JOHN BOY. DOE. PRESTER ~. LITTLE ~ (Robin *Hood*). LONG ~ SILVER (*Stevenson*). LOO.

JOINT FORK, HINGE, JUNCTION, SEAM, T(EE), TENON. BARON, LEG, SIDE (beef, lamb etc). DIVE, NIGHTCLUB. *CIGARETTE*, *REEFER* (*drug*). ANKLE, ELBOW, FINGER, HIP, KNEE, KNUCKLE, SHOULDER, TOE, WRIST. COMBINED.

JOKER WILD CARD. *CLOWN, JESTER*, WAG.

JOLLIFICATION *DO*, FIESTA, PARTY.

JOLLY HAPPY, LIVELY. MARINE, RM.

JOLT *Anag.* JERK, SHAKE, SHOCK, SURPRISE.

JONES *INIGO* (*archit*). PAUL (US Navy).

JONSON BEN (The Alchemist, Epicoene, Volpone).

Jor Jordan.

JOSEPH 1. Bibl s of *Jacob* and Rachel, who made him a 'coat of many colours'. ~ was sold into slavery in Egy, but rose to be chief minister and mar Osnath (d of Potiphar, a priest of *On*). 2. A *carpenter* of Nazareth, s of Heli; mar to Mary who was m of *Jesus*; ~ was also f of James, Joses, Simon and *Judas*, either by Mary after Jesus was born, or by a previous mar. 3. ~ of Arimathea; bibl Jew who went to *Pilate* after the d of Jesus and begged for his body, which he laid in a tomb.

JOSHUA Bibl s of Nun, ~ was the lieutenant of *Moses* who took Jericho by '*compassing*' the city seven times and blowing on seven rams' horns; ~ eventually took the whole Promised Land.

JOURNALIST *REPORTER* **Union** = NUJ [*newspaper*; Clark *Kent*; *Superman*].

JOURNEY BUMMEL (Three Men on the ~), *TRIP*, VOYAGE.

JOVE = *JUPITER*, Rom chief *god* (**Gk** = *Zeus*).

JOY DELIGHT, GLEE, PLEASURE; SATISFACTION (**opp** = *dolour*). GIRL.

JP JUSTICE OF THE PEACE, MAGISTRATE.

JUDAS 1. ~ Maccabaeus; the eldest s of Mattathias who d 161 B.C. 2. ~ Iscariot (A.D. 30). *Apostle* (treasurer) who betrayed *Jesus* for '30 pieces of silver', which were later used to buy the *Potter's* Field, a plot of land known as Aceldama, which became the burial ground for Jews who did not live in the city. 3. Thaddeus (A.D. 30). Another *Apostle*, possibly the author of the Epistle of Jude. 4. Br of *Jesus*, another possible author of Jude's Epistle. 5. *WINDOW*.

JUDGE J. ARBITER, ASSESS, *LAW* OFFICER; CADI, KADI, QADI (Mos). CENSURE, CONSIDER, CRITICIZE, DECIDE, DECREE, SENTENCE, SUPPOSE, TRY. **Celeb:** *DANIEL*, *ELI*, ~ JEFFRIES, RHADAMANTHUS (Gk myth), *SAMUEL*, *SOLOMON*.

JUDGEMENT MISFORTUNE, SENTENCE. ASSESSMENT, DISCERNMENT, ESTIMATE, OPINION. 20 (*tarot*).

JUG *GAOL*. *EWER*. *NIGHTINGALE* SONG.

JUGGERNAUT 1. Krishna idol (Ind), wheeled in procession on *chariot*; frenzied devotees threw themselves under the wheels. Any destroying force. 2. HGV, *LORRY*, TRUCK (comm).

JULY (7th) MONTH, M, JUL (Julius *Caesar*). **Birthstone** = *cornelian*.

JUMPER CARDIGAN, GUERNSEY, JERSEY, PULLOVER. **Animal** ~s: *ANTELOPE*, CICADA, *CRICKET*, FLEA, *FROG*, *GRASSHOPPER*, HARE, KANGAROO. (STEEPLE)CHASER. PARA(CHUTIST). *BOUNCER*, *BOUNDER*, LEAPER [*Gorgon*].

JUNCTION *JOINT*.

JUNE 1. GIRL. 2. (6th) MONTH, M, JUN (Juno). **Birthstone** = *agate*.

JUNK *DRUG*. *BOAT* (Ch), LORCHA. SALT MEAT (naut). RUBBISH.

JUNO 1. BEAUTIFUL/STATUESQUE WOMAN. 2. Rom myth Q of the *gods* and of mar; w of *Jupiter*. **Gk** = *HERA*. 3. *Shak* (Temp).

JUPITER 1. Rom myth K of the *gods*; also JOVE, PLUVIUS (rain) or TONANS (thunder). Son of *Saturn* and Ops, he mar his sis *Juno*. **Gk** = *ZEUS* (*seven wonders*). 2. Largest of the sun's *planets*.

JUST DESERVED, EQUITABLE, *FAIR*, WELL-GROUNDED. BARELY. EVEN, EXACTLY, PRECISELY, QUITE, RECENTLY. Also = JOUST.

JUSTICE JP; SHALLOW, SILENCE (*Shak*). THE LAW. FAIR TREATMENT. 8 (*tarot*). Fifth age (*Shak's seven ages*; AYLI). **Goddess**, **Gk** = ASTRAEA.

JUST SO SIC. STORIES (*Kipling*).

JUVENTAS Rom *goddess* of YOUTH. **Gk** = *HEBE*.

K KELVIN. KILO(METRE). KING. KOCHEL (mus). POTASSIUM (*chem*). 1,000 (hence M).

k Killed. *Int unit*.

KAIKAS Gk myth NE *WIND* (**Rom** = AQUILO).

KALI Ind *goddess* of destruction, to whom practising *Thugs* sacrificed their victims; she is the consort of Shiva, and is depicted with many arms.

KANGAROO 1. *MARSUPIAL*, Macropus genus: BRUSH ~, GREAT GREY ~, POTOROO, QUOKKA, RAT ~, ROCK ~, TREE ~, WALLABY. **Assembly** = *mob*; **male** = BOOMER. [*Kipling*, *Lear*, pouch]. HOPPER, *JUMPER* (crypt). 2. ~ **court** = lynch mob, rough justice.

KC KILOCYCLE. KING'S COUNSEL.

KEEN *ACUTE*, SHARP, STRONG, VIVID. EAGER,
WILLING; DETERMINED, SET UPON. *CRY*, DIRGE,
FUNERAL SONG, WAIL (Sc).

KEEN-EYED SHARP-EYED, FAR-SIGHTED, GIMLET, X-
RAY. **Celeb**: *ARGUS*, LYNCEUS (Gk myth); *CAT*, *EAGLE*,
HAWK, *LYNX*, *OWL*.

KEEP INNER FORT, STRONGHOLD, TOWER (*castle*).
CONFINE, DEFEND, DETAIN, GUARD, HOLD, POSSESS,
RETAIN, STOCK, STORE. LOOK AFTER, MAINTAIN
(dog; mistress). PRESERVE, RESERVE, WITHHOLD
(judgement). ASSOCIATE (~ company). OBSERVE (e.g.
Christmas, Ramadan). REMAIN, STAY IN/ON (place, seat).
(TAKE) CARE, CHARGE, WATCH. BOARD, LIVING,
LODGE, LODGING, MAINTENANCE, SUPPORT.

~ **OFF** AVERT, FORFEND, WARD OFF. STAY CLEAR.

KELVIN K.

KENT *Division* of UK, SE, GARDEN (of Eng); UNIVERSITY.
ARCHITECT; *CABINET-MAKER*; GARDENER. CLARK
~ (*SUPERMAN* ® [*Krypton*; Lois Lane; reporter,
Daily Planet]). CIGARETTE. *PAINTER*. **Pl** = BUFFS (mil).

KERNEL (s/l *colonel*). NUT CENTRE (hence U) [shelling].

KETCH EXECUTIONER, HANGMAN. (SAIL)BOAT.

KEY (s/l *quay*). A, B, C, D, E, F or G (mus). CLEF, CLEVIS,
MAJOR, MINOR, NOTE; TONIC (mus). CLUE,
SOLUTION. HYPE. IMPORTANT, CENTRAL. TAP.
WARD; *LOCKER* (crypt). **Pl** = *LEGISLATIVE ASSEMBLY*.

KEYHOLDER *GAOLER*.

KG KNIGHT OF THE GARTER [Edward III, Countess of
Salisbury, Honi soit qui mal y pense].

KHAN CARAVANSERAI (Arab), INN, WAYPOST. RULER
(Ch, Mong, Turk); **celeb**: AGA ~, BATU, GENGHIS ~,
HULEGU, KUBLAI ~, MONGKE, OGEDEI.

KICK *PUNT*, HACK (with foot) [*Sciron*]. RESILIENCE,
STIMULUS, THRILL. RECOIL. DENT IN BOTTLE.

KID DUPE, FOOL, HOAX, HUMBUG. TUB. LEATHER.
CHILD, TOT. *Offspring* of goat.

KIDDED FOOLED, HOAXED. GAVE BIRTH,
PARENTHOOD (crypt).

KILL CULL, DEADEN, DESTROY, DISPATCH,
EXTERMINATE, FINISH, WASTE (sl). BAG (game).

KILO K (*int units*).

KIND OF *Anag.* KIDNEY, SORT, TYPE. AMIABLE OF, GENEROUS OF.

KINEMOPHILE *Lover* of the cinema.

KING 1. (COURT) *CARD. CHESSPIECE. SNAKE.* Pl = RIVER (Ire). 2. HM, K, R, REX; male *MONARCH* (q.v. for ~s of UK), SOVEREIGN, e.g. CR (Charles), GR (George), etc. [and see *emperor, pharaoh*]; **celeb** (**bibl**): AGAG, AGRIPPA, *AHAB*, AHAZ, AMON, ARTAXERXES, ASA, BAASHA, BALAK, *BELSHAZZAR*, BERA, CYRUS, DARIUS, *DAVID*, EGLON, ELAH, EVI, GOG, HADAD, *HEROD*, HEZEKIAH, HIRAM, HOHAM, HORAM, HOSEA, HUR, JABIN, JAPHIA, JEHORAM, JEHOSHAPHAT, *JEHU, JEROBOAM, JESUS*, JORAM, JOSIAH, JUDAH, LEMUEL, MAGOG, MANASSEH, MELCHIZEDEK, NABAT, *NEBUCHADNEZZAR*, *OG*, OMRI, *PHARAOH*, PIRAM, *PTOLEMY*, PUL, *REHOBOAM*, REZIN, *SALMANAZAR*, SARGON, *SAUL*, SENNACHERIB, *SO, SOLOMON*, TOI, TRYPHON, UZZIAH, *XERXES*, ZACHARIAH, ZEBAR, ZEDEKIAH, ZIMRI; **celeb** (**fict**): ~ of Barataria (LUIZ, Gondoliers, *G & S*), ~ of Hearts (*Alice*), HILDEBRAND (Ida, *G & S*), LEAR (*Shak*), OBERON (MND, *Shak*), PANDION (Ode, Barnfield), PARAMOUNT (Utopia, *G and S*), Red and White ~s (*Alice*); **celeb** (**early Eur**): ALFRED, ARTHUR, ATHELSTAN, CANUTE/CNUT/KNUT, CARA(C)TACUS, CHARLEMAGNE, CHARLES the Bald, ~ the Bold, ~ the Fat, *DAVID*, EADRID, EADWIG, E(C)GFRITH, EDGAR, EDMUND (Ironside), EDWARD (the Confessor), EDWIN, EGBERT, (A)ETHELBALD, (A)ETHELBERT, (A)ETHELRED (the Unready), (A)ETHELWULF, GODWIN, GUTHRUM, HARALD (Barefoot; Hardrada), MALCOLM, OFFA, OLAF, OLEG, SWEIN/SWEYN. **Celeb, various**: CROESUS (~ of Lydia; rich); CROSBY (~ of swing; film); GABLE (~ of Hollywood; film); MIDAS (Gk myth ~ of Phrygia; gold); PRESLEY (~ of rock 'n' roll; theat); CETEWAYO (Zulus).

~ **ARTHUR** King of Silures in Ancient Britain. Son of Uther Pendragon (br of Morgana), mar *Guinevere*. Wounded fighting Mordred (his nephew) at Camlan in Cornwall, and d Isle of Avalon [*Camelot, Round Table*].

~ **EDWARD** POTATO. ED, RED, REXED, RTED, KTED (crypt).

~ **OF ARMS** CHIEF HERALD: BATH, *GARTER*, LORD LYON, *ULSTER* (St Patrick), CLARENCIEUX (thistle), NORROY.

~'s **COUNSEL** KC. RICHELIEU.

~s **of UK** See *MONARCHS* for list.

KINGSWAY REGALLY, ROYALLY (crypt).

KIPLING Rudyard, writer; b Bombay 1865, d 1936 [Nobel (lit)]. **Works**: Actions and Reactions; Barrack Room Ballads; A Book of Words; The City of Dreadful Night; The Day's Work; Debits and Credits; Departmental Ditties; A Diversity of Creatures; The Five Nations; Gunga Din (watercarrier); If; The Jungle Book (animals); The Just So Stories [The Alphabet; Armadilloes; *Butterfly*; *Camel*, (hump); The *Cat* that Walked by Himself; *Crab*; The Elephant's Child ('satiable curiosity; trunk); The First Letter; The Kangaroo (Yellow-Dog Dingo); The Leopard (spots); The Rhinoceros (skin); The *Whale* (throat)]; Kim (Anglo-Indian orphan); The Light that Failed; The Phantom Rickshaw; Plain Tales from the Hills; Puck of Pook's Hill; Rewards and Fairies; Schoolboy Lyrics; The Seven Seas; Soldiers Three; Stalky & Co (schoolboys); The Story of the Gadsbys; Traffics and Discoveries; Under the Deodars; Wee Willie Winkie; The Years Between.

KIPPER *SALMON*, SMOKED HERRING. SLEEPER (sl).

KISS BUSS, OSCULATE, *SALUTE*, X; **comp** = *tell*. BRUSH, TOUCH. CANNON (billiards). [Blarney Stone].

KIT *BAGGAGE*, EQUIPMENT, GEAR, RIG. CHRISTOPHER. KITCHENETTE, SMALL KITCHEN (crypt).

KITCHENER C IN C, EARL, GENERAL. CHEF, COOK, GALLEY SLAVE (crypt).

KITTY FUND, POOL. *CAT*, PUSS(Y). GIRL.

KLEPTOMANIA *Obsession* with stealing.

KNAP (s/l *nap*). CHIP, WORK FLINT.

KNIGHT (s/l *night*). 1. BART, BT, CHEVALIER, KG, KT, SIR; PALADIN. *Chaucer* char. [Round Table]. *CHESSPIECE*. *PAINTER*. 2. **Orders of knighthood, with motto**:

THE GARTER (KG)	Honi soit qui mal y pense
THE THISTLE (KT)	Nemo me impune lacessit
ST PATRICK (KP)	Quis separabit?
THE BATH (KB)	Tria juncta in uno
THE STAR OF INDIA (ex)	Heavens light our guide

ST MICHAEL & ST GEORGE (KMG)	Auspicium melioris aevi
THE INDIAN EMPIRE (ex)	Imperatricis auspiciis
ROYAL VICTORIAN ORDER	Victoria
THE BRITISH EMPIRE	For God and the Empire

KNIT (s/l nit). ENTANGLE, *KNOT*. CROCHET, PURL, PLAIN, STITCH [*jersey*; Mme Defarge, 2 Cities, *Dickens*].

KNOCK RAP, *STRIKE*. CRITICIZE. ASTONISH. INNINGS. *CASTLE*.

KNOCKOUT *Anag*. KO. EMPTY (pipe). KONCK, NOCKK etc (crypt).

KNOCK UP WAKEN. SLEEP WITH (US). PAR (dn, crypt).

KNOT (s/l *not*). KT, *MEASURE* (naut), NMPH, RATE, SPEED (naut). *BIRD*, DUNLIN. PROBLEM. CLUSTER, GROUP. BEND, HITCH, LOOP: BECKET, *BOW*, BOWLINE, *CLOVE* HITCH, *FISHERMAN'S* BEND, GRANNY, HALF HITCH, REEF ~, SHEEPSHANK, SHEET BEND, STOPPER ~, TIMBER HITCH. SPLICE: *CROWN*, MATTHEW WALKER, MONKEY'S FIST, TURK'S HEAD, WALL ~. TIE; KNIT.

KNOW (s/l *no*). BE AWARE, RECOGNIZE. SLEEP WITH (bibl). **Pl** = (s/l noes, *nose*); REALIZES, *UNDERSTANDS*.

KOCHEL K, SCORE (mus) [Mozart].

KOP (s/l *cop*). *FOOTBALL* GROUND (Anfield, Liverpool).

KR KRYPTON (*chem*).

KRAKEN Nor myth sea *monster*.

KRISHNA Ind *god* of *fertility*. **Idol** = *juggernaut* chariot.

KRYPTON KR (*chem*). GASEOUS ELEMENT. PLANET (fict; *Superman*).

KT KNIGHT OF THE THISTLE [James II, St Andrew, Queen Anne, Nemo me impune lacessit]. *KNOT* (naut).

L (s/l ell). *LAKE*. LARGE. LATIN. *LEARNER. LEFT. LIBERAL*. LIRA. LITTLE. *LONG. LOVE*. LUXEMBOURG (*car plate*). FIFTY. POUND.

£1,050 CLASSIC, ONE THOUSAND GUINEAS.

£2,100 CLASSIC, TWO THOUSAND GUINEAS.

LA *LAKE*. LANTHANUM (*chem*). LOS ANGELES.

LOUISIANA. NOTE (mus; also LAH).

LAB LABORATORY. LABOUR.

LABOUR LAB. CHILDBIRTH. ELABORATE. EXERTION, TRAVAIL, TOIL, WORK [*Hercules*]. JOB CENTRE.

LABYRINTH 1. Complicated irregular structure in Gk myth, designed by *Daedalus* to house the *Minotaur* at King *Minos'* palace in Cnossos, hence any MAZE. 2. INNER *EAR*.

LACE CORD, TIE. BEAT, DEFEAT, LASH, WHIP. FLAVOUR, SPIKE. FINE FABRIC, *MATERIAL*, ORRIS; *anniversary* (13th).

LACKING 1. WITHOUT, UN-. 2. Put letters NO or UN (or similar) in front of word indicated, e.g. **Corner lacking approval** (4) = NO·OK. 3. Delete *ing* from clue-word, e.g. **Ingrate lacking speed** (4) = ···RATE. Note that this clue could also imply that a synonym for **speed** should be dropped, i.e. omit **rate** = ING····.

LADDER STEPS; CLIMBING FRAME. PATH, ROUTE. RUN (*tights*). **Pl comp** = *snakes*.

LADY WOMAN. Title (dame; d of earl; w of lord etc).

LADYBIRD Coleopterous insect of genus coccinella. LADYBUG (US), LADYCOW, LADYFLY (Bishop Barnaby, Cushcow Lady; nickname, e.g. Lucie (to Miss Pross, 2 Cities, *Dickens*); Mrs L. B. Johnson (to h, President ~). Also (crypt) any female bird, e.g. hen, pen, reeve (see *Male and Female*) ['~, ~ fly away home . . . ' (trad)].

LADY OF THE LAKE 1. ELAINE (*Lancelot*). 2. NIMIANE, NIMUE, VIVIEN, VIVIENNE [*Merlin*]. 3. ELLEN DOUGLAS (~, Sir Walter Scott). 4. LADY WINDERMERE (crypt).

LAERTES 1. Father of *Ulysses* [see *Penelope*]. 2. Son of Polonius (Hamlet, *Shak*).

LAID UP ABED, ILL, SICK. HAULED OUT, WINTERING (naut). DIAL (dn, crypt).

LAKE L, LA, LOCH, LOUGH, TARN. PIGMENT; *COLOUR* (red). INLAND WATER [*Great* ~s]; **world's principal large ~s:**

2-letters

NO (Af)

3-letters

| TOP (CIS) | XAU (Af) | ZUG (Swi) |

4-letters

ARAL (salt) (CIS)
CHAD (Nig)
ERIE (Can/US)

EYRE (salt) (Aus)
NESS (Sc)
TANA (Ethiopia)

5-letters

ABAYA (Ethiopia)
FROME (salt) (Aus)
HURON (Can/US)
LEMAN (Swi)
MWERU (Zam)
NEAGH (N Ire; largest Br
  Is)

NYASA (Af; ex)
ONEGA (CIS)
POOPO (Bol)
RUKWA (Tanz)
TAUPO (NZ)
VOLTA (Ghana)

6-letters

BAIKAL (CIS; deepest)
GENEVA (Swi)
KARIBA (Zimbabwe)
KISUMU (Af)
LADOGA (CIS)
MALAWI (Mal)

MOBUTU (Ug/Zaire)
NASSER (Egy)
RUDOLF (salt) (Ken)
ZARAKA (Gk myth;
  Stymphalus)

7-letters

AGASSIS (N Am,
  primeval)
CASPIAN (Pers/CIS;
  largest salt)
DERWENT (Eng)
ICHKEUL (Af)

KOKO-NOR (salt) (Ch)
LUCERNE (Swi)
ONTARIO (Can/US)
TORRENS (salt) (Aus)
TURKANA (salt) (E Af)

8-letters

BALKHASH (CIS)
CONISTON (Eng)
CUYABENO (S Am)
ISSYK-KUL (CIS)
MICHIGAN (US)
REINDEER (Can)

SUPERIOR (Can/US;
  largest fresh)
TITICACA (Peru/Bol)
VICTORIA (Ken/Tan/Ug)
WINNIPEG (Can)

9+ letters

ATHABASCA (Can)
DISAPPOINTMENT (Aus)

GITCHE-GUMEE
  (*Hiawatha*)

GREAT BEAR (Can)
GREAT SLAVE (Can)
MARACAIBO (Venez)
NICARAGUA (Nic)
STYMPHALUS (Gk,
  Hercules)

TANGANYIKA
  (Tan/Zam/Z)
THIRLMERE (Eng)
ULLSWATER (Eng)
WINDERMERE (Eng)

LAMB (s/l lam). *JOINT*, MEAT; **comp** = mint (sauce). *Offspring* of sheep. SKIPPER (crypt). YEAN. *ISLAND*. INNOCENT. ELIA, ESSAYIST, *WRITER*. 'AGNES'.

LAMBETH *PALACE* (eccles). *THAMES BRIDGE.*

LAME *CRIPPLED*, DISABLED, HALT. IMPERFECT, UNCONVINCING. GOLD/SILVER-THREADED *MATERIAL*, ORRIS.

LANCELOT Kt of the *Round Table*; mar Elaine (*Lady of the Lake*), f of *Galahad*. Seduced *Guinevere*. [*Camelot, King Arthur*].

LANCING CUTTING, PIERCING, PRICKING. DANCING (quadrille). *PUBLIC SCHOOL.*

LAND *COUNTRY*, EARTH; ACRES, SPACE [*measure*]. ALIGHT, COME DOWN, PITCH, SETTLE [Huma, myth bird which never ~s]. SET DOWN. GET, OBTAIN (job).

LANDING ALIGHTING, PANCAKE (av sl), SETTLEMENT (crypt) [*Fido*]. PLATFORM, PONTOON. BETWEEN FLIGHTS (stairs – crypt).

LANDLADY Keeper of boarding-house, inn, lodgings; **celeb**: MRS BOUNCER (Box and Cox, Morton), MRS CRUPP (Copperfield, *Dickens*), MRS MACSTINGER (Dombey, *Dickens*), MRS PIPCHIN (Dombey, *Dickens*), MISTRESS QUICKLY (Boar's Head, H.iv, H.v, *Shak*), MRS TODGERS (Chuzzle, *Dickens*).

LANDLORD LESSER, LETTER; **comp** = *tenant*. *HOST*, INN-KEEPER, PUBLICAN; **celeb**: HARRY BAILEY (The Tabard, Canterbury Tales, *Chaucer*), BENDIT (La Bohème, Puccini), BONIFACE (Beaux' Stratagem, Farquhar), JOHN WILLET (The Maypole, Rudge, *Dickens*).

LAND'S END D or S (crypt). Tip of Cornwall. SW.

LANSDOWNE ROAD *FOOTBALL/RUGBY* GROUND.

LAPIS LAZULI GEM (blue). *COLOUR* (blue).

LARES Rom HOUSEHOLD *gods*; **comp** = penates. GIBBON, *MONKEY.*

LARGE M, L. BIG, GRAND, GREAT. BROAD, FREE,

SWEEPING. **Comp** = *by*.
LARK GAME, HORSEPLAY; HOAX, JAPE, JOKE. *BIRD*;
   assembly = bevy, exaltation [singing].
LASER (s/l *lazer*). RADIATION, RAY.
LASS GAL, *GIRL*, MISS.
LAST 1. OMEGA, Z, ZED, ZEE (US). ENDURE, END,
   FINAL, FINALLY, LATEST, LOWEST (**opp** = *first*). [*Holmes*
   case]. MATRIX, SHOE MOULD. *MEASURE* (wool). 2. Last
   letter of word(s) concerned, e.g. **Last will and testament** = LDT.
  ~ **MONTH** DECEMBER; ULT. H (crypt). Any abbreviation for
   the current previous month.
  ~ **VEHICLE** E (crypt). HEARSE (crypt).
  ~ **WORDS** EPITAPH, OBITUARY. AMEN. PS, YOURS
   (FAITHFULLY/SINCERELY/TRULY). COBBLER, SHOE,
   UPPER, WELT etc (crypt).
LAT LATIN. *LATITUDE* [navigation].
LATE D, DEAD, EX, FORMER. RECENT. BACKWARD,
   OVERDUE, TARDY. EVENING, SMALL HOURS.
  ~ **NEWS** EPITAPH, OBIT(UARY).
LATIN 1. L, LAT [school]. 2. Put word(s) indicated into Latin,
   e.g. **I am Latin in total** (3) = SUM.
LATITUDE MOVEMENT, *PLAY*, SCOPE. CLIME, REGION,
   TROPIC [parallel]. BREADTH, LEEWAY, ROOM.
LAUGH BE AMUSED, CHORTLE, CHUCKLE, GIGGLE,
   GRIN, SMILE; HA-HA [*funny*, ludicrous, risible].
   RIDICULE, SCORN. [donkey, hyena, jackass (~ penguin),
   kookaburra, mockingbird].
LAUNCHER ROCKET PAD, *WEAPON* FIRER.
   ORIGINATOR, STARTER. COXSWAIN (naut).
LAUREL 1. *TREE*; BAY. **Comp**: Hardy. 2. In Gk myth,
   DAPHNE was changed into a laurel to escape *Apollo*.
LAVA *AA*, IGNEOUS ROCK, MAGMA, TUFA, TUFF.
LAW REGULATION, RULE; INJUNCTION. JUDICIAL
   REMEDY, LITIGATION. **Comp** = *order*. LEGAL
   KNOWLEDGE/PROFESSION; **celeb practitioners**: Aedile
   (Rom); Sampson and Sally Brass (OC Shop, *Dickens*); Sgt
   Buzfuz (Pickwick, *Dickens*); Dodson and Fogg (Pickwick,
   Dickens); Draco (Gk); Fang (magistrate, Oliver, *Dickens*); Fips
   (legal agent, Chuzzle, *Dickens*); Miss Flite (Bleak Ho, *Dickens*);
   Fury (dog, *Alice*); Jaggers (advocate, Great Ex, *Dickens*); Portia
   (M of V, *Shak*); Reeve (*Chaucer*); Serjeant of Law (*Chaucer*);
   Justice Shallow (H.iv and Merry Wives, *Shak*); Justice Silence

(H.iv, *Shak*); Snagsby (Bleak Ho, *Dickens*); Spenlow and
Jorkins (proctors, Copperfield, *Dickens*); Tulkinghorn (lawyer,
Bleak Ho, *Dickens*); George Warrington (barrister, Pendennis,
Thackeray); Mr Whymper (Animal Farm, *Orwell*); Mr Wickfield
(lawyer, Copperfield, *Dickens*).

LAWFUL APPOINTED, PERMITTED, QUALIFIED,
RECOGNIZED. LEGAL, LICIT.

LAX LOOSE, REMISS, SLACK. LACROSSE (sl).

LAY AMATEUR, NON-PROFESSIONAL. NON-CLERICAL,
NOT IN ORDERS (hence UNORDERED – crypt). DEPOSIT,
PLACE, PUT DOWN; ARRANGE, DISPOSE, PREPARE.
PRODUCE (egg). LIE, TWIST (rope). POEM, *SONG.*
COPULATE WITH, BED (US).

LAYER COATING, FILM; *COURSE*, STRATUM. *BIRD*, HEN
(crypt). BETTER, BOOKIE, GAMBLER, PUNTER (crypt).

LAYMAN AMATEUR, NON-EXPERT, UNPROFESSIONAL.
NON-CLERICAL; UNORDERED (crypt).
EGG-PRODUCER, CHICKEN FARMER (crypt).
CROONER, SINGER (crypt). BOOKIE, GAMBLER.

LAZER (s/l *laser*). *LOAFER*, IDLER.

LB *MEASURE*, POUND WEIGHT.

LEAD *METAL*; PB (*chem*), BASE METAL. DEPTH
SOUNDER (naut). CHANNEL, CONDUCT, *DIRECT*,
GUIDE; DIRECTION, GUIDANCE. PASS, SPEND.
OPEN; PLAY CARD. STARRING ROLE. GO FIRST; VAN.
WATERCOURSE.

LEADER (s/l Leda, *lieder*). 1. DUCE, FUHRER. CO
DIRECTOR, GUIDE, TOP PERSON [*military* ~]. COVER
STORY, LEADING ARTICLE. 2. First letter of word(s)
indicated, e.g. **Military leader** = M.

LEAGUE ASSOCIATION, CLIQUE. THREE MILES (arch).

LEAN *BANK*, BEND, INCLINE, LIST, *TILT*. FAT-FREE,
SLENDER, SLIM (**opp** = fat, obese) [diet. Jack Sprat].

LEANDER 1. Gk myth lover of *Hero*, drowned when the
lighthouse failed as he was swimming the *Hellespont* from
Abydos to visit her at Sestos. 2. Rowing club.

LEANING ASLANT, LISTING, OBLIQUE, *TILTED* (**opp** =
upright). BENT, INCLINATION, WISH.

LEAR 1. *MAD KING* (3 d: Cordelia, Goneril, Regan [*Shak*]).
2. Edward ~, writer. **Books/rhymes**: The Book of Nonsense,
More Nonsense Rhymes, Laughable Lyrics; The Dong with the
Luminous Nose, The Duck and the Kangaroo, The Jumblies, The

Owl and the Pussycat, The Pobble Who Has No Toes, The Quangle-Wangle's Hat, The Two Old Bachelors, The Akond of Swat, The Pelican Chorus, Mr & Mrs Discobbolos. 3. Aircraft company.

LEARNER L, PUPIL; APPRENTICE, BEGINNER. TIRO, TYRO (**opp** = expert).

LEARNING KNOWLEDGE, LORE. FINDING OUT. EDUCATION.

LEATHERNECK JOLLY, MARINE, RM.

LEAVE ABANDON, *DESERT*, GET OUT, PART, QUIT (**opp** = *enter*). MAKE *WILL*, TESTIFY. EXEAT, FURLOUGH, HOLIDAY [AWOL]. **Pl** = FOLIAGE. FF, FOLIOS, SHEETS.

LEAVING 1. Indicates word or letter(s) removed from clue, e.g. **Ship leaving Moscow** = MO; or **Animal doctors leaving Moscow** (3) = COW. 2. **Pl** = DREGS, LEES, ORT, REMAINS.

LECTURE *LESSON*, READING, TALK. TAKE TO TASK, TALKING TO.

LEDA (s/l *leader*, *lieder*). Q of Sparta, m of *Helen*, *Clytemnestra*, Castor, Pollux by *Zeus* (who *transformed* himself into a *swan* to seduce her).

LEE SHELTER (**opp** = *open*, windward). *MILITARY LEADER* (US). **Pl** = DREGS, *LEAVINGS*, ORT, REFUSE, REMAINS, SEDIMENT.

LEFT L, P; LARBOARD, PORT (naut), *RED*, *SINISTER* (*herald*). NOT RIGHT. ABANDONED, OVER, REMAINING. DEPARTED, GONE, WENT. COMMUNIST, LABOUR.

LEG CRUS (**Pl** = Crura). LIMB, MEMBER [*bone*]. PROP, SUPPORT; UNDERSTANDING (crypt). WALK, HOP, LENGTH, RUN, SECTION, SPAN, STAGE, TACK. ON (*cricket*; **opp** = *off*).

LEGEND 1. CAPTION, EXPLANATION (chart, map); INSCRIPTION, TITLE (*coin*, *herald*). 2. POPULAR STORY, TRADITION (for lands and cities of ~, see *COUNTRY*, **fict** and *Lost City*). 3. ANKLE, FOOT (crypt).

LEGISLATIVE ASSEMBLY BOARD, *CABINET*, COUNCIL, DEBATING CHAMBER, FORUM, *HOUSE*, SENATE, e.g. BUNDESTAG (W Ger), CONGRESS (House of Representatives, Senate, US), CORTES (Port, Sp), DÁIL (Seanad, Eire), DIET (Holy Roman Empire), DUMA (Russia), FOLKETING (Denmark), FORUM (Senate, Rom), *HOUSES* OF PARLIAMENT (*Commons*, *Lords*, UK), PNYK

(Athenian), REICHSRAT (A-Hung), REICHSTAG (Ger), RIKSDAG (Swe), STORMONT CASTLE (N Ire), STORTING (Nor), THING (ON), TYN(E)WALD (House of Keys, IOM), WITENAGEMOT (Sax). [Iolanthe (*G & S*)].

LEMON *FRUIT. TREE. COLOUR* (yellow). ANSWER (crypt).

LEMUR Nocturnal mammal; **types**: ANGWANTIBO, BABACOOTE, BABAKATO, BROWN ~, BUSHBABY, COLUGO (flying ~), GALAGO, (WOOLLY) INDRI(S), KINKAJOU, KUKANG, LEPI, LORIS, MAKI, MALMAG, MOUSE ~, POTTO, QUANACO, RACOON, RED-BELLIED ~, RED-FRONTED ~, RINGTAIL ~, SIFAKA, *SLOTH*, TANA, TARSIER [Madagascar, *monkey*; *ghost*].

LENGTH *MEASURE*. ELL, PERCH, POLE, ROD. FOOT, FT, IN, INCH, YARD, YD etc. LEAGUE, METRE, VERST.

LENT (s/l leant). ABSTAIN, FAST TIME [Easter]. ADVANCED, LOANED (**opp** = borrowed).

LEOTARD DOUBLET (hence TT, crypt), TIGHTS [*ballet*].

LEPIDOPTERA WINGED *INSECTS*; BUTTERFLIES, MOTHS, BUGS; **breeds (butterflies)**: Autumn Blue, Birdwing, Blue Crow, Brimstone, Cabbage White, Camberwell Beauty (Grand Surprise, White Petticoat), Comma, Common Blue, Common White, *Copper*, Crow ~, Diadem, *Emperor*, *Footman*, Fritillary, Green Hairstreak, Green-veined white, Greyling, Hairstreak, Heliconid, Holly Blue, Large Blue, Large Skipper, Large White, Leaf ~, Meadow Brown, *Monarch*, Orange Tip, Owl ~, Painted Lady, Peacock, Pearl Bordered Fritillary, Red Admiral, Ringlet, Satyr(id), *Skipper*, Small Copper, Small Heath, *Tiger*, Tortoiseshell, Wall Brown, Woodnymph, Yellow Brimstone [sea butterfly-pteropod, sea slug]; **breeds (moths)**: Buff Tip, Burnet, Cinnabar, Drinker, Eggar, Elephant Hawkmoth, *Emperor*, Eyed Hawkmoth, Hawkmoth, Hummingbird Hawkmoth, Kentish Glory, Lackey, *Magpie*, *Psyche*, Pussmoth, Silver Y, Six-spot Burnet, Tigermoth, Vapourer, White Ermine, Yellowtail, Yellow Underwing.

LES LESLIE. THE FRENCH.

LESSEN (s/l *lesson*). 1. *DECREASE*, DIMINISH, REDUCE. 2. Delete letters EN, e.g. **If you lessen Penates, on your heads be it** (5) = P**ATES.

LESSER 1. MINOR, SMALLER. *LANDLORD*. 2. Delete letters ER, e.g. **Lesser copper ice-wood** (7) = COPP**ICE.

LESSON (s/l *lessen*). 1. INSTRUCTION, TEACHING [*study*]. READING, SCRIPTURE. ADMONISH, EXAMPLE,

OCCURRENCE, PUNISHMENT, REBUKE. 2. Delete ON from clue, e.g. **Mutton lesson is stupid** (4) = MUTT**.

LESS THAN 1. UNDER. NOT SO MUCH. 2. Drop one or two letters from word indicated, e.g. **Inside is less than an evening meal** (5) = *INNER.

LET LEASE, RENT. *ALLOW*, PERMIT (**opp** = *hinder*). *HINDER*, PREVENT (arch; **opp** = *allow*).

LETHE Gk myth personification of oblivion; the *underworld* river from which souls of the departed drank and thereby forgot everything of the upper world [*Styx*].

LETTER MAIL, MESSAGE, MISSIVE, POST. CHARACTER: A, B, C etc. For Gk and Heb ~s, see *alphabet*. *LANDLORD*. HINDRANCE, PREVENTER (arch).

~ **OPENER** L (crypt). KNIFE. DEAR MADAM/SIR (crypt).

~ **SENDER** CORRESPONDENT, WRITER, POSTER. YOURS FAITHFULLY/SINCERELY/TRULY (crypt).

LEVEL *EVEN*, HORIZONTAL. DRAWN, EQUAL, TIED. STRAIGHT. HEIGHT.

LEVY *COLLECT*, EXTORT, IMPOSE, RAISE; DUTY, RATE, SCOT, TAX, TOLL. CONSCRIBE, *ENLIST*, ENROL; CONSCRIPT, PRESSED MAN.

LIAR (s/l *lyre*). FIBBER, STORY TELLER. **Celeb**: ANANIAS (bibl); DE TOTT (Baron); MATILDA (Belloc); MUNCHAUSEN (Baron); OBLOMOV (Gonchorov).

LIB LIBERAL. LIBERATION.

LIBER = *BACCHUS*.

LIBERA = *PROSERPINE*.

LIBERAL L, LIB; POLITICIAN. ABUNDANT, AMPLE (**opp** = *mean*), CANDID, *FREE*, GENEROUS, OPENHANDED.

LICK TASTE [tongue]; **comp** = promise. *BEAT* (sl). *SPEED* (sl).

LID *HAT. COVER*.

LIED FIBBED, TOLD STORY. *SONG* (Ger).

LIEDER (s/l *leader*). *SONGS* (Ger).

LIFE PAYMENT RANSOM. PENSION. CAPITAL PUNISHMENT.

LIFT RAISE, TAKE UP (**opp** = *lower*) [hitch hike]. ELEVATOR, PATERNOSTER [Otis, inventor]. CHARGE, EXHILARATION, KICK. *STEAL* [robber].

LIGHT NOT DARK, BLOND(E), PALE. NOT HEAVY, UNLADEN; TRIVIAL. *BEAM*, FLOOD ~, *RAY*, SPOT ~, LAMP; ILLUMINE. 'PHOEBE'. *FIRE*, *MATCH*. GIDDY, NIMBLE, *NIPPY*. CLUE, PRINCIPLE, TENET.

PORTHOLE, WINDOW (naut). EYE (poet). SHORT,
UNDERSUBSCRIBED. **Pl** = INNARDS, KIDNEYS, LIVER,
LUNGS, OFFAL.
LIGHTER MATCH, SPILL. PALER. LESS BURDENED.
BARGE. GLAZIER (crypt). LAMP, SUN (crypt).
LIGHTNING 1. DISCHARGE (met); **comp** = *thunder*. SPEEDY.
AIRCRAFT. 2. **God: Rom** = FULMINATOR; **goddess: Rom** =
MINERVA.
LIKE *AS*, EQUAL, SIMILAR. CONSENT. FIND
AGREEABLE.
LIKING FANCY, FONDNESS, REGARD, TASTE (**opp** =
aversion). See also *Lover of*.
LILY *FLOWER* of genus LILIUM: ARUM, BELLADONNA,
CALLA, *GUERNSEY*, *IRIS*, LENT, MADONNA, RED-HOT
POKER, TORCH ~, TRITOMA, WATER ~, WHITE ~.
'SUSAN'. [~ Langtry (Jersey ~); ~ Marlene (song)]. **Pl** =
ROYAL ARMS (Fr Bourbon).
LIMIT *BOUNDARY*. CONTROL. END, TERMINUS.
MAXIMUM SPEED.
LIMITED LTD, PLC. RESTRICTED (**opp** = *free*).
~ **FRENCH** SA.
~ **GERMAN** AG, GMBH.
LINCOLN 1. ABE. *AIRCRAFT*. GREEN. *PIG*. *RACETRACK*
(horses). *UNIVERSITY COLLEGE*. USS ~ (Mme *Butterfly*).
2. LINDUM (Rom). US *state* capital.
LINCOLN'S INN *INN OF COURT*, LAW SOCIETY.
LINE FILE, *ROW*, TIER. LETTER. BOAST. RAILWAY: GWR,
LMS, LNER, SR etc (often as 'old ~'). FISHING TACKLE,
GUT, PATERNOSTER; **comp** = *rod*. FIGURE. **Pl** = BR,
RLY, RY. ODE, POEM, POETRY, VERSE. IMPOT (sl),
PUNISHMENT.
LINER 1. *BOAT*, SHIP, *STEAMER*. PROTECTION,
SLEEVE. COTTON, LINEN, LINING, SILESIA. ARTIST,
CARTOONIST, DRAUGHTSMAN, DRAWER (all crypt).
ACTOR, PLAYWRIGHT (crypt). RULER (crypt). 2. Put word
inside another, e.g. **Bag with thin liner is popular in the sea** (7)
= BA*THIN*G.
LINESMAN FOOTBALL OFFICIAL, TOUCHJUDGE.
SOLDIER (crypt). CONDUCTOR, ENGINE DRIVER,
GUARD, RAILWAYMAN, TRAIN DRIVER (all crypt).
AUTHOR, POET, WRITER (all crypt). ELSMAN (crypt:
L*in*ESMAN).

LINE UP ALIGN, DRESS. PARADE. REPRESENTATIVES,
TEAM. ENIL (dn, crypt).

LING *FISH. HEATHER.*

LINKS (s/l *lynx*). CONNECTIONS, TIES. CUFF BUTTONS.
GOLF COURSE. KLS (crypt: L*in*KS).

LION 1. BIG *CAT*, KING OF BEASTS, LEO; **assembly** = pride,
offspring = cub, lioncel (*herald*); **comp** ≙ unicorn. [Alfred
(Stanley Holloway); Androcles (Rom slave); *Daniel* (bibl);
Holmes case]; *Shak* (Snug in MND). 2. BRAVE PERSON,
HERO. *CELEBRITY*, STAR, VIP. **Pl** = *Football* team (US).
RUGBY PLAYERS. 3. One of the labours of *Hercules.*
4. *Constellation*; (5th) sign of the *Zodiac* (Leo). 5. Char in *Alice*
and in *The Wizard of Oz.*

LIONHEART COEUR DE LION, RICHARD [Blondel,
Durnstein castle]. *IO* (crypt).

LIP CHEEK, IMPUDENCE, INSOLENCE. EDGE, RIM, TIP.
Pl = 1. MOUTH; SPEAKERS. 2. Gk myth SW *wind* (**Rom** =
AFRICUS).

LIQUEUR ALCOHOL, AFTER-DINNER DRINK; **types**
(most ®): ABSINTHE (wormwood), ANISETTE
(aniseed), BENEDICTINE (brandy), CHARTREUSE (herbs
& flowers), CHERRY BRANDY (cherries), COINTREAU
(orange), CRÈME DE MENTHE (mint), CURAÇAO
(orange), DRAMBUIE (whisky), KIRSCH (cherry),
KUMMEL (caraway), GRAND MARNIER (brandy/orange),
MARASCHINO (cherry), NOYAU (fruit kernels), RATAFIA
(*almonds*), SLOE GIN (sloes), TIA MARIA (coffee).

LIRA L.

LIST *BOOK*, CATALOGUE, INDEX, ROLL, *TABLE. HEEL,*
LEAN, TILT. BORDER, EDGE, HEM. ATTENTION,
HARK, HEED, LISTEN. **Pl** = TILTING GROUND
(jousting).

LISTENER AUDITOR, HEARER; *EAR* (crypt). **Pl** =
AUDIENCE.

LIT ILLUMINATED, ILLUMINED, LIGHTED. DRUNK.
STRUCK; SET FIRE TO.

LITTER BROOD, FARROW (piglets); and see *offspring.*
RUSHES, STRAW. RUBBISH. BED, BIER, HURDLE,
STRETCHER; PALANQUIN (Ind) [Sedan chair].

LITTLE 1. L; DIMINUTIVE, *DWARF*, MINI, PYGMY,
SMALL, WEE (**opp** = *big*). *THEATRE.* 2. Use abbreviated or
shortened version, e.g. **Each little** = EA. 3. **Celeb (fict)**: ~ Billee

(Trilby, du Maurier); Bingo ~ (*Wodehouse*); ~ Bo-peep (trad); ~ Boy Blue (trad); ~ Dorrit (*Dickens*); ~ Em'ly (Copperfield, *Dickens*); Eric or ~ by ~ (Farrar); ~ Foxes (Hellman); ~ Jack Horner (trad); ~ John (Robin *Hood*); ~ Lord Fauntleroy (Burnett); ~ Men (Alcott); ~ Mildred (*Kipling*); ~ Nell (OC Shop, *Dickens*); ~ Princess (Burnett); ~ Red Riding *Hood* (trad); ~ Tim (Xmas Carol, *Dickens*); ~ Women (Alcott). 4. Hidden word, e.g. **Little Corporal lied and regrouped his troops** (7) = RAL*LIED.

~ **BOY** 1. LAD, YOUNGSTER. 2. Use abbreviated or familiar version of boy's name, e.g. **A little boy is a handsome youth** (6) = A*DON*IS.

~ **BY** ~ ERIC (Farrar). LL (crypt).

~ **GIRL** 1. LASS, YOUNGSTER. 2. Use short or familiar form of girl's name, e.g. **Laughing little girl joins the monarch** (6) = JO*KING.

~ **MAN** 1. *DWARF*, MIDGET. 2. Use abbreviated form of name, e.g. **Little man joins little particle to make lots** (7) = BILL*ION.

~ **MONEY** C, D, P etc. CENT, PENNY. SMALL CHANGE.

~ **TIME** HR, MIN, MO, SEC, TICK, TIM (crypt).

~ **WOMAN** 1. *DWARF*, MIDGET. *WIFE*. 2. Use abbr form of name, e.g. **Is the little woman a child?** (5) = IS*SUE. 3. AMY, BETH, JO, MEG (Louisa May Alcott).

LIVE EXIST. DOSS, HANG OUT, INHABIT. QUICK (**opp** = *dead*). INSTANT; SPONTANEOUS, UNRECORDED. CHARGED, ON, SHOCKING (elect). **Pl** = EXISTS, IS.

LIVER SURVIVOR. ORGAN, OFFAL [*Prometheus*]; **comp** = bacon.

LIVING ALIVE, EXISTING, QUICK (**opp** = *dead*). EXISTENCE, LIVELIHOOD [Saturday's *child*]; CAREER. BENEFICE, PARISH (eccles).

LIZARD *REPTILE* (*dinosaur*, lacertilia); AGAMA, ANOLIS, BASILISK, BEADED MONSTER, BLIND WORM, BLUE-TONGUED ~ (Aus), CHAMELEON, DRACO, *DRAGON*, FLYING DRAGON, GECKO, GILA, GREEN ~, GUANA, HATTERIA (NZ), IGUANA, KOMODO DRAGON, *MOLOCH* (Aus), *MONITOR*, OLM, SALAMANDER, SAND ~, SEPS, SKINK, SWIFT ~, TUATERA (NZ), UTA, WATER DRAGON, WORREL, ZONURE [loses tail; newt]. **Celeb**: BILL (*Alice*).

LLAMA (s/l lama). Domesticated ruminant 2-toed quadruped (S Am); **breeds**: ALPACA, GUANACO, HUANACO, PACO,

VICU(G)NA [*camel*].
LLOYDS *BANK* ®. INSURERS, MARINE
UNDERWRITERS [coffee house; Lutine bell]. SHIP
SURVEYORS; REGISTER [A1; yachts]. *REFERENCE
WORK* (ships).
LO BEHOLD, LOOK, SEE.
LOAF IDLE, SLACK (**opp** = *beaver*). BREAD, *COB*,
COTTAGE. HEAD (*rh sl*).
LOAFER IDLER, *LAZER*, SLACKER. *BAKER* (crypt).
LOBSTER CRUSTACEAN (10-footed); CRAWFISH, CRAYFISH
[langouste, langoustine, prawn, shrimp; quadrille (*Alice*)].
UNDERARM BOWLER (*cricket*). BRITISH SOLDIER,
REDCOAT (arch).
LOCAL BELONGING TO, PECULIAR TO; NEAR BY,
NEIGHBOURING, VICINITY. PARTLY, RESTRICTED.
PUB. TRAIN. ANAESTHETIC.
LOCH L, LAKE, LOUGH (Ire); NESS.
LOCK BOLT, KEY, WARD. CURL, *HAIR*, TRESS.
LOCKER CUPBOARD. CHEST, COMPARTMENT (naut).
KEY; GAOLER, TURNKEY, WARDER (crypt). BARBER,
HAIRDRESSER (crypt).
LOCK-KEEPER CANAL GATE OPERATOR. COMB, HAIR-
GRIP, HAIRPIN, SLIDE (all crypt). *HAIRDRESSER* (crypt).
LOCO-MEN RAILWAY MEN (**Unions** = ASLEF, NUR).
CRANKS, IDIOTS, MADMEN, NUTTERS.
LODGE DEPOSIT, LAY DOWN. PUT UP, RESIDE, STAY.
Habitation (*beaver*, otter). BRANCH MEMBERS. COTTAGE,
DWELLING, *HOUSE*.
LOFTING 1. LOBBING (sport). STORING, WAREHOUSING
(comm). 2. Laying-out full-scale lines of a hull (naut). 3. Hugh
~, WRITER. **Books**: Dr Dolittle's Caravan, ~'s Circus, ~'s
Garden, ~'s Post Office, ~'s Zoo, Story of ~, Voyages of
~, Story of Mrs Tubbs, Porridge Poetry. **Characters**: Dr John
Dolittle (talked with animals), Barbary *Dragon*, Ben-Ali (*pirate*),
Chee-Chee (*monkey*), Dab-Dab (*duck*), Gub-Gub (*pig*), Jabizri
(*beetle*), Jip (*dog*), Jolliginki (*African tribe*, Queen Ermintrude,
Prince Bumpo), Polynesia (*parrot*), Pushmipullyu (2-headed
animal), Tommy (*cobbler's* son), Too-Too (*owl*), Tripsitinka
(*Fairy* Queen); Spidermonkey Island. See also *Doolittle*.
LOG ENTER, *RECORD*, REGISTER; *LIST*. LOGARITHM
[Napier]. BILLET (wood).
LOGGER LUMBERJACK, SAWYER. DIARIST, RECORDER

(crypt).

LOKI Nor *god* of FIRE; m Angurboda; f of Fenris (*wolf*), *Hel* and Midgard (*serpent*).

LONDON 1. CAPITAL, SMOKE [*Gates. Thames bridges*]. *BOXER. UNIVERSITY. WRITER.* 2. LONDINIUM (*Rom*).

LONDON DISTRICT EC, SW, WC etc; hence N*ONE, W*EIGHT (i.e. N1, W8 – crypt).

LONG L; ENDURING, LENGTHY (**opp** = *short*). CRAVE, LANGUISH, PANT, *PINE*, YEARN. LONGITUDE [meridian, navigation]. ISLAND (Eng, Ire, US).

LONGING CRAVING, YEARNING, YEN. BELONGING TO (arch).

LONG LIFE UHT. OCTOGENARIAN; METHUSELAH. [*cat*].

~ **PANTS** SLACKS, TROUSERS, COMBS, ~ JOHNS. *LONGING* (crypt).

LOOK *CON*, GLANCE, LEER, LO, *PEER*, PRY, REGARD, SEE, STARE, SURVEY; BUTCHERS (*rh sl*); DEKKO (sl). AIR, ASPECT, *BEARING*, MIEN.

~ **BACK** 1. REFLECT, REMINISCE. TURN HEAD, TURN ROUND [*Eurydice, Lot, Orpheus*]. 2. Word reads backwards, e.g. **Royal looks back for his beer** (5) = LAGER.

~ **FOR** SEARCH, SEEK; *FISH*.

~ **OUT** *CAVE* (hence CAVEMAN – crypt), FORE, TAKE CARE, WARE. OBSERVER, *SENTRY, WATCHER* [crow's nest].

LOON *BIRD*, DIVER, GREBE. IDLER, SCAMP. DOLT, IMBECILE, LUNATIC.

LORD *NOBLE*, PEER. DOMINATE, DOMINEER. Thomas ~ (cricket). **Pl** = *LEGISLATIVE ASSEMBLY*, ANOTHER PLACE. PEERAGE. *CRICKET* GROUND; TEST(ING) GROUND (crypt). 12th day of *Christmas* in song.

LORRY (s/l Laurie). 1. FLAT CAR, FLOAT, *JUGGERNAUT*, PANTECHNICON, (MOTOR) TRUCK, VAN, WAG(G)ON. 2. BANKER (2 Cities, *Dickens*).

LOSE 1. GET RID OF, MISLAY, MISPLACE (**opp** = *discover*). BE/GET DEFEATED (**opp** = *beat*, win); SURRENDER. BECOME SLOW. IMMERSE. 2. Delete letter(s) indicated, e.g. **Encourage to lose no ace** (4) = ****UR*GE.

~ **HEART** 1. DESPAIR. ADORE, FALL IN LOVE. 2. Omit middle letter(s), e.g. **Peter loses heart, the noble fellow** = PE*ER.

LOSING ONE Omit letter I, e.g. **I'm a rat, losing one French Revolutionist** (5) = *M*A*RAT.

LOST CITY, *EL DORADO*, LYONESSE. [Mu (Continent)].
LOT 1. HIGH NUMBER, LASHINGS, MANY hence C, D,
  M. SALE ITEM. CHANCE, DRAW, FATE, SORT, STRAW.
  PLOT. TAX DUE. DEPARTMENT, *RIVER* (Fr). *AIRLINE*
  (Pol). 2. Abraham's nephew, s of Haran. His w was turned into
  a pillar of salt, on *looking back* as she fled from the destruction
  of Sodom and Gomorrah. Ancestor of Ammon and Moab.
LOUD F, FF; DIN, NOISE, *ROW* (**opp** = *quiet*).
LOUGH L, IRISH LAKE.
LOVE 1. L, O, DUCK, EGG, NIL, ZERO, ZILCH. ADORE,
  DEAR, HONEY; ALOHA. 'Charity'. [Friday's *child*].
  2. **Gods: Gk** = EROS, **Rom** = AMOR, *CUPID*; **goddesses: Gk** =
  APHRODITE, **Rom** = VENUS, **Bab** = ISHTAR, **Egy** = *ISIS*,
  Nor = *FREYA*, **Phoen** = ASTARTE.
~ **APPLE** TOMATO.
LOVER 1. AMANT, AMOUR, GIRL/BOY FRIEND,
  INAMORATA, SWEETHEART; [*companion*; *inspiration*;
  patron saint; *seven ages* (*Shak*)]; **Pl** = 6 (*tarot*); **celeb**:
  CASANOVA (It); DON JUAN (~, Byron); LOCHINVAR
  (Marmion, Scott); LOTHARIO (The Fair Penitent, Rowe);
  TOM JONES (~, Fielding). **Pl** = ABELARD/HELOISE
  (Fr); ANTONY/CLEOPATRA (Rom/Egy and *Shak*);
  CELADON/AMELIA (The Seasons, Thomson);
  CHOPIN/GEORGE SAND; DARBY/JOAN (trad ballad);
  HENRY II/FAIR ROSAMOND (Talisman, Scott);
  LEANDER/HERO (Gk myth); NAPOLEON/JOSEPHINE
  (Fr); NELSON/EMMA (UK); PYRAMUS/THISBE (Bab
  myth and MND, *Shak*); ROMEO/JULIET (~, *Shak*). 2. One
  who is keen on a subject (**opp** = one who has an *aversion* to a
  subject), e.g.

Books	BIBLIOPHILE
Cinema	KINEMOPHILE
Death	NECROPHILE
Dogs	CYNOPHILE
English ways	ANGLOPHILE
Feet	PODOPHILE
Foreigners	XENOPHILE
French ways	FRANCOPHILE
God	THEOPHILE
Horses	HIPPOPHILE
Learning	PHILOMATH

Pain	ALGOPHILE
People	GENOPHILE
Russian ways	RUSSOPHILE
Wine	OENOPHILE
Women	PHILOGYNIST

3. In dn clue, put L before (or 'over') word indicated, e.g.
Oaf-lover sounds needed (4) = L*OAF.

LOVE-SICK AMOROUS; LOST HEART, hence (crypt) omit
middle letter(s) as in *LOSE HEART* above.

LOW ABJECT, *BASE*, DEJECTED, DISPIRITED, DOWN,
HUMBLE (**opp** = high). COARSE, DEGRADED,
MEAN, VULGAR (**opp** = U). QUIET. COL, CYCLONE,
DEPRESSION (met). BELLOW, MOO. *CARTOONIST*
(Blimp, TUC horse).

~ **CREATURE** *BULL*, *COW*, *OX* (crypt). SNAKE. TUC
HORSE (crypt).

LOWER DEBASE, DEGRADE, DIMINISH, DISGRACE;
BENEATH, NETHER. DESCEND, LET DOWN, SINK (**opp**
= *hoist*, *lift*). FROWN, LOUR. BOVINE, *COW*, *OX*, NEAT
etc (crypt).

LOW-LYING DEPRESSED. IN HIDING (crypt).

LP RECORD.

LSD (OLD) MONEY. *DRUG*.

LUCIFER 1. *MATCH* (arch). *DEVIL*. 2. Rom name for *VENUS*
as the MORNING STAR; **Gk** = PHOSPHORUS (**opp** =
Hesperus).

LUG PULL. PAWL. EAR.

LUGGAGE *BAGGAGE*.

LUNA (s/l *lunar*). Rom myth *goddess* of the *MOON* (**Gk** =
SELENE).

LUNAR (s/l *luna*). MONTHLY. *MOON*. MOONIE (crypt).

LUNATIC *FOOL*, IDIOT, MADMAN, *NUTCASE*.

LYDIA 1. GIRL. 2. Part of Asia Minor, MAEONIA (**King** =
Croesus).

LYNX (s/l *links*). *CAT*. HELICOPTER.

LYON (s/l *lion*). *HERALD*. RIVER (Sc). TOWN (Fr). **Pl** =
CAFE (*Nippy*).

LYRE (s/l *liar*). 1. *BIRD*. INSTRUMENT (mus) [*Hermes*,
Orpheus]. 2. *Constellation* (Lyra).

M *MAIDEN*. MALTA (*car plate*). *MARK*. *MARRIED*. *MALE*, MASCULINE. MEDIUM. MEGA (*Int unit*). *MEMBER*. MERIDIEM, NOON. METRE. MILLION. MONDAY. MONSIEUR. *MOTHER*. Head of MI5. THOUSAND.

MA MASTER OF ARTS; DEGREE. *MOTHER*, MUM. MASSACHUSETTS (US *state*). MOROCCO (*car plate*). *Goddess* of Truth (Egy).

MACBETH THANE; THE SCOTTISH PLAY [damned spot; *Shak*].

MACE NUTMEG, *SPICE*. SPIKED CLUB, *WEAPON*. STAFF OF OFFICE [House of Commons; Speaker].

MACRON ACCENT (¯ = long sound).

MAD *Anag*. ANGRY, ANNOYED, BATS, CRAZY, *CROSS*, DOTTY, IDIOTIC, LUNATIC, NUTS, *NUTTY*, SCREWY; **celeb**: Bertha *Mason* (Jane Eyre, *Brontë*); *Caligula* (Incitatus); Mr Dick (Copperfield, *Dickens*); Giselle (*Adam*); Hamlet (*Shak*); ~ Hatter (*Alice*); Landseer (*painter*); Dr Manette (2 Cities, *Dickens*); Mignon (Goethe); Nijinski (ballet); Ophelia (Hamlet, *Shak*); *Saul* (1); Schumann (*composer*); van Gogh (*painter*); and see *Mad King*.

MADE (s/l *maid*). BUILT, CONSTRUCTED, CREATED, *FASHIONED* (**opp** = *broke*, destroyed). ARRIVED, REACHED.

MAD KING CHARLES VI (Fr), GEORGE III (Eng), LEAR (*Shak*), LUDWIG (Bavaria), *SAUL* (bibl).

MADMAN IDIOT, LUNATIC, *NUTCASE*.

MAGELLAN *EXPLORER*. *STRAIT*.

MAGI Bibl wise men of Chaldaea, ASTROLOGERS, MAGICIANS, PRIESTS (Zoroastra), especially the three ~ of the Nativity: *Balthazar*, Caspar and Melchior.

MAGICIAN *CONJUROR* (q.v.), NECROMANCER, *SORCERER* (q.v.), THAUMATURGE, VOODOO, *WITCH*, *WIZARD*; **celeb fact**: PAUL DANIELS, DR JOHAN FAUST(US), HOUDINI, MASQUELINE & DEVANT; **celeb fict**: FAUST (Goethe, Marlowe), MANDRAKE (bot, legend), MEDEA (Gk myth), MEPHISTOPHELES (Goethe, Marlowe), MERLIN (*King Arthur*) PROSPERO (*Shak*, Temp).

MAGISTRATE (A)EDILE (Rom), JP, *LAW PRACTITIONER*, STIPENDIARY; BEAK(sl). **Celeb**: DRACO (Gk); FANG (*Dickens*). And see *Judge* and *Law*.

MAGNESIUM *METAL*; MG (*chem*).

MAGNUM *BOTTLE* (double size).

MAGPIE TARGET RING (penultimate). CHATTERER, GOSSIP. COLLECTOR, *KLEPTOMANIAC*. *LEPIDOPTERA* (moth). *BIRD* (pica pica or crow family); (1) sorrow, (2) joy, (3) girl, (4) boy, (5) letter, (6) something better, (7) greeting, (8) wish, (9) kiss, (10) meeting; [bad luck, stealing; *Pierides* (Gk myth); Thieving ~ (mus)]. **Pl** = NOTTS COUNTY (*football* team).

MAIA 1. Gk myth d of *Atlas* and Pleione; eldest of the *Pleiades*; m by *Zeus* of *Hermes*. 2. Rom myth *goddess* of Earth; the first fruits were offered in *May*.

MAID (s/l *made*). DAMOSEL, DAMSEL, *GIRL*, LASS; SPINSTER, UNWED. SERVANT, SERVING GIRL, WENCH, TWEENY. **Celeb**: ABIGAIL (The Scornful Lady, Beaumont and Fletcher), FAIR ~ (of Kent), *JOAN* (of Arc), KEZIA (Mill on the Floss), MARIA (12th N, *Shak*), MISS MIGGS (Rudge, *Dickens*), CLARA PEGGOTTY (Copperfield, *Dickens*), GUSTER (Bleak Ho, *Dickens*), ~ MARION (Robin *Hood*), NERISSA (M of V, *Shak*), RUTH (Pirates, *G & S*), SUZUKI (Madam *Butterfly*) [Yeoman, Mikado (3 pretty ~s) *G & S*].

MAIDEN M, UNMATED, UNWED, VIRGIN; [~ over, *cricket*]. FIRST. GUILLOTINE (hist Sc). 'CORA'. *CASTLE*. MALCOLM (Sc king).

MAIL (s/l *male*). LETTERS, POST. ARMOUR. NEWSPAPER ®.

MAIN (s/l *mane*). CHIEF, PRINCIPAL; **comp** = *might*. SUPPLY (drains, electricity, gas, water). *SEA*.

~ **COURSE** SHIP'S HEADING. PRINCIPAL DISH (*course*). SEAFOOD (crypt).

MAJOR PRIME MINISTER. PRINCIPAL (**opp** = *minor*). PITCH, SCALE (mus). MAJ, OFFICER, SOLDIER (crowned – crypt); **celeb**: BAGSTOCK (Dombey, *Dickens*); BRIDGENORTH (*Scott*); PENDENNIS (Thackeray); PENTO (Thackeray); PIG (*Orwell*); THOMPSON (Les Carnets du Major ~; Pierre Daninos).

MAKE *Anag.* BUILD, CONSTRUCT, FABRICATE, FASHION. COMPEL, FORCE, IMPEL(L). SUCCEED; **comp** = break. BRAND, MARQUE, MODEL, TYPE. CONSORT, PEER (arch).

MAKER *Anag. GOD.* FABRICATOR, MANUFACTURER.

MAKE UP *Anag.* IMAGINE, INVENT. CONCOCT, COMPOSE. COMPENSATE; COMPLETE. RECONCILE, *SETTLE*. CHARACTER, TEMPERAMENT. COSMETICS; WAR-

PAINT (sl). EKAM (dn, crypt).

MALE AGNATE, *FATHER*, MASCULINE, SPEAR; **opp** = distaff, *female*; STAG. INTERNAL FITTING (mech).

~ **AND FEMALE** There are many special words for denoting male or female genders for various animals. These are sometimes used misleadingly, to lure the solver into an incorrect train of thought, e.g. **Pen, pot and pan is nutty** (3) = COB ('pot and pan' being *rhyming slang* for 'old man', or husband; the husband of a pen (swan) is a 'cob', which also means a nut). Therefore particular note should be taken of those genders which offer a second meaning or cryptic clue, such as **tup** (put back), **queen** (*monarch*), **drake** (*military leader*), **doe** (**pl** = does), **ewe** (you sound . . .) and so on. **Genders include:**

Genus	Male	Female
Ass	JACKASS	*JENNY*
Bird	COCK	HEN
Bovine	*BULL*	*COW*
Canine	*DOG*	BITCH
Cat	*TOM*	*QUEEN*
Cattle	*BULL*	*COW*
Chicken	COCK	HEN
Child	BOY	GIRL
Crab	COCK	HEN
Deer	BUCK, HART, *STAG*	DOE, HIND
Donkey	*JACK*	*JENNY*
Duck	*DRAKE*	*DUCK*
Elephant	*BULL*	*COW*
Ferret	*BUCK*	*DOE*, GILL
Fox	*DOG*	VIXEN
Goat	BILLY	*NANNY*
Goose	GANDER	*GOOSE*
Hare	*BUCK*	*DOE*
Hawk	T(I)ERCEL	
Horse	STALLION	MARE
Human	MAN	WOMAN
Hunting dog	*HOUND*	BRACH
Lobster	COCK	HEN
Monarch	*KING*	*QUEEN*
Monastic recluse	ABBOT, *MONK*	ABBESS, NUN
Ox	*BULL*	*COW*

Pig	BOAR	SOW
Rabbit	*BUCK*	*DOE*
Rat	*BUCK*	*DOE*
Ruff	RUFF	REEVE
Salmon	COCK	HEN
Sandpiper	RUFF	REEVE
Sheep	RAM, TUP	*EWE*
Sovereign	*KING*	*QUEEN*
Swan	*COB*	*PEN*
Turkey	COCK, *STAG*	HEN
Walrus	*BULL*	*COW*

Male	Genus
Abbot	MONASTIC RECLUSE
Billy	*GOAT*
Boar	*PIG*
Boy	CHILD
Buck	CATTLE, *DEER, RABBIT,* RAT
Bull	BOVINE, CATTLE, ELEPHANT, OX, WALRUS
Cob	*SWAN*
Cock	*BIRD, CHICKEN*, CRAB, LOBSTER, SALMON, TURKEY
Dog	CANINE, *FOX*
Drake	*DUCK*
Gander	*GOOSE*
Hart	*DEER*
Hound	HUNTING DOG
Jack	*DONKEY*
Jackass	ASS
King	MONARCH, SOVEREIGN
Man	HUMAN
Monk	MONASTIC RECLUSE
Ram	*SHEEP*
Ruff	SANDPIPER (RUFF)
Stag	*DEER*, TURKEY
Stallion	*HORSE*
T(i)ercel	*HAWK*
Tom	*CAT*
Tup	*SHEEP*

Female	Genus
Abbess	CONVENT/MONASTIC RECLUSE
Bitch	CANINE
Brach	HUNTING DOG
Cow	BOVINE, CATTLE, ELEPHANT, *WALRUS*
Doe	*DEER*, FERRET, HARE, *RABBIT*, RAT
Duck	*DUCK*
Ewe	*SHEEP*
Gill	FERRET, POLECAT
Girl	CHILD
Goose	*GOOSE*
Hen	*BIRD, CHICKEN*, CRAB, LOBSTER, *SALMON*
Hind	*DEER*
Jenny	ASS, *DONKEY*
Mare	*HORSE*
Nanny	*GOAT*
Nun	CONVENT/MONASTIC RECLUSE
Pen	*SWAN*
Queen	*CAT, MONARCH*, SOVEREIGN
Reeve	RUFF (SANDPIPER)
Sow	*PIG*
Vixen	FOX
Woman	HUMAN

MALLARD *DUCK*; **assembly** = flock, flush.
MAMBA *DANCE. SNAKE.*
MAN HE, HOMO SAPIENS, HUMANITY [Heidelberg ~, Java ~, Peking ~, Piltdown ~]; ONE, PERSON. *MALE,* MASCULINE GENDER. HUSBAND. BOB, TOM, WILL etc. *CREW, SAILOR.* FILL, FURNISH. SOLDIER. *CHESS*/GAMES PIECE. IOM, *ISLAND.* MANITOBA (*Province*, Can).
MANAGE ORGANIZE, *RUN. HANDLE.*
MANAGING DIRECTOR MD (**Union** = ASTMS).
MANDARIN OFFICIAL (Ch). BUREAUCRAT, ESTABLISHMENT FIGURE, GURU, PARTY LEADER

(hence P – crypt). CHINESE LANGUAGE. *DUCK*. CITRUS *FRUIT*.

MANGANESE *METAL*; MN (*chem*). HARD METAL.

MANIA CRAZE, EAGER PURSUIT, EXCESSIVE ENTHUSIASM, *OBSESSION*.

MANLY BUTCH, MASCULINE, VIRILE (crypt).

MANOEUVRE *Anag*. MANEUVER (US). EXERCISE, PLAN (mil). FIGURE, MOVEMENT. HANDLE, MOVE, STEER, TURN (aero; naut).

MAN WOULD HED.

MANX CAT *CAT* (breed); it has no tail, hence CA (crypt).

MANX RACE TT, BIKE RACE. DOUBLET (crypt).

MANY LOTS, hence C, D, M.

~-ARMED ARMY, WELL-ARMED (crypt). **Celeb:** AEG(A)EON, BRIAREUS, COTTUS, *DEVI*; ENCELADUS; *GY(G)ES; KALI*; STARKADDER (Nor myth); *URANIDS*.

~-DAUGHTERS Celeb: DANAUS, *NEREUS, SELENE*.

~-EYED *Keen-eyed*. **Celeb:** *ARGUS*; DRAGONFLY; LYNCEUS.

~-HEADED MIRV (mil *missile*). **Celeb:** *CERBERUS* (dog); CRATAEIS; GERYON (*Hercules*); *GY(G)ES; HYDRA*; LADON (dragon of *Hesperides*); ORTHRUS (dog); *SCYLLA*; *TYPHON*; *URANIDS*.

~-LEGGED Insect. **Celeb:** CRATAEIS; SLEIPNIR (*horse*).

~-LOVERS/WIVES Polygamist. **Celeb:** CASANOVA; *DAVID*; DON JUAN; LOTHARIO; *SOLOMON*; ZEUS.

~-SONS Celeb: AEGYPTUS, *PRIAM*.

MAR (s/l *ma*). DISFIGURE, *HINDER, IMPAIR, RUIN, SPOIL. MARRIED. MARCH*. **Pl** = Rom *god* of war.

MARBLE LIMESTONE, POLISHED STONE. **Pl** = BRAINS (sl). *GAME; AGATE*, ALLY, BONCE, *TAW*.

MARCH 1. MEASURED TREAD, PARADE, *STEP, TRAMP*, TRUDGE, WALK. DISTANCE, PROGRESS. BORDER, *BOUNDARY*, FRONTIER; TERRITORY. 2. (3rd) MONTH, M, MAR (*Mars*). **Birthstone** = *bloodstone*.

MARE *HORSE* (fem) [labour of *Hercules*]. SEA (Lat); CRATER (moon).

MARGIN BORDER, BRIM, EDGE. ROOM, SPACE. CLEARANCE. LEEWAY.

MARINE JOLLY, LEATHERNECK, RM. MARITIME, NAUTICAL, SEA.

MARK BLAZE, DENT, IMPRESS, SCRATCH, SOIL, SPOT, STAIN. BRAND, *CROSS*. PUNTER, SUCKER (sl).

TARGET. *COIN*. *ANTONY*; TWAIN. **Pl comp** = Spencer.

MARKER CHALKER, SCORER. PYLON, SIGNPOST. IOU (US sl).

MARKET DEMAND. BARTER, BUY, SELL. EXCHANGE, SALES/TRADE PLACE; **London ~s**: BILLINGSGATE (fish); COVENT GARDEN (fruit, vegetables, flowers); LEADENHALL (meat); NINE ELMS (fruit, vegetables, flowers); SMITHFIELD (cattle); PETTICOAT LANE (street ~); PORTOBELLO ROAD (antiques). FLEA ~ (Paris), SOUK (Arab).

MARRIAGE 1. MATRIMONY, WEDDING; SPLICING, *UNION* [Darby and *Joan*]. 2. **Gods: Gk** = *HYMEN*, **Rom** = GENIUS. ~ **LICENCE** MATE'S TICKET; UNION CARD (crypt).

MARRIED M, *MAR*. COUPLED, HITCHED, JOINED, MATED, PAIRED, SPLICED, *WED*(DED).

MARRY COUPLE, HITCH, JOIN, MATE, PAIR, SPLICE, TAKE THE PLUNGE, WED. CORRELATE, UNITE. GOLLY, GOSH, GRACIOUS (arch).

MARS 1. Rom *god* of WAR; mar Bellona (**Gk** = Enyo); f by *Rhea* (Silvia) of *Romulus* and Remus [*March*]. **Gk** = ARES. 2. RED *PLANET*. *SPACECRAFT*.

MARSUPIAL POUCHED MAMMAL: BANDICOOT, GLIDER, KANGAROO, KOALA, OPOSSUM, PHALANGER, THYLACINE, TASMANIAN DEVIL, WALLABY, WOMBAT.

MARTIAL ART SELF-DEFENCE, UNARMED COMBAT; **types**: AIKIDO (Jap), CH BOXING, JUDO (Jap), JU-JITSU (Jap), KARATE (Jap), KENDO (Jap), KUNG FU (Ch), TAEKWONDO (Korean), THAI BOXING, WUSU (Ch). WAR PAINTING (crypt).

MARXIST COMMIE, RED. KARL [Highgate cemetery]. CHICO, HARPO, GROUCHO, GUMMO, ZEPPO (all crypt).

MASCOT *PET*, TOTEM.

MASCULINE M; BUTCH, MANLY, VIRILE (and see *male and female*).

MASK (s/l masque). FACE COVERING/PROTECTION. FACE PACK. FACE (cat, dog, fox). CONCEAL, COVER, DISGUISE. LIKENESS (in death). **Celeb ~ed men**: BATMAN (comics, film, TV), *COMUS* (Rom god), LONE RANGER (TV), MAN IN IRON ~ (Dumas), PHANTOM OF THE OPERA (Leroux), ZORRO (McCulley).

MASON 1. STONEWORKER. 2. Member of fraternity of Free

and Accepted ~s [Grand Master, lodge, ritual]. 3. Bertha ~,
mad w of Mr Rochester (Jane Eyre, *Brontë*).
MASS CONVOCATION, LITURGY, (MUSICAL) *SERVICE*.
AGGREGATION, AMOUNT, EXPANSE; MATTER.
MASSACHUSETTS (*state* of US).
~ **MEETING** CONVOCATION, RALLY, SYMPOSIUM,
TEACH-IN. CHURCH SERVICE (crypt).
MASTER MA. MFH. DOMINIE, MR CHIPS, MONITOR,
SCHOOLMASTER (q.v.), TEACHER, TUTOR (**Union** =
NUT). DOMINATE, DEFEAT, OVERCOME. CAPTAIN,
SKIPPER (naut). EMPLOYER; SAHIB, TUAN. HEAD OF
HOUSE. CRAFTSMAN, *PAINTER*. MATRIX.
MATCH CONGREVE, FUSEE, LUCIFER, STRIKER,
VESTA ®. COMPARE, COPY, EQUAL, MATE,
PAIR, TALLY. CONTEST, FRIENDLY, GAME, *TEST*.
ENGAGEMENT, MARRIAGE, UNION, WEDDING.
MATCHBOX CONTAINER; **coll** = phillumenist. BOTTOM
DRAWER, WEDDING PRESENT (crypt).
MATCHED ENGAGED, MARRIED, *WED*. FITTED, TONED.
CONTESTED, PLAYED. *FIRED*, LIT (crypt).
MATCHLESS INCOMPARABLE, PEERLESS. BACHELOR,
SPINSTER, UNWED (crypt).
MATE HUSBAND, *MATCH*, PAIR, WIFE. JOIN. ALLY,
COMPANION. CHINA (rh sl).
MATERIAL 1. CLOTH, COTTON, DRAB, FABRIC, FLAX,
KNITWEAR, POLYESTER, STUFF, WEAVE, WOOL
[*measure*]. **Types** (many ®): ACRILAN, BARATHEA,
BALDACHIN, BAYADERE, BOMBASINE, -ZINE,
BROCADE, BURLAP, CALICO, CHIFFON, CORDUROY,
CORPORAL (eccles), DACRON, DAMASK, DIMITY,
DREADNOUGHT, DUPION, FELT, FICHU, GABARDINE,
GEORGETTE, GINGHAM, HARRAT(T)EEN, HESSIAN,
JUTE, LAMÉ, LAWN, LENO, LINSEY, LOCKRAM,
LUSTRE, MOREEN, MUNGO, MUSLIN, NAINSOOK,
NANKEEN, NET, NYLON, ORGANDIE, ORGANZA,
ORGANZINE, ORRIS, PARRAMATTA, PERCALE,
PETERSHAM, PLAID, PLUSH, PONGEE, RATINE,
RAT(T)EEN, REP, SACKCLOTH, SAMITE, SARSANET,
SATIN, SHALLOON, SHODDY, SILK, TAMIN, -IS, -NY,
TARLATAN, TERYLENE, TULLE, TWEED, VELVET,
WORSTED. 2. ELEMENTS. CORPOREAL, IMPORTANT.
JOKES, LINES (theat).

MAUSOLEUM TOMB, especially that one built by Artemisia in memory of her husband K Mausolus. One of the *Seven Wonders of the World*.

MAXWELL GAUSS, MAGNETIC FLUX.

MAY 1. IS ALLOWED, CAN, MIGHT, PERMITTED (**opp** = *cant*). HAWTHORN. *CASTLE*. Pl = EXAMS (C); BOAT RACES. 2. GIRL. 3. (5th) MONTH, M (Rom *Maia*); **birthstone** = *emerald*.

MAYA *Am Ind* tribe inhabiting Yucatan, with cities Merida (capital), Chichen Itza and Uxmal. Ancient culture incl human sacrifice, and gods Chac (rain), Quetzalcoatl (feathered serpent).

MAYBE *Anag.* 1. MYTHICAL, PERHAPS. 2. Sounds like, e.g. **Massage may be wanted** (5) = KNEAD.

MAYFAIR WEST END. WI.

MB BACHELOR OF MEDICINE, DOCTOR.

MBE *DECORATION*, MEDAL.

MC MASTER OF CEREMONIES. MILITARY CROSS; DECORATION, MEDAL. MONACO (*car plate*).

MD DOCTOR (OF MEDICINE). MANAGING DIRECTOR. MENDELEVIUM (*chem*). MUSICAL DIRECTOR, *CONDUCTOR*. MARYLAND (US *state*). 1,500.

ME I, NUMBER ONE, PERSONAL PRONOUN, SELF. MAINE (US *state*). MIDDLE EAST. MIDDLE ENGLISH. AIRCRAFT (Ger); MESSERSCHMITT. HALF TIME (crypt). NOTE (mus; also MI).

MEAL FEAST, PICNIC, REPAST, SPREAD: BREAKFAST, BRUNCH, *DINNER*, LUNCH, SUPPER, TEA. GRAIN, MAIZE, PULSE. Pl = *BOARD*, KEEP.

MEAN (s/l *mien*). INTEND, IMPLY. AVERAGE, *PAR*. NEAR, MISERLY, NIGGARDLY, PARSIMONIOUS, STINGY (**opp** = *liberal*). Pl = FACILITIES, WHEREWITHAL.

MEANING DRIFT, EXPLANATION, INTENTION, SIGNIFICANCE. EXPRESSIVE.

MEASURE 1. *DANCE*. ACTION, LAW, LEGISLATION. *COMPARE*, EVALUATE, ESTIMATE, *GAUGE*. *DEGREE*, EXTENT; *STANDARD*; TRAVERSE. *ROD*, TAPE. MARK OFF; QUANTITY, SIZE. CC, CM, FT, IN, LB, MM etc; CUBIT; DRAM, FIFTH, FINGER, SLUG, TOT. *FOOT*, METRE, RHYTHM. 2. In the following lists of types of measure, the figures in parentheses between different units of measurement represent the quantity of the first unit which is required to make up one of the second:

Area: SQ IN (144) SQ FT (9) SQ YD (30¹/₄) SQ *ROD/POLE/ PERCH* (40) ROOD (4) ACRE (640) SQ MILE [SQ CHAIN, HECTARE].

Capacity: GILL or *NOGGIN* (4) PINT (2) QUART (4) GALLON (2) *PECK* (4) BUSHEL (8) *QUARTER* (4¹/₂) CHALDRON.

Beer: GILL (4) PINT (2) QUART (4) GALLON (4¹/₂) PIN (2) FIRKIN (2) KILDERKIN (2) BARREL (1¹/₂) HOGSHEAD (2) BUTT or *PIPE* (2) TUN [PUNCHEON, TIERCE].

Fish: BARREL, QUINTAL, *BOX*, WARP.

Timber: LOAD, STACK, CORD.

Wine: SPLIT (2) PINT (2) *BOTTLE* (2) MAGNUM (2) JEROBOAM (1¹/₂) REHOBOAM (1¹/₃) METHUSELAH (1¹/₂) SALMANAZAR (1¹/₃) BALTHAZAR (1¹/₄) NEBUCHADNEZZAR (= 20 bots).

Weight:

  Avoirdupois: DRAM (16) OUNCE/OZ (16) POUND/LB (14) *STONE* (2) *QUARTER* (4) HUNDREDWEIGHT/CWT (20) TON [GRAINS (7,000 = 1 LB)].

  Apothecaries: GRAIN (20) SCRUPLE (3) DRACHM (8) OUNCE/OZ (12) POUND.

  Troy: GRAIN (24) PENNYWEIGHT/DWT (20) OUNCE/OZ (12) *POUND*/LB.

  Hay: LB (56) TRUSS (36) LOAD.

  Wool: LB (7) *CLOVE* (2) *STONE* (2) TOD (6¹/₂) WEY (2) SACK (12) *LAST*.

Length: NAIL (2¹/₄) *INCH*/IN (12) *FOOT*/FT (3) YARD/YD (22) CHAIN (10) FURLONG (8) MILE.

  Cloth: *INCH*/IN (2¹/₄) NAIL (4) QUARTER (5) *ELL*.

  Land: LINK (25) *ROD/POLE/PERCH* (4) CHAIN (80) MILE.

  Naut: *FOOT*/FT (6) FATHOM (100) CABLE (10) NAUTICAL MILE [degree; knot].

Paper size: FOLIO (F), QUARTO (4to), OCTAVO (8vo), DUODECIMO (12mo). CROWN, DEMY, ELEPHANT, FOOLSCAP, IMPERIAL, LARGE POST, MEDIUM, *POST, ROYAL*.

Paper qty: SHEET (24) QUIRE (20) REAM (2) BUNDLE (5) *BALE*.

Biblical: DIGIT (4) PALM (3) SPAN (2) CUBIT (4) FATHOM (2) ARABIAN POLE (10) MEASURING LINE (3) STADIUM (5) SABBATH JOURNEY (2) EASTERN MILE

(24) DAY'S JOURNEY.

Foreign: PICUL (Ch weight); LI (Ch mile); VERST (Russ mile).

MED MEDICAL, MEDICINE. MEDITERRANEAN. MEDIUM.

MEDAL VC, GC, GM, DSO, DSC, MC, DFC, CGM, DSM, MM, DFM, TD etc. GONG (sl). **Coll** = numismatist.

MEDEA Gk myth magician who mar *Jason*. She k their children when he remar, and then also k the new w.

MEDIA COUNTRY (Pers). VEIN (insect). CONSONANT (phonetics). *PRESS* (q.v.), NEWSAGENCIES, RADIO, TV. And see *MEDIUM*.

MEDICAL *MO*.

MEDICINE 1. DOCTORING, HEALING, MEDICAL ART. ELIXIR, NOSTRUM, PILL, POTION. CHARM, FETISH, INCANTATION, SPELL. 2. **Gods: Gk** = *ASCLEPIUS*; **Rom** = AESCULAPIUS.

MEDIUM M, MED, MIDDLE QUALITY. CONDITIONS, ENVIRONMENT. AGENCY, MEANS. SPIRITUALIST, MADAME ARCATI (Blithe Spirit, Coward). NEWS SYSTEM. **Pl** (media) = *PRESS, RADIO, TV, WIRELESS*. COUNTRY (Pers).

MEDUSA 1. 'The Ruler'. In Gk myth, one of the *Gorgons*, m of Chrysaor and *Pegasus* by *Poseidon*. Anyone who looked at her head, even after it was cut off by *Perseus*, was turned to stone [*Andromeda, Athene, Atlas*]. 2. JELLYFISH (Port man o'war; sea nettle).

MEDWAY TOWNS CHATHAM, GILLINGHAM, *ROCHESTER*.

MEET (s/l *meat*, mete). ENCOUNTER. FITTING, PROPER, SUITABLE. HUNT, RACE DAY [*fox, hounds*].

MEGA M (*int units*).

MEGAERA *FURY* (myth).

MEGALOMANIA *Obsession* with grandiose ideas.

MELPOMENE Gk myth; one of the nine *Muses* (Tragedy).

MEMBER M, MEP, MBE, MP. ARM, FINGER, HAND, LEG.

MEMORY RECALL, RECOLLECTION, REMEMBRANCE [Munin (*raven*)]; REPUTATION [rosemary]. ACCUMULATOR, COMPUTER CELL, RETRIEVAL BANK, STORAGE.

MENDER *Anag.* REPAIRER, RESTORER.

MENELAUS Gk myth K of Sparta; br of *Agamemnon*, mar to *Helen*, whose abduction led to the siege of *Troy*.

MEPHISTOPHELES *DEVIL* (Goethe). SORCERER (Marlowe).

MERCILESS *IRON*, PITILESS, RUTHLESS, UNPITYING.

MERCURY 1. *METAL*; HG (*chem*). LIQUID METAL, QUICKSILVER. 2. Rom *messenger* of the *gods*, s of *Jupiter* and *Maia*; he wore a winged cap (petasus) and winged sandals, and carried the caduceus. **Gk** = HERMES. 3. A *PLANET*. 4. *SPACECRAFT*.

MERCY COMPASSION, FORBEARANCE, PITY, QUARTER, RUTH [*sisters* of ~].

MERE *LAKE. SIMPLE.* MAORI WAR-CLUB, *WEAPON*.

MERIT DESERVE, EARN. OM.

MERLIN *BIRD*. AIRCRAFT ENGINE. *MAGICIAN* [*King Arthur*].

MERMAID 1. Myth sea creature, half-woman, half-fish, possibly inspired by the *manatee* [dugong, halicore, sea-cow; *Miranda*]. 2. *TAVERN* at Cheapside, burned in the Great Fire of London. *THEATRE*.

MERMAN Male counterpart of *mermaid*; **celeb**: TRITON (s of *Poseidon* and *Amphitrite*).

MESH *NET*, WEAVE. [gears].

MESOLITHIC *AGE*.

MESS *Anag.* MIX-UP, MUDDLE. POTTER. *FOOD, MEAL* [*Esau; Jacob*; officers' ~].

MESSAGE *CABLE, LETTER, NOTE.* MEANING, SIGNIFICANCE.

MESSENGER 1. *ANGEL*, FORERUNNER, *HERALD*, NUNCIO (papal). HAIGHA, HATTA (*Alice*), SALERIO (*Shak*, M of V). 2. **Gods: Gk** = HERMES; **Rom** = *MERCURY*. **Goddess: Gk** = ARTEMIS.

METAL QUALITY, WORTH, RAILS (rly); TARMAC (roads). BROADSIDE (mil); HEAVY ~; ARMOUR, TANKS (mil). ELEMENT (*chem*); ALLOY, GLASS, ORE (and see *mineral*) e.g.

3-letters

TIN (SN)

4-letters

GOLD (AU)
IRON (FE)
LEAD (PB)
ZINC (ZN)

5-letters

CUPRO-(CU) FERRO-(FE) PLUMB (PB)

6-letters

BARIUM (BA) *COPPER* (CU) RADIUM (RA)
CHROME (CR) *NICKEL* (NI) *SILVER* (AG)
COBALT (CO) OSMIUM (OS) SODIUM (NA)

7-letters

ARGENTO-(AG) GALLIUM (GA) THORIUM (TH)
BISMUTH (BI) IRIDIUM (IR) URANIUM (U)
CADMIUM (CD) LITHIUM (LI) *WOLFRAM* (W)
CALCIUM (CA) *MERCURY* (HG)

8-letters

ANTIMONY (SB) TITANIUM (TI)
CHROMIUM (CR) TUNGSTEN (W)
PLATINUM (PT) VANADIUM (V)
THALLIUM (TL)

9+ letters

ALUMINIUM (AL) *PHOSPHORUS* (P)
BERYLLIUM (BE) POTASSIUM (K)
MAGNESIUM (MG) STRONTIUM (SR)
MANGANESE (MN) YTTERBIUM (YB)
MOLYBDENUM (MO) ZIRCONIUM (ZR)
PALLADIUM (PD)

METHUSELAH 1. *BOTTLE* (wine) = 8 normal ~s. 2. The s of *Enoch* and Lamech, a bibl *wise man* who is said to have lived for 969 years; f of *Noah*.
METRE DISTANCE, *MEASURE. BEAT. FOOT.*
METRIC PREFIX See *International Units.*
METROPOLITAN *CAPITAL*, CENTRAL; HOME COUNTRY. *CHURCHMAN* (Gk). *THEATRE.*
Mex MEXICO.
MG MAGNESIUM (*chem*). *CAR*, MORRIS GARAGE.
MID 1. AMID; CENTRAL, MIDDLE. 2. Use middle letter(s), e.g. **Mid Sussex** = ss.
MIDAS 1. Gk myth king of Phrygia. All he touched turned to *gold*, even his food. He gained relief by bathing in the river Pactolus [Croesus, Dives]. 2. *SPACECRAFT.*

MIDDAY 1. NOON. TWELVE. A (crypt). 2. Put letter or word into synonym for day, e.g. **Airs nitrogen midday** (5) = TU*N*ES.

MIDDLE COURT *INN OF COURT*, LAW SOCIETY. U (crypt).

MIDNIGHT 00.00. TWELVE. DARKNESS. G (crypt).

MIDSHIPMAN P (crypt). BRASS-BOUNDER (merchant navy), ENSIGN (US), MIDDY (sl), SNOTTY (sl); EASY (Marryat), MIDSHIPMITE (Nancy Bell, *G & S*). *FISH*.

MIEN (s/l *mean*). APPEARANCE, *BEARING, LOOK*.

MIGHT COULD, MAY. *MAIN*, POWER, STRENGTH.

MIL *CURRENCY* (Cyprus). MILITARY (abbr). 1/1000th part (abbr).

MILANION Gk myth m of *Atalanta* [*apples*].

MILITARY CROSS *DECORATION*, MC, MEDAL.

MILITARY LEADERS Celebrated soldiers, sailors and airmen, e.g.

Air

BADER, G/C Sir D.	GOERING, F/M Hermann
BALBO, Gen (It)	MANNOCK, Major VC
BALL, Capt Albert VC	RICHTOFEN, Baron von
BISHOP, Col VC	RICKENBACKER, Capt
CHESHIRE, G/C VC	SPAATZ, Gen Carl
DOOLITTLE, Gen J.	TEDDER, MRAF Lord
DOWDING, A/M Lord	TRENCHARD, MRAF
GALLAND, Gen Adolf	Lord
GIBSON, W/C Guy VC	

Land

ALEXANDER, q.v.	*LEE*, Gen Robert E.
ANTIPATER, Macedon	MACARTHUR, Gen
CAESAR, Julius	MONTGOMERY,
CUSTER, Gen George	F/M Lord
EISENHOWER, Gen	NAPOLEON
GENGHIS KHAN	PATTON, Gen George
HANNIBAL	ROMMEL, F/M Erwin
JACKSON, Gen	SLIM, F/M Lord
KESSELRING, F/M	WELLINGTON, Duke of

Sea

BLIGH, Capt Wm.	HAWKINS, Sir John
DOENITZ, Gd Adm Karl	JONES, Capt John Paul
DRAKE, Sir Francis	MOUNTBATTEN,
HALSEY, Adm William	Adm Lord

NELSON, Adm Lord	RODNEY, Adm Lord
NIMITZ, Adm Chester	SHOVEL, Adm Sir C.
POUND, Adm Sir Dudley	SPRUANCE, Adm
RALEIGH, Sir Walter	YAMAMOTO, Adm
RAEDER, Gd Adm	

MILITARY POLICE MP, SP, REDCAP (hence R, crypt).

MILK NOURISHMENT, PAP [Poppaea (asses' ~)]; **comp** = sugar. EXTRACT. *COLOUR* (white). RIVER (US).

MILLION M.

MILNE A. A., *WRITER* (*Alexander* Beetle, *Alice*, Edward Bear, Christopher *Robin*, Eeyore, Heffalump, Kanga, Piglet, Pooh, Roo, *Rabbit*, Rabbit's Friends and Relations, Tigger, Winnie the Pooh, Wol).

MINCE (s/l *mints*). MINCED MEAT; SWEETMEAT (~ pie). CUT SMALL; RESTRAIN. WAGGLE, WALK AFFECTEDLY. **Pl** = EYES (*rh sl*).

MIND (s/l *mined*). ATTENTION, FEELING, THINKING. NURSE, TAKE CARE. BRAIN, INTELLECT, SOUL [*study*]. OPINION; CONCERN, TAKE NOTE. MEMORY, REMEMBRANCE. FUSS, OBJECT, WORRY.

MINE EXCAVATION, PIT, SAP; *BURROW*, DIG, UNDERMINE. POSSESSIVE (**opp** = theirs, yours). *BANGER*, EXPLOSIVE, *WEAPON*.

MINER (s/l *minor*). COLLIER (**Union** = NUM), *PITMAN* (crypt). *WORKER. DIGGER*, FORTY-NINER, PROSPECTOR.

MINERAL 1. WATER naturally impregnated with ~, or artificially carbonated; MIXER, SODA, TONIC. 2. Inorganic matter, especially crystalline; extracted or mined *ORE* (**comp** = animal, vegetable, abstract) e.g.

3-letters

JET	*ORE*

4-letters

CLAY	LIME	PEAT	TALC
COAL	MARL	*SALT*	
COKE	MICA	*SPAR*	

5-letters

BORON (B)	EMERY

6-letters

BARITE	IOLITE	SILICA
CARBON (C)	PUMICE	SPINEL
GARNET	PYRITE	
GYPSUM	QUARTZ	

7-letters

ARSENIC (AS)	LIGNITE	SILICON
ASPHALT	OLIVINE	TRIPOLI
AZURITE	PERLITE	ZEOLITE
BAUXITE	PYRITES	
BITUMEN	REALGAR	

8-letters

ANTIMONY (SB)	CRYOLITE	PYROZENE
ASBESTOS	FELDSPAR	SIDERITE
CHROMITE	FLUORITE	SILICATE
CINNABAR	GRAPHITE	TINSTONE
CORUNDUM	OBSIDIAN	

9-letters

ALABASTER	IRONSTONE	MARCASITE
BRIMSTONE	LIMESTONE	WULFENITE
FLUORSPAR	LODESTONE	
FOOL'S GOLD	MALACHITE	

10+ letters

CHALCEDONY	MEERSCHAUM	*PHOSPHORUS* (P)
IRON PYRITES	MOLYBDENITE	PITCHBLENDE

MINERVA 1. Rom myth *goddess* of Invention, Wisdom and the Arts (**Gk** = PALLAS *ATHENE*), and later of War. 2. A minor *PLANET*.

MINI *LITTLE*, SMALL (**opp** = mega). SKIRT. *CAR*.

~ **STATES Celeb**: ANDORRA, LIECHTENSTEIN, LUXEMBOURG, MONACO, MONTENEGRO (ex), SAN MARINO, TONGA.

MINOR (s/l *miner*). 1. *CHARGE*, INFANT, JUNIOR, WARD; UNDER 18/21. THE YOUNGER. PITCH, *SCALE* (mus). INFERIOR, LESSER (**opp** = *major*). 2. Use diminutive, abbreviation, e.g. **Minor operation** = OP.

MINOS Gk myth K of Crete; s of *Zeus* and *Europa*, he mar

Pasiphae. His palace at Cnossos contained the *labyrinth* (designed by *Daedalus*), where the *Minotaur* was kept until k by *Theseus*.

MINOTAUR Gk myth Cretan *monster* (half man, half bull) of *Minos*. Kept in the *labyrinth*, which was designed by *Daedalus*, it was fed on human flesh in the form of seven youths and seven maidens sent yearly as tribute from Athens, until *Theseus* volunteered to be included and he k it.

MINSTREL ENTERTAINER, MUSICIAN, SINGER; LAYMAN (crypt) [Blondel (*Lionheart*). Mikado (*G & S*)]. **Pl** = NEGRO SINGERS.

MINT AROMATIC *HERB* (see *MINTHA*); **comp** = *lamb*. CANDY, SWEET. COIN, MAKE MONEY, UTTER. LOT OF MONEY.

MINTHA Gk myth d of *Cocytus*, *transformed* by *Demeter* into the *mint herb*.

MINX *BAGGAGE*, HUSSY, JADE.

MIRAGE ILLUSION, REFLECTION, REFRACTION; **celeb**: BROCKEN (Harz Mt, Ger); DELIBAB (Hung); FATA MORGANA (Messina, It) [*ignis fatuus*. Desert, water]. AIRCRAFT (Fr).

MIRANDA 1. Girl's name, especially the d of Prospero (Temp, *Shak*). 2. *Mermaid* (theat). 3. Satellite of *planet* Uranus. 4. Carmen ~, film star (Port).

MIRROR NEWSPAPER ®. 1. LOOKING GLASS, POLISHED SURFACE; REFLECT, REVERSE IMAGE, hence read backwards, or sometimes form a palindrome, e.g. **Midday mirror** (4) = NOON. 2. Used by *Perseus* so as not to look directly at *Medusa* when he slew her.

MIS- Added as prefix to mean 'amiss', 'badly' or 'wrongly'. In crosswords, is often used to mean *anag*., e.g. **Mistake** (4) = KATE or TEAK. It can also be included into the answer, e.g. **Lure** (7) = MISRULE.

MISER *BORE* (tech). HOARDER; NIGGARD, STINGY PERSON; **celeb**: EUCLIO (Plautus), GRANDET (Balzac), HARPAGON (Molière), SCROOGE (*Dickens*), SHYLOCK (M of V, *Shak*).

MISO- *HATRED* OF –

MISS (s/l *mis-*). *GIRL*, MAIDEN. [**near** ~ = *chaperone* (crypt)]. SCHOOLMISTRESS. Any girl's name. AVOID, DODGE, FAIL (**opp** = *hit*) [mile]. MISSISSIPPI (US *state*).

~ **FRENCH** MLLE.

MISSILE *ARROW*, BULLET, DART, FLECHETTE, ROCKET, SLINGSHOT; WEAPON. **Celeb**: CRUISE, ICBM, MIRV, PERSHING, POLARIS, MX, SAM, SS 10, SS 20, TRIDENT, *VI*.

MIST (s/l missed). FRET, HAZE, VAPOUR. DIM, FILM, FOG.

MISTAKEN 1. *Anag.* IN ERROR, AT FAULT; GAFFED (crypt). *ROB*, STEAL, THIEVE (crypt). 2. Take 'mis' as indicated, e.g. remove the letters 'mis', as in: **Lock the mistaken courtesan** (5) = ***TRESS.

MISTER ADDRESS, TITLE; MASTER, MR, SIR; BWANA (Af), EFFENDI (Turk), HERR (Ger), MASTER (Ch), MIJNHEER (NL), MIRZA (Pers), *MONSIEUR* (Fr), SAHIB (Arab, Ind), SARDAR (Sikh), SENHOR (Port), SENOR (Sp), SIGNOR (It), TUAN (Malay).

MISTRESS *COURTESAN* (q.v.). COMMANDING, CONTROLLING. SCHOOL TEACHER; **celeb**: JOYCE GRENFELL (film), MISS MABLETHORPE (*Wodehouse*).

MISUSE *Anag.* ABUSE, ILL-TREAT. SUE (crypt).

MITHRAS *God* of the SUN (Pers). Sacrificed a *bull* to fertilize the world.

MIX *Anag.* COMBINE, JOIN, MINGLE, SCRAMBLE. FIX. 1009 (crypt, Lat).

MIXER *Anag.* BITTER LEMON, SODA, TONIC; *DRINK*. *BEATER*, FOOD PROCESSOR, WHISK.

MIXTURE *Anag.* MEDICINE. AMALGAMATION, COMBINATION.

MIX-UP *Anag.* CONFUSION, INVOLVEMENT. XIM (dn, crypt).

MLLE MADEMOISELLE; MISS FRENCH; FRENCH GIRL.

MM FRENCHMEN, MESSIEURS. MILITARY MEDAL. MILLIMETRE. 2,000.

MME MADAME; MRS FRENCH.

MNEMOSYNE 1. Mother by *Zeus* of the nine Gk *Muses* [memory]. 2. A minor *PLANET*.

MO MEDICAL OFFICER. MODUS OPERANDI. MOLYBDENUM (*chem*). MOMENT. *DOCTOR*. MISSOURI (US *state*).

MOA *BIRD* (ex; flightless; NZ) [cassowary, dinornis (NZ, ex), emu, nandoo, ostrich].

MOB GANG, RABBLE. ATTACK, MOLEST. CAP, *HAT*. *Assembly* of *kangaroos*.

MOBY DICK *WHALE* [Ahab, Herman Melville. Vessel: Pequod].

MODEL FIGURE, PUPPET, REPRESENTATION. CARVE, FASHION, *FORM*, SHAPE. MANNEQUIN, POSER, SITTER. NORM, *PAR, STANDARD. DESIGN*, MARK, MARQUE, MATRIX, PATTERN, STYLE, TEMPLATE, -LET, TYPE; real life persons reportedly used as ~s for fict characters:

Alice (Carroll) modelled on	Alice Lidell
Alice (nanny, *Milne*)	Olive Brockwell
Anna (and the King of Siam)	Anna Leonowens
Beatrice (Dante)	Bice Portinari
Bunthorne (G & S)	Oscar *Wilde*
William Boot (Scoop, Waugh)	Lord Deedes
Father Brown (*Chesterton*)	Father O'Connor
Buggins (~ turn)	Admiral Fisher (coined)
Bulldog Drummond (Sapper)	Gerard Fairley
David Copperfield (*Dickens*)	Charles Dickens himself
Dotheboys Hall (*Dickens*)	Bowes Hall
Dracula (Bram Stoker)	Prince Vlad of Wallachia
Drones Club (*Wodehouse*)	Pelican Club
Fine lady on a white horse (trad)	Celia Fiennes
Falstaff (*Shak*)	Sir John Oldcastle
Hiawatha (Longfellow)	Haiohratha (Mohawk chief)
Robin *Hood* (trad)	Robert FitzOoth of Locksley
Robinson *Crusoe* (Defoe)	Alexander Selkirk
Sherlock *Holmes* (Conan Doyle)	Dr Joseph *Bell*
Humpty Dumpty	Duke of Gloucester (1640)
Jack (and the beanstalk)	Tom Hickathrift (of Ely)
King of Siam (Anna and ~)	King Maha Mungkut
'M' (James Bond's boss)	Max Knight (MI5)
Laura (Petrarch)	Laure de Noves
Mr Micawber (*Dickens*)	John Dickens (f of Charles ~)
Wackford Squeers (*Dickens*)	W Shaw Bowes
Stalky (~ & Co, *Kipling*)	Rudyard Kipling himself
Toby Jug	Harry Elwes
Winnie the Pooh (*Milne*)	Sir Owen Seaman
Mrs Worthington's d (Coward)	Angela Fox (née Lonsdale)

MODEST *BASHFUL*, COY, DIFFIDENT, HUMBLE,

RETIRING, SELF-EFFACING (**opp** = *bragging*). CHASTE,
DECOROUS (**opp** = *arch*). RESTRICTED, SMALL.
MOHAMMED MOHAMET, MUHAMID, MUHAMMED etc.
Founder of Islam, mar Ayesha; 1 d Fatima. Qur'an (Koran)
tells of Allah, *Adam, Abraham*, Gabriel, *Isaac, Jesus, Moses,
Noah*. **Priests**: Ayatollah, Muezzin, Mufti; **caliphs**: Abu Bekr,
Omar, Ali; **sects**: Shiite, Sunni. Pilgrimage (haj) to Mecca; holy
war (jehad); heretics, Druses (**opp** = Maronites). Leader Aga
(Khan); M (crypt). **Comp**: mountain.
MOIRAI Gk *goddesses* of the three *FATES* (q.v.). **Rom** =
PARCAE.
MOLE BREAKWATER, JETTY, QUAY. *AGENT*, SPY.
DIARIST. BURROWING RODENT [*Grahame*]. BLEMISH,
SPOT.
MOLOCH Fire-god (Jew) to whom children were sacrificed.
LIZARD (Aus).
MOLYBDENUM *METAL*; MO (*chem*).
MOMENT MO. INSTANT, MINUTE. IMPORTANT. TORQUE,
TWIST.
MONACO MC (*car plate*). *RACETRACK* (cars).
MONARCH 1. BUTTERFLY (*lepidoptera*). 2. EMPEROR,
EMPRESS, KING, RULER, QUEEN, SOVEREIGN
[*governor; regent*; viceroy]. ~s **of England and Britain**:

England
Saxons and Danes

Egbert	827–839
Ethelwulf	839–858
Ethelbald	858–860
Ethelbert	860–865
Ethelred	865–871
Alfred the Great	871–899
Edward the Elder	899–924
Athelstan	924–939
Edmund	939–946
Edred	946–955
Edwig	955–959
Edgar	959–975
Edward the Martyr	975–978
Ethelred the Unready	978–1016
Edmund Ironside	1016–1016
Canute (Knut)	1017–1035

Harold I   1035–1040
Hardicanute   1040–1042
Edward the Confessor   1042–1066
Harold II   1066–1066

Normans
William I   1066–1087
William II   1087–1100
Henry I   1100–1135
Stephen   1135–1154

Plantagenets
Henry II   1154–1189
Richard I   1189–1199
John   1199–1216
Henry III   1216–1272
Edward I   1272–1307
Edward II   1307–1327 (deposed)
Edward III   1327–1377
Richard II   1377–1399 (deposed)
Henry IV ⎫   1399–1413
Henry V ⎬ **Lancaster**   1413–1422
Henry VI ⎭   1422–1461 (deposed)
Edward IV ⎫   1461–1483
Edward V ⎬ **York**   1483–1483
Richard III ⎭   1483–1485

Tudors
Henry VII   1485–1509
Henry VIII   1509–1547
Edward VI   1547–1553
Jane (9 days)   1553–1553
Mary   1553–1558
Elizabeth I   1558–1603

Britain
Stuarts
James I (VI of Scotland)   1603–1625
Charles I   1625–1649 (beheaded)

Commonwealth
Oliver Cromwell   1649–1658

Richard Cromwell	1658–1659

Stuarts

Charles II	1660–1685
James II (VII of Scotland)	1685–1688 (deposed)
William and Mary	1689–1702
Anne	1702–1714

Hanovers

George I	1714–1727
George II	1727–1760
George III	1760–1820
George IV	1820–1830
William IV	1830–1837
Victoria	1837–1901

Windsors

Edward VII	1901–1910
George V	1910–1936
Edward VIII	1936–1936 (abdicated)
George VI	1936–1952
Elizabeth II	1952–

Celeb monarchies: Bhutan, Cook Is, Denmark, Liechtenstein (Principality), Luxembourg (Grand Duchy), Nepal, Norway, Monaco (Principality), Spain, Swaziland, Sweden, Tonga, United Kingdom. **Recently extinct**: Afghanistan, Albania, Bulgaria, Egypt, Ethiopia, Germany, Greece, Hungary, Iran, Iraq, Italy, Romania, Russia, Siam (Thailand) and various Indian States.

MONDAY MON. DAY OF THE MOON. ~s **child** = fair of face. [Solomon *Grundy*].

MONEY C, D, L, P, S; CENTS, DOLLARS, POUNDS, SHILLINGS. BRASS, CASH, *COIN, CURRENCY* (q.v.), LOOT, PELF, READY, RHINO, TIN. RESOURCES, SHINERS, MINT. BEES AND (*rh sl*). [~ *spider*].

MONGREL *Anag*. CROSSBREED, IMPURE, MIXED [heinz].

MONITOR LIZARD. PREFECT. GUNSHIP, WARSHIP, *WEAPON. CONTROL*, EAVESDROP, TAP.

MONK MONASTIC RECLUSE (male), HERMIT; *Chaucer* character. CELLIST (crypt). BENEDICTINE, BUDDHIST, CARTHUSIAN, CISTERCIAN, ESSENE, TRAPPIST (silence); [*friar* (mendicant)]. Monks are not *friars*.

MONKEY 1. FIDDLE, INTERFERE, PLAY. £500. MACHINE HAMMER. WATER VESSEL. APE, MIMIC, MOCK. 2. MAMMAL, *PRIMATE; PUG* (Sc); APE; **breeds**: BABOON (Af, Arab), BARBARY (Gibraltar), BOONDER (Rhesus), BUSHBABY (Af), CAPUCHIN (Af), CEBUS (S Am), CHACMA (Af), CHIMPANZEE (Af), COAITA (S Am), COLOBUS (Af), DOUC (Asia), DRILL (Af), ENTELLUS (Ind), GALAGO (Af), GELADA (Af), GIBBON (Asia), GORILLA (Af), GRIVET (Ethiopia), GUENON (Af), HANUMAN (Ind), HOWLER (S Am), HYLOBATE (Ind), LANGUR (Asia), *LAR(ES)* (Asia), LEAF ~ (Asia), *LEMUR* (Madagascar), MACAQUE (Asia), MACQUES (Af), MAGOT (Af), MANDRILL (Af), MANGABEY (W Af), MARMOSET (Am), MURIQUI (Braz), ORAN(G)-OUTAN(G) (SE Asia), OUAKARI (S Am), *OWL* ~ (S Am), PONGO/PONGID (Af), PROBOSCIS ~ (S Am), RHESUS ~ (Asia), SAGOIN (-UIN) (S Am), SAI (Braz), SAKI (S Am), SAPAJOU (Am), SATYRUS, SIAMANG (Malay), SIMPAI (Sumatra), *SPHINX* ~ (Af), SPIDER ~ (S Am), SQUIRREL ~ (S Am), TAMARIN (S Am), TEE-TEE, TITI (S Am), TELAPOIN (E Ind), UAKARI (S Am), VARI (Madagascar), VERVET (Af), WANDEROO (Ind), WEEPER; **celeb**: BANDERLOG (*Kipling*), CHEE-CHEE (*Lofting*), CHETA (*Tarzan*), KING KONG (Edgar Wallace) [*Ch calendar*; PG Tips].
MONOMANIA *Obsession* with one idea.
MONSIEUR M; MR FRENCH (crypt).
MONSTER 1. ENORMOUS, HUGE. CRUEL, WICKED. ABORTION, MIS-SHAPEN. 2. IMAGINARY ANIMAL (incongruous, deformed or large);

celebrated monsters

ABOMINABLE	
SNOWMAN/YETI	(Himalayas)
ARGUS	(100 eyes)
BIGFOOT/SASQUATCH	(N American Yeti)
BUNYIP	(Aus)
CENTAUR	(head human, body horse)
CHIM(A)ERA	(head lion, body goat, legs dragon)
CRATAEIS	(12 feet, 6 heads; barked)
CYCLOPES	(one eye)
DRACULA	(Bram Stoker)

DRAGON	(fire-breathing)
ECHIDNA	(half woman, half serpent)
FRANKENSTEIN'S CREATION	(manufactured humanoid)
GAMA	(Ida, *G & S*)
GERYON	(Labours of *Hercules*)
GIGANTES	(winged; legs ending in snakes)
GOG & MAGOG	(British giants)
GOLIATH	(bibl)
GORGONS	(winged; snakes for hair)
GRIFFIN/GRYPHON	(winged; head eagle, body lion)
HARPY	(head woman, body vulture)
HYDRA	(nine heads)
IDRIS	(Welsh mountain giant)
KRAKEN	(Nor sea monster)
MAGOG	(See GOG above)
MINOTAUR	(Head bull, body man)
NESSIE	(Loch Ness, Sc)
ODIN	(Nor; one eye)
PAN	(head and body man, legs goat)
POLYPHEMUS	(one eye)
PYTHON	(serpent)
SASQUATCH/BIGFOOT	(N American Yeti)
SCYLLA & CHARYBDIS	(six-headed sea monsters)
SPHINX	(head human, body lion)
TYPHON	(100 heads; fire-breathing)
URANIDS	(100 arms, 50 heads)
WODEN	(A-Sax; one eye)
WYVERN	(*herald*)
YAMINSKAY	(S Andes Yeti)
YETI/ABOMINABLE SNOWMAN	(Himalayas)
YMIR	(frost, Nor)

MONTH *Calendar* ~: JAN, FEB, MAR etc; *lunar* ~: 4 WEEKS, 28 DAYS; *TIME*. LIKING, INCLINATION (arch).
MONUMENT COMMEMORATION, MEMORIAL, (TOMB)STONE; **celeb**: ALBERT MEMORIAL (Prince Albert), ARC DE TRIOMPHE (French Army), BRANDENBURG GATE (Berlin), CENOTAPH (World Wars dead; Lutyens), CLEOPATRA'S NEEDLE (Embankment; Heliopolis), INVALIDES (Napoleon), MENIN GATE (Ypres),

THE MONUMENT (Great Fire, London), PYRAMIDS
(Gizeh; sacred rites), NELSON'S COLUMN (Trafalgar),
QUEEN VICTORIA (The Mall, Brock), RUNNYMEDE
(Commonwealth Air Forces), SOMME (Lutyens), UNKNOWN
WARRIOR (Westminster Abbey/UK; Arc de Triomphe/Fr;
Santa Maria degli Angeli/It; Arlington Cemetery/USA).
MOON 1. *MOPE.* EARTH SATELLITE, LUNAR BODY
[Nokomis (d of the ~) *Hiawatha*]. 18 (*tarot*). *Wodehouse* char.
[Monday; over the ~ = delighted (**opp** = sick as a *parrot*)].
2. **Goddesses: Gk** = *ARTEMIS, PHOSPHORUS*, SELENE; **Rom**
= *DIANA*, JUNO, LUNA.
MOOR FEN, HEATHLAND, OPEN LAND; MARSH. MAKE
FAST, TIE UP (naut). *GAOL.* BACKROOM (crypt). BLACK
MAN; **celeb**: AARON (Titus Andronicus), OTHELLO (*Shak*),
LAILA (Southey).
MOPED WAS BORED, DEPRESSED, LISTLESS, MOONED.
(MOTOR) SCOOTER.
MORE WORK UTOPIA (crypt).
MORNING (s/l mourning). 1. AM, FORENOON. 2. ~ **star** =
Lucifer (Rom), *Phosphorus* (Gk); **opp** = *Hesperus*.
MORPHEUS Rom myth s of Sleep and *god* of Dreams. [Hypnos].
MORSE *WALRUS.* CLASP. ALPHABET CODE, SIGNAL
(dot, dash).
MOSES 1. Bibl lawgiver; s of Amram and Jochebed, br of
Aaron and Miriam (*c.* 15th cent B.C.). At ~'s birth, *Pharaoh*
ordered all infants to be k. Jochebed hid ~ in some reeds (or
bullrushes), watched over by Miriam, and he was found by
Pharaoh's d (possibly Merrhis); Miriam suggested Jochebed as
a nurse. He grew up in the royal house and became a *shepherd*;
mar Zipporah and was f of Gershom and Eliezer. When cast
down before *Pharaoh*, his rod was transformed into a *serpent*.
Despite a rebellion by his br Aaron, ~ led the Israelites out
of Egy with *Joshua* as his lieutenant, across the Red Sea to the
Promised Land. Because of disobedience to divine command,
he was not vouchsafed entry to the Promised Land, but he saw
it before he d on Mt Pisgah. 2. *PAINTER* ('Grandma' ~).
RAVEN (Orwell).
MOSQUITO ANOPHELES, CULEX. GNAT, *INSECT*;
BLOODSUCKER. *AIRCRAFT.* **Pl** = GULF.
MOSTLY 1. MAINLY, PRINCIPALLY. 2. Nearly (e.g.) anag,
e.g. **Material which is mostly a masked product** (6) = DAMASK
(the E is omitted from **a masked**).

MOTH *INSECT, LEPIDOPTERA* (q.v. for **breeds**). **Coll** =
lepidopterist. RIVER (NZ). *Shak* char (MND).
MOTHER ABBESS. DAM, MA, MATER, MATERNAL
PARENT, MUM; OLD LADY (sl); BEARER (crypt);
and see *Male and Female*. **celeb**: ~ Goose, ~ Hubbard, ~
Riley, ~ Shipton. *ISIS* (Egy myth). VINEGAR PRODUCT.
HYSTERIA. BUG HUNTER, LEPIDOPTERIST (crypt).
MOTOR RACE GRAND PRIX; TT. CAR*NATION (crypt). For
~ **tracks**, see *Racetrack*.
MOTORWAY MI, MIV, MV etc.
MOULD DECAY, MILDEW, ROT. *CAST, FORM*, MATRIX,
PATTERN, SHAPE, TEMPLATE, -LET.
MOUNT ASCEND, CLIMB. EMINENCE, HILL, MOUND,
TOR. GET ON; SADDLE. STEED. CARD, MARGIN;
DISPLAY, SET OFF. STAMP HINGE. ARRANGE,
PRODUCE, STAGE (theat).
MOUNTAIN HEAP, PILE. ELEVATION, HILL, *MOUNT*; **pl** =
range; **celeb**: ALASKA RANGE (US), ANDES (S Am), ALPS
(Eur), APENNINES (It), APPALACHIANS (US), ATLAS
~ (N Af), BLUE RIDGE ~ (US), BROOKS RANGE (US),
ETHIOPIAN HIGHLANDS (E Af), FLINDERS RANGE
(Aus), GREAT DIVIDING RANGE (Aus), HAMMERSLEY
RANGE (Aus), HIMALAYAS (Asia), HINDU KUSH (Asia),
KUN LUN SHAN (Ch), LOMONDSOV RIDGE (Arctica),
MACDONNEL RANGE (Aus), PAROPAMISUS (Asia),
ROCKY ~s (Can/US), SIERRA MADRE (Mex), SIERRA
NEVADA (N Am), TIBESTI (N Af), TIEN SHAN (Asia),
TOUBKAL (N Af), TRANSANTARCTIC ~s (Antarctica),
URALS (CIS), VINSON PLATEAU (Antarctica). **Comp** =
Mohammed.
MOUNTED ASCENDED, CLIMBED. ASTRIDE, HORSED,
RIDING, SADDLED, UP. HILLY (crypt). CARDED,
DISPLAYED, SET OFF. PRODUCED, STAGED (theat).
MOUNT OLYMPUS DIVINE ABODE, HEAVEN. See *Olympus.*
MOUTH FACE, GOB, KISSER, LIPS, NORTH AND SOUTH
(*rh sl*), TRAP (sl). CHATTER; CHEEK, IMPUDENCE.
OPENING. RANT, RAVE, SPEAK, UTTER. GRIMACE.
MOUTHORGAN HARMONICA, *INSTRUMENT* (mus).
TONGUE (crypt).
MOVING *Anag*. EMOTIONAL, TENDER. AFOOT, AGATE,
MOBILE (**opp** = *still*). SHIFTING; CHANGING HOUSES.
MP MEMBER OF PARLIAMENT, REPRESENTATIVE.

MILITARY POLICE, REDCAP. **Pl** = *MEMBERS; POLICE; CHEMIST.*
MR 1. MISTER. 2. *Male* of species named, e.g. **Mr Swan** = COB.
MRS 1. MISTRESS, MISSUS, WIFE. 2. *Female* of species named, e.g. **Mrs Fox** = VIXEN.
~ **FRENCH** MADAME, MME.
MUCH 1. IMPORTANT, IMPRESSIVE, LOT, NEARLY, OFTEN, PRACTICALLY. 2. One of Robin *Hood*'s men. Plays the *clown* in morris dancing.
MUFTI CHURCHMAN (Mos). CIVILIAN CLOTHES, CIVVIES (*mil*; **opp** = *uniform*).
MUG BEAT UP (hence TAEB, dn crypt), COSH [GBH]. CUP, TROPHY. *FACE, MOUTH.* FOOL. CRAM, SWOT.
MULE HYBRID; *offspring* of donkey and horse, hence DON or KEY (crypt); [*Absalom; Silenus*]; **celeb**: MUFFIN. OBSTINATE. DOLT, *FOOL.* MACHINE, SPINNER. *SHOE*, SLIPPER.
MULL CONSIDER, PONDER, THINK. HUMUS. MESS, MUDDLE. *MATERIAL*, MUSLIN. *ISLAND.* MAKE PUNCH, DRINK. PROMONTORY (Sc). SNUFFBOX.
MURMURATION *Assembly* of starlings.
MURPHY POTATO, SPUD, TUBER.
MURRAYFIELD *RUGBY* GROUND.
MUSE (s/l mews). 1. PONDER, THINK. POET. 2. *PIERIDES* Gk myth (**Rom** = CAMENAE) nine *goddesses* of song, who presided over the arts, sciences and poetry. They were dd of *Zeus* and *Mnemosyne*, and lived on Parnassus, being the companions of *Apollo*: CALLIOPE (epic poetry), CLIO (history), ERATO (love songs), EUTERPE (lyric poetry), MELPOMENE (tragedy), POLYHYMNIA/POLYMNIA (singing), TERPSICHORE (choral dance), THALIA (comedy) and URANIA (astronomy); **fountain nymph** = Aganippe. [*theat*].
MUSEUM BM.
MUSHROOM *FUNGUS* (q.v. for list). GROW RAPIDLY.
MUSIC 1. SONG. NOTES, SCORE, SHEETS [*instrument; patron saint; tempo*]; **comp** = words. 2. **Gods, Gk** = *Apollo* [*Muses*]; **other** = Bes (Egy). 3. ~ **terms; notes** (each is twice as long as its successor): breve, semi-breve, minim, crotchet, quaver, semiquaver, demi-semiquaver, hemi-demi-semiquaver; **opus**: cantata, concerto, fugue, neume, nocturne, oratorio, scherzo, sonata, suite, symphony, toccata; **tempi**: adagietto, adagio,

allegretto, allegro, animato, comodo, largamente, largo, lento, maestoso, pressando, prestissimo, presto, rallentando, rubato, stringendo, vivace; **voices**: alto, bass, basso profundo, contralto, counter tenor, mezzo-soprano, soprano, tenor, treble; **all terms** (incl inflexion, intensity and marks):

1-letter

f (loudly)

p (quietly)

2-letters

ff (very loudly)
fz (with strong attack)
mf (fairly loudly)

mp (fairly quietly)
pp (very quietly)

3-letters

bis (repeat)

rit (hold back)

4-letters

alto (voice)
bass (voice)
brio (spirit)

capo (start)
flat

5-letters

breve (note)
forte; f (loud)
fugue (opus)
largo (slow)
lento (tempo)
minim (note)

mosso (moved)
piano; p (quiet)
sharp
suite (opus)
tacet (is silent)
tenor (voice)

6-letters

adagio (slowly)
comodo (moderate)
da capo (from start)
legato (legato)
presto (fast)
quaver (note)

rubato (flexibly)
sonata (opus)
suivez (follow)
treble (voice)
vivace (briskly)

7-letters

agitato (agitated)
allegro (lively)
amoroso (lovingly)

andante (walking
  pace)
animato (animated)

cadenza (flourish)
calando (lowering)
cantata (secular opus)
con brio (with spirit)
forzato (forced)
morendo (dying)

natural
soprano (voice)
toccata (opus)
tremolo (rapid repeat)
vibrato (pitch
   fluctuation)

8-letters

animando (animating)
arpeggio (split chord)
calcando (slow
   acceleration)
castrato (voice)
concerto (opus)
con mosso (movingly)
crotchet (note)
falsetto (voice)

maestoso (majestically)
nocturne (opus)
obbligato (obligatory)
oratorio (opus)
ritenuto (held back)
sforzato (forced)
staccato (clipped)
symphony (opus)

9-letters

a capella
   (unaccompanied)
adagietto (slow)
cantabile (singingly)
contralto (voice)
crescendo (getting
   louder)
glissando (sliding run)

obbligato (obligatory)
pizzicato (plucked)
pressando (faster)
semibreve (note)
sforzando (forcing)
sostenuto (sustained)
sotto voce (barely
   audible)

10+ letters

accelerando
   (accelerating)
allargando (slower
   & fuller)
allegretto (pretty
   lively)
counter-tenor (voice)
decrescendo (getting
   softer)
demisemiquaver (note)
diminuendo
   (diminishing)
fortissimo; ff (v loud)

largamente (broadly)
mezzo forte; mf
   (medium loud)
mezzo piano; mp
   (medium quiet)
mezzo-soprano (voice)
mezzo staccato
   (semi-clipped)
pianissimo; pp
   (v quiet)
prestissimo (v quick)
rallentando (slowing)

ritardando (holding	stringendo
back)	(quickening)
semiquaver (note)	

MUSICIAN B MUS; BANDSMAN, *INSTRUMENTALIST*, PLAYER; **celeb**: APOLLO (Gk); ASAPH (bibl); CHIBIABOS (*Hiawatha*); *DAVID* (bibl); TERPANDER (Gk) [*composer; conductor; instrument; Muses; music* (q.v.)].

MUSIC-MAKER 1. BANDSMAN; *COMPOSER* (q.v.); *CONDUCTOR* (q.v.) INSTRUMENT(ALIST); *MUSICIAN*, (ORCHESTRA) PLAYER. 2. Any of several audio systems e.g. AMPLIFIER, AUDIO (BINAURAL, MONO, STEREO), BUG, COMPACT DISC, GRAMOPHONE, HI-FI, JUKEBOX, (LOUD)SPEAKER, MICROPHONE, MIKE, NICKELODEON, PHONOGRAPH, PIANOLA, PICK-UP, PUBLIC ADDRESS (PA, TANNOY), RADIO(GRAM), RECORD PLAYER, SOUND TRACK, STEREO, TAPE RECORDER, TURNTABLE, TV, VICTROLA, VIDEO, WIRELESS, WOOFER.

MUST HAVE TO. NEW WINE. MOULD. FRENZY.

MUSTANG *AIRCRAFT. HORSE.*

MUSTER *GATHERING* (mil). LIST, ROLL (mil). ENROL. SUMMON. *ASSEMBLY* (peacocks).

MYTH Mythology, especially the legends which grew up in Greece and Rome, played a large part in the lives of the ancients. Various poets and writers wove stories to account for natural phenomena such as volcanoes, whirlpools, cloud-capped mountains etc; they also sought to explain the Creation itself and some of the everyday events of life such as love, childbirth and the harvest, through personification in the form of *gods* and *goddesses* (q.v.). Most ancient civilizations and peoples developed their own folklore and mythology.

N NAME(D). NAPOLEON. NEUTER. NITROGEN (*chem*). NOON. NORWAY (*car plate*). NORTH; POINT. NOUN. BRIDGE PLAYER.

NA *SODIUM* (*chem*).

NAG *HORSE*, PONY, SCREW. HARP, SCOLD.

NAIAD (water) *NYMPH*. LARVA (insect). PLANT (water).

NAIL FINGER-TIP, TOE-TIP; HORN; CLAW, TALON; **comp**

= *tooth*. [fingerplate]. FASTENING, SPIKE: BRAD, CLOUT, HOB, OVAL. CATCH, ENGAGE, FASTEN, FIX, SECURE. *MEASURE* (cloth).

NAKED NUDE.

NAME N. CALL, CHRISTEN. REPUTATION, REPUTE. N*OR*M (catechism – crypt).

NANDOO BIRD (S American) [cassowary, dinornis (NZ, ex), emu, moa (ex), ostrich].

NANNY *GOVERNESS* (q.v. for **celeb**), NURSE. GRANNY (sl). Fem *goat*; *BUTTRESS* (crypt).

NAP (s/l *knap*). NAPOLEON; BONEY. DOZE, KIP, *SLEEP*. PILE (cloth). *CARD GAME*. CERT, SURE THING.

NAPOLEON N, NAP, BONEY. *CARD GAME*. GOLD PIECE (Fr). PIG (Animal Farm, Orwell). [*Bellerophon*, *Corporal*, *Emperor*, First Consul. *Chesterton*. Macavity (*cat*, Eliot). Moriarty (*Holmes*)].

NARCISSUS 1. *FLOWER*. 2. Gk myth youth, for whom *Echo* bore unrequited love, so that she pined away. He fell in love with his own reflection and also pined away, so that he turned into the flower which bears his name [self-admiration].

NATIVE ABORIGINE; BORN, INDIGENOUS. BIVALVE, *OYSTER*. DOMESTIC. WILD MAN, SAVAGE. ~ **of Australia** = ABORIGINE, *EMU*; ~ **of Britain** = CELT; ~ **of Ireland** = PICT, CELT; ~ **of N Britain** = PICT, CELT; ~ **of NZ** = KIWI, MAORI; ~ **of USA** = *REDSKIN*; ~ **of Wales** = CELT.

NATURE 1. CHARACTER, INCLINATION. MOTHER EARTH. 2. **Goddesses: Gk** = *ARTEMIS*, *DEMETER*; **Rom** = *CERES*, *DIANA*, OPS; **Egy** = *ISIS*, UPIS. [*Pleiades*].

NAUT NAUTICAL, NAVAL, MARITIME [*measure*].

NAVIGATE CON, *SAIL*, STEER [Henry. *Pytheas*].

NAVY *FLEET*, MARINE, NAUTICAL, RN, TARS, USN. *COLOUR* (blue).

NAY (s/l *neigh*). CONTRADICTION, DENIAL, NO, REFUSAL. AND MORE, EVEN, MOREOVER, RATHER, WELL, WHY.

NB NORTH BRITAIN. NOTA BENE, TAKE NOTE. NEW BRUNSWICK (*Province*, Can). NIOBIUM (*chem*).

NCO CPL, RSM, SGT.

ND NO DATE, UNDATED. NEODYMIUM (*chem*).

NE *NEON* (*chem*). NEAR EAST. NORTH-EAST (i.e. Tyneside etc).

NEAR BY; *CLOSE*. MEAN, *STINGY*.
NEARLY 1. ALMOST, NIGH. 2. Word less one or two letters,
 e.g. **The cricketer is nearly done** (3) = DON* (Bradman).
NEAR MISS CLOSE THING, NARROW SHAVE.
 CHAPERONE, DUENNA, HONOUR GUARD (crypt).
NEAT UNDILUTED. ORDERED, TIDY; *CHIC*, DEFT,
 ELEGANT, SMART. *CATTLE*, OX(EN); LOWER (crypt).
NEB NATIONAL ENTERPRISE BOARD. *BEAK* (Sc). HILL-
 CLIMB (dn, crypt).
NEBUCHADNEZZAR 1. LARGE *BOTTLE*. 2. K of Babylon who
 carried the Jews to Chaldea.
NECESSITY COMPULSION, CONSTRAINT,
 INDISPENSABILITY, NEED.
NEEDLE IRRITATE, PROVOKE. KNIT, *SEW*. **Pl** = ROCKS
 (geog, IOW).
NEEDLER IRRITANT. ANAESTHETIST, ACUPUNCTURIST;
 NUMBER (crypt). SEAMSTRESS, *SEWER* (crypt).
 TATTOOIST. DRUG ADDICT (crypt).
NEEDLEWOMAN KNITTER, MIDINETTE, SEAMSTRESS,
 SEWER, TRICOTEUSE. ACUPUNCTURIST (crypt).
 ANAESTHETIST (crypt). *CLEOPATRA* (crypt).
NEEDLEWORK IRRITATION, PROVOCATION.
 ACUPUNCTURE; ANAESTHETICS, DEADENING,
 NUMBING (crypt). *TATTOO. KNITTING, SEWING*.
NEGLIGÉE NIGHTIE, PEIGNOIR, UNDRESS.
NEIGH (s/l *nay*). WHINNY (*horse*).
NEMESIS 1. Gk *goddess* of retribution (similar to *Ate*); d of *Nyx*
 without benefit of a father. 2. A minor *PLANET*.
NEOLITHIC *AGE*.
NEON NE (*chem*). *GAS*.
NEPTUNE 1. Rom *god* of the SEA (**Gk** = *POSEIDON*). On the
 overthrow of *Saturn*, his realm was divided: the heavens to
 Jupiter, the underworld to *Pluto* and the seas to Neptune.
 2. *PLANET* (q.v.).
NEREID 1. Gk myth sea-nymph (as opposed to fresh water
 nymphs), dd of *Nereus* and *Doris*. Propitious to sailors
 (especially to the *Argonauts*), one of them was Thetis, m of
 Achilles [*Andromeda*]. 2. A satellite of the *planet Neptune*.
 3. SEA WORM (zool).
NEREUS Gk myth *god* of the sea, s of Pontus and *Ge*, he had 50
 d's by *Doris*, who were the *Nereids*. Also *POSEIDON*. **Rom** =
 NEPTUNE, OCEANUS.
NERO The last Rom *Caesar* (A.D. 54–68) and *Emperor* of Rome,

he mar (1) Octavia (div and later ass by ~), (2) Poppaea (d
as the result of a kick from ~), and (3) Statilia Messalina.
In a reign of terror he ass his adopted br Britannicus, his m
Agrippina, and two of his wives. The burning of Rome, at which
he is said to have 'fiddled' (idled), he blamed on the Christians,
and he massacred thousands. Piso's conspiracy was put down
with brutality, but eventually ~ committed sui to escape
from Galba.

NESS CAPE, *HEAD*, POINT. LOCH [*monster*].

NET *GIN*, MESH, SNARE, *TRAP*, WEB. CLEAN, CLEAR
(comm); **opp** = *gross. BARRIER*, DIVIDER (*tennis*).
PRACTICE AREA (*cricket*).

NETHERLANDS NL (*car plate*).

NETTLE ANNOY, *BOTHER*, IRK, IRRITATE, WORRY. *WILD
PLANT, STING.*

NEUTER 1. N. ASEXUAL, NO SEX, CASTRATE. 2. Remove
letters 'sex' from clue, e.g. **Neuter Middlesex** = MIDDLE.

NEVER-ENDING 1. CONTINUOUS, ENDLESS. CIRCLE,
RING. 2. Word with last letter(s) removed, e.g. **Disapproval of
the never-ending book** (3) = BOO(k).

NEVER NEVER EASY TERMS, HIRE PURCHASE. PAN
COUNTRY (*Barrie*; crypt).

NEVERTHELESS DESPITE THAT, *NOTWITHSTANDING.*
EVERMORE (crypt).

NEW (s/l knew). *Anag.* CHANGED, DIFFERENT, FRESH,
FURTHER, NOVEL, RECENT (**opp** = *old*). *DISCOVERED,
INVENTED. FOREST. THEATRE.* **Pl** = INFORMATION,
TIDINGS [*media*]. ALL POINTS, ALL QUARTERS, FOUR
QUARTERS (crypt).

NEWSPAPER *DAILY*, JOURNAL, *PRESS*, RAG, SHEET,
TABLOID, WEEKLY [Fleet Street].

NEW TESTAMENT BIBLE. NT (**opp** = OT).

NEXT MONTH PROX, PROXIMO; name of the current next
month.

NI NICKEL (*chem*). NORTHERN IRELAND, PROVINCE.

NICK *GAOL*. ARREST, DETAIN. *STEAL*. NOTCH, *SCORE*.
THE *DEVIL*. NICHOLAS (abbr). SMALL BOY.

NICKEL *METAL*; NI (*chem*). *COIN* (US).

NICKNAME 1. *PRISON* (crypt). 2. Abbreviated or familiar
name given to anyone, often associated with their surname or
occupation, e.g.

American	= YANK
Arab	= WOG
Australian	= DIGGER
Englishman	= BRIT, GRINGO (S Am),
	LIMEY (US), POM (Aus),
	WHITEY
Frenchman	= FROG
German	= FRITZ, HUN, KRAUT
Irishman	= MICK, PADDY
Italian	= WOP
Scot	= JOCK, MAC
Welshman	= TAFFY
Bell	= DINGER
Clark	= NOBBY
Dean	= DIXIE
Grey	= DOLLY
Lane	= SHADY
Miller	= DUSTY
Smith	= SMUDGER
White	= CHALKY
Wilson	= TUG

NIGHT (s/l *knight*). 1. Darkness (**opp** = *day*). 2. **Gk goddess** = *HECATE*, *NYX*. **Rom** = NOX.

NIGHTCLUB CLIPJOINT, *DIVE*, SPEAKEASY. COSH, TRUNCHEON (crypt).

NIGHTFLIER BAT, MOTH, OWL.

NIGHTINGALE *BIRD*; SINGER [Hans *Andersen*; jug]. JENNY LIND (Swe). INSTRUMENT (mus). FLORENCE ~, LADY OF THE LAMP, *NURSE*, PHILOMELA (Gk myth), SANTA FILOMENA (Longfellow).

NIKE Gk *goddess* of VICTORY (**Rom** = VICTORIA); d of *Pallas* and *Styx*.

NIL O, *DUCK*, *LOVE*, ZERO.

NIMROD 1. Bibl s of Cush and descended from *Noah* (grand-s of *Ham*); 'a mighty hunter.' 2. Maritime aircraft based on the de Havilland Comet.

NINE See *number*. IX; ONE OVER THE EIGHT. *MUSES*. DAYS WONDER. ~ GODS (Lars Porsena, Macaulay). ~ LIVES (*cat*). ~ Drummers drumming in *Christmas* song; ~ Bright Shiners in *song*. ~ of diamonds = curse of Scotland. **Pl** = ELABORATELY, TO PERFECTION (dress).

~ **ANGELIC ORDERS** *ANGELS*, ARCHANGELS, CHERUBIM, DOMINATIONS, *POWERS*, PRINCIPALITIES, SERAPHIM, THRONES, VIRTUES.

~ **WORTHIES** MEDIAEVAL HEROES: JOSHUA, DAVID, JUDAS MACCABAEUS, *HECTOR*, *ALEXANDER* THE GREAT, JULIUS *CAESAR*, *KING ARTHUR*, CHARLEMAGNE, GEOFFREY OF BOUILLON.

NIOBE 1. Gk myth d of Tantalus, w of the K of Thebes. She turned to stone at the death of her children and shed incessant *tears*. 2. A minor *PLANET*.

NIPPY BITING, COLD, CHILLY, PARKY. AGILE. WAITRESS (Lyons).

NITROGEN N (*chem*).

NL NETHERLANDS, HOLLAND (and *car plate*).

NO (s/l *know*). 1. NAY, NEGATIVE; REFUSAL; O, LOVE, NIL. Nobelium (*chem*). NORTH. NOT OUT (*cricket*). LAKE (Af). Classic drama (*Jap*). NUMBER, NUMERO. NEIN (Ger), NIET (RUSS), NON (Fr); **opp** = *yes*. 2. Omit letter or word indicated, e.g. **No right turn for VAT** (3) = TU*N. 3. Opposite of word indicated, e.g. **No matter** (4) = MIND. 4. Reflection on . . . (crypt = NO).

~ **BETTER** NOT WORSE, STATIC, THE SAME. *WINNER* (crypt). ANTI-GAMBLING (crypt).

~ **CHARGE** *FREE*, GRATIS. *FLAT*, RUN DOWN (elect). DEFENDING, NO ATTACK.

NOAH Bibl grand-s of *Methuselah* and s of Lamech; and f of Shem, *Ham*, (grand-f of *Nimrod*) and Japheth; ~ built the ark to escape the flood. Towards the end, he sent out a *raven* (which did not return), and then a dove (twice), which came back the second time with an olive leaf; the ark then came to rest on Mt Ararat (c.f. *Deucalion*). Another legend makes ~ the first vintner.

NOBLE 1. GOLD COIN (OE). FALCON. VILLAIN (Dornford Yates). DIGNIFIED, *EXCELLENT*, *GRAND*, *IMPOSING*; **opp** = ignoble. 2. Resistant to oxydization (*chem*). 3. ARISTOCRAT, ARMIGER, *PEER* [*emperor*, *monarch*]; **UK** = DUKE/DUCHESS, EARL/COUNTESS, LORD/LADY, MARQUIS/MARCHIONESS, VISCOUNT/VISCOUNTESS, BARON/BARONESS [*knight*, baronet]; **others** = AG(H)A (Turk); ATHELINE (A-Sax); BEG, BEY (Turk); BEGUM (Ind); BOYAR (Russ); COMTE/-ESSE (Fr); CONTE/-ESSA (It); COUNT/-ESS (Eur); DAIMYO (Jap); DATO (Malay); DAUPHIN/-E (Fr); EMIR (Islam); GRAF/-INE (Ger, Swe);

GRANDEE (Sp); HIDALGO (Sp); INFANTE/-A (Port, Sp);
KHAN (Ch, Turk); KHEDIVE (Egy); LANDGRAF/-GRAVE
(Ger); MAHARAJA/-RANI (Ind), MARGRAF/-GRAVINE
(Ger); MIRZA (Pers); NABOB (Ind); NAWAB (Ind);
PALSGRAVE/-GRAVINE (Ger); PASHA (Turk);
RAJAH/RANEE (Ind, Malay); SEIGNEUR (Fr); SEIGNIOR
(OE); SHEIK(H) (Arab); VICOMTE/-ESSE (Fr);
WALDGRAVE/-GRAVINE (Ger).
NODDY SIMPLETON. SEA-BIRD. [Toyland].
NOGGIN *HEAD. DRINK. MEASURE*: GILL, 1/4 PINT hence P,
I, N or T.
NO GOOD 1. *BAD*, DUFF, DUD. NE'ER-DO-WELL, RAKE.
2. Delete any reference to 'good' or its synonym from the clue, e.g.
No-good racecourse (4) = ****WOOD.
NOISELESS QUIET, SILENT, SOUNDLESS. *ODIN* (crypt).
NOISY F, FF. ROWDY [DB] (**opp** = *quiet*).
NO LONGER EX, LATE, WAS. SHORTER.
NONCONFORMIST *Anag.* DISSENTING, FREE CHURCH.
NONPLUS AMAZE, ASTOUND. MINUS (crypt).
NON-U 1. *COMMON*. 2. Delete letter 'U' from clue, e.g. **Non-U
guy** = G*Y.
NOON 1. N; MERIDIEM, MIDDAY, M. 2. Delete letters 'On',
e.g. **Noon Monday** = M**DAY.
NO-ONE 1. NOBODY. NOI (crypt). 2. Delete letter 'I' from clue,
e.g. **Landlords no-one hoists** (5) = HO*STS.
NO QUARTER 1. *MERCILESS*, *PITILESS*. 2. Delete letters E,
N, S and W from clue, e.g. **No quarter for Wales man in battle**
(4) = *AL**MA*.
NOR Norse, Norway.
NO RIGHT 1. NO ENTITLEMENT. *LEFT*. NOR (crypt).
2. Delete letters 'R' or 'RT' from clue, e.g. **Reward no right party**
(3) = PA**Y.
NORM ACCEPTED STANDARD, *PAR*; AVERAGE.
NORMAN, NAME (catechism, crypt).
NORMAN BOY, MAN. INVADER, NORTH FRENCH (hence
NORD, crypt). [*stone*].
NORTH 1. N; POINT; *BRIDGE PLAYER*. POLE. *SEA*.
2. Reads upwards (dn).
~ **AND SOUTH** NS, NANDS. MOUTH (*rh sl*). BRIDGING
TEAM (crypt).
~ **WIND Gk** = BOREAS, **Rom** = SEPTENTRIO.
NORVIC *Episcopal sig* of NORWICH.

NORWAY N (*car plate*). *WRITER*; NEVIL SHUTE.

NORWICH Episcopal sig = NORVIC.

NOSE (s/l *knows*, noes). FEATURE; BREATHER, HOOTER, SCHNOZZLE (sl). *AIRPORT*, AIRWAY (crypt). AROMA, BOUQUET; SENSE OF SMELL.

NOT (s/l *knot*). 1. NEGATIVE. 2. Omit word referred to, e.g. **Hire character is not billed** (7) = CHAR**TER.

NOTABLE WELL KNOWN. EMINENT, REMARKABLE, STRIKING. BUSTLING, CAPABLE, HOUSEWIFELY (arch). INCAPABLE (crypt). MUSICAL (crypt).

NOTE *NOTICE. CASH*, MONEY [*currencies*]: *BUCK*, FIVER, ONCER, *QUID*, TENNER. *KEY*, PITCH, SOUND, TONE, *TONIC*: FLAT, NATURAL, SHARP; A, B, C, D, E, F, G; DO/DOH, RAY/RE, ME/MI, FA/FAH, SO/SOH, LA/LAH, TE/TI; BREVE = 2 SEMI-BREVES = 4 MINIMS = 8 CROTCHETS = 16 QUAVERS. COMPOSE (crypt, e.g. **He noted** = name of any composer).

NOTED 1. FELT, NOTICED, REGISTERED, REMARKED, SEEN. KEYBOARD; MUSICAL; SCORE (crypt). 2. Remove letters ED or TED from clue, e.g. **Noted Te Deum** = T**EUM or ***EUM. 3. Add any note to word indicated, e.g. **Is hesitantly noted before** = ER*E, or **Anger is noted for giving illusion** = MI*RAGE. 4. COMPOSER (crypt: 'he noted').

NOT EVEN NOT ONLY. *ODD*.

NOTHING *LOVE*, O, NIL, ZERO, e.g. **Is nothing to me** = IS*O*ME.

~ LESS 1. AT LEAST, IN TRUTH. 2. Omit synonym for nothing from clue, e.g. **Shocking Olive, nothing less** (4) = *LIVE.

NOTICE *AD*, POSTER, PROCLAMATION. REMARK, *SEE*, *SPOT*. MELTED, WARM (crypt).

NOTOS Gk myth SOUTH WIND (**Rom** = AUSTER).

NOT OUT AT HOME, *IN*. BATTING (*cricket*). BLACKLEG.

NOT RIGHT INCORRECT. LEFT. WRONG. See also *NO RIGHT* (2).

NOTWITHSTANDING ALL THE SAME, ALTHOUGH, NEVERTHELESS. SEATED, SITTING, LYING (crypt). GIVING WAY, YIELDING (crypt).

NOUN N.

NOVEMBER (11th) MONTH, M, NOV (Rom ninth month until *Caesar* reorganized the calendar). **Birthstone** = *topaz*.

NOWADAYS AT PRESENT. AD.

NT NEW TESTAMENT (**opp** = OT); BIBLE.

NUDE 1. NAKED (**opp** = *dressed*). [Hans *Andersen*]. 2. Remove synonym for clothes from clue, e.g. **Nude lawsuit** = LAW or, more cryptically, **Nude Ursula** = AN(dress).

NUMBER EDITION, ISSUE, SUPPLEMENT. *ANAESTHETIC*, DEADENING, DRUG, NEEDLE (all crypt). AGGREGATE, *NO*, QUANTITY, SUM; *COUNT*, RECKON, TELL. V = 5, X = 10, L = 50, C = 100, B = 300, D = 500, M = 1,000. **Pl** = BOOK (bibl, OT). **Specific ~s:**

0 = CYPHER, DUCK, EGG, LOVE, NIL, NIX, NOTHING, ROUND, ZERO, ZILCH; A- [calm (Beaufort scale), fool (*tarot*)].

1 = A, I; *FIRST*, MONAD, ONCE(-R), *ONE*, ONLY, SELF, *SINGLE*, SOLO, UNITY; EIN (Ger), UN, -E (Fr); MONO- [paper (*anniversary*), sorrow (*magpie*), red ball (*snooker*), all alone (*song*), partridge (*song*), juggler (*tarot*), First Letter (*Kipling*)].

2 = II; BIS (Fr), DEUCE, DUET, DUO, DYAD, ENCORE, SECOND, *TWICE*, *TWO*; DEUX (Fr), ZWEI (Ger); BI- [cotton (*anniversary*), cannon (*billiards*), joy (*magpies*), conversion (*rugby*), yellow ball (*snooker*), lilywhite boys (*song*), turtledoves (*song*), female pope (*tarot*), ~ bits].

3 = III; TER, *THIRD*, *THREE*, THRICE, TRIAD, TRIO; DREI (Ger), TROIS (Fr); TRI- [feather (*anniversary*), red ball (*billiards*), gables (*Holmes*), Garridebs (*Holmes*), ~quarters (*Holmes*), students (*Holmes*), Soldiers ~ (*Kipling*), girl (*magpie*), try (was *rugby*), green ball (*snooker*), French hens (*song*), rivals (*song*), empress (*tarot*), ~ estates]. **Quotes:** 'There are ~ kinds of lies: lies, damned lies and statistics' (Disraeli); '~ little *maids* from school' (Mikado, *G & S*); 'Come the ~ corners of the world in arms, and we shall shock them' (John, *Shak*); '~ ravens sat on a tree' (ballad).

4 = IV; *FOUR(TH)*, QUARTET, TETRAD; VIER (Ger); QUAD(R)- [flower (*anniversary*), boundary (*cricket*), try (*rugby*), Sign of ~ (*Holmes*), boy (*magpie*), brown ball (*snooker*), calling birds (*song*), gospel makers (*song*), emperor (*tarot*); bissextile (leap year)]. **Quotes:** '~ essential human freedoms . . . speech . . . worship . . . from want . . . from fear' FDR Jan 41).

5 = V; *FIFTH*, *FIVE*, PENTA, PENTAD, QUINQUE, QUINTET; **Pl** = ballgame [wood (*anniversary*), orange pips (*Holmes*), Nations (*Kipling*), letter (*magpie*), lustrum, quinquennium (period), ~ *towns* (potteries), gold rings (*song*), symbols (*song*), pope (*tarot*), ~ *classic orders.* **Quote**: 'Full fathom ~ thy father lies' (Temp, *Shak*).

6 = VI; HEXAD, SEXTET, SICE, *SIX*(TH); SEX- [~ *nations* (*American Indians*), candy (*anniversary*), boundary (*cricket*), ~ Napoleons (*Holmes*), ~ honest serving men (*Kipling*), something better (*magpie*), pink ball (*snooker*), geese a-laying (*song*), proud walkers (*song*), lovers (*tarot*)]. **Quote**: '~ days shalt thou labour' (Exodus).

7 = VII; HEPTAD, SEPTAD, *SEVEN*(TH); SEPTO-; **Pl** = *rugby* [copper or wool (*anniversary*), near gale (Beaufort scale), ~ Seas (*Kipling*), greeting (*magpie*), septenary (period), ~ hills (Rom), black ball (*snooker*), stars in the sky (*song*), swans a-swimming (*song*), chariot (*tarot*), ~ *ages* (*Shak*), ~ *deadly sins*, ~ *hills*, ~ *sages*, ~ *sisters*, ~ *wonders of the world*]. **Quotes**: 'If ~ maids with ~ mops swept for half a year' (*Alice* thro' the Looking-Glass); 'His acts being ~ ages' (AYLI, *Shak*).

8 = VIII; EIGHT(H), OCTAD, OCTET; OCTO-; ROWING CREW, BLUE, GOLDIE (C reserve ~), ISIS (O reserve ~) [bronze (*anniversary*), gale (Beaufort scale), wish (*magpie*), maids a-milking (*song*), bold rangers (*song*), justice (*tarot*)]. **Quote**: 'Pieces of ~' (parrot, *Stevenson*).

9 = IX; *NINE*, NINTH, NONAD, NONET; NONA-, NOV-. **Pl** = ELABORATELY, TO PERFECTION (dress) [pottery (*anniversary*), kiss (*magpie*), bright shiners (*song*), drummers drumming (*song*), ~ of diamonds (curse of Scotland), hermit (*tarot*), ~ *Muses*, ~ points of the law, ~ *angelic orders*]. **Quote**: '~ bean rows will I have there' (Innisfree, Yeats).

10 = X; DECIMAL, TEN(TH), DECA- [tin (*anniversary*), storm (Beaufort scale), decade (period), *commandments* (*song*), green bottles (*song*), pipers piping (*song*), wheel of *fortune* (*tarot*)].

11 = II, XI; ELEVEN(TH); HENDECA-; IMPAIRED (crypt); **Pl** = SNACK [steel (*anniversary*), side/team (cricket, hockey etc), ladies dancing (*song*), ~ who went to Heaven (*song*), strength (*tarot*)].

12 = XII; DOZEN, DUODECIMAL, TWELFTH, TWELVE; DODECA- [silk (*anniversary*), hurricane (Beaufort scale), *apostles* (*song*), lords a-leaping (*song*),

hanged man (*tarot*), glorious ~th (grouse shooting), ~th
Night (*Shak*)].

13 = XIII; BAKER'S DOZEN, THIRTEEN(TH),
UNLUCKY [lace (*anniversary*), side/team (rugby league),
death (*tarot*)].

14 = XIV; FOURTEEN(TH) [ivory (*anniversary*),
temperance (*tarot*)].

15 = XV; FIFTEEN(TH) [crystal (*anniversary*), side/team
(rugby union), *devil* (*tarot*), rebellion (Old Pretender)].

16 = XVI; SIXTEEN [*tower* (*tarot*)].

17 = XVII; SEVENTEEN [*star* (*tarot*)].

18 = XVIII; EIGHTEEN [*moon* (*tarot*)].

19 = XIX; NINETEEN [*sun* (*tarot*)].

20 = XX; JACKSON (sl), *SCORE*, TWENTY [china
(*anniversary*), day of *judgement* (*tarot*)]. **Quote**: '~
love-sick maidens we' (Patience, *G & S*).

21 = XXI; MAJORITY, VINGT-ET-UN (Fr) [world
(*tarot*)].

25 = XXV; PONY (sl), QUARTER CENTURY [*silver*
(*anniversary*)].

30 = XXX; THIRTY; 2nd XV (rugby) [*pearl* (*anniversary*),
~ Years' War]. **Quote**: 'And they covenanted with him for
~ pieces of silver' (St Matthew).

35 = XXXV [*coral* (*anniversary*)].

40 = XL: FORTY, TOPS (darts) [ruby (*anniversary*),
roaring ~s (*winds*), ~ winks (sleep)].

45 = XLV [sapphire (*anniversary*), rebellion (Young
Pretender)].

50 = L; HALF CENTURY, HALF TON (sl) [gold
(*anniversary*), bullseye (darts)].

52 = LII; PACK (cards).

55 = LV [*emerald* (*anniversary*)].

60 = LX [*diamond* (*anniversary*), ~ glorious years].
Quote: 'If you can fill the unforgiving minute with ~
seconds worth of distance run' (If, *Kipling*).

70 = LXX [*platinum* (*anniversary*)].

75 = LXXV [diamond (*anniversary*)].

76 = TROMBONES (song).

78 = TAROC, *TAROT* (pack).

100 = C; CENTURY, *HUNDRED*, TON (sl); HECTO-
[Old ~th (All people that on earth do dwell; was psalm
100); Chiltern ~s (stewardship, MP's resignation)].

101 = CI. DALMATIANS (Disney film).
105 = CV. NORTH TOWER (2 Cities, *Dickens*).
144 = GROSS.
180 = MAXIMUM (darts).
200 = CC; DOUBLE CENTURY, TWO TON (sl).
300 = B (Rom).
500 = D; *MONKEY* (sl).
600 = DC [Balaclava, Cardigan, Light Brigade]. **Quote**:
'Into the valley of death rode the ~' (Charge of the Light
Brigade, Tennyson).
1,000 = K, M; *GRAND* (sl), MIL (meas); KILO- [chiliad,
millennium (period), ~ Guineas (*classic* horserace)].
1,009 = M*IX, AD*M*IX (crypt).
1,500 = *MD*.
1,760 = MILE (yards).
1,976 = ASCOT MILE (yards).
2,000 = KK, MM [~ Guineas (*classic* horserace)].
6,100 = VI*C (crypt).
6,350 = VI*TRIO*L (crypt).
6,500 = PENNSYLVANIA (*song*, Glenn Miller).

NUMBER OF PLAYERS DUET, OCTET, QUARTET etc.
ELEVEN, FIFTEEN, *SIDE*, TEAM.
~ **ONE** *ME*, I, SELF; NO*I.
NUN (s/l none). *CHURCHWOMAN*; CONVENT GIRL, *SISTER*;
Chaucer character. *BIRD*: BLUE TIT, *PIGEON*, SMEW. The f
of *Joshua*. CHAOS (Egy god); FRANCISCA (*Shak*); MARIA
(Sound of Music).
NURSE DEVELOP, FOSTER, HARBOUR. WORKER
(insect). *FISH*, *SHARK*. CARE, COSSET, LOOK AFTER,
TEND; SUCKLE. AMAH (Asia), AYAH (Ind), MIDWIFE,
NANNY, NOURICE, *SISTER*, SRN (**Union** = COHSE); **celeb**
(**fiction**): SARAH GAMP (Chuzzle, *Dickens*); LYCHORIDA
(*Shak*, Per); MARCHIONESS (OC Shop, *Dickens*); MRS
POOLE (Jane Eyre, C. *Brontë*); BETSY PRIG (Chuzzle,
Dickens); MISS PROSS (2 Cities, *Dickens*); RUTH (Pirates,
G & S); TILLY SLOWBOY (Cricket on the Hearth, *Dickens*);
celeb (**fact**): EDITH CAVELL, FLORENCE *NIGHTINGALE*.
NURSERY HOTHOUSE, PROPAGATION PLOT. HOSPITAL,
WARD (crypt). CHILD'S BEDROOM; ROCKERY (crypt).
~**MAN** MARKET GARDENER. BOY BLUE, JACK
HORNER, SIMPLE SIMON etc (crypt, from ~ rhymes).

NUT FASTENING [bolt]. ENTHUSIAST, FAN; FOOL. Egy *goddess*. HEAD (sl). COAL LUMP. FRUIT (shell [kernel]); **types**: ACORN, ALMOND, BRAZIL, CASHEW, FILBERT, GROUNDNUT, HAZEL, PEANUT, PECAN, PISTACHIO, WALNUT. TEACHERS (*union*). **Pl** = *MAD*. **Pl comp** = bolts.
~-**CASE** LUNATIC, MADMAN. *SHELL* (crypt).
NYM CORPORAL, SOLDIER (*Shak*).
NYMPH 1. *INSECT* (immature), PUPA: DAMSELFLY, DRAGONFLY. GIRL, HOURI (Mos). YOUNG WOMAN. 2. Gk myth Naiad, one of the fresh water maidens (as opp to the salt water *Nereids*, or the Oceanides of the great oceans). Nymphs are distinct from *goddesses*, in that they belong to one particular spot, as opp to the goddesses' overall domain. **Mountain nymphs** = OREADS; **tree nymphs** = DRYADS and HAMADRYADS; **nymphs of the groves and glens** = NAPAEAE; **fountain** ~s = AGANIPPE, CAMENAE, EGERIA [K Numa].
NYMPHOMANIA Obsession (in women) with sex.
NYX Gk *goddess* of NIGHT (**Rom** = NOX); d of *Chaos* and m, without benefit of husband, of many *gods* and *goddesses*, including the *HESPERIDES*, *HYPNOS*, *MOIRAE*, MOMOS, THANATOS and *NEMESIS*, also by Erebus of *Charon*.
NZ NEW ZEALAND (and *car plate*).

O OHIO. OXFORD. OXYGEN (*chem*). DUCK, LOVE, NIL, ROUND, ZERO. CRY, EXCLAMATION.
OAK *TREE* [*Absalom*; Charles I]. **Pl** = *CLASSIC*.
OAR (s/l *or*, ore). GALLEY SLAVE, *ROWER*. PADDLE.
OARSMAN *ROWER*: *BOW*, *STROKE*. *CHARON*.
OAST HOUSE DRIER, HOP DRIER, *HOPPER*.
OATH APPEAL, ASSERT, PROMISE, SWEAR [*Hippocrates*, Witness]. CURSE, PROFANITY: BLAST, BLOW, BOTHER, DAMN, DASH, DRAT etc.
OB *DIED*, OBIT. ALUMNUS, OLD BOY [Tom Brown's Schooldays, T. Hughes' pseudonym]. OUTSIDE BROADCAST.
OBJECT 1. *AIM*, *END*, *POINT*. THING. *BAR*, COMPLAIN, DISAPPROVE. 2. Accusative case, e.g. **I object** = ME.
OBSERVE *NOTE*, *SEE*, *WATCH*.

OBSESSION EAGER PURSUIT, EXCESSIVE ENTHUSIASM, MANIA e.g.:

ANGLOMANIA	= **English customs**
BIBLIOMANIA	= **books**
EROTOMANIA	= **sexual passion**
KLEPTOMANIA	= **stealing**
MEGALOMANIA	= **grand ideas**
MONOMANIA	= **one idea**
NECROMANIA	= **death**
NYMPHOMANIA	= **sexual desire (in women)**
PYROMANIA	= **fire-raising**

OBTAINABLE *Anag.* e.g. **Camp follower obtainable from Ulster** (6) = SUTLER. ACQUIRABLE; AVAILABLE, ESTABLISHED, PREVALENT.
OBVERSE FACE, FRONT; HEAD (*coin*; **opp** = reverse). COUNTERPART.
OC ONLY CHILD. OFFICER COMMANDING.
OCCIDENT(AL) W, WESTERN (**opp** = oriental).
OCEAN One of the main areas of sea water: ARCTIC, ANTARCTIC, ATLANTIC, INDIAN, PACIFIC [*Pluto* (acronym); seven seas].
OCEANIDES Gk myth *NYMPHS* of the great oceans.
OCEANUS Gk myth river flowing round the (supposedly circular flat) earth, and also the associated *god*, mar to Tethys; later came to mean the Atlantic (i.e. the water beyond the known Mediterranean sea).
OCTOBER 1. BEER. 2. (10th) MONTH, M; OCT (8th Rom month, before *Caesar* reorganized the calendar). **Birthstone** = *opal*.
ODD *Anag.* e.g. **How odd** = WHO. 1. UNEVEN. CASTING, *EXTRA*, ORRA (Sc), OVER. REMAINING, ADDITIONAL, CASUAL, UNCONNECTED. *ECCENTRIC*, EXTRAORDINARY, QUEER, REMARKABLE, SINGULAR, STRANGE, UNCO (Sc). 2. **Pl** = ADVANTAGE, BALANCE, CHANCES, HANDICAP, PROBABILITIES, SP (betting). REMNANTS. DIFFERENCE, INEQUALITIES, STRIFE, VARIANCE. [**Comp**: ends.]
ODIN 1. Nor myth chief warrior *god* (br of Ve), who mar (1) *Frigg* (s = *Balder*) and (2) *Freya* (s = Tyr). One-eyed, he lived in Valhalla; his horse Sleipner had eight legs; his two *ravens*

Hugin (*reflection*) and Munin (*memory*) conveyed news of
the outside world. (**Gk** = *ZEUS*, **Rom** = *JUPITER*, **A-Sax** =
WODEN/WOTAN). 2. NOISELESS, QUIET (crypt).

ODYSSEUS = *ULYSSES*.

OEDIPUS Gk myth s of K Laius and Q Jocasta of Thebes.
Banished as a baby because an oracle prophesied that Laius
would be k by his own son, who would then marry his mother.
Returning, Oedipus fulfilled the prophecy by slaying his
unrecognized f on the way. He then relieved the Thebans by
solving the riddle of the *Sphinx*, so that he was made K and mar
his own m. When the facts were revealed, Jocasta killed herself
and Oedipus blinded himself. [~ complex; **opp** = *Electra*].

OF OLD FRENCH. FROM.

~ **COURSE** NATURALLY, OBVIOUSLY. [crypt = *golfing*;
meals; *racing*].

OFF *Anag.* 1. APART, AWAY. NOT ON. *GO*, START. LOOSE,
SEPARATE. CANCELLED. *BAD*, MOULDY. THE
COVERS (*cricket*; **opp** = *on*, *leg*). ASLEEP (crypt). 2. Delete
word or letters indicated, e.g. **Hit it off** = H(it).

OFFHAND CASUAL, INFORMAL. DIGITAL (crypt).

OFFICE BUREAU, QUARTERS. APPOINTMENT, DUTY,
JOB, POSITION, POST, TASK. ATTENTION, KINDNESS,
SERVICE. WORSHIP.

OFFICER FUNCTIONARY, MINISTER, SERVANT: BAILIFF,
CHAIRMAN, CONSTABLE, HERALD, PRESIDENT,
SECRETARY, TREASURER. Commissioned rank in mil
services: CAPT, CDR, *CO*, *COL*, LT, PO etc; ENSIGN,
GENERAL, SUBALTERN etc. **Comp** = gentleman.

OFFING DISTANCE. TOPPLING, UNSEATING, UPSETTING
(crypt).

OFFSPRING DIVE (crypt). BROOD, CHILD(REN),
DESCENDANT, PROGENY, LITTER, YOUNG, **specifically**:

Adult	Young
Ass/mare	MULE
Bear	*CUB*
Bird	CHICK
Camel	*COLT*
Cat	KITTEN
Cow	*CALF*
Deer	*FAWN*
Dog	PUP

Duck	DUCKLING
Eagle	EAGLET
Eel	ELVER
Elephant	*CALF*
Fish	*FRY*
Fox	*CUB*
Frog	TADPOLE
Goat	*KID*
Goose	GOSLING
Hare	LEVERET
Hawk	BOWET, EYAS, NYAS
Hen	CHICK
Heron	CHICK
Horse	COLT (masc), FILLY (f), FOAL
Human	BABY, CHILD
Lion	*CUB*
Pig	PIGLET, SHOAT
Salmon	PEAL, GRILSE, SMOLT
Sheep	*LAMB*
Stallion/Ass	HINNY
Swan	CYGNET
Tiger	*CUB*
Turkey	POULT
Walrus	*CALF*
Whale	*CALF*
Wild boar	GRICE
Wolf	*CUB*
Yak/Cow	DZHO, DZO
Young	**Adult**
Baby	HUMAN
Bowet	*HAWK*
Calf	*COW, ELEPHANT, WALRUS, WHALE*
Chick	*BIRD*, HEN, HERON
Child	HUMAN
Colt	*CAMEL, HORSE* (masc)
Cub	*BEAR, FOX, LION, TIGER, WOLF*
Cygnet	*SWAN*
Duckling	*DUCK*
Dzho, dzo	YAK/COW

Eaglet	*EAGLE*
Elver	*EEL*
Fawn	*DEER*
Filly	*HORSE* (f)
Foal	*HORSE*
Fry	*FISH*
Gosling	*GOOSE*
Grice	WILD BOAR
Grilse	*SALMON*
Hinny	STALLION/*ASS*
Kid	*GOAT*
Kitten	*CAT*
Lamb	*SHEEP*
Leveret	HARE
Mule	*ASS*/MARE
Peal	*SALMON*
Piglet	*PIG*
Poult	TURKEY
Pup	*DOG*
Shoat	*PIG*
Smolt	*SALMON*
Tadpole	*FROG*

OG OLD GERMAN. GO BACK (crypt). KING (bibl). ORIGINAL GUM (stamps). OWN GOAL. GOD (Celt; chief, death, fertility).

OH CALL, *CRY*. OHIO (US *state*).

OILER GREASER, MECHANIC. BRIBER. **Pl** = TEAM (US *football*). OPEC (crypt).

OLD 1. ANCIENT, EX, FORMER, ONCE (**opp** = *new*). AGED, GREY [*study*]. **Comp** = *young*. 2. Use old form of word indicated, e.g. **Old enough** = ENOW; **the old** = YE. 3. Use Roman name, e.g. **Old Exeter** = ISCA.

~ **BOY** ALUMNUS, *OB* (author of Tom Brown's Schooldays).

~ **FASHIONED** *DATED*, OUT OF DATE, SQUARE (**opp** = *in*); use arch words, e.g. **Are** ~ = ART; **If** ~ = AN. COCKTAIL, *DRINK*.

~ **FLAME** EX, PAST LOVE. ASH, EMBER (crypt).

~ **FRENCH** OF. VIEUX (trans).

~ **GERMAN** OG. ALT (trans).

~ **LADY** *MOTHER*. CRONE.

~ **MAN** *HUSBAND*; POT AND PAN (*rh sl*). GAFFER.

~ **RAILWAY** GWR, LMS, LNER, SR etc.

~ **STYLE** *OS*.

~ **TESTAMENT** OT.

~ **TRAFFORD** *CRICKET GROUND*, TESTING GROUND.

~ **WOMAN** *WIFE*.

OLIVER NOLL. CROMWELL. *PAINTER*. ~ TWIST ('more'). *Shak* char. **Comp** = Roland.

OLYMPIC 1. GAMES. MAGNIFICENT, SUPERIOR. 2. Of *Olympus*, hence relating to Gk myth *gods* and *goddesses*.

OLYMPUS Thessalian mountain, dwelling place of *Zeus* and the principal Gk *gods* and *goddesses*. [*Seven Wonders*].

OM ORDER OF MERIT.

OMAR KHAYYAM, TENT MAKER [astronomy, maths, poetry].

OMIT 1. *CUT*, FAIL, LEAVE OUT, NEGLECT. 2. Omit letter(s) or word(s) from clue as indicated, e.g. **Lord Peter omits tea apparently** (4) = PE*ER.

ON *BET*, WAGERED. AHEAD. POSSIBLE. *CONNECTED*. CITY, HELIOPOLIS (Egy). LEG (*cricket*; **opp** = *off*). *OVER*. No reflexion . . . (crypt = ON).

~ **BOARD** 1. EMBARKED, LOADED, SHIPPED; NAUTICAL. FOOD, ON THE TABLE. SURFER (crypt). 2. Put letter(s) or word(s) into synonym for boat or ship (often into letters s . . . s), e.g. **Pool on board rolls** (6) = S*POOL*S. 3. Any object which is normally used on a board, e.g. **Food on board** = CHEESE; **piece on board** = CASTLE, PAWN, ROOK etc, and (crypt) DRAUGHTSMAN; also any *boardgame* (q.v. for types).

ONCE 1. ARCHAIC, EX. ONE TIME. 2. Put into Lat or old Gk, e.g. **But ~** = SED.

ONE 1. See *number*. A, ACE, I, MONAD, UNIT. RED BALL (snooker). 2. All *alone* in *song*; *partridge* in a peartree (*Christmas song*).

~**-ARMED** Single-handed (crypt). **Celeb:** ~ BANDIT (slot machine); NELSON (*mil leader*); CAPT HOOK (Peter Pan, *Barrie*).

~ **BY** ~ IN ORDER, SERIATIM, SINGLY. ELEVEN, II (crypt).

~ **CARD** *ACE*.

ONE-EYED INEFFICIENT (sl). Singularly observant (crypt). MONOCULAR; **Celeb:** *CYCLOPES* (monsters); DAVY GAM(M) (k at Agincourt); *GRAEAE*; HANNIBAL; KING HAROLD (k at Hastings); HORATIUS; MARSHLAND SHALES (19th cent horse); NELSON (*mil leader*); *ODIN*;

POLYPHEMUS; PHILIP (of Macedon, f of *Alexander*); POPEYE (Disney); SQUEERS (*schoolmaster*, *Dickens*); *WODEN*; WOTAN (and see *blind*) ['~ man is king' (Country of the Blind, H. G. Wells)].

~-LEGGED One-sided, unequal (sl). **Celeb**: Capt *AHAB* (Melville); BERCHTA (Ger myth); LONG JOHN SILVER (*Stevenson*).

~ THOUSAND GUINEAS CLASSIC.

ON SHOW 1. DEMONSTRATED, EXHIBITED, EXPOSED. 2. Hidden word, e.g. **Fit for a king on show at the picture gallery** (5) = RE*GAL.

ONWARD FORWARD, FURTHER ON, PROGRESSING. IN HOSPITAL (crypt).

ONYX *GEM*, SEMI-PRECIOUS STONE; *CHALCEDONY*; *AGATE*.

OO EXCLAMATION, OH. BIRD (Hawaiian). *DUCKS*, EGGS, *LOVES*, OVA (all crypt). PAIR (cricket).

OOH EXCLAMATION, OH. BACKWATER (H_2O backwards, crypt – but *chem* inaccurate).

OP OBSERVATION POST. (MINOR) OPERATION, OPUS, WORK. OPPOSITE PROMPT, STAGE RIGHT (theat). ORDER OF PREACHERS (DOMINICANS). OUT OF PRINT. OPTICAL. **Pl** = Rom *goddess* of *NATURE*.

OPAL *GEM*, PRECIOUS STONE; GIROSOL (fire ~). *Birthstone* (October). HYALITE (clear); SILICA QUARTZ.

OPEN OVERT. WINDWARD, WINDY (**opp** = *lee*). CRACK, UNDO, UNWRAP; **comp** = shut. TAKE STRIKE (*cricket*). *UNIVERSITY*. GOLF CHAMPIONSHIP, TOURNAMENT; PRO-AM (crypt).

~ AIR AL FRESCO, OUTSIDE. CANDOUR.

OPENER 1. DOOR, GATE. *KEY*. (FIRST) BAT (*cricket*). TIN OPENER. **Pl** = QUALIFYING HOLDING (cards). 2. First letter, e.g. **Letter opener** = L.

OPENING 1. CRACK, FISSURE, GAP, HOLE [Sesame]. OVERTURE. GAMBIT. 2. First letter, e.g. **Clever opening** = C.

OPERATING THEATRE SURGERY. WORK ROOM. WORKSHOP.

OPERATION MANIPULATION, WORKING. OP. SURGERY. *BATTLE*; ACTION, ENGAGEMENT (mil).

OPERATOR MANIPULATOR, WORKER. SURGEON (crypt).

OPPORTUNITY CHANCE. PAT, TIMELY.

OPPOSITE ANTONYM. CONTRAST; FACING. [~ **sides** = EW, HC, LR (crypt)]. **Pl** = BACK/FRONT, CHALK/CHEESE, IN/OUT, ON/OFF.

OPS 1. WORKS. 2. Rom *goddess* of *NATURE*.

OPTION CHOICE; REFUSAL.

OR (s/l *oar*, ore). *GOLD* (*herald*). BEFORE, ERE (arch). EITHER (arch). ALTERNATIVE.

ORACLE 1. ADVISER, AUTHORITY, DIVINE INSPIRATION, JUDGEMENT. *PROPHET*. TELETEXT (ITV); **opp** = Ceefax (BBC). 2. Sacred place of divine response, given by a priest or priestess to enquiry by a votary. Often with a carefully worded double meaning. Two celebrated oracles were at Delphi (*Apollo*) and Dodona (*Zeus*); others were at Branchidae and Patara [*Sibyl*]. 3. **God: Gk/Rom** = *APOLLO*; **goddess: Rom** = *MAIA*.

ORAL (s/l *aural*). EXAM(INATION), VIVE VOCE. SAID, SPOKEN, VERBAL. BY MOUTH.

ORANGE *COLOUR*. FRUIT, *TREE* [*Holmes* case]; **Pl comp** = *lemons*. *RIVER* (SA). TOWN (Fr). ROYAL FAMILY (NL).

ORCUS Rom equivalent of *HADES*. Synonymous with *PLUTO* (q.v.).

ORDER ASSOCIATION, *CLUB*, FRATERNITY, MOVEMENT. CLASS, KIND, RANK, SORT. DECREE, EDICT; BULL (papal), UKASE (Russ). **Comp** = *law*. ADJUST, ARRANGE, TIDY; ARRANGEMENT, *ROW*, SEQUENCE, SUCCESSION. DECORUM (**opp** = *chaos*) [*Speaker*]. NEATNESS, *SERIES*. COMMISSION, INDENT, SEND FOR. COMMAND, DO, INSTRUCT. AWARD, DECORATION, HONOUR: CBE, DSO, KBE, MBE, OBE, OM etc. **Pl** = CLERICAL STATUS, ORDINATION. [*five* classical ~s; *nine* angelic ~s].

ORDERED *Anag.* ARRANGED, TIDIED. SENT FOR. COMMANDED, INSTRUCTED. *CHURCHMAN* (crypt). Also CBE, DSO etc as *ORDER* (crypt).

ORDER OF MERIT OM. MITRE, TIMER etc (crypt).

ORDNANCE MOUNTED CANNON/GUNS, *WEAPONS*; **types:** BASILISK, BASSE, CANNON DOUBLE, CANNON ROYAL, CARRONADE, CULVERIN, DEMI-CANNON, DEMI-CULVERIN, DEMI-SLING, FALCON, FIELD-GUN, HOWITZER, MINION, MORTAR, SAKER, SLING, STERN-CHASER. *WEAPON*.

ORE (s/l *oar*, *or*). CURRENCY (Dan, Nor, Swe). *MINERAL* (q.v. for types).

OREAD *NYMPH* (mountain).

ORESTES Gk myth s of *Agamemnon* and *Clytemnestra*. With his sis *Electra*, he k his adulterous mother. [**Comp**: Pylades].

ORGAN 1. PART OF BODY (hence B, O, D or Y – crypt), e.g. APPENDIX, COLON, also *mouthorgan* = TONGUE (crypt). MAGAZINE, MEDIUM, MOUTHPIECE, NEWSPAPER. 2. HARMONIUM, MUSICAL INSTRUMENT; **parts**: backfall, bellows, diapason, feeder, keyboard, pallet, pipe, slider, sticker, stop, swell-box, tracker, wind-chest; **stops**: bourdon, diapason, flue, gamba, mixture, musette, mutation, reed, string-toned, tremulant.

ORGANIZATION *Anag*. ASSOCIATION, CLUB, FRATERNITY, MANAGEMENT, MOVEMENT, SCHEME, SET-UP.

ORIENT(AL) E, *EAST*, EASTERN (**opp** = occidental).

ORIGINAL 1. EARLIEST, FUNDAMENTAL, INITIAL, INNATE, PRIMITIVE, PRIMORDIAL. MATRIX, PATTERN. CREATIVE, INVENTIVE. 2. First letter, e.g. **Original sin** = s.

ORION Gk myth *HUNTER*. When k in Crete with *Artemis*, he became a *constellation* [belt; sword; *dog*; Sirius].

Ork Orkneys.

ORPHEUS Gk myth poet, who charmed all Nature with his *lyre*; he accompanied the *Argonauts* [*siren*]. He mar *Eurydice* and, when she d, followed her to *Hades* and won her back with his music; but when he *looked back* to see if she was following, she was taken back again. His grief angered the Thracian women, who tore him to pieces, and his lyre was placed among the stars as a *constellation* (Lyra).

ORT LEAVING, *REFUSE*, SCRAP.

ORWELL 1. RIVER (Eng). 2. GEORGE (Eric Blair), writer. Animal Farm **chars**: dogs = Bluebell, Jessie, *Pitcher*; donkey = Benjamin; farmer = Mr Jones; goat = Muriel; horses = *Boxer*, Clover, Mollie; pigs = *Major*, Minimus, *Napoleon*, Snowball, *Squealer*; raven = Moses; solicitor = Mr Whymper. 1984 **chars**: Big Brother (BB), Julia, O'Brien, Parsons, Syme, Winston Smith; **words**: Airstrip One, doublethink, Ingsoc, Miniluv, Minipax, Miniplenty, Minitrue, newspeak, prole, thought police, unperson, Eastasia, Eurasia, Oceania.

OS OSMIUM (*chem*). OLD STYLE. BIG, LARGE, OUTSIZE.

OSCAR *AWARD*® (US film; the original statuette reminded a secretary 'of her uncle Oscar').

OSIRIS Gk form of Egy *god* of death and eternal life. Mar *Isis*, br of *Set*.

OSP OBIIT SINE PROLAE (d without issue).

OSTRICH BIRD genus RATITAE STRUTHIO (Af; flightless; head in sand) [aepyornis (ex), cassowary, dinornis (NZ ex), emu, moa, mooruk, nandoo, rhea].

OT OLD TESTAMENT (**opp** = NT); BIBLE.

OTHELLO MOOR (*Shak*).

OTHERS ET AL, REST.

OTTER ~ BOARD (fishing). Aquatic musteline animal of *weasel* family; **celeb**: MIJ (Ring of Bright Water, Maxwell), TARKA (Williamson).

OUNCE *CAT. MEASURE*, OZ.

OUR TIME AD, NOWADAYS.

OUT *Anag*; e.g. **Eats out** = TEAS, or **outpost** = STOP. 1. NOT AT HOME, NOT IN. READY (e.g. **pan out** = READY TO COOK). AT FAULT, IN ERROR. FINISHED; **comp** = *down*. BLOOMING, FLOWERING. B, CT, LBW (*cricket*). EMERGED, HATCHED, e.g. **Chickened out?** (7) = HATCHED. 2. Word outside another, e.g. **Directed me to help out** (5) = AI*ME*D. 3. Letter or word omitted, e.g. **Criminal, caught out, fleeced** (6) = (C)ROOKED. 4. Decide against, e.g. **No holidays under canvas** (7,3) = CAMPING OUT.

OUTDOORS AL FRESCO. EXITS (crypt).

OUTER EXTERNAL. OBJECTIVE. BOWLER (crypt). *CRICKET GROUND* (Melbourne). TARGET RING [*bullseye, inner, magpie*].

OUTING EXPEDITION, TRIP. BOWLING, WICKET TAKING (*cricket*, crypt). BLOOMING, FLOWERING (crypt).

OUTLANDISH ODD. ABROAD, FOREIGN (crypt). Trans (crypt).

OUTLAW DISQUALIFY, FORBID, PROHIBIT. BADDIE, BADMAN, LAW-BREAKER (crypt **opp** = in-law); **celeb**: BILLY THE KID, THE CISCO KID, THE CLANCEYS, THE DALTONS, DOC HOLLIDAY, THE DOONES, JESSE JAMES, NED KELLY (Aus) [*cowboy, highwayman, robber*]. (JUST) WILLIAM (BROWN), DOUGLAS, GINGER, HENRY [Violet Elizabeth]; Richmal Crompton.

OUT OF 1. EX. FOALED BY (mare). 2. Hidden word, e.g. **Horses out of form are stabled** (5) = M*ARE*S. 3. One word or letter placed outside another, e.g. **He is out of work with**

optimism (4) = H*OP*E.

OUTPOST *SETTLEMENT.*

OUTRIGHT 1. ALTOGETHER, ENTIRELY, OPENLY. DIRECT, DOWNRIGHT, THOROUGH. 2. Remove letters RIGHT, RT or R from word, e.g. **Print outright for a drink** (4) = P*INT.

OUTSIDE 1. EXTERIOR, FIELDER (*cricket*, crypt). WINGER (*football*). 2. Word placed round another, e.g. **When in, he is outside the order** (4) = H*OM*E.

~ **BROADCAST** OB.

OUTSIDER 1. *BOUNDER*, CAD. FIELDER (*cricket*, crypt). 2. **Pl** = first and last letters, e.g. **Complete outsiders** = C*E.

OUTSIZE BIG, OS.

OUTSTANDING CONSPICUOUS, EMINENT, REMARKABLE, SIGNAL. *OVERDUE*, UNPAID, UNSETTLED. GROYNE, JETTY, PIER (crypt). *CAMEO*, FRIEZE, TRIGLYPH (crypt).

OUTWARDLY 1. APPARENTLY, EXTERNALLY, VISIBLY. 2. One word round another, e.g. **He is outwardly feline, the deceiver** (5) = C*HE*AT.

OVA (s/l *over*). EGG, O.

OVAL EGG-SHAPED, ELLIPTICAL. *CRICKET GROUND*, TESTING GROUND. *NAIL.*

OVER (s/l *ova*). 1. ABOVE [~ the *moon* = delighted (**opp** = sick as a *parrot*)]. ENDED; LEFT, REMAINING. *CONCERNING*. REVERSED. SIX BALLS/DELIVERIES (*cricket*). ON. 2. In down clue, word preceding another, e.g. **Residuum form of rise overdue** (7) = RESI*DUE.

OVERDRAWN OD, IN THE RED, hence word in RED, e.g. **Overdrawn State stayed behind** (8) = RE*MAINE*D.

OVERDRESS FLAMBOYANCY [Beau Brummel]. APRON, *PINAFORE* (crypt).

OVERDUE LATE. *OUTSTANDING*, UNPAID, UNSETTLED.

OVERHAUL OVERTAKE, *PASS*. EXAMINE, PATCH, REPAIR, *SERVICE.*

OVERHEAD FIXED COST, STANDING CHARGE. HAT (crypt); ROOF (crypt); UMBRELLA (crypt). **Opp** = under foot, understanding (crypt).

OVERLOOK FORGET, TAKE NO NOTICE. OVERSEE, SUPERINTEND. GIVE ONTO, HIGHER THAN. BEWITCH.

OVERMAN *BOSS*, FOREMAN, MANAGER, SUPERINTENDENT. BOWLER (crypt).

OVERSIGHT OMISSION. EYEBROW, EYELASH, FOREHEAD (crypt).

OVERTURE 1. OPENING (mus). FEELER, PROPOSAL. 2. First letter, e.g. **Handel's overture** = H.

OVERWEIGHT 1. FAT, OBESE. 2. In down clue, word preceding, or over, synonym for weight, e.g. **Foolish Herb is overweight** (9) = SIMPLE*TON.

OWE (s/l O, *Oh*). DEBT, DUE, *OVERDRAW*.

OWL BIRD; NIGHT-FLYER; **breeds**: BARN ~, BUBO, BURROWING ~, EAGLE ~, ELF ~, FISH ~ (Jap), FROGMOUTH ~ (Aus), (GREAT) GREY ~, HAWK ~, HOOT ~, HORNED ~, LITTLE ~, LONG-EARED ~, MOPOKE, MOREPORK (Aus, NZ), SAWWHET (Arcadia), SCREECH ~, SHORT-EARED ~, SNOWY ~, TAWNY ~, URAL ~, WOOD ~ [eyesight, wisdom]; **comp** = nightingale (OE, de Guildford); pussycat (*Lear*). **Celeb**: TOO-TOO (*Lofting*), *BUNTER*, OLD BROWN ~ (*Potter*), ASCALAPHUS (myth), WOL (*Milne*). BUTTERFLY (lepidoptera). **Pl** = football team.

OWN POSSESS. *ADMIT*, CONFESS. ALONE, INDEPENDENT, PERSONALLY, UNRIVALLED; TOD SLOAN (*rh sl*).

OX BOVINE ANIMAL (genus Bos): ANOA (SE Asia), AUROCHS (ex, and = URUS), BISON, BUFFALO, GAYAL (Ind), KOUPREY (SE Asia), MITHAN (Ind), MUSK-OX, SAPI(O)UTAN (SE Asia), SELADANG (Malay), TAKIN (Asia), TAMARAU (Pac), UNICORN (myth), WISENT, YAK, ZEBU.

OXFORD Episcopal sig = OXON. *UNIVERSITY* (q.v. for colleges); **comp** = Cambridge. *CASTLE*. *COLOUR* (dark blue). *SHOE*. *BOSPHORUS*. *Shak* char.

OXON *Episcopal sig* of OXFORD. *UNIVERSITY*.

OXYGEN O (*chem*). *GAS*.

OYSTER BIVALVE, *NATIVE* [*Colchester*, Whitstable]; *SHELL* (*close, silent*). Alice char.

OZ *OUNCE* [*measure*]. WIZARD [Emerald City; Yellow Brick Road; Lion etc]. *Aus* (sl).

P (s/l pea, pee). PAGE. PARK(ING). PENNY. PHOSPHORUS (*chem*). PIANO, QUIET, SUBDUED. PORT. PORTUGAL (*car plate*). *PRESIDENT*. **Pl** = PP, PS.

PA (s/l *par*). *FATHER*. PANAMA (*car plate*). PROTACTINIUM (*chem*). PENNSYLVANIA (US *state*).

PACK 1. BUNDLE, KNAPSACK, *MEASURE*, PACKET, RUCKSACK; LOT, SET (cards). BAG, BOX, *COVER*, WRAP, CROWD, CRUSH, FILL. CARRY (gun). STACK (jury). ~*ICE*. CAKE (cosmetics, *medicine*). 2. *Assembly* of *brownies*, *cards*, *cubs*, *grouse*, *hounds*, *hyenas*, Rugby forwards, submarines, wolves.

PACKMAN PEDLAR (arch); BOB JAKIN (Mill on the Floss, Eliot). JACK, KING, KNAVE; DEALER (cards, crypt).

PAGE ATTENDANT, BUTTONS, BELL-BOY, BELL-HOP; (*Chaucer*). CALL, SUMMON. P, FOLIO, LEAF, RECTO, (RE)VERSO, VO. BOOKMAKER (crypt). Mistress ~ (Merry Wives, *Shak*). ROBIN (*Shak*). **Pl** = FF, PP.

PAIN (s/l *pane*). AGONY, HURT; STITCH. **Aversion to** ~ = ALGOPHOBIA; **lover of** ~ = ALGOPHILE. FRENCH BREAD (trans, crypt).

PAINTED *MADE UP*. *COATED*, COLOURED, PIGMENTED; PINXIT. [La Creevy, *Dickens*].

PAINTER MOORING LINE/ROPE; BOW-TIE (crypt). BEAUTICIAN, COSMETICIAN, MAKE-UP ARTIST (crypt). DECORATOR; HITLER. RA; *ARTIST*, MASTER; CUBIST, DADAIST, EXPRESSIONIST, FAUVE, FUTURIST, IMPRESSIONIST, LANDSCAPE ~, MINIATURE ~, MODERNIST, ORPHIST, PORTRAIT ~, RENAISSANCE ~, STILL-LIFE ~, SURREALIST, SYNCHRONIST, VORTICIST; CANVASSER, EXHIBITIONIST (crypt). **Goddess, Gk** = *Athene*, **Rom** = *Minerva*. In classic Gk times (*c*.400 B.C.), Zeuxis and Parrhasius competed for superiority in still-life painting. The former painted a bunch of grapes which deceived the birds, who tried to eat them; he then called upon the latter to unveil his painting so it could be judged – but the curtain covering it was the painting, which won because it had deceived a fellow artist [*Athene*, Minerva, fine arts, *Company* (livery)]; **celeb**:

3-letters

COX, David	Eng	*FRY*, Roger	Eng
DOU, Gerard	NL		

4-letters

BELL, Robert Anning	Eng	
BONE, Sir Michael	Eng	
COPE, Sir Arthur	Eng	
CUYP, Albert	NL	
DALI, Salvador	Sp	
DORÉ, (Paul) Gustave	Fr	
DUFY, Raoul	Fr	
DYCK, Anthony van	NL	
ETTY, William	Eng	
EYCK, Hubert van	NL	
GOGH, Vincent van	NL	
GOYA, Francisco de	Sp	
GRIS, Juan	Sp	
HALS, Frans	NL	
HEEM, David van	NL	
HUNT, William Holman	Eng	
JOHN, Augustus Edwin	Eng	
KENT, William	Eng	
KLEE, Paul	Swi	
LELY, Sir Peter	Eng	
LENS, Bernard	Eng	
MAES, Nicolaes	NL	
MARC, Franz	Ger	
MIRÓ, Joan	Sp	
NASH, Paul	Eng	
RENI, Guido	It	
RITT, Augustus	Russ	
ROSA, Salvator	It	
SHEE, Sir Martin Archer	Ire	
WEST, Benjamin	US	
WINT, Peter de	Eng	
WOOD, Christopher	UK	
ZORN, Anders Leonhard	Swe	

5-letters

BACON, Francis	Ire	
BAYEU, Francisco	Sp	
BLAKE, William	Eng	
BROWN, Ford Madox	Eng	
COROT, Jean-Baptiste	Fr	
CUNEO, Terence Tenison	Eng	
DANBY, Frances	Eng	
DAVID, Jacques	Fr	
DAYES, Edward	Eng	
DEGAS, Hilaire Germain Edgar	Fr	
DULAC, Edmond	Fr	
DURER, Albrecht	Ger	
ENSOR, James	Belg	
ERNST, Max	Ger	
FRITH, William Powell	Eng	
GOYEN, David van	NL	
GRECO, El	Gk	
GROSZ, George	Ger	
HOOCH, Pieter de	NL	
JACON, Max	Fr	
JONES, George	Eng	
KLIMT, Gustav	A	
KLINE, Franz	US	
LÉGER, Fernand	Fr	
LEWIS, Wyndham	US	
LIPPI, Fra Filippo	It	
LOWRY, Lawrence Stephen	Eng	
MANET, Edouard	Fr	
MARIN, John	US	
MARIS, Jacob	NL	
MONET, Claude	Fr	
MOSES, Anna 'Grandma'	US	
MUNCH, Edvard	Nor	
NOLDE, Emil	Ger	
ORPEN, Sir William	Ire	
REDON, Odilon	Fr	
ROCHE, Hippolyte (Paul) de la	Fr	

ROSSI, Giovanni	It	TOBEY, Mark	US
SARTO, Andrea del	It	VELDE, Jan van de	NL
SCOTT, Sir Peter	Eng	VELDE, Willem van de	NL
SMART, John	Eng	VINCI, Leonardo da	It
SPEAR, Ruskin	Eng	WATTS, George	
STEEN, Jan	It	Frederick	Eng

6-letters

ANCHER, Michael	Dan	LÁSZLÓ, Philip de	Hung
ARCHER, James		LAVERY, Sir John	Ire
Wykeham	Eng	LEBRUN, Marie	Fr
BODINI, Giambattista	It	MCEVOY, Ambrose	Eng
BRAQUE, Georges	Fr	MABUSE, Jan	NL
BUFFET, Bernard	Fr	MATSYS, Quentin	NL
CLAUDE, Lorrain		MILLET, Jean	
(Gelée)	Fr	Francois	Fr
COOPER, Alexander		*OLIVER*, Isaac	
& Samuel	Eng	& Peter	Eng
COPLEY, John	US	OROZCO, José	Mex
COSWAY, Richard	Eng	PLIMER, Andrew	
COTMAN, John Sell	Eng	& Nathaniel	Eng
COZENS, John Robert	Eng	RENOIR, Pierre-	
DERAIN, André	Fr	Auguste	Fr
DE WINT, Peter	Eng	RIVERA, Diego	Mex
EVENOR	Ancient Gk	ROMNEY, George	Eng
FOSTER, Miles	Eng	ROTHKO, Mark	US
GIBSON, Charles		RUBENS, Peter Paul	NL
Dana	US	SEURAT, Georges	
GIBSON, Richard	Eng	Pierre	Fr
GIOTTO (di		SIGNAC, Paul	Fr
Bondone)	It	SISLEY, Alfred	Fr
GIRTON, Thomas	Eng	TITIAN (Tiziano	
GREUZE, Jean-		Vecellio)	It
Baptiste	Fr	TURNER, Joseph	
HAYDON, Benjamin		Mallord Wm	Eng
Robert	Eng	VARLEY, John	Eng
HEARNE, Thomas	Eng	VERNET, Claude	Fr
HUYSUM, Jan van	NL	WARHOL, Andy	US
INGRES, Jean	Fr	WEYLER, Jean-	
KNIGHT, Dame		Baptiste	Fr
Laura	Eng	WILKIE, Sir David	Sc
KROYER	Dan	WILSON, Richard	Wal

WYLLIE, William Lionel	UK	ZEUXIS	Ancient Gk

7-letters

APELLES	Ancient Gk	LAUTREC, Henri de Toulouse	Fr
BARTOLI, Taddeo	It	LEONARD, Michael	Eng
BELLINI, Gentile & Giovanni	It	LIEVENS, Jan	NL
BONNARD, Pierre	Fr	LINNELL, John	Eng
BORDONE, Paris	It	LORRAIN, Gelée (Claude)	Fr
BOUCHER, François	Fr		
BRUEGEL, Jan (Velvet)	NL	MALBONE, E. G.	US
CASSATT, Mary	US	MATISSE, Henri	Fr
CÉZANNE, Paul	Fr	MILLAIS, Sir John	Eng
CHAGALL, Marc	Russ/Fr	MORISOT, Berthe	Fr
CHARDIN, Jean-Baptiste Siméon	Fr	MURILLO, Bartolome	Sp
		NASMYTH, Alexander	Sc
CHIRICO, Giorgio de	Gk/It	NATTIER, Jean	Fr
COLLIER, John	Eng	PICASSO, Pablo (Ruiz)	Sp
COURBET, Gustave	Fr	POLLOCK, Jackson	US
DAUMIER, Honoré	Fr	POUSSIN, Nicholas	Fr
DA VINCI, Leonardo	It	RAEBURN, Sir Henry	Sc
DE HOOCH, Pieter	NL	RAPHAEL (Sanzio)	It
EL GRECO	Gk	ROBERTS, William	Eng
FRANCIA, Francesco	It	ROUAULT, Georges	Fr
GAUGUIN, Paul	Fr	SARGENT, John Singer	Eng
GILBERT, Sir John	Eng	SICKERT, Walter	Eng
GUTHRIE, Sir James	Sc	SINGRAY, Jean-Baptiste	Fr
HEBBORN, Eric (forger)	Eng	*SOLOMON*, Solomon Joseph	UK
HOBBEMA, Meindert	NL		
HOGARTH, William	Eng	SOUTINE, Chaim	Fr
HOKUSAI, Katsushuka	Jap	SPENCER, Sir Stanley	Eng
HOLBEIN, Hans	Ger	TENIERS, David	NL
HOPPNER, John	Eng	TENNANT, Stephen James Napier	Eng
HOSKINS, John	Eng		
JANSSEN, Cornelius	Ger	THAULOW, Frits	Nor
KEATING, Tom (forger)	Eng	TIEPOLO, Giovanni	It
KNELLER, Sir Godfrey	Eng	UCCELLO, Paolo	It
KOONING, Willem de	NL/US	UTRILLO, Maurice	Fr
LARSSON, Carl	Swe	VAN DYCK, Anthony	NL
		VAN EYCK, Hubert	NL

VAN GOGH, Vincent	NL	WATTEAU, Antoine	Fr
VAN HEEM, David	NL	WOOTTON, Frank	Eng
VERMEER, Jan	NL	ZOFFANY, John	Eng

8-letters

ANGELICO, Fra Guido	It	MULREADY, William	Ire
ANNIGONI, Pietro	It	MUNNINGS, Sir Alfred	Eng
BOCCIONE, Umberto	It	PERUGINO (Pietro	
BOUGHTON, George		Vannucci)	It
Henry	Eng	PISSARRO, Camille	Fr
BRUEGHEL, Pieter		REYNOLDS, Sir	
(*Hell*)	NL	Joshua	Eng
CARRIERA, Rosalta	It	RICHMOND, Sir William	
DE LASZLO, Philip	Hung	Blake	Eng
DELAUNAY, Robert	Fr	RICKETTS, Charles	Eng
DEL SARTO, Andrea	It	ROSSETTI, Dante	
HILLIARD, Nicholas		Gabriel	Eng
& Laurence	Eng	ROUSSEAU, Henri	Fr
JAMESON, George	Sc	RUYSDAEL, Jakob	
KOLLWITZ, Kathe	Ger	van	NL
LANDSEER, Sir Edwin		SALBREUX, Louis	
Henry	Eng	Lie Perin	Fr
LAWRENCE, A. K.	Eng	SOHLBERG, Harald	Nor
LAWRENCE, Sir		STOTHARD, Thomas	Eng
Thomas	Eng	VAN GOYEN, David	NL
LEIGHTON, Lord		VERONESE, Paola	It
Frederick	Eng	VLAMINCK, Maurice	
MANTEGNA, Andrea	It	de	Fr
MASACCIO (Tommaso		VUILLARD, Jean-	
Giovanni)	It	Edouard	Fr
MEEGEREN, Hans van		WHISTLER, James	US
(forger)	NL	ZURBARÁN, Francisco	
MONDRIAN, Piet	NL	de	Sp

9-letters

CANALETTO,		DE CHIRICO, Giorgio	Gk/It
Giovanni	It	DE KOONING, Willem	NL/US
CHURCHILL, Sir		DELACROIX, Eugène	Fr
Winston	Eng	DE LA ROCHE, Hippolyte	
CONSTABLE, John	Eng	(Paul)	Fr
CORREGGIO, Antonio		DONATELLO, Donato	It
da	It	EDELFELT, Albert	Finn

FEININGER, Lyonel	US	LLEWELLYN, Sir	
FRAGONARD, Jean	Fr	William	Eng
GIORGIONE, Giorgio	It	MCTAGGART,	
GREENAWAY, Kate	Eng	William	Sc
HONTHORST, Gerrit		REMBRANDT (van	
van	NL	Rijn)	NL
KANDINSKY, Vasili	Russ	SANSOVINO, Andrea	It
KAUFFMANN,		SIQUEIROS, David	
Angelica	Swi	Alfaro	Mex
KOKOSCHKA, Oskar	A	VAN HUYSUM, Jan	NL
LAVREINCE, Nicolas/		VELASQUEZ, Diego	Sp
LAFRENSEN, Nils	Swe	or	
		VELAZQUEZ, Diego	Sp

10+letters

ARCHER-SHEE, Sir		MODIGLIANI,	
Martin	Ire	Amedeo	It
BARTOLOMMEO, Fra	It	PARRHASIUS	Ancient Gk
BOTTICELLI, Sandro	It	ROTHENSTEIN, Sir	
BUONARROTI		William	Eng
(Michelangelo)	It	SUTHERLAND,	
CARAVAGGIO,		Graham	Eng
Michelangelo da	It	TINTORETTO (Jacopo	
DA CORREG(G)IO,		Robusti)	It
Antonio	It	TOULOUSE-LAUTREC,	
DE ZURBARÁN,		Henri de	Fr
Francisco	Sp	VAN DE VELDE,	
GAINSBOROUGH,		Jan & Willem	NL
Thomas	Eng	VAN HONTHORST,	
GHIRLANDAIO bros	It	Gerrit	NL
GIACOMETTI,		VANMEEGEREN, Hans	
Alberto	Swi	(Vermeer forger)	NL
MACWHIRTER, John	Sc	VAN RUYSDAEL,	
MICHELANGELO		Jakob	NL
(Buonarroti)	It		

PAIR (s/l *pear, pare*). PR. OO (cricket sl). BRACE, COUPLE,
TWO (**pigeon** ~ = one of each sex); **comp** = *carriage.*
AFFIANCE, *ENGAGE*, MARRY, MATE, *WED.*
Pak Pakistan.
PALACE BISHOP'S/PRESIDENT'S/SOVEREIGN'S
RESIDENCE. Any grand building, *THEATRE* etc, **such as:**

ALEXANDRA (Eng)
ALHAMBRA (Sp)
BILSKIRNIR (Nor myth)
BLENHEIM (Eng)
BUCKINGHAM (Eng)
CAESAR'S (US)
CNOSSOS (*Minos*)
CRYSTAL (Eng)
DALKEITH (Sc)
DOGE'S (It)
ELYSÉE (Fr)
HAMPTON COURT (Eng)
HATFIELD (Eng)
HOLYROOD (Sc)
KENSINGTON (Eng)
LAMBETH (Eng)

NONSUCH (Eng)
PINK (Arg)
ST JAMES'S (Eng)
SANS SOUCI (Ger)
SCONE (Sc)
STRELSAU (fict, *Hope*)
ST STEPHEN'S (Eng)
TOWER OF LONDON
(Eng)
UFFIZI (It)
VERSAILLES (Fr)
VICTORIA (Eng)
WESTMINSTER (Eng)
WHITEHALL (Eng)
WINDSOR (Eng)

PALAEOLITHIC *AGE*.
PALATIAL GRAND, SPLENDID; like a *palace*.
PALLADIUM 1. *METAL*; PD (*chem*). *THEATRE*. 2. Any image of Pallas Athene, conferring safety on the town which possessed it, but especially that held at *Troy* until it was removed by *Odysseus* and Diomedes.
PALLAS 1. = *ATHENE* [*Palladium*]. 2. A *TITAN*, s of Orius and Eurybia, mar *Styx* and f of *Nike*. 3. A minor *PLANET*.
PALM 1. *HAND*. CONCEAL. LAUREL, VICTORY GARLAND. 2. TREE; **types**: ARECA, ARENG, BACTRIS, BAMBOO ~, CALUMNUS, CARNAUBA, COCO(A)NUT, COHUNE, COKERNUT, CURYPHA, DATE ~, DOUM, EJOO, ELAEIS, FAN ~, GOMUTI, -O, GRU-GRU, JUPATI, KITOOL, -TUL, MORICHE, NARGIL, NIKAU, NIPA, OIL ~, PALMETTO, PALMYRA, PAXIUBA, *PHOENIX*, PIASSABA, -VA, RAPHIA ~, RATTAN ~, RHAPSIS, SAGO ~, TALIPAT, -ET, -OT, -UT, TUCUM, WAX ~, WINE, ZALACCA, ZAMIA [frond, raffia].
~ **OIL** FAT, GREASE (candles, soap). BRIBE (crypt).
PAN 1. DISH, POT. BERATE, CRITICIZE. WASH *GOLD* [*digger*]. SWING (photo). PETER [*Barrie*; Never Never *Land*]. 2. Gk *god* of *shepherds*; chief *satyr*. 3. With hyphen = all-embracing, universal, e.g. pan-American.
PANDORA 1. STRINGED INSTRUMENT. 2. Gk myth first woman on earth. She opened the box containing all human ills,

and only Hope remained inside. 3. A minor *PLANET*.

PANE (s/l *pain*). *SHEET*. HAMMERHEAD (hence H), PEEN.

PANIC ALARM, *FEAR*, FRIGHT, TERROR. *GRASS*.

PAPER PRESS, RAG **names** (all ®): HERALD, MIRROR,
STAR, SUN, TELEGRAPH, TIMES, TRIBUNE etc.
DECORATE. BUMF, DOCUMENT, RECORD. WRAPPER.
PAPYRUS [*measure*, origami (*Jap*)]; *anniversary* (1st).

PAPERWORK ADMINISTRATION, ARCHIVES, BUMF (sl),
RECORDS, RED TAPE. ORIGAMI (Jap, crypt).

PAR (s/l *pa*). *EQUAL*, *EVEN*, LEVEL. *AVERAGE, MEAN*.
BOGEY, NORM, STANDARD (*golf*).

PARADISE EDEN, ELYSIUM, *HEAVEN*, UTOPIA,
VALHALLA [Asphodel meadows].

PARASITE Animal or plant living on another [host, commensal],
e.g. **bot**: DODDER, EPIPHYTE, *FUNGUS*, GALL-NUT,
MISTLETOE, SAPROPHYTE, YEAST; **zool**: ACARNO,
BACTERIUM, FLEA, GUINEA-WORM, ICHNEUMON
FLY, LEECH, LOUSE, TAPE-WORM, TRICHINA; hence
HANGER-ON, TOADY. DROPPING-ZONE (mil, crypt).

PARCAE Rom *goddesses* of the three *FATES*. **Gk** = MOIRAI.

PARE (s/l *pair, pear*). *CUT, PEEL*, SHAVE, *TRIM*, WHITTLE.

PARENTAL GUIDANCE A, *CENSORSHIP* (film).

PARIS 1. *Capital* of France, hence (crypt) F. PLASTER. 2. Gk
myth s of *Priam*. He judged *Aphrodite* the fairest against *Athene*
and *Hera* for a coveted golden apple. Loved Oenone before he
ran off with *Helen*, who was mar to Menelaus, and thus started
the war of *Troy*. He k Achilles by shooting him in the heel.
3. *Shak* character(s).

PARKING P. [Mansfield Park, *Austen* (crypt)].

PARLIAMENT COUNCIL, DEBATING CHAMBER,
LEGISLATIVE ASSEMBLY [Commons, Lords, the House].

PARNASSUS Gk myth mountain home of the *Muses*.

PARROT COPY, MIMIC, REPEAT. RIVER. *BIRD*
(Psittaciformes). **Types**: BUDGERIGAR, BUDGIE,
COCKATIEL, COCKATOO, CONURE, CORELLA,
KAKA (NZ), KAKAPO (NZ), KEA (NZ), LORIKEET,
LORY, MACAW, NESTOR, PAR(R)AKEET, PAROQUET,
ROSELLA, ZATI. **Celeb**: Capt Flint (*Stevenson*), POLYNESIA
(*Lofting*). [Sick as a ~ = disappointed, *upset* (**opp** = over the
moon)]. **Sea** ~ = puffin.

PARSON 1. *CHURCHMAN*, INCUMBENT, PADRE (mil),
RECTOR, VICAR; GOD-BOTHERER, SKY-PILOT (sl);

celeb (fict): ~ Adams (Fielding); Amos Barraclough (*Kipling*); Boanerges (Mrs Oliphant); Brocklehurst (Jane Eyre, *Brontë*); Father Brown (*Chesterton*); Vicar of Bray (18th-cent song); Caponsacchi (Browning); Chadband (Bleak Ho, *Dickens*); Evans (*Shak*); Elmer Gantry (Sinclair Lewis); Archdeacon Grantly (Trollope); Harding (Trollope); Charles Honeyman (Thackeray); Friar John (Rabelais); Dr Middleton (Meredith); Primrose (Goldsmith); Quiverful (Trollope); Dominie Samson (*Scott*); ~ Samson (Thackeray); Obadiah Slope (Trollope); Shepherd Stiggins (Pickwick, *Dickens*); Dr Syntax (Coombe); Friar Tuck (Ivanhoe, *Scott*); Vicar of Wakefield (Goldsmith); and char in *Chaucer*. 2. BIRD, TUI [~'s nose].

PART 1. *Anag. GO, LEAVE*, QUIT. ROLE. PIECE, SOME (**opp** = *all*). COMPONENT, SPARE. **Comp** = parcel. SPLIT HAIRS (crypt). 2. Hidden word, e.g. **Love is part of Much Ado re Nothing** (5) = ADO*RE. 3. **Pl** = word split, e.g. **Romantic in parts about Talia** (7) = I*TALIA*N.

PARTNER ASSOCIATE, *COMPANION*, FELLOW, OPPO. WIFE/HUSBAND. **Pl** = EW, NS, HC, RL. MAST GATE (naut). DARBY & JOAN, NOW & THEN, PROP & COP etc.

PARTRIDGE GAME BIRD; **assembly** = covey. [1st day of Christmas].

PARTY AT HOME, BALL, *DANCE*, *DO*, FUNCTION, RECEPTION, SHINDIG. SIDE (leg). **Politics**: ALLIANCE, CON, DEM, L, LAB, LIB, REP, SDP, TORY, WHIG.

PASS *HAND*. OVERHAUL, OVERTAKE. ACCEPT, APPROVE, LET GO BY. *COL*, DEFILE. GRADUATE, SUCCEED; NO HONOURS (crypt). AMOROUS ADVANCE. LUNGE, THRUST (*fencing*); VERONICA (*bullfighting*).

PASSENGER FARE. (FELLOW) TRAVELLER. BURDEN, LIABILITY.

PAST (s/l passed). 1. ANTIQUE, BYGONE, *EX*, FORMER, GONE BY. 2. Use past tense, e.g. **Past art** = WERT.

PASTE CONFECTION, MIXTURE. GLUE, STICK. IMITATION *DIAMOND/GEM*.

PATIENCE ENDURANCE, PERSEVERANCE [*Job*]. CARD GAME. PLANT.

PATRICK *PATRON SAINT* (Ire). [Bishop, Pope Celestine, 17 March].

PATRON SAINT TUTELARY PROTECTOR; **celeb (with feast day)**: AGATHA (bellfounders, nurses; 5 Feb), ANDREW

(Scotland, 30 Nov), ANNE (Brittany; 26 Jul), ANTONY (lost property; poor; 13 Jun), BARBARA (*firemen*; *gunners*; 4 Dec), BLAISE (woolcombers; 3 Feb), BRIDGET (*Ireland*; 1 Feb), CATHERINE (attorneys; *scholars*; wheelwrights; 25 Nov), CECILIA (church music; 22 Nov), CHRISTOPHER (wayfarers; 25 Jul), CRISPIN(IAN) (leatherworkers; 23 Oct), *DAVID* (Wales; 1 Mar), DENYS (*France*; 9 Oct), ELMO/ERASMUS (*sailors*; 2 Jun), EUSTACE (*hunters*; Madrid; 20 Sep), FRANCIS OF ASSISI (animals; 4 Oct), *GEORGE* (England; *Portugal*; armourers; 23 Apr), GILES (*beggars*; blacksmiths; *cripples*; 1 Sep), HUBERT (*huntsmen*; 3 Nov), JOAN OF ARC (*France*; 30 May), JOHN OF GOD (*booksellers*; printers; 8 Mar), JOSEPH (*workers*; 1 May), JUDE (afflicted; 28 Oct), LEONARD (*prisoners*; 6 Nov), LUKE (physicians; 18 Oct), MARGARET (women in travail; 20 Jul), MAURUS (charcoal burners; 15 Jan), MENAS (merchants; 11 Nov), MONICA (Christian mothers; 27 Aug), NICHOLAS (*children*; *sailors*; 6 Dec), PANTALEON (physicians; 27 Jul), *PATRICK* (*Ireland*; 17 Mar), SABAS (Serbia; 14 Jan), TERESA (foreign missions; 3 Oct), URSULA (*schools*; 21 Oct), VALENTINE (lovers; 14 Feb), VITUS (*sickness*; 15 Jun), WENCESLAS (Bohemia; 28 Sep).

PATTERN (s/l pattern). EXAMPLE. DESIGN, MATRIX, *MODEL*, MOULD, TEMPLATE, TEMPLET.

PAUL SAUL; *apostle*; b in Tarsus c.a.d. 3, ~ was anti-Christian until converted by *Jesus* in a vision, and became travelling missionary to the Gentiles (c.f. *Peter* ditto to Jews). Imprisoned by Rom *governor* Felix, and later shipwrecked at Malta; martyred by *Herod c*. a.d 65 under *Nero*.

PAUL'S LETTERS COLOSSIANS, CORINTHIANS, EPHESIANS, GALATIANS, PHILEMON, PHILIPPIANS, *ROMANS*, THESSALONIANS, TIMOTHY, TITUS. P, A, U and L (crypt).

PAUSE (s/l paws). BREVE, *REST* (mus). BREAK, HESITATION, INACTION, *INTERVAL*. AWAIT, LINGER, TARRY (**opp** = *go*on*).

PAWNBROKER POP, UNCLE [*pledge*; *weasel*]. *PAWNEE* (crypt).

PAWNEE *AMERICAN INDIAN*. *PAWNBROKER* (crypt).

PAX 1. PEACE. TRUCE! 2. Rom *goddess* of PEACE: **Gk** = *IRENE*.

PAY PAYMENT, *SALARY*, *SCREW*, WAGES. DISCHARGE,

RECOMPENSE, RETURN, REWARD, *SETTLE*. CAULK,
STOP (naut).
PAYER PAYMASTER; *SETTLER* (crypt).
PB *LEAD* (*chem*). PAPERBACK.
PC PARISH COUNCIL. PER CENT. POLICE CONSTABLE.
POST CARD. PRIVY COUNCILLOR.
PD PALLADIUM (*chem*). POLICE DEPARTMENT.
PE PHYSICAL EXERCISE; GYMNASTICS, PT. PERU
(*car plate*).
PEACE (s/l *piece*). 1. ORDER, QUIET, TRANQUILLITY (**opp**
= *war*); RIVER (Can). 2. **Gk goddesses** = *HORAE*, especially
IRENE (**Rom** = *PAX*).
PEACH *FRUIT*; *TREE*. BETRAY. DOLLY-BIRD, SMASHER.
PEAK (s/l pique). *HEAD*; HOLD; TILT (naut). BRIM, APEX,
SUMMIT. PINE, WASTE AWAY.
PEAL (s/l *peel*). *RING*. CLAP, LOUD NOISE (thunder).
GRILSE.
PEAR (s/l *pair*, *pare*). FRUIT/TREE (genus Pyrus communis); **pl
comp** = *apples* (*rh sl*). [**beverage**: perry]; **types**: BARTLETT,
BERGAMOT, COMICE, CONFERENCE, FERTILITY,
JOSEPHINE DE MALINES, LOUISE BONNE, WILLIAMS
BON CHRETIEN, WINTER NELIS; ALLIGATOR,
AVOCADO; ANCHOVY; PRICKLY ~.
PEARL *GEM* [oyster]; *anniversary* (30th); 'MARGARET'.
PRECIOUS THING. *COLOUR* (white). BEAD, DROP.
PICOT (lace). *BUCK* (films). RIVER (US). *TYPEFACE*.
PECK KISS; STAB WITH BEAK/BILL. *MEASURE*.
GREGORY ~ (films).
PECULIAR *Anag*. PARTICULAR, SPECIAL. ODD,
STRANGE. EXEMPT. PRIVILEGED (eccles).
PEEL (s/l *peal*). PARE, *SKIN*. JOHN ~ (*huntsman*; *dogs*).
RIVER (*Can*). *ROBERT* ~ (*police*). SHOVEL. TOWER.
PEELED (s/l pealed). 1. PARED, SKINNED. 2. Remove first and
last letters, e.g. **Called peeled orange** (4) = *RANG*.
PEELER SKINNER (crypt). *POLICEMAN*.
PEER (s/l *pier*). NOBLEMAN: *BARON*, DUKE, EARL, *LORD*,
MARQUIS, VISCOUNT. EQUAL, *FELLOW*. APPEAR;
LOOK, PEEP, PRY. ~ GYNT (mus, Grieg). [Iolanthe
(*G & S*)].
PEERESS FEM *PEER*. LADY LOOKER (crypt).
PEGASUS 1. Gk myth winged *horse* of *Bellerophon*.
2. *Constellation*. 3. Badge of the Airborne Forces.

PELT *SHY*, THROW. *SKIN*.

PEN BALLPOINT, BIRO, QUILL, STYLO, WRITE(R); **comp** = ink. SCRIBBLE. CAGE, CORRAL, ENCLOSURE, *FOLD*, STY, TORIL (*bullfighting*). SWAN (*fem*).

PENELOPE 1. Gk myth wife of *Ulysses* and m of Telemachus who, to deter suitors in her husband's absence, said she could not answer them until she had finished making a *cloak* for Laertes, her f-in-law; each night she undid the previous day's work. 2. A minor *PLANET*. BIRD.

PENNILESS 1. BROKE; BORACIC LINT (*rh sl*). 2. Remove letters D or P from word, e.g. **Encourage to clean out – penniless** (4) = (p)URGE.

PENNY D, P. *COIN, COPPER*.

PENNYWEIGHT DWT, *MEASURE*.

PENSION LIFE PAYMENT, RETIREMENT PAY. BOARDING HOUSE. [*football* team].

PENULTIMATE LAST BUT ONE, hence Y (crypt).

PEP *GO*, *SPIRIT*, VIGOUR, ZIP. ENCOURAGE, GINGER. INVESTMENT PLAN.

PEPYS (s/l peeps). *DIARIST*, NAVY SECRETARY, SAM(UEL), *WRITER* [Evelyn].

PERCH LENGTH, *MEASURE, POLE, ROD* (5$\frac{1}{2}$ yds). BASS, FISH. BALANCE; BAR, RAIL, ROOST. ALIGHT, *REST, SETTLE*.

PERFORM ACT, PLAY, *SING*. CARRY OUT, *DO, EXECUTE*.

PERFORMING ACTING, ON STAGE; *TURNING* (crypt). DOING.

PERI FAIRY, GOBLIN (Pers myth; Jamshid), IMP, *SPIRIT*, SPRITE [Iolanthe, *G & S*].

PERIOD CLASS, TUITION. FULL STOP (US). PORTION OF TIME (hence TIM, ME etc, crypt), e.g. YEAR, LUSTRUM (5 yrs), QUINQUENNIUM (5 yrs), SEPTENARY (7 yrs), DECADE (10 yrs), CENTURY (100 yrs), MILLENNIUM (1,000 yrs).

PERIODICAL RECURRING, REGULAR. MAGAZINE, WEEKLY. [astronomy; chemistry].

PERIPHITES Gk myth *giant*, too large for his own legs to carry, who beat travellers to death with a massive *club*; he was finally k by *Theseus*.

PERMANENT LASTING, INDEFINITE. MARCEL, *WAVE*.

~ **WAY** *RAILWAY*; IRON WAY, *TRACK*.

Pers Persian.

PERSE (s/l purse). 1. COLOUR, BLUE (*herald*). COLLEGE (C). *POET* (Fr). IN ITSELF, INTRINSICALLY (Lat, 2 words). 2. An *Oceanid*, m of *Circe* by *Helios*.

PERSEPHONE Also CORA. Gk myth Q of the *Underworld*; d of *Zeus* and *Demeter*, she was carried off by *Pluto*. Hermes finally got her back, but she had eaten (a pomegranate seed) in the lower world, so she was permitted to spend only 8 months each year in the upper world – in order that Demeter would allow it to produce its fruits. **Rom** = PROSERPINE.

PERSEUS 1. Gk myth s of *Zeus* (who *transformed* into a shower of gold to visit *Danae* in her prison cell and f ~). ~ k *Medusa*, helped by *Athene*, the magic sword Herpe, the helmet of *Hades*, winged sandals, a magic bag and a mirror (he looked at Medusa only in the mirror, put her severed head in the bag, and escaped on winged heels, wearing the helmet which made him invisible). Mar to *Andromeda*, he eventually fulfilled a prophecy by (accidentally) killing Acrisius, his own grandfather. 2. *Constellation*.

PERSIAN IRANIAN [Xerxes, Darius, Satrap]. *CAT*, CATTY, FELINE; MIAOW.

PERT *ARCH*, JAUNTY, SAUCY (**opp** = *retiring*).

PET CARESS, PAT; *DARLING*, FAVOURITE, MASCOT. FONDLE, TAME (animal). TANTRUM, TIFF; ILL-HUMOURED, OFFENCE.

PETER 1. CORDITE, DYNAMITE, EXPLOSIVE, TNT. PRISON CELL; SAFE, STRONGBOX; WITNESS BOX (all sl). FADE, GIVE OUT. BLUE ~ (flag). BOY'S NAME; 'A ROCK'; **celeb**: ~ the Great (Russ *emperor*, tsar); ~ the *Hermit* (Fr monk); ~ Pan (*Barrie*); *Shak* chars. 2. Known as Simon originally, St ~ was the s of Jonas and br of Andrew; he was a fisherman. A leading disciple who became a missionary (to the Jews; c.f. *Paul*), and one of the 12 *apostles*, he was the first Pope. Probably martyred in Rome *c.* A.D. 66 under *Nero*.

PETERBOROUGH Episcopal sig = PETRIBURG.

PETRIBURG *Episcopal sig* of PETERBOROUGH.

PG PARENTAL GUIDANCE (film *censorship*). LODGER, PAYING GUEST. [*monkey*].

PH ACIDITY, ALKALINITY (Sorensen).

PHAETON 1. CARRIAGE. BIRD. 2. Gk myth s of *Helios* and Clymene. He drove his f's *chariot* so dangerously that *Zeus* struck him down with a thunderbolt. [*Jehu*].

-PHAGY Eating of . . . , e.g. **hippophagy** = horses, **ichthyophagy** = fishes.

PHALANX INFANTRY, LINE, *SOLDIERS* (Gk; hoplite). *BONE*. STAMENS (bot).

PHANTOM *GHOST*, SPECTRE. *AIRCRAFT*. ~ of the Opera (Leroux).

PHARAOH (s/l faro). KING OF EGYPT (= GREAT HOUSE) [*Ptolemy* (q.v. for list)].

PHIL (s/l fill). PHILADELPHIA. PHILHARMONIC (mus). PHILOSOPHY. PHILIPPIANS. FLUTER.

PHILOGYNIST *Lover* of women.

PHILOSOPHER WISDOM SEEKER; MORALIZER, THEORIZER; **celeb**: ANAXAGORAS (Gk), ANISTHENES (Gk), APEMANTHUS (*Shak*), THOMAS AQUINAS (It), ARISTIPPUS (Gk), ARISTOTLE (Gk), ARTEMIDORUS (*Shak*), CATO (Rom), CHRYSIPPUS (Gk), DEMOCRITUS (Gk), DESCARTES (Fr), DIDEROT (Fr), DIODOTUS (Rom), *DIOGENES* (Gk), EPICTETUS (Gk), EPICURUS (Gk), ERASMUS (NL), EURIPIDES (Gk), HEGEL (Ger), HYPATIA (Gk, fem), JANET (Fr), KANT (Ger), LEUCIPPUS (Gk), MONTAIGNE (Fr), NEWTON (Eng), NIETZSCHE (Ger), PASCAL (Fr), *PLATO* (Gk), PROTAGORAS (Gk), RUSSELL (Eng), SANTAYANA (Sp), SCHOPENHAUER (Ger), SCHWEGLER (Ger), SCHWEIZER (Swi), SENECA (Rom), SOCRATES (Gk), SPINOZA (NL), SWEDENBORG (Swe), *SWIFT* (Eng), THALES (Gk), VOLTAIRE (Fr), XENOCRATES (Gk), ZENO (Gk). [~'s stone, alchemy; metaphysical ~, moral ~, natural ~].

PHLEGETHON *PYRIPHLEGETHON*.

PHOBIA *AVERSION*.

PHOEBE 1. A Titaness, Gk d of *Uranus* and *Ge*. 2. Associated with Artemis/*Diana* as goddess of the *moon* (MND, *Shak*). 3. A minor *planet*, the smallest satellite of *Saturn*. *BIRD*.

PHOEBUS Rom *god* of the *SUN*; also SOL. **Gk** = *APOLLO*, HELIOS; **Egy** = HORUS, RA; **Nor** = FREY; **Pers** = MITHRA; **Phoen** = BAAL.

Phoen Phoenicia, ~n.

PHOENIX 1. Fabulous bird which, every 500 years, built a pyre and burned itself to death; it was then reborn from the ashes. The ~ Generation (*Williamson*). FUM (Ch). 2. A *constellation*. 3. DATE *PALM*. *THEATRE*. 4. US *State* capital.

PHOSPHORUS 1. Gk name for *VENUS* when seen as the *MORNING STAR* (**Rom** = Lucifer); **opp** = *Hesperus*.
2. *MINERAL*, P (*chem*).

PI (s/l *pie*). 1. DEVOUT, OVER-RELIGIOUS, PIOUS. 2. Gk letter; in maths, the ratio of the circumference of a circle to its diameter.

PIANO P, *QUIET* (mus); and see *music* (3). INSTRUMENT (mus).

PIE (s/l *pi*). *Anag.* COTTAGE ~, PIZZA, SHEPHERD'S, TART. *BIRD*, MAGPIE. *DOG*, MONGREL. CHAOS.

PIECE (s/l *peace*). 1. *BIT*, MORSEL; **pl comp** = *bits*. 2. Hidden word, e.g. **Piece of Spanish amateur pretence** (4) = SH*AM.
3. Constituent part of object indicated, e.g. **Dollar piece** = CENT.

PIER (s/l *peer*). *JETTY*. BRIDGE SUPPORT.

PIG POLICEMAN (sl). BILLET, LUMP (iron). GLUTTON. Quadruped (genus Suidae), SWINE, TUSKER; **assembly** = drove, herd; **male** = BOAR; BARROW (castrated ~); **female** = SOW; **offspring** = PIGLET, SHOAT/SHOTE. [*Ch calendar*]. **Celeb**: MAJOR, MINIMUS, *NAPOLEON*, SNOWBALL, *SQUEALER* (Animal Farm, *Orwell*); BLAND, ROBINSON (*Potter*); BLANDINGS, Empress of (*Wodehouse*). **Breeds**:

BABIRUS(S)A	*LINCOLN*
BERKSHIRE	RAZORBACK
BUSH	SADDLEBACK
ESSEX	TAMWORTH
LANDRACE	WARTHOG
LARGE BLACK	WESSEX
LARGE WHITE	WILD BOAR

PIGEON BIRD; HOMER (crypt); CUSHAT, NUN ~, POUTER ~, TURBIT; **assembly** = flock, loft. MARK, SUCKER.
[~ **pair** = one of each (boy and girl)].

PIGS EAR BEER (*rh sl*).

PIKE *FISH*, GAR, JACK. HILLTOP. ROAD, TOLL, TOLL-BAR. BILL, HALBERD, *WEAPON*. *DIVE* (swim).

PILATE PONTIUS. Mar to Procula; a bibl Rom *judge* and *governor* of Judea and Samaria, who tried *Jesus*. Ruled harshly, recalled to Rome, sui.

PILE CASTLE, HEAP, STATELY HOME. *POST*, STAKE. *NAP*. NUCLEAR FURNACE. **Pl** = HAEMORRHOIDS.

PILE-UP ACCIDENT, COLLISION, SMASH. CARPET (crypt).

ELIP (dn, crypt).

PILGRIM 1. HOLY VOYAGER, TRAVELLER, VOYAGER [Haj (Mos); Islam; Mecca. Canterbury Tales (*Chaucer*); scollop/scallop]. MAYFLOWER SETTLER [~ Fathers (Plymouth, Mass, 1620)]. 2. From Bunyan's Pilgrim's Progress (from City of Destruction to Celestial City): CHRISTIAN, FAITHFUL, HOPEFUL [Apollyon (angel), Greatheart (guide to Christiana), Giant Despair (lord of Doubting Castle), Slough of Despond].

PILLAGE LOOT, PLUNDER, *SACK*. DISPENSARY (crypt).

PILLARS OF HERCULES Old name for ABYLA (CEUTA) and CALPE (GIBRALTAR).

PILOT AVIATOR, FLIER (**Union** = BALPA). *DOG* (Brontë). GUIDE, NAVIGATOR, *STEERSMAN*. TEST PRODUCT. *FISH*.

PINAFORE FROCK, PINNY; GREMIAL (*church dress*); OVERDRESS (crypt). LIGHT OPERA (*G & S*).

PINCH *STEAL* [*robber*]. GRIP, NIP, SQUEEZE. SMALL QUANTITY. EMERGENCY. ARREST. DRUDGE (Martin Chuzzlewit, *Dickens*); *SCHOOLMASTER* and *CONJUROR* (C of Errors, *Shak*).

PINE LANGUISH, LONG, YEARN; PEAK, WASTE. *TREE*; DEAL, TIMBER.

PINK *FLOWER*, CARNATION; *COLOUR*, PALE RED, *ROSE*. *SNOOKER* BALL (score 6). RED HUNTING COAT. PERFECT. PRICK, WOUND. KNOCK, PRE-IGNITION. *BOAT* (sailing).

PINKERTON Lieutenant Benjamin Franklin ~, USS *Lincoln* (Mme *Butterfly*, Puccini). *DETECTIVES* (US).

PIOUS *PI*, RELIGIOUS.

PIPE BRIAR, CHURCHWARDEN, CLAY, COB, MEERSCHAUM [*Holmes*]. TUBE [*Pluto*]. DRESS, TRIM. *MEASURE* (beer, port). REED (mus). CONDUIT, *SEWER*.

PIPER BAGPIPE PLAYER, MUSICIAN [10th day of *Christmas* in song]. BOATSWAIN (crypt). HANDKERCHIEF (crypt). *SMOKER*, SHERLOCK *HOLMES* (crypt). PAN (crypt).

PIRATE COPY, PLUNDER, STEAL; *BORROW*. *SPIDER*. BUCCANEER, CORSAIR, FREEBOOTER, PRIVATEER, ROVER [*cat. G & S*], SEA WOLF; **notorious**:

JOHN AVERY (LONG BEN)
JEAN *BART*

BEN-ALI (*Lofting*)
BLACKBEARD (EDWARD TEACH)
BLACK DOG (Treasure Island, *Stevenson*)
BLIND PEW (Treasure Island, *Stevenson*)
BILLY BONES (Treasure Island, *Stevenson*)
BONITO (BENNETT GRAHAM)
ANNE BONNY (mar Rackham)
CALICO JACK (JOHN RACKHAM)
LORD CONRAD (Byron)
WILLIAM DAMPIER
FRANCIS *DRAKE*
JOHN ESQUEMELING
HENRY EVERY
FLINT (Treasure Island, *Stevenson*)
FREDERIC (*G & S*)
BEN GUNN (Treasure Island, *Stevenson*)
DIRK HATTERAICK
HOOK (Peter Pan)
PAUL JONES
WILLIAM KIDD
LAFITTE
SIR HENRY MORGAN
JOHN RACKHAM (CALICO JACK)
MARY *READ*
BASIL RINGROSE
BLACK BART ROBERTS
LONG JOHN *SILVER* (Treasure Island)
BARTHOLOMEW SHARP
SMEE (Peter Pan)
SWAN
EDWARD TEACH (or THATCH)
EDWARD THATCH (or TEACH)
CAPT THOMPSON
LIONEL WAFER
WILLIAM WALKER
Pl = *Football* team (US). ~s of Penzance (*G & S*).

PISTOL (s/l pistil, pistole). DERRINGER, FIREARM,
HANDGUN, *WEAPON*. *Shak* char (Merry Wives, H.iv, H.v;
mar Ms *Quickly*).
PITCH GROUND, PLAYING FIELD (*cricket*, *football* etc).
CAST, THROW; **comp** = toss. ASPHALT, BITUMEN, *TAR*.

BLACK (*colour*).

PITCHER *EWER*, URN. DELIVERER, BASEBALL PLAYER. UNSTEADY ONE. ROADMAN, ROAD WORKER (crypt). STALLHOLDER (crypt). DOG (*Orwell*).

PITCHFORK HAYFORK. *CAST*, THRUST. TUNING FORK (mus, crypt).

PITMAN *MINER* (**pl** and **union** = NUM). SHORTHANDED (crypt).

PITY COMPASSION, MERCY; RUTH (arch). *ALAS*; REGRET, SORROW, SORRY.

PL PLURAL. POLAND (*car plate*).

PLACE (s/l *plaice*). PUT, *SET*. SPOT. COUNTRY HOUSE, SEAT, STATELY HOME.

PLACED PUT, SET. SEATED. LANDED GENTRY (crypt).

PLAGUE AFFLICTION, PESTILENCE, PUNISHMENT. *ANNOY*, BOTHER, NUISANCE, *TROUBLE*. **Gk** and **Rom god** = *APOLLO*. **Bibl** ~s: water into blood; frogs; lice; flies; murrain; boils; hail; locusts; darkness; death of firstborn.

PLAICE (s/l *place*). FLAT *FISH*.

PLAIN (s/l *plane*). 1. CLEAR, EVIDENT, SIMPLE. STITCH (knitting; **opp** = purl). MOURN. 2. LEVEL/OPEN TRACT: KIRGHIZ (CIS), LLANO (S Am), PAMPAS (S Am), PRAIRIE (N Am), PUSZTA (Hung), SAVANNAH (tropics), SERENGETI (Tanz), STEPPES (CIS), TUNDRA (Arctic) [*grass*].

PLAN *Anag*. *CHART*, DESIGN, DIAGRAM, DRAWING, LAYOUT, MAP. ARRANGE, PLOT, METHOD, SCHEME. TIMETABLE.

PLANE (s/l *plain*). *TREE*. SCRAPER, SMOOTHER, TOOL. LEVEL, SURFACE. *AIRCRAFT*; GLIDE.

PLANET 1. CHASUBLE, VESTMENT (eccles). Daily ~, fict *newspaper* (*reporter*: Clark *Kent*, *Superman*). 2. Heavenly body, revolving round a star, as a satellite. **Major planets** of our own Sun (in order of increasing distance and with their own satellites or moons): *MERCURY, VENUS, EARTH* (Luna/Moon), *MARS* (Deimos, Phobos), *JUPITER* (Callisto, *Europa*, *Ganymede*, *Io*), *SATURN* (Dione, Enceladus, Hyperion, *Iapetus*, Janus, Mimas, *Miranda*, *Phoebus*, *Rhea*, Tethys, *Titan*), *URANUS* (Ariel, Oberon, Titania, Umbriel), *NEPTUNE* (Triton, *Nereid*), *PLUTO*. There are also thousands of smaller bodies orbiting the Sun, mainly between Mars and Jupiter, and most of them lumps of rock. Some 2,000 are large enough to be

identified and named as asteroids or **minor planets**, including:
CERES (the largest; dia 1,000 km), *VESTA* (dia 530 km),
PALLAS (dia 600 km) and *JUNO* (dia 240 km), plus *CHIRON*,
HERMES, *HYGEIA, ICARUS, IRIS, ISIS*, KRYPTON (fict),
*MINERVA, MINOS, MNEMOSYNE, NEMESIS, NIOBE,
PENELOPE, TROJANS*.
PLANT 1. FACTORY, MILL, WORKS; MACHINERY, TOOLS.
CONCEAL. HOAX. EMBED, FIX, SET. 2. *FLOWER* (q.v.),
FRUIT (q.v.), *HERB* (q.v.), REED, SHRUB, *SPICE, TREE*
(q.v.), *VEGETABLE* (q.v.), *WEED, WILD FLOWER/PLANT*
(q.v.); **parts**: carpel (ovary, ovule, stigma, style), nectary, petal,
pistil, root, sepal, stalk, stamen (anther, filament, pollen sac),
stem (bud, leaf, shoot), tendril, torus; and see **alternative names**
under *Flower*; **types**:

3-letters

BOX	*FOG*	IVY	UDO (Ch)
ERS	HOP	*RYE*	

4-letters

AIRA	DOOB	LING	TORE
ALFA	DURA	LYME	TUTU
ANIL	FERN	MOSS	VINE
ARUM	*FLAG*	REED	WEED
BENE	GILL	*RHEA*	WELD
BENT	*HEBE*	RUSA	WHIN
BLUE	HEMP	RUSH	WOAD
COCA	*HERB*	SEGO	WORT
COIX	IRID	SUNN	YARR
DISS	KANS	TARE	
DOCK	KAVA	TEFF	

5-letters

ABACA	BUNCH	FURZE	NAIAD
ANISE	*CAPER*	GORSE	ORACH
AROLD	CAREX	*GRASS*	ORYZA
BHANG	CHIVE	GUACO	OSHAC
BOHEA	COUCH	HALFA	PANAX
BRIER	CUTCH	HAULM	*PANIC*
BRIZA	DURRA	KEMPS	RHYNE
BROOM	DWALE	LIANA	SEDGE
BUGLE	ERICA	MELIC	SISAL

SPEAR	THORN	VETCH	VIOLA
SUMAC			

6-letters

ALSIKE	COCKLE	HEDERA	PHLEUM
ARNICA	COFFEE	HYPNUM	PRIVET
ARRACH	COMFRY	IBERIS	PROTEA
ARUNDO	CONIUM	KALMIA	PTERIS
BAJREE	COTTON	KNAWEL	QUITCH
BARLEY	COWAGE	KOUSSO	RADISH
BEDDER	CROTON	LOLIUM	RAMSON
BEJUCO	CUMMIN	LUPINE	REDTOP
BETONY	DARNEL	MADDER	RICCIA
BIBLUS	DESMID	MALLOW	RUPPIA
BLINKS	DODDER	MARRAM	SABINE
BOCAGE	FESCUE	MATICO	SESAME
BORAGE	FILAGO	MEDICK	SESBAN
BRIONY	FIMBLE	MYRTLE	SESELI
BRYONY	FIORIN	NARDUS	SMILAX
BURNET	FRUTEX	NETTLE	SPURGE
CACTUS	FUNGUS	ORACHE	SUMACH
CASSIA	GARLIC	ORCHIL	THRIFT
CEREUS	GERVAO	ORPINE	TWITCH
CICELY	GERVAS	OX-HEEL	UNIOLA
CICUTA	GINGER	PAIGLE	URTICA
CISSUS	GNETUM	PAMPAS	VISCUM
CITRUS	GROMEL	PEPPER	

7-letters

ACANTHA	BOG-RUSH	CLIVERS
ACONITE	BRACKEN	COMFREY
ALE-HOOP	BRAMBLE	CONEINE
ALFALFA	BUGLOSS	COWBANE
ALL-GOOD	BUG-WORT	COWSLIP
ALLSEED	BURDOCK	CUDWEED
ALYSSUM	CALUMBA	DIONAEA
AMELLUS	CAMPION	DITTANY
ASH-WORT	CARAWAY	DOGWOOD
ATROPIN	CARDOON	ELF-WORT
AWL-WORT	CARLUUS	ESPARTO
BLAWORT	CASSAVE	EULALIA
BOG-BEAN	CATMINT	FESTUCA

Plate 383

FOGGAGE	MALACCA	SKIRRET
FOXTAIL	MILFOIL	SORGHUM
GENISTA	MUGWORT	SPIGNEL
GINSENG (Ch)	MUSTARD	SQUITCH
HOGWEED	NAVETTE	THISTLE
HEATHER	OREGANO	TIMOTHY
HEDEOMA	OSMUNDA	VETIVER
HEMLOCK	POP-WEED	WAGWANT
HENBANE	RAGWORT	WHANGEE
JASMINE	SAFFRON	ZIZANIA
LUCERNE	SEA PINK	

8-letters

ABSINTHE	CINQFOIL	PLANTAIN
ACANTHUS	CLEAVERS	PONDWEED
AGRIMONY	COWBERRY	PUFFBALL
ANGELICA	DEMERARA	PUSS-TAIL
BANEWORT	DOG-GRASS	STAR-WORT
BEDSTRAW	DOG-WHEAT	TURMERIC
BERBERRY	ELEUSINE	VALERIAN
BINDWEED	FLAX-WORT	VERONICA
BULLRUSH	FLEABANE	VIRGINIA
CAMOMILE	FLEA-WORT	WORMWOOD
CANWABIS	GYNERIUM	XANTHIUM
CAPSICUM	MANDRAKE	

9+ letters

ARROWROOT	CROSSWORT	MARIJUANA
ARTEMISIA	DANDELION	MONKSHOOD
BALDMONEY	FORSYTHIA	PEPPERMINT
BELLADONNA	GILLYFLOWER	PUSSY WILLOW
BLACKBERRY	GOOSEBERRY	*RASPBERRY*
BLACKTHORN	HOREHOUND	SAGEBRUSH
BLUEBERRY	HORSETAIL	SPEARMINT
CHICKWEED	HUCKLEBERRY	SPEEDWELL
CHOKEBERRY	LADY'S THUMB	STINKWEED
CORIANDER	LIVERWORT	TUMBLEWEED
CRANBERRY	LOGANBERRY	WINTERGREEN

PLATE COVER, ENCASE, PROTECTION, VENEER. ENGRAVING (print). FILM (photo). RAILROAD. CUTLERY, EPNS, SHEFFIELD. GOLD/SILVER TROPHY.

ASHET (Sc), DISH, PLATTER. FALSE TEETH. *RIVER* (Braz). **Pl** = FEET (*rh sl*).

PLATINUM *METAL*; PT (*chem*); WHITE METAL; *anniversary* (70th). BLONDE.

PLATO 1. Gk *poet* of the Old Comedy (*c*.400 B.C.). 2. Gk *philosopher* (*c*.400 B.C.), the s of Aristo and Perictione. Pupil of *Socrates* (who, the night before ~ arrived, dreamed that a *swan* flew into his lap); ~ later travelled widely and associated with the *tyrant* Dionysius, who imprisoned him. Freed later by a friend, ~ taught philosophy in his garden, or the Academy; pupils incl Aristotle and Xenocrates.

PLAY ACT, DO, DRAMA, *PERFORM*, PIECE, REP, SHOW, STAGE, BUSK, STRUM. GAMBOL, HAVE FUN. *LATITUDE*, MOVEMENT, SLAP (mech). BOWL, *PITCH*, SERVE (games).

PLAYERS ACTORS, *CAST*, THESPIANS; [*Shak* chars]. BAND, MUSICIANS, OCTET, ORCHESTRA, QUARTET, SEXTET. *SIDE*, *TEAM*. *CIGARETTE*.

PLAYFUL *ARCH*. FROLICSOME, HUMOROUS, SPORTIVE.

PLAYGROUND COURSE, COURT, DIAMOND, FIELD, *LINKS*, *PITCH*, RINK, WICKET (all crypt). STAGE (crypt). NURSERY (crypt). SCHOOL COURTYARD, QUADRANGLE. And see *cricket*, *football*, *rugby* etc.

PLAYGROUP KINDERGARTEN, NURSERY SCHOOL. *CAST* (theat, crypt). *BAND*, ORCHESTRA, *PLAYERS* (crypt). *SIDE*, TEAM, XI, XV (crypt).

PLAYTIME CURTAIN-UP (crypt). RHYTHM, TEMPO (crypt). BULLY-OFF, FIRST BALL, KICK-OFF, START, WHISTLE (crypt). BREAK (school).

PLAY VIOLIN *BOW*, *FIDDLE*.

PLEASE (s/l pleas). BEGUILE, *CHARM*, GIVE PLEASURE (**opp** = *annoy*). THINK FIT. BE GOOD ENOUGH, KINDLY.

PLEDGE BAIL, PROMISE, SURETY. TOAST. ABSTINENCE (TT). HOCK, *PAWN*, *POP* [*weasel*].

PLEIADES Seven d of *Atlas*, placed among the stars and associated with *rain* and *nature*; **names**: ALCYONE, CELAENO, *ELECTRA*, *MAIA* (the eldest), STEROPE and TAYGETE, with one who was invisible, MEROPE.

PLIERS PINCERS. CABDRIVERS, TAXIS (crypt).

PLOT CABAL, *CONSPIRACY*; CONSPIRE, INTRIGUE, *PLAN*. *CHART*, NAVIGATE. ALLOTMENT, BED, GARDEN, GREEN, LAWN, PATCH, YARD (US).

PLOUGH 1. DIGGER, EARTH-MOVER, FARM IMPLEMENT, PLOW (US), SPIT TURNER, TILL(ER). SNOW CLEARER. PLANE. FAIL (exam). 2. CONSTELLATION; BIG DIPPER, CHARLES'S WAIN, URSA MAJOR [north star].

PLOVER WADING *BIRD*; **types**: AVOCET, CURLEW, DOTTEREL, KILLDEER, LAPWING, OYSTERCATCHER, PE(E)WIT, SNIPE, STILT, TURNSTONE, WHAUP, WHIMBREL.

PLUM (s/l plumb). BEST, GOOD. *COLOUR*. FRUIT TREE genus Prunus; **types**: CATALONIA, GREENGAGE, MIRABELLE, VICTORIA.

PLUTO 1. *DOG* (Disney). Pipe-line under the ocean (acronym); FUEL SUPPLY. 2. Gk and Rom *god* of the *UNDERWORLD* (**Gk** = HADES), br of *Jupiter* and *Neptune*, he carried off Proserpine (**Gk** = *Persephone*). Synonymous with AIDONEUS and DIS. 3. A *PLANET*.

PLUTUS Gk *god* of WEALTH.

PLUVIUS Rom *god* of *RAIN*. **Gk** = *JUPITER*.

PM AFTERNOON, POST MERIDIEM. *PRIME MINISTER*. PROMETHIUM (*chem*). POST MORTEM. PROVOST MARSHAL.

POET BARD, *WRITER*; LINESMAN (crypt); SWAN (of Avon). **Muses** = Calliope (epic ~), Euterpe (lyric ~), Thalia (bucolic ~). [*Argonaut*]. **Celeb** (PL = Poet Laureate):

3-letters

POE, Edgar Allen	US	PYE, Henry James (PL9)	Eng

4-letters

GRAY, Thomas	Eng	LI-PO (8th cent)	Ch
GUNN, Thomson William	Eng	MUIR, Edwin	Sc
		OWEN, Wilfred	Eng
HILL, Geoffrey William	Sc	POPE, Alexander	Eng
HOOD, Thomas	Eng	ROWE, Nicholas (PL4)	Eng
HUNT, James Henry Leigh	Eng	SADI	Pers
		TATE, Nahum (PL3)	Eng
LEAR, Edward	Eng	WAIN, John	Eng

5-letters

AUDEN, Wystan Hugh	Eng	LEWIS, Alun	Wal
BLAKE, William	Eng	LEWIS, Cecil Day (PL16)	Eng
BYRON, Lord George Gordon	Eng	LORCA, Federico	Sp
CRANE, Harold Hart	US	LUCAN, M Annaeus (A.D. 39–65)	Rom
DANTE (Alighieri)	It	MOORE, Marianne	US
DAVID (bibl)	Heb	NOYES, Alfred	Eng
DONNE, John	Eng	OLSON, Charles	US
ELIOT, Thomas Stearns	US/Eng	OPPEN, George	US
		PATER, Walter	Eng
FROST, Robert	US	PERSE, Jean St	Fr
GOSSE, Sir Edmund William	Eng	PLATH, Sylvia	US
		PLATO (428–389 B.C.)	Gk
GOWER, John	Eng	*POUND*, Ezra Loomis	US
HARDY, Thomas	Eng	SAADI	Pers
HOMER (*c*.1000 B.C.)	Gk	*SCOTT*, Sir Walter	Sc
KEATS, John	Eng	TASSO, Torquato	It
KEYES, Sidney	Eng	WATTS, Isaac	Eng
		YEATS, William Butler	Ire

6-letters

AUSTIN, Alfred (PL13)	Eng	JONSON, Ben (unofficial PL1)	Eng
BINYON, Robert Laurence	Eng	LARKIN, Philip	Eng
BISHOP, Elizabeth	US	LOWELL, Amy	US
CIBBER, Colley (PL6)	Eng	LOWELL, Robert	US
DOBSON, Henry Austin	Eng	MILTON, John	Eng
		PINDAR (522–442 B.C.)	Gk
DRYDEN, John (PL1)	Eng	*PORTER*, Peter	Aus
EUSDEN, Laurence (PL5)	Eng	RUSKIN, John	Eng
FULLER, Roy	Eng	SAPPHO (*c*.600 B.C.; fem)	Gk
GOETHE, Johann von	Ger	SEXTON, Anne	US
GRAVES, Robert Ranke	Eng	THOMAS, Dylan	Wal
		VIRGIL, Maro (70–19 B.C.)	Rom
HENLEY, William Ernest	Eng	WARTON, Thomas (PL8)	Eng
HORACE (65–8 B.C.)	Rom		
HUGHES, Ted (PL18)	Eng		

7-letters

ADDISON, Joseph	Eng	JOHNSON, Lionel	
BENTLEY, Edmund		Pigot	Eng
Clerihew	Eng	KHAYYAM, Omar	Pers
BLUNDEN, Edmund		*KIPLING*, Rudyard	Eng
Charles	Eng	LYDGATE, John	Eng
BRIDGES, Robert		MARVELL, Andrew	Eng
Seymour (PL14)	Eng	NEWBOLT, Sir Henry	
CARROLL, Lewis		John	Eng
(see *Alice*)	Eng	PLAUTUS, T Maccius	
CHAUCER, Geoffrey	Eng	(*c*.250 B.C.)	Rom
CORNISH, Sir		SHELLEY, Percy	
William	Eng	Bysshe	Eng
DARYUSH, Elizabeth	Eng	SITWELL, Dame Edith	Eng
DOUGLAS, Keith	Sc	SITWELL, Sacheverell	Eng
EUPOLIS (446–411		SKELTON, John	Eng
B.C.)	Gk	SOUTHEY, Robert	
FLECKER, James		(PL10)	Eng
Elroy	Eng	STEVENS, Wallace	US
GILBERT, Sir		TENNANT, Stephen	
William Schwenck	Eng	James Napier	Eng
HERBERT, George	Eng	TERENCE (190–158	
HERRICK, Robert	Eng	B.C.)	Rom
HOPKINS, Gerard		WHITMAN, Walt	US
Manley	Eng		

8-letters

BERRYMAN, John	US	MENANDER (342–291	
BETJEMAN, Sir John		B.C.)	Gk
(PL17)	Eng	PETRARCH,	
CRATINUS (519–422		Francesco	It
B.C.)	Gk	PHILAMON (myth)	Gk
DAVENANT, Sir Wm		PHILEMON (*c*.360	
(unofficial PL2)	Eng	B.C.)	Gk
FLETCHER, John	Eng	SHADWELL, Thomas	
GINSBERG, Allen	US	(PL2)	Eng
LANGLAND, William	Eng	TENNYSON, Alfred	
LAWRENCE, David		Lord (PL12)	Eng
Herbert	Eng	WILLIAMS, William	
MALLARMÉ,		Carlos	US
Stéphane	Fr		

9+ letters

AESCHYLUS
  (525–456 B.C.)   Gk
ARISTOPHANES
  (*c*.444 B.C.)   Gk
CAECILIUS
  (230-168 B.C.)   Rom
CHESTERTON, Gilbert
  Keith   Eng
COLERIDGE, Samuel
  Taylor   Eng
CUNSTANCE, Olive   Eng
DOOLITTLE, Hilda   US
FITZGERALD,
  Edward   Eng
GOLDSMITH, Oliver   Ire
LONGFELLOW, Henry
  Wadsworth   US

MASEFIELD, John
  (PL15)   Eng
PHILAMMON (myth)   Gk
PHRYNICHUS
  (*c*.500 B.C.)   Gk
SHAKESPEARE,
  William   Eng
SOPHOCLES
  (495–406 B.C.)   Gk
SWINBURNE, Algernon
  Charles   Eng
WHITEHEAD, William
  (PL7)   Eng
WORDSWORTH, William
  (PL11)   Eng

POETRY 1. LINES, ODE, *VERSE* (**opp** = prose). 2. **Gk myth Muse** = *CALLIOPE, ERATO*, EUTERPE.
POINT AIM, GIST, OBJECT. INDICATE, SHOW. HEADLINE, *NESS*, PT. APEX, *TIP*, TOE. NEEDLE, PIN. *CRICKETER*, FIELDER. E, N, S OR W, EAST, NORTH, SOUTH or WEST. PUNCTUATE. REFACE (bricks and mortar). SWITCH (rly).
POINTER *ARROW, DIRECTOR*, INDICATION. *DOG*.
POINTLESS 1. MEANINGLESS. NO SCORE. BATED, BLUNT. 2. Remove letters indicating cardinal points from word(s) indicated, e.g. **Type of communication that's read is now pointless** (5) = R*ADI**O*.
POISON DRINK (sl). CORRUPT, DEFAME, DESTROY, EMBITTER, ENVENOM, FESTER, INFECT, INJURE, KILL, MURDER, PERVERT, RANKLE, SPOIL, TAINT. DISCHARGE (med), DISEASE, EVIL, PUS, TOXICANT, TOXIN, VENOM (DEFOLIANT, FUNGICIDE, GERMICIDE, HERBICIDE, INSECTICIDE, PESTICIDE). **Types** = ANTIMONY, ARSENIC, ATROPINE, CARBON MONOXIDE, CHLORINE, CURARE, CYANIDE, DDT, HYOCINE, MUSTARD GAS, NABEE, NERVE GAS, NICOTINE, PHENOL, POTASSIUM CYANIDE, PRUSSIC ACID, PTOMAINE ~, RICIN, SCOPOLOMINE,

SULPHURIC ACID, STRYCHNINE, WARFARIN.
~ **plants**: ACONITE, ANTIAR, BANEWORT, BELLA
DONNA, DATURA, DEADLY NIGHTSHADE, DEATH
CAP *FUNGUS*, DEVIL'S BOLETUS, DIGITALIS,
EARTHY INOCYBE, FLY AGARIC, FOXGLOVE,
HEMLOCK, HENBANE, LOCOWEED, MONKSHOOD,
PANTHER CAP, POISON *IVY*, POKEWEED, SICKENER,
STINKHORN, TOADSTOOL (*fungus*), *UPAS*,
WOLF(S)BANE, WOOLLY MILK CAP, YELLOW
STAINING MUSHROOM.

Pol Poland (*car plate* = PL). Political.

POLE (s/l *poll*). N, S, NORTH, SOUTH. *MEASURE* (length):
PERCH, ROD. EAST EUROPEAN, SLAV. PILLAR, *POST*,
MAST. QUANT.

POLICE CAR BLACK MARIA, PANDA-CAR, SQUAD-CAR,
Z-CAR.

POLICEMAN BOBBY (Sir Robert Peel), BOW STREET
RUNNER (Henry Fielding), COP, DICK, PEELER (Sir
Robert Peel), *PIG*, ROZZER (all sl). *MP*, PC, SP. **Pl** = CID,
FBI, FEDS, PD, CONSTABLE, FORCE, FUZZ, GESTAPO,
SPECIALS [*detective*]. **Celeb**: DAY (*Kipling*), DIXON (TV),
MR PLOD.

POLISH *BUFF*, CLEAN, RUB; SHEEN, VENEER. OF
POLAND.

Polit Political.

POLL (s/l *pole*). HEAD. VOTE. *PARROT*. SAMPLE. CUT
OFF, LOP.

POLLUX 1. Gk myth *twin* of *Castor*. Skilful boxer and patron of
seamen. 2. One of the *Argonauts*.

POLY(HY)MNIA 1. Gk myth; one of the nine *Muses* (hymns).
2. A minor *PLANET*.

POMPEY 1. PORTSMOUTH (sl). FOUR (*rh sl*). 2. Roman leader
and general (106–48 B.C.). Maintained an uneasy alliance with
Caesar (with Crassus, they formed the first triumvirate in 60
B.C.); a great warrior. Mar Julia (d of Caesar). Political ambition
finally brought him into open conflict with Caesar, and civil war
followed. After being defeated at Pharsalus in 48 B.C., he fled to
Egypt, where he was ass by Septimus on the orders of Ptolemy's
ministers as he was being rowed ashore. 3. *Shak* chars (A and
C); and *clown* in M for M.

PONY *HORSE*, NAG. GLASS. £25 (sl).

POOL KIT BALLS, CUE, CHALK, REST, TABLE. DIVING

BOARD, FILTER.
POP *FATHER*. BANG. MUSIC. PAWN, PLEDGE (*weasel*).
DRINK. SOCIETY (*Eton* prefects).
PORCELAIN *CERAMICS*.
PORPOISE 1. UNDULATE. *CETACEAN* MAMMAL; WHALE
(genus Phocaena). **Assembly** = school. 2. Char in *Alice*.
PORT P, LARBOARD (arch), *LEFT*. *WINE*. *GATE*(WAY),
HARBOUR. *BEARING*, CARRIAGE. LIGHT, OPENING,
WINDOW.
Port Portugal (*car plate* = P). [*patron saint*].
PORTER BEER, *DRINK*. DOOR-KEEPER, GATE-KEEPER.
BAGGAGE CARRIER. *POET, WRITER*.
PORTUGAL P (*car plate*). [patron saint = St George].
POSEIDON Gk god of the sea (**Rom** = *NEPTUNE*), allied to
Nereus (**Rom** = Oceanus). Son of Cronos (**Rom** = *Saturn*) and
Rhea; br to *Zeus* and *Hades*. On dividing the universe with his
two brs, ~ got the Seas, Zeus the *Heavens*, and Hades the
Underworld. Mar *Amphitrite* and f of Proteus (*prophet* who
tended the *seals*) and Triton (*merman*); ~ was also god of
horses.
POSER PROBLEM. *MODEL*, SITTER.
POSSESSIVE 1. GRASPING, *MISERLY*, RAPACIOUS.
OWNING. 2. Put into the possessive case, e.g. **He is possessive**
= HIS.
POST *PILE*, *POLE*, STAKE. *DELIVERY*, MAIL; SEND.
APPOINTMENT, JOB, *SITUATION*. *MEASURE* (paper size).
POSTER *AD*, *BILL*, HOARDING, NOTICE, PLACARD.
LETTER SENDER (crypt).
POSTHOLDER INCUMBENT. ENVELOPE, LETTERBOX,
MAILBAG, MAILBOX, PILLARBOX (all crypt).
POST HOLE LETTER/PILLAR BOX (crypt).
POST SCRIPT AFTERTHOUGHT, PS.
POT COOKPOT, PAN. *DRUG*. POCKET, SINK (billiards, pool,
snooker).
POTASSIUM *METAL*; K (*chem*).
POTATO EARTH-APPLE (arch); MURPHY, SPUD, YAM;
KING EDWARD (hence R*ED or R*TED [eyes]).
POTENTIALLY *Anag*. CAN BE, MAYBE; CAPABLE,
POSSIBLY. CHARGED (elect).
POTTER 1. DAWDLE, LOITER, WANDER. WORK
(desultorily). BILLIARD/POOL/SNOOKER PLAYER
(crypt). CLAY WORKER, hence any maker of *ceramics* (q.v.);

BOWLER, THROWER (crypt); KHNUM (Egy), ~ who created the human race on his ~'s wheel (Anukis and Satis were his consorts). *CONDUCTOR* (mus). ~'s Field, see *Judas* (2). 2. Stephen ~, WRITER (humorist; Lifemanship; One-upmanship). 3. Beatrix ~, WRITER (children's); **books**: Appley Dapply's Nursery Rhymes; Benjamin Bunny; Cecily Parsley's Nursery Rhymes; A Fierce Bad Rabbit; The Flopsy Bunnies; Ginger and Pickles; Jemima Puddle-Duck; Johnny Town-Mouse; Little Pig Robinson; Miss Moppet; Mr Jeremy Fisher; Mr Tod; Mrs Tiggy-Winkle; Mrs Tittlemouse; Peter Rabbit; The Pie and the Patty Pan; Pigling Bland; Samuel Whiskers; Squirrel Nutkin; The Tailor of Gloucester; Timmy Tiptoes; Tom Kitten; Two Bad Mice; **characters**: Babbity Bumble (bee); Cousin Ribby, Mittens, Moppet, Simpkin, Tabitha Twitchit, Tom Kitten (*cats*); Chippy Hackee (chipmunk); John Joiner, Kep (*dogs*); *Drake*, Jemima & Rebecca Puddle-Duck (*ducks*); Mr Jackson, Jeremy Fisher (*frogs*); Mrs Tiggy-Winkle (hedgehog); Farmer *Potatoes*, Mr & Mrs McGregor, Tailor of Gloucester (humans); Johnny Town-Mouse, Thomasina, Mrs Tittlemouse (mice); Old Brown (*owl*); Bland, Robinson (*pigs*); Benjamin, Flopsy, Mopsy, Cottontail & Peter (*rabbits*); Aunt Maria, Samuel Whiskers (rats); Nutkin, Silvertail, Timmy & Goody Tiptoes, Twinkleberry (squirrels).

POTTERY *CERAMICS*; *anniversary* (9th). BILLIARD/POOL/SNOOKER HALL or TABLE (crypt). **Pl** = Staffs area producing china (*five towns*).

POUCHED BAGGED, CAUGHT, POSSESSED. *MARSUPIAL*.

POUND L, LB, *MEASURE* (weight). COIN, *CURRENCY* (UK); QUID, SOVEREIGN. PULSATE, THROB; *BEAT*, HAMMER, PUMMEL. CAGE, ENCLOSURE, PEN. *MILITARY LEADER*. POET, *WRITER*.

POUT *FISH*, WHITING. PROTRUDE, SULKY. [pigeon].

PP *PAGES*. PER PRO, PROXY. PAST PARTICIPLE.

PR PUBLIC RELATIONS, ADVERTISING.

PRASUTAGUS h of *Boadicea*.

PREACHER ADVOCATE, EVANGELIST, GOSPELLER, MORALIZER, PULPITEER, SERMONIZER, TUB-THUMPER; CLERGYMAN, *CHURCHMAN*. **Celeb**: BOANERGES (James & John, bibl); CALVIN (Fr); ECCLESIASTES (Koholeth, bibl); *EDDY*, Mary Baker (US); KNOX, John (Sc); LUTHER, Martin (Ger); MOSES (bibl); SPURGEON, Dr (Eng); WESLEY, John (Eng).

PRECIOUS STONE *GEM*, JEWEL.

PRECIS *SUMMARY*.
PREFIX HANDLE, TITLE. ADD, QUALIFY; INTRODUCE.
  [metric ~, see *International units*].
PREMISE INFERENCE, INTRODUCE [logic]. AFORESAID,
  FOREGOING. **Pl** = *BUILDING*, HOUSE, OFFICES.
PREPARED *Anag*. COMPOSED, FIT, READY. MIXED (*chem*).
  ALREADY PEELED (crypt).
PRESENT NOW; EXISTING, OCCURRING. READY
  (arch). AT HAND, ON SITE, THERE. DONATION,
  GIFT; EXHIBIT, OFFER. APPEAR, INTRODUCE,
  RECOMMEND. AIM, SALUTE (mil). *PUT UP* (petition). **Pl**
  = DOCUMENT (leg).
~ **DAY** NOW, *AD*. *ANNIVERSARY*, BIRTHDAY,
  CHRISTMAS etc (crypt).
PRESIDENT P. MANAGING DIRECTOR (US). GOVERNOR
  (arch), HEAD (of Board, State, Country); **~s of the USA since
  independence**:

*GEORGE WASHINGTON	Fed	1789–97
JOHN ADAMS	Fed	1797–1801
*THOMAS JEFFERSON	Rep	1801–09
JAMES MADISON	Rep	1809–17
JAMES MONROE	Rep	1817–25
JOHN QUINCEY ADAMS	Rep	1825–29
ANDREW JACKSON	Dem	1829–37
MARTIN VAN BUREN	Dem	1837–41
WILLIAM H. HARRISON	Whig	1841 (d in office)
JOHN TYLER	Whig	1841–45
JAMES K. POLK	Dem	1845–49
ZACHARY TAYLOR	Whig	1849–50 (d in office)
MILLARD FILLMORE	Whig	1850–53
FRANKLIN PIERCE	Dem	1853–57
JAMES BUCHANAN	Dem	1857–61
*ABRAHAM LINCOLN	Rep	1861–65 (ass)
ANDREW JOHNSON	Rep	1865–69
ULYSSES S. GRANT	Rep	1869–77
RUTHERFORD B. HAYES	Rep	1877–81
JAMES A. GARFIELD	Rep	1881 (ass)
CHESTER A. ARTHUR	Rep	1881–85
GROVER CLEVELAND	Dem	1885–89
BENJAMIN HARRISON	Rep	1889–93

GROVER CLEVELAND	Dem	1893–97
WILLIAM McKINLEY	Rep	1897–1901 (ass)
*THEODORE ROOSEVELT	Rep	1901–09
WILLIAM HOWARD TAFT	Rep	1909–13
WOODROW WILSON	Dem	1913–21
WARREN G. HARDING	Rep	1921–23 (d in office)
CALVIN COOLIDGE	Rep	1923–29
HERBERT C. HOOVER	Rep	1929–33
FRANKLIN D. ROOSEVELT	Dem	1933–45 (d in office)
HARRY S. TRUMAN	Dem	1945–53
DWIGHT D. EISENHOWER	Rep	1953–61
JOHN F. KENNEDY	Dem	1961–63 (ass)
LYNDON B. JOHNSON	Dem	1963–69
RICHARD M. NIXON	Rep	1969–74 (resigned)
GERALD R. FORD	Rep	1974–76 (nominated)
JIMMY CARTER	Dem	1976–80
RONALD REAGAN	Rep	1980–88
GEORGE BUSH	Rep	1988–92
BILL CLINTON	Dem	1992–

* = Head is carved at Mt Rushmore.

PRESS FOURTH *ESTATE*, NEWSPAPERS, *PAPERS*, *MEDIUM*. PRINTING MACHINE. API, BUP, GRUB STREET, REUTER, TASS, UPI, XINHUA. *IRON*; SQUASH, SQUEEZE. CONSCRIBE, SHANGHAI (naut arch). *URGE*.
~ **CHIEF** ED, PRO.
~ **GANG** RECRUITING PARTY [Andrew Miller, conscription, draft, national service, **opp** = *volunteer*]. EDITORS, NUJ, PRINTERS, *REPORTERS* (crypt).
~ **MAN** ED(ITOR), REPORTER. IRONER, LAUNDRYMAN (crypt).
PRETENDER CLAIMANT, OLD ~, YOUNG ~ (s, grandson of James II). ACTOR (crypt).
PRIAM Gk myth last K of *Troy*; mar (1) Arisbe, (2) Hecuba, and f of *Cassandra*, and 50 ss, incl *Hector* and *Paris*. [T and C (*Shak*)].
PRICKLY SPINY, THORNY. HEDGEHOG, PORCUPINE, URCHIN (crypt). TINGLING, UP-TIGHT.
PRIDE 1. AMOUR-PROPRE, ARROGANCE [*herald*]. HUBRIS. BEST, PICK. [~ and Prejudice (*Austen*); fall].

2. *Assembly* of lions.

PRIEST CANON, *CHURCHMAN* (q.v. for list), MINISTER; TQADDIK (Heb) [*Chaucer*]. *AARON, ELI, ELIJAH, ELISHA,* EZEKIEL; THOMAS A BECKET (this turbulent ~, Hii); HUME (*Shak*). *ISLAND.*

PRIMARY COLOURS GREEN, RED, VIOLET (in painting: BLUE, RED, YELLOW).

PRIMATE SENIOR *CHURCHMAN.* APE, HIGH MAMMAL, MAN, *MONKEY.*

PRIME MINISTER PRINCIPAL MINISTER OF STATE, PM; CABINET MAKER (crypt). **British ~s since 1900**:

MARQUIS OF SALISBURY	Cons	1895–1902
A. J. BALFOUR	Cons	1902–05
SIR H. CAMPBELL-BANNERMAN	Lib	1905–08
H. H. ASQUITH	Lib	1908–15
H. H. ASQUITH	Coaln	1915–16
D. LLOYD GEORGE	Coaln	1916–22
A. BONAR LAW	Cons	1922–23
STANLEY BALDWIN	Cons	1923–24
J. RAMSAY MACDONALD	Lab	1924
STANLEY BALDWIN	Cons	1924–29
J. RAMSAY MACDONALD	Lab	1929–31
J. RAMSAY MACDONALD	Nat	1931–35
STANLEY BALDWIN	Nat	1935–37
NEVILLE CHAMBERLAIN	Nat	1937–39
NEVILLE CHAMBERLAIN	War Cab	1939–40
WINSTON S. CHURCHILL	War Cab	1940–45
CLEMENT ATTLEE	Lab	1945–51
SIR WINSTON CHURCHILL	Cons	1951–55
SIR ANTHONY EDEN	Cons	1955–57
HAROLD MACMILLAN	Cons	1957–63
SIR ALEC DOUGLAS-HOME	Cons	1963–64
HAROLD WILSON	Lab	1964–70
EDWARD HEATH	Cons	1970–74
HAROLD WILSON	Lab	1974–76
JAMES CALLAGHAN	Lab	1976–79
MARGARET THATCHER	Cons	1979–90
JOHN MAJOR	Cons	1990–

PRIMUS ELDEST, FIRST. BISHOP (Sc).
PRINCE(SSE)S ROYALS. *THEATRE.*

PRINCIPAL (s/l *principle*). CHIEF, *HEAD*, MAIN. *CAPITAL*.

PRINCIPLE (s/l *principal*). *LIGHT*, STANDARD, TENET.

PRISE (s/l *prize*). *FORCE*, LEVER, PURCHASE. Also = *PRIZE*.

PRISON *GAOL* (q.v. for list) [M for M (*Shak*); Yeomen (*G and S*)].

PRISONER GAOLBIRD, LAG, *CONVICT* (q.v.), HOSTAGE; [*patron saint*]; *CELLIST* (crypt); **celeb**: COL ALTAMONT (Pendennis, Thackeray); BERNADINE (*Shak*); SAMUEL BURTON (Kingsley); COUNT OF MONTE CRISTO (Dumas); *LIONHEART* (Eng king); MAGWITCH (Great Ex, *Dickens*); DR MANETTE (shoemaker, 105 North Tower, 2 Cities, *Dickens*); MAN IN THE IRON MASK (Dumas); JEAN VALJEAN (Les Misérables, Victor Hugo); ~ OF ZENDA (Elphberg, *Hope*).

PRIVATE PERSONAL, RESTRICTED, RETIRED, SECLUDED, SECRET; ARCANE, ESOTERIC (**opp** = public). GI, PFC (US), RANKER, SOLDIER, TOMMY (ATKINS).

PRIZE (s/l *prise*). *AWARD* (q.v. for list), CUP, *REWARD*, TROPHY. CAPTIVE. Also = *PRISE* (arch).

PRO PUBLIC RELATIONS OFFICER, ADMAN. PROFESSIONAL (**opp** = amateur). FOR (**opp** = *anti*, con). PUBLIC RECORD OFFICE (Kew).

PROCEED GO, GO ON, MAKE WAY. *ACT*, SUE. *ISSUE*, ORIGINATE. **Pl** = *Anag*. MONEY, RECEIPTS.

PROCESSED *Anag*. *TREATED*. PROGRESSED, TRAVELLED.

PROCRUSTES Gk myth *robber*, who tailored his victims to his *bed* (by amputation or stretching, as appropriate); k by *Theseus*.

PRODUCT *Anag*., e.g. **Nuclear product** = UNCLEAR. GOODS, LINE, OUTPUT, RESULT. MULTIPLIED.

PROFIT (s/l *prophet*). ADVANTAGE, BENEFIT, GAIN, RETURN.

PROMETHEUS Gk myth *TITAN*, who stole fire from Mt *Olympus* to give to mankind. Chained by *Vulcan* to a rock, where a vulture (Ethon) fed daily on his liver, only for it to grow again each night. Rescued by *Hercules*.

PRONOUNCED DECIDED, MARKED. DELIVERED, SOUNDED, UTTERED. See *Pronunciation* below.

PRONUNCIATION Many words sound like others which are spelled differently, and this can affect the meaning of a clue, or otherwise lead to the correct answer. 'Court' and 'caught' can introduce an obvious play on courtship and being caught in matrimony; sometimes there are three different interpretations, such as 'cruise', 'crews' and 'cruse'. Such words are often hinted at by use of phrases like ' . . . we listen to . . . ', ' . . . it sounds as though . . . ', ' . . . a pronounced . . . ', or some such in the clue. Thus: **We hear of a sea voyage – unending for widows** (5) means that, when read aloud, the answer sounds like a sea voyage, or cruise; **unending for widows** reveals that it should be the widow's CRUSE which, in biblical times, never emptied.

But don't necessarily think that all is as straightforward even as this. If the puzzle setter can turn a word to his advantage, he will do so. An obvious example is 'flower' which, besides meaning a plant, can mean something which flows, i.e. a river. Even if you are prepared for this kind of deviousness, you may allow your mind to be programmed to accept the wrong pronunciation. The clue **Rows of beans cultivated by our forefathers?** (6, 4) may lead to the following train of thought: 'Rows could be tiers, ranks, lines or files; beans could be haricot, runner or broad.' But the popular phrase 'a row of beans' has been deliberately suggested in order to mislead, for rows can also mean 'dins, noises, battles, fights, or shindies'. This clue requires the answer FRENCH WARS.

The moral is to examine clues for words or phrasing which might imply alternative spelling to produce a similar sound, or alternative sound to produce a different meaning. Where an entry in this Companion sounds like another word, its explanation starts (s/l . . .). Those words capable of unusual interpretation, not always through different pronunciation (but frequently), are too many to list separately but they have been noted in their individual entries, usually by the addition of the word (crypt) to show that a cryptic interpretation is necessary. Besides **flower** = plant and river, and **row** = tier or din mentioned above (or paddle), examples include **banker** = financier or river (between two banks), **sewer** = drain or seamstress, **number** = digit or anaesthetic (makes one numb), **fast time** = high speed or lent/ramadan, **crew** = ship's complement or the past tense of crow (like a cockerel). There are many, and the puzzle setter will usually be one jump ahead of you, so be alert. See also *punctuation*.

PROOF OF DEBT BILL, INVOICE, IOU, MARKER.
PROPERTY ATTRIBUTE, CHARACTERISTIC, *QUALITY.*
BELONGINGS, CHATTELS, POSSESSIONS; OWNING;

REAL ESTATE. COSTUME, FURNITURE (theat).
PROPHECY FORETELLING. **Gk god** = *APOLLO* [*Cassandra*;
Macbeth (*Shak*), A and C (*Shak*); *Oedipus; Perseus*].
PROPHET (s/l *profit*). AUGUR, AUSPEX, CHALDEAN,
CLAIRVOYANT, DIVINER, FORECASTER, FORTUNE
TELLER, ORACLE, PALMIST, *SEER*, SHADOWER,
SOOTHSAYER, *SORCERER* (q.v.), VISIONARY [Old
Moore]. **Celeb**: AMPHIARUS (*Argonaut*); CALCHAS (Troy;
he d when, as foretold by oracle, he met Mopsus, a superior
~); MELAMPOS (1st doctor); *MOHAMMED*, MOPSUS
(*Argonaut*); PETER (of Pomfret, *Shak*); PHINEAS (*blind* ~
[*Harpies*]); PROTEUS (Gk myth, s of *Poseidon*); TIRESIAS
(*blind* [gold staff]). **Celeb bibl**:

ABRAHAM	JEREMIAH
AMOS	JEREMY
DANIEL	JOEL
ELI	JONAH
ELIJAH (ELIAS)	*JOSEPH*
ELISHA	*JOSHUA*
ENOCH	MALACHI
EZEKIEL	MICAH
HABBAKKUK	*MOSES*
HAGGAI	NAHUM
HOSEA	OBADIAH
IDDO	*SAMUEL*
ISAAC	URIJAH
ISAIAH	ZACHARIAH
JACOB	ZEPHANIAH

PROPHETESS Fem *Prophet*, *SIBYL* (q.v.), SOOTHSAYER
[*oracle*]; **celeb (bibl)**: ANNA (Luke 2); DEBORAH (Judges
4, 5); **celeb (myth)**: AMALTHEA; *CASSANDRA*; SIBYL (of
Cumea); **celeb (other)**: MOTHER SHIPTON; *JOAN* (of Arc).
PROSERPINE 1. Rom eq of *PERSEPHONE*. 2. A minor *PLANET*.
PROSPERITY God: Gk = AGATHODAEMON. **Rom** =
GENIUS.
PROUD 1. ARROGANT, HAUGHTY. GRATIFIED,
HONOURED, PLEASED, SATISFIED. DISTINGUISHED,
STATELY. 2. PROJECTING, PROTRUDING, IN RELIEF
[*cameo*].
PROVERB ADAGE, APHORISM, BYWORD, MAXIM, SAW,

SAYING. **Pl** = BOOK (bibl). GAME.
PROVINCE 1. AREA, BRANCH, BUSINESS, DEPARTMENT, FIELD, SPHERE. 2. DISTRICT (eccles), ADMINISTRATIVE *DIVISION*, TERRITORY, in particular N Ireland or NI. 3. **Specifically of Canada**:

ALBERTA	AL
BRITISH COLUMBIA	BC
MANITOBA	MAN
NEW BRUNSWICK	NB
NEWFOUNDLAND	NF
NW TERRITORIES	NWT
NOVA SCOTIA	NS
PRINCE EDWARD ISLAND	PEI
ONTARIO	ONT
QUEBEC	Q
SASKATCHEWAN	SAS
THE YUKON	YUK

PS POST SCRIPT, AFTERTHOUGHT. POLICE SERGEANT. PRIVATE SECRETARY. PROMPT SIDE. PSALM.
PSYCHE 1. MIND, SOUL, SPIRIT. 2. MOTH. 3. Gk and Rom myth maiden; *Venus* envied her *beauty* and sent *Cupid* with instructions to make ~ fall for the most contemptible of all men but Cupid fell in love with ~ himself. Enslaved by a jealous Venus, ~ eventually became a goddess and was reunited with Cupid. Is often represented with *butterfly* wings. 4. A minor *PLANET*.
PT PHYSICAL TRAINING; PE, GYMNASTICS. PLATINUM (*chem*). *POINT*.
PTOLEMY KING OF EGYPT. Successive kings (I–IX) reigned from 323–81 B.C., notable chiefly for their cruelty, incest (they regularly married their sisters or mothers, who were as regularly called *Cleopatra* and as cruel as their husbands), and the loss of territory. Particularly notable were ~ V (Epiphanes; 205–181 B.C.) who is the subject of the *Rosetta Stone*; ~ X (Alexander II; 81 B.C.) who married his cousin Cleopatra Berenice and immediately had her ass, whereupon rioters did the same for him; ~ XI (Auletes; 80–51 B.C.) who was expelled to Rome, where he bribed *Pompey* to reinstate him in 55 B.C. (he k his own daughter Berenice); ~ XII (son of ~ XI; 51–47 B.C.) who

reigned jointly with his sis Cleopatra (the well-known one) with whom he quarrelled and, when *Caesar* took her side, he was drowned escaping; ~ XIII (br of ~ XII; 47–43 B.C.) who was appointed by Caesar to marry his sis Cleopatra and rule jointly, but she had him ass during the Alexandrine war.

PUB *BAR*, BISTRO(T), INN, *LOCAL*, PH (abbr), *TAVERN*. *PUBLIC*. PUBLISHED.

PUBLICAN *HOST*, INNKEEPER, *LANDLORD*. TAX-GATHERER (bibl).

PUBLICATION *ISSUE*. BOOK, MAGAZINE, PAPER, WEEKLY.

PUBLIC SCHOOL BOARDING-, ENDOWED-, PRIVATE-SCHOOL; **celeb:**

ALLEYN'S	founded 1619
ALLHALLOWS	16th century
AMPLEFORTH	(Fr 1608) 1802
ARDINGLY	1858
BEDALES	1893
BLOXHAM	1860
BLUECOAT	1553
BLUNDELLS	1604
BRYANSTON	1928
CANFORD	1923
CHARTERHOUSE	1611
CHRIST'S HOSPITAL	1552
CHURCHER'S	1722
CLIFTON	1862
CRANLEIGH	1863
DAUNTSEY'S	1543
DOUAI	(Fr 1615) 1903
DOWNSIDE	(Fr 1606) 1789
DULWICH COLLEGE	1619
EPSOM	1853
ETON	1440
FELSTED	1564
GORDONSTOUN	1934
GRESHAM'S	1555
HABERDASHERS'	1690
HAILEYBURY	1862
HARROW	1571
HURSTPIERPOINT	1849

LANCING	1848
THE LEYS	1875
LORETTO	1862
MALVERN	1862
MARLBOROUGH	1843
MERCHANT TAYLOR'S	1561
MONKTON COMBE	1868
OSWESTRY	1407
OUNDLE	1556
RADLEY	1847
REPTON	1557
ROSSALL	1844
RUGBY	1567
SAINT PAULS	1509
SEDBERGH	1525
SHERBORNE	1550
SHREWSBURY	1552
STONYHURST	1593
STOWE	1923
TONBRIDGE	1553
UPPINGHAM	1584
WELLINGTON	1841
WESTMINSTER	1560
WHITGIFT	founded 1596
WINCHESTER	1382
WORKSOP	1890
WREKIN	1880
WYCLIFFE	1882

PUCK 1. *SPIRIT* (MND, *Shak*); IMP. 2. Ice hockey disc.
PUDDING *Anag*. AFTERS, *COURSE*, SWEET; **types**: APPLE ~,
   BLACK ~, FRUIT ~, HASTY ~, MILK ~, PLUM ~,
   SPONGE ~, STEAMED ~, YORKSHIRE ~, ROLY POLY,
   SPOTTED DICK. FAT PERSON. PAD, PROTECT (naut).
PUG BEAT, GRIND; CLAY. BOXER, PUGILIST. DARLING,
   DEAR. *DOG* [~ engine; ~ moth; ~ nose]. *FOX*.
   FOOTPRINT, TRACK. GOBLIN (obs). HARLOT. *MONKEY*
   (Sc). PULL, THIEVE, TUG (dial). SERVANT (arch obs).
PULLER DRAWER, EXTRACTOR; DENTIST (crypt).
   TOWER, TUG.
PUMP BALE, DISCHARGE, EMPTY. *SHOE*.
   INTERROGATE, QUESTION.

PUNCH *DRINK*, NEGUS. BLOW, HOOK, JAB, KNOCK,
SWING, UPPERCUT. [~ and Judy].

PUNCTUATION Commas and even full stops are ruthlessly used
by the puzzle setter to mislead. The object, as with use of words
with different *pronunciation* (q.v.), is to brainwash the reader
into putting a certain interpretation on a word, particularly
one which may have two or more meanings. Note how the clue
Offers more doubt, is uncertain (7) points to lack of sureness
or confidence, but moving the comma (and this has to be done
mentally, because the puzzle setter won't do it for you) from
after the word 'doubt' to before it, changes the complexion of
things: 'Offers more, doubt is uncertain' gives a word which
must mean 'offers more' and is an 'uncertain' rendering (thus
an anagram) of 'doubt is'; the answer = OUTBIDS. See also
Question mark.

PUNT *BET*, WAGER. *BOAT*; QUANT. COUNTRY (pre-bibl
[Queen Hatshepsut]). KICK. CURRENCY (Ire).

PUP PUPPY; *offspring* of dog. DUD. *AIRCRAFT*.

PUPIL L, STUDENT, SCHOLAR [*class, form*]. IRIS, EYE
CENTRE (hence Y, crypt); *SEER* (crypt).

PURPLE *COLOUR*; *PURPURE* (*herald*). [Idmon of Colophon, a
dyer of ~ and f of Arachne].

PURPURE *COLOUR*; *PURPLE* (*herald*).

PUSSYFOOT LURK, PROWL, SNEAK. OVERCAUTION. *TT*,
PROHIBITIONIST [W. E. Johnson]. CATSPAW (crypt).

PUT *PLACE, SET*.

~ **BACK** DEMOTE, REPLACE. DEFER. TES, TUP (crypt).

PUTTER *CLUB*; *GOLFER*. PLACER, SETTER.

PUTTING *GOLF*, HOLING. PLACING, SETTING.

PUT UP BUILD, CONSTRUCT, ERECT. TOLERATE.
EMPLOY (jockey). *FLUSH* (game bird). *LODGE* (guest).
OFFER (fight, prayer). *PRESENT* (petition). PROPOSE
(candidate). *RAISE* (price). SHEATHE (sword). TUP (dn).

PYGMALION Gk myth K of Cyprus, who fell in love with the
ivory statue he had sculpted. He persuaded *Aphrodite* to give it
life, and mar her as *Galatea*. [G. B. Shaw].

PYRIPHLEGETHON Gk myth underworld river; literally: flaming
with fire.

PYROMANIA *Obsession* with fire-raising.

PYROPHOBIA *Aversion* to fire.

PYTHEAS Gk navigator, 4th cent B.C. Sailed the N coast of Eur,
incl Britain and Thule (possibly derived from tales of Nor and

its frozen seas), in two voyages, reaching a river he called Tanais
(possibly the Elbe), which ~ took to be the division between
Eur and Asia (c.f. the Don/Volga). Originated derivation of
latitude through sun's shadow.

PYTHON 1. *SNAKE*. 2. Gk myth *DRAGON* or *SERPENT* which
was formed from primeval ooze after the *Deucalion* deluge. Slain
by *Apollo*, who founded the Pythian *games* in commemoration.

Q (s/l queue). QUEBEC (*Province*, Can). QUEEN. QUESTION.
HEAD OF MI5.

QC QUEEN'S COUNSEL, SILK.

QT ON THE QUIET, QUIET(LY).

QUAIL FLINCH. GAME *BIRD*; **assembly** = bevy.
INSTRUMENT (mus).

QUAKE ROCK, SHAKE, SHIVER, TREMBLE.
EARTHQUAKE [Richter]. *GRASS*.

QUAKER FRIEND, REFORMER, **celeb**: FOX, FRY, PENN;
pl = FRIENDLY SOCIETY [Fox]. EARTHQUAKE,
TREMBLER (crypt) [Richter]. DUMMY GUN, GUNPORT.
SOOTY ALBATROSS (~ bird).

QUALITY ACCOMPLISHMENT, APTITUDE, ATTRIBUTE,
CHARACTERISTIC, FACULTY, *PROPERTY*, SKILL,
TIMBRE. DEGREE, EXCELLENCE. GENTRY, *RANK*,
STANDING.

QUARREL *Anag*. ARGUE, -MENT, CONTEND, DISPUTE,
FALL OUT, FIGHT, FIND FAULT, SCRAP, WAR. *ARROW*,
BOLT (arbalest, cross-bow). Diamond-shaped pane in *window*.

QUARTER E, N, S, W, NE, SE, *NORTH*, *EAST* etc. MERCY,
PITY. TRAVERSE. FOURTH PART, *MEASURE*. COIN
(US). AREA, NEIGHBOURHOOD. **Pl** = BILLET,
LODGING.

~ **DAYS** D, A, Y or S (crypt). **England/Ireland**: LADY DAY
(25 Mar), MIDSUMMER (24 Jun), MICHAELMAS (29 Sep),
CHRISTMAS (25 Dec); **Scotland**: CANDLEMAS (2 Feb),
WHITSUN (15 May), LAMMAS (1 Aug), MARTINMAS
(11 Nov).

~ **HOUR** H, O, U or R (crypt).

~ **PINT** P, I, N or T (crypt). GILL, *MEASURE*.

QUAY (s/l key). BUND, *DOCK*, *JETTY*, *MOLE*, PIER,
WHARF.

QUEEN 1. CARD (*Alice*). *CAT* (fem). CHESSPIECE. 2. King's wife, *MONARCH* (fem; q.v.), REGINA, SOVEREIGN (fem); EII, ER, HM, Q, R; **celeb**: AETHELFLED (Mercia), ANNE (Eng), BESS (Eng), BILKIS (Sheba), *BOADICEA*, CANDACE (bibl), CATHERINE (Eng, Fr, Russ), *CLEOPATRA, CLYTEMNESTRA, CORA*, ELEANOR (Eng [Charing Cross, Waltham Cross, etc]), ELIZABETH (Eng), ESTHER (bibl), GERTRUDE (*Shak*), *GUINEVERE*, HATSHEPSUT (Egy [Punt]), *HECUBA, HELEN, HERA*, HEPHZIBAH (bibl), HERMIONE (*Shak*), *HIPPOLYTE*, ISABELLA (Sp), JEZEBEL (bibl), *JOCASTA, JUNO*, LEDA (*Helen*), MARIA THERESA (A), MARIE ANTOINETTE (Fr), MICHAL (bibl), NEFERTITI (Egy), *NIOBE*, PASIPHAE (*Minos*), *PERSEPHONE, PROSERPINE*, TITANIA (*Shak*), VASHT (bibl), *VICTORIA*. **Pl** = *THEATRE*.

QUEENS OF ENGLAND *See* Monarchs.

QUEER *Anag. ODD*, PECULIAR [*Chesterton*]. *FAIRY*, GAY.

~ **STREET** BANKRUPTCY, INSOLVENCY; CAREY STREET. DEAD END (crypt). Anag. of 'street', e.g. TESTER.

QUESTION Q; PROBLEM (**opp** = answer). INTERROGATE, GRILL, *PUMP*.

~ **MARK** A question mark is used when the puzzle setter is feeling benevolent and wishes to draw attention to a double meaning. In effect, it warns that the answer, while relating well to one half of the clue, only responds to the other half in a punning or cryptic way. One of the shortest examples is **Regal liner**? (5) = RULER (where the answer = 'regal' because it means a king, but it = 'liner' because it may be said to help in ruling lines); another instance is **Bulls-eye at the mortuary**? (4, 6) = DEAD CENTRE (where the answer = 'bulls-eye' happily enough, but must be looked at cryptically to arrive at a centre for dead people, or 'mortuary').

It can also be used to indicate that a different meaning should be put on a word by giving it a different spelling, e.g. **Purchaser for the old cow shed**? (4) = BYRE (where the answer is an old-fashioned word for 'cowshed', but it has to be turned into BUYER before it can mean 'purchaser'). See also *pronunciation* and *punctuation*.

QUEUER (s/l *cuer*). ONE WHO QUEUES/WAITS IN LINE; WAITER.

QUICK *ALIVE*. RAPID, *SMART*. SUBCUTANEOUS

404 *Quickly*

TENDERNESS.
QUICKLY RAPIDLY, *SMARTLY*, SPEEDILY. *ALIVE* (crypt).
Shak char.
QUID *NOTE, POUND*. TOBACCO WAD.
QUIET P, PP, SH; HUSH, LOW, PIANO, SILENT, WHIST (**opp**
= *loud*). EASE, REST, TRANQUIL.
QUIETLY P, PP, QT, SH.
QUINCE *FRUIT* (tree). CARPENTER (MND, *Shak*).
QUIT DEPART, *GO*, LEAVE, PART. SHOT.
QUIXOTIC IDEALISTIC, LOFTY, VISIONARY [Cervantes;
Rosinante (horse)].
QUOD *GAOL*. WHICH (Lat).
QV QUOD VIDE, WHICH SEE.
Q without U There are many place names (mostly Arab, but some
Ch) that use the letter Q without a following U. The following
list, however, is of words, abbreviations or acronyms that are
more everyday. CINQ (five); CINQFOIL (*plant*, bot); COQ
(*jester*); DARRACQ (Fr *car*); IRAQI; LUQA (*airport*); NQA,
NQING, NQONG (Aus gods, *Kipling*); QADI (Mos *judge*);
QANAT (Tunnel); QANTAS (Aus *airline*); QARANC (mil
acronym, med); QAT (*plant*; obs Egy weight); Q-BOAT (mil);
QC (leg abbr); QED (math, Lat abbr); QIANA (US material);
QIBLA (direction of Mecca); QIGONG (Ch healthy breathing);
QING (*Ch dynasty*); QINTAR (*currency*, Albania); QOPH
(Heb *alphabet*); QORAN (koran); Q-SHIP (mil); QT (abbr,
quart/quiet); QTO (abbr, paper *measure*); QTY (abbr, quantity);
QV (Lat abbr); QWERTY (typewriting); SUQ (Arab market);
TQADDIK (Heb *priest*).

R (s/l are). *RAILWAY*. RAND. REAMUR. RECTO.
REGIMENT. *REGINA*. *RESTRICTED* (film *censorship*).
REVEREND. REX. RIGHT. *RIVER*. *ROYAL*. ROMANIA
(*car plate*). RUNS. KING (= EDWARD, GEORGE,
HENRY etc).
RA RADIUM (*chem*). ROYAL ARTILLERY, GUNS. ROYAL
& ANCIENT (*golf club*). ROYAL ACADEMICIAN, ARTIST,
PAINTER (q.v. for list) [Burlington House; Tate]. SUN *GOD*
(Egy) [Cleopatra's needle]. **Pl** = Abyssinian king.
RABBIT (s/l rabbet, rarebit, rebate). CHATTER, TALK (sl).
DUFFER, POOR PLAYER. BOTHER, CONFOUND, DRAT.

ISLAND. BURROWING RODENT, HARE; BUNNY, CONEY; **male** = BUCK; **female** = DOE; **assembly** = warren; **breeds**: ANGORA, LOP-EARED; **celeb**: BENJAMIN BUNNY (Beatrix *Potter*); BRER RABBIT (Uncle Remus; Joel Chandler Harris; Brer Fox, Tar-Baby); BUGS BUNNY ® (cartoon); FIVER; HAZEL (Watership Down); FLOPSY, MOPSY, COTTONTAIL, PETER (Beatrix *Potter* [Mr McGregor]); HARVEY (invisible, Mary Chase); RABBIT (*Milne* [Friends and Relations]); MARCH HARE, WHITE RABBIT (*Alice in Wonderland*); THUMPER ® (Bambi ®) [*Ch calendar*; *habitation*; myxomatosis; playboy].

RAC ROYAL ARMOURED CORPS. ROYAL AUTOMOBILE CLUB [AA, cars].

RACE *BREED*, ETHNIC GROUP. *TIDE-RIP*. GINGER ROOT, *SPICE*. *CLASSIC*, COMPETITION, EGG AND SPOON ~, EVENT, GRAND PRIX, INDY, MARATHON, OBSTACLE ~, RELAY ~, *TT*, SACK ~. [*Atalanta*].

~ OF MAN HOMO SAPIENS. *TT* (crypt).

RACETRACKS 1. **Celeb (horses)**:

AINTREE (Eng)
ASCOT (Eng)
AUTEUIL (Fr)
AYR (Sc)
BANGOR ON DEE (Wal)
BATH (Eng)
BEVERLEY (Eng)
BRIGHTON (Eng)
CARTMEL (Eng)
CAMPTOWN (US)
CATTERICK (Eng)
CHANTILLY (Fr)
CHELTENHAM (Eng)
CHEPSTOW (Wal)
CHESTER (Eng)
CHURCHILL DOWNS
 (US)
CRAVEN (Ire)
CURRAGH (Ire)
DEVON & EXETER
 (Eng)
EDINBURGH (Sc)

EPSOM (Eng)
FOLKESTONE (Eng)
FONTWELL PARK (Eng)
GOODWOOD (Eng)
HAMILTON (Sc)
HAYDOCK PARK (Eng)
HEREFORD (Eng)
KEMPTON (Eng)
LEICESTER (Eng)
LINCOLN (Eng)
LONGCHAMPS (Fr)
LOUISVILLE (US)
LUDLOW (Eng)
MAISONS-LAFITTE (Fr)
MARKET RASEN (Eng)
NAAS (Ire)
NETHERHAMPTON
 (Eng)
NEWBURY (Eng)
NEWMARKET (Eng)
NEWTON ABBOT (Eng)
PERTH (Sc)

RIPON (Eng)
SAINT-CLOUD (Fr)
SANDOWN PARK (Eng)
STRATFORD (Eng)
UTTOXETER (Eng)
WARWICK (Eng)

WINDSOR (Eng)
WOLVERHAMPTON
  (Eng)
YARMOUTH (Eng)
YORK (Eng)

2. **Celeb (motor cars):**

BRANDS HATCH (Eng)
BROOKLANDS (ex Eng)
DAYTONA BEACH (US)
GOODWOOD (Eng)
IMOLA (It)
LE MANS (Fr)
MONACO (Fr)
MONTLHÉRY (Fr)
MONZA (It)

NURNBURGRING (Ger)
OULTON PARK (Eng)
RICHMOND (US)
SAN MARINO (It)
SILVERSTONE (Eng)
SPA (Belg)
THRUXTON (Eng)
ZANDVOORT (NL)

RACKET DIN, NOISE, UPROAR. *DODGE*, SCHEME. ORDEAL. *BAT*; Pl = *GAME*.
RADIO *BROADCAST*, WIRELESS; *MEDIUM*.
RADIUM *METAL*; RA (*chem*).
RAFFIA PALM FIBRE, *PALM* [bass].
RAFFLE LUMBER, RUBBISH. DRAW, LOTTERY. DICE GAME. Pl = Colonial Administrator (Singapore); gentleman burglar and cricketer (fict; E. W. Hornung).
RAF TYPE AC, AIRMAN, FO, *PILOT* etc.
RAG CHAFF, RIB, *TEASE*. FROLIC, GAMBOL. CLOTH, SCRAP; comp = *bone*. BAD PRESS, GUTTER PRESS. SLATE; STONE. *CLUB* (sl: Army & Navy).
RAIL BR, RLY, RY; IRON WAY; TRACK; HARD LINES (crypt). LOCOS, ROLLING STOCK. *BIRD*. ABUSE, RAGE, RANT, RAVE, *THUNDER*. BAR, FENCE, GUIDE, PERCH, ROD. [Bluebell, Severn Valley, Volks (elect), Watercress. *cat*].
RAIL GUIDE ABC ®, BRADSHAW ®.
RAILWAYMAN DRIVER, FIREMAN, GUARD, LOCOMAN, PORTER; PLATER, TRAINER (crypt); **Unions** = ASLEF, NUR. TOBY VECK (The Chimes, *Dickens*).
RAIN (s/l *reign*, *rein*). 1. PRECIPITATION, DELUGE, DOWNFALL, DOWNPOUR, *SHOWER*; DRENCH [piano wires, stair-rods]. 2. Put RA in word indicated, e.g. **Rainbox for**

crystalline salt (5) = BO⁺RA⁺X. 3. **God: Gk** = JUPITER, *ZEUS*;
Rom = PLUVIUS; **Egy** = OSIRIS; **Ind** = INDRA; **Mayan** =
CHAC; **Goddess, Gk** = *HORAE* [Hyades; Pleiades].

RAINBOW 1. ARCH [REFRACTION] (**colours in order**: red,
orange, yellow, green, blue, indigo, violet). 2. **Goddess: Gk** =
IRIS. [Bifrost (~ bridge of Nor gods from Asgard to earth)].

RAISE (s/l raze). 1. ELEVATE, ERECT, HOIST, *PUT UP*
(**opp** = *lower*). 2. Word in dn clue, written up, e.g. **Raise Cain**
= NIAC.

RALLY BANTER, *CHAFF*. REASSEMBLE, RECOVER,
REVIVE. *RACE*. DEMONSTRATION, PARADE.

RAM SHEEP (male), TUP; sign of *Zodiac* (1st, ARIES). BEAK,
PROD (battering, mil). PISTON, PLUNGER (mech). BEAT
DOWN, CRAM, DASH, DRIVE, PACK, PUSH, SHOVE,
STRIKE, STUFF, TAMP. ROYAL ACADEMY OF MUSIC.
Pl = *Football* team (UK/US).

RANGER GIRL GUIDE. FORESTER, PARK WARDEN.
COMMANDO (US). COWBOY (crypt). **Pl** = CAVALRY.
8 in *song*.

RANK *CLASS*, GRADE, QUALITY, STANDING; **mil** = CAPT,
COL, LT etc. LINE, QUEUE, *ROW*, *TIER* (**opp** = file);
ARRAY, ORDER. COARSE, CORRUPT, FOUL, GROSS,
INDECENT, LOATHSOME, OFFENSIVE. LUXURIANT.

RAPT (s/l rapped, wrapped). ABSORBED, CARRIED AWAY,
ENGROSSED, ENRAPTURED, INTENT.

RASH HASTY, IMPETUOUS, OVERBOLD, RECKLESS.
ERUPTION, *GATHERING*, *SPOTS*.

RASPBERRY BRAMBLE, SOFT *FRUIT*; *PLANT*. BIRD,
DERISION, DISAPPROVAL.

RAT 1. *RODENT* (q.v. for list) [*Ch calendar*]. 2. CAD, *HEEL*,
NEERDOWELL, RENEGADE, ROTTER, *SWINE*,
TRAITOR, TURNCOAT; BLACKLEG, SCAB, STRIKE-
BREAKER. ABANDON, CHANGE SIDES, CROSS THE
FLOOR, *DESERT*. 3. *BETRAY* (q.v.). 4. **Pl** = NONSENSE!
ROT! RUBBISH!

RATE *LEVY*, LOCAL TAX. MPH, SPEED. COST, VALUE;
CONSIDER, ESTIMATE, *RANK*, REGARD. CLASS;
MAN OF WAR (arch naut). DRESS DOWN, *REPRIMAND*,
SCOLD, *SLANG*.

RATING AB, JACK, *SAILOR*, TAR. ABC, TAM, GALLUP ®.
HANDICAP (naut). (HOUSE) TAX.

RAVEN 1. PILLAGE, PLUNDER, LOOT. BOLT, DEVOUR,

408 Raw

WOLF (food). *BLACK*. 2. BIRD, family corvidae (ill-omen);
N Am god of *tricky* deceit; **celeb**: GRIP (*Dickens*); HUGIN
(*reflection*) and MUNIN (*memory*; *Odin*; poem by E A Poe);
MOSES (*Orwell*). [*Elijah*; *Noah*; Tower of London].

RAW UNRIPE. UNCOOKED (**opp** = *done*). *GREEN*,
UNTRAINED. PART-MADE (hence MAD). BITING,
CHILLY. SKINNED, SENSITIVE, SORE.

RAY *BEAM*, *LIGHT*, SHAFT [hope]. *FISH*: MANTA, *SKATE*,
STING. NOTE (mus; also RE).

RC RED CROSS. ROMAN CATHOLIC. **Pl** = Royal College of
Surgeons.

RD BOUNCE, DUD CHEQUE [refer to drawer]. RURAL
DEAN. ROAD. RNR DECORATION.

RE RHENIUM (*chem*). *ABOUT*, CONCERNING,
DESCRIBING. AGAIN. ROYAL ENGINEERS, SAPPERS.
NOTE (mus; also RAY). Egy *god*.

REACTOR 1. Nuclear power plant; **types**: AGC, BWR,
PWR: **celeb**: CALDER HALL, CHERNOBYL (USSR),
CULCHETH, CULHAM, DOUNREAY, HARWELL,
RISLEY, SELLAFIELD, SIZEWELL, SPRINGFIELDS,
THREE-MILE ISLAND (US), THURSO, WINDSCALE,
WINFRITH. 2. REAGENT (chem). COIL (elect). [allergy].

READ (s/l reed, *red*). 1. INTERPRET, STUDY, UNDERSTAND
[books]. *PIRATE*. 2. Word reads differently if split (or read
differently), e.g. **A measure of justice, we read** (8, 5) = FREEZING
POINT (just*ice).

READY APT, FACILE, INCLINED, PREPARED, PROMPT,
QUICK, WILLING. *CASH*. OUT (e.g. **Happen to be ready to
cook** (3,3) = PAN OUT).

RECEDING 1. DECLINING, SHRINKING, WITHDRAWING.
2. Answer reads backwards, or partly backwards, e.g. **The
Hittite's top hair is receding** (5) = U*RIAH.

RECEIVER BANKRUPTCY OFFICIAL. RADIO,
HEADPHONES, TV SET. FENCE. HOST. ACCEPTER,
TAKER (**opp** = giver, donor).

RECKONING AC, *ACCOUNT*, *BILL*, *NOTE*, SUM, TOTAL.
THINKING.

RECLUSE *HERMIT* (q.v.), INTROVERT. **Celeb**: MISS
HAVISHAM (*Dickens*); HOWARD HUGHES.

RECORD DISC, EP, LP. ANNAL, ARCHIVE, *CHART*,
DIARY, *ENTER*, ENTRY, LIST, *LOG*, *NOTE*, REGISTER,
ROLL, TAPE, WRITE. BEST PERFORMANCE,

CHAMPIONSHIP. TIE AGAIN (crypt). **Pl** = ALBUM.
RECORDER TAPE. *DIARIST*. LOGGER. CHAMPION, *WINNER*. FLUTE. *INSTRUMENT* (mus). JUDGE.
RED (s/l *read*). BILLIARD/SNOOKER BALL (score 3/1). BOLSHEVIK, COMMIE, COMMUNIST, LEFTIE, REVOLUTIONARY, RUSSIAN; MARX(IST), STALIN, *TROT*(SKY); IVAN. *SEA*. ERIC. *COLOUR*; GULES (*herald*) [*blush*; Elphberg (*Hope*); *Esau*]. *CASTLE*. OVERDRAWN. RIVER (Can; US; Viet). **Pl** = (*football* team).
REDCAP MILITARY POLICEMAN, MP, SP. *BIRD*.
REDCOAT HUNTING PINK. HOLIDAY CAMP GUIDE (Butlins). SOLDIER (arch); **pl** = BRITISH ARMY, LOBSTERS (arch).
REDHEAD COPPERNOB; **celeb**: ELPHBERGS (*Hope*); *ESAU*. COMMUNIST LEADER (crypt); hence C. R (crypt).
RED INDIAN See *AMERICAN INDIAN* for **tribes**.
REDSKIN *AMERICAN INDIAN* (q.v. for **tribes**). **Pl** = *football* team (US).
REEFER JOINT (*drug*). *SAILOR* (crypt). JACKET.
REEL *Anag*. DANCE, LURCH, STAGGER, SWAY. COIL, SPOOL: *WIND*.
RE-ENACTED *Anag*. REPEATED, REPLAYED, RE-RUN.
REEVE MAGISTRATE, SHERIFF. THREAD (naut). *FEMALE* RUFF (*bird*). *Chaucer* char.
REFERENCE MARK Direction sign referring reader to note, e.g. ASTERISK (*), DAGGER/OBELISK (†), DOUBLE OBELISK (‡), PARAGRAPH (¶), PARALLEL (‖), SECTION (§). DATUM.
REFERENCE WORK BOOK, CONSULTATION DOCUMENT, FILE; *DEVILRY* (crypt); **celeb** (**many** ®): ABC (rly), ALMANACH DE GOTHA (genealogy and statistics), BAEDEKER (countries and travel), MRS BEETON (cook), BLUE BOOK (US aristocracy), BRADSHAW (rly), BRITANNICA (encyclopaedia), BURKE'S (aristocracy), CHAMBERS (dictionary), COLLINS (dictionary), CROCKFORDS (*churchmen*), DEBRETT'S (aristocracy), *LLOYDS* (shipping, yachts), MEDICAL REGISTER (doctors), NAUTICAL ALMANAC (naut tables and ephemera), OED (dictionary), OLD MOORE (statistics, prophecy), REEDS (naut ephemera), ROGET (thesaurus), STUD BOOK (racehorses), WHITAKER'S ALMANACK (statistics), WHO'S WHO (people).

REFLECTION 1. CENSURE. RECONSIDERATION,
THOUGHT [Hugin (*raven*)]. (MIRROR) IMAGE. *ECHO.*
2. Word reads backwards, or is a palindrome, e.g. **On reflection,
I lead to a certain amount of evil-smelling** (7) = NO•I•SOME.
REFORM *Anag.* ABOLISH, CORRECT, CURE. FORM AGAIN
(hence FROM, crypt).
REFRAIN ABSTAIN, CURB, DESIST, RESTRAIN.
(RECURRING) PHRASE/*TUNE.*
REFUSE 1. *DECLINE*, DENY, REJECT, SAY NAY, SHUN,
SHY (**opp** = *allow*). GARBAGE, LEAVINGS, ORT,
RUBBISH, SCRAP, TRASH. 2. In Gk myth, suitors were ~d
by: *Atalanta, Cassandra, Daphne, Dido, Narcissus, Penelope.*
REGENT 1. Ruler in absentia or minority, e.g. ANTIPATER
(Macedonia), ADMIRAL HORTY (Hung), and for George III
(Eng), LOUIS XV (Fr). 2. *THEATRE.*
REGINA QUEEN, R.
REGIONS OF SCOTLAND See *Divisions.*
REGRET APOLOGIZE, BE SORRY, GRIEVE, REPENT,
RUE; [Miss Otis].
REHOBOAM 1. *BOTTLE* (wine = 6 normal). 2. Bibl s of *Solomon*
and Naamah, who mar Maacah. When K of Isr (975–957 B.C.),
~ refused reform ('my f chastised you with whips, I shall
chastise you with scorpions'), so that ten N tribes seceded to
Jeroboam.
REIGN (s/l *rain, rein*). RULE, SOVEREIGNTY, SWAY;
REALM, SPHERE. HOLD ROYAL OFFICE, BE
EMPEROR/KING/QUEEN/MONARCH/SOVEREIGN.
REIN (s/l *rain, reign*). 1. *CONTROL*, CURB, GOVERN,
RESTRAIN. *HARNESS.* 2. Put RE in word indicated, e.g. **The
little man's horserein** (4) = G•RE•G. 3. Pl = KIDNEYS, LOINS
(arch). CONTROLS.
REINDEER CARIBOU, SUBARCTIC DEER; **celeb**: BLITZEN,
COMET, CUPID, DANCER, DASHER, DONDER,
PRANCER, *VIXEN* (Moore); *RUDOLF. LAKE.*
REJECT 1. EVACUATE, VOMIT. *DECLINE, REFUSE*, TURN
ASIDE. 2. Letter or word dropped, e.g. **Treaty rejecting the
French fever** (4) = (le)AGUE. 3. In Gk myth, suitors were ~ed
by *Atalanta, Cassandra, Daphne, Dido, Narcissus* and *Penelope.*
RELATED AGNATE; ALLIED, KIN, KITH. NARRATED,
TOLD.
RELATION CONNECTION, FAMILY, KIN, KITH; **e.g.**
AUNT, *BROTHER*, COUSIN, *DAUGHTER, FATHER,*

GRANDDAUGHTER, ~FATHER, ~MOTHER, ~SON,
HUSBAND, IN-LAW, *MOTHER, SIBLING, SISTER,
UNCLE, WIFE*. ACCOUNT, NARRATIVE, STORY, TALE.
RELIEF WORK AID TO POOR, OXFAM, UNICEF. CAMEO
(**opp** = intaglio), ENGRAVING; BAS, FRIEZE. BRAILLE
(crypt). LINOCUT, STENCIL.
RELIGION DIVINE RECOGNITION, FAITH, PIETY,
WORSHIP; MONASTIC LIFE [*church, friar, monk*]. **Celeb
vedantisms**: HINDUISM (**gods**: Shakti, Shiva, Vishnu;
goddesses: Durga, Lakshmi; **priest**: brahmin); BUDDHISM
(**versions**: Mahayana, Theravada, Ch'an (Ch), Zen (Jap);
founder: Gautama; Nirvana (bliss); **priests**: monks); BABISM;
BAHAISM, JAINISM (non-violence); LAMAISM (Tibet);
PARSISM (**founder**: Zoroaster); SAKTIISM (Tantras);
SIKHISM (**founder**: Guru Nanak); ZOROASTRIANISM.
Celeb oriental: CONFUCIANISM (**concepts**: chan-tza,
hsiao, jen, li, shu, tao, t'ien); SHINTOISM (**concept**:
kami); TAOISM (**concepts**: tao, te, we, wei, yang, yin).
Celeb Judaisms: CHRISTIANITY (**founder**: Jesus); ISLAM
(**founder**: *MOHAMMED*; **prophets**: Abraham, Adam, *Jesus*,
Moses, *Mohammed*, Noah); ZIONISM (**founders**: Abraham,
Isaac, Jacob [**Israel**]). **Celeb paganisms/atheisms**: MARXISM
(communism); SATANISM (black magic); VOODOO (ju-ju);
WITCHCRAFT (magick, wicca).
RELIGIOUS HOLY, *PI*.
REMEDY *Anag. CURE*, NOSTRUM, PALLIATIVE.
REMOVE 1. ABSTRACT, TAKE AWAY/OFF. DISMISS.
CHANGE, DEPARTURE, DISTANCE, DISTANT,
REMOTE. DISH. DEGREE. PROMOTION (school); *CLASS*,
FORM [*Bunter*]. 2. Take away letters indicated, e.g. **Remove the
courtesan's curves in this joint** (5) = MI(S)TRE(SS).
REMOVED 1. APART. TAKEN AWAY. 2. Remove letter D from
clue, e.g. **Dart removed skill** (3) = *ART. 3. Remove letters RE
from clue, e.g. **Refuse removed igniter** (4) = **FUSE.
REMUS 1. Uncle ~ (book, Joel Chandler Harris; Brer *Fox*, Brer
Rabbit, Brer Terrapin, Tar-Baby). 2. Rom myth *twin* br of
Romulus, s of *Mars* and *Rhea* (Silvia). They were suckled by
wolves, and Romulus later k Remus.
RENT CLEAVE, RIP, TEAR; CLEFT, FAULT, FISSURE. LET;
HIRE CHARGE, PAYMENT.
REP *MATERIAL*. REPERTORY. REPRESENTATIVE;
CONGRESSMAN, MP. *CHAPMAN*, DRUMMER,

SALESMAN, TRAVELLER, REPUBLICAN.

Rep Republican [donkey].

REPAIR *Anag.* MEND, OVERHAUL, PATCH, *SERVICE*.
GO, HIE.

REPEAT 1. BIS, ENCORE. DO/SAY AGAIN, IMITATE,
RECITE, REHEARSE, REPRODUCE. RECUR. BELCH,
BURP. 2. Write word/letter again, e.g. **Flower is repeated** (4)
= IS*IS.

REPEATER FIREARM, *WEAPON*. CLOCK, *WATCH*.
DUPLICATE DIAL/SIGNAL; RELAY, RETRANSMITTER.
ACTOR, RECITER, REPETITEUR, SOLILOQUIST (crypt).

REPEL 1. BEAT BACK, REPULSE, WARD OFF. DISPLEASE,
BE DISTASTEFUL (**opp** = *attract*). 2. Word(s) read backwards,
e.g. **Little Sarah is repellent to Eliot's weaver** (5) = SI*LAS
(Marner).

REPORTER ACCOUNTANT, NARRATOR. ED,
JOURNALIST. DAILY ~ (fict newspaper, *Superman*).
BANGER, BOMB, EXPLOSIVE, GUN, RIFLE (crypt).

REPRIMAND *CARPET*, DRESS DOWN, REPROVE, *ROCKET*,
TELL OFF (**opp** = praise).

REPTILE Coldblooded vertebrate of genus reptilia: *ALLIGATOR*,
CHAMELEON, *CROCODILE*, *DINOSAUR*, GECKO,
KOMODO *DRAGON*, *LIZARD* (q.v. for list), *MONITOR*,
SKINK, *SNAKE* (q.v. for list), TERRAPIN, *TORTOISE*,
TUATARA, TURTLE.

REPUBLICAN PRO-REPUBLIC. POLITICIAN [donkey].
SOCIAL.

RE-ROW REPECHAGE. RE-ARGUE.

RESERVE *BOOK*. POSTPONE, WITHHOLD. SERVE
AGAIN [let; tennis]. COOLNESS, RETICENCE. **Pl** =
REINFORCEMENTS; TERRITORIALS (mil).

RESOLVE *Anag.* ANALYSE, SOLVE, *SETTLE*; DISSIPATE,
DISSOLVE. DECIDE, DETERMINE.

REST (s/l wrest). DREGS, LEES, REMAINS. HOLIDAY;
BREAK, PAUSE. *BAR* (mus). BRIDGE, CUE-PROP,
SPIDER (pool/snooker).

RESTRICTED CONFINED, LIMITED, NUMBERED. OFF-
LIMITS. R (film *censorship*).

RESUME CARRY ON, CONTINUE. *SUMMARY*.

RETAIL NARRATE, RECOUNT, RELATE. SELL, TRADE.

RETIRED 1. *LEFT*, RECEDED, RETREATED,
WITHDRAWN. PENSIONED. ABED, SLEEPING. 2. Word

reads backwards, e.g. **Retired officer is sweet** (3) = JAM.
3. Word/letter is put into 'bed', e.g. **Retired woman is disbarred** (6)
= B*ANN*ED. 4. Because ~ can mean 'in bed', it thus refers crypt
to gardening.

RETIRING As *Retired* and: SHY, UNSOCIABLE,
WITHDRAWN (**opp** = *pert*).

RETORT 1. CHEMICAL VESSEL, *STILL*; ALEMBIC (arch).
COMEBACK, REPARTEE, REPLY, RETALIATE. 2. Word
reads backwards, e.g. **Mad retort stops the flow** = DAM.

RETRIBUTION 1. RECOMPENSE, REQUITAL,
VENGEANCE. 2. **Goddess: Gk** = ATE, NEMESIS; **Other** =
MENI (Bab).

RETURN 1. COME/GO/SEND BACK (hence EMOC/OG/DNES,
crypt); CONVEY/GIVE/PAY/PUT BACK (do). DIVIDEND,
INTEREST, PAY, PROFIT. COME-AND-GO, DOUBLE
JOURNEY. [boomerang; Miolnir (*Thor*)]. 2. Reads backwards,
e.g. **Beat in return game** (4) = FLOG. 3. Turn letters RE = ER,
e.g. **Go and return for a quick one** (4) = GO*ER.

REVEALS 1. BETRAYS, DISCLOSES, DIVULGES, MAKES
KNOWN, *SHOWS*. 2. *Hidden word.*

REVERSE 1. DEFEAT, MISFORTUNE. CAPSIZE. VERSO,
TAIL (coin); **opp** = obverse, head. CONTRARY. ANNUL,
REVOKE. TRANSPOSE. 2. Reads backwards, e.g. **Gained
some ground? Now reverse** (3) = WON.

REVISE *Anag*, AMEND, CORRECT, EDIT, IMPROVE.
CHANGE, RECONSIDER. SECOND SIGHT (crypt).

REVOLUTIONARY *Anag*. AGITATOR, REBEL, *RED*; CHE.
SPINNER, *TOP*, *WHEEL* (crypt).

REVOLVER COLT ®, PISTOL, *WEAPON*, WEBLEY ®. *TOP*,
TURNSTILE, WHEEL [*Ixion*], (WIND)MILL (all crypt).
SWING DOOR.

REWRITE *Anag*. EDIT, *REVISE*, SUB-EDIT.

REX KING, R.

RHEA (s/l rear). 1. Gk *goddess* of FERTILITY; d of Uranus and
Ge; mar *Cronos*, m of *Hades*, *Poseidon* and *Zeus*. In Rom myth
(as ~ Silvia) m by *Mars* of *Romulus* and Remus. Synonymous
with **Gk** = CYBELE, *DANAE*; **Rom** = *CERES*, *DIANA*, OPS.
2. A satellite of the planet Saturn. 3. *BIRD* (*ostrich*).

RHINESTONE IMITATION *DIAMOND* [paste].

RHINO PACHYDERM, TOXODON (ex); **assembly** = crash.
NOSE. MONEY (sl).

RHYMING SLANG Form of cockney slang code, which involves

paired words, the second of which rhymes with the meaning
(and is often not spoken – this is indicated below by the use of
parentheses)

Slang	Meaning
Apples (and pears)	STAIRS
Ball of chalk	WALK
Bangers and mash	CASH
Barnet (Fair)	HAIR
Bees and (honey)	MONEY
Bird (lime)	TIME
Boat race	FACE
Boracic lint	SKINT
Bull and cow	ROW
Burnt cinder	WINDOW
Butcher's (hook)	LOOK
Cain and Abel	TABLE
Cherry (Ripe)	PIPE
Cobbler's (awls)	BALLS
Dicky (dirt)	SHIRT
Dog (and bone)	PHONE
Frog and toad	ROAD
Jam roll	DOLE
Lady Godiva	FIVER
Loaf (of bread)	HEAD
Mince (pie)s	EYES
Mutt and Jeff	DEAF
North and south	MOUTH
Pen and ink	STINK
Pig's ear	BEER
Plates (of meat)	FEET
Pompey (whore)	FOUR
Pot and pan	OLD MAN
Rosie (Lee)	TEA
Rub a dub (dub)	PUB
Sexton (Blake)	FAKE
Square (and round)	POUND
Tea leaf	THIEF
Titfer (tat)	HAT
Tod (Sloan)	OWN
Trouble (and strife)	WIFE
Whistle (and flute)	SUIT

Meaning	Slang
Balls	COBBLER'S (awls)
Beer	PIG'S EAR
Cash	BANGERS AND MASH
Deaf	MUTT AND JEFF
Dole	JAM ROLL
Eyes	MINCE (pie)s
Face	BOAT RACE
Fake	SEXTON (BLAKE)
Feet	PLATES (of meat)
Fiver	LADY GODIVA
Four	POMPEY (whore)
Hair	BARNET (fair)
Hat	TITFER (tat)
Head	LOAF (of bread)
Husband	POT AND PAN
Look	BUTCHER'S (hook)
Money	BEES AND (honey)
Mouth	NORTH AND SOUTH
Old Man	POT AND PAN
Own	TOD (Sloan)
Phone	DOG (and bone)
Pipe	CHERRY RIPE
Pound	SQUARE (and round)
Pub	RUB A DUB (dub)
Road	FROG AND TOAD
Row	BULL AND COW
Shirt	DICKY (dirt)
Skint	BORACIC LINT
Stairs	APPLES (and pears)
Stink	PEN AND INK
Suit	WHISTLE (and flute)
Table	CAIN AND ABEL
Tea	ROSIE (Lee)
Thief	TEA LEAF
Time	BIRD (lime)
Walk	BALL OF CHALK
Wife	TROUBLE (and strife)
Window	BURNT CINDER

RHYTHM *BEAT*, SEQUENCE [scan verse for each *foot*].
RI RELIGIOUS INSTRUCTION. RHODE ISLAND. ROYAL

INSTITUTION.
RIB BONE [*Eve*]. CHAFF, *TEASE*. RIVER (Eng).
RICH ABUNDANT, COSTLY, FATTY, SPLENDID, SUGARY,
WEALTHY (**opp** = *broke*); VALUABLE [*Croesus*, Mammon,
Midas, Nabob, Plutus, Dives]. LAUGHABLE, LUDICROUS.
RIDER ABACK, BACKED, UP (crypt), EQUESTRIAN,
JOCKEY, *MOUNTED*. ADDITION, CODICIL, EXTRA, PS.
HAGGARD (writer).
RIG *DRESS*, GEAR. PROVIDE. DODGE, FIX,
MANIPULATE. *STAY*. BARK, BARQUE, BERMUDAN,
BRIG, CUTTER, GAFF, GUNTER, KETCH, LATEEN,
LUG, SCHOONER, SLOOP, SPRIT, SQUARE, YAWL.
RIGGING FIXING, MANIPULATION, TRICKERY. STAYS,
WIRES: BACKSTAY, BRAIL, BUNTLINE, CLUELINE,
FORESTAY, *GARNET*, *JUMPERS*, MARTNET, REEF,
RUNNERS, SHROUND, TRIATIC.
RIGHT (s/l *rite*, write). R, RT, S; DEXTER, STARBOARD (**opp**
= *left*, port, larboard, *sinister*). **Comp** = left. CORRECT (**opp**
= *wrong*). OP (theat). UPTURN, LIEN. TORY. *WHALE*. Pl
= CHARTER.
~ **AWAY** 1. IMMEDIATELY, NOW. 2. Delete letter(s) R or RT,
e.g. **Smooth part right away** (3) = PA•T.
~ **ONE** *CASE*, CAUTION, WAG. R*ONE, R*I (crypt).
RING O (crypt). BUZZ, *CALL*, *DIAL*, PHONE, TOLL [STD].
ARENA, CIRCLE, CIRCUS. CARTEL, CLIQUE, GANG,
SET. *CASTLE*. ENGAGED SIGNAL (crypt). AUREOLE,
CORONA, DISC, GLORIOLE, HALO, NIMBUS. HOOP.
[Wagner].
RINGED CIRCLED, MARKED. AFFIANCED, ENGAGED
(crypt).
RINGER *BELL*; CAMPANOLOGIST. COPY, DOUBLE,
DUPLICATE. QUOIT. FIANCE (crypt).
RINGING 1. CALLING, PHONING. MARKING. TINNITUS.
2. Word round another, e.g. **Hot and bothered, Fred's ringing the
First Lady** (7) = F•EVE•RED.
RINGLEADER AGITATOR, INSTIGATOR. R (crypt).
DIALLING (crypt).
RINGMASTER CIRCUS MC. *BOXER*, CHAMPION, PRIZE
FIGHTER, PUGILIST (crypt). JEWELLER (crypt).
RITE (s/l *right*, write). CEREMONY, PROCEDURE, LORE.
RIVAL 1. COMPETITOR, COMPETE, VIE. COMPARABLE.
2. Three in *song*. Pl = BOB ACRES & CAPT ABSOLUTE/

ENSIGN BEVERLEY (The ~s, Sheridan).
RIVER R; BECK, *BOURN*, BROOK, BURN, CREEK, EA, ESTUARY, RILL, RIVULET, STREAM, TRIBUTARY, WATERCOURSE; crypt: *BANKER*, CURRENCY, *FLOWER*, *RUNNER*; myth: *ACHERON*, COCYTUS, LETHE, *OCEANUS*, PYRIPHLEGETHON, *STYX*. [Alpheus; Cebren (god), *Cerberus*, Charon]. **Comps** = ABANA & PHARPAR (bibl ~s of DAMASCUS). **Pl** = *Shak* char. **Celeb:**

1-letter

E (Sc)

2-letters

AA (Fr, CIS)   OB (CIS)
II (Finn)   PO (It)

3-letters

AAR (Sw)   LEA (Eng)
AHI (Ger)   LEK (NL)
ALN (Eng)   LIM (Y)
ALT (Eng)   *LOT* (Fr)
AXE (Eng)   LYD (Eng)
AYR (Sc)   MOY (Ire)
BUG (Pol, CIS)   NAR (Eng)
CAM (Eng) [Granta] OBI (CIS)
CAN (Eng)   OKA (CIS)
CHU (CIS)   ORD (Aus)
DAL (Swe)   PIC (Can)
DEE (Ire, Sc, Wal) PUR (CIS)
DJA (Cam)   *RED* (Cam, US, Viet)
DON (Eng, Sc, CIS) *RIB* (Eng)
DUA (Z)   ROE (Ire)
ELY (Eng)   *RYE* (Eng)
EMS (Ger)   SIR (CIS)
ESK (Eng)   TAF (Wal)
EXE (Eng)   TAW (Eng)
FAL (Eng)   TAY (Sc)
FLY (Papua)   TYE (Eng)
HAY (Aus, Can)   USK (Wal)
ILI (CIS)   VÁH (Cz)
JIU (Rum)   VAR (Fr)
KUR (Iran)   VER (Eng)

WEY (Eng)   YEO (Eng)
WYE (Eng)

4-letters

AARE (Swi)   GLAN (Ger)
ADUR (Eng)   GLEN (Eng)
AGRA (Sp)   *GREY* (NZ)
AGRI (It)   HASE (Ger)
AIRE (Eng)   HULL (Eng)
ALPH (Gk)   IRIN (A)
ALTA (N)   *ISIS* (Thames, Eng)
AMOO (CIS)   ISLA (Sc)
AMUR (CIS)   JUBA (Som)
ARNO (It)   KAMA (CIS)
ARUN (Eng)   LEAF (Can)
AUBE (Fr)   LECH (Ger)
AUDE (Fr)   LENA (CIS)
AVON (Eng, Sc)   LIMA (Port)
BACK (Can)   LUNE (Eng)
BANN (Ire)   LYON (Sc)
BENI (Bol)   MAAS (NL)
BRUE (Eng)   MAIN (Ger)
BURE (Eng)   MEON (Eng)
BUSH (Ire)   META (Venez)
CARY (Eng)   *MILK* (US)
CHER (Fr)   MOLE (Eng)
CHEW (Eng)   *MOTH* (NZ)
CHIR (CIS)   NENE (Eng)
COLN (Eng)   NILE (Egy)
CREE (Sc)   ODER (Pol)
DART (Eng)   OHIO (US)
DOON (Sc)   OISE (Fr)
DOVE (Eng)   ORNE (Fr)
EARN (Sc)   OUSE (Eng)
EBRO (Sp)   OXUS (CIS)
EDEN (Eng, Sc)   *PEEL* (Can)
ELBE (Ger)   PLYM (Eng)
ELWY (Wal)   QENA (Egy)
ERNE (Ire)   RENO (It)
EURE (Fr)   ROCK (US)
FINN (Ire)   RUHR (Ger)
GILA (US)   SAAR (Ger)

SEAL (Can)
SPEY (Sc)
STYX (myth)
SUIR (Ire)
SWAN (Aus)
TARA (CIS, Y)
TAVY (Eng)
TAWE (Wal)
TEES (Eng)
TEST (Eng)
TONE (Eng)
TOWY (Wal)
TYNE (Eng, Sc)
TYWI (Wal)

UGIE (Sc)
URAL (CIS)
VAAL (SA)
VIRE (Fr)
WAAL (NL)
WEAR (Eng)
WICK (Sc)
WOLF (US)
WYRE (Eng)
YALU (Ch)
YARE (Eng)
YORK (US)
YSER (Belg)
ZORN (Fr)

5-letters

ABANA (bibl)
ADIGE (It)
ADOUR (Fr)
AERON (Wal)
AFTON (Sc)
AGANO (Jap)
AISNE (Fr)
ALDAN (CIS)
ANNAN (Sc)
APURE (Venez)
AVOCA (Ire)
BOVEY (Eng)
BOYNE (Ire)
BRORA (Sc)
BRIDE (Ire)
CAIRN (Sc)
CAMEL (Eng)
CEDAR (US)
CLARE (Ire)
CLWYD (Wal)
CLYDE (Sc)
COLNE (Eng)
CONGO (Zaire)
CONWY (Wal)
DEBEN (Eng)
DERRY (Ire)

DOURO (Port)
DOVEY (Wal)
DVINA (CIS)
ELLEN (Eng)
FLEET (Eng, Sc)
FLINT (US)
FORTH (Sc)
FOWEY (Eng)
FOYLE (Ire)
FROME (Eng)
GABON (Gab)
GARRY (Sc)
GRAND (Can)
GREEN (US)
HONDO (Mex)
INDRE (Fr)
INDUS (Pak)
ISERE (Fr)
ISHIM (CIS)
JUMNA (Ind)
JURVA (Braz)
KINGS (Ire)
LETHE (myth)
LIPPE (Ger)
LOIRE (Fr)
LOTTA (CIS)

MARNE (Fr)
MEUSE (Belg)
MIAMI (US)
MOSEL (Ger)
NAIRN (Sc)
NEATH (Wal)
NEGRO (Arg, Braz)
NIGER (Nig)
PAYNE (Can)
PEACE (Can)
PEARL (US)
PELLY (Can)
PIAVE (It)
PLATE (Braz)
PRUTH (Rum)
PURUS (Braz)
RHINE (Ger)
RHÔNE (Fr)
ROPER (Aus)
SARRE (Fr)
SEINE (Fr)
SIONT (Wal)
SLAVE (Can)
SNAKE (US)
SNOWY (Aus)
SOMME (Fr)
SPREE (Ger)

STOUR (Eng)
SWALE (Eng)
TAGUS (Port)
TAMAR (Eng)
TARIM (Ch)
TEIFI (Wal)
TEIGN (Eng)
THAME (Eng)
TIBER (It)
TRENT (Eng)
TWEED (Eng)
VITIM (CIS)
VOLGA (CIS)
WAHGI (Papua)
WESER (Ger)
WHALE (Can)
WHION (Wal)
WHITE (US)
XINGU (Braz)
YANDA (Aus)
YAQUI (Mex)
YARTY (Eng)
YONNE (Fr)
YTHAN (Sc)
YUKON (Can, US)
ZAIRE (Af)

6-letters

ALBANY (Can)
AMAZON (Braz)
ANGARA (CIS)
ARAGON (Sp)
BARCOO (Aus)
BARROW (Ire)
BIO-BIO (Chile)
BOURNE (Eng)
BUCHAN (Sc)
BULLOO (Aus)
CALDER (Eng)
CARRON (Sc)
CONWAY (Wal)

COQUET (Eng)
CUIABA (Braz)
DANUBE (Aus)
ESCAUT (Belg, Fr)
FRASER (Can)
GAMBIA (Gam)
GANGES (Ind)
GRANDE (Mex)
GRANTA (Cam, Eng)
HUDSON (US)
HUELVA (Sp)
HUMBER (Eng)
HWAN-HO (Ch)

IRTYSH (CIS)
ITCHEN (Eng)
JAPURA (Braz)
JAVARI (Peru)
JORDAN (Jor)
KENNET (Eng)
KIKORI (Papua)
KOLYMA (CIS)
LIDDEL (Sc)
LIFFEY (Ire)
MAMORE (Bol)
MEDINA (Eng)
MEDWAY (Eng)
MEKONG (Viet)
MERSEY (Eng)
MOHAWK (US)
MOISIE (Can)
MOSKVA (CIS)
MURRAY (Aus)
NADDER (Eng)
NECKAR (Ger)
NEISSE (Ger, Pol)
NELSON (Can)
NOATAK (US)
ORANGE (SA)
ORWELL (Eng)
OTTAWA (Can)
PARANÁ (Arg, Braz)

PARROT (Eng)
PRIPET (CIS)
QUOILE (Ire)
RIBBLE (Eng)
ROTHER (Eng)
RUPERT (Can)
SABINE (US)
SALMON (US)
SEIONT (Wal)
SEVERN (Can, Eng)
TANANA (US)
TEVIOT (Sc)
THAMES (Eng) [Isis]
THURSO (Sc)
TIGRIS (Iraq)
TUGELA (SA)
TUMMEL (Sc)
TURKEY (US)
UMPQUA (US)
USSURI (CIS)
VIENNE (Fr)
VILYNY (CIS)
WABASH (US)
WEAVER (Eng)
WENSUM (Eng)
YAMUNA (Ind)
YARROW (Sc)
YELLOW (Ch)

7-letters

ACHERON (myth)
ALABAMA (US)
ALPHEUS (Gk)
ANALONG (Ire)
BERMEJO (Arg)
BIG HORN (US)
CLEDDAU (Wal)
COCYTUS (myth)
DARLING (Aus)
DERWENT (Aus, Eng)
DEVERON (Sc)
DNIEPER (USSR)

DOUGLAS (Eng)
DURANCE (Fr)
ETTRICK (Sc)
EUROTAS (Gk)
GARONNE (Fr)
GIRONDE (Fr)
HOANG-HO (Ch)
LA PLATA (Braz)
LIMPOPO (Moz)
MADEIRA (Braz)
MEANDER (Turk)
MERANON (Peru)

MOSELLE (Fr)
OCEANUS (myth)
ORINOCO (Venez)
OWENBOY (Ire)
PHARPAR (bibl)
POTOMAC (US)
RED DEER (Can)
ROANOKE (US)
SALWEEN (Bur/Ch)
SCHELDE (Belg, Fr)
SELENGA (Mong)
SHANNON (Ire)

SUNDAYS (SA)
SUNGARI (CIS)
TAPAJOS (Braz)
TRINITY (US)
UCAYALI (Peru)
WELLAND (Eng)
XANTHUS (Turk)
YANGTSE (Ch)
YENISEI (CIS)
YSTWYTH (Wal)
ZAMBESI (Zam)

8-letters

AMU-DARYA (CIS)
ARAGUAIA (Braz)
COLORADO (Arg; US)
COLUMBIA (US)
DELAWARE (US)
EVENLODE (Eng)
FINDHORN (Sc)
FLINDERS (Aus)
GUIVIARE (Venez)
HAMILTON (Can)
ILLINOIS (US)
MISSOURI (US)

MITCHELL (Aus)
PACTOLUS (Gk; *Midas*)
PARAGUAY (Arg)
PARNAIBA (Braz)
PUTUMAYO (Braz)
SAVANNAH (US)
STINCHOR (Sc)
SUWANNEE (US)
TORRIDGE (Eng)
TUNGUSKA (CIS)
VICTORIA (Aus)
WANSBECK (Eng)

9+ letters

BLACKWATER (Ire)
BRA(H)MAPUTRA (Pak)
CHANGJIANG (Ch)
ESSEQUIBO (Guy)
EUPHRATES (Iraq)
HACKENSACK (US)
HELMSDALE (Sc)
INDIGIRKA (USSR)
IRRAWADDY (Bur)
MACKENZIE (Can)
MADRE DE DIOS (Bol)
MISSISSIPPI (US)
PILCOMAYO (Arg/Para)

PYRIPHLEGETHON
(myth)
QU'APPELLE (Can)
RICHELIEU (Can)
RIO GRANDE (Mex)
ROOSEVELT (Braz)
ST LAWRENCE (Can)
SÃO FRANCISCO (Braz)
TENNESSEE (US)
TOCANTINS (Braz)
TROMBETAS (Braz)
YANGTSEKIANG (Ch)

RIVERSIDE *BANK*; ON EDGE.
RLY *RAILWAY*.
RM ROYAL MARINES; JOLLIES. [Irish ~, Major Yeates].
Malagasy Rep (*car plate*).
ROACH *CARP*, *FISH*. CONVEX PART OF SAIL.
COCKROACH.
ROAD (s/l rowed). AVE, RD, MI, MIV, ST. DRAG,
HIGHWAY, PIKE, STREET, *WAY* (q.v.). FROG AND
TOAD (*rh sl*).
ROBBER BANDOLERO, BURGLAR, CRACKSMAN,
PILFERER, SHOPLIFTER, *STEALER*, SWAGMAN, THIEF,
YEGG; TEA LEAF (*rh sl*); [cat]. **Gk god** = *Hermes*; **celeb**:
AUTOLYCUS (Gk myth); *BARABBAS* (bibl); *CACUS* (Rom
myth); COL BLOOD (Crown Jewels); DANE, WILLIAM
(Silas Marner, Eliot); DIDDLER, JEREMY (Raising of the
Wind, Kenny); DODGER, ARTFUL (Oliver, *Dickens*);
DOONES (Lorna Doone, Blackmore); FAGIN (Oliver,
Dickens); FILCH (Beggars Opera, Gay); KAMAL (East and
West, Kipling); MEG MERRILIES (Guy Mannering, Scott);
PROCRUSTES (Gk myth); *SCIRON* (Gk myth); *SINIS* (Gk
myth); SIKES, BILL (Oliver, *Dickens*); *TOM* (Piper's son);
WILD, JONATHAN (~, Defoe, Fielding).
ROBERTSON WILLIAM I (crypt).
ROBIN *BIRD*, REDBREAST, RUDDOCK. CHRISTOPHER
(*Milne*). GOODFELLOW, PUCK (page, *Shak*, Merry Wives).
HOOD, *OUTLAW*. **Pl** = BRISTOL CITY, CHARLTON
ATHLETIC (*football* teams).
ROCHESTER Episcopal sig = ROFFEN. *CASTLE. MEDWAY
TOWN*. Char in Jane Eyre, who goes *blind* [*Mason*] (*Brontë*).
ROCK 1. BOULDER, CARBONIFEROUS ~, COAL, CRAG,
FLINT, GNEISS, GRANITE, LAPIDIFIED, LATERITE,
LIMESTONE, METAMORPHIC ~, MINERAL, ORE,
PETRIFACTION, RUBBLE, SANDSTONE, SCREE,
SEDIMENTARY ~, STONE, VOLCANIC ~ (AA, IGNEUS
~, LAPILLUS, LAVA, MAGMA, MANTLE, MONOLITH,
PAHOEHOE, SARSEN STONE, SCORIA, SLAG). **Celeb**:
~ of Ages; Brighton ~; Gibraltar; St Peter. 2. CRYSTAL,
DIAMOND, *GEM*, JEWEL (all sl). FIRM, STEADFAST.
CANDY, SWEET. REEL, SHAKE, SWAY. *DANCE*, POP
MUSIC (**comp** = roll).
ROCKERY GARDEN (ROCK/STONE). QUARRY (crypt).
CRADLE, NURSERY (crypt).

ROCKET BANGER, BAZOOKA, CONGREVE, FIREWORK, FLARE, FLYING BOMB, *SPACECRAFT*, *WEAPON*. *CARPET*, *REPRIMAND*. RAILWAY ENGINE [Stevenson].

ROCK SINGER ELVIS. LORELEI, SIREN (crypt). NANNY, NURSEMAID [Lullaby] (crypt).

ROD SYMBOL; BAR, CANE, *POLE*, SWITCH, WAND [*Aaron's* and *Moses'* ~s. *Garter*]; **comp** = *line*. SHAFT. GUN, PISTOL, REVOLVER (sl). EYEPIECE, RETINA. *PERCH*, *MEASURE*.

RODENT GNAWING. Mammalian order, (vermin), **incl**: agouti, *beaver*, capybara, carpincho, cavy, chipmunk, coypu, dormouse, fieldmouse, gerbil, gopher, guinea-pig, hamster, house mouse, jerboa, lemming, marmot, mouse, muskrat, musquash, nutria, porcupine, prairie dog, prairie marmot, *rat*, squirrel, vole, water rat, woodchuck.

ROFFEN *Episcopal sig* of *ROCHESTER*.

ROLLING STONE NOMAD, WANDERER [no moss; *Sisyphus*]. **Pl** = POP GROUP.

Rom *Roman*; (and see *Roman Place Names*).

ROMAN 1. LATIN. *TYPEFACE*. UPRIGHT TYPE. OF ROME (**Noblest** ~ = Brutus). 2. Put into Latin, e.g. **He is Roman** (3) = EST.

~ **COIN** AS, DENARIUS, SOLIDUS, TALENT.

~ **GOD** DEUS (Lat). LAR (and see *god* for full list).

~ **GODDESS** See *goddess* for full list.

~ **PLACE NAME** The following are some of the better known names of Roman towns in Britain, with their modern equivalents.

4-letters

DEVA *Chester*	~ (Dumnuniorum) *Exeter*
ISCA Caerleon	MONA Anglesey

5-letters

BANNA Bewcastle	RATAE Leicester
DANUM Doncaster	SARUM *Salisbury*
ITIIS (Ins) St Michael's Mount	VENTA Caistor
NIDUM Neath	~ (Belgarum) *Winchester*
	~ (Silurium) Caerwent

6-letters

ABONAE Sea Mills	ALABUM Llandovery

ALAUNA Learchild
ARBEIA South Shields
BREMIA Llanio
DUBRIS Dover
GLEVUM Gloucester
LINDUM *Lincoln*

MAGNIS Kenchester
MONAVA (Ins) *Isle of Man*
OTHONA Bradwell
SPINIS Speen
VECTIS (Ins) *Isle of Wight*

7-letters

BINOVIA Binchester
BURRIUM Usk
CALLEVA Silchester
CAONIUM Rivenhall
CICUTIO Y-Glaer

CONDATE Northwich
CUNETIO Mildenhall
ISURIUM Aldborough
LEMANIS Lympne
SALINAE Droitwich

8-letters

AD PONTEM East Stoke
ANDERITA Pevensey
BLESTIUM Monmouth
CANOVIUM Caerhun
CARINIUM Cirencester
EBORACUM *York*

LINDINIS Ilchester
MAMUCIUM Manchester
RUTUPIAE Richborough
SEGENTUM Caernarfon
VERLUCIO Sandy Lane

9-letters

LAGENTIUM Tadcaster
LONDINIUM *London*
MORIDUNUM
  Carmarthen

REGULBIUM Reculver
URICONIUM Wroxeter
VAGNIACAE Springhead
VONDOMORA Ebchester

10-letters

AQUAE SULIS Bath
BRANODUNUM
  Brancaster
CLAUSENTUM
  Southampton
DORNOVARIA
  Dorchester
DURNOVARIA *Chesterton*
DUROBRIVAE *Rochester*
DUROLIPONS *Cambridge*
DUROVERNUM
  Canterbury

GORBANNIUM
  Abergavenny
LACTODORUM
  Towcester
LUGUVALIUM Carlisle
MEDIOLANUM
  Whitchurch
NOVIOMAGUS *Chichester* ~
  Crayford
VERULAMIUM *St Albans*
VIROCONIUM Wroxeter

11+ letters

CAESAROMAGUS
  Chelmsford
CAMULODUNUM
  Colchester
CATARACTONIUM
  Catterick
DUROCOBRIVAE
  Dunstable
DUROVIGUTUM
  Godmanchester

LONGOVICIUM
  Lanchester
MAGIOVINIUM
  Dropshort
SERVIODUNUM
  Old Sarum
VINDOCLADIA Badbury

ROMAN ROAD VIA (Lat). The following are some of the better-known Roman roads in Britain:

AKEMAN'S ST
ASHWELL ST
DERE ST
DEVIL'S CAUSEWAY
ERMINE ST
FOSSE WAY
ICKNIELD WAY

PEDLAR'S WAY
PILGRIM'S WAY (path)
PORTWAY
RIDGE WAY
RYKNILD ST
STANE ST
WATLING ST

~ **SOLDIER** CENTURION etc. See *SOLDIER*.
~ **TRIBES** See *TRIBES*.
ROME (s/l roam). 1. ETERNAL CITY, SPQR [*Aeneas, AUC, Romulus* and *Remus*, Seven Hills; A and C, Cor, Titus (*Shak*)].
  2. Implies Latin, e.g. **They go out in Rome** (6) = EXEUNT.
ROMULUS Rom myth *twin* br of *Remus*, s of *Mars* and *Rhea* (Silvia), suckled by wolves, founded *Rome*. Slew his br.
ROOK *BIRD, CROW. CHEAT, ROB. CHESSPIECE* (*CASTLE*).
ROOKERY HABITATION (penguins, *rooks*, seals). BURGLARY, *ROBBERY* (crypt).
ROSE (s/l roes, rows). *FLOWER, TREE*; [St Dorothy; St *Elizabeth* of Hungary (bread into ~s); *Abraham* (fire into bed of ~s in Mos faith)] 'RHODA'. ASCENDED, *MOUNTED*, SOARED; GOT UP (hence TOG, dn crypt). REBELLED. SPRINKLER. BADGE (polit; Lab). *WINDOW. WORLD-GIRDLER. WRITER.* WALKWAY (Chester). **Comp** = *crown*.
~ **BOWL** FLOWER VASE. *FOOTBALL* GROUND/ COMPETITION (US college).

ROSETTA STONE Memorial inscription to *Ptolemy* V (205–181
B.C.) in hieroglyph, demotic (coptic) and Greek languages on a
slab of black basalt, discovered in 1799 by a French officer in the
Nile delta. It proved the key to the meaning of hieroglyphics.

ROSE WATER SCENTED WATER, COMPLIMENT [gentle
handling]. *SHOWER*, SPRAY (crypt).

ROSIE LEE TEA (*rh sl*).

ROSINANTE NAG, *HORSE*, *SCREW* (Don *Quixote*).

ROT DECAY, PUTREFACTION. BOSH, NONSENSE,
RUBBISH. BANTER, CHAFF, *TEASE*.

ROUGH (s/l *ruff*). *Anag.* CRUDE. SHAGGY, UNEVEN.
BOISTEROUS, RIOTOUS, SEVERE, VIOLENT.

ROUND 1. O (crypt). DRINKS, TURN, TREAT. SANDWICH.
CONTINUOUS, ENTIRE, UNBROKEN. CANDID,
GENUINE. CIRCULAR, REVOLVING, ROTUND,
SPHERICAL. BULLET, SHELL. GAME (golf). **Pl** =
INSPECTION ROUTE, VISITS (med). 2. Word round another,
e.g. **He's round at the sports eliminators** (5) = HE·AT·S. 3. **A**
~ = letter A before any synonym for 'round', e.g. A*BOUT,
A*WHEEL, A*NIL (crypt).

ROUNDABOUT 1. C, CA, CIRCUMLOCUTION. ROAD
JUNCTION. CONVOLUTED. MERRYGOROUND
(fairground). 2. Word round synonym for 'about', e.g. **The
roundabout between two and four** (5) = TH·RE·E. 3. Word or
letter plus synonym for 'round' placed about word or letter
indicated, e.g. **When roundabout fifty, too** (4) = A·L·S·O.

ROUNDHEAD 1. PARLIAMENTARIAN (**opp** = Cavalier).
SKINHEAD. R (crypt). 2. Place letter o before synonym for
'head', e.g. OHEAD, OPATE, ONUT. 3. Place letter o before any
word or letter indicated, e.g. **At Roundhead fodder** (3) = O·AT.

ROUNDSMAN *DELIVERY MAN*: MILKMAN, PAPERBOY,
POSTMAN. GOLFER (crypt).

ROUND TABLE BUSINESS ASSOCIATION, ROTARY CLUB.
ORDER OF CHIVALRY (hist) [*Camelot*, *King Arthur*;
knights: Bedivere (Tennyson), Bors (Tennyson), Calidore
(Spenser), *Galahad* (Tennyson), Gawain (Tennyson), Geraint
(Tennyson), *Lancelot* (Tennyson), Launfal (Lowell), Mordred
(Tennyson), Pelleas (Tennyson), Percivale (Tennyson), Tristram
(Malory); **Ladies**: Elaine (loved Sir *Lancelot*), Enid (wife of
Geraint), Ettarre (loved Gawain, loved by Pelleas), Guinevere
(wife of *King Arthur*, loved *Lancelot*), Iseult (Tristram), *Lady
of the Lake* (Vivien), Lady of Shalott (*weaver*), Morgan le Fey

(*sorceress*)].

ROUSE (s/l rows). AWAKEN, INFLAME, PROVOKE,
STARTLE, STIR (UP), WAKEN. BUMPER, DRAUGHT;
DRINKING BOUT, REVEL, TOAST. HAUL. CURE FISH.

ROW (s/l roe). OAR, PULL, SCULL. ALIGNMENT,
DRESSING, FILE, LINE, RANGE, RANK, TERRACE,
TIER. BATTLE, DISAGREEMENT, FIGHT, WAR. DIN,
NOISE, *RACKET*, SHINDY.

ROWER OARSMAN, SCULLER, *STROKE*, WET-BOB.
ARGUER, FIGHTER, SCOLD, SHREW (all crypt). DRILL
SERGEANT (crypt).

ROWING SCULLING, STROKING; PADDLING.
ALTERCATION, ARGUING, DISAGREEING, FIGHTING.
ALIGNING, DRILLING, LINING-UP (crypt).

ROYAL R; MAJESTIC, REGAL. *COLOUR* (blue). *THEATRE.
ANTELOPE. SAIL. MEASURE* (paper). **Pl** = ROYAL
FAMILY. HORSEGUARDS, HOUSEHOLD CAVALRY.

~ **AIR FORCE** RAF. *AIRMEN.*

~ **AND ANCIENT** RA. *GOLF CLUB.*

~ **ARMOURED CORPS** RAC. TANKERS (crypt).

~ **ARTILLERY** RA. *GUNMEN*, GUNNERS.

~ **AUTOMOBILE CLUB** RAC. CARMEN.

~ **ENGINEER** RE. SAPPER. EMINENCE GRISE (crypt;
Richelieu).

~ **FAMILY** *HOUSE*, RULING LINE [court cards; *Ch dynasty*;
mad king; *monarch*; *noble*]; **celeb**:

Country	Family
Abyssinia	MENELUK (Solomon/Sheba)
Austria	HABSBURG/HAPSBURG
Bavaria	WITTELSBACH
Belgium	COBURG
China	HWAN, MANCHU, MING, TANG
Denmark	OLDENBURG
France	BOURBON, CAPET, VALOIS
Franks	CHARLEMAGNE
Germany	HOHENZOLLERN
Greece	SCHLESWIG-HOLSTEIN
Holy Roman Empire	HABSBURG/HAPSBURG, HOHENSTAUFEN

Hungary	HABSBURG/HAPSBURG
India	GUPTA
Ireland	DESMOND, MCCARTHY, O'BRIEN, O'CONNOR, O'NEILL
Italy	*SAVOY*
Monaco	GRIMALDI
Morocco	ALAOUITE
Netherlands	*ORANGE*
Poland	JAGELLON
Portugal	BRAGANZA
Prussia	HOHENZOLLERN
Rumania	HOHENZOLLERN
Ruritania	ELPHBERG (fict)
Russia	ROMANOFF
Scotland	STUART
Spain	BOURBON, HAPSBURG
Sweden	BERNADOTTE, VASA
UK	HANOVER, PLANTAGENET, STUART, TUDOR, WINDSOR
Wales	GLYNDWR, LLEWELLYN, MORTIMER, TUDOR

ROYAL SOCIETY RS. THE *COURT*, PALACE ENTOURAGE (crypt).

RR RIGHT REVEREND, hence *BISHOP*.

RRR BASIC EDUCATION, THREE R'S.

RT RIGHT. RADIO TELEPHONE.

RUBBISH BOSH, *ROT. REFUSE*.

RUBY *GEM*, PRECIOUS STONE; BALAS, CORUNDUM; *anniversary* (40th). *COLOUR* (red). *DOG* (John Peel). *TYPEFACE*.

RUDE COARSE, IMPOLITE, INSOLENT, OFFENSIVE, UNCIVILIZED. CRUDE, PRIMITIVE, SIMPLE. ABRUPT, SUDDEN, VIOLENT. HEARTY, VIGOROUS.

RUDOLF *LAKE. REINDEER*. RASSENDYLL (Prisoner of Zenda, *Hope*).

RUFF (s/l *rough*). FRILL, NECK-PIECE, PARTLET. *BIRD*, PIGEON, SANDPIPER (**female** = reeve). *FISH*. TRUMP (cards), hence *TRUMPERY* (crypt).

RUGBY FOOTBALL. RUGGER [**Grounds**: Cardiff Arms Park

(Wal), Lansdowne Road (Ire), Murrayfield (Sc), Twickenham (Eng)]. [2 for conversion; 4 for try]. *PUBLIC SCHOOL.* *SERVANT* (to Dr Caius, Merry Wives, *Shak*).

~ **MAN** FOOTBALLER. SCHOOLBOY. DR ARNOLD, TOM BROWN, FLASHMAN. W. W. ELLIS. **Pl** = ALL-BLACKS, LIONS, SPRINGBOKS, WALLABIES.

RUIN *Anag*. 1. DOWNFALL. REMAINS, RESIDUE. HAVOC, IMPAIR, MAR, SPOIL. BANKRUPT, BREAK, WRECK. 2. Put RU in word before or after, e.g. **Did ruin Welsh priest** (5) = D*RU*ID.

RULER AMEER, AMIR, *EMPEROR*, *KING*, *MONARCH*, SOVEREIGN, SULTAN; CHIEF (**opp** = *subject*). *MEASURE*, STRAIGHT-EDGE; LINER (crypt). *GORGON*.

RUM *DRINK*, LIQUOR, SPIRIT; NELSON'S BLOOD, TOT. DANGEROUS, DIFFICULT. *ODD*, QUEER, STRANGE. *ISLAND*.

Rum Rumania, ~n.

RUN DOUBLE, LOPE, SCAMPER, SPEED, STREAK; **comp** = hit. COURSE, FLOW. MANAGE, ORGANIZE. R, SINGLE (*cricket*). CAGE, PEN. SMUGGLE. SCHEDULED SERVICE, SHUTTLE, TRIP. PUT UP, STAND (for office). *LADDER*. CRESTA. **Pl** = SCORE (*cricket*).

RUNNER *FLOWER*, RIVER, R (crypt). SMUGGLER. ATHLETE. BEAN.

~ **UP** *SECOND*, SILVER MEDALLIST. DRESSMAKER. NAEB (dn, crypt).

RUN UP APPROACH, INTRODUCTION. (DRESS) MAKE. NUR (dn, crypt).

RURAL DEAN RD. *CHURCHMAN*.

RUSH ADVANCE PRINT, CLIP (film). MARSH PLANT, REED, STRAW (and see *GRASS*). ASSAULT, CHARGE, DASH, DRAG, FORCE, IMPEL, STAMPEDE, SWARM. OVERCHARGE. FALL, FLOW, HURRY. **Pl** = see *song*.

Russ Russia, ~n (as opposed to USSR).

RUSSIAN RED. IVAN, SERGE.

RUSTLER CATTLE-THIEF, HORSE-THIEF; STEERSMAN (crypt). FORAGER. *SILK*, TAFFETA (crypt).

RUTH 1. COMPASSION, PITY. 'A FRIEND'. BABE (*baseball*). *G & S*. 2. Moabite who mar (1) Mahlon (2) Boaz [Naomi (Mara) mother-in-law. *Tears* amid the alien corn (Keats)].

RV REVISED VERSION, BIBLE. RENDEZ-VOUS, MEETING PLACE, TRYST.

RYE *DRINK*, WHISKY. CORN. *GRASS*. CINQUE PORT.
RIVER (Eng).

S *SAINT*. SAN, SANTA. SATURDAY. *SECOND*. SINGULAR.
SMALL. SOCIETY. SOLIDUS, SHILLING. SON. *SOUTH*.
ST. STARBOARD. SULPHUR (*chem*). SUNDAY. SWEDEN
(*car plate*). BRIDGE PLAYER. DOLLAR.
SA SEX APPEAL; *CHARM*; IT. SOUTH AFRICA.
SABLE BLACK (*herald*). DREAD, DUSKY, GLOOMY.
MARTEN. PAINTBRUSH.
SABRE CUTLASS, SWORD, *WEAPON*. AIRCRAFT.
SACK *DISCHARGE*. PILLAGE, PLUNDER. *BAG*. DRESS.
FABRIC, *MATERIAL*. *MEASURE* (wool). SHERRY, *WINE*.
SADDLE *MOUNT*, RIDE (**in the** ~ = UP); BACK-SEAT (crypt).
BURDEN. *COL*.
SADLY *Anag*. REGRETFULLY, RUEFULLY,
SORROWFULLY.
SAGE DISCREET, JUDICIOUS, WISE; MAGUS (**Pl** = MAGI),
MAHATMA (Ind), MENTOR, SAVANT, WISEACRE,
WISEMAN [Nestor (*Argonaut*), Solomon, Solon]. *HERB*.
CHEESE. *COLOUR* (green). And see *Seven* ~s.
SAID 1. RECITED, SPOKEN, UTTERED; ORAL; **comp** =
done. PORT (Egy). 2. *Sounds like* another word.
SAIL (s/l sale). CANVAS, PROPELLANT (naut), **types**:
BONNET, COURSE, DRABBLER, DRIVER, FLYING
JIB, FORESAIL, GENOA, JIB, GAFF ~, GUNTER,
LATEEN, LUG, MAINSAIL, MIZZEN, ROYAL, SKYSAIL,
SPANKER, SPINNAKER, SPRIT ~, SQUARESAIL,
STAYSAIL, STUDDING SAIL, TOPGALLANT, TOPSAIL,
YANKEE (and see *rig*). COLLECTION/*ASSEMBLY* OF
SHIPS, SHIP; JOURNEY, NAVIGATE, VOYAGE (**opp**
= *steam*). DORSAL FIN (fish). BLADE (windmill [Don
Quixote]). SOAR (aero).
SAILOR AB, CREW, DECKHAND, GOB (US), *HAND*,
JACK, LASCAR, OS, RATING, SALT, TAR; (**Union** =
NUS), CRAFTSMAN (crypt), *REEFER* (crypt). RN, USN.
YACHTSMAN. **Celeb**: CAPT *AHAB* (*Moby Dick*), ANCIENT
MARINER (Coleridge), TOM BOWLING (Smollett),
BILLY BUDD (Melville), CHUCKS (Marryat), LONG TOM
COFFIN (Fenimore Cooper), CAPT CUTTLE (*Dickens*),

DICK DEADEYE (*Pinafore, G & S*), MIDSHIPMAN EASY (Marryat), LEMUEL GULLIVER (*Swift*), RAPHAEL HYTHLODAY (More), DANIEL & HAM PEGGOTTY (*Dickens*), LT *PINKERTON* (Mme *Butterfly*, Puccini), SHIPMAN (*Chaucer*), SIN(D)BAD (Arabian Nights), DISCO TROOP (Kipling), SALVATION YEO (Kingsley); [*military leaders, world-girdlers, patron saint*].

SAINT S, ST. *ANGEL.* GOODMAN (crypt). [*patron* ~]. Pl = *Football* teams (UK & US).

ST ALBANS 1. **Episcopal sig** = ALBAN. 2. VERULAMIUM (*Rom*).

ST CATHERINE Virgin martyr of Alexandria (4th century). Tradition represents her as tied to a *wheel* [*firework*].

ST ELMO'S FIRE CORPOSANT. Glowing corona, like fire, caused by elect discharge around ch spires and ship masts (and more lately aircraft wings or propellers), associated in Gk myth with *Dioscuri* and *Helen.* Derived from *Elijah* = Elias = Elmo, who confounded the priests of *Baal* and *Astarte*, when only he was able to call down to Mt Carmel fire from heaven; c.f. *ignis fatuus* (which is chem different).

ST LEGER *CLASSIC* (horserace).

SALAMIS Site of a great sea *battle* near Athens in 480 B.C., in which 300 Gk ships under Themistocles defeated over five times their number of *Xerxes'* invading fleet.

SALARY EMOLUMENT, INCOME, PAY, *SCREW*, STIPEND, WAGE.

SALISBURY 1. **Episcopal sig** = SARUM. 2. HARARE (ex-*capital* of Rhodesia/Zimbabwe. SARUM (*Rom*). *Shak* char (R.ii, H.v, H.vi).

SALLY BELL ROPE. COCONUT SHY. OUTBURST, WIT. SALVATION ARMY. SORTIE. STONE-FLY. WREN. SARAH. ~LUNN [tea-cake].

SALMANAZAR 1. *BOTTLE* (wine = 12 normal). 2. Bibl K of Assyria *c.* 725 B.C., who conquered Isr and captured Samaria.

SALMON RIVER (US). *FISH* (genus salmonidae); **stages:** ALEVIN (fry), BAGGIT (after spawning), KELT (spent), SAMLET (young), SMOLT (1st sea migration), SPRAG (young), SPROD (2nd year); **types:** BARRAMUNDI (Aus, NZ), BLUE-BACK, BLUE-CAP, CAPLIN, COHO(E) (Pacific), FORKTAIL, GWINIAD (fresh water), KIPPER, KOKANEE (N Am), NERKA (US), OUANANICHE (Can), PALLAN (Ire), PARR, QUINNAT (King ~), RED

~, SEWIN (Wal), SMELT, SOCKEYE, SPARLING; **male** = cock, **fem** = hen, **offspring** = grilse, peal. **Celeb**: SALAR (Williamson).

SALOME 1. Bibl sis of Mary (m of *Jesus*) and mar to Zebedee. 2. Herodias' d (bibl), who danced (seven veils) before her step-f *Herod* Antipas and, at her m's behest, exacted the head of John the Baptist. 3. Play by *Wilde*.

SALT SEASONING; BRINE, *MINERAL*, SODIUM CHLORIDE (NACL, *chem*) [*Lot's* wife]. ARMS TALK. *ISLAND*. PUNGENCY, STING, WIT. *SAILOR*. ~ meat = *JUNK*.

SALUTE *BOW, GREET, HAIL, KISS*; ACCOST (Aloha, Ave, Hallo, Hi). HOMAGE; GUNFIRE.

SAM BROWNE (mil). SMALL (theat). MISSILE (*rocket*), *WEAPON*.

SAME DITTO, DO, IDEM. MONOTONOUS, UNIFORM, SIMILAR.

~ **PLACE** IB(ID).

SAMPHIRE *HERB*; CLIFFHANGER (crypt), CLIMBER (crypt).

SAMSON 1. Bibl Jew s of Manaoh, he mar a Phil, trad enemies of Isr. Endowed with great *strength*, he was betrayed by the *courtesan* Delilah, who sapped his powers by cutting off his hair. Captured and blinded by the Phil, his strength was miraculously restored so he could pull down the temple of Dagon. 2. Servant (R & J, *Shak* [Sampson]). 3. ~ Agonistes; blind wrestler (Milton). 4. Guillotine operator (2 Cities, *Dickens*). *PARSON*. 5. Mooring post for *painter* (naut).

SAMUEL Bibl s of Elkaneh and Hannah, who lived with *Eli* and travelled widely as a *judge* and *prophet*; he defeated the Phil and established Isr as a nation (*c*.1000 B.C.). In response to demand for a K, ~ chose *Saul* (q.v.), but the latter's qualities did not last, so ~ chose *David* to succeed him. Before his final overthrow, Saul consulted the prophecy of ~'s *ghost* via the Witch of Endor.

SANDHURST ACADEMY, RMA (mil).

SANDWICH PICNIC LUNCH, SNACK; SQUARE MEAL (crypt); SARNIE (sl). LAYER CAKE. INSERT, SQUEEZE IN. *CASTLE. CINQUE PORT. GOLF COURSE*.

SAN(TA) S. SPANISH SAINT. (FATHER CHRISTMAS).

SAPPER RE; ENGINEER. LEECH (crypt).

SAPPHIRE *GEM*, PRECIOUS STONE (blue), CORUNDUM; *anniversary* (45th). *COLOUR* (blue).

SARAH *SAL(LY)*.
SARD *GEM*; SEMI-PRECIOUS STONE, CORNELIAN
(orange).
SARDINE FISH, SARDELLE, YOUNG PILCHARD [herring].
GEM, SEMI-PRECIOUS STONE. **Pl** = *GAME* [tight-packed].
SARDONYX *GEM*, mix of *sard* and *onyx* (orange and white);
birthstone (August).
SARK CI, CHANNEL ISLAND. SHIRT. ROOFBOARDING.
SARUM SALISBURY *(Rom)*. *Episcopal sig* of SALISBURY.
SAS SPECIAL AIR SERVICE. SCANDINAVIAN AIR
SERVICE *(airline* ®).
SATAN *DEVIL*, IMP, LUCIFER, OLD NICK (lit = adversary).
SATELLITE 1. FOLLOWER, HANGER-ON, HENCHMAN.
DEPENDENT COUNTRY. 2. Moon or other body orbiting a
planet or star. 3. *SPACECRAFT*.
SATIRIST CYNIC, LAMPOONIST [irony, ridicule, sarcasm];
celeb: BUTLER (Eng), BYRON (Eng), DRYDEN (Eng),
HOGARTH (Eng), HORACE (Rom), JUVENAL (Rom),
LA BRUYÈRE (Fr), POPE (Eng), RABELAIS (Fr), *SWIFT*
(Eng), VOLTAIRE (Fr).
SATURDAY S, SA, SAT. Day of *Saturn*. ~'s child = works hard
for its living. [Solomon *Grundy*].
SATURN 1. Rom *god* of agriculture, after whom Italy was called
Saturnia at one time; mar to Ops. **Gk** = CRONOS. [Saturday].
2. *PLANET*.
SATYR 1. BUTTERFLY, RAKE, ROUÉ, WOMANIZER.
MONKEY. 2. Gk myth woodland deities, half man half *goat*,
with horned head, pointed ears and a tail. Chief among them
was *Pan*. Representatives attended *Bacchus*, at the feasts staged
by humans to him. **Rom** = FAUN.
SAUCE (s/l *source*). CHEEK, IMPERTINENCE, IMPUDENCE.
RELISH, KETCHUP: HP ®, PARSLEY, TOMATO,
WORCESTERSHIRE ® etc. DRINK (US sl).
SAUCY *ARCH*, CHEEKY, IMPUDENT (**opp** = *retiring, shy*).
SEASONED (cook, crypt).
SAUL 1. Bibl s of Kish and f of Ishbaal and Jonathan, whom
Samuel chose as first K of Isr (*c*.1000 B.C.). Power corrupted
him and he went *mad*, so that *David* was chosen to succeed, but
~ retained much influence. ~ persuaded the Witch of Endor
to call up the *ghost* of Samuel for a prophecy before the fateful
battle of Gilboa, at which both ~'s ss were k, and ~ suffered
severe defeat by the Phil; sui. 2. Name of *Paul* (q.v.) before his

conversion.

SAVE DELIVER, PRESERVE, PROTECT, RESCUE. BUT, EXCEPT, UNLESS.

SAVOY CABBAGE. HOTEL. *ROYAL FAMILY* (It).

SAW (s/l sore). NOTICED, SPOTTED. SERRATED/TOOTHED TOOL; **types**: BAND ~, COPING ~, CROSS-CUT ~, CIRCULAR ~, FRET ~, HACK ~, JIG ~, TENON ~; CUT, RIP. ADAGE, MAXIM, PROVERB, *SAYING*.

Sax Saxon.

SAY E.G., FOR INSTANCE. *Shak* char (H.vi).

SAYING ADAGE, APHORISM, BON MOT, BYWORD, DEFINITION, MAXIM, MOTTO, PROVERB, QUOTATION, *SAW*.

Sc Scotland, ~ish. For ~ regions, see *Division*. SCANDIUM (*chem*).

SCALE 1. CLIMB, *MOUNT*. CLASSIFICATION, GRADUATION [vernier]. PITCH ARRANGEMENT (chromatic, diatonic, *major, minor*, pantatonic; A–G). FLAKE, HUSK, PLATE, POD, SCAB. INCRUSTATION, RUST. BALANCE, WEIGHING INSTRUMENT. 2. A *constellation* (Libra); sign of the *Zodiac* (7th).

SCAMPER *DASH, RUN*.

SCAN CON, EXAMINE, LOOK AT, OVERLOOK. RESOLVE. READ RHYTHMICALLY (test verse by examining each metric *foot*). SCANDINAVIA.

SCARF 1. FISH, JOINT (carpentry). 2. *Material* worn at head or neck: BANDANA, BOA, COMFORTER, CRAVAT, DUPATTA (Ind), FICHU, FUR, GUIMPE, HEAD~, KERCHIEF, MUFFLER, NECKBAND, -CLOTH, -ERCHIEF, -TIE, RUFF, SHAWL, STOCK, TALLITH, TIPPET, TUCKER, WIMPLE.

SCENE (s/l *seen*). *STAGE. ACTION*, INCIDENT. LANDSCAPE, LOCATION, PAINTING, *PLACE*, VIEW, VISTA. LIFESTYLE. QUARREL, *ROW*.

SCENT (s/l *cent*, sent). AROMA, FRAGRANCE, ODOUR, PERFUME, SMELL. SPOOR, TRACK, TRAIL. CLUE, DETECT, SNIFF, SUSPECT.

SCH *SCHOOL*.

SCHOLAR BA, MA, L; SCHOOLBOY/GIRL. SECOND AGE (AYLI, *Shak*). LEARNED PERSON, CHELA (Ind), DISCIPLE, SAVANT [*patron saint*]; *Chaucer* char, ERASMUS.

SCHOOL DISCIPLINE, TAME, TEACH, TRAIN. DISCIPLES,

FOLLOWERS, IMITATORS, SECT. *Assembly* of cardplayers, fish, porpoises, whales. ALMA MATER, CLASS, PLACE OF EDUCATION, SCH [*patron saint*]; **celeb (fiction)**: BROOKFIELD (Goodbye Mr Chips, James Hilton), DOTHEBOYS HALL (Nich Nick, *Dickens*), GRANGE HILL (TV), GREYFRIARS (*Famous Five*, Frank Richards), LOWOOD (Jane Eyre, C. *Brontë*), ST TRINIANS (Ronald Searle), SALEM HOUSE (Copperfield, *Dickens*); **celeb (public)**: see *Public Schools*.

SCHOOLMASTER BEAK, DOMINIE (Sc), *MASTER*, TEACHER, TUTOR; SIR (**opp** = *miss*); **celeb**: DR ARNOLD (*Rugby*); DR BLIMBER (Dombey, *Dickens*); BROCKLEHURST (Jane Eyre, C. *Brontë*); CAMBIO (Taming, *Shak*); CHIPPING (Goodbye Mr Chips, James Hilton); CREAKLE (Copperfield, *Dickens*); GRADGRIND (Hard Times, *Dickens*); HOLOFERNES (LLL, *Shak*); PARTRIDGE (Tom Jones, Fielding); PINCH (C of Errors, *Shak*); QUELCH (*Greyfriars*, Richards); SQUEERS (Nich Nick, *Dickens*); DR STRONG (Copperfield, *Dickens*); WATERBURY (*Wodehouse*).

SCHOONER *BOAT*, (SAILING) VESSEL, SHIP; **celeb**: Cutty Sark (tea clipper); *Hesperus* (Longfellow); Pequod, (*Moby Dick*). GLASS (sherry).

SCIRON (s/l *Skiron*). Gk myth *robber* who kicked all strangers over a cliff where they were devoured by a *tortoise*; k by *Theseus*.

SCOFF GIBE, MOCK, TAUNT. EAT, *WOLF*; FOOD, GRUB, MEAL (sl).

SCOLD NAG, RAIL, REBUKE, *UPBRAID*; *SHREW*, SPITFIRE, TERMAGANT, VIRAGO [Kate (*Shak*). *Xanthippe*].

SCORE BLAZE, *MARK, NICK*, NOTCH, SCRATCH, SLASH. TWENTY, XX. COMPOSE, *MUSIC, NOTED*. (MAKE) *RUNS*, POINTS, POT, TOTAL.

SCOREBOARD DISPLAY, TALLYWAG. MUSIC STAND (crypt). DARTBOARD.

SCORPION 1. ARACHNID (*insect*). BALLISTA (hist). GIBRALTARIAN (sl). TANK (mil). *WHIP* (bibl).
2. *Constellation* (Scorpio); sign of the *Zodiac* (8th).

SCOT NATIVE OF SCOTLAND; IAN, JOCK, MAC, MC, MON. *TAX*. **Pl** = Scottish (for ~s Regions, see *Division*).

SCOTCH SCOTS, SCOTTISH; GAELIC; CELTIC. DRINK,

WHISKY. BRAKE, WEDGE (mech). MARK, *SCORE*,
WOUND. END, FRUSTRATE, STOP.

SCOTT (s/l *scot*). 1. Sir Giles Gilbert ~; archit. 2. Capt Robert
Falcon ~; *explorer*. 3. Sir Walter ~; *poet, writer;* **books**: Bride
of Lammermoor, Guy Mannering, Ivanhoe, Kenilworth, *Lady
of the Lake*, Lay of the Last Minstrel, Marmion, Rob Roy,
Rokeby, Talisman, Two Drovers, Waverley novels. 4. Gloria ~
(*Holmes* case). 5. Sir Peter ~, s of (2); naturalist and *painter*.

SCOUT SERVANT, VALET (Oxford [C = gyp]). REJECT,
RIDICULE. ADVANCE PARTY, FORAGER, RANGER,
RECCE, RECONNOITRE, TRAIL-BLAZER, VANGUARD
(mil). FIGHTER (*aircraft*). CHAP, FELLOW. BOY, CADET.
PATROLMAN. BIRD.

SCRAMBLE *Anag.* e.g. **Scrambled eggs** = GEGS, SEGG etc.
CLAMBER, CRAWL. *MIX, STIR. FLY*, TAKE OFF (av sl).

SCRAP *BATTLE*, CONTEST, DISPUTE, FIGHT, QUARREL,
ROW, SCRIMMAGE. *REFUSE*, WASTE. DISCARD.
FRAGMENT, ODDMENT, PIECE, *RAG*, REMNANT.

SCRATCH NOTCH, *SCORE*. ITCH, SCRAPE. PAR,
UNHANDICAPPED. ERASE, WITHDRAW. *DEVIL*.

SCREEN DISPLAY, PROJECT (films, radar, TV). *BLIND*,
PARTITION, REREDOS, SHADE. GRID, MESH, SIEVE.
CHECK, *TEST. CONCEAL*, HIDE, PROTECT.

SCREW *GAOLER*. PAY, *MONEY*, SALARY, WAGES.
COUPLING, FASTENING. PROPELLER [Archimedes].
REVOLVE. CONTORT, DISTORT. SQUEEZE. NAG,
POOR *HORSE* [Rosinante].

SCRIBE AMANUENSIS, ARCHIVIST, CLERK, COPYIST,
SCRIVENER, SECRETARY, *WRITER*. MARKER, STYLE.
JURIST, TEACHER, THEOLOGIAN (bibl, Jew) [Pharisee];
celeb: EZRA.

SCULL (s/l *skull*). OAR, *ROW. BIRD*, SKUA.

SCULLERY KITCHEN, WASHROOM. ROWING [Henley]
(crypt).

SCULPTOR 1. ARTIST, CARVER, GLYPTOGRAPHER,
(STONE)MASON, MODELLER, WOODCUTTER;
FIGURER (crypt); **celeb**: ARP, CALDER, CANOVA,
DAEDALUS, DONATELLO, EPSTEIN, FRENCH,
GHIBERTI, GIBSON, GILBERT, LEONARDO DA VINCI,
MODIGLIANI, MAROCHETTI, MICHELANGELO,
MILLES, MOORE, PHIDIAS, PISANO, PRAXITILES,
RODIN, TALUS. 2. *CONSTELLATION*.

SCYLLA 1. Six-headed sea monster on a rock which, with *Charybdis*, formed a hazard for seafarers in the Straits of Messina. 2. A minor *PLANET*.

SE SELENIUM (*chem*). SOUTH EAST; HOME COUNTIES, KENT (crypt).

SEA (s/l *see*). 1. MAIN, SALT WATER. *COLOUR* (blue). **The Seven Seas** = ANTARCTIC, ARCTIC, INDIAN, N. ATLANTIC, S. ATLANTIC, N. PACIFIC, S. PACIFIC OCEANS. 2. **Gods: Gk** = NEREUS, *POSEIDON;* **Rom** = NEPTUNE; **Nor** = AEGIR. **Goddess: Gk** = *AMPHITRITE*. **Celeb seas:**

3-letters
RED

4-letters
ARAL	*DEAD*	KARA	SULU
AZOV	JAVA		

5-letters
BANDA	*CORAL*	JAPAN	*WHITE*
BLACK	CRETE	*NORTH*	
CERAM	*IRISH*	TIMOR	

6-letters
AEGEAN	CELTIC	IONIAN	TASMAN
BALTIC	FLORES	LAPTEV	WADDEN
BERING			

7-letters
ANDAMAN	BARENTS	GALILEE	OKHOTSK
ARABIAN	CASPIAN	MARMARA	SOLOMON
ARAFURA	CELEBES	MOLUCCA	

8-letters
ADRIATIC	HEBRIDES
AMUNDSEN	LIGURIAN
BEAUFORT	*SARGASSO* (weed)
BISMARCK	

9+ letters
CARIBBEAN	EAST CHINA

EAST SIBERIAN
HUDSON BAY
MEDITERRANEAN
NORWEGIAN
SCAPA FLOW

SOUTH CHINA
TRANQUILLITY
(moon)
TYRRHENIAN

SEAFOOD Any fish or shellfish eaten at a meal: CLAMS,
COCKLES, CRABS, *FISH, LOBSTER*, MUSSELS,
OYSTERS, PRAWNS, SHRIMPS, SQUID, WINKLES
[*crustacean*]. MAIN COURSE, MAIN MEAL, HARD TACK
(crypt).

SEAL 1. *CLOSE*, FASTEN, PLUG, SECURE, *STOP*,
WATERPROOF. APPROVE, ATTEST, CLINCH,
FINALISE, RATIFY, SETTLE, SIGN, VALIDATE;
AUTHENTICATION, *AUTHORITY*, IMPRIMATUR,
INSIGNIA, SIGNET (RING), *STAMP*; *WAX* [Great ~ (Mark
Twain)]. 2. Pinniped aquatic mammal, eared or earless; **male**
= bull, **fem** = cow, **offspring** = pup, **assembly** = herd, pod,
rookery; **breeds**: Atlantic ~, bladder-nose ~, Californian ~,
Caspian ~, common ~, crabeater, elephant ~, fur ~, grey ~,
harbour ~, hooded ~, Lake Baikal ~, leopard ~, Monk ~,
otary, ringed ~, silkie (Sc), Weddel ~; sealion [Proteus
(herdsman); walrus].

SEASON AUTUMN, *FALL, SPRING, SUMMER*, WINTER;
Gk goddesses = *HORAE*. (PROPER) TIME; PERIOD.
ACCLIMATIZE. ADD PIQUANCY (jests, wit; pepper,
salt etc).

SEASONAL SUITABLE, TIMELY. CONDIMENTS, MUSTARD,
PEPPER, *SALT* (crypt).

SEAT BENCH, CHAIR, STOOL, THRONE; BOTTOM,
BUTTOCKS. POSTURE. SIT. ABIDING PLACE, *COUNTRY
HOUSE*, PLACE, *STATELY HOME*.

SEATED ASTRIDE; *CHAIRED, MOUNTED* (crypt). SAT
(UPON). LANDED GENTRY (crypt).

SEAWEED ALGA(E); **types**: AGAR, BLADDERWRACK,
BROWN, CARRAGEEN, CEYLON MOSS, CLADOPHORA
RUPESTRIS, CORALLINE, CORAL WEED, DEVIL'S
APRON, DIATOM, GRASS KELP, IRISH MOSS,
(PURPLE) LAVER, NULLIPORE, OARWEED, OREWEED,
SARGASSO, SEA LETTUCE, SUGAR KELP, THONG
WEED, BLADDER-, CHANNELLED-, FLAT-, KNOTTED-,

SERRATED-WRACK, ZOSTERA [eelweed, grasswrack, pondweed].

SEC SECANT, SECOND(ARY). SECRETARY. *DRY* (Fr).

SECOND 1. S, SEC, TIC, TIME. B; AFTER FIRST, LATTER, NEXT BEST, NUMBER TWO, RUNNER UP, SECUNDUS; SILVER MEDALLIST. TRANSFER. ATTENDANT. D (mus). *BACK, SUPPORT.* FAULTY GOODS, SUB-STANDARD. 2. Second letter of previous or following word, e.g. **Second rate** = A.

~ **CLASS** B. E (*Lloyds*). L (crypt).

~ **HAND** USED, PART-WORN. MATE (naut, crypt). A (crypt).

SECRET ARCANE, CLOSE, DARK, ESOTERIC, *HIDDEN*, MYSTERY, PRIVATE, PRIVY, RETICENT. RESTRICTED, CONFIDENTIAL.

~ **AGENT** BOND, *MOLE*, SPY.

~ **POLICE** Secret force allegedly to combat subversion, but usually to maintain dictatorship, much given to ruthless cruelty. **Notorious examples**: *BOSS* (S Af); CHEKA, GPU, OGPU, NKVD, MVD, NKGB, KGB (CIS); GESTAPO (Ger); PSB (Ch); TON-TON MACOUTE (Haiti).

SECURE CLOSE, FORTIFY, LATCH, LOCK. CONFIDENT; IMPREGNABLE, RELIABLE, SAFE. GET, OBTAIN.

SEE (s/l *sea*). 1. DESCRY, DISCERN, ESPY, LO, LOOK, *NOTE*, NOTICE, OBSERVE, REFLECT, *SPOT, WATCH*; **comp** = wait. REFER TO, VIDE. BISHOPRIC, DIOCESE, hence CHESTER, ELY etc [*episcopal sig*]. 2. Means that the answer is then visible, i.e. if you . . . you will see . . . , e.g. **Miss Chan is outside to see the President** (8) = CHA*IRMA*N.

SEED GRAIN, MILT, PIP, SEMEN. DESCENDANTS, *OFFSPRING*, PROGENY. BEGINNING, CAUSE, GERM, ORIGINS. SCREENED COMPETITOR (tennis).

SEEDSMAN *SOWER*. MILLER (crypt). HANDICAPPER, SCREENER (crypt, tennis).

SEEN (s/l *scene*). *NOTED*, NOTICED, REMARKED, *SPOTTED*.

SEER (s/l sear, sere). *PROPHET. FISH* (Ind). *MEASURE* (Ind). EYE, PUPIL; SPECTATOR, VIEWER (crypt). SEE RIGHT (crypt).

SEE RIGHT ENSURE FAIRNESS. OBSERVE CORRECTLY. *SEER* (crypt).

SEETHE BOIL, COOK, FESTER, SIMMER. NOTE THE . . . (crypt).

SELECT CHOICE, ELITE, PICK. CHOOSE, ELECT.

SELENE Gk *goddess* of the *Moon* (**Rom** = LUNA); d of Hyperion and sis of *Helios* (Sun) and Eos (Dawn). Loved Endymion, who f 50 dd by her. Identical with *ARTEMIS*.

SELF I, ME, NUMBER ONE. INDIVIDUALITY, PERSON. *UNIFORM*, SAME, ALL ONE (colour). **Pl** = FLOWERS (natural coloured).

~ HELP DIY. SELF-SERVICE. BURGLARY, *ROBBERY*, SHOP-LIFTING (crypt).

SENSE APPRECIATION, JUDGEMENT, MEANING, PERCEPTION, SENTIMENT, WISDOM. Any of the five senses: HEARING, SIGHT, SMELL, TASTE, TOUCH (**sixth** = INTUITION). SANITY, WIT. DIRECTION. [~ and Sensibility, *Austen*].

SENTENCE CONSIGN. BIRD (sl), GAOL TERM, PORRIDGE (sl), STRETCH, *TIME*, PUNISHMENT; DEATH, FINE, LIFE. GRAMMATICAL CONSTRUCTION, QUOTATION; *SAYING*.

SENTRY *GUARD*, LOOK-OUT, SENTINEL, *WATCH*, WATCH-KEEPER. BOXED, *BOXER*, BOXMAN, CAVEMAN (crypt). CAPT ~ (Addison).

SEPTEMBER 9th month, M, SEPT (seventh Rom month, before *Caesar* reorganized the calendar). **Birthstone** = chrysolite.

SEPTENTRIO Rom myth N *WIND* (**Gk** = BOREAS).

SERGEANT NCO, RSM, SGT. **Celeb**: BUZFUZ (*Dickens*), CUFF (Moonstone, Collins), KITE (Farquhar), ~ AT LAW (*Chaucer*), TROY (Hardy). ['This fell ~ Death' (Hamlet, *Shak*)].

SERIES (s/l *Ceres*). *ORDER*, *ROW*, SEQUENCE, *SET*, SUCCESSION [seriatim].

SERPENT REPTILE, *SNAKE* (q.v.); **celeb**: APEP (Egy god); KAA (*Kipling*); MIDGARD (*Loki*); *PYTHON*; QUETZALCOATL (*Mayan* god); URAEUS (Egy god); *WYVERN* (*herald*) [caduceus; Cadmus and Harmonia; *Moses* and *Aaron* (*Pharaoh*)]. *Constellation. DEVIL*; TEMPTER. FIREWORK. *INSTRUMENT* (mus).

SERVANT *AGENT*, FACTOR. BUTLER, *COOK*, *DOMESTIC*, FLUNKEY, *FOOTMAN*, *GARDENER*, *GOVERNESS*, *MAID*, *NANNY*, *PUG* (arch), *SEWER*, TWEENY, VALET. *CONSTABLE*, FACTOTUM, LACKEY, MAJOR DOMO, (MAN) FRIDAY. GYP (C sl), *SCOUT* (O sl). [*Six*]. **Celeb**: ADAM (AYLI); ADMIRABLE CRICHTON (Barrie);

AMPHITRYON (Molière); CALEB BALDERSTONE
(Scott); *BALTHAZAR* (*Shak*); *BUNTER* (Dorothy Sayers);
HUMPHREY CLINKER (Smollett); CROMWELL (H.viii);
JOHN GRUEBY (*Dickens*); GUMBO (Thackeray);
HUDSON (TV); JEEVES (*Wodehouse*); JOSEPH (E.
Brontë); LITTIMER (*Dickens*); LUCETTA (*Shak*); BETTY
MUXWORTHY (Blackmore); PANTHINO (Shak); SANCHO
PANZA (Cervantes); PAROLLES (All's Well); PASSE-
PARTOUT (Jules Verne); CLARA PEGGOTTY (*Dickens*);
PETER (R & J); PETO (H.iv); RUGBY (Merry Wives);
SCAPIN (Molière); SIMPLE (Merry Wives); SPEED (2 G of
V); STEPHANO (*Shak*); CPL TRIM (Sterne); JOB TROTTER
(*Dickens*); SAM WELLER (*Dickens*).

SERVICE *ACE*, FAULT (tennis). DEAL. ARMED FORCE: AIR
FORCE, ARMY, NAVY, RAF, RN, USAF, USN. CHURCH
MASS, MASS-MEETING, WORSHIP; BAPTISMAL ~,
(HOLY) COMMUNION, COMPLINE, (SUNG)
EUCHARIST, EVENSONG, FUNERAL ~, LITANY, LITURGY,
MAT(T)INS, SACRAMENT, WEDDING ~. MAINTAIN,
OVERHAUL, REPAIR. *CHINA*, DISHES, PLATES. TREE.

SERVICEMAN *AIRMAN*, *SAILOR*, *SOLDIER* (**opp** = civilian,
civvy). PARSON, PRIEST, VICAR, *CHURCHMAN* (crypt).

SESAME *HERB*, PLANT. PASS-WORD [open ~].

SET 1. FIRM, GO OFF, RIGID. GAME. CABAL, CLIQUE,
COTERIE, ESTABLISHMENT, GROUP, *SERIES [tennis]*.
DANCE. BATCH, CLUTCH. EQUIPMENT. PLACE, PUT.
BOX, RADIO, TELLY, TV. SCENE, STUDIO (film, theat).
2. *Habitation* of badgers. 3. Egy *god* of DARKNESS.

SETH ADAMSON (crypt).

SET OFF *Anag*. BEGIN, *START*. *Anag*. of 'set', e.g. STE, TSE.
COMPLEMENT, ENHANCE, FOIL, *GRACE*. CARDED,
MOUNTED, ORNAMENT.

SET ON ENCOURAGE, SICK, *URGE*.

SET OUT *Anag*. BEGIN, *START*. *Anag*. of 'set', e.g. STE, TSE,
EST etc.

SETTER One who finds a thief's or a trickster's victim; SPY.
DOG (Gordon ~, Irish ~, Red ~). COMPOSITOR,
PRINTER. ADJUSTER. CLUB MEMBER, *COLLECTOR*,
PLASTERER, SQUARE DANCER, STAGE MANAGER,
TENNIS PLAYER (all crypt). TREAT (with Seton; med).
COMPILER (crosswords).

SETTLEMENT *AC*, *BILL*; PAYMENT. LANDING (crypt).

CAMP, COLONY, OUTPOST, HOMESTEAD.
SUBSIDENCE.

SETTLER COLONIST, HOMESTEADER, IMMIGRANT.
ARBITER, COMPOSER, JUDGE, PEACEMAKER. *COIN*,
CHECK (US), CHEQUE, PAYER (crypt).

SEVEN See *number*. HEPTAD. BLACK BALL (snooker). *Stars*
in the sky (song). *Swans* a-swimming (*Christmas* song) [~ maids
with ~ mops (*Alice*; Walrus)].

~ **AGES** (AYLI, *Shak*): (1) INFANT (mewling and puking);
(2) SCHOOLBOY (whining; snail); (3) LOVER (sighing like
furnace); (4) SOLDIER (bubble reputation); (5) JUSTICE
(full of wise saws); (6) PANTALOON (lean and slipper'd);
(7) SECOND CHILDISHNESS (oblivion; sans teeth, sans eyes,
sans taste, sans everything).

~ **DEADLY SINS** ANGER, AVARICE, ENVY, GLUTTONY,
LUST, PRIDE, SLOTH.

~ **HILLS** (of Rome): AVENTINE, CAELIAN, CAPITOLINE,
ESQUILINE, PALATINE, QUIRINAL, VIMINAL.

~ **SAGES** BIAS (of Priene), CHILON (of Sparta), CLEOBULUS
(of Lindus), PERIANDER (of Corinth), PITTACUS (of
Mitylene), SOLON (of Athens), THALES (of Miletus).

~ **SEAS** ANTARCTIC, ARCTIC, N and S ATLANTIC,
INDIAN, N and S PACIFIC *OCEANS*.

~ **SISTERS** HILLS, WHITE CLIFFS (of Dover).

~ **WONDERS** COLOSSUS (of Rhodes), HANGING GARDENS
(of Babylon), *MAUSOLEUM* (at Helicarnassus), PHAROS (at
Alexandria), STATUE OF *JUPITER* by Phidias (at *Olympus*),
PYRAMIDS (of Egypt), TEMPLE OF DIANA (at Ephesus).

SEWER CONDUIT, DRAIN. MACHINE, *SINGER* (*invention*);
NEEDLE(R), SEAMSTRESS (*Dickens*; guillotined, 2 Cities);
MIMI (Puccini -- crypt). BUTLER, FOOD TASTER, PLACE
SETTER, *SERVANT*, TABLE LAYER (arch). *GAS*.

~ **COVER** MANHOLE LID. THIMBLE (crypt).

SEWN STITCHED, *NEEDLED* (crypt). COMPASS POINTS
(crypt).

SEX APPEAL CHARM, IT, OOMPH, *SA*.

SEXY ATTRACTIVE, PROVOCATIVE, SENSUOUS. X (film
censorship).

Sh Shetlands. HUSH, QUIET.

SHADE *COLOUR*, HUE. BLIND, *SCREEN*; UMBRAGE.
GHOST.

SHADOW 1. SHADE, UMBRA; (DARK) IMAGE, HINT,

OUTLINE, REFLECTION, SEMBLANCE, SILHOUETTE;
BLIGHT, *GHOST*, PHANTOM, SPECTRE, THREAT;
PREMONITION, TRACE, UNREAL; PROTECTION,
SHELTER. OPPOSITION (polit). 2. *DOG*, FOLLOW, TAIL,
TRACK(ER); DETECTIVE, PRIVATE EYE, SLEUTH;
COMPANION. 3. *Shak* char (H.iv)
SHAKESPEARE THE BARD, DRAMATIST, SWAN OF AVON
(1564–1616), mar Ann Hathaway (2 dd: Susanna, Judith; 1 s:
Hamnet). Fake play = VORTIGERN (W. H. Ireland). **Chars:**

2-letters
WH Dedication, Sonnets

3-letters
ARC Joan of; H.vi
BOY Banquo's s; MacB
ELY Bishop of; H.v, R.iii
NYM Servant of Falstaff; H.v, Merry Wives
SAY Lord; H.vi
SLY Christopher ~, tinker; Taming
TOM ~ Snout; MND. Poor ~, disguise of Edgar; Lear

4-letters
ADAM Servant; AYLI
AJAX General; T & C
ANNE Lady; R.iii. ~ Bullen, Q to H.viii; H.viii
BEAR Pursues Antigonus; W Tale
BONA Sis to Fr Q; H.vi
BOYS Sir Rowland de ~; AYLI
CADE Rebel; H.vi
CATO Friend of Brutus; Caesar
DAVY Servant; H.iv
DICK Butcher and rebel; H.vi
DION Lord; W Tale
DOLL Tearsheet, a bawd; H.iv
DULL *Constable*; LLL
EROS Friend of Antony; A & C
FANG Sheriff's officer; H.iv [*Dickens*]
FOOL See *clown*
FORD Alice ~; Merry Wives. Frank ~, gent; Merry Wives
GREY Sir Thomas; H.v. Lord; R.iii. Lady; H.vi
HERO d to Leonato (disguise: Margaret); Much Ado

HOST of Garter Inn; Merry Wives
HUME *Priest*; H.vi
IAGO Villain; Othello
IDEN Alexander ~, Kentish gent; H.vi
IRAS Attendant on Cleopatra; A & C
IRIS Spirit; Tempest
JAMY Sc *soldier*; H.v
JOAN of Arc, La Pucelle; H.vi
JOHN K ~; John. Prince ~, Duke of Bedford; H.iv, H.v,
    H.vi. ~ of Gaunt; R.ii. Don ~, *bastard*; Much Ado. Rebel;
    H.vi. Friar, R & J
JUNO Spirit; Tempest
KATE d of Baptista Minola, shrew; Taming
KENT Earl; H.iv, Lear
LEAR *Mad king*; ~
LENA Popilius, Senator; Caesar
LION Play char (Snug); MND
LUCE Servant; C of E
LUCY Sir William ~, Knight; H.vi
MOTH Fairy; MND. Page; LLL
NICK ~ Bottom, *weaver*; MND
PAGE George ~, gent; Mistress Meg ~; d Anne and s
    William; Merry Wives. *Robin* (a ~); Merry Wives
PETO Servant & humorist; H.iv
PRAT Falstaff's fem disguise; Merry Wives
PUCK Goodfellow, *Spirit*; MND
ROSS Lord; R.ii. Sc noble; MacB
SNUG Joiner, plays lion; MND
TROY K of ~, Priam; T & C
TYRE Pericles, prince of ~; Per
VAUX Messenger; H.vi. Sir Nicholas ~, Knight; H.viii
WALL Play char (Snout); MND
WART Recruit; H.iv
YORK Duke of ~; R.ii, H.v, H.vi, R.iii. Duchess of ~;
    R.ii, R.iii. Archbishop Scroop of ~; H.iv. Thomas
    Rotherham, Archbishop of ~; R.iii

5-letters
AARON Moor; Titus
ALICE Fr lady; H.v
ANGUS Sc noble; MacB
ANJOU Duke Reignier; H.vi

ARIEL Spirit; Tempest
BAGOT Toady; R. ii
BATES Soldier; H.v
BELCH Sir Toby ~, Uncle of Olivia; 12 N
BEVIS George ~, rebel; H.vi
BIGOT Earl; John
BIRON Fr lord; LLL
BLUNT Sir Walter ~; H.iv
BOULT Servant; Per
BOYET Fr lord; LLL
BROOK Ford's disguise; Merry Wives
BUSHY Toady; R.ii
BUTTS *Doctor*; H.viii
CAIUS *Doctor*; Merry Wives. Titus' kinsman; Titus.
  ~ Marcius (Cor); Cor
CASCA *Conspirator*; Caesar
CELIA d of Duke Frederick (disguise: Aliena); AYLI
CERES Spirit; Tempest
CINNA *Conspirator*; Caesar. Poet; Caesar
CLEON *Governor*; Per
CLOWN Costard; LLL. Gobbo; M of V. and in All's Well,
  M for M, 12 N, W Tale, A & C, Hamlet, Lear
CORIN *Shepherd*; AYLI
COURT Soldier; H.v
CUPID Timon
CURAN Courtier; Lear
CURIO Gent; 12 N
DENNY Sir Anthony ~; H.viii
DERBY Earl; R.iii
DIANA Goddess; Per. Widow's d (place taken by Helena);
  All's Well
EDGAR s of Gloucester; Lear
EGEUS f of Hermia; MND
ELBOW Constable; M for M
ESSEX Earl; John
EVANS Sir Hugh ~, Wal parson; Merry Wives
EXTON Sir Pierce of ~; R.ii
FESTE *Jester*; 12 N
FLUTE Francis ~, *bellows maker* (plays Thisby); MND
FROTH Foolish gent; M for M
GAUNT John of ~, K's uncle; R.ii
GHOST Hamlet's f; ~. Banquo; MacB. Victims of R.iii; ~

GOBBO *Clown* (and his f); M of V
GOFFE Matthew ~; H.vi
GOWER Eng soldier; H.v. King's man; H.iv. Chorus; Per
GREEN Toady; R.ii
HELEN Beauty; T & C. Maid; Cymb
HENRY Prince; John, H.iv. King; H.iv, H.v (disguise: Harry
   Leroy, H.vi, H.viii. Bolingbroke; R.ii. Richmond; H.vi, R.iii.
   Percy; H.iv. Hotspur; R.ii, H.iv
HERNE the Hunter, disguise of Falstaff; Merry Wives
HYMEN God of marriage; AYLI
JULIA Beloved of Proteus (disguise: a page); 2 G of V
LAFEU Lord; All's Well
LEROY K's disguise; H.v
LEWIS Dauphin; John, H.v, H.vi
LICIO Music teacher alias of Hortensio; Taming
LOUIS K of France; H.vi. Dauphin; John, H.v, H.vi
LOVEL Lord; R.iii (and see Lovell)
LUCIO A fantastic; M for M
MARCH Edmund Mortimer, Earl of ~; H.iv, H.vi
MARIA Maid; 12 N. Lady; LLL
MELUN Fr lord; John
MENAS Friend of Pompey; A & C
MILAN Duke of ~; 2 G of V, Tempest
MOPSA *Shepherdess*; W Tale
NEVIL Earl of Warwick; H.vi
OSRIC Courtier; Hamlet
PARIS Noble; R & J. s of Priam; T & C
PEDRO Don ~, prince; Much Ado
PERCY Hotspur; R.ii, H.iv. Thomas ~, Earl of Worcester;
   H.iv. Henry ~; R.ii, H.iv. Lady ~; H.iv
PETER Servant; R & J. *Prophet*; John. Friar; M for M.
   Armourer's assistant; H.vi. ~ Quince; MND
PHEBE *Shepherdess*; AYLI
PHILO Friend of Antony; A & C
PINCH Conjuror and *schoolmaster*; C of Errors
POINS Servant & humorist; H.iv
PRIAM K of *Troy*; T & C
REBEL Cade, Dick, George, John, Michael and Smith the
   weaver; H.vi
REGAN Graceless d; Lear
ROBIN Page; Merry Wives. ~ Goodfellow, Puck; MND
ROMEO Montague (disguises with a mask); R & J

RUGBY John ~, servant; Merry Wives
SANDS Lord; H.viii
SMITH Weaver and rebel; H.vi
SNARE Sheriff's officer; H.iv
SNOUT Tinker (plays Wall); MND
SPEED Servant and *clown*; 2 G of V
TIMON Noble; Timon
TITUS ~ Andronicus, noble; Titus. Servant; Timon.
    ~ Lartius General; Cor
TOPAS Sir ~ (disguise of clown); 12 N
TUBAL Jew; M of V
VARRO Servant; Caesar. Servant's master (unseen); Timon
VENUS ~ and Adonis (poem)
VIOLA *Twin* of Sebastian (male disguise: Cesario); 12 N

6-letters
ADONIS *Venus* and ~ (poem)
ADRIAN Lord; Tempest. A Volscian; Cor
AEGEON Merchant; C of Errors
AENEAS Commander; T & C
ALBANY Duke; Lear
ALEXAS Attendant on Cleopatra; A & C
ALIENA Disguise of Celia; AYLI
ALONSO K of Naples; Tempest
AMIENS Lord; AYLI
ANGELO Lord; M for M. Goldsmith; C of Errors
ANTONY Triumvir; Caesar, A & C
ARMADO Don ~, a Sp fantastic; LLL
ARTHUR Duke of Bretagne; John
ATHENS Theseus, Duke of ~; MND
AUDREY Country wench; AYLI
BANQUO General and *ghost*; MacB
BASSET Red-rose supporter; H.vi
BIANCA Sis to Kate; Taming. *Courtesan*; Othello
BISHOP Ely; H.v, R.iii. Winchester; H.vi, H.viii. Carlisle;
    R.ii
BLANCH of Spain, niece to K John; John
BLOUNT Sir James; R.iii
BOTTOM Nick ~, *weaver* (plays Pyramus); MND
BRUTUS Decius ~, *conspirator*; Caesar. Junius ~, tribune;
    Cor, Rape of Lucrece (poem); Marcus ~, conspirator; Caesar
BULLEN Anne, Q of England; H.viii

CADWAL Alias Arvirasus, s of Cymb; Cymb

CAESAR Julius ~, general, orator; Caesar, A & C. Octavius
~, triumvir; Caesar, A & C

CAMBIO Lucentio's disguise (*schoolmaster*); Taming

CAPHIS Servant; Timon

CASSIO Othello's lieutenant; Othello

CHIRON s of Tamora; Titus

CHORUS H.v. R & J. Gower; Per. Hymen; AYLI.
Prologue; MND, T & C, Hamlet. Time; W Tale. Rumour;
H.iv

CICERO Senator, orator; Caesar

CIMBER *Conspirator*; Caesar

CLITUS Servant; Caesar

CLOTEN s of the Q; Cymb

COBHAM Eleanor ~, Duchess of Gloucester; H.vi

COBWEB *Fairy*; MND

CURTIS Servant; Taming

DE BOIS/BOYS Sir Rowland, unseen f of Jaques, Oliver,
Orlando; AYLI

DENNIS Servant; AYLI

DORCAS *Shepherdess*; W Tale

DORSET Marquis; R.iii

DROMIO *Twin* servants; C of Errors

DUBOIS see DE BOIS/BOYS

DUMAIN Fr lord; LLL

DUNCAN K of Sc; MacB

EDMUND Earl of Rutland; H.vi. Duke of York; R.ii.
Bastard; Lear

EDWARD K; R.iii. Prince of Wales; H.vi, R.iii. Earl of
March; H.vi

ELINOR Queen; John

EMILIA w of Iago; Othello. Lady; W Tale

EXETER Duke; H.v, H.vi

FABIAN Servant; 12 N

FEEBLE Recruit; H.iv

FENTON Gent; Merry Wives

FIDELE Male disguise of Imogen; Cymb

FULVIA Unseen w of Antony; A & C

GALLUS Friend of Caesar; A & C

GEORGE Duke of Clarence; H.vi, R.iii. ~ Bevis, rebel;
H.vi

GREMIO Suitor to Bianca; Taming

GRUMIO Servant; Taming
GURNEY Servant; John
HAMLET Prince of Denmark and *ghost* of his f ~; ~
HECATE Goddess of *witchcraft*; MacB
HECTOR s of Priam; T & C
HELENA Lady (takes place of Diana); All's Well. In love
    with Demetrius; MND
HERMIA d of Egeus; MND
HORNER Thomas, armourer; H.vi
IMOGEN Princess (disguise: Fidele, boy); Cymb
ISOBEL Fr Q; H.v
JAQUES Lord and Cynic; AYLI. s of Sir Rowland de
    Boys; AYLI
JULIET Capulet; R & J. Minor lady; M for M
LAUNCE Clownish servant; 2 G of V
LE BEAU Courtier; AYLI
LENNOX Sc noble; MacB
LOVELL Sir Thomas ~; H.viii (and see Lovel)
LUCIUS Lord; Timon. s of Titus; ~. General; Cymb.
    Servant; Caesar
MARCUS Andronicus, tribune; Titus
MARINA d of Per; Per
MINOLA Baptista, f of Kate & Bianca; Taming
MORGAN Alias of Belarius; Cymb
MORTON John, *Bishop* of Ely; R.iii. Retainer; H.iv
MOULDY Recruit; H.iv
MUTIUS s of Titus; ~
NAPLES Alonso, K of ~; Tempest. Reignier, K of ~; H.vi
NESTOR Commander; T & C
OBERON K of the fairies; MND
OLIVER Gent; AYLI
OLIVIA Countess; 12 N
ORSINO Duke of Illyria; 12 N
OSWALD Steward; Lear
OXFORD Earl of ~; H.vi, R.iii
PHILIP Fr K; John. ~ the bastard; John
PIERCE of Exton; R.ii
PISTOL Cowardly servant of Falstaff; Merry Wives,
    H.iv, H.v
POMPEY General; A & C. *Clown*; M for M
PORTIA Belmont heiress (disguise: Dr of law); M of V. w of
    Brutus; Caesar

QUINCE Peter ~, *carpenter* (plays Prologue); MND
RIVERS Lord; H.vi, R.iii
ROBERT Starveling; MND
RUMOUR Chorus; H.iv
SANDYS Lord; H.viii
SCALES Lord Governor of Tower; H.vi
SCARUS Friend of Antony; A & C
SCROOP Archbishop of York; H.iv. Lord; H.v. Sir Stephen
    ~; R.ii
SEXTUS Pompeius; A & C
SEYTON Officer; MacB
SHADOW Recruit; H.iv
SILIUS Officer; A & C
SILVIA Beloved of Valentine; 2 G of V
SIMPLE Peter ~, servant; Merry Wives
SIWARD Eng earl & son; MacB
SPIRIT Ariel; Tempest. Raised by *conjuror*; H.vi
STRATO Servant; Caesar
SURREY Duke; R.ii. Earl; H.iv, R.iii, H.viii
TALBOT Lord and s; H.vi
TAMORA Q of Goths; Titus
TAURUS General; A & C
THAISA d of Simonides; Per
THISBE-Y Play char (Flute); MND
THOMAS Friar; M for M. Duke of Clarence; H.iv
THURIO Foolish rival; 2 G of V
TRANIO Servant; Taming
TYBALT Capulet; R & J
TYRREL Sir James; R.iii
URSULA Lady; Much Ado
VENICE Duke; M of V, Othello
VERGES *Constable*; Much Ado
VERNON Sir Richard; H.iv. White rose supporter; H.vi
WOLSEY *Cardinal*; H.viii
YORICK *Jester* and skull; Hamlet

7-letters
ABRAHAM Servant; R & J
ADRIANA w of Antipholus; C of E
AEMILIA Abbess, and m of twins; C of E
AGRIPPA Friend of Cor; ~. Friend of Caesar; A & C
ALARBUS s of Tamora; Titus

ALENCON Fr duke; H.vi
AMAZONS In a mask; Timon. Q of ~; MND
ANTENOR Commander; T & C
ANTONIO A merchant of Venice; ~. Also minor parts
   Much Ado, Tempest, 12 N, 2 G of V
ARRAGON Prince of ~; M of V. Much Ado (Don Pedro)
AUMERLE Duke of ~; R.ii
AUSTRIA Archduke of ~; John
BASTARD ~ of Orleans; H.vi. Don John; Much Ado. Philip
   Falconbridge; John. Margarelon; T & C. ~ of Gloster; Lear
BEDFORD Duke; H.iv, H.v, H.vi
BERKLEY Earl; R.ii. Gent; R.iii
BEROWNE Fr lord; LLL
BERTRAM Fr Count of Rousillon; All's Well
BOUCHER Cardinal, Archbishop of Canterbury; R.iii
BOURBON Fr duke; H.v
BRANDON Sir William ~; R.iii. Officer; H.viii
CALCHAS Priest; T & C
CALIBAN *Monster*, s of Sycorax; Tempest
CAMILLO Lord; W Tale
CAPILET Diana; All's Well
CAPULET Feuding head of house (& lady); R & J
CASSIUS *Conspirator*; Caesar
CATESBY Sir William; Riii
CERIMON Lord; Per
CESARIO Disguise of Viola and of Sebastian; 12 N
CHARLES Fr K; H.v, H.vi (and Dauphin). *Wrestler*; AYLI
CLAUDIO Gent; M for M. Lord; Much Ado
CONRADE Follower of Don John; Much Ado
COSTARD *Clown*; LLL
CRANMER Archbishop of Canterbury; H.viii
DAUPHIN of France; John, H.v, H.vi
DE BURGH Chamberlain; John
DIONYZA w of Cleon; Per
DON JOHN *Bastard*; Much Ado
DOUGLAS Archibald, Earl; H.iv
ELEANOR Duchess of Gloster; H.vi
EPHESUS Solinus, Duke of ~; C of E
ESCALUS Prince; R & J. Lord; M for M
ESCANES Lord of Tyre; Per
FLAVIUS Steward; Timon. Tribune; Caesar
FLEANCE s of Banquo; MacB

FRANCIS ~ Flute; MND. Friar ~; Much Ado. Drawer;
    H.iv

GLOSTER Richard, Duke of ~; H.vi, R.iii. Humphrey
    Duke of ~; H.iv, H.v, H.vi. Earl of ~; Lear. Duchess of ~;
    R.ii, H.vi. All also spelled Gloucester.

GONERIL Graceless d; Lear

GONZAGO Murder of, sub-play; Hamlet

GONZALO Counsellor; Tempest

GREGORY Servant; R & J

HELENUS s of Priam; T & C

HERBERT Sir Walter; R.iii

HOLLAND Rebel; H.vi

HORATIO Friend of Hamlet; ~

HOTSPUR Henry Percy; R.ii, H.iv

IACHIMO Friend of Philario; Cymb

ILLYRIA Orsino, Duke of ~; 12 N

ISIDORE Unseen master of servant; Timon

JESSICA d of Shylock; M of V

LAERTES s of Polonius; Hamlet

LANGLEY Duke of York; R.ii

LARTIUS Titus ~, general; Cor

LAVACHE *Jester*; All's Well

LAVINIA d of Titus; Titus

LEONATO Governor of Messina; Much Ado

LEONINE Servant; Per

LEONTES K of Sicily; W Tale

LEPIDUS Triumvir; Caesar, A & C

LINCOLN Bishop of ~; H.viii

LORENZO In love with Jessica; M of V

LUCETTA Servant; 2 G of V

LUCIANA Sis of Adriana; C of E

LUCRECE Rape of ~ (poem)

LYMOGES Duke of Austria; John

MACBETH General (and Lady ~); ~

MACDUFF Sc noble (and Lady ~); MacB

MALCOLM s of Duncan; MacB

MARCADE Lord; LLL

MARCIUS Coriolanus; ~

MARDIAN Attendant on Cleopatra; A & C

MARGERY ~ Jourdain, *witch*; H.vi

MARIANA Betrothed to Angelo (takes place of Isabella); M
    for M. Friend of widow; All's Well

MARTEXT Sir Oliver ~, vicar; AYLI
MARTIUS s of Titus; ~
MERCADE Lord; LLL
MESSALA Friend of Brutus and Cassius; Caesar
MESSINA Governor of ~, Leonato; Much Ado
MICHAEL Gent; H.iv. Rebel; H.vi
MIRANDA d of Prospero; Tempest
MONTANO Predecessor of Othello as Governor; Othello
MONTJOY Fr *herald*; H.v
MOROCCO Prince of ~; M of V
MOWBRAY Duke of Norfolk; R.ii, H.iv
NAVARRE Fr K of ~; LLL. Princess of ~; LLL
NERISSA *Maid* (disguise: clerk of law); M of V
NICANOR A Roman; Cor
NORFOLK Duke of ~; R.ii, H.vi, R.iii, H.viii
OCTAVIA Sis of Caesar & w of Antony; A & C
OPHELIA d of Polonius; Hamlet
ORLANDO Rosalind's lover; AYLI
ORLEANS Fr duke; H.v. Maid of ~; H.vi. *Bastard* of
    ~; H. vi
OTHELLO *Moor*; Othello
PAULINA Lady; W Tale
PERDITA Princess of Sicily; W Tale
PHRYNIA Mistress of Alcibiades; Timon
PISANIO Servant; Cymb
POMFRET Peter of ~; John
POOR TOM Disguise of Edgar; Lear
PROTEUS One of the 2 G of V; ~
PROVOST Officer; M for M
PUBLIUS Senator; Caesar. s of Marcus; Titus
PUCELLE La ~, Joan of Arc; H.vi
PYRAMUS Play char (Bottom); MND
QUICKLY *Landlady*; H.iv (and Pistol's wife); H.v. Servant
    to Dr Caius; Merry Wives
QUINTUS s of Titus; ~
RICHARD K; R.ii, R.iii. Duke of York (2 ss); H.vi. Duke of
    Gloster; H.vi, R.iii
RUTLAND Edmund, Earl of ~; H.vi
SALERIO *Messenger*; M of V
SAMPSON Servant; R & J
SHALLOW *Justice*; Merry Wives, H.iv
SHYLOCK *Jew*; M of V

SILENCE *Justice*; H.iv
SILVIUS *Shepherd*; AYLI
SIMPCOX Imposter; H.vi
SLENDER Cousin of Shallow; Merry Wives
SOLANIO Friend of Antonio; M of V
SOLINUS Duke of Ephesus; C of E
STANLEY Sir John & Sir William; H.vi, R.iii
SUFFOLK Earl of ~; H.vi, H.viii
SYCORAX *Witch* (unseen); Tempest
TARQUIN or Superbus; Rape of Lucrece (poem)
THESEUS Duke of Athens; MND
THYREUS Friend of Caesar; A & C
TITANIA Q of the fairies; MND
TRAVERS Retainer; H.iv
TRESSEL Gent; R.iii
TROILUS s of Priam; T & C [*Chaucer*]
TULLIUS Servius ~; Rape of Lucrece (poem)
ULYSSES Commander; T & C
URSWICK Christopher ~, priest; R.iii
VALERIA Woman friend of Virgilia; Cor
VARRIUS Friend of Pompey; A & C. Gent; M for M
VAUGHAN Sir Thomas; R.iii
VELUTUS Tribune; Cor
WARWICK Yorkist Earl (Nevil); H.iv, H.v, H.vi, R.iii
WILLIAM Country fellow; AYLI

8-letters
ABHORSON *Hangman*; M for M
ACHILLES Commander; T & C
AEMILIUS Noble; Titus
ANTONIUS Marcus ~, triumvir; Caesar
ARCHDUKE Lymoges of Austria; John
AUFIDIUS General; Cor
AUVERGNE Fr countess; H.vi
BAPTISTA ~ Minola, f of Kate & Bianca; Taming
BARDOLPH Lord; H.iv. *Cowardly* follower of Falstaff;
   Merry Wives, H.iv, H.v
BASSANIO Friend of Antonio; M of V
BEATRICE Niece of Leonato; Much Ado
BEAUFORT Duke of Exeter; H.vi. Cardinal ~, Bishop of
   Winchester; H.vi
BELARIUS Banished lord, disguised as Morgan; Cymb

BENEDICK Lord; Much Ado
BENVOLIO Friend of Romeo; R & J
BERKELEY Earl; R.ii. Gent; R.iii
BERNARDO Officer; Hamlet
BORACHIO Follower of Don John; Much Ado
BRETAGNE Arthur, Duke of ~: John, H.v
BRITAINE Duke of ~; John, H.v
BULLCALF Recruit; H.iv
BURGUNDY Fr duke; H.v, H.vi, Lear
CAMPEIUS Cardinal; H.viii
CANIDIUS General; A & C
CAPUCIUS Ambassador; H.viii
CARDINAL Boucher; R.iii. Campeius, Wolsey; H.viii.
   Pandulph, Pope's *Ambassador*; John
CARLISLE Bishop; R.ii
CHARMIAN Lady attending Cleopatra; A & C
CLARENCE Thomas, Duke of ~; H.iv. George, Duke of
   ~; H.vi, R.iii
CLAUDIUS K of Denmark; Hamlet
CLIFFORD Lord; H.vi
COLVILLE Sir John; H.iv
COMINIUS General; Cor. Servant; Caesar
CORDELIA Dutiful d; Lear
CORNWALL Duke; Lear
CRESSIDA d of Calchas; T & C [*Chaucer*]
CROMWELL Servant; H.viii
DARK LADY Sonnets
DERCETAS Friend of Antony; A & C
DE NARBON Helena; All's Well
DIOMEDES General; T & C. Attendant on Cleopatra;
   A & C
DISGUISE See after **10+ letters**
DOGBERRY *Constable*; Much Ado
DON PEDRO Prince; Much Ado
EGLAMOUR Helps Silvia; 2 G of V
FALSTAFF Sir John ~, a drunken knight; H.iv, Merry Wives
   (disguise: Mrs Prat)
FASTOLFE Sir John ~; H.vi
FLORENCE Duke; All's Well
FLORIZEL Prince of Bohemia; W Tale
FLUELLEN Wal Soldier; H.v
GADSHILL Servant & humorist; H.iv

GANYMEDE Rosalind's male disguise; AYLI
GARDINER Bishop of Winchester; H.viii
GARGRAVE Sir Thomas ~; H.vi
GERTRUDE Q of Denmark, m of Hamlet; ~
GRANDPRE Fr lord; H.v
GRATIANO Desdemona's uncle; Othello. Friend of
  Antonio; M of V
GRIFFITH Usher; H.viii
HARCOURT K's man; H.iv
HASTINGS Lord; H.iv, H.vi, R.iii. Poursuivant; R.iii
HERMIONE Q of Sicily; W Tale
HISPERIA Attendant to Rosalind (unseen); AYLI
HUMPHREY Prince; H.iv, H.v, H.vi
ISABELLA Sis of Claudio (Mariana takes her place);
  M for M
JOURDAIN Margery ~, *witch*; H.vi
KEEPDOWN Kate, unseen woman; M for M
LAWRENCE Friar; R & J
LEONARDO Servant; M of V
LEONATUS Posthumus ~, gent; Cymb
LIGARIUS *Conspirator*; Caesar
LODOVICO Kinsman of Brabantio; Othello
LODOWICK Friar ~, disguise of Vincentio; M for M
LUCENTIO In love with Bianca (disguise: Cambio); Taming
LUCILIUS Servant; Timon. Friend of Brutus; Caesar
LUCULLUS Lord; Timon
LYSANDER In love with Hermia; MND
MALVOLIO Steward; 12 N
MARGARET Queen; H.vi, R.iii. Disguise of Hero;
  Much Ado
MARULLUS Tribune; Caesar
MECAENUS Friend of Caesar; A & C
MENELAUS Br of Agamemnon; T & C
MENTEITH Sc noble; MacB
MERCUTIO Friend of Romeo; R & J
MONTAGUE Marquis; H.vi. Feuding head of house (and
  Lady ~); R & J
MORTIMER Edmund ~, Earl of March (& 2 ss); H.iv,
  H.vi. Sir Hugh ~ and Sir John ~; H.vi. Lady ~; H.iv
OVERDONE Mistress & bawd; M for M
PANDARUS Cressida's uncle; T & C
PANDULPH Cardinal ~, Pope's *Ambassador*; John

458

PANTHINO Servant; 2 G of V
PAROLLES Servant; All's Well
PATIENCE Lady in waiting; H.viii
PEMBROKE Earl; H.vi, John
PERICLES Prince of Tyre; Per
PHILARIO Friend of Posthumus; Cymb
PHILEMON Servant; Per
PHILOTUS Servant; Timon
PINDARUS Servant; Caesar
POLONIUS Lord Chamberlain; Hamlet
POLYDORE Alias of Guiderius; Cymb
POMPEIUS Sextus ~; A & C
PRINCESS of France; LLL, H.v
PROLOGUE See Chorus
PROSPERO Duke of Milan, *magician*; Tempest
RAGOZINE (unseen) executed pirate; M for M
RAMBURES Fr lord; H.v
RATCLIFF Sir Richard ~; R.iii
REIGNIER Duke of Anjou; H.vi
REYNALDO Servant; Hamlet
RICHMOND Henry, Earl of ~; H.vi, R.iii
RODERIGO Gent; Othello
ROSALIND d of banished duke (disguise: Ganymede); AYLI
ROSALINE Fr lady; LLL. Romeo's first love (unseen); R & J
SELEUCUS Attendant on Cleopatra; A & C
SOMERSET Duke; H.vi
STAFFORD Sir Humphrey (& br); H.vi
STEPHANO Servant; M of V. Drunken butler; Tempest
SUPERBUS Tarquin; Rape of Lucrece (poem)
THALIARD Lord; Per
TIMANDRA Mistress; Timon
TITINIUS Friend of Brutus; Caesar
TRINCULO Fool; Tempest
VALERIUS Publius ~; Rape of Lucrece (poem)
VIOLENTA Friend of widow; All's Well
VIRGILIA w of Corialanus; ~
VOLUMNIA m of Corialanus; ~
WHITMORE Walter (Gaultier); H.vi
WILLIAMS Soldier; H.v

9-letters
AGAMEMNON General; T & C

AGUE-CHEEK Sir Andrew ~; 12 N
ALEXANDER Servant; T & C
ANTIGONUS Lord ('exit, pursued by a bear'); W Tale
ANTIOCHUS K of Antioch; Per
APEMANTUS *Philosopher*; T & C
ARCHIBALD Earl of Douglas; H.iv
ARVIRAGUS (alias Cadwal), s of Cymb; ~
AUTOLYCUS Rogue salesman; W Tale
BALTHASAR Merchant; C of E. Servant; Much Ado,
   M of V, R & J
BASSIANUS br of Saturninus; Titus
BIONDELLO Servant; Taming
BOURCHIER Cardinal, Archbishop of Canterbury; R.iii
BRABANTIO Senator; Othello
CAITHNESS Sc noble; MacB
CAMBRIDGE Earl, *conspirator*; H.v
CASSANDRA Prophetess; T & C
CHATILLON Fr ambassador; John
CLEOMENES Lord; W Tale
CLEOPATRA Q of Egypt; A & C
COLEVILLE Sir John; H.iv
COLLATINE Rape of Lucrece (poem)
CONSTABLE of France; H.v
CONSTANCE m of Arthur; John
CORNELIUS Physician; Cymb. Courtier; Hamlet
CYMBELINE K of Britain; Cymb
DARDANIUS Servant; Caesar
DEIPHOBUS s of Priam; T & C
DEMETRIUS Loves Hermia; MND. Antony's friend;
   A & C. s of Tamora; Titus
DESDEMONA w of Othello; ~
DOLABELLA Friend of Caesar; A & C
DONALBAIN s of Duncan; MacB
ELIZABETH Q of Ed iv; R.iii
ENOBARBUS Friend of Antony; A & C
ERPINGHAM Sir Thomas ~; H.v
FERDINAND Noble; Tempest. K of Navarre; LLL
FITZ-PETER Earl of Essex; John
FITZWATER Lord; R.ii
FLAMINIUS Servant; Timon
FRANCISCA *Nun*; M for M
FRANCISCO Lord; Tempest. Soldier; Hamlet

FREDERICK Usurping duke; AYLI
GENTLEMAN Proteus & Valentine; 2 G of V. Petruchio, a
  gent of Verona; Taming
GLANSDALE Sir William; H.vi
GLENDOWER Owen, H.iv
GRANDPREE Fr lord; H.v
GUIDERIUS (alias Polydore), s of Cymb; ~
GUILDFORD Sir Henry ~; H.viii
HELICANUS Lord; Per
HIPPOLYTA Q of Amazons; MND
HORTENSIO Suitor to Bianca (disguise: Licio); Taming
KATHERINA Shrew, d of Baptista; Taming
KATHARINE Fr princess; H.v. Fr lady; LLL.
  Q of H.viii; ~
LANCASTER John of Gaunt, Duke of ~; R.ii
LA PUCELLE Joan of Arc; H.vi
LONGSWORD Earl of Salisbury; John
LUCRETIUS Lucrece's f; Rape of Lucrece (poem)
LYCHORIDA *Nurse*; Per
MACMORRIS Ire soldier; H.v
MAMILLIUS Prince of Sicily; W Tale
MARCELLUS Officer; Hamlet
MARESHALL Earl of Pembroke; John
MOONSHINE Play char (Starveling); MND
NATHANIEL Sir ~, curate; LLL
PATROCLUS General; T & C
PETRUCHIO Tames Kate; Taming
POLIXENES K of Bohemia; W Tale
POSTHUMUS Leonartus ~; Cymb
ROTHERHAM Thomas ~, Ebor; R.iii
ROUSILLON Count Bertram & Countess (his m); All's Well
SALISBURY Earl of ~; John, R.ii, H.v, H.vi (Yorkist)
SEBASTIAN Noble; Tempest. Br of Viola (disguise:
  Cesario); 12 N. Julia's male disguise; 2 G of V.
SERVILIUS Servant; Timon
SIMONIDES K of Pentapolis; Per
SOUTHWELL Priest; H.vi
TEARSHEET Doll ~, a bawd; H.iv
THERSITES Deformed; T & C
TREBONIUS *Conspirator*; Caesar
VALENTINE One of the 2 G of V; ~. Gent; 12 N. Kinsman
  of Titus; ~

VENTIDIUS Friend of Antony; A & C. False friend of
Timon; ~
VINCENTIO Duke (disguise: friar Lodowick); M for M. Old
gent of Pisa; Taming
VOLTIMAND Courtier; Hamlet
VOLUMNIUS Friend of Brutus; Caesar
WOODVILLE Officer of the Tower; H.vi

10+ letters
ABERGAVENNY Lord; H.viii
ALCIBIADES General; Timon
AMBASSADOR John; H.v, H.viii, A & C, Hamlet
ANDROMACHE Hector's w; T & C
ANDRONICUS Marcus ~, tribune; Titus. Titus ~,
general; Titus
ANTIPHOLUS ~ of Ephesus, and ~ of Syracuse, *twins*;
C of E
ARCHBISHOP Cantab: H.v, R.iii, H.viii. Ebor: H.iv, R.iii
ARCHIDAMUS Lord; W Tale
ARTEMIDORUS *Philosopher*; Caesar
BERNARDINE *Prisoner*; M for M
BOLINGBROKE Henry ~, duke; R.ii. Roger ~, *conjuror*;
H.vi
BRACKENBURY Sir Robert, officer of the Tower; R.iii
BUCKINGHAM Duke; H.vi, R.iii, H.viii
CALPHURNIA w of Caesar; ~
CANTERBURY Archbishop (Cantuar); H.v, R.iii, H.viii
CORIOLANUS Caius Marcus ~, noble; Cor
EUPHRONIUS *Ambassador*; A & C
FAULCONBRIDGE Sir Robert ~, Robert ~, Philip ~
(*bastard* of R.i), Lady ~; John
FORTINBRAS Prince of Norway; Hamlet
GLANDSDALE Sir William ~; H.vi
GLOUCESTER See Gloster
GOODFELLOW Robin ~ or Puck; MND
GUILDENSTERN Courtier; Hamlet
HOLOFERNES *Schoolmaster*; LLL
HORTENSIUS Servant; Timon
JANQUENETTA Country wench; LLL
LONGAVILLE Fr lord; LLL
LORD MARSHALL; R.ii
LYSIMACHUS *Governor*, Per

MARGARELON *Bastard* s of Priam; T & C
MENECRATES Friend of Pompey; A & C
MONTGOMERY Sir John ~; H.vi
MUSTARDSEED *Fairy*; MND
NORTHUMBERLAND Earl; R.ii, H.iv, H.vi. Lady ~; H.iv
PEASEBLOSSOM *Fairy*; MND
PHILOSTRATE Master of the Revels; MND
PLANTAGENET Richard ~, Duke of York; H.vi
PROCULEIUS Friend of Caesar; A & C
ROSENCRANTZ Courtier; Hamlet
SATURNINUS Emperor; Titus
SEMPRONIUS Lord; Timon. Kinsman of Titus; ~
SOMERVILLE Sir John ~; H.vi
STARVELING Robert ~, *tailor* (plays Moonshine); MND
TARQUINIUS Sextus; Rape of Lucrece (poem)
TOUCHSTONE *Jester*; AYLI
WESTMINSTER Abbot of ~; R.ii
WESTMORELAND Earl; H.iv, H.v, H.vi
WILLOUGHBY Lord; R.ii
WINCHESTER Bishop of ~; H.vi, H.viii

Disguises: Many of *Shak*'s plays use disguises and aliases
(sometimes charmingly penetrable) to put across their point.
These include:

Character	Disguise	Play
Arviragus	Cadwal	Cymb
Belarius	Morgan	Cymb
Celia	Aliena	AYLI
Clown	Sir Topas	12 N
Edgar	Poor Tom	Lear
Falstaff	Prat (fem) and Herne	Merry Wives
Ford	Brook	Merry Wives
Guiderius	Polydore	Cymb
Helena	Diana	All's Well
Hero	Margaret	Much Ado
King Henry	Harry Leroy	H.v
Hortensio	Licio	Taming
Imogen	Fidele (male)	Cymb
Julia	Sebastian (male)	2 G of V
Lucentio	Cambio	Taming
Mariana	Isabella	M for M

Nerissa	Clerk of Law (male)	M of V
Portia	Dr of Law (male)	M of V
Romeo	masked	R & J
Rosalind	Ganymede (male)	AYLI
Sebastian	Cesario	12 N
Vincentio	Friar Lodowick	M for M
Viola	Cesario (male)	12 N

Shakespeare's Plays:

ALL'S WELL THAT ENDS WELL (abbr: All's Well). Comedy set in France. Helena cures the K of France of an illness; as reward she mar Bertram, who refuses to consummate the union. He won't accept her until she conceives his child and wears his ring, and then he goes off to the wars. Helena follows, secretly takes Diana's place in his bed, and the gullible Bertram exchanges rings in the night. Helena eventually displays his ring, and Bertram must accept her as she has also shared his bed.

ANTONY AND CLEOPATRA (abbr: A & C). Tragedy set in Rome and Egy. Mark Antony is besotted with Cleopatra, but is forced by reports of his dalliance to report to Rome, where he is made to mar Octavia, sis of Caesar. Cleopatra is furious but eventually Antony returns to Egy. War follows, with Octavia's br Octavius leading the Romans against A & C. At the sea battle of Actium, C withdraws her fleet, and A goes from defeat to defeat. To test A's love, C sends false news of her d, whereupon A commits sui; C follows suit with a poisoned asp.

AS YOU LIKE IT (abbr: AYLI). Comedy set in and around the Forest of Arden. Frederick has usurped the ducal realm of his br, the rightful duke, who now lives in the Forest of Arden. Each duke has a d: Celia is that of the usurping Duke Frederick, while Rosalind is her cousin. Oliver, Jaques and Orlando are the ss of the late Sir Rowland de Boys, whose estate is managed by Oliver for his own interest and to the almost inhuman discomfort of his youngest br Orlando. Duke Frederick's wrestler Charles is beaten by Orlando, who attracts the attention of Rosalind. This angers Duke Frederick, because Sir Rowland was a supporter of the exiled Duke; Rosalind is banished. She dresses as a boy (Ganymede) and, with her inseparable cousin Celia disguised

as Ganymede's sis Aliena, goes to live in the Forest of Arden.
They meet Orlando, who has finally been driven from home
to join the exile but, as ever with Shak's devices, he fails to
recognise Rosalind in Ganymede; indeed, he tells 'him' of his
love for her. Wit is contributed by Rosalind, with broader
comedy coming from the clown Touchstone; Jaques provides
melancholy. Meanwhile, Duke Frederick has sent Oliver to k
Orlando; he is attacked by a lion and saved by his younger br.
Repentance and reconciliation follow, as Oliver mar Aliena,
Orlando mar Rosalind, and Frederick sees the error of
his ways.

THE COMEDY OF ERRORS (abbr: C of E). Comedy set
in Ephesus. Twin boys both called Antipholus had twin slaves
called Dromio. A shipwreck split the family, and the f Aegeon
ended up in Syracuse with one s and his slave; his w Aemilia
disappeared with the other s and his slave. On reaching
manhood, Antipholus of Syracuse set off with his slave
Dromio to seek his br, and never returned. Aegeon thereupon
went to look for both his ss, and the play starts with his arrest
in the enemy city of Ephesus, where he is condemned to d.
Needless to say, the first Antipholus lives in Ephesus, and
his twin br arrives on the day of their f's arrest. After much
mix-up among the two pairs of twins, all is sorted out and the
family reunited.

CORIOLANUS (abbr: Cor). Tragedy set in Rome and
Antium. After the Volscian wars, the arrogant Caius Marcius
~ is urged by Menenius to seek the consulship; he is opposed
by the tribunes Sicinius and Brutus, who inflame the people.
~ deserts to the Volscian general Aufidius, and later
advances on Rome. Menenius pleads in vain for the city, and
it takes pleas from ~'s mother Volumnia and his w Virgilia
to make him relent. On his return to Antium, ~ is k by the
Volscian mob, angry because Rome has been spared.

CYMBELINE (abbr: Cymb). Tragedy set in Br and It. K
~'s d Imogen mar Posthumus Leonatus, against the wishes
of her f and step-mother the Q (who want her to mar Cloten,
her unpleasant s by a former h). Posthumus is banished to
Rome, where Iachimo challenges his belief in Imogen's virtue;
the Roman goes to Br with letters from Posthumus to his w,
and he persuades her to take a travelling chest into her room.
Iachimo is concealed in the chest, and he slips out at night,
notes the layout of the room, and steals a bracelet. Posthumus

is persuaded of his w's infidelity and orders her ass. Imogen disguises as a boy (Fidele), meets her long-lost brs Guiderius and Arviragus (disguised as Polydore and Cadwal), and is made a page to the Roman invader Lucius (they go on to be captured). Amid a welter of recognition and forgiveness, all ends happily ever after.

HAMLET, PRINCE OF DENMARK (abbr: Hamlet). Tragedy set in Denmark. ~, s of the late K of Denmark of the same name, is disgusted by his mother Gertrude's hasty mar to Claudius, his f's br. He sees the ghost of his f, who tells him how he was k by Claudius (poisoned in the ear as he slept). ~ once courted Ophelia, d of Polonius, but now spurns her, and seems to be going mad. By getting a troupe of strolling players to re-enact the murder scene, ~ causes Claudius to betray himself. A bloody ending starts with ~ killing Polonius; Ophelia goes really mad and drowns, Gertrude drinks poison meant for ~, Laertes and ~ k each other, and ~ has just enough strength left to k Claudius.

JULIUS CAESAR (abbr: Caesar). Tragedy set in Roman It. Cassius and Brutus add their voices to others jealous of ~'s popularity, and they join a conspiracy with Casca, Cinna and others. Brutus strikes the final blow when ~ is ass; Mark Antony swears vengeance. Brutus and Cassius flee, and the former decides (against the latter's advice) to confront Antony's army at Philippi; they are defeated and commit sui.

KING HENRY THE FOURTH (abbr: H.iv). Historical play in 2 parts. Part 1 is set in Eng and Wal. H.iv (the usurper Bolingbroke, of R.ii) wants peace. Henry Percy (Hotspur) defeats the Sc and won't release his prisoners until the K ransoms Mortimer, prisoner of Owen Glendower; H.iv refuses. Meanwhile the Prince of Wal roisters with Falstaff and Co, but rallies to his f, when Hotspur joins Glendower. At the battle of Shrewsbury, the prince k Hotspur and finds Falstaff seemingly d; but the fat kt is shamming and, on seeing Hotspur's body, claims to have k him.

H.iv Part 2 is set in Eng. Hal, Prince of Wal, returns to his drunken friends. Falstaff meets Justices Shallow and Silence. The civil war now goes in favour of the K, but he is soon seen to be dying. When Prince Hal becomes K, Falstaff is delighted and borrows money on his expectations; but H.v is a changed man, and spurns his old drinking companion.

KING HENRY THE FIFTH (abbr: H.v). Historical

play set largely in Fr. A very regal H.v confirms the change seen at the end of H.iv; he determines on war with Fr and, after dealing leniently with the plot of Cambridge, Grey and Scroop, he sets forth on the invasion. After capturing Harfleur ('once more unto the breach, dear friends'), he leads his ragged army to victory at Agincourt and mar Princess Katherine of Fr. Comedy is provided by Ancient Pistol, Nym and Bardolph, erstwhile companions of the now-d Falstaff.

KING HENRY THE SIXTH (abbr: H.vi). A trilogy of historical plays. Part 1 is set in Eng and Fr. H.v's death sets the scene for a power struggle. While the Dukes of Bedford and Gloster act as regents for the infant H.vi, the Fr, led by Joan of Arc, re-open the war with Eng. Richard Plantagent (later Duke of York) quarrels with the K's faction (who trace their Lancaster connections through H.iv - Bolingbroke - back to John of Gaunt; Shak invented the selection of white and red roses in the Temple garden). A diplomatic mar between H.vi and the d of the Fr Count of Armagnac is set aside in favour of one with Margaret, d of the Duke of Anjou.

H.vi Part 2 is set in Eng. The Earl of Suffolk and Q Margaret are lovers, and plot to ass the Duke of Gloster, uncle and protector of the K; Suffolk is discovered and k. The Duke of York claims the throne by direct descent from Ed.iii, and foments Jack Cade's rebellion. On York's return from Ire, he starts a civil war by defeating the K's army at St Albans.

H.vi Part 3 is set in Eng and Sc. The Duke of York allows H.vi to stay on the throne during his lifetime, but his s is disinherited. Q Margaret raises an army and defeats York at Wakefield (and impales his head on York city gates). His ss Ed, Earl of March (later Ed.iv) and Richard, Duke of Gloster (much later R.iii) force the K and Q to flee to Sc. H.vi is captured and imprisoned in the Tower. The battle of Tewkesbury confirms the York victory and Ed.iv on the throne; H.vi is ass in the Tower by the Duke of Gloster, whose future role as R.iii is foreshadowed.

KING HENRY THE EIGHTH (abbr: H.viii). Historical play set in London and Kimbolton. After the Field of the Cloth of Gold, the Duke of Buckingham fails to ward off the ambitions of Cardinal Wolsey, who has the Duke ass. The K wants a divorce from Q Katherine so as to mar Ann Bullen; Wolsey opposes, is arrested and d. The existing royal mar is annulled by Cranmer (whom the nobles fail to discredit), ex-Q Katherine d, and Princess Elizabeth is b to the new Q. The play ends with a paeon to the baby, so recently in real life a memorable Q of Eng (Eliz.i d 1603; the play was first produced 1613).

KING JOHN (abbr: John). Historical play set in Eng and Fr. Arthur, Duke of Britaine (Britanny), has a strong claim to the Eng throne through his f, late elder br of John, and he has the support of K Philip of Fr. John orders that his nephew Arthur be taken and blinded, but Hubert de Burgh is moved to pity by the young man's pleas. However, Arthur d attempting a later escape. Throughout, Philip Faulconbridge, the bastard, remains steadfast to Eng. The play ends with John's d.

KING LEAR (abbr: Lear). Tragedy set in Br. Lear, K of Br, wants to divide his kingdom between his three dd, Goneril, Regan and Cordelia, according to their professed love of him. The first two flatter fulsomely, but Cordelia is unable to be cloying - she loves him as a dutiful d; so she gets nothing, while her unctuous ss divide the spoils. As a sub-plot, the Duke of Gloster's bastard s Edmund tries to supplant his half-br Edgar, and persuades their f that Edgar is plotting his d. Edgar flees and becomes the simpleton Poor Tom. Meanwhile, Lear's maintenance is becoming irksome to Goneril and Regan, who seek to set him aside; he leaves in a rage which develops into madness, and is sheltered by Edgar. There follows much intrigue, ass and putting out of eyes, which brings d to the three dd, their two hh, the bastard Edmund, the evil steward Oswald and even the faithful fool; Lear d of grief.

THE LIFE AND DEATH OF KING RICHARD THE SECOND (abbr: R.ii). Historical play set in Eng and Wal. Thomas Mowbray, Duke of Norfolk, quarrels with Henry Bolingbroke, Duke of Hereford (and s of John of Gaunt); they are both banished and R.ii confiscates the latter's lands to finance the war in Ire. On his return, R.ii is captured by Bolingbroke, who has landed to claim the throne as H.iv. R.ii is ass, and Harry Hotspur makes his first appearance on the troubled scenes, prior to the two parts of H.iv.

THE LIFE AND DEATH OF KING RICHARD THE THIRD (abbr: R.iii). Historical play set in Eng. The events follow the trilogy of H.vi. Richard, as Duke of Gloster, is

triumphant at the victory of the Yorkists; his br is K as Ed.iv
and he means to succeed him. He mar the widow of the
Prince of Wal (whom he had k at Tewkesbury), ass his own
elder br George, Duke of Clarence (drowned in a butt of
malmsey). When his br Ed.iv d, Richard imprisons Ed.v and
his br Richard Duke of York as the Princes in the Tower, and
later has them k. Now R.iii, the K quarrels with the Duke
of Buckingham, who thereafter rallies to the cause of the
Earl of Richmond (who has landed with an army to claim
the throne). Buckingham is k, but Lord Stanley, Earl of
Derby, gives his support to Richmond, who wins the battle of
Bosworth, k R.iii and becomes H.vii.

LOVE'S LABOURS LOST (abbr: LLL). Comedy set in
Navarre, Fr. Ferdinand, K of Navarre, resolves with three
of his nobles to abstain for three years from the company of
women, for the better advancement of art and learning in
the court. The Princess of France arrives with three ladies-
in-waiting, and disturbs this plan; Ferdinand falls in love with
the Princess, and his three nobles fall for the three ladies. The
court enjoys a season of flirtation, with humour provided by
Holofernes the schoolmaster, Dull the constable, and Costard
the clown. The K of Fr (f of the Princess) d, and she must
leave; she and her ladies promise to return in a year.

MACBETH (abbr: MacB). Tragedy set in Sc and Eng.
MacB and Banquo, generals of K Duncan of Sc's army, hear
three witches prophesy that the former will become Thane of
Cawdor and K; the latter will beget Ks, but be none himself.
The first prophecy is immediately fulfilled, and starts ~
thinking about the throne. Lady ~ provides the steel for
the ass of K Duncan, but his ss Malcolm and Donalbain flee
to Eng. ~ assumes the crown and ass Banquo, who then
haunts his killer. ~ believes himself invulnerable, but he is
k by Macduff (who was delivered by caesarian and was thus
'not of woman born'), after his army had caused Birnam
Wood to move against ~ because they used the branches
for camouflage. Malcolm accedes to the throne; Banquo was
ancestor to the Stuart line, thus fulfilling the second part of
the witches' prophecy.

MEASURE FOR MEASURE (abbr: M for M). Comedy
set in Vienna. Vincentio, Duke of Vienna, pretends to leave
on a voyage, but remains in disguise as Friar Lodowick, in
order to observe how Angelo his deputy adminsters the

harsh laws relating to morality. Claudio has got his fiancée
Juliet pregnant before their wedding, and is condemned
to die; he appeals for help to his sis Isabella, a nun. She is
unable to move Angelo except to lust; as she tells her br in
his cell, she would give her life for him, but not her virginity.
Meanwhile the bogus Friar Lodowick (Duke of Vienna) has
been watching, and he now moves to restore freedom and the
lovers to each other.

THE MERCHANT OF VENICE (abbr: M of V). Comedy
set in Venice and Belmont. Antonio is the merchant who
goes surety in Venice for his friend Bassanio to borrow
money from Shylock the jew, so that Bassanio can mar Portia;
the bond is a pound of flesh. Bassanio can now voyage to
Belmont to win Portia (by correctly choosing the last-named
between caskets of gold, silver and lead); they mar, as do his
friend Gratiano and Portia's maid Nerissa. The two ladies
give their hh a ring each, which they swear never to surrender.
Meanwhile Antonio's ships do not come in, and Shylock
demands his bond. Portia and Nerissa disguise themselves as
advocate and clerk to defend Antonio. The jew is told that he
may have only his pound of flesh, but not one drop of blood;
he gives in. Bassanio and Gratiano are so glad that they yield
their rings to the two defence counsels (whom, of course, they
fail to recognise), and there is much sport by the ladies about
this towards the end of the play.

THE MERRY WIVES OF WINDSOR (abbr: Merry
Wives). Comedy set at Windsor. Sir John Falstaff has his eyes
on the money which the two Mistresses Ford and Page control
through their hh. He sends them letters in order to woo them,
but Nym and Bardolph tell the hh; the ladies compare letters,
and plan to play a trick on Sir John, who has to hide among
the dirty linen, is thrown into the mud, and is beaten by
Ford while in disguise as Mrs Prat. Falstaff is finally lured to
Windsor Forest, where he is pushed and pinched by the Page
and Ford families dressed as fairies. Mistress Page's d Anne
eludes the attentions of Dr Caius and of Slender, and she is
won by Fenton; Falstaff is forgiven and comforted by a posset
of drink. In modern parlance, any resemblance between Sir
John Falstaff, Nym and Bardolph, and any other Shak chars is
purely coincidental (they formed a convenient group of names
for the playwright to use in comedy).

A MIDSUMMER NIGHT'S DREAM (abbr: MND).

Comedy set in Athens. Theseus, Duke of Athens, plans his
mar to Hippolyta, Q of the Amazons. Hermia is the d of
Egeus, who wants her to mar Demetrius, but she refuses
because she loves Lysander; the Duke orders her to obey
her f or die. Hermia and Lysander flee from Athens and are
followed to a nearby wood by Demetrius and Helena, a friend
of Hermia. The wood is inhabited by fairies, whose K Oberon
is quarreling with his Q Titania. He gets a potion from the
sprite Puck, to drop in the Q's eyes; on waking, she will fall in
love with the first creature she sees. In a series of mischances
and mishaps, the potion is used on both Demetrius and
Lysander. Bottom the Weaver (who is in the woods with
his friends Flute, Quince, Snout, Snug and Starveling, to
rehearse a play for the K's mar) is given the head of an ass
by the mishievous Puck; and it is him that Titania sees first
on waking, so she falls in love with him, ass's head and all.
To sort it all out, Oberon has to shroud in a mist, but this is
duly done.

MUCH ADO ABOUT NOTHING (abbr: Much Ado).
Comedy set in Messina. Leonato, Governor of Messina,
receives Don Pedro, Prince of Arragon, returning from the
wars together with Claudio and Benedick, lords of Florence
and Padua respectively; the former is particularly praised for
his recent deeds, which arouses the jealousy of Don Pedro's
bastard br Don John. Claudio falls in love with Governor
Leonato's d Hero, and Don John plans to spoil their wedding.
Meanwhile, Benedick and the Governor's niece Beatrice
engage in much witty crosstalk, to the point where they too
fall in love. By disguising the maid Margaret as Hero, Don
John persuades Don Pedro and Claudio that Hero is secretly
meeting his follower Borrachio. There follows the typical
Shak confusion as the chars fail to spot the obvious, but all
is eventually cleared up so that the two young couples are
reconciled.

OTHELLO, THE MOOR OF VENICE (abbr:
Othello). Tragedy set in Venice and Cyprus. ~ secretly
mar Desdemona, d of the senator Brabantio, but Roderigo
secretly longs for her. Iago, a long service soldier, sees
the young Cassio preferred to himself for lieutenancy in
the service of ~, who now commands the Venetian force
defending Cyprus from a Turkish attack. All the chars
find themselves in Cyprus, and Iago tells Roderigo that

Desdemona secretly lusts after Cassio; Cassio is as easily
fooled. By much dissembling, including planting on Cassio
one of Desdemona's handkerchiefs, ~ is persuaded of his w's
infidelity, so he k her. In the aftermath, Roderigo and Iago's
w Emilia are also k. The truth comes out, and ~ commits sui
in despair.

PERICLES, PRINCE OF TYRE (abbr: Per). A romance,
set in various places (Antioch, Pentapolis, Ephesus, Tyre).
In seeking the hand of the d of the K of Antioch, Per realises
that the K himself loves her incestuously, so he flees back
to Tyre. He is pursued by Thaliard, who has instructions to
k him, so he flees again. This time he is shipwrecked on the
shore of Pentapolis as the only survivor. He mar Thaisa, d of
K Simonides and soon receives a call from Helicanus, a lord of
Tyre, that Antiochus has d, and Per must take the throne. Per
sets out for Tyre with Thaisa, who gives birth to a d, Marina,
during a storm; Thaisa seems to die, and is cast overboard in a
chest, but is revived at Ephesus by Cerimon. Per puts Marina
in the care of Cleon, Governor of Tarsus. Sixteen years later,
Dionyza (w of Cleon) becomes jealous of Marina's beauty and
tries to k her; the young girl is captured by pirates and sold to
a brothel, where her innocence protects her from the seemingly
inevitable consequences. Per arrives, is reunited with his d,
who mar the local Governor, and he also finds his long-lost w
Thaisa.

ROMEO AND JULIET (abbr: R & J). Romantic tragedy
set in Verona and Mantua. To heal a family feud with the
Montagues, Lord Capulet gives a party, where Count Paris is
expected to woo his d Juliet. Romeo, s of Montague, attends
hoping to see his love Rosaline, but he and J fall in love at
first sight; though she is only 14, the couple mar secretly.
After more family fights (and killings), R is banished. Lord
Capulet insists that J mar Count Paris, so Friar Lawrence
(who had mar R & J) gives her a potion which will simulate
d; he says he will tell R. The information does not reach R
before he hears that J is 'dead'. He goes to the vault where
she lies, k Count Paris, says his farewells and drinks poison.
J wakes to see him d, and stabs herself. The two families are
reconciled.

THE TAMING OF THE SHREW (abbr: Taming).
Comedy set in and around Padua. There is a somewhat
meaningless Induction, in which Christopher Sly (a drunken

tinker) is taken in by a lord, who pretends to him that he, Sly, is also a lord. The play proper then starts at Padua, where Baptista Minola is f of 2 dd, Katherina and Bianca. Their f has ruled that the latter may not mar until her elder sis is wed; the snag is that Katherina is ill-mannered, rude and unloved – until Petruchio comes from Verona in search of a rich w. He chooses Katherina, despite her bad temper. By giving as good as he gets (and more) he gradually tames his shrewish w, so that she is later adjudged the most obedient and quiet of them all.

THE TEMPEST (abbr: Tempest). Comedy set on a lonely island. Twelve years before the start of the play, Prospero the rightful Duke of Milan was cast adrift with his infant d Miranda, eventually to wash up on a lonely island. The play opens on board a ship in a tempest, which has been raised by Prospero's art in order to bring his br Antonio (the usurping duke), with the K of Naples and various attendants, to the island, the only other inhabitants of which are Caliban (a savage and deformed slave) and Ariel (an airy spirit). Miranda falls in love with the s of the K of Naples. Prospero uses his magic to frustrate the evil designs of the shipwrecked mariners, who eventually recognise him and repent. They all return to Milan and Naples in the magically restored ship.

TIMON OF ATHENS (abbr: Timon). Tragedy set in and around Athens. Timon, a noble Athenian, is over-generous to his friends, so that he goes broke and has to ask them for money in his turn; but they spurn him. He gives a dinner party at which only bowls of warm water are served, as though to the dogs he consider them; he then storms out to go and live in a cave, where he uncovers a hoard of gold. He gives some to Alcibiades, an Athenian officer exiled by the lawless factions, some to Apemanthus a philosopher, and some to his faithful steward Flavius. Word gets out and the sycophants return, but ~ is d; Alcibiades restores law and order to the city.

TITUS ANDRONICUS (abbr: Titus). Tragedy set in and around Rome. Titus captures Tamora, Q of the Goths, and brings her and her three ss to Rome, where the eldest is ass. The Emperor Saturninus wants the d of ~ (Lavinia) for his w, but is also drawn to Tamora; his br Bassanius seizes Lavinia for himself. Emperor Saturninus mar Tamora, who, aided by her lover Aaron, a moor, sets about revenge by k Bassanius

while her surviving two ss rape Lavinia, before cutting off
her hands and tearing out her tongue. Two of the ss of ∼
are accused of the murder and executed; Lucius the eldest is
banished. In an orgy of blood, ∼ k Tamora's two ss (whom
he serves up to their mother for dinner), and Lavinia, before
he k Tamora herself. Saturninus k ∼ and is k himself by
Lucius, who has returned at the head of a Gothic army and
now becomes Emperor. The moor Aaron is buried up to his
neck to starve to d.

TROILUS AND CRESSIDA (abbr: T & C). Tragedy set
in and before Troy. In a truce during the siege of Troy, T (s
of K Priam) loves C, d of Calchas (Trojan priest who deserts
to the Gk camp); her uncle Pandarus arranges what turns out
to be a mutually satisfactory liaison between the two (hence
pander). An exchange of prisoners somehow includes C, who
now becomes the property of Diomedes, a Gk commander
(her sensuous nature accepts the situation happily). There
is some interplay involving a few more classical Gk heroes,
during which Achilles k the noble Hector, and the war starts
up again.

TWELFTH NIGHT; or, WHAT YOU WILL (abbr: 12
N). Comedy set in Illyria (E Adriatic). Orsino Duke of Illyria
has unrequited love for Olivia. Twins Viola and Sebastian
are shipwrecked nearby, and Viola thinks her br drowned.
She dresses as a man (Cesario) and becomes a page to Duke
Orsino where, as Cesario, she is urged by her master to
intercede with Olivia on his behalf; Olivia falls for Cesario.
Sebastian has survived and arrives in the same town. But the
twins don't meet yet, and there is much play on mistaken
identity of one twin for the other, as even Sebastian's best
friend Antonio fails to notice that Cesario is not her br. The
play is full of well-drawn minor chars such as the rumbustious
Sir Toby Belch, Sir Andrew Aguecheek, the preening
Malvolio gulled into cross-gartering, and Feste the clown
(who sings 'O mistress mine' among other songs). All is sorted
out when the twins find each other, and the Duke mar Viola
while Sebastian claims Olivia.

TWO GENTLEMEN OF VERONA (abbr: 2 G of V).
Comedy set in N It. The two friends Valentine and Proteus
separately make their way to Milan, where the former falls in
love with Silvia, the Duke's d; the latter (who has left his love
Julia behind in Verona) arrives later and also falls for Silvia.

Valentine plans an elopement but Proteus tells the Duke, so that his friend is banished. Impatient for Proteus, Julia arrives dressed as a man and, conveniently unrecognised by her lover, becomes his page Sebastian. Humour is added to wit by the clownish servants Speed and Launce. Meanwhile Silvia runs off to look for Valentine, is captured by robbers and rescued by Proteus, who then tries to seduce her. The sudden interruption of Valentine makes Proteus contrite, so that unbelievably he is quickly forgiven and given the go-ahead by his friend. Julia (present as the page Sebastian) swoons at this, and is finally recognised; Proteus quickly switches his affections back to her. Valentine and Silvia are united.

THE WINTER'S TALE (abbr: W Tale). Comedy set in Sicily and Bohemia. Polixenes, K of Bohemia, is guest of Leontes and Hermione, K and Q of Sicily. Polixenes declines to prolong his stay at Leontes' urging, but eventually yields to Hermione's pleas. This causes her h to become jealous, and he orders Camillo to poison his erstwhile friend, but Camillo flees with Polixenes instead. Leontes throws Hermione into prison, where she bears him a d, which her h orders to be abandoned to die; Antigonus casts her safely away on the shores of Bohemia, but is k by a bear before he can return ('exit, pursued by a bear'). The baby is taken in by a shepherd. News of Hermione's d causes Leontes to repent; humour is contributed by the rogue Autolycus (who is 'a snapper-up of unconsidered trifles'). 16 years pass, and Florizel (s of Polixenes) loves Perdita, a lovely shepherdess, but the K won't agree to the mar with a commoner, so the couple flee to Sicily, followed by Polixenes. Perdita's identity as the castaway princess is revealed, so all is clear for the young couple. Q Hermione is still alive (she has been hidden by Paulina and is now first revealed pretending to be a statue). Leontes and Polixenes are reconciled.

SHANGHAI CARRY OFF, IMPRESS, PRESS. CITY (Ch).
SHAPE *FASHION, FORM*, FIGURE. MAKE, MOULD. HQ, HEADQUARTERS (mil).
SHARK 1. ADVENTURER, SWINDLER. 2. *FISH*; breeds: *ANGEL* ~, BASKING ~, *BLUE* ~, BUTTERFLY ~, GREAT WHITE ~, GREY *NURSE*, HAMMERHEAD, HORN ~, MACKEREL ~, MAKO, MAN-EATING ~, *NURSE*, PENNY-DOG, PORBEAGLE, PORT

JACKSON ~, RHIN(E)DON, SELACHE, SPUR-DOG,
SUNFISH, SWORDFISH ~, THRESHER ~, *TIGER*
~, TOPE, *WHALE* ~ (biggest fish), WHITE ~,
WHITE POINTER, WOBBEGONG (Aus), *ZEBRA* ~,
ZYGAENA [pilot fish, remoru, shagreen, squaloid].

SHARP-EYED see *KEEN-EYED*.

SHARPSHOOTER 1. MARKSMAN, SNIPER. *GUN*.
2. Crooked dicer, hence CIDER, RICED etc (crypt).

SHAW (s/l shore, sure). 1. THICKET, WOOD (arch).
2. George Bernard ~, Irish dramatist. **Plays**: Androcles
and the Lion, The Apple Cart, Buoyant Billions, Caesar
and Cleopatra, Candida, Doctor's Dilemma, Heartbreak
House, Pygmalion, Saint Joan, Too True to be Good.
3. Aircraftsman ~ = Lawrence of Arabia = Ross.

SHE FEMALE SUBJECT, WOMAN. [~ who must be
obeyed, *Haggard*].

SHEBA 1. Kingdom of S Arabia; modern Yemen. 2. SABA,
the kingdom of Joktan. AAZIZ; BILKIS, a Queen of ~,
visited *Solomon* to check on the rumours of his wealth;
'Behold the half was not told unto me.' The Abyssinians
adopted her as the Cushite or Ethiopian ~, making
her and Solomon joint ancestors of the *royal family* of
Ethiopia. 3. Bibl s of Bichri, who rose against *David* and
exhorted ' . . . every man to his tents O Israel.' Pursued to
the city of *Abel* and k by *Joab*.

SHED CAST, DOFF(ED), DROP(PED), HIVE(D) OFF,
PART(ED) WITH, SPILL(ED). DIFFUSE(D), DISPERSE(D).
REDUCE(D). HUT, SHELTER, STORE. *FOOTBALL
GROUND* (Chelsea). SHE WOULD (crypt).

SHEEP 1. BASHFUL/DOCILE PERSON, NONENTITY.
ISLAND. 2. Horned ruminant, genus ovis. HOGGET,
RAM, TEG, TUP, WETHER. *Constellation*; sign of Zodiac
(9th). **Breeds**: AMMON, AOUDAD (N Af), ARGALI
(Asia), BHARAL (Ind), BLACKFACE, BORDER,
CARACUL, CHEVIOT, COTSWOLD, DORSET,
HAMPSHIRE DOWN, HERDWICK, HIGHLAND, JACOB'S
JUMBUK, LEICESTER, MANX, MERINO, MUFFLON
(wild), ROMNEY MARSH, ROUGH FELL, SCOTTISH
BLACKFACE, SOAY, SOUTHDOWN, SUFFOLK,
SWALEDALE, ST KILDA, URIAL (Asia), WELSH
MOUNTAIN, WENSLEYDALE, ZUNA (Angola) (**assembly**

= flock, herd; **male** = ram; **female** = ewe, theave; **offspring** = lamb).

SHEER (s/l shear). PERPENDICULAR, PLUMB, VERTICAL. HOIST, JURY CRANE; RISE OF DECKLINE; YAW (naut). MERE, OUT AND OUT, SIMPLE, UNDILUTED. BREAK, SNAP. DEPART, PART COMPANY. RAKE, WOMANIZER (crypt).

SHEET *LAYER*, STRATUM. ROPE (naut). PANE. *MEASURE* (paper); F, FOLIO, PAGE. COVERING. **Pl** = BED LINEN, COVERS.

SHELF LIFE STAY-FRESH PERIOD, STORAGE TIME. SPINSTERHOOD (crypt).

SHELL BOMBARD, FIRE AT, LAY BARRAGE, STONK. CARTRIDGE, PROJECTILE, *WEAPON*. PETROL; OIL COMPANY ®. SHE WILL (crypt). *FORM*, SEMBLANCE, SHOW. CARAPACE, CASE, CRUST, HUSK, *NUTCASE* [*kernel*], POD; [*collector*; *crustacean*, *study*]; **types** (**marine**): ABALONE, BARNACLE, CLAM, COCKLE, CONCH, COWRIE, GAPER, LAVER, LIMPET, MUSSEL, ORMER, *OYSTER*, PERIWINKLE, RAZOR, SCALLOP (pilgrim), SEA EAR, SEA SNAIL, SNAIL, SPIRAL LAVER, SPIROBIS, WAMPUM, WHELK, WINKLE [mollusc]. **Comp** = *shot*.

SHEPHERD 1. FARMER, *TENDER*; MARSHAL, TEND; **celeb**: Astrophel (Spenser); *Abel*; Corin, Silvius (*Shak*); *David*; Lycidas (Milton); *Moses*; Stiggins (Pickwick, *Dickens*); in Winter's Tale (foster-f of Perdita, *Shak*); in H.iv (f of Joan of Arc, *Shak*). CHURCHMAN, MINISTER, PARSON, VICAR. 2. **Gk god** = PAN. 3. *Constellation* (Bootes).

SHEPHERDESS Fem *shepherd*; *COWGIRL* (crypt); GIRL GUIDE (crypt); **celeb**: BO-PEEP (trad); CELIA (AYLI, *Shak*); DORCAS (W Tale, *Shak*); MARY (had a little lamb, trad); MOPSA (W Tale, *Shak*); PERDITA (W Tale, *Shak*); PHEBE (AYLI, *Shak*).

SHIELD PROTECT, *SCREEN*. *ARMOUR*, BUCKLER; AEGIS (*Athene*). *ACHIEVEMENT*, BADGE, ESCUTCHEON [coat of arms (*herald*)].

SHIFT *Anag*. MOVE. GANG, SPELL, TURN, WATCH. DODGE, TRICK. CONTRIVE. CHEMISE, SARK, SHIRT.

SHINER BLACK EYE. *FISH* (US). Nine bright, in *song*. **Pl** = *MONEY*.

SHIP SS; *BOAT* (q.v.), SQUARE RIGGER, *VESSEL*

(q.v.). *AIRCRAFT* (US). STOW, TAKE ABOARD.
DELIVER, SEND. EMBARK.
SHIPMAN *Chaucer's* sea captain. *SAILOR*.
SHIPWRECK FOUNDERING, SINKING, STRANDING.
Any anag of SHIP.
SHIRT CHEMISE, JERSEY, SARK, SHIFT.
SHIVA Chief Ind *god*; mar to Devi.
SHOCKER ELECTRICITY (crypt). *JAR*, JERK, JOLT.
MURDER MYSTERY, THRILLER.
SHOCKING DISGUSTING, HORRIFYING, IMPROPER,
SENSATIONAL. ELECTRIC, LIVE. STOOKING.
SHOE (s/l *shoo*). *BOOT*, BROGUE, CLOG, FOOTWEAR,
MULE, *OXFORD*, *PUMP*, SABOT, SLIPPER,
TOPBOOT, *TRAINER*, *WELLINGTON*, ZORI (Jap)
[cobbler, heel, last, snob, sole, tongue, upper, vamp].
HORSE ~. FERRULE, SOCKET. KEEL-BAND,
MAST-STEP (naut). IRON STRAP; SPRIG, WHEEL
DRAG. CONTACT (elect mech). CARD DISPENSER
(casino). **Pl** = SHOON (arch).
SHOOT (s/l chute). DISCHARGE, EMIT, *FIRE*, LOOSE
OFF. KILL. BUD, SUCKER. *FILM*, PHOTOGRAPH,
TURN. SCORE. SPEAK!
SHOP BUY, PURCHASE. EMPORIUM, SALEROOM,
SUPERMARKET. BUSINESS. *BETRAY*. WOOLWICH (mil sl).
SHOPPER PURCHASER. *BETRAYER*.
SHORN (s/l Sean). 1. CLIPPED, CUT; DISTRESSED
(crypt). 2. Remove synonym for hair from word, e.g.
German shorn huntress (3) = HUN(tress).
SHORT 1. BRIEF, CONCISE, CURTAILED, CUT,
RUNT, SMALL (**opp** = *long*, tall). CURT. OWING,
SHY. BREAK INSULATION, UNEARTH (elect).
CRUMBLING, FRIABLE (cook). **Pl** = BERMUDAS.
DRINKS, SPIRITS. 2. Use any abbr, short or diminutive
word, e.g. **Short ton** = T; **Short test** = EXAM; **Short
measure** = TOT.
SHORT TIME HR, MIN, MO, SEC (crypt). QUICKLY.
SHOT CANNON, CUT, DRIVE, GLANCE, MASSE,
POT, PULL, PUTT (games). *FIRED*, LOOSED OFF,
POTSHOT; KILLED. FILMED, SNAPPED; VIEW
(photo). *GO*, TURN. **Comp** = *shell*.
SHOUT BAWL, CALL, *CRY*, HAIL (**opp** = whisper).
TREAT, TURN.

SHOW *CONDUCT*, GUIDE, INDICATE, POINT.
DEMONSTRATE, PROVE. DISCLOSE, DISPLAY,
EXHIBIT, EXPO, MANIFEST, OFFER. EXHIBITION,
PAGEANT, PANTO, *PLAY*, RODEO, SPECTACLE.
PROJECT, SCREEN.

SHOWER DOWNPOUR, HAIL, PEPPER,
PRECIPITATION, RAIN; DOUCHE, ~ BATH
[*Danae*]. DEMONSTRATOR, EXHIBITOR (crypt);
CONDUCTOR, DRAGOMAN (crypt).

SHOWPLACE CINEMA, *THEATRE* (crypt). SIGHT,
TOURIST SPOT.

SHREW INSECTIVORE (~ mouse). GRIMALKIN,
SCOLD, SPITFIRE, TERMAGANT, VIRAGO; **celeb**:
EPICOENE (Ben Jonson), KATE (Taming, *Shak*),
XANTHIPPE (Gk).

SHRUB *DRINK*. PLANT (q.v.), *WILD PLANT* (q.v.).

SHUN AVOID, ESCHEW, EVADE. CUT, SNUB.
ATTENTION (mil).

SHUT *BAR*, CLOSE, FASTEN. GAG, *SILENCE*. **Comp**
= *open*.

SHUTTLE BOBBIN, WEFT-CARRIER. BIRD
(badminton). BRANCH LINE, COMMUTE, FEEDER
SERVICE, TRAVEL TO AND FRO. *SPACECRAFT*
(Challenger, Columbia).

SHY *ARCH*, CHARY, COY, NEBBISH, RETIRING, TIMID.
REAR UP. ELUSIVE, UNEASY. *CAST*, FLING, *PELT*,
THROW; AUNT SALLY. OWING, *SHORT*.

SI SYSTEME INTERNATIONALE, *INTERNATIONAL
UNITS*. SILICON (*chem*). STAR OF INDIA (*order*). **Pl** =
SISTER.

SIB(LING) AKIN, RELATED; *BROTHER*, *SISTER* (one of
two or more children with the same parent or parents).

SIBYL FORTUNE TELLER, *PROPHETESS* (q.v.),
ORACULAR MOUTHPIECE; **celeb**: AMALTHEA (cornucopia),
~ of CUMEA (Tarquinius and the Sibiline books),
DEIOPHOBE, DEMO, DEMOPHILE, HEROPHILE,
PHEMONOE. HAG, *WITCH*. Girl's name.

SIC (s/l *sick*). SO, THUS.

SICK (s/l *sic*). AEG(ROTAT), *ILL*, INDISPOSED [*patron
saint*]. VOMIT. ENCOURAGE, SET ON, *URGE*. [~ as
a parrot = *upset* (**opp** = over the moon)].

SIDE 1. ELEVEN, FIFTEEN, II, XI, XV; PLAYERS,

TEAM. BOASTING, SWANK. 2. Use either or both
sides (i.e. ends) of word indicated, e.g. **Both sides of some
Kentish area** = s**E; **This side of the moon** = MO**. 3. **Pl**
= any common pair of items which may be on either side,
e.g. ON and OFF, L and R, E and W.

~ **LINE** ALTERNATIVE, SECOND STRING
[moonlighting]. *BAY*, SIDING; TOUCH, TRAMLINES (games).

SIDING SWITCH-LINE (rly). PARTISANSHIP.

Sig Signature.

SIGN (s/l sine). CROSS, MARK; GUARANTEE,
PASSWORD, *SEAL*, TOKEN. OMEN, PORTENT.
SYMPTOM. PLUS, MINUS, MULTIPLY etc. *ARROW*,
BOARD, POSTER. UNDERWRITE. [*Zodiac*].

SIGNAL *SIGN*, INDICATION. *ARROW*, *DIRECTOR*.
MORSE, SEMAPHORE [aldis, flag code]. FLARE,
PYROTECHNIC, ROCKET. OUTSTANDING,
REMARKABLE.

SILENCE NOISELESS, PEACE, QUIET. P, PP, SH;
HUSH, MUM, WHIST [*oyster, Shak char*]. [**Pl** = Les ~s
du Col Bramble; Maurois].

SILICON SI (*chem*).

SILK 1. KC, QC; BARRISTER, COUNSEL. GOWN; RACING
COLOURS. *MATERIAL*: BOMBAZINE, TAFFETA,
TULLE; RUSTLER (crypt). 2. *Anniversary* (12th).

SILVER *METAL*; AG (*chem*). *ARGENT* (*herald*).
Anniversary (25th). CHANGE, *COINS* (nickel) [*Judas*].
HORSE. *PIRATE* (Treasure Island, *Stevenson*).

SIMPLE ARTLESS, *ATTIC*, BASIC, EASY, PLAIN,
UNCOMPLICATED (**opp** = *involved*). ABSOLUTE.
MERE. FOOLISH. HUMBLE, LOWLY. HERBAL
REMEDY, HERB. SERVANT (*Shak*).

SIN 1. DO WRONG, ERR, SLIP, TRANSGRESS. 2. **Seven
deadly, or mortal, sins**: ANGER, AVARICE, ENVY,
GLUTTONY, LUST, PRIDE, SLOTH. 3. Bibl city (Egy);
wilderness. 4. Moon god (Ur).

SINGER DIVA, CROONER, *SONGSTER*,
TROUBADOUR, VOCALIST; ALTO, BARITONE,
BASS, CONTRALTO, SOPRANO, TENOR; **celeb**:
BLONDEL (minstrel), CARUSO, GIGLI, *JENNY* LIND,
LORELEI, MELBA, ORPHEUS (*Argonaut*), *SIREN*
(myth). *BETRAYER* (sl). BURNER, TOASTER (crypt).
SEWER (crypt).

SINGLE 1. *ACE*, I, ONE, UNIT. BACHELOR, SPINSTER, UNMARRIED, UNWED. R, RUN (cricket). **Pl** = game of tennis. 2. Remove indication of marriage (i.e. letters 'm' or 'wed') from clue, e.g. **Secure single wedlock** (4) = ***LOCK.

SINGULAR S. ODD, PECULIAR, STRANGE. INDIVIDUAL, UNIQUE; ONE ONLY (**opp** = plural).

SINIS Gk myth *robber* who tied his victims to twin bent fir trees, and split them on release. Slain by *Theseus*.

SINISTER EVIL, MALIGNANT, VILLAINOUS. *LEFT* (**opp** = *dexter*); BASTARDY (*herald*).

SIRE *FATHER*, GOVERNOR (arch), PA, POP. BEGET. LORD, MASTER, MAJESTY.

SIREN 1. HOOTER, SIGNAL, WARNING [*police*]. SINGER, TEMPTRESS. 2. Sea nymphs whose sweet singing lured sailors to shipwreck. *Ulysses* filled his sailors' ears with wax and had himself tied to the mast. *Orpheus* surpassed them in singing, so they threw themselves into the sea and were turned into rocks. A siren also lured sailors at Lorelei on the Rhine.

sis Sister.

SISERA Bibl general, defeated by Barak and Deborah at Kishon. He fled to Heber the Hittite, but Heber's w Jael took advantage of ~ and k him.

SISTER *CHURCHWOMAN*, NUN. *SIB*, SIBBE, SIBLING [uterine] (**opp** = *brother*). *NURSE*. **Pl** = CONVENT, NUNNERY; ~ OF MERCY. **Celeb:** ANDREWS, BEVERLEY, NOLAN (all theat), DANAIDS, *MUSES, NEREIDS*, PIERIDES.

SISYPHUS Gk myth king of Corinth, condemned to atone for his sins in the *Underworld*, by rolling a boulder uphill, at the top of which it always rolled down again. [*Autolycus*].

SITTER EASY, FACILE. *MODEL*, POSER. BABYMINDER.

SITUATION APPOINTMENT, JOB, POSITION, *POST*. LOCATION. PASS.

SIX See *number*. HEXAD, SICE, VI. BOUNDARY, UNBOUNCING (*cricket*). *PINK BALL* (*snooker*). *Proud walkers* (*song*). *Geese* a-laying (*Christmas song*). [*Holmes* case; ~ honest serving men: What, Why, When, How, Where, Who (*Kipling*)].

~ **FOOTER** ANT, *INSECT* (crypt).

~ **NATIONS** Iroquois confederation of *American Indian* tribes, west of New York (1770).

SKATE ICE ~, ROLLER ~. *FISH, RAY.*
SKIN FELL, FLEECE, *HIDE,* PELT. PARE, PEEL, RIND,
  CICATRIZE, FLAY. PLANKING, PLATING (naut).
  Comp = *bones.*
SKINNER FURRIER. *PEELER.* [~'s Horse (mil)].
SKINT BROKE; BORACIC LINT (*rh sl*); **opp** = *flush.*
SKIPPER *BOSS,* CAPT. *BUTTERFLY. DEER. FISH.*
  ABSCONDER, RUNAWAY (crypt). *LAMB* (crypt).
  [bowls, curling].
SKIRON (s/l *Sciron*). Gk myth NW *WIND* (**Rom** = CAURUS).
SKULK 1. LURK, SHIRK DUTY. 2. *Assembly* of foxes.
sl Slang.
s/l *Sounds like* (and see *Pronunciation*).
SLACK IDLE, LAZE, LAZY. LATITUDE, MARGIN,
  PLAY. COAL DUST. **Pl** = TROUSERS.
SLANG 1. ARGOT (Fr), IDIOM, JARGON (denoted in this
  Companion by the abbr: 'sl'); *common* or vulgar speech [Shelta
  (Ire tinkers)]. ABUSE, BERATE, INSULT, RAGE, *RAIL,*
  RANT, RAVE, *THUNDER* AT. 2. The solver should be
  prepared for clues which seek to divert attention through the
  use of words which have a ~ meaning different from their
  more usual interpretation, e.g. **He's got plenty of coppers to
  afford the drug** (4) = HE·MP (note the use of **afford**, which
  encourages consideration of coppers as money, rather than **to
  provide** the answer. 3. The answer itself may be a ~ word,
  not necessarily indicated in the clue, e.g. **Point to a fish with
  some hesitation, and run for it** (7) = S·CARP·ER. 4. Employ
  ~ for word(s) in clue, e.g. **Slang talk for fast breeder** (6) =
  RABBIT.
SLAVE DEPENDENT UNIT (mech/tech). SUBORDINATE
  ANT. DRUDGE; VICTIM; BONDSMAN, ESNE(OE),
  HUMAN CHATTEL, SERF, UNPAID SERVANT;
  celeb: AESOP (when young; fables), ANDROCLES
  (lion, thorn), CALIBAN (Tempest, *Shak*), GUMBO (Virginians,
  Thackeray), JIM (Huckleberry Finn, *Twain*), MORGIANA
  (Arabian Nights), SPARTACUS (Rom), TOPSY, UNCLE
  REMUS (*Harris*), TOUSSAINT L'OUVERTURE (Haiti
  'Napoleon'), UNCLE TOM (Topsy = 'I 'spects I growed',
  Uncle Tom's Cabin, H. B. *Stowe*). HELOT (Gk). RIVER
  (Can).
SLEEPER KIPPER, NAPPER (sl) [*Morpheus*]. EAR-RING.
  RAILBED.

SLEEPY DOZY, DROWSY, SOMNOLENT.
INATTENTIVE, INDOLENT, UNOBSERVANT.
DWARF (Snow White).
SLIGHT LITTLE, SLIM, *SMALL*. INSULT.
SLING BALLISTA, CATAPULT [David and Goliath (bibl)].
DRINK. HOIST, SUPPORT, SUSPEND. BANDAGE,
BELT, STRAP.
SLIP *FALL*, SLIDE. ESCAPE. ERROR, FAULT, GAFFE,
MISTAKE. LANDING, QUAY, RAMP, WAY (naut).
PETTICOAT, UNDERSKIRT. DROP. *CRICKETER*,
FIELDER.
SLIPPER INDOOR *SHOE, MULE*. BEAT, CHASTISE,
LEATHER, WALE. BRAKE, SKID (mech). CLAY.
EEL, SKATE, SKI, SLEDGE, TOBOGGAN (all crypt).
SLOPING *INCLINED*, LEANING, LISTING, SLANTING.
ITALIC.
SLOTH IDLENESS, INDOLENCE, LAZINESS. TREE
MAMMAL; **2-toed**: CHOLEOPUS, UNAU; **3-toed**: AI,
BRADYPUS. ~ BEAR (Ind); ~ MONKEY (loris). [And
see *lemur*].
SLOUGH 1. BACKWATER, BOG, HOLLOW, MARSH. 2.
DESPAIR, DESPOND [Pilgrim's Progress]. 3. DISCARD
(cards). CAST OFF, SHED; COATING, DEAD
SKIN/TISSUE (zool). 4. TOWN (Home Counties).
SMACK BLOW, SLAP. *BOAT*. HEROIN, *DRUG*. TASTE;
LICK (lips).
SMALLHOLDING ACRE, ALLOTMENT. MINORITY
SHARE. BRIEFCASE, ETUI, RETICULE (crypt).
SMALL VOLUME CC, VOL (crypt). QUIET (crypt), hence P.
SMART A LA MODE, CHIC, DAPPER, FASHIONABLE,
IN, MODISH, SWELL, TONISH. HURT, STING.
CLEVER, EFFICIENT [Alec]. QUICK. *PAINTER*.
SMASHED BROKEN, SHATTERED. *DRUNK* (sl).
SMEE (s/l It's me). *DUCK. PIRATE* (*Barrie*).
SMELT FISH, *SALMON*. EXTRACT, MELT (tech).
SNIFFED; STANK.
SMITH METAL WORKER; FORGER (crypt); *IRONER*
(crypt); **celeb**: JAMES BURTON (Kingsley); JOE
GARGERY (Great Ex, *Dickens*); THE VILLAGE
BLACKSMITH (Longfellow); FE ~ (Lord Birkenhead);
weaver, (*Shak*). SMUDGER (*nickname*).
SMOKER COMPARTMENT (rly). CIGARETTE, CIGAR,

PIPE(R), *DRAWER* (crypt). CHIMNEY, FIREPLACE, FLUE, FUNNEL, LUM, STACK (all crypt).

SMUGGLE AVOID DUTY, RUN; CONCEAL, *HIDE*, STASH [contraband, Customs].

SN *TIN* (*chem*).

SNAFFLE *STEAL. BIT, HARNESS.*

SNAKE 1. SWAY, WIGGLE. EMF (European Monetary Fund). RIVER (US). 2. Limbless *reptile*, ASP, OPHIDIA; **breeds:** *ADDER,* ANACONDA, BASILISK, BOA, BOLOBI, BUSHMASTER (S Am), COBRA, COCKATRICE, CORAL, CRIBO, DABOIA, FER-DE-LANCE (S Am viper), GARTER ~, GLASS ~ (lizard), *GRASS,* GWARDAR, HABU, JIBOYA, KARUNG (water ~), KING, KRAIT, *MAMBA,* MOCCASIN, *PYTHON,* RATTLER, RING-HALS, SEPS, SURUCUCU (S Am), TAIPAN (Aus), VIPER, WHIP ~ (Aus). **Celeb:** KAA (Kipling), A and C (*Shak*), MIDGARD (*Loki*), and see *SERPENT*; **k by ~ bite:** *Cleopatra, Eurydice,* Laocoon (*Troy*) [*Ch calendar*]. **Pl comp** = *ladders.* 3. *Constellation* (Serpens).

SNAP *BREAK. CARD* GAME. PHOTO, PICTURE. QUICK, SPUR OF THE MOMENT.

SNEAK *BETRAY. CREEP.*

SNEEZY *DWARF* (Snow White).

SNIP AMBUSH, ATTACK [*sharpshooter*]. GAMEBIRD; **assembly** = wisp.

SNOOKER POOL [billiards; pyramids; *black, blue, brown, green, pink, red, yellow* balls]; BLOCK, OBSTRUCT. DEFEAT, THWART. GESTICULATOR (crypt).

SNOW ICE CRYSTALS. COCAINE, *DRUG. BOAT.* SILVER/NICKEL *COINS.*

SNUB CUT, *SHUN.* PULL, TUG (naut).

SO SOUTH. STANDING ORDER. STATIONERY OFFICE. ERGO, SIC, THUS; AS. NOTE (mus; also SOH). KING (bibl). **Pl** = MAYDAY.

SOCIETY S. ASSOCIATION, *CLUB,* ORGANIZATION.

SOCRATES Gk philosopher, mar *Xanthippe* in self-penance. Condemned to death, he chose to drink hemlock in front of his friends.

SODIUM *METAL*; NA (*chem*).

SOFA SETTEE, UPHOLSTERED SEAT; ~ TABLE; and see *furniture.*

SOFT B (pencil); P, PP (mus), SH; HUSH, QUIET;
DULCET. EASY, GIVING (**opp** = *hard*).

SOILED DIRTY, UNWASHED. EARTHY; BEDDED,
LAID OUT, PLANTED (crypt).

SOL Rom *god* of the SUN; also PHOEBUS (**Gk** =
APOLLO, HELIOS).

SOLDIER 1. Any rank in the Army, usually abbreviated, e.g.
BRIG, CAPT, *COL*, CPL, *GEN*, LT, MAJ, RSM, SGT.
ANT. 2. POILU (Fr); HOPLITE (Gk); BERSERKER
(ON); KERNE (Ire); CENTURION, LEGIONARY,
PRIMUS PILUS (Rom); LOBSTER (arch), PBI,
PONGO, REDCOAT (arch), SWADDY, TOMMY
ATKINS (UK); DOUGHBOY, GI, PFC (US). **Celeb**:
ALEXANDER (the Great), ANTIPATER (Macedon),
BEN BATTLE (Faithless Nelly Gray, Hood), *CLUBS*
(*Alice*), FOURTH AGE (The *Seven Ages* of Man,
Shak), MONTY (Lord Montgomery), OLD BILL (Bruce
Bairnsfather), and, all from H.v (*Shak*): BARDOLPH,
BATES, COURT, FLUELLEN (Wal), GOWER (Eng),
JAMY (Sc), MACMORRIS (Ire), NYM, PISTOL and
WILLIAMS; [*military leaders*]. **Pl** = ARMY, INFANTRY,
MEN, TROOPS, ~s of the Queen. **Gk** = *PHALANX*,
Rom = LEGIONARY (100) CENTURY, MANIPLE (6)
COHORT [eagle, vexillum] [10] LEGION (commanded by a
Legatus); **Irregulars** = AUXILIA (Rom); FENCIBLES, HOME
GUARD, LDV, MILITIA, TA, TERRIERS, VIGILANTES.

SOLE EXCLUSIVE, ONLY. UNMARRIED (leg). *FISH*,
FLAT-FISH. BASE, BOTTOM, FOUNDATION;
SHOE-TREAD. **Comp** = *heel*.

SOLICITOR BEGGAR, IMPORTUNER, TOUT.
LAWYER [Sampson and Sally Brass, *Dickens*]. See *law*.

SOLIDARITY COMMUNITY INTEREST,
INTERDEPENDENCE. *UNION* (Pol).

SOLIDUS S. *COIN* (Rom) [£ s d]. OBLIQUE STROKE,
VIRGULE.

SOLOMON 1. Second s of *David* and Bathsheba (bibl),
third king of Isr (*c*.990–930 B.C.). He then had his half-br Adonijah
(who coveted his step-m Abishag) ass, and also *Joab*. Endowed
with great *wisdom* (decision on custody of baby), ~ is renowned
for the number of his 'wives' or concubines, incl the Queen
of *Sheba* (by whom he started the *royal family* of Abyssinia).
[Rider *Haggard*]. 2. ~ Pross, alias John Barsad, prison *spy* who

lets Carton into Darnay's cell (2 Cities, *Dickens*). 3. ~ *Grundy*.
4. Br *painter*. 5. Musician.

SOLUTION ANSWER, *KEY*, RESOLUTION, SOLVING,
DISSOLUTION, SEPARATION.

SOLVE ANSWER, PUZZLE OUT. DISSOLVE, LOOSEN,
UNTIE.

Som Somalia.

SOME (s/l *sum*). 1. A FEW, APPROXIMATELY. A
QUANTITY, AT LEAST. WONDERFUL. 2. Hidden
word, as *part* (2). 3. Part of word following, e.g. **Some
money for my Scots friend** (3) = MON**.

SON (s/l *sun*). 1. S; BOY, LAD. 2. Used after a name to indicate
'the son of', e.g. **Adamson** = CAIN or ABEL or SETH [*Ap*].

SONG 1. AIR, ARIA, *CATCH*, CHANSON, DITTY, *GLEE,
LAY, LIED*, SHANTY, TUNE. CHEAP. 2. **Gk goddess** =
TERPSICHORE. 3. **Celeb**: Green grow the rushes-oh:
  (1) All *alone* and evermore shall be so;
  (2) Lilywhite *boys*;
  (3) *Rivals*;
  (4) *Gospel* makers;
  (5) *Symbols* at your *door*;
  (6) Proud *walkers*;
  (7) *Stars* in the sky;
  (8) Bold *rangers*;
  (9) Bright *shiners*;
  (10) *Commandments*;
  (11) Who went to *Heaven*;
  (12) *Apostles*.

Twelve days of *Christmas*:

  (1) *Partridge* in a pear-tree;
  (2) Turtle *doves*;
  (3) French *hens*;
  (4) Calling *birds*;
  (5) Gold *rings*;
  (6) *Geese* a-laying;
  (7) *Swans* a-swimming;
  (8) *Maids* a-milking;
  (9) *Drummers* drumming;
  (10) *Pipers* piping;
  (11) *Ladies dancing*;

(12) *Lords* a-leaping.

SONGSTER *BIRD*. CROONER, *SINGER*; POET; COMPOSER, LYRICIST.

SOON 1. *ANON*, PRESENTLY, SHORTLY. WILLINGLY. ETC (crypt). 2. Add 'so' to word, e.g. **Lace and so on brings comfort** (6) or **Lace soon brings comfort** (6) = SO•LACE.

SOOTHSAYER See *PROPHET*.

SORCERER One who controls supernatural powers. ASTROLOGER, CHALDEAN (arch), ENCHANTER, -TRESS, FAMILIUS, *MAGICIAN*, MAGUS, SPELLBINDER, SPELLER (crypt), WARLOCK, *WITCH* (q.v.), WIZARD. See also *prophet* [gramarye (arch), incantation, juju, obi, philtre, rune, sortilege, talisman, voodoo. *G & S*; Paul Dukas; Glubbdubdrib (*Swift*)].

SORCERESS Fem equivalent of *Sorcerer* (q.v.). **Celeb:** *CIRCE*, *GORGON*, *MEDEA*, *MEDUSA*, *SIREN*, *WITCH* OF ENDOR.

SORRY APOLOGIZE, CARE, DEJECTED, LAMENTATION, PENITENT, REGRETFUL, REPINING, RUEFUL, SELF-REPROACH, UNHAPPY. PALTRY, SHABBY, WRETCHED.

SORT SIEVE, SIFT. *LOT*. KIND, TYPE. MANNER, WAY. **Pl** = HEALTH, SPIRITS, TEMPER.

SOUND 1. DIN, NOISE, *RACKET*, *ROW*, TONE. *DIVE*, FIND DEPTH, PLUMB (naut). *FIRM*, *FIT*, HALE. 2. Implies that the sound invoked by the following word is required, e.g. **Sound asleep** = SNORE or ZZ.

SOUNDER MORE STABLE. FITTER. LEAD-LINE (naut). *Assembly* of swine.

SOUNDS LIKE Indicated in this Companion by use of the letters s/l at the appropriate entries, it means that other spellings may sound similar, e.g. BORN, BORNE, BOURNE all have *pronunciation* (q.v.) which is similar. Can also require the sound made by . . . (onomatopoeic), e.g. **Sounds like a sheep** = BAA.

SOUP *Anag*. BOUILLON, BROTH, CONSOMME, STEW, STOCK; *COURSE*. NITRO-GLYCERINE (sl).

SOURCE (s/l *sauce*). *Anag*. EMITTER, ORIGIN. FOUNTAINHEAD, SPRING, *WELL*.

SOUTH S, SO; POINT, POLE. *BRIDGE PLAYER* (crypt). ~ **WIND Gk** = NOTOS, **Rom** = AUSTER.

SOVEREIGN GOLD *COIN*, POUND. *MONARCH*.

SP SERVICE POLICEMAN. STARTING PRICE; BETTING ODDS.

SP Spain, ~ish.

SPA (s/l *spar*). 1. HEALTH RESORT, SPRING, WATERING PLACE (town in Belgium). *RACETRACK* (cars). 2. **Celeb resorts**: AIX LES BAINS, BADEN BADEN, BATH, BUXTON, CONTREXEVILLE, CHELTENHAM, DROITWICH, HARROGATE, OSTEND, TUNBRIDGE WELLS, VICHY, WIESBADEN.

SPACECRAFT *ROCKET*, *SPACE TRAVELLER*, SPACE VEHICLE [NASA]. SCIENCE OF SPACE. **Celeb (US)**: *APOLLO*, AQUARIUS, ARIEL, *ATLAS*, CHALLENGER, COLUMBIA, COURIER, *DISCOVERER*, *ECHO*, *EXPLORER*, *GEMINI*, MARINER, *MARS, MERCURY, MIDAS*, NIMBUS, PIONEER, RANGER, SAMOS, SHUTTLE, SKYLAB, SPACELAB, TELSTAR, VANGUARD, VIKING, VOYAGER. **Celeb (CIS)**: COSMOS, LUNA, LUNIK, SALYUT, SOYUZ, SPUTNIK, TIROS, VOSHKOD, VOSTOK.

SPACE TRAVELLER ASTEROID, COMET, METEORITE, *MOON, PLANET*, SHOOTING STAR. *SPACECRAFT*. ASTRONAUT, COSMONAUT. **Celeb (US)**: ALDRIN (2nd on moon), ARMSTRONG (1st on moon), BORMAN, CARPENTER, CERNAN, COLLINS, CONRAD, COOPER, GLENN (1st US), GORDON, GRISSOM, LOVELL, MCDIVITT, SALLY RIDE (1st US fem), SCHIRRA, SCOTT, STAFFORD, *WHITE, YOUNG*. **Celeb (CIS)**: BELYAEV, BYKOVSKY, FEOKTISTOV, GAGARIN (1st man in space), LAIKA (*dog*; 1st space traveller), LEONOV (1st *EVA*), NIKOLAYEV, POPOVICH, TERESHKOVA (1st woman), TITOV, YEGOROV [Jules Verne; H. G. Wells].

SPAIN SP. E (*car plate*).

SPANIARD DON, SENOR, SR.

SPANNER TOOL, WRENCH. *ARCH, BRIDGE* (crypt).

SPAR (s/l *spa*). BOOM, GAFF, MAST, SPRIT, *YARD. BOX*, FIGHT. *MINERAL*. HOOP, STAPLE (thatching).

SPEAKER *ORATOR* (q.v.) (chairman; Commons). *LIP*, MOUTH, TONGUE (crypt). AMPLIFIER, HI-FI, STEREO, TWEETER, WALKMAN, WOOFER (radio).

SPEAR HALBERD, HARPOON, JAVELIN (Meleager), PIKE, *WEAPON*. RUN THROUGH, SPIKE, SPIT. *MALE* (**opp** = distaff). EAR, SPRIG [asparagus (bot)]. *GRASS. PAINTER*.

SPECTACLE EXHIBITION, *SHOW*, SIGHT. **Pl** = BIN(N)S, GLASSES [*Company* (livery)].

SPECTATOR ONLOOKER, VIEWER, WATCHER. **Pl** = *CROWD*.

SPECULATOR *BEAR*, PUNTER, *STAG* (comm).

SPEECH *ADDRESS*, *DELIVERY*, LECTURE, TALK. LANGUAGE.

SPEED KNOT, KPH, LICK, MPH, *RATE*, *TEMPO*. DRUG. SERVANT/JESTER (2 G OF V, *Shak*).

SPELL ATTRACTION. CANTRIP, CHARM, INCANTATION. DUTY, PERIOD, TURN, *WATCH*. RELIEVE. INVOLVE, PRESAGE, RESULT. MAKE or FORM WORDS.

SPELLER *WITCH* (crypt).

SPELLING 1. CHARMING, INCANTATION, WITCHCRAFT (crypt). RELIEVING (naut watch). INVOLVING. ABC, WORD FORMATION. 2. The clue setter will sometimes vary the breakdown of letters in an answer, so as to offer a different meaning (which should be alluded to in the clue) e.g. **Cheeky aroma some puddings possess** (5, 5) = AFTER SHAVE; this responds to the first two words of the clue, whereas changing the position of the letter 'S' from the second word to the first (to give AFTERS HAVE) responds to the last three clue words – thus providing the secondary indication.

SPENT *TIRED*. PASSED (time), STAYED, BLEW, BLUED, EXPENDED, SQUANDERED.

SPHINX 1. Egy male *monster* (head human, body lion; strangler) representing the god Horamkhu. Also Gk female counterpart who put a riddle to the Thebans and killed all who could not solve it. *Oedipus* solved it and the Sphinx committed suicide. The riddle was 'A being with 4 feet has 2 feet and 3 feet, and only one voice; but its feet vary, and when it has most it is weakest. Who or what is it?' Oedipus' answer was 'Man, who in infancy crawls on all fours, then stands up on two feet, and in old age supports himself with a stick.' 2. Monkey (strangler).

SPICE FLAVOUR, MALICE, ZEST: ABSINTHE, *ARTEMISIA*, CAPSICUM, CARAWAY, CARDOMOM, -ON, -UM, CAYENNE, CHIL(L)I, CHIVE, CINNAMON, *CLOVE*, CORIANDER, CROSSWORT, CURRY, GARLIC, GILLYFLOWER, GINGER, *MACE*, MOULI, MUGWORT, MUSTARD, NUTMEG, OREGANO, PAPRIKA, PEPPER, PIMENTO, *RACE*, SAFFRON, SAGEBRUSH, TURMERIC, WORMWOOD [*herb*].

SPIDER ARANEIDA. 8-LEGGED ARTHROPOD: BLACK
WIDOW, BOLUS ~, *CARDINAL* ~, *COB*, GOLIATH
~, HARVESTER ~, KARAKURT, MITE, MONEY ~,
PIRATE ~, SEA ~, SOLPUGA, TANT, TARANTULA,
TICK, *WOLF*, *ZEBRA* ~ ; *SPINNER*, WEBSTER (crypt).
[Anansi (W Af ~ god), *Arachne*, Robert the Bruce]. CUE-
REST. CRAB. CARD GAME. *MONKEY*.
~ **GIRL** *ARACHNE*. MISS MUFFET.
SPILL *Anag.* LIGHTER, TAPER. SHED, UPSET.
SPINNER FISHERMAN, TROLLER; BAIT, LURE, SPOON.
TOP. DRIER. GYROSCOPE. *SPIDER*. SCHEHERAZADE
(crypt). RUMPELSTILTSKIN (Grimm).
SPIRIT 1. *DRINK* (q.v.); HARD STUFF (sl); AQUAVIT,
ARAK, ARRACK, BOURBON, BRANDY, COGNAC,
GIN, GRAPPA, HOLLANDS, RUM, RYE, SAKE, -I,
SCHIEDAM, SCHNAPPS, SCOTCH, VODKA, WHISKEY
(Ire), WHISKY (Sc) [*liqueur*]. 2. ÉLAN, *GO*, LIFE,
MORALE, *PEP*, VERVE, VIM. 3. *GHOST*, SHADE,
SOUL. AFREET, AFRIT, *ANGEL*, BANSHEE, *BROWNIE,
DEMON*, DJINN, ELF, *FAMILIAR* (*witch*), GENIE,
GOBLIN, HOBGOBLIN, *IMP*, KELPIE, KOBOLD (Ger),
PERI, PIXIE, -EY, *SPRITE*, TROLL (Nor). **Celeb**: ARIEL
(*Shak*), *CERES* (*Shak*), *IRIS* (*Shak*), *JUNO* (*Shak*), WILI
(Giselle ballet).
SPITFIRE *SHREW*, TERMAGANT. *AIRCRAFT*; **comp** =
Hurricane.
SPLIT *CLEAVE*, DIVIDE. CLEFT, CRACK, FISSURE, RENT.
BREACH, RUPTURE, SCHISM. *BETRAY*. *DRINK*,
MIXER. *BOTTLE*. DISH. TOWN (Y). And see *read* for
~ words.
SPOIL DAMAGE, *MAR*, *RUIN*. BOOTY, LOOT.
SPONDEE *FOOT*.
SPOON UTENSIL; **comp** = fork. SCOOP. BILL AND COO,
CANOODLE, WOO. *GOLF-CLUB*.
SPORT 1. JOKING, PLAYFUL; MOCKERY. FROLIC,
GAMBOL, SKIP. MUTATION (biol, zool). COBBER, FRIEND,
MATE, PAL (Aus sl). GOOD LOSER, FAIR PLAYER.
2. (competitive) ACTIVITY, EXERCISE, *GAME*. PASTIME.
GREYHOUND-, HORSE-RACING (the ~ of kings; and
see *racetrack*); CAR-, MOTOR-RACING (and see *racetrack*),
CYCLING, CYCLO-CROSS, DIRT-TRACK, SPEEDWAY
RACING. *BOXING* (q.v. for weights); *WRESTLING* (q.v.

for types). BLOOD ~ (for so-called pleasure): COURSING,
FISHING, HUNTING, SHOOTING, STAG-HUNTING.
Pl = *ATHLETICS* (q.v. for field and track events), *GAMES*
(Asian ~, Commonwealth ~, Olympic ~) e.g. **Indoor** ~:
any *GAME* or EXERCISE played or taken indoors, usually
competitively and often with a *ball* (q.v.) or on a *board* (q.v.).
CANOODLING, LOVE-MAKING, PETTING (sl). **Outdoor**
~: any *GAME* (q.v.) or EXERCISE played or taken outdoors,
usually competitively with a *ball* (q.v.); any blood ~. And
see *BALL GAME* and *GAME* for lists of such ~. **Water**
~: AQUALUNG, *DIVING* (q.v. for positions), *SAIL*
(and see *rig*), SKIN DIVING, SUB-AQUA, SURFING,
SWIMMING (q.v. for styles), WATER POLO, YACHTING.
Winter ~: BOBSLEIGH, CURLING, LUGEING, SKATING,
SKIING (cross-country, down-hill, jumping, langlauf, slalom),
SLEDGING, TOBOGGANING (Cresta Run).
SPORTING CLUB FA, MCC, RFU etc. BAT, *RACKET* (crypt).
~ **JUDGE** REFEREE, UMPIRE.
~ **SET** *SIDE*; TEAM.
SPOT 1. PLACE, LOCALITY. ACNE, PIMPLE. MARK, SOIL,
STAIN. CIRCLE, PATCH. *DASH*, DROP, *LITTLE*. BEAM,
FLOOD (light). DETECT, ESPY, LOCATE, *NOTICE*, SEE.
2. May indicate a location connected with the following word(s)
in the clue, e.g. **Spot of gambling** (5, 5) = MONTE CARLO.
SPOTTED SEEN. DAPPLED, SPECKLED.
SPRING BOUND, JUMP, LEAP. COIL ~, LEAF ~. *SEASON*.
FLOW, WELL [*spa*]; FOUNTAIN [Arethusa *transformation*;
nymphs]. *Assembly* of teal.
SPRINGBOK *ANTELOPE*. *RUGBY* PLAYER.
SPRINGTIME SEASON; MARCH, APRIL, MAY.
SPRITE *SPIRIT*; PUCK (MND, *Shak*), ARIEL (Temp, *Shak*).
SPRUCE *TRIM*. *TREE*.
SPUR *URGE*. **Pl** = *FOOTBALL* TEAM.
SPY *AGENT* (q.v.). SEE, SPOT. SNOOP. *CARTOONIST*.
SQUARE 1. *DATED*, OLD FASHIONED. PLACE, PIAZZA.
RIGHTANGLED. T-, SET-. 2. Any square number, 9, 100 etc,
hence IX, C. [*measure*].
~ **MEAL** GOOD SPREAD. BISCUIT, SANDWICH (crypt).
SQUASH CORDIAL, *DRINK*. VEGETABLE. CRUSH,
SQUEEZE. *GAME*.
SQUEALER *BETRAYER*, *GRASS*, SNEAK, TELL-TALE. PIG
(*Orwell*).

SS *SAINTS. SHIP.* Hitler's bodyguard, élite troops. Gestapo, *Secret* police.

ST *SAINT*; GOODMAN (crypt). *STREET. STONE.* STUMPED (cricket).

STABLE 1. *FIRM*, SOUND, STEADY. RACEHORSE. STRING; *habitation* of horses. 2. Gk myth stable of *Augeus*, the subject of one of the labours of *Hercules*.

STAFF 1. *ROD*, VERGE (eccles), WAND [authority, office; Black Rod, Gold Stick; *Aaron*; Tiresias (*prophet*)]; CADUCEUS [*Asclepius* (medicine); *Hermes, Mercury*]; PEDUM (*shepherd*); THYRSUS (*Bacchus, Dionysus*). QUARTER ~, STAVE, STICK [Kendo (Jap), Little John (Robin *Hood*)]. 2. Framework for written *music* (STAVE).

STAG 1. Male *DEER*, BROCKET (2nd year), CERVUS [The Old ~, *Williamson*]. MALE (party). BEETLE. SHARE BUYER, SPECULATOR. **Pl** = *Football team*. 2. Gk myth *ACTAEON*. 3. One of the labours of *Hercules*.

STAGE DAIS, PLATFORM, SCAFFOLD, STEP, SUERTE (bullfighting). ACTING PROFESSION, *BOARDS*, DRAMA, THEATRE. ARRANGE, PRESENT, PRODUCE. BUS-STOP, LEG, PERIOD, POINT, STATION, STOP-OVER. *CARRIAGE*, COACH.

STAIRS FLIGHT, STEPS [ladder]. APPLES (*rh sl*).

STAKE (s/l steak). ANTE, *BET*, RISK, *WAGER*. POST, SPIT, STICK. *ANVIL*. FASTEN, *SECURE*.

STAMP FRANK, IMPRESS(ION), IMPRINT; (HALL)MARK, *SEAL*. BANG, CLUMP, THUMP, TRAMPLE, TREAD, TRUDGE. POSTAGE ~; **coll** = philatelist. [Roland *Hill*].

STANDARD BANNER, EAGLE, ENSIGN, *FLAG*, FLIER (crypt), PENNANT. DEGREE, LEVEL, *MEASURE*, NORM, PAR, QUALITY, REGULAR, YARDSTICK.

STANDING ORDER SO. ATTENTION, GET UP (crypt).

STAR 1. ASTERISK, *MARK*; 17 (tarot). *CASTLE*. ACTOR, ACTRESS, CELEBRITY, *LION*, VIP; ACT, FEATURE, PLAY LEAD. MAIN, OUTSTANDING, PRINCIPAL. *DECORATION*. 2. NEBULA; CELESTIAL/HEAVENLY BODY, NOVA, SUN; ESTOILE (*herald*); SKYLIGHT (crypt): (binary-, day-, double-, *evening-*, falling-, *morning-*, multiple-, pole-, shooting- [black hole, *planet*, pulsar, quasar, white dwarf]). 'ESTHER'. 3. **Pl** = *CONSTELLATION*. Seven ~s in the sky in *song*.

STARBOARD S; RIGHT (**opp** = *port*, larboard). PLAYBILL
(crypt).

STARLING *BIRD (assembly)*. YOUNG ACTOR (crypt).

START FRIGHT, JUMP. SCRATCH. BEGIN, FOUND,
INITIATE (**opp** = *end*). OPENING. *GO*, OFF, *REPAIR*.
EASE, LOOSEN (naut).

STARTER 1. *BEGINNER*. APPETIZER, *COURSE*, ENTREE
(cook). JUMPER (crypt). GUNMAN (sports, crypt). A,
ALPHA (crypt). ADAM, EVE (crypt). 2. First letter of word
concerned, e.g. **Race starter** = R; note that this could also be
GUNMAN or ADAM/EVE.

STARTING 1. BEGINNING. JUMPING (crypt). 2. First letter,
e.g. **Starting time** = T; but note **Failure starting with a cry** (7) =
W*A*SHOUT, which is revealed by the secondary word **failure**.

STAR TURN MAIN ITEM, LEAD PART. Anag. 'star' as RATS,
TSAR etc.

STATE ANNOUNCE, SAY. CONDITION. ANXIOUS,
EXCITED, UNTIDY. DIGNITY, POMP, RANK.
COMMUNITY, GOVERNMENT, NATION. **Pl** =
LEGISLATIVE BODY (CI). **Division of Aus**:

Aus State	Nickname
NEW SOUTH WALES	Ma ~
NORTHERN TERRITORY	White Ant ~
QUEENSLAND	Bananaland
SOUTH AUSTRALIA	Wheat ~
TASMANIA	Apple Isle
VICTORIA	Cabbage Patch
WESTERN AUSTRALIA	Groperland

Division of the USA:

State	Abbr	Abbr	Capital
ALABAMA	ALA	AL	Montgomery
ALASKA	ALAS	AK	Juneau
ARIZONA	ARIZ	AZ	Phoenix
ARKANSAS	ARK	AR	Little Rock
CALIFORNIA	CALIF	CA	Sacramento
COLORADO	COLO	CO	Denver
CONNECTICUT[13]	CONN	CT	Hartford
DELAWARE[13]	DEL	DE	Dover

DISTRICT OF COLUMBIA		DC	Washington
FLORIDA	FLA	FL	Tallahassee
GEORGIA[13]		GA	Atlanta
HAWAII		HI	Honolulu
IDAHO	IDA	ID	Boise
ILLINOIS	ILL	IL	Springfield
INDIANA	IND	IN	Indianapolis
IOWA		IA	Des Moines
KANSAS	KANS	KS	Topeka
KENTUCKY		KY	Frankfort
LOUISIANA		LA	Baton Rouge
MAINE		ME	Augusta
MARYLAND[13]		MD	Annapolis
MASSACHUSETTS[13]	MASS	MA	Boston
MICHIGAN	MICH	MI	Lansing
MINNESOTA	MINN	MN	St Paul
MISSISSIPPI	MISS	MS	Jackson
MISSOURI		MO	Jefferson City
MONTANA	MONT	MT	Helena
NEBRASKA	NEBR	NE	Lincoln
NEVADA	NEV	NV	Carson City
NEW HAMPSHIRE[13]		NH	Concord
NEW JERSEY[13]		NJ	Trenton
NEW MEXICO	N MEX	NM	Santa Fe
NEW YORK[13]		NY	Albany
NORTH CAROLINA[13]		NC	Raleigh
NORTH DAKOTA	N DAK	ND	Bismarck
OHIO	O	OH	Columbus
OKLAHOMA	OKLA	OK	Oklahoma City
OREGON	OREG	OR	Salem
PENNSYLVANIA[13]	PENN	PA	Harrisburg
RHODE ISLAND[13]		RI	Providence
SOUTH CAROLINA[13]		SC	Columbia
SOUTH DAKOTA	S DAK	SD	Pierre
TENNESSEE	TENN	TN	Nashville
TEXAS	TEX	TX	Austin
UTAH		UT	Salt Lake City
VERMONT		VT	Montpelier
VIRGINIA[13]		VA	Richmond
WASHINGTON	WASH	WA	Olympia
WEST VIRGINIA	W VA	WV	Charleston

| WISCONSIN | WISC | WI | Madison |
| WYOMING | WYO | WY | Cheyenne |

13 = one of the original 13 states.

STATECRAFT DIPLOMACY. PRESIDENTIAL YACHT, ROYAL *BARGE* (crypt).

STATELY HOME *COUNTRY HOUSE* (q.v. for **celeb**, *fict*), PLACE, SEAT (dignified, grand, imposing; open to the public); **celeb (fact)**:

APSLEY HOUSE	HEVER CASTLE
ARUNDEL CASTLE	HOLKHAM HALL
BEAULIEU	KNEBWORTH HOUSE
BELVOIR CASTLE	LEEDS CASTLE
BERKELEY CASTLE	LONGLEAT
BLAIR CASTLE	LUTON HOO
BLENHEIM PALACE	PETWORTH HOUSE
BODIAM CASTLE	POWDERHAM CASTLE
BROADLANDS	SCARISBRICK HALL
BURGHLEY HOUSE	SCONE PALACE
CAWDOR CASTLE	STRATFIELD SAYE
CHARTWELL	SUDELEY CASTLE
CHATSWORTH HOUSE	TATTON PARK
COMPTON WYNYATES	UPPARK HOUSE
FALKLAND PALACE	WARWICK CASTLE
GLAMIS CASTLE	WILTON HOUSE
HAMPTON COURT	WINDSOR CASTLE
HAREWOOD HOUSE	WOBURN PLACE
HATFIELD HOUSE	WOOLATON HALL

STATESMAN POLITICIAN. AMERICAN (crypt).

STAUNCH FIRM, LOYAL, TRUSTWORTHY. CHECK, DAM, STEM, STOP. AIRTIGHT, WATERTIGHT.

STAY AVAST (naut); REMAIN, STOP (**opp** = *go*, *go on*). PREVENT. GUY (ROPE), PROP, RIG, *SUPPORT*. **Pl** = CORSET.

STEAL (s/l *steel*). *BONE* (sl), BURGLE, FILCH, NICK, PINCH, PURLOIN, *ROB*, SNAFFLE, THIEVE. CREEP, GLIDE (AWAY).

STEAMER *BOAT*, LINER, SS (**opp** = *sailing* craft) [see *Comet* (2)]. ENGINE, TRAIN. COOKER, COOKPOT.

STEEL (s/l *steal*). 1. METAL [Bessemer]. HONE, SHARPENER.
BRACE, HARDEN, RESOLVE. 2. Alloy of carbon, iron and
manganese, hence (crypt) letters CFEMN. 3. *Anniversary* (11th).
STEEP PRECIPICE, SHEER, VERTICAL. IMMERSE.
DRENCH, SOAK. DEAR, EXPENSIVE.
STEEPLECHASER *HORSE*; JUMPER; FENCER (crypt).
STEER *CON*, CONDUCT, DIRECT, DRIVE, HELM. *COW*,
STOT (ox, zool).
STEERSMAN HELMSMAN, NAVIGATOR, PILOT, TILLER-
MAN; CONMAN, WHEELER (crypt). *COWBOY* (crypt).
GLAUCUS (*Argonaut*).
STELLA GIRL, 'STAR'. *AWARD* (Br film) ®.
STEM CHECK, DAM, *STA(U)NCH*, *STOP*. BOW, FRONT
(naut). ADVANCE. LINE, ORIGIN, STALK.
STEP (s/l *steppe*). MARCH, PACE. DANCE. RISER, TREAD.
Pl = FLIGHT, LADDER, STAIRS.
~ **DOWN** DECLINE, GIVE WAY, CEDE. DESCEND.
RESIGN. DEMOTION.
STEPPE (s/l *step*). PLAIN (q.v.).
STERLING L, POUND. HIGH QUALITY.
STEVENSON (s/l Stephenson). 1. Engineer (Sc), lighthouse
builder (not steam engines – he was -ph-); Bell Rock. 2. Robert
Louis, writer; **celeb books**: The Black Arrow, Catriona (sequel
to Kidnapped), Inland Voyage (his first), Kidnapped (sequel:
Catriona), The Master of Ballantrae, The Strange Case of Dr
Jekyll and Mr *Hyde*, Travels with a Donkey in the Cevennes,
Treasure Island (ex The Sea Cook) [Benn Gunn (marooned),
Billy Bones, Black Dog, Blind Pew, Capt Flint (*parrot/*; *pirate*),
Israel Hands (coxswain), Jim Hawkins, Dr Livesey, Long
John *Silver* (one-legged *pirate*, cook 'Barbecue', *parrot*), Capt
Smollett, Squire Trelawney; the black spot (death sentence),
Hispaniola (ship), Admiral Benbow (inn), the Spyglass (inn)].
STEW *Anag.* BOIL, COOK, FERMENT, *SEETHE*. DISH.
STUDY. ANGER, ANXIETY, BOTHER, FUSS, WORRY.
BROTHEL (*sl*). FISH-POND.
STICK ADHERE, *CLEAVE*, GLUE, UNITE. ABIDE,
TOLERATE. BAFFLE, CONFUSE, PUZZLE. *BRANCH*,
TWIG; BATON, *ROD*, STAFF, WAND. CONTROL
COLUMN (av); MAST, *SPAR*, *YARD* (naut). GROUP, LINE
(bombs, paratroops). PIERCE, PUSH, STAB, THRUST,
TRANSFIX. **Pl** = COUNTRY, HILLS, OUTBACK, WOODS.
STILL EVER, YET. DISTILLERY, RETORT [moonshine (*sl*)].

CALM, MOTIONLESS (**opp** = *moving*). EVEN.
STILTED BOMBASTIC, POMPOUS. AWKWARD,
  GRALLATORIAL, HIGH-STANDING, TALL (crypt).
STING NETTLE, HURT, PROVOKE. OVERCHARGE.
  FISH, RAY.
STINGY MEAN, MISERLY, NEAR, TIGHT. HURTFUL,
  INSULTING, WOUNDING. BEE, WASP (crypt).
STIR *Anag.* AROUSE, INFLAME. *ADMIX*, *MIX*, WHIP.
  COMMOTION, EXCITEMENT, TO-DO. *GAOL* (sl).
STOAT ERMINE, *WEASEL*.
STOCK CREDIT, REPUTATION. PROVIDE, RESERVE,
  STORE. BREED, BLOOD, FAMILY, *STRAIN*; ANIMALS,
  CATTLE. BASE, BUTT, HANDLE, STUMP. *FLOWER*.
  SHIPYARD WAY/SLIP. CRAVAT, SCARF, TIE. BRICK. **Pl**
  = wooden punishment device. **Pl comp** = shares.
STOCKTAKING COUNTING, REVIEW. RUSTLING (crypt).
STOIC 1. AUSTERE, COURAGEOUS, SELF-CONTROLLED.
  2. *Philosopher* of Athens school founded by ZENO;
  celeb: ANISTHENES, ANTIGONUS, *BRUTUS*, *CATO*,
  CHRYSIPPUS, *CICERO*, CLEANTHES, DIODOTUS,
  EPICTETUS, MARCUS AURELIUS, SENECA.
STOLEN *ROBBED*; HOT [*steal*].
STONE COBBLE, GRANITE, PEBBLE, ROCK (Norman,
  Portland) [*Andromeda*, *Atlas*, *Medusa*, *Niobe*, *Perseus*].
  AGATE, *GEM*. AGE. *MEASURE* (weight), *ST*.
STONED DRUGGED, DRUNK. PELTED. SCULPTED (crypt).
STOOL PIGEON *BETRAYER*, GRASS, SNEAK, SHOPPER.
STOP 1. ARREST, BAR, CLOSE, CUT OFF, GAG,
  OBSTRUCT, PARRY, PREVENT, STAUNCH, STIFLE.
  CEASE, CHECK, DESIST, GIVE OVER, HALT, PAUSE.
  CALL AT, REMAIN, SOJOURN, *STAY*. HALT, STATION
  (rly). APERTURE, DIAPHRAGM, ORGAN CONTROL,
  VALVE. PUNCTUATE: COLON, COMMA etc. MAKE
  FAST. CAULK, PAY (naut). *CARD GAME*. 2. Word with last
  letter(s) removed, e.g. **Drink stops play** (4) = DRAM(a).
~ **TALKING** BUTTON UP, CLAM UP. GAG, SILENCE.
STOREY (s/l *story*). FLOOR, LEVEL.
STORM *Anag.* 1. ASSAULT. RAGE. SHOWER. GALE,
  HAILSTORM, HURRICANE, RAINSTORM,
  SNOWSTORM, TEMPEST, THUNDERSTORM, TORNADO.
  2. **Rom god** = FULGURATOR. **Gk goddesses** = *HARPIES*.
STORY (s/l *storey*). ACCOUNT, NARRATION, NARRATIVE,

RELATION. FIB, LIE, TALE.

STOUT *BRAVE*, DOUGHTY, RESOLUTE, STAUNCH, STUBBORN, STURDY [Cortes]. BULKY, CORPULENT, FAT, OBESE (**opp** = *thin*). *BEER*, GUINNESS ®.

STOVE COOKER [oven]. BREACHED, BROKEN.

STOWE (s/l stow). 1. *PUBLIC SCHOOL*. TOWN. 2. Harriet Beecher ~, writer; **book**: Uncle Tom's Cabin (Legree, *bully*; Li'l Liza; Topsy [*slave*; I 'spects I growed]).

STRAIN AIR, MUSIC, SONG, TONE, TUNE. INJURE, OVER-TASK, PULL, RICK, STRESS, STRETCH. FILTER. BREED, *STOCK*.

STRAIT (s/l straight). RIGOROUS, STRICT. CONFINE, LIMITED, NARROW. **Pl** = DISTRESS, NEED. PASSAGE OF WATER; **celeb**:

4-letters

BASS	*COOK*	PALK

5-letters

BANKS	DOVER	KOREA	NARES
CABOT	KERME	LUZON	SUNDA
DAVIS			

6-letters

BERING	HORMUZ	HUDSON	TORRES

7-letters

DENMARK	FOVEAUX	OTRANTO
FLORIDA	MALACCA	
FORMOSA	MESSINA	

8+ letters

BELLE ILE	LA PEROUSE	SINGAPORE
BONIFACIO	*MAGELLAN*	SKAGERRAK
BOSPHORUS	MAKASSAR	
GIBRALTAR	PENTLAND	

STRANGER ALIEN, FOREIGNER. TEA LEAF (fig). MORE PECULIAR, RUMMER.

STREAK BAND, LINE, STRIPE. ELEMENT, SERIES, SPELL, STRAIN. DASH, RUN; RUN NAKED.

STREET ST; DRAG, *ROAD*.

~ MARKET BRICK LANE, FLEA-MARKET, MARCHE DES PUCES (Fr), MIDDLESEX STREET, PETTICOAT LANE, PORTOBELLO ROAD; AGORA (Gk), SOUK (Mos), MONOPOLY ® (crypt, game).

STRENGTH QUALITY. COGENCY; INTENSITY: NUMBERS, SUCCESS (mil); FIRMNESS, FORCE, POTENCY, POWER; **celeb possessors (male)**: ANTAEUS, CHARLES *ATLAS*, BROBDINGNAGIANS (*Swift*), BRIAREUS, COLOSSUS, CRATOS, *CYCLOPES*, GOLIATH, HERACLES/*HERCULES*, KWASIND (*Hiawatha*), MILO(N) (of Crotona), POLYPHEMUS, *SAMSON*, SANDOW, *SUPERMAN*, *TARZAN*, *TITAN*; **~ (fem)**: *AMAZONS*, STHENO (*Gorgon*).

STRIKE BAT, HIT, INNINGS, *KNOCK*, RAM, SMACK, SWING. IMPRESS. DIVERGE. LEVEL. FIND (gold/oil). LOWER FLAG, SURRENDER. STOP WORK, TAKE (industrial) ACTION. KNAP (flint).

STRIKER BATTER, HITTER. FLINT, FUSEE, LUCIFER, MATCH (crypt). PROSPECTOR. YIELDER. NON-WORKER. LIGHTNING (crypt).

STRIKING BATTING, HITTING, INNINGS (*cricket*). LIGHTING (match). YIELDING. IDLING, OUT. EYE-CATCHING. UNCO (Sc).

STRING CORD, PULL, TAG, TIE. *STABLE* (racehorses). **Pl** = OBLIGATION.

STRIP DENUDE, DOFF, UNDRESS (**opp** = *dress*). SHEAR.

STROKE CARESS, FONDLE. OARSMAN, *ROWER*. APPROACH, CHIP, DRIVE, HOOK, LOFT, PUTT, SLICE, SWING (golf); BLOCK, CUT, DRIVE, HOOK, GLANCE, LOFT, PULL, SLASH, SWING (*cricket*). BRAIN STORM.

STUCK UP SUPERCILIOUS, SUPERIOR. BILLED, POSTED (crypt).

STUDENT L, LEARNER, *PUPIL* (**Union** = NUS).

STUDIO WORK ROOM (artist/painter/cinema/film/movie/music/photographic/radio/sculptor's/TV); and see *FILM* ~ for list.

STUDY DEN, SANCTUM. *CON*, EXAMINE, EYE, READ, *SCAN*, SCRUTINIZE; OVERLOOK (arch and crypt). Any subject thus investigated, e.g.

animals	ZOOLOGY
antiquities	ARCHAEOLOGY
beetles	COLEOPTEROLOGY

birds	ORNITHOLOGY
blood (med)	H(A)EMATOLOGY
bones (med)	OSTEOLOGY
caves	SPEL(A)EOLOGY
character	ETHOLOGY
China (geog)	SINOLOGY
clouds	NEPHOLOGY
coins	NUMISMATOLOGY
culture	SOCIOLOGY
disease (body)	PATHOLOGY
disease (mental)	PSYCHOLOGY
~ (female)	GYNAECOLOGY
earth's crust	GEOLOGY
Egypt (ancient)	EGYPTOLOGY
ferns	PTERIDOLOGY
fossil life	PAL(A)EONTOLOGY
handwriting	GRAPHOLOGY
heart	CARDIOLOGY
insects	ENTOMOLOGY
languages	PHILOLOGY
life (fossil)	PAL(A)EONTOLOGY
mankind	ANTHROPOLOGY
medals	NUMISMATOLOGY
mind (med)	PSYCHOLOGY
minerals	MINERALOGY
mountains	OROLOGY
old age	GERONTOLOGY
religion	THEOLOGY
shells (zool)	CONCHOLOGY
sleep	HYPNOLOGY
soil management	AGRONOMY
teeth	ODONTOLOGY
tissue (med)	HISTOLOGY
weather	METEOROLOGY
weevils	COLEOPTEROLOGY
wine	OENOLOGY
words	ETYMOLOGY
writing	GRAPHOLOGY
~ (ancient)	PAL(A)EOGRAPHY

STUFF CRAM, FILL, *FORCE*, PACK, SHOVE, SQUEEZE
[taxidermy]. GORGE, OVEREAT. GREASE (tannery). *RIG*

(ballot box). *MONEY* (sl). *DRUG* (sl). CLOTH, FABRIC, *MATERIAL* (q.v. for list).

STUVW S*TO*W (crypt).

STY (s/l *stye*). ENCLOSURE, PEN; *habitation* (pigs).

STYE (s/l *sty*). *EYESORE*, IRITIS.

STYX Gk myth principal river of the Underworld, d of *Oceanus* and Tethys [*Acheron, Charon, Cocytus, Lethe, Pyriphlegethon*].

SU SUNDAY. SOVIET UNION (*car plate*).

SUBJECT SUBDUE; VASSAL (**opp** = *ruler*). EXPOSE, INFLICT, TREAT. LIABLE TO. NOUN, NOMINATIVE (e.g. **My subject** = ɪ). THEME. EGO, MIND. PHOTO, PIC, POSER, MODEL, STILL LIFE.

SUBMIT *BOW*, GIVE WAY, SURRENDER, YIELD. OFFER, PRESENT, RENDER.

SUBSCRIBE CONTRIBUTE, ENGAGE, RAISE (money). SIGN, UNDERWRITE (arch).

SUBSOLANUS Rom myth EAST *WIND* (**Gk** = APELIOTES).

SUBSTITUTE 1. DEPUTY, EXCHANGE, REPLACE(MENT), SURROGATE. 2. Exchange a letter, usually in anag, e.g. **I substitute a revision of pure ideas for a dramatist** (9) = EURIPIDES (anag of 'pure ideas' with 'a' substituted by 'I').

SUCCEED ENSUE, FOLLOW, INHERIT. ACCOMPLISH, GET ON, PROSPER, WIN.

SUCCESSOR One who succeeds, e.g. HEIR, FOLLOWER, WINNER.

SUCKER (s/l *succour*). BARNACLE, LEECH, LIMPET. BUD, SHOOT. GREENHORN, GULLIBLE FELLOW, MARK, PIGEON.

SUIT ADAPT, FIT, SATISFY; *BECOME*. SET (*armour*, clothes, sails). ACTION, CLAIM, COURT CASE, ISSUE, PETITION. CLUBS, DIAMONDS, HEARTS, SPADES. WHISTLE (*rh sl*).

SUITABLE 1. APPROPRIATE, FITTED, FITTING, MEET, PROPER. 2. In a *suit* [*bridge, cards*].

SUITED CLOTHED, DRESSED. COURTED, WOOED (crypt). ACCOMMODATED, SATISFIED. FLUSH (*cards*).

SULKY MOROSE, PET(ULANT), POUTING, SULLENLY. *CARRIAGE*.

SULLIVAN Sir Arthur ~, *COMPOSER*, MUSICIAN (Eng); co-op with *Gilbert* in operettas (for details, see *G & S*).

SULPHUR S (*chem*).

SULTRY *HOT*. PROVOCATIVE, PASSIONATE, SENSUAL.

SUM (s/l *some*). *ADD UP*, TOT, TOTAL. AMOUNT. SUBSTANCE, SUMMARY. I AM (Lat).

SUMMARY (s/l summery). ABSTRACT, DIGEST, PRECIS, RESUME, SUBSTANCE, SYNOPSIS.

SUMMER SEASON. HORIZONTAL BEAM, JOIST, RAFTER. ADDER, CALCULATOR, COUNTER (crypt).

SUN (s/l son). 1. *SUNDAY*. STAR; SKYLIGHT (crypt); 19 (*tarot*). NEWSPAPER ®. YEAR (crypt). SUNBATHE, TAN. 2. **Gods: Gk** = APOLLO, HELIOS; **Rom** = PHOEBUS, SOL.

SUNDAY S, SU, *SUN*. Day of the *Sun*; day of rest. *ISLAND*. ~'s **child** = bonny & blithe, good & gay [Solomon *Grundy*]. **Pl** = RIVER (SA).

SUPERIOR ABOVE, HIGHER, UPPER. BETTER, MORE, U. (GREAT) LAKE; GITCHE-GUMEE, BIG SEA WATER (*Hiawatha*).

SUPERMAN IDEAL/SUPERIOR MAN. CLARK *KENT* [Krypton; Lois Lane].

SUPPLIED *Anag*. 1. FUNDED, FURNISHED, PER, PROVIDED (BY). 2. Hidden word, e.g. **Food is supplied by great ingenuity** (6) = (gr)EAT·ING(enuity).

SUPPLY FURNISH, MEET, PROVIDE; **comp** = *demand;* **pl** = PROVISIONS, STOCKS, STORES. FLEXIBLY, PLIANTLY.

SUPPORT 1. CARRY, CONFIRM, HOLD UP, *SECOND*. BRA, CORSET, TRUSS. BACK, BRACKET, GUY, LEG, PROP, SLING, STAY. 2. Directs attention to second half of dn answer, e.g. **Age supports us by custom** = US·AGE.

SUPPORTER BACK, FOOT, LEG, PROP, SLING, STAY. BELT, BRA, BRACES, SUSPENDERS. FAN, FOLLOWER.

SWAGMAN AUSSIE, DIGGER. *ROBBER* (crypt).

SWALLOW 1. ABSORB, DOWN, EAT, ENGULF. GULLET, WEASAND. REPRESS, SUPPRESS. *BIRD* [Sea ~ = tern]; Procne transformation. 2. Word put into another, e.g. **We are swallowed by me, a patron of the arts** (4) = M·US·E; the same answer is given more cryptically by **A patron of the arts, I engulf** (or, **swallow**) **America. Pl comp** = *Amazons*.

SWAN 1. RUBBER-NECK, SIGHT-SEEING (RAF sl). *RIVER*. *THEATRE*. *ISLAND*. *PIRATE*. *Constellation* (Cygnus). **Comp** = Edgar. 2. Waterbird of genus CYGNUS; BEWICK ~, BLACK ~, MUTE ~; **assembly** = wedge; **male** = COB; **fem** = PEN; **offspring** = CYGNET. [*Graeae. Leda/Zeus* (qq.v.). *Plato*. Ugly Duckling (Hans *Andersen*)]. 3. Seven ~s a-swimming in *Christmas* song. ~ of Avon (*Shak*).

SWARM 1. CLUSTER, LARGE GROUP. CONGREGATE.
ABOUND, BE OVERRUN, CLAMBER, CLIMB,
SCRAMBLE. 2. *Assembly* of bees; e.g. TUC, WORKERS
(crypt).

Swe Sweden, ~ish.

SWEDEN S (*car plate*). Swe (abbr).

SWEETHEART DONAH, FLAME, *LOVER*, POPSIE (RAF sl).
HARD/SOFT CENTRE (crypt). E (crypt).

SWELL *SMART*, TOFF. HEAVE, SCEND, SURGE, WAVES.
BULGE, CRESCENDO, DILATE, EXPAND, RISE [*organ*].

Swi Switzerland, Swiss. For ~ cantons, see *Swiss canton*.

SWIFT 1. FAST, PROMPT, QUICK, RAPID, SOON. FRAME
(winding yarn). *LIZARD*. *BIRD* [*swallow*, martin]; DEVIL'S
BIRD (arch). 2. Jonathan ~, Ire writer and *satirist*; ordained.
Books: Battle of the Books, The Drapier's Letters, Journal to
Stella, Meditation on a Broomstick, Tale of a Tub, (and esp)
Gulliver's Travels, the Journals of Lemuel Gulliver, Surgeon
and Captain; Book 1: Lilliput (dwarfs), Big-endians (catholics),
Little-endians (protestants), blundercrad (book of lore); Book 2:
Brobdingnag (tall and strong people); Book 3: Laputa (flying
island, science), Balnibarbi (projectors), Luggnagg (Struldbrugs,
immortal), Glubbdubrib (sorcerers and magicians), Japan; Book 4:
Houyhnhms (intelligent horses), Yahoos (degenerate humans).

SWIMMER *FISH* (crypt). BATHER [natation]; **celeb**: *LEANDER*
(Gk), 7 swans (*Christmas* song), ESTHER WILLIAMS (films),
TARZAN (Edgar Rice Burroughs), CAPT WEBB (Eng
Channel 1875). And see *dive* and *sport* (*water*).

SWIMMING *Anag*. DRENCHED, STEEPED. BATHING,
NATATION, WATER *SPORT;* **styles**: back stroke, breast
stroke, *butterfly*, crawl (trudgen), dogpaddle, freestyle, medley,
overarm, sidestroke. And see *DIVE; SPORT*.

SWINDLE *Anag*. *CHEAT*, CON, COZEN, *DO, FIDDLE,
RACKET, RAMP*.

SWINE BEAST, BRUTE, CAD, GLUTTON, HEEL, LOUT,
SCOUNDREL. HOG, *PIG;* **assembly** = herd, sounder; **male** =
BOAR; **fem** = SOW; **offspring** = PIGLET. [pearls before ~].
Patron saint = Anthony.

SWISS CANTON Division of Switzerland: AARGAU,
APPENZELL, BASEL-LAND, BERNE, FRIBOURG,
GRAUBUNDEN, GLARUS, LUCERNE, NEUCHÁTEL,
OBWALDEN, ST GALLEN, SCHWYZ, SOLOTHURN,
THURGAU, TICINO, UNTERWALDEN, VALAIS, VAUD,

ZURICH.
SWITCHED *Anag.* DEVIATED, EXCHANGED, SWAPPED (rly lines). TURNED OFF/ON (elect). BEATEN, CANED (rod).
SWITZERLAND CH (*car plate*). Swi (abbr). For cantons of ~, see *Swiss canton*.
SYMBOL (s/l cymbal). ANALOGY, ASSOCIATION. CHARACTER, LETTER, NOTATION, SIGN. CREED. 5 ~s at your door in *song*.
SYNOPSIS *SUMMARY*.

T (s/l *te, tea, tee*). TENANT. TERA (*Int unit*). *TIME*. TON. TUESDAY. TURN. JUNCTION, SQUARE. CAR, FORD. SHIRT.
TA (s/l *tar*). TITANIUM (*chem*). TERRITORIAL ARMY. THANKS.
TABARD *CLOAK* (knight), COAT (*herald*). INN (*Chaucer*).
TABLE DUMMY (*bridge*). FACET. COLUMN, LIST, SCHEDULE. *FURNITURE* (q.v. for **types**), CAIN AND ABEL (*rh sl*); BOARD, FOOD, KEEP, MEALS.
TACITUS Cornelius, Rom historian b A.D. 55, d A.D. 120. A friend of Pliny, ~ mar the d of Agricola. Only five of his works survive.
TACK BOARD, COURSE (naut). BISCUIT, FOOD (naut). GEAR, *HARNESS*. FASTENING, PIN. STITCH.
TAIL BACKSIDE, BOTTOM, REAR. SCUT, WAGGER. FIN AND RUDDER (av). WAKE. DOG, SHADOW, TRACK. RAIL, TRAIN. REVERSE (coin **opp** = obverse). DOCK. **Pl** = EVENING DRESS (**opp** = heads).
TAILED FOLLOWED, TRACKED; hence *COMET* (crypt). FADED. EVENING DRESS, WHITE TIE (crypt). DOCKED; hence remove last letter, e.g. **Pete is tailed, the dear boy** (3) = PET*.
TAIL ENDER SCUT; RABBIT. L (crypt). LAST MAN.
TAILOR (s/l tailer). 1. ADAPT, CUT, FIT, SUIT, TRIM. 2. A person who makes or repairs clothes; **celeb**: STARVELING (*Shak*); ~ of Gloucester (*Potter*); Tinker, ~, Soldier, Sailor etc (trad rhyme).
TAKE OVER 1. BUY OUT, COMMANDEER, SEQUESTER. RELIEVE. *BOWL* (crypt). 2. Add OVER to word, e.g. **Sir Thomas takes over, besides** (8) = MORE*OVER.

TALENT ABILITY, APTITUDE, FACULTY, GIFT. *COIN*,
MONEY; WEIGHT (Gk, Rom).

TALK CHATTER, COMMUNICATE, DICTATE, LECTURE,
MOUTH, NARRATE, NATTER, ORATE, RELATE,
SPEAK, SPEECH [summit ~s].

TAN BRONZE, BROWN, SUNBURN, SUNTAN. *COLOUR*
(brown). BEAT, CANE, THRASH, WHIP. BARK. CURE.
TANGENT.

TANNER SIXPENCE; hence SHIL or LING (crypt). LEATHER-
WORKER, -CURER. SUN(SHINE), UV rays (crypt).

TANTALUS Gk myth s of *Zeus*. Stood to his neck in water, which
receded when he tried to drink; food above his head wafted out
of reach when he tried to take it. Father of *Niobe* and Pelops
(tantalize).

TAP DRAW OFF, SIPHON. FAUCET (US). BUG,
EAVESDROP, MONITOR. BROACH, PENETRATE.
SOLICIT. CUT THREAD. KNOCK, RAP, STRIKE. **Pl** =
LIGHTS OUT (US mil). *AIRLINE* (Port).

TAPESTRY NEEDLEPOINT, WALL-HANGING, *WEAVE*;
ARRAS, AUBUSSON, BAYEUX, GOBELIN (*carpet*).

TAR (s/l *ta*). AB, JACK, GOB (US), *SAILOR*, SALT.
ASPHALT, BITUMEN, PITCH.

TAROT TAROC; card game; fortune telling cards; 78 in pack, 22
trumps.

0 = *fool/jester*	11 = *strength*
1 = juggler	12 = *hanged* man
2 = female pope	13 = *death*
3 = *empress*	14 = temperance
4 = *emperor*	15 = *devil*
5 = pope	16 = *tower*
6 = *lovers*	17 = *star*
7 = *chariot*	18 = *moon*
8 = *justice*	19 = *sun*
9 = *hermit*	20 = day of *judgement*
10 = wheel of *fortune*	21 = *world*

TART ACID, BITING, CUTTING. PROSTITUTE. PASTRY,
PIE, SWEET; **celeb**: apple, Bakewell, cherry, custard, fruit,
jam, mince, peach, walnut.

TARTAN PATTERN, PLAID (Sc); *MATERIAL*. *BOAT*.
GENERAL (bibl).

TARZAN Jungle-dwelling character of Edgar Rice Burroughs, 'real' name Lord Greystoke [Jane. Cheta (monkey)].

TATTOO NEEDLEWORK (crypt). MARK, STAIN; DECORATE. DRUMMING, SIGNAL. PAGEANT.

TAUNT RAG, REPROACH, RIB, *TEASE*, UPBRAID.

TAVERN *BAR*, INN, PH (abbr), PUB; **celeb**: Admiral Benbow (Treasure Island, *Stevenson*); Boar's Head (H.iv, H.v, *Shak*); Garter (Merry Wives, *Shak*); *Mermaid* (Cheapside 1666); Spyglass (Treasure Island, *Stevenson*); Tabard (Canterbury Tales, *Chaucer*). *CRICKET CROWD* (Lord's).

TAW LEATHER, *WHIP*. MARBLE (game). RIVER (Eng).

TAX (s/l *tacks*). DUTY, EXCISE, LEVY, PAYE, SCOT, TOLL, VAT [*customs, smuggle*]. ASSESS, DEMAND, DRAIN, *TEST*, TRY. [~ **gatherer** = PUBLICAN (bibl)].

TB TERBIUM (*chem*). TORPEDO BOAT (mil). TRIAL BALANCE. TUBERCULOSIS.

TE (s/l *tea, tee*). NOTE (mus; also TEE, TI). TELLURIUM (*chem*). Jap karate term.

TEA (s/l t, *tee*). *MEAL*. DRINK (genus camellia); CHA, CHAR, CUPPA, ROSIE LEE (*rh sl*); **types**: CEYLON, CHINA (BOHEA, CONGOU, EARL GREY, JASMINE, KEEMUN, LAPSANG, OOLONG, ORANGE PEKOE, SUCHONG); INDIAN (DARJEELING, KASHMIRI, NILGIR). [Jap ~ ceremony (Chanoyu, Koicha, Ususha)].

TEA GIRL *ALICE*; POLLY (nursery rhyme).

TEAM (s/l teem). 1. II, XI, XV, ELEVEN etc. GANG, PLAYERS, *SIDE*, SQUAD. YOKED OXEN. 2. *Assembly* of young ducks, oxen.

TEA-MAKER KETTLE, POT, SAMOVAR. POLLY. ATE, EAT (crypt).

TEA-PARTY AT-HOME, ENTERTAINMENT. FRACAS (sl). CHAR-LADY, POLLY (crypt) [Mad Hatter (*Alice*); Boston].

TEAR (s/l tare, *tier*). *DASH*, HURRY, *RUN*. PULL, REND, *RIP*. DRIP, DROP, LACHRYMA [*Niobe, Ruth*]. ~ GAS.

TEASE (s/l t's, *teas, tees*). CHAFF, CHIP, *RAG*, RIB, TAUNT, TWIT. PICK FIBRES. IRRITATE, VEX.

TEASING *ARCH*, COY. *CHAFF*, TAUNTING. PICKING, SEPARATING FIBRES.

TED EDWARD. TEDDY BOY. DRY/MAKE HAY. HEATH (Prime Minister).

TEE (s/l *te, tea*). PROP, SUPPORT (golfball). PIPE JOINT, ROAD JUNCTION (as letter T). NOTE (mus; also TE, TI).

TARGET (curling, c.f. bowls jack).

TEETH CHAMPERS, MASHERS, MOLARS [*study*]; DENTURES (see *bone, tooth*). COGS (mech).

TEETOTAL AA, ABSTAINER, TT; RECHABITE. [Richard *Turner*].

TEG *SHEEP* (young). GET UP (dn). GET BACK.

TELEPHONE BELL (sl), CALL, DIAL, DOG (rh sl), PHONE, RING [STD].

TELEVISION BOX, MEDIUM, SET, TV. [BBC, IBA, ITA, ITV; ABC, CBS, NBC (US)].

TELL RECOUNT, RELATE, NARRATE. *COUNT.* BOWMAN (crypt), WILLIAM [Rossini]. LINTEL (crypt: L*in*TEL).

~ **OFF** CARPET, *REPRIMAND.* COUNT, *NUMBER.*

~ **TALE** FIBBER, LIAR. *BETRAY.* INDICATOR, SIGNAL. RELATE, NARRATOR.

TELLUS Rom eq of *GE* (also TERRA).

TEMPER ANGER, IRE. HARDEN. MITIGATE, RESTRAIN; TUNE.

TEMPEST STORM, *WIND. AIRCRAFT*, FIGHTER. Play by *Shak*.

TEMPLE 1. Part of head/skull. STRETCHER (weaving). SHIRLEY ~ (film). 2. *INNS OF COURT* (Knights Templar). 3. FANE, PLACE OF WORSHIP (*oracle*); **architecture**: adytum, cella, mecaron, naos, portico, posterula, propylaeum, propylon, sekos, thalamos, vestibule; **celeb**: ABU SIMBEL (Nile), *APOLLO* (Delphi; Palatine), *ARTEMIS* (Ephesus; *seven wonders*), *DELPHI* (*Apollo*), *DIANA* (Aricia), KARNAK, LUXOR, MICAH (Jewish), PARTHENON (Athens), PHILAE (Aswan Dam), SOLOMON'S ~ (Jerusalem), THE TEMPLE (Jerusalem, Solomon).

TEMPO RHYTHM, TIME (mus): ACCELERANDO, ADAGIO, ALLEGRETTO, ALLEGRO, ANDANTE, ANIMATO, COMODO, LARGAMENTE, LARGO, LENTO, MAESTOSO, MORENDO, MOSSO, PRESTO, PRESTISSIMO, RALLENTANDO, RUBATO, STRINGENDO, VIBRATO. **Pl** = TEMPI. And see *Music* (3).

TEMPTRESS ENCHANTRESS, HOURI, SEDUCTRESS, *SIREN*, VAMP.

TEMU Egy *god* of gods, Creator. **Gk** = *ZEUS*; **Rom** = JOVE, JUPITER.

TEN See *number.* DECADE, IO, VV, X. TWE or NTY (crypt). [tithe]. *Commandments* in *song*; pipers piping, in Christmas *song.* ~ green bottles.

TENANT T. HOLDER, LESSEE, OCCUPANT; **comp** = *landlord.* [*Brontë*].

TEN COMMANDMENTS Spoken by God to Moses: (1) Thou shalt have no other gods before me. (2) Thou shalt not make unto thee any graven image. (3) Thou shalt not take the name of the Lord thy God in vain. (4) Remember the sabbath day, to keep it holy. (5) Honour thy father and thy mother. (6) Thou shalt not kill. (7) Thou shalt not commit adultery. (8) Thou shalt not steal. (9) Thou shalt not bear false witness against thy neighbour. (10) Thou shalt not covet thy neighbour's house, his wife . . . nor anything that is his.

TEND *APT*, CONDUCE, INCLINE, SERVE. CARE, *NURSE*, WAIT ON.

TENDER OFFER, PRESENT, PROFFER. SOFT, SORE. NEEDING CARE, TICKLISH. AFFECTIONATE, CONSIDERATE, FOND, LOVING, SOLICITOUS. ATTENDANT BOAT/WAGON, GUARDIAN. SHEPHERD (crypt). MATRON, NANNY, *NURSE*, SISTER (crypt).

TENNE/TENNY BROWN (*herald*).

TENNIS BALL GAME; **venues**: Forest Hills, Flushing Meadows, Queen's Club, Stade Roland Garros, Wimbledon. DECK ~, LAWN ~ [WCT], REAL ~ [dedans, grille, hazard side, penthouse, service side, tambour], RING ~, TABLE ~.

TENT CANOPY, (CANVAS) SHELTER, LODGE, TEE-PEE, WIGWAM. DILATE, PLUG, PROBE; WOUND PLUG, WAD. (RED) WINE. HEED, NOTICE. FRAME (embroidery).

~ **MAKER** CANVAS WORKER. BREWER, VINTNER; OMAR (KHAYYAM). NETT (crypt, anag).

TERM BOUNDARY, LIMIT, PERIOD, *SENTENCE*, SPAN. CONDITION, FOOTING, RELATION, STIPULATION. CALL, DENOMINATE; LANGUAGE. HALF, SEMESTER: Easter (C), Hilary (O), Lent (C, O), Michaelmas (C, O), Trinity (O). For music terms, see *Music* (3).

TERMITE *INSECT*, (WHITE) ANT. SCHOLAR, SCHOOLBOY, -GIRL (crypt).

TERPANDER The first historical *musician*, who lived at Antissa in Lesbos 700–650 B.C.

TERPSICHORE Gk myth, one of the nine *Muses* (*dance* and *song*).

TERRA Also TELLUS. Rom eq of *GE*, *goddess* of EARTH.

TERRITORIAL ARMY TA, TERRIERS (hence *football team*). *RESERVES.*

TERRY BOY, MAN. TOWEL.

TEST EXERCISE, TAX, TRIAL, *TRY*; EXAMINE. ASSAY, REFINE. *MATCH* (games). *RIVER.*

TESTER ANALYST, ASSAYER, EXAMINER. (BED) CANOPY. *COIN* (Eng). CRICKETER (crypt).

TESTING GROUND LABORATORY, LAB, WIND TUNNEL. *CRICKET GROUND.*

TH *THORIUM* (*chem*). *THURSDAY.*

THALIA 1. Gk myth, one of the nine *Muses* (comedy and bucolic poetry). 2. A minor *PLANET.*

THAMES RIVER. *ISIS.* LONDON BANKER (crypt). CAPITAL CURRENCY (crypt). **Bridges of the** ~ (in order from the sea):

Barrier	Charing Cross (rly)
Tower	*Westminster*
London	*Lambeth*
Cannon St (rly)	Vauxhall
Southwark	Grosvenor Rd (rly)
Blackfriars (rly)	Chelsea
Blackfriars	Albert
Waterloo	Battersea
Hungerford (foot)	Battersea (rly)
Wandsworth	Chiswick
Putney (rly)	Kew (rly)
Putney	Kew
Hammersmith	*Twickenham*
Barnes (rly)	Richmond

THANKS *GRACE*, GRATITUDE, TA.

THANKSGIVING Expression of gratitude, usually to God; specifically 4th Thursday in Nov (US) and 2nd Mon in Oct (Can).

THAT YON.

~ **FRENCH** ÇA, CELA.

~ **IS** ID EST, IE.

~ **LATIN/ROMAN** ID, ILLE.

~ **ONE** HE, SHE.

THAT'S ID EST, IE.

~ **RIGHT** IER (crypt).

THEATRE 1. ARENA, FIELD, SCENE, BATTLE-, WAR-ZONE (mil). OPERATING ROOM (med). LECTURE HALL;

STUDIO. 2. AUDITORIUM, MUSIC-HALL, PLAYHOUSE, STAGE. ART, DRAMA, REP, SHOW BIZ, THE STAGE, VAUDEVILLE [*awards. Apollo, Athene, Minerva, Muse* (all q.v.)]; **celeb**:

ABC	LA SCALA (It)
ADELPHI	LIBERTY
ALBERY	*LITTLE* ~
ALDWYCH	LYCEUM
ALHAMBRA	LYRIC
AMBASSADORS	LYTTLETON
APOLLO	MARQUIS (US)
BARBICAN	MAYFAIR
COLISEUM	*MERMAID*
COMEDY	*METROPOLITAN*
CONNAUGHT	MUSIC HALL
COTTESLOE	NATIONAL ~
COVENT GARDEN	*NEW* ~
CRITERION	NEW LONDON ~
CURZON	NEW OXFORD ~
DALYS	ODEON
DOMINION	OLD VIC
DRURY LANE	OLIVIER
DUCHESS	OPERA HOUSE
DUKE OF YORK'S	*PALACE*
EMPIRE	*PALLADIUM*
ESSOLDO	PAVILION
EVERYMAN	*PHOENIX*
FORTUNE	PICCADILLY
GAIETY	PIT
GARRICK	PLAYHOUSE
GAUMONT	PRINCE EDWARD
GLOBE (OE)	PRINCE OF WALES
GRANADA	*PRINCE'S*
GRAND	PROMENADE (US)
GREENWICH	*QUEEN'S*
HAYMARKET	*REGENT*
HER MAJESTY'S	RIALTO
HIPPODROME	ROSE (OE)
HIS MAJESTY'S	*ROYAL*
HOLBORN EMPIRE	ROYAL COURT
KINGSWAY	ROYALTY

SADLER'S WELLS	TROCADERO
ST JAMES	*VARIETY*
ST MARTIN'S	VAUDEVILLE
SAVOY	*VICTORIA* PALACE
SHAFTESBURY	VIRGINIA (US)
STOLL	*WESTMINSTER*
STRAND	WHITEHALL
STRATFORD	WINTER GARDEN
SWAN	WYNDHAM'S
THEATRE ROYAL	YOUNG VIC
TIVOLI	YVONNE ARNAUD

THEATRE GOER PLAY-WATCHER. PATIENT, SURGEON (crypt).

~ **WORK** ACTING, PLAYING. MEDICINE. OPERATION, SURGERY (crypt).

THE FRENCH LA, LE, LES.

~ **GERMAN** DER, DAS, DIE.

~ **ITALIAN** IL.

THEOLOGIAN *See CHURCHMAN* for list.

THERMOPYLAE Narrow defile in the mountains 100 miles north of Athens, where 300 Spartans under Leonidas withstood *Xerxes* and his army of about 1,000,000 men for three days. They only failed in the end because the treachery of Ephialtes revealed a secret path through the hills to their rear. The sole Gk survivor was received in Athens with reproaches for having fled.

THESE TIMES AD, NOW(ADAYS).

THESEUS Gk myth hero, to whom *Ariadne* (d of king *Minos*) gave a ball of string so he could find his way back out of the labyrinth after he had killed the *Minotaur.* He was one of the *Argonauts* and, on his successful return to *Attica*, he neglected to hoist the white sail which was the signal of his triumph; Aegeus, his father, thought him dead so he leaped into the sea and was drowned – thus jumping to a *conclusion.* [*Cercyron*; *Periphites*; *Procrustes*; *Sciron*]. And *Shak* char.

THE SPANISH EL.

THEY PEOPLE, PERSONS. AUTHORITY, THE ESTABLISHMENT. OPPONENTS (*bridge*).

THIEF *ROBBER* (q.v.); TEA LEAF (*rh sl*). [Ali Baba].

THIN CULL, DILUTE. LEAN, SKINNY, SLENDER (**opp** = fat, *stout*). FINE, NARROW. BALDING. INSUBSTANTIAL, INSUFFICIENT. FLIMSY, SCANTY, SHALLOW,

TRANSPARENT (**opp** = thick).

THING OBJECT; RES (Lat). CONVENTION. OBSESSION. LIFESTYLE. *LEGISLATIVE ASSEMBLY* (ON). **Pl** = BELONGINGS, PROPERTY.

THIRD Next to second, hence 'a second before'; BRONZE. E (mus). INTERVAL (mus). DIVISION, RIDING.

~ **CLASS** C. A (crypt).

~ **MAN** ABEL (crypt). *CRICKETER*. HARRY LIME. N (crypt).

~ **PERSON** CAIN (crypt). HE, SHE, THEM. R (crypt).

THIS 1. Indicates near at hand (**opp** = that). EXISTING, PRESENT. 2. Ancient Egy town (TINI). 3. Answer is added to preceding or following word, to make a further word as also indicated, e.g. **Play no to this remedy** (5) = (no)STRUM; or **Elevated this way for the main road** (4) = HIGH(way). 4. This side of . . . indicates the first part of the next word, e.g. **Musical instrument this side of violence** (4) = VIOL(ence).

~ **MONTH** INST. Current month, as JAN, FEB etc.

THOR (s/l thaw). 1. Nor *god* of THUNDER, s of *Odin*. He possessed a magic throwing hammer called Miolnir. **Rom** = TONANS. [Thursday]. 2. HEYERDAHL (Kon-Tiki).

THORIUM TH (*chem*).

THOROUGHBRED HIGH-SPIRITED, METTLESOME, PURE-BRED (**opp** = mongrel) [original horse studbook ancestors = BYERLY TURK, DARLEY ARABIAN, GODOLPHIN BARB].

THOUSAND See *number*. K, KILO; M (Lat). CHILIAD.

~ **GUINEAS** *CLASSIC*: LML (crypt).

THREE See *number*. TRIAD. GREEN BALL (snooker). *Rivals* in *song*. French *hens* in *Christmas song*. [*Holmes* cases]. ~ Men in a Boat (George, Harris, J and the dog Montmorency) by Jerome K. Jerome.

~ **ESTATES** COMMONS, LORDS SPIRITUAL, LORDS TEMPORAL [**fourth estate** = *press*].

~ **FEET** YARD, *MEASURE*. TRIPOD.

~ **QUARTERS** BACKS, WINGS (*rugby*) [*Holmes* case]. 75%. Any 3 of E, N, S and W (crypt).

THRICE TER, THREEFOLD, THREE TIMES.

THRILL FRISSON, PULSATION, THROB, TREMOR; EXCITE, WOW.

THROUGHWAY BY-PASS, FLYOVER. ARCH, TUNNEL (crypt).

THROWER BALLISTA, CATAPULT, SLING, TREBUCKET.

GARDENER; POTTER (crypt). *THOR.*

THUG 1. ROUGHNECK, RUFFIAN, TOUGH GUY, YAHOO
(*Swift*). 2. Indian religious fanatic of 19th century, who garotted
victims as sacrifice to *Kali,* Hindu *goddess* of Destruction.

THUNDER 1. CLAP, CRASH, LOUD NOISE; **comp** = *lightning.*
ADVANTAGE, CREDIT. RAIL, THREATEN. 2. **Gods: Gk**
= *ZEUS*; **Rom** = JOVE/*JUPITER*, *TONANS*; **Nor** = *THOR.*
3. BOANERGES (James and John, sons of ~; bibl).

THUNDERBOLT DESTRUCTION, LIGHTNING, SHAFT,
THREAT. *AIRCRAFT.* [Jove, *Jupiter, Tonans, Zeus*].

THUNDERER *THOR, TONANS.* THE TIMES ®.

THURSDAY TH, THURS; day of *Thor.* ISLAND (Aus). ~'s
child = far to go [*Chesterton*, Solomon *Grundy*].

TI *TITANIUM* (*chem*). BACK IT (crypt). NOTE (mus, also TE).
TREE (Polynesia, NZ).

TICK CR, CREDIT. CHECK OFF, MARK. CASE, COVER.
BLOODSUCKER, *INSECT*, PARASITE. CLICK. INSTANT,
MO, MOMENT, SEC. GROUSE, GRUMBLE (sl).

~ **OFF** 1. CHECK, MARK. BERATE, CHASTISE,
REPRIMAND. STOPWATCH. 2. Delete any synonym for 'tick'
from clue, e.g. **Tick off sector hill (3)** = ***TOR.

~ **OVER** IDLE, RUN SLOWLY. STOPPED CLOCK (crypt).

TIER (s/l *tear*). LINE, RANGE, RANK, *ROW.* DRAWER,
EQUAL WINNER. BINDER, KNOTTER.

TIGER TANK, *WEAPON.* CHEER. *LEPIDOPTERA* (moth).
SHARK. MANELESS FELINE; BIG CAT; SHERE KHAN
(Kipling); **offspring** = cub. [*Ch calendar*; Tora (*Jap*)]. **Pl** =
Football team.

TIGHT CLOSE, FIRM. IMPERMEABLE (**opp** = porous).
NEAR, MEAN, MISERLY. STRETCHED, TAUT, TENSE,
TENSIONED. *DRUNK.* **Pl** = HOSE, UNDERWEAR;
CATSUIT, LEOTARD.

TILBURY *DOCK. CARRIAGE. CASTLE.*

TILDE ACCENT (ñ = ny).

TILL UNTIL, UP TO. CASHBOX. CULTIVATE, FARM,
PLOUGH, TURN UP. CLAY.

TILLER SALESMAN/WOMAN (crypt). *FARMER* (crypt).
HELM. DANCING GIRL.

TILT AWNING. *CANT, LEAN,* LIST, SLOPE. JOUST.

TIM BOY. SPEAKING CLOCK. LITTLE TIME (crypt).

TIMBER (s/l timbre). *FOREST*, TREES, WOOD [*measure*].
FRAME, RIB (naut).

TIME T; *DATE*, HOUR, MOMENT, SECOND. EST, GMT etc.
ENEMY (sl). CLOCK, RECORD, REGISTER. PERIOD;
DAY, *MONTH*, *SEASON*, *WEEK*, *YEAR*; *AGE*, AEON,
EON, ERA. BIRD, GAOL TERM, PETER, PORRIDGE,
SENTENCE, STRETCH. *TEMPO*. **Pl** = PAPER ®,
THUNDERER (was Daily Universal Register; founder John
Walter). *TYPEFACE*. X, MULTIPLY BY. [O tempora, O
mores (Cicero)].
~ **OUT** BREAK, BREATHER, INTERVAL. EMIT, ITEM
(crypt, anag).
~ **WARP** FOURTH DIMENSION [Einstein]. EMIT, ITEM
(crypt, anag).
TIN 1. *METAL*; SN (*chem*); *anniversary* (10th). CAN. MONEY.
2. Put letter 't' in word(s) following, e.g. **Tin spoon precisely**
(4, 2) = SPO*T*ON.
TINY 1. MINUTE, SMALL, WEE (**opp** = *giant*). [*Dickens*].
2. Use diminutive or offspring of, e.g. **Tiny Tom** = KITTY or TH.
TIP 1. EDGE, END, POINT, RIM. CUE, HINT. WRINKLE.
CANT, TILT, TOPPLE. GRATUITY. 2. First or last letter of
word, e.g. **Asparagus tip** = A or S.
~ **OFF** 1. CUE, HINT. WRINKLE. 2. First or last letter
removed, e.g. **Communist Fred's tip-off** (3) = *RED.
TIRE (s/l *tyre*). BORE, EXHAUST, FATIGUE, WEARY. US =
TYRE (UK). ATTIRE, DRESS.
TISIPHONE One of the *Furies*.
TIT NIPPLE. CONTROL, KNOB (av). BIRD; bearded ~,
blue ~, coal ~, crested ~, great ~, longtailed ~, marsh ~,
willow ~.
TITAN (s/l tighten). 1. Gk myth children of *Uranus* and *Ge*
(sometimes incorrectly confused with the *giants* or *monsters*
called Gigantes): OCEANUS and TETHYS (sea), HYPERION
and THEA (sun and moon), COCUS and PHOEBE (light),
CREIOS and EURYBIA (strength), CRONOS and RHEA
(heaven and earth), THEMIS and MNEMOSYNE (law and
memory), IAPETUS (father of mankind). 2. A satellite of the
planet SATURN.
TITANIUM *METAL*; TI (*chem*).
TITFER HAT (*rh sl*).
TITLE HANDLE, NAME. BARON, COUNT, DUKE, EARL,
LORD, VISCOUNT etc. DEED, RIGHT.
TO (s/l too, two). 1. AS FAR AS. TOWARDS; **comp** = fro.
COMPARED WITH. BY WAY OF, FOR. CONTAINED,

INCLUDED, INVOLVED. 2. Letters or word put before word indicated, e.g. **As to this, it's in pieces below** (5) = (as)UNDER.

TOAD (s/l toed, towed). 1. BOOTLICKER, CAD, FAWNER, FLATTERER, LICKSPITTLE, SPONGER, SYCOPHANT, *TOOL*, YES-MAN; **celeb**: LORD VERISOPHT (*Dickens*). 2. Amphibian genus BUFO, PIPA etc (does not leap); **breeds**: CANE ~ (Aus); COMMON ~; FIREBRAND ~; MIDWIFE ~; PADDOCK, PUDDOC (Sc); SPADEFOOT ~; SURINAM ~ (S Am). **Offspring**: pollywog, tadpole [~ of ~ Hall, cars, *Grahame* (q.v.); banner of King Clovis].

TOADSTOOL See *FUNGUS* for list.

TOAST BROWN, COOK, HEAT, SCORCH, SINGE, WARM; COOKED BREAD; **comp** = butter, marmalade. CHEERS, CHIN CHIN, PROSIT, SANTE, SKOLL; ROUSE.

TOASTER COOKER; *SINGER* (crypt). HEALTH-DRINKER (crypt).

TOBACCO Plant genus Nicotiana: TURKISH, VIRGINIA. QUID, SNOUT (sl), TWIST [chewing, snuff].

TOD *MEASURE* (wool). ALONE (*rh sl*).

TODAY MON, TUES, WED etc according to date. A.D.

TOM *CAT*. ~ *BROWN*; ~, DICK and HARRY; ~ SAWYER (*Twain*); ~ THUMB. *BELL* (Oxford). DR or UM (half of tom-tom).

TOMMY LAD, SMALL BOY. BAR. GUN. TUCKER. ATKINS, SOLDIER.

TON (s/l *tun*). C, T. 100 (mph). CENTURY, HUNDRED. *FASHION*.

TONANS Rom *god* of THUNDER.

TONE PITCH, QUALITY, MODULATION; SOUND. FITNESS, CHARACTER. HARMONIZE. SHADE, TINT.

TONIC BRACING, INVIGORATING. TREATMENT. KEYNOTE, TONAL (mus). *DRINK*, MIXER; **comp** = *gin*.

TONY *AWARD* [Antoinette Perry] (theat) ®. ANT(H)ONY.

TOOL 1. SYCOPHANT, *TOAD*. GUN (sl). 2. HAND ~, IMPLEMENT, MACHINE ~; CUT, SHAPE, WORK. **Types (garden)**: CHOPPER, DIBBER, FORK, HOE, MATTOCK, PICK, PRUNING HOOK, SCYTHE, SHOVEL, SICKLE, SLEDGEHAMMER, SPADE, TROWEL. **(workshop)**: ADZE, AWL, BENCHDRILL, BIT, BRADAWL, CHISEL, CROWBAR, DIVIDERS, DRAWKNIFE, DRILL, FILE, GRINDSTONE, HAMMER, JACK, LATHE, LEVEL, MALLET, MAUL, PINCERS,

PLANE, PLIERS, PUNCH, ROUTER, SAW (BAND, BOW,
BUZZ, CHAIN, CIRCULAR, COPING, ELECTRIC, FRET,
HACK, JIG, KEYHOLE, POWER, PRUNING, RIP ~s),
SCREWDRIVER, STAPLER, VICE, VISE (US), WRENCH.

TOOTH *BONE* (q.v.), CHAMPER, *FANG*, IVORY, MASHER.
MOLAR [caries]; **comp** = *nail*. COG, SPROCKET.

TOP 1. ACE, ACME, APEX, *HEAD*, SUMMIT, UPPER, U.
COVER, PIECRUST. BEST, OVERCOME. BEHEAD,
EXECUTE. DIABOLO, SPINNING TOY. BEST, FIRST
CLASS. *LAKE* (CIS). 2. Omit first letter, e.g. **Top gear for
listener** (3) = EAR. 3. **Pl** = DOUBLE TWENTY, hence FORTY,
XL (darts).

TOPAZ *GEM* (blue, green, white, yellow). *Birthstone* (November).
Sir ~ (*Chaucer* char).

TOPAZOLITE *GEM* (green, yellow); GARNET.

TOPE *DRINK*, TIPPLE. MANGO-GROVE. *SHARK*. SHRINE.

TOPLESS 1. BALD. BAREBREASTED. 2. Remove letters 'bra'
from word, e.g. **Topless bravery is extreme** (4) = ***VERY. 3. No
first letter in dn answer.

TOPMAN CHAIRMAN, C-IN-C, DICTATOR, *EMPEROR*,
KING, MD, *MONARCH*, OC, *PRESIDENT*, *PRIME MINISTER*,
SOVEREIGN, SUPREMO. CIRCUS
ARTISTE. EXECUTIONER, *HANGMAN* (crypt). SAILOR,
YARDMAN.

TOPPING AI, FIRST CLASS, FIRST RATE. HALO, *HAT*,
ROOF, TIARA (crypt). EXECUTION (crypt).

TORTOISE 1. *Reptile* with carapace or shell; land version of
TURTLE or TERRAPIN [Achilles and ~ (Zeno); Aeschylus (k
by ~); hare and ~ (Aesop); *Sciron's* ~ (myth)]. 2. Tank-like
formation of Rom soldiers protected by shields held overhead or
alongside; TESTUDO.

TORY C, POLITICIAN, RIGHT WING. *ISLAND* (Ire).

TOT CHILD. *DRINK*, MEASURE. SUM; *COUNT*, TELL.
SCAVENGE.

TOUCH *SENSE*; BRUSH, CONTACT, FEEL. REACH.
INJURE, MARK. AFFECTED, CRAZY. SYMPATHY.
SIDE-LINE (games).

TOWED (s/l *toad*, toed). DRAWN, PULLED, TUGGED.
HEMPEN. TO *MARRY* (crypt).

TOWER TALL BUILDING, SKYSCRAPER. 16 (*tarot*).
CITADEL, FORTRESS. SOAR. *DRAWER*, PULLER, TUG
(crypt). *THAMES* BRIDGE.

TOXIPHOBIA *Aversion* to poisons.

TOYMAKER MASTER CHERRY (Pinocchio), DR COPPELIUS (Coppelia, Delibes), CALEB PLUMMER (Cricket, *Dickens*), TACKLETON (Cricket, *Dickens*). OTY, YOT etc (crypt, anag).

TRACE *SIGN*, VESTIGE. DELINEATE, *MARK*, SKETCH, WRITE; *COPY*, FOLLOW. ASCERTAIN, OBSERVE, PURSUE, TRACK. *HARNESS*, STRAPS.

TRACT COURSE, FOOTPRINTS, PATH, SCENT. *RACECOURSE. DOG*, FOLLOW, TAIL, TRACE. GROOVE (disc, EP). TREAD (tank, tractor). GAUGE, WIDTH; *EM, TT*, Z (wheels, rails); BR, IRON WAY, RLY, RY: HARD LINES (crypt).

TRACT (s/l tracked). GROUND, PLOT, STRETCH. HAND-OUT, PAMPHLET.

TRADE TERMS DISCOUNT. GATT. CIF, EX WORKS, FAS, FOB (crypt).

TRADING COMPANIES MUSCOVY ~ (1555), EASTLAND ~ (1579), LEVANT ~ (1581), AFRICA ~ (1588), EAST INDIA ~ (1600), HUDSON BAY ~ (1670).

TRAGEDY 1. CALAMITY, DRAMA. 2. Any celebrated play of tragic nature, e.g. KING LEAR. 3. **Gk Muse** = MELPOMENE.

TRAIN KEEP FIT [PE, PT]. *COACH, DRILL*, INSTRUCT, PREPARE. CORTEGE, RETINUE, SKIRT, STRING, TAIL. APT, BR, HST, RLY, RY ENGINE, *LOCAL* [commuting]. EXPLOSIVE CHARGE, *FUSE*.

TRAINEE APPRENTICE, LEARNER. COMMUTER, PASSENGER, RAILMAN, TRAINER (all crypt).

TRAINER *COACH*, TEACHER. COMMUTER (crypt). *SHOE*. Pl = RAILMEN (**Unions** = ASLEF, NUR).

TRAINING COACHING, LEARNING, TEACHING. EXERCISING, KEEPING FIT, REGIME. COMMUTING (crypt).

TRAITOR DESERTER, RAT, RENEGADE, TURNCOAT. SIR MORDRED (Knight of the *Round Table*, Tennyson). [Quisling].

TRAMP BAGLADY (US sl), BUM, DERO (Aus), HOBO, SUNDOWNER, VAGRANT. *BOAT*, CARGO SHIP. FOOTSLOG, *MARCH*, STAMP, TRAMPLE, TREAD, TRUDGE, WALK, YOMP. *GOLDDIGGER*.

Trans Translate.

TRANSFER *Anag.* CONVEY, HANDOVER, REMOVE. CHANGE, MOVE, SWITCH. WATERCOLOUR.

TRANSFORMATION *Anag.* ALTERATION, CHANGE,

METAMORPHOSIS; e.g. *insects* (caterpillar's ~ into pupa, into imago); *ballet* or pantomime actors' ~ into players in subsequent harlequinade or play-within-a-play, e.g. in Nutcracker ballet); also in Gk myth, esp ~s of *Zeus* (q.v., usually for amatory purposes). **See also**: *Aaron's* rod (into *serpent*, and to almond tree; bibl); *Acheron* (into river; myth); *Actaeon* (into *stag*; myth); Alpheus into underground river (while chasing Arethusa; myth); *ants* (into men; Myrmidons, myth); *Arachne* (into *spider*; myth); Arethusa by Artemis into *fountain* (escaping Alpheus; myth); *Argus* (eyes to peacock's tail; myth); *Atlas* (into stone; myth); *Autolycus* (all he touched; myth); bread (into roses; St *Elizabeth*); Cadmus and Harmonia (into *serpents*; myth); *Daphne* (into laurel; myth); dragon's teeth (into soldiers; Cadmus, myth); father (into son; Vice Versa, Anstey); fire (into roses; *Abraham*, bibl); frog (into prince; trad); *Galatea* (from ivory statue to life; myth); hand (withered; *Jeroboam*, bibl); head (into that of an ass; Bottom, *Shak*); Io (into heifer; myth); ivory statue (into *Galatea*; myth); Dr Jekyll (into Mr *Hyde; Stevenson*); *Lot's* wife (into a pillar of salt; bibl); *Medusa* (others to stone; myth); mice and pumpkin (into coach and horses; Cinderella, trad); *Midas* (all to gold; myth); *Moses'* rod (into *serpent*; bibl); *Narcissus* (into flower; myth); *Niobe* (into stone; myth); Philomela (into *nightingale*); Procne (onto *swallow*); *Sirens* (into rocks; myth); son (into father; Vice Versa, Anstey); stones (into people; *Deucalion*, myth); Ugly Duckling (into *swan; Andersen*); water (into wine; *Jesus*, bibl); *witch* (into black cat; trad).

TRANSLATION *Anag.* 1. *TRANSFER, TRANSFORMATION.* INTERPRET. 2. Put into foreign language, e.g. **My French translation at the beginning of the week** (3) = MON. 3. Reverse the syllables, **Translate the German stable** (6) = MAN·GER.

TRANSPORT EMOTION, RAPTURE. CONVEY, MOVE; *AIRLINE*, BR, BUS, CAB, *CAR, CARRIAGE, LORRY*, RLY, *TRAIN*, TRAM, VAN (**Union** = TGW).

TRAP CATCH, *GIN*, SNARE. *CARRIAGE*. **Pl** = *BAGGAGE*, CASES, GRIPS, LUGGAGE. DRUMS, *INSTRUMENTS* (mus).

TRAPPIST BENEDICTINE, CISTERCIAN MONK [silence]. HUNTER (crypt). DRUMMER (crypt).

TREAT *Anag.* MANIPULATE, MINISTER, NEGOTIATE, PROCESS. REGALE, ROUND, SHOUT, STAND. EXCURSION; PLEASURE.

TREBLE ALTO; CLEF. *BET.*
TREE 1. ANCESTORS, GENEALOGY. FRAME-WORK.
BOOT-BLOCK. Celeb actor. 2. PERENNIAL PLANT;
[*branch*, sapling, stem; *Absalom*, Charles I] **types** (and see *fruit*).

2-letters

BO	TI

3-letters

ASH	*BOX*	GUM	SAL
ASP	ELM	JAK	YEW
BAY	FIG	KOA	
BEN	FIR	OAK	

4-letters

ACER	GEAN	*PALM*	SHEA
AKEE	HOLM	*PEAR*	SORB
BAEL	ILEX	*PINE*	TEAK
COCO	JALA	*PLUM*	TEIL
DALI	KOLA	POON	TITI
DATE	LANA	RATA	TOON
DHAK	LIME	*ROSE*	*UPAS*
DOUM	MORA	SAGO	
EJOO	NIPA	SAUL	

5-letters

ABELE	EDONY	*PEACH*
ABIES	ELDER	*PLANE*
ALDER	HAZEL	ROHAN
APPLE	HOLLY	ROWAN
ARECA	IROKO	SALIX
ARENG	JAMBU	TAXUS
ASPEN	JUDAS	TIKUL
BALSA	KAURI, -Y	TILIA
BEECH	LARCH	TINGI
BIRCH	*LEMON*	TUCUM
BODHI (sacred)	LILAC	WITHY
BUNYA	MAPLE	YACCA
CACAO	OLIVE	ZAMIA
CAROB	OSIER	ZANTE
CEDAR	PAPAW	

6-letters

ACACIA
ACAJOU
ALMOND
ANTIAR
BAMBOO
BANANA
BANIAN
BANYAN
BAOBAB
BOG-OAK
BOMBAX
CARAPA
CARICA
CASHEW
CERRIS
CHERRY
COHUNE
CONKER
COWDIE
DEODAR (sacred)
ELAEIS
FUSTIC

GINGKO
GINKGO
GOMUTI
GOMUTO
GOPHER
JARRAH
JUJUBE
JUPATI
KITOOL
KITTUL
LAUREL
LINDEN
LOCUST
LONGAN
MABOLA
MACACO
MALLEE
MASTEL
MIMOSA
NARGIL
OBECHE
ORANGE

PEEPUL (sacred)
PLATAN
POPLAR
PRUNUS
QUINCE
RATTAN
RED-BUD
RED-GUM
RED-OAK
RHAPIS
SAPELE
SAPIUM
SISSOO
SORBIN
SORBUS
SPRUCE
TUPELO
WALNUT
WATTLE
WILLOW
YARRAH

7-letters

AILANTO (sacred)
ARBUTUS
BACTRIS
BAY-TREE
BAYWOOD
BEBEERU
BEE-TREE
BURR-OAK
CAJEPUT
CALAMUS
CAMPHOR
CANELLA
CARYOTA
CATALPA
CEDRELLA
CHAMPAC
COCONUT

COG-WOOD
CONIFER
COQUITO
CORYPHA
CYPRESS
DURMAST
ELK-WOOD
EMBLICA
FAN-PALM
FILBERT
HICKORY
HOLM-OAK
JUGLANS
JUNIPER
MORICHE
MORINGA
OIL-PALM

PALMYRA
PAXIUBA
PHOENIX
PLATANE
QUERCUS
REDWOOD
ROBINIA
SAPLING
SEQUOIA
SERVICE
SHITTAH
SUNDARI
TALIPAT
TALIPET
TALIPOT
TALIPUT
TANGHIN

WALLABA	WYCH-ELM	ZALACCA
WAX-PALM	YEWTREE	

8-letters

AGUE-TREE	*DATE-PALM*	PALMETTO
ALGAROBA	GUAIACUM	PIASSABA
BEDEWEEN	HAWTHORN	PIASSAVA
BLACK-GUM	HEMP-PALM	PINASTER
BOURTREE	HORNBEAM	ROSEWOOD
CARNAUBA	JACKWOOD	SAGO-PALM
CASTANEA	KINGWOOD	SCRUB-OAK
CHESTNUT	LABURNUM	SWEETSOP
COCOANUT	MAGNOLIA	SYCAMORE
COKERNUT	MAHOGANY	WITCH-ELM
CORKWOOD	MANGROVE	ZIZYPHUS
CRABWOOD	MULBERRY	

9+ letters

BLACKTHORN	MONKEY PUZZLE
BREADFRUIT	SILVER BIRCH
CLUSTER-PINE	SPINDLETREE
COPPER BEECH	SUGAR APPLE
CUSTARD APPLE	TURKISH OAK
FLAME OF THE	*WELLINGTON*
FOREST	YGGDRASIL
FRANGIPANI	(Nor myth)

TREMBLER VIBRATOR (elect). *BIRD* (W Ind).
EARTHQUAKE (crypt).
TRENT BRIDGE *CRICKET GROUND*.
TRESPASSER EVIL DOER, SINNER. INTRUDER [~s William,
Piglet's grandfather, *Milne*].
TRIANGLE FIGURE (geom); **types**: EQUILATERAL ~,
ISOSCELES ~, SCALENE ~, OBTUSE/ACUTE ANGLED
~, [Bermuda; eternal]. INSTRUMENT (mus).
TRIBE GROUP (zool). FAMILY, NUMBER, SET. CLAN,
DIVISION [see *African*; *American Indian*; *Israel*; and see
TRIBESMAN]. **Roman Britain**: ATREBATES, BELGAE,
BRIGANTES, CANTII, CARVETII, CATUVELLAUNI,
CORITANI, CORNOVII, DECEANGLI, DEMETAE,
DOBUNNI, DUMNONII, DUROTRIGES, ICENI,
ORDOVICES, PARISI, REGENSES/REGNI, SILURES,

TRINOVANTES; chiefs: *Boudicca*, Cara(c)tacus, Cartimandua (f); Cunobelinus, Epilus, Togodumnus, Verica (masc).

TRIBESMAN BARBARIAN, NOMAD, SAVAGE, JOLLIGINKI (Lofting), YAHOO (Gulliver's Travels, Swift). CLANSMAN, NATIVE, **celeb**: AMHARA (Af), ANGLE (Eur), ARAB (Af), ASHANTI (Af), BANTU (S Af), BARI (Af), BASUTO (Af), BEJA (Af), BELGA (Eur), BERBER (NW Af), CHAOUIA (Af), COSSACK (Russ), DINKA (Af), DORDAN (Gk), FRANK (Eur), GAUL (Fr), GOTH (Eur), HAUSA (Af), HITTITE (bibl), HOTTENTOT (Af), HUN (Asia), HYKSOS (Egy), IBO (Af), JUTE (Eur), KABYLES (Af), KHOI (Af), KIKUYU (Af), LINGALA (Af), MAGYAR (Eur), MASAI (Af), MEDE (bibl), MONGOL (Asia), MOOR (NW Af [Othello]), NAMA (Af), NILOTES (Af), NUBIAN (Af), NUER (Af), OSTROGOTH (Eur), PARTHIAN (Asia), PHOENICIAN (bibl), PYGMY (Af), SAN (Af), SAXON (Eur), SOMALI (Af), SOTHO (Af), SPARTAN (Gk), SWAHILI (Af), TARTAR (Russ), TUAREG (Af), TURKANA (Af), VANDAL (Eur), VISIGOTH (Eur), XHOSA (Af), YORUBA (Af), ZOUAVE (Af), ZULU (Af) [*American Indian*; impi; *Israel*; and see *TRIBE*].

TRICKY ADROIT, CRAFTY, DECEITFUL, DELICATE, TICKLISH; **N Am god** = *raven*. RESOURCEFUL. *CARD GAME* (bridge, solo, whist etc; crypt).

TRIFLE BAGATELLE, CIPHER, MODICUM [*Autolycus*]. NEGLECT, PLAY/TOY WITH, SKIMP. CONFECTION, PUDDING, SWEET. PEWTER.

TRILBY *HAT*. BOOK (Gerald du Maurier, *inspiration*).

TRIM NEAT, SMART, *SPRUCE*, TIDY. ADORNMENT, DECORATION, PIPING. BALANCE, BALLAST; *TUNE*. CUT, PARE, PRUNE, WHITTLE. FIT, GOOD SHAPE. *SERVANT* (Sterne).

TRIP EXPEDITION, JOURNEY, OUTING, TOUR, VOYAGE. FALL, STUMBLE. RELEASE, TRIGGER. HALLUCINATION (drugs).

TRIPOD STAND, STOOL, TABLE (3 feet; hence YARD, crypt). ALTAR (*Delphi*).

TRIPPER GROCKLE, HOLIDAYMAKER, RUBBERNECK, TOURIST. DANCER (crypt). TRIGGER (crypt). PROJECTION, SNAG (crypt). DRUG TAKER.

TROCHEE *FOOT* (–).

TROJAN 1. FIGHTER. CITIZEN OF TROY. 2. **Pl** = minor *planets*.

TROT GAIT, PACE, RUN. FISHING LINE. PRODUCE. COMMIE, *RED*, REVOLUTIONARY. DAVID COPPERFIELD (*Dickens*).

TROUBLE *Anag*. ADO, BOTHER, DO, FUSS, RIOT, TO-DO. AIL, FIX. WIFE (*rh sl*).

TROUSERS BAGS, DUCKS, PANTS (US), SHORTS, SLACKS.

TROY 1. System of weight *measure* (precious metals). 2. HISSARLAK, also ILIUM. According to *Homer's* Iliad, a city of Asia Minor, scene of 10 years' war (*c.* 1250 B.C.), when Gks under *Agamemnon* beat the Trojans under King Priam's s Paris (whose abduction of *Helen*, w of Menelaus, started it all), by means of hiding soldiers (as suggested by *Ulysses*) in a wooden horse, which was taken into the city by the unsuspecting defenders. 3. Scene of T and C (*Shak*).

TRUE ACCURATE, GENUINE, REAL; STRAIGHT. CONSTANT, HONEST, LOYAL (**opp** = *false*). *DOG* (John Peel). 'VERA'.

TRUMPERY BRIC-A-BRAC, NONSENSE, RUBBISH. DELUSIVE, SHALLOW, WORTHLESS. BRIDGE, WHIST (crypt); RUFFING (crypt).

TRUMPETER BUGLER, MUSICIAN. AGAMI, *BIRD*, CRANE, ELEPHANT, *FISH*, HERON, HOOPOE, PIGEON, *RAIL*, SWAN.

TRURO Episcopal sig = TRURON. CITY (SW Eng).

TRURON *Episcopal sig* of TRURO.

TRUTH 1. ACCURACY, HONESTY, LOYALTY. 2. **Egy god** = MAAT.

TRY FOUR POINTS (hence E, N, S and W, crypt); SCORE, TOUCHDOWN. ATTEMPT, EXPERIMENT, ESSAY, GO, STAB, TEST. INVESTIGATE. ARRAIGN, JUDGE.

TRYING ATTEMPTING. IRRITATING. *RUGBY* (crypt). IN COURT, JUDGING (crypt).

TT ABSTAINER, DRY, *PUSSYFOOT*, RECHABITE, TEETOTAL [Richard *Turner*; W. E. Johnson]. BIKE RACE, MANX RACE. GAUGE (model rly). MILK. DOUBLET (crypt).

TUB FATSO, FATTY. BATH. BARREL, VAT [*Diogenes*].

TUC TRADES *UNION* CONGRESS, WORKERS [Ruskin College]. Dn = CUT UP, hence CHOPSTICKS (crypt). CUT BACK (crypt).

TUESDAY TUES. Day of Tiw, A-Sax *god* of war. ~'s **child** = full
of grace. [Shrove ~; Solomon *Grundy*].

TUN (s/l *ton*). *MEASURE* (beer, wine).

TUNA *FISH*, TUNNY. EEL (NZ). PRICKLY PEAR.

TUNE AIR, CATCH, LILT, REFRAIN, *SONG*, STRAIN.
ADJUST, BREATHE ON, *TRIM*, TWEAK (mech).

TUP *SHEEP* (male), RAM. PUT UP (dn, crypt).

TUPPENCE DD, PP (crypt).

TURK Turkey, ~ish (abbr); (**car plate** = TR).

TURKISH OFFICIAL AG(H)A, BEG, BEY, DEY, EGA, EMIR,
PASHA, SATRAP, WALI [*Eastern official*].

TURN (s/l tern). 1. T, TN. U ~. ADAPT, CONVERT, DIVERT,
INVERT, REVERSE, REVOLVE, TWIST, *WHEEL*.
BEND, CORNER, DEFLECTION. CHANGE, CURDLE,
NAUSEATE, SHOCK. SPASM, STATE. CHARACTER,
DISPOSITION, TENDENCY. DRIVE, RIDE, STROLL,
WALK. ACT, PERFORMANCE. *GO*, OCCASION,
OPPORTUNITY, PRIVILEGE, PURPOSE, SPELL, *TIME*,
TRICK [Buggins' ~ (*unseen*)]. COIL, WRITHE. 2. Word reads
backwards, e.g. **Gratuities for the turnspit** (4) = TIPS; or, in
conjunction with another word, e.g. **It turns colour when sleepy**
(5) = TI*RED.

TURNER 1. ACROBAT, ACTOR, ARTISTE, GYMNAST,
PERFORMER, TUMBLER. CARPENTER, *PAINTER*,
WOODWORKER [*Company* (livery)]. AXLE, LATHE,
ROTOR, SPINNER, TOP, WHEEL (crypt). BIRD. 2. Reverse,
or turn, word, e.g. **Jolly Mr Turner** = RM. 3. Richard ~, who
coined the word *teetotal*, because he stammered when describing
t-total abstinence.

TURNING CORNER, JUNCTION; T. MACHINING,
WOODWORKING. ACTING, PERFORMING (crypt). **Pl** =
SHAVINGS (mech).

TURNKEY *GAOLER*. YEK (crypt).

TURN-OUT APPEAR. PRODUCE. DRESS, GEAR, KIT,
OUTFIT, RIG. TOU, UTO (anag, crypt); RUNT, TRUN
(anag, crypt).

TURNOVER *Anag*. ROLL, UPSET. BUSINESS,
THROUGHPUT. PIE, TART. REVO, ROVE, VORE etc
(crypt).

TURN UP APPEAR, ARRIVE. [Micawber, *Dickens*]. PLOUGH,
PLOW (US), TILL. CUFF (clothes). PU (crypt). NRUT
(dn, crypt).

TURQUOISE *GEM*, PRECIOUS STONE (blue/green). *Birthstone* (December). *COLOUR* (blue/green).

TV BOX, BROADCASTING, IDIOT'S LANTERN, MEDIUM, SET, TELEVISION, TELLY. BBC, IBA, ITA, ITV.

TWAIN Mark (pseudonym of Samuel Langhorne Clemens); *writer* (US) b 1835; became riverboat pilot, then took to journalism ('mark ~' indicates the two fathoms' necessary depth for riverboats); mar Olivia Langdon (2 d, Susy and Jean). **Books**: The Celeb Jumping *Frog* of Calaveras County (first); The Innocents Abroad; Roughing It (autobiographical); The Gilded Age (with C. D. Warner); A Tramp Abroad; The Prince and the Pauper (Prince Ed – later ED VI – changes place with Tom Canty, his *double*, and only regains the throne when he can produce the Great *Seal* – which Tom has been using as a nutcracker); The Adventures of Tom Sawyer (with Huckleberry Finn, Tom witnesses a murder by Injun Joe, and they hide; later the Indian is found dead and they obtain his money); Life on the Mississippi (autobiographical); The Adventures of Huckleberry Finn (Tom and Huck escape on a raft down the Mississippi with Jim the *slave*); Pudd'nhead Wilson; Personal Recollections of *Joan* of Arc (as though written by 'Sieur Louis de Comte' and translated by 'Jean François Alden'); Following the Equator; The American Claimant; Tom Sawyer Abroad; Tom Sawyer Detective; The Mysterious Stranger.

TWELVE See *number*. DODECA, DOZEN, XII. *Apostles* in song. *Lords* a-leaping in *Christmas song*.

TWENTY See *number*. SCORE, XX, JACKSON (sl).

TWENTY-FIVE See *number*. £~ (PONY). XXV.

TWICE 1. BIS, ENCORE. TWO TIMES, DOUBLY. 2. Letter or word repeated, e.g. **The priest is twice a small boy** = A*A*RON; but beware **Is twice the river**, which is not THE*THE, but = IS*IS.

TWICKENHAM *RUGBY GROUND*; TRYING PLACE (crypt). *THAMES BRIDGE*.

TWIN 1. DUPLICATE, EXACT *COPY*, FACSIMILE, MIRROR IMAGE, REPLICA. TWO-ENGINED (Av). COUPLE, PAIR. 'THOMAS'. 2. Two children born at the same time; **celeb**: AMOREL/BELPHOEBE (Faerie Queene, Spenser), ANTIPHOLUS bros (C of E, *Shak*), *APOLLO/ARTEMIS* (myth), *CASTOR/POLLUX* (myth), CHEERYBLES (Nich Nick, *Dickens*), CORSICAN BROS (Dumas), DROMIO bros (C of E, *Shak*), ESAU/JACOB (bibl), DIOSCURI, *GEMINI* (stars), *HELEN/CLYTEMNESTRA*

(myth), *ROMULUS/REMUS* (myth), TWEEDLEDUM/
TWEEDLEDEE (*Alice* in Wonderland, Lewis Carroll),
VALENTINE/ORSON (Legends of Charlemagne),
VIOLA/SEBASTIAN (12 N, *Shak*). 3. *Constellation* (*Gemini*);
sign of the *Zodiac* (3rd).

TWIST *Anag.* CHANGE, DISTORT, WARP. CURL. *DIVE.*
INTERWEAVE, SPIRAL. ROPE, TWINE. *DANCE.*
SWINDLE. TOBACCO. OLIVER ~ [ask for more; *Dickens*].

TWISTER *Anag.* CHEAT, SWINDLER. ROPE-, THREAD-
MAKER. BALL, DELIVERY, SPINNER. TORNADO,
WIND (US). EEL, *SERPENT*, *SNAKE* (crypt).

TWO See *number*. BIS, DUO, TWAIN. YELLOW BALL
(snooker). Lilywhite *boys* in *song*. Turtle *doves* in *Christmas song*.

~ **BITS** 25 cents (US), from two bits, or pinches, of gold dust as
payment in a bar during the gold rush.

~ **HUNDRED** CC, TWO TON.

~ **PENCE** DD, PP.

~ **THOUSAND** See *number*. MM. KK (crypt).

~ **GUINEAS** *CLASSIC*: LMMC.

TYNESIDE NE (crypt).

TYPE CHARACTERISTIC, EXAMPLE, GENUS, KIND,
SORT. TAP, WORD-PROCESS. GOTHIC, ITALIC, PICA,
ROMAN.

TYPEFACE Design, size or style of printing; *FACE*, LOWER/
UPPER CASE; **sizes** (in order, smallest first): EXCELSIOR,
BRILLIANT, *GEM*, *DIAMOND*, *PEARL*, *AGATE*
(US), *RUBY*, NONPAREIL, MINION, BREVIER,
BOURGEOIS, ELITE, LONG PRIMER, SMALL PICA,
CICERO, *ENGLISH*, COLUMBIAN, GREAT PRIMER,
PARAGON, *CANON*; **styles**: ANTIQUE, *BASKERVILLE*,
BOLD, CASLON, CENTURY, CLARENDON, CURSIVE,
DORIC, *ELECTRA*, FUTURA, GARAMOND, GOTHIC,
GRANJON, IONIC, ITALIC, JANSON, OLD ENGLISH,
ROMAN, SANS SERIF, SCRIPT, *TIMES*, TYPEWRITER.

TYPHON Gk myth *monster* with 100 heads; embodiment of
earthquakes and volcanoes, breathing fire and hurricane winds.
Father of *Chim(a)era* and the inclement *winds*.

TYPHOON STORM, *WIND. AIRCRAFT*, FIGHTER.

TYPICAL CHARACTERISTIC, SYMBOLIC. PRINTING,
TYPESETTING (crypt).

TYRANT *BULLY*, OPPRESSOR, THUG; **celeb**: *ATTILA*;
CALIGULA; *CERCYON*; DIONYSIUS; GELON, HIERO

(Syracuse); *NERO*; PHALARIS (Rom).
TYRE (s/l *tire*). CROSSPLY, RADIAL, SOLID. *BIBLICAL
TOWN*, PORT (Phoen) [Sidon].

U (s/l *ewe*, you). URANIUM (*chem*). UNIVERSAL (film
censorship). UPPER CLASS; ACCEPTABLE, DONE,
SUPERIOR, TOP (**opp** = *low*). BEND, *TURN*.
UD UT DICTUM; AS DIRECTED.
UGLY (s/l ugli). *Anag.* DISCREDITABLE, UNPLEASANT,
VILE; THREATENING, UNPROMISING. REPULSIVE,
UNPLEASING; DUCHESS (*Alice*); ~ DUCKLING (*swan*,
Andersen) (**opp** = *attractive*). BONNET, SHADE.
UHT ULTRA HEAT TREATED (milk).
UK UNITED KINGDOM.
ULSTER *HERALD.* KING OF ARMS. COAT. NI, N
IRELAND. *UNIVERSITY.*
ULT ULTIMO. LAST MONTH.
ULTIMATE FINAL, LAST, OMEGA, Z. MAXIMUM.
FUNDAMENTAL, PRIMARY.
ULYSSES (Gk = ODYSSEUS). 1. Rom myth s of Laertes, mar to
Penelope. In the Odyssey, *Homer* describes his return from the
Trojan war, how he blinded Polyphemus, one of the *Cyclopes*,
then navigated between the *monsters* on the rocks *Scylla* and
Charybdis, and was tempted by the *sirens*. Only he could bend
the black bow of Eurytus. 2. T and C character (*Shak*).
UMBRAGE INJURY, OFFENCE, SLIGHT. SHADE.
UMLAUT ACCENT (¨).
UN 1. UNITED NATIONS, A FRENCH (crypt). 2. As prefix
indicates 'lacking'. 3. Often implies anag when used as a prefix,
e.g. 'undone', 'uneven' or 'unwrapped'. 4. Remove synonym for
word indicated, e.g. **Uncertain gratification** (4) = PLEA(sure) or
Uncatalogued medallist (5) = MEDAL****.
UNCIVIL ILL-MANNERED, IMPOLITE, RUDE. MILITARY
(crypt).
UNCLE RELATION [*Remus*; Sam]. PAWNBROKER; POPIST,
POPPER (crypt) [pledge, three balls]. BOB (catchphrase).
UNDER 1. BELOW, BENEATH, LESS THAN, LOWER.
2. Word under another in dn clue, e.g. **Little man has under 100**
(4) = C*HAS. 3. Indicates what goes under, or beneath, the word

indicated, e.g. **Underclothes** (4) = BODY or SKIN; or **Underrider** (6) = SADDLE.

~ **CANVAS** CAMPING. SAILING. INTENT (crypt), hence TE . . . NT.

UNDERCURRENT 1. INFLUENCE. HIDDEN ACTIVITY. 2. **Any of the rivers of the Underworld** = *ACHERON, COCYTUS, LETHE, PYRIPHLEGETHON, STYX.*

UNDERSTANDING 1. COMPREHENSION, *GRIP*, INTELLIGENCE. AGREEMENT, CONVENTION, HARMONY. 2. Anything beneath the legs (crypt), e.g. DAIS, FEET, *FOOT*, PAWS, PLATFORM, SHOES, SOLES, *STAGE.*

UNDERTAKER BURIAL/FUNERAL DIRECTOR; **celeb**: WILLIAM BANTING (dietician), MOULD (Chuzzle, *Dickens*), OMER (Copperfield, *Dickens*). DOER, GUARANTOR (crypt). PROCUROR (arch).

UNDERWEAR UNDERCLOTHES; e.g. BELT, *BLOOMERS*, BRA, BRIEFS, BUST-BODICE, CAMISOLE, COMBS, CORSET, *DRAWERS*, *GIRDLE*, HOSE, KNICKERS, PANTS, PANTIES, SHIFT, SOCKS, SPENCERS, STOCKINGS, *TIGHTS*, UNDERPANTS, VEST. But also: PANTS, SHOES, SKIRT, SOCKS, TROUSERS or any garment worn on nether part of the body (crypt).

UNDERWORLD ABODE OF THE DEAD, *HELL*, NETHER REGIONS, **specifically**: ABADDON (Hebr), ABYSM, ABYSS (Heb), EBLIS (Asia), EREBUS (Gk myth), GEHENNA (bibl), *HADES* (Gk myth), INFERNO (Dante), ORCUS (Rom myth), TARTARUS (Gk myth) [asphodel meadows; *Cerberus, Charon, Hecate* and, for all ~ rivers, see *Styx*]. **Gods: Gk** = *HADES;* **Rom** = *DIS*, ORCUS, *PLUTO*; **Egy** = OSIRIS, SERAPIS; **goddesses: Gk** = *HECATE, PERSEPHONE*; **Rom** = PROSERPINE; **judges** = AEACUS, MINOS, RHADAMANTHYS. **Hebr** = BOR, SHAHAT, SHEOL; **Nor** = HEL; ANTIPODES. ATLAS (crypt). GANGLAND, ORGANIZED CRIME.

UNDERWRITE ACCEPT LIABILITY. SIGN (crypt).

UNEARTH DISCLOSE, DISCOVER, FIND (**opp** = *hide*). DIG UP. FUSE, SHORT CIRCUIT (crypt).

UNEATABLE BAD, INEDIBLE. *FOX* [*unspeakable* (Wilde)].

UNFAIR BIASED, CHEATING. ROUGH, UNEVEN. *UGLY.* BRUNETTE, DARK, REDHEAD (crypt).

UNIFORM CONSTANT, SAME, UNVARYING.

CONFORMING. MILITARY/SCHOOL DRESS (**opp** = mufti, civvies). *SELF.*

UNION 1. COALITION, JUNCTION. *MARRIAGE,* MATRIMONY, WEDDING, WEDLOCK. ENGLAND/SCOTLAND; GB/IRELAND. AGREEMENT, CONCORD. PIPE JOINT. 2. WORKERS' ASSOCIATION; **celeb**: APEX (professional and executive), ASLEF (locomotive *engineers* and *firemen*), ASTMS (scientific technical and *managerial*), AUEW (*engineering* workers), BALPA (air line *pilots*), COHSE (health service), ETU (*electricians*), GMBU (boilermakers), ISTC (iron and steelworkers), NALGO (local government officers), NATSOPA (operative printers), NFU (farmers), NGA (printers), NUJ (*journalists*), NUM (*miners*), NUPE (public employees), NUR (*railwaymen*), NUS (seamen, students), NUT (teachers), POEU (Post Office engineers), SLADE (graphical and allied trades), SOLIDARITY (Polish workers), TGW (*transport* and general workers), *TUC* (Trades Union Congress). **Foreign** ~s: ARTEL (USSR co-op); TEAMSTERS (US). [*Livery* companies. Trade guilds. Ruskin College (Tolpuddle Martyrs)].

~ **CARD** MARRIAGE LICENCE (crypt).

~ **MAN** TRADE UNIONIST, WORKER. (BRIDE) GROOM, BEST MAN, USHER (crypt).

UNIT I, INDIVIDUAL, *ONE.* FACTORY. And see *International units.*

UNIVERSAL *U* (film *censorship*). GENERAL, WIDESPREAD. PAN-.

UNIVERSITY FURTHER EDUCATION ESTABLISHMENT. BAs. **Celeb**:

	3-letters	
CUA (US)	MIT (US)	USC (US)

	4-letters	
BATH (Eng)	IOWA (US)	UCLA (US)
CITY (Eng)	*KENT* (Eng)	UWCM (Wal)
CUNY (US)	*OPEN* (Eng)	YALE (US)
HULL (Eng)	*OXON* (Eng)	YORK (Can, Eng)

	5-letters	
ASTON (Eng)	KEELE (Eng)	LEEDS (Eng)
ESSEX (Eng)	LAVAL (Can)	PADUA (It)

POONA (Ind)   UMIST (Eng)   WALES (Wal)

6-letters

ACADIA (Can)
BANGOR (Wal)
BOMBAY (Ind)
BRUNEL (Eng)
DUBLIN (Ire)
DUNDEE (Sc)
DURHAM (Eng)
EXETER (Eng)
LONDON (Eng)
MCGILL (Can)

OTTAWA (Can)
OXFORD (Eng)
PRAGUE (Cz)
QUEBEC (Can)
QUEEN'S (Can, Ire)
SURREY (Eng)
SUSSEX (Eng)
ULSTER (Ire)
VASSAR (US)

7-letters

ALBERTA (Can)
BELFAST (Ire)
BOLOGNA (It)
BRISTOL (Eng)
CALGARY (Can)
CARDIFF (Wal)
CHICAGO (US)
CORNELL (US)
FLORIDA (US)
GLASGOW (Sc)
HARVARD (US)

LEIPZIG (Ger)
LOUVAIN (Belg)
LUCKNOW (Ind)
MONCTON (Can)
NEW YORK (US)
READING (Eng)
SALERNO (It)
SALFORD (Eng)
SWANSEA (Wal)
TORONTO (Can)
WARWICK (Eng)

8-letters

ABERDEEN (Sc)
ADELAIDE (Aus)
AUCKLAND (NZ)
BRADFORD (Eng)
CALCUTTA (Ind)
CAPE TOWN (SA)
CARLETON (Can)
CARNEGIE (US)
COLUMBIA (US)
FLINDERS (SA)
FREIBURG (Ger)

ILLINOIS (US)
MANITOBA (Can)
MICHIGAN (US)
MONTREAL (Can)
ST DAVID'S (Wal)
SORBONNE (Fr)
STAMFORD (Eng)
STIRLING (Sc)
SYRACUSE (US)
TASMANIA (Aus)
VICTORIA (Aus)

9-letters

CAMBRIDGE (Eng)   DALHOUSIE (Can)

EDINBURGH (Sc)
FRANKFURT (Ger)
GOTTINGEN (Ger)
JAMES COOK (Aus)
LANCASTER (Eng)
LEICESTER (Eng)
LIVERPOOL (Eng)
MELBOURNE (Aus)
MINNESOTA (US)

NEWCASTLE (Eng)
NOTRE DAME (Can)
PRINCETON (US)
ROCHESTER (Eng)
ST ANDREWS (Sc)
SHEFFIELD (Eng)
SINGAPORE (S'pore)
WISCONSIN (US)

10+ letters

ABERYSTWYTH (Wal)
BIRMINGHAM (Eng)
BUCKINGHAM (Eng,
   pte)
CALIFORNIA (US)
CANTERBURY (NZ)
CINCINNATI (US)
CITY COLLEGE (US)
CONNECTICUT (US)
EAST ANGLIA (Eng)
GOETTINGEN (Ger)
HEIDELBERG (Ger)
HERIOT-WATT (Sc)
LETHBRIDGE (Can)
LOUGHBOROUGH
   (Eng)

MANCHESTER (Eng)
MASSACHUSETTS (US)
MILTON KEYNES (Eng)
MOUNT ALLISON (Can)
NEW BRUNSWICK (Can)
NEW ENGLAND (Aus)
NOTTINGHAM (Eng)
PENNSYLVANIA (US)
PITTSBURGH (US)
SASKATCHEWAN (Can)
SHERBROOKE (Can)
SIMON FRASER (Can)
SOUTHAMPTON (Eng)
S CALIFORNIA (US)
STRATHCLYDE (Sc)
WASHINGTON (US)

UNIVERSITY COLLEGE Colleges of Cambridge (C) and Oxford
(O):

3-letters

NEW (O)

5-letters

CAIUS (C)
CLARE (C)

JESUS (C, O)
KEBLE (O)

KINGS (C)
ORIEL (O)

6-letters

DARWIN (C)
EXETER (O)
GIRTON (C)

MERTON (O)
QUEENS' (C)
QUEEN'S (O)

SELWYN (C)
WADHAM (O)

7-letters

BALLIOL (O)	*LINCOLN* (O)	ST HUGH'S (O)
CHRIST'S (C)	NEWNHAM (C)	ST JOHN'S (O)
DOWNING (C)	ST ANNE'S (O)	TRINITY (C, O)

8-letters

ALL SOULS (O)	MAGDALEN (O)
EMMANUEL (C)	PEMBROKE (C, O)
GONVILLE (C)	ROBINSON (C)
HERTFORD (O)	ST HILDA'S (O)
HOMERTON (C)	ST PETER'S (O)

9-letters

BRASENOSE (O)	MAGDALENE (C)
CHURCHILL (C)	*WORCESTER* (O)

10+ letters

CHRISTCHURCH (O)	ST CATHARINE'S (C)
CORPUS CHRISTI (C, O)	ST EDMUND HALL (O)
FITZWILLIAM (C)	SIDNEY SUSSEX (C)
LADY MARGARET	SOMERVILLE (O)
HALL (O)	TRINITY HALL (C)
PETERHOUSE (C)	UNIVERSITY (O)

UNIVERSITY GRANT BURSARY, EXHIBITION, SCHOLARSHIP. DEGREE (crypt).

UNKNOWN STRANGE, UNFAMILIAR. X,Y (maths).

UNLIMITED 1. GREAT, UNRESTRICTED, VAST. 2. Delete both end letters, e.g. **Old money is unlimited cash** = *AS*.

UNLOCKED OPENED, UNBOLTED, UNFASTENED. *CUT*. DISTRESSED, SCALPED, SHORN (crypt).

UNMARRIED 1. BACHELOR, SINGLE, SPINSTER. 2. Delete **m** or **wed** from clue, e.g. **Unmarried man** = *AN (crypt).

UNORDERED *Anag.* HIGGLEDY-PIGGLEDY, RANDOM, SCATTERED, UNTIDY. SPONTANEOUS, VOLUNTARY. LAY, NON-CLERICAL (crypt).

UNQUALIFIED 1. UNRESTRICTED. INCOMPETENT. UNTRAINED. COMPLETE, PERFECT, UTTER. 2. Remove any letters implying technical or educational qualification (BA, FCA, MB etc), e.g. **Early South African unqualified bomber** (4) = BO**ER.

UNQUIET 1. UNEASY. NOISY, F. 2. Delete any indication of quiet from clue (e.g. **p**, **sh** etc), e.g. **Unquiet tipper leads to row** (4) = TI**ER.

UNREADY UNPREPARED. LACKING ADVICE, RASH; ETHELRED.

UNSAINTLY 1. UNHOLY. 2. Delete letters **st** from word, e.g. **Ernest is unsaintly bird** (4) = ERNE**.

UNSEEN 1. INVISIBLE, NOT NOTICED, NOT READ [*eminence grise*]. 2. ~ characters in literature: BUGGINS (~ turn); BUNBURY (The Importance of Being Earnest, *Wilde*); *MRS GRUNDY* (Thos Morton); MRS HARRIS (Chuzzle, *Dickens*); HARVEY (*rabbit*, Mary Chase); INVISIBLE MAN (H. G. Wells); LT KIJE (Troika, Prokofiev); MACAVITY (*cat*, T. S. Eliot); MRS PARTINGTON (Sydney Smith), and (all *Shak*) DARK LADY, DE BOYS, FULVIA, KEEP DOWN, HISPERIA, ISIDORE, RAGOZINE, ROSALINE, SYCORAX, VARRO.

UNSPEAKABLE OBJECTIONABLE, REPULSIVE. HUNT, HUNTERS, HUNTSMEN [*uneatable* (*Wilde*)].

UNSUPPORTED 1. SECONDARY, SOLO, UNAIDED, UNSUBSTANTIATED. DESTITUTE. CANTILEVER. 2. Remove synonym for 'support' (bra, guy, prop, stay), e.g. **Prohibit unsupported staybar** (3) = ****BAR.

UNWATERED 1. DRY, PARCHED; DESERT, NOT IRRIGATED. NEAT, UNDILUTED. 2. Delete synonym for **water** from clue (hoo, sea etc), e.g. **Volume of unwatered choochoo** = C***C***.

UNWILLING RELUCTANT. INTESTATE (crypt).

UP 1. ON HIGH, TO HIGHER PLACE (**opp** = *down*). AT UNIVERSITY. FINISHED. RISEN. MOUNTED, RIDING, SADDLED. UTTAR PRADESH (*India*). 2. Dn answer reads backwards, or upwards, e.g. **Dickens lived up** (5) = DEVIL.

UPAS ANTIAR, *TREE*. EVIL INFLUENCE, MALEVOLENCE. SA (dn, crypt).

UPBRAID CHIDE, SCOLD. PUT UP HAIR [bun] (crypt).

UPHOLD 1. CONFIRM, MAINTAIN, *SUPPORT*. 2. In dn answer, word holds another inside, and one or both reads backwards, e.g. **Every account he upholds** (4) = E*AC*H.

UPIS 1. Egy chief *goddess*, and of *NATURE*. 2. *SI* (dn, crypt).

UP-MARKET SOPHISTICATED. TRAM (dn, crypt).

UPPER HIGHER, TOP. SHOE TOP, VAMP. REP (dn, crypt).

UPPER CLASS U; ARISTOCRACY, GENTRY. FIRST FORM, SIXTH FORM, SENIOR.

UPRIGHT CORRECT, RIGHTEOUS. VERTICAL (**opp** =
leaning). PIANO. ROMAN TYPE. TR (dn, crypt).
UPSET *Anag.* 1. CAPSIZE, DISTURB, OVERTURN, SPILL.
ANXIOUS, WORRIED [*parrot*]. TES (dn, crypt). 2. Answer
reads up (dn). 3. RIDING SCHOOL (crypt).
UPSTART NOUVEAU RICHE. U (crypt).
URANIA 1. Gk myth, one of the 9 *Muses* (astronomy). 2. A minor
PLANET.
URANIDS Gk myth sons of *Uranus* and *Gaea*, identified with the
GIGANTES, who conquered the *Titans* when the latter made
war on the gods; they were *monsters* with 100 arms and 50 heads:
AEGAEON or BRIAEREUS, COTTUS and GYGES or GYES.
URANIUM *METAL*; U (*chem*).
URANUS Gk *god* of HEAVEN, f (by Ge) of the *Titans* and the
Uranids. When he was k, *Aphrodite* sprang from the sea foam
where his limbs were thrown.
URGE ABET, ADVOCATE, EGG, ENCOURAGE, ENTREAT,
EXHORT, IMPEL, SET ON, SICK, SPUR, STIMULATE.
DRIVE, DESIRE, WISH, YEARNING.
URIAH HEEP (David Copperfield, *Dickens* ['umble]). HITTITE.
US WE (**opp** = them). UNITED STATES OF AMERICA.
USA UNITED STATES OF AMERICA (*car plate*).
USS US SHIP, *BOAT*.
USSR SOVIET RUSSIA (as opposed to **Russ** = Russia).
UTHERSON *KING ARTHUR* (son of Uther Pendragon)
[*Guinevere, Lancelot, Round Table*].
UTTER EXPRESS, SAY, SPEAK. CIRCULATE, ISSUE
(money). COMPLETE, TOTAL, *UNQUALIFIED*.
UTTERLY COMPLETELY, TOTALLY. *Sounds like* . . . ,
pronounced like . . . (crypt).

V VANADIUM (*chem*). VATICAN CITY (*car plate*). VERSUS,
VS; AGAINST. VICTORY SIGN. SEE, VIDE. VOL(UME).
VOLTS. *FIVE*.
VALE CHANNEL, VALLEY (**opp** = *hill*). FAREWELL.
VALHALLA Nor myth; *Odin's* great hall, the house of warriors
slain in battle [*Valkyries*].
VALKYRIES Nor myth; *Odin's* handmaidens, who selected those
to be slain in battle and thus go to *Valhalla*.
VAMP ADVENTURESS, FLIRT. ALLURE, EXPLOIT,

SEDUCE. UPPER (shoe). FURBISH, REPAIR.
IMPROVISE, STRUM (mus).
VANADIUM *METAL*; V (*chem*).
VARIETY *Anag.* DIVERSITY, CHANGE. SPECIMEN, TYPE.
SHOWBIZ, *THEATRE*, VAUDEVILLE. [spice of life].
VAT CISTERN, CONTAINER, TANK, TUB, VESSEL. TAX.
VAULT JUMP, LEAP, *SPRING*. *ARCH*, CELLAR, CRYPT,
FIRMAMENT.
VEGETABLE 1. MONOTONOUS, UNEVENTFUL.
APATHETIC, CATALEPTIC, INCAPACITATED.
2. PLANTLIFE (**comps** = animal, mineral or abstract).
Pl = GREENS. **Types:**

3-letters

COS	OCA	SOY	YAM
DAL	PEA	UDO	ZEA

4-letters

BEAN	DOHL	KOHL	RAPE
BEET	EDDO	LEEK	SOYA
COLE	FABA	OKRA	SPUD
CORN	KALE	*PEAR*	

5-letters

APIUM	CRESS	ONION	PULSE
CHARD	MAIZE	ORACH	SWEDE
CHICH	NAVEW	PEASE	TUBER

6-letters

BATATA	ENDIVE	PORRET	SPROUT
CARROT	LENTIL	*POTATO*	*SQUASH*
CELERY	LOMENT	PYROLA	TOMATO
CYNARA	MARROW	RADISH	TURNIP
DAUCUS	PHASEL	RUNNER	

7-letters

CABBAGE	LETTUCE	SALSIFY	SHALLOT
CHICORY	PARSNIP	SEAKALE	SPINACH
GHERKIN	PUMPKIN	*SEAWEED*	TRUFFLE

8-letters

BEETRAVE	BEETROOT	BORECOLE

BRASSICA	CHOW-CHOW	CUCUMBER
CELERIAC	COLERAPE	EGG-PLANT
CHICK-PEA	COLEWORT	

9 + letters

ARTICHOKE	COURGETTE
ASPARAGUS	FRENCH BEAN
AUBERGINE	JERUSALEM
BROAD BEAN	ARTICHOKE
BRUSSELS SPROUT	MANGE-TOUT
CAULIFLOWER	RUNNER BEAN
COLOGASSI	SWEET CORN

VEHICLE AUTO, CAB, *CAR*, *CARRIAGE*, LORRY. BUS, CHARABANC, MINI-BUS, MINI-CAB. TRUCK, VAN. AIRBUS, AIRCRAFT, PLANE. *BOAT*.

VENETIAN OF VENICE; MARCO (POLO). BLIND.

Venez Venezuela.

VENUE RENDEZVOUS. GAME PARK, MATCH SITE; AWAY, HOME. GROUND (*cricket*, *football*, *rugby*, *tennis*).

VENUS 1. Rom *goddess* of *LOVE*; m of *Aeneas* by Anchises and of *Cupid* by Jupiter. **Gk** = *APHRODITE*, HESPER (US); **Phoen** = ASTARTE; **Nor** = *FREYA*; **Bab** = ISHTAR; **Egy** = *ISIS*. 2. *PLANET*. As *evening star* = *HESPERUS*; as *morning star* = *LUCIFER*.

VERSE POEM, POETRY, STANZA. FURROW. VERSICLE (bibl).

VERSED EDUCATED, SCHOOLED, *TRAINED*. POETIC, IN POETRY (crypt).

VERSION *Anag*. ACCOUNT. BOOK. VARIANT. TURNING (crypt).

VERSUS V, VS; AGAINST.

VERT VERTICAL. GREEN (*herald*).

VERY BIG OS.

VERY LOUD FF.

VESSEL *BOAT* (q.v.), *CRAFT*, SHIP; HMS, SS, USS. **Celeb**: ARK (Noah), BEAGLE (*Darwin*), *BELLEROPHON* (Napoleon), BOUNTY (Bligh), *CINQUE PORTS* (*Crusoe*), *DISCOVERY* (Cook, Scott), ENDEAVOUR (Cook), FRAM (Nansen), GOLDEN HIND (ex Pelican, *Drake*), HISPANIOLA (Treasure Island), USS LINCOLN (*Pinkerton*), MARY ROSE (Henry VIII), MAUD (Amundsen), NINA

(Columbus), PELICAN (later Golden Hind, *Drake*), PEQUOD
(*Ahab*), PINTA (Columbus), RESOLUTION (Cook),
REVENGE (Grenville), *VICTORY* (Nelson). *BOWL*, CROCK,
CRUSE, CUP, DISH, *EWER*, FLAGON, GLASS, LAVER,
PAN, POT, STOUP, URN.
VESTA 1. MATCH ®, LUCIFER. 2. Rom *goddess* of the
HEARTH; **Gk** = *HESTIA*. 3. A minor *PLANET*.
VESTMENT *CHURCH DRESS* (q.v.), GARMENT, ROBE.
BLOCKADE, SIEGE (mil; arch).
VETO BAN, BAR. WRONG VOTE (crypt).
VI SIX. VIOLET. BUZZBOMB, DOODLEBUG, FLYING
BOMB, *ROCKET*, *WEAPON*.
VICTOR CONQUEROR, WINNER. *AIRCRAFT*, BOMBER.
VICTORIA 1. *QUEEN*; REGINA; *EMPRESS*. RLY STATION.
CARRIAGE. *LAKE*. *RIVER* (Aus). *STATE* (Aus).
THEATRE. *UNIVERSITY*. 2. Rom *goddess*, eq of *NIKE*.
3. A minor *PLANET*.
VICTORY 1. TRIUMPH, WIN. WARSHIP [Nelson].
CIGARETTE. 2. **Goddesses: Gk** = *NIKE*; **Rom** = VICTORIA.
~ **SIGN** LAUREL, MEDAL, PALM, GARLAND; V.
Viet Vietnam.
VIGORN *Episcopal sig* of WORCESTER.
VINTNER TENTMAKER, WINE MERCHANT; **celeb**:
Benedictines (Dom Pérignon, champagne); Carthusians
(chartreuse); *Chaucer's* f; LEIF ERICSSON (Vinland, N Am);
OMAR KHAYYAM; Romans; CAPT MCARTHUR (Aus);
NABOTH (bibl); NEBUCHADNEZZAR (bibl); NOAH (bibl);
SOLOMON (bibl).
VIOLIN *FIDDLE*, *INSTRUMENT*, ROCTA (mus) [viol, viola];
parts: back, bass bar, belly, block, bout, bridge, button,
fingerboard, fret, head, neck, nut, peg-box, rib, scroll, sound-
hole, string, tail-piece, waist. [Amati, Cremona, Guadagnini,
Guarneri(us), Rocta, Strad(ivarius)].
VIOLINIST FIDDLER; *BOWER*, BOWMAN, SCRAPER
(crypt). *HOLMES*. [Amati, Strad(ivarius)].
VIP VERY IMPORTANT PERSON; *CELEBRITY*, LION,
NOTABLE, *STAR*.
VIPER *ADDER*.
VIRGINITY 1. INNOCENCE (patron saint: Agnes). FLORIMEL
(Faerie Queene, Spenser). 2. **Goddess: Gk** = ARTEMIS.
3. *Constellation* (Virgo); sign of the *Zodiac* (6th).
VIRGO *Constellation* (Virgin); sign of the *Zodiac* (6th).

ASTRAEA (justice).

VIRTUE EXCELLENCE, MORALITY, QUALITY, RIGHTEOUSNESS; CHASTITY; **celeb cases**: *Atalanta, Cassandra, Daphne, Dido, Narcissus, Penelope*. **Cardinal** ~s: FORTITUDE, JUSTICE, PATIENCE, PRUDENCE, TEMPERANCE; **theological** ~s: CHARITY, FAITH, HOPE. **Pl** = 5th of the nine orders of angelology.

VISIT CALL, GO TO SEE, STAY. ATTACK; PUNISH (bibl). BLESS, COMFORT (arch).

VIXEN FOX (*female*). SCOLD, TERMAGANT. *REINDEER*.

VO/VOL VOLUME. BOOKLET, SHORT BOOK (crypt).

VOLCANO ERUPTING MOUNTAIN; HOT SPOT (crypt). [active, dormant, extinct; igneous rock; magma; lava; crater]. **Celeb**: ETNA, FUJIYAMA, MT ST HELENS, KRAKATOA, MAHARA, MAUNA LOA, PARICUTIN, MT PELEE, STROMBOLI, SURTSEY, SUSWA, TANGSHAN, VESUVIUS.

VOLTS V; SHOCKING (crypt).

VOLTURNUS Rom myth SE *WIND*; **Gk** = EUROS.

VOLUME BOOK, TOME, VOL. CAPACITY, CC, CL, GAL, *MEASURE, PECK*.

VOLUNTEER OFFER, UNDERTAKE; ENLIST, JOIN UP (**opp** = conscribe, conscript, *press gang*). Type of snooker. **Pl** = DAD'S ARMY, HOME GUARD, LDV, TA, TERRIERS [*soldiers*].

VOTE BALLOT, CROSS, POLL, X; CHOOSE, ELECT, SUGGEST, VOICE.

VOWEL A, E, I, O, U (Y). Open sound of speech capable of forming a syllable. Word with all ~s in correct order: FACETIOUS; 5-letter word with only vowels: AEAEA (see *Circe*); word with five ~s consecutively: QUEUEING; 6-letter word with no ~s: CRWTHS (instrument), RHYTHM; 9-letter word with only one ~: STRENGTHS. **Opp** = consonant.

VS V; AGAINST, VERSUS. FIVES (crypt).

VULCAN 1. *AIRCRAFT*, BOMBER. 2. Rom *god* of *FIRE*; **Gk** = HEPHAESTUS.

VULGAR 1. COARSE, COMMON, LOW, PLEBEIAN (**opp** = U). FREQUENT, PREVALENT, POPULAR. 2. Use slang or abbreviation, e.g. **Quiet! Isn't Edward vulgar made up like that** (7) = P*AINT*ED.

W WATTS. WED, WEDNESDAY. WEST. WHITE. WICKET.
WIDE. WIFE. WITH. WOLFRAM (*chem*). WOMEN'S (size).
TUNGSTEN (*chem*). *BRIDGE PLAYER.*

WAGE CARRY ON, CONDUCT. REQUITAL. PAY, *SCREW*
[salary].

WAGER COMBATANT (crypt). *BET.* PAID WORKER (crypt).

WAIF ABANDONED CHILD, MITE, SCRAP. TINY TIM.

WAIT (s/l *weight*). ATTEND, AWAIT, REMAIN, *STAY*; **comp** =
see. CAROL SINGER. AMBUSH.

WAITER ATTENDANT, COMMIS, GARÇON, MAITRE
D'HOTEL. RUNNER (Stock Exchange). CAROL SINGER
(crypt). QUEUER (crypt).

Wal Wales, Welsh. The Principality. Cambria, ~n. [*patron saint*].
For ~ counties, see *Division.*

WALK BALL OF CHALK (*rh sl*), FOOTPATH,
PERAMBULATE, PROMENADE, PATH;
CONSTITUTIONAL, OUTING; AMBLE, TRAIPSE. [*Enoch*
'~ed with God'].

WALKER PEDESTRIAN, PERAMBULATOR; 6 proud ~s in
song. WALKING AID.

WALRUS SEA-MAMMAL, MORSE; **male** = *bull*; **female** =
cow; **offspring** = *calf* [seal, sealion]. *Alice* character; **comp** =
carpenter.

WANDERING *Anag.* ERRING, MEANDERING, WINDING
[*Jew*].

WAR *BATTLE*, BELLIGERENCE, CONTENTION, FIGHT,
HOSTILITIES, STRIFE, STRUGGLE (**opp** = *peace*).
Gods: Gk = *ARES*, **Rom** = MARS, **Ger** = TIW; **goddesses**:
Gk = *ATHENE*, PALLAS, **Rom** = *MINERVA*, **Nor** =
BRUNHILDA.

WAR CRY 1. Salvation Army broadsheet. 2. Battlecry used in
action, e.g. BANZAI (Jap); GERONIMO (US para); GUNG
HO (Ch, US); HARAMBEE (Kenya); TO ARMS (gen);
TORA TORA (Jap, Pearl Harbor); VAE VICTIS (Rom); UP
GUARDS AND AT 'EM (*Wellington* at Waterloo).

WARD (s/l *warred*). CONFINEMENT, CUSTODY. CHARGE,
MINOR. LOCK FLANGE. DEPARTMENT, DISTRICT,
DIVISION; ROOM; NURSERY (crypt). DEFENCE;
BAILEY. AVERT, PARRY. DRAWBACK (crypt).
CARTOONIST.

WARDER *GAOLER.* DOCTOR, HOUSEMAN, INTERN (US),
NURSE, PATIENT (all crypt).

WAR OFFICE WO; BUNKER, COMMAND POST, OPS ROOM.

WASP *INSECT*; STINGER (crypt). WOMEN'S AIR FORCE (US).

WATCH ATTENTION, GUARD, LOOK-OUT, OBSERVATION, VIGILANCE; CAVE-MAN (crypt). CARE FOR, OBSERVE. DUTY SPELL. STREET PATROL. VIGILANTE [posse]. *CLOCK* (q.v.), (HALF) HUNTER, REPEATER, TIMEPIECE. *Assembly* of nightingales.

WATCH CASE SENTRY BOX (crypt).

WATCHMAN 1. GUARD(IAN), SENTINEL, SENTRY [cave, curfew]. PEEPING TOM, VOYEUR (crypt). SAILOR. HOROLOGIST, JEWELLER (crypt). SPECTATOR (crypt). 2. ~ **of the gods** = HEIMDAL (Nor) [*Cerberus*].

WATER *GULF*, LAKE, RAIN, *RIVER*, *SEA*, SPRING, STREAM, WELL; ADAM'S ALE: HOO (crypt) [Thales, Gk *philosopher*]. DRIBBLE, SALIVATE. DILUTE. **Comp** = *fire*.

~ **CARRIER** 1. AQUEDUCT, GOURD, MAINS, PIPE [Gunga Din (Kipling)]. 2. *Constellation* (Aquarius); sign of the *Zodiac* (11th).

WATERFALL CASCADE, CATARACT, FALLS, RAPIDS [Minnehaha]; **celeb falls:** *ANGEL* (S Am), ANGRABIES (S Af), BOYOMA (W Af), CEDAR (USA), CHURCHILL (Can), *GRAND* (Can), IGUACA (S Am), IROQUOIS (Can), KABALEGA (Af), NGONEYE (Af), NIAGARA (Can/USA), OWEN (Af), PARK (USA), REICHENBACH (Swi, *Holmes*), SIOUX (USA), SMITHS (Can), VICTORIA (Af). RAIN(DROP) (crypt). TEARS (crypt).

WATERLOO *BATTLE*; FINISH, UNDOING. STATION (rly); ~ and City Line = THE DRAIN. THAMES BRIDGE.

WATER SPORTS See *SPORT*.

WATER TOWER MAIN SUPPLY, TANK. TUG (crypt).

WATTS W.

WAVE BREAKER, BRINY, COMBER, FOAM, RIPPLE, ROLLER, SEA, SURF, WHITE HORSE; BORE, EAGRE. CURL, HAIR, LOCK, MARCEL [permanent]. BRANDISH, FLUTTER, VIBRATE; CURVE, UNDULATE.

WAVING OSCILLATION, SIGNALLING. HAIRDRESSING (crypt). SURFING, SWIMMING (crypt).

WAX (s/l whacks). BEESWAX, RESIN [*Daedalus*, Icarus]. *SEAL*. POLISH. GROW, INCREASE. FIT OF ANGER, TEMPER.

WAY (s/l weigh). AVENUE, CUL-DE-SAC, LANE, PASSAGE,

PATH, RAIL, *ROAD* (q.v.), ROUTE, STREET, TRACK
[Appian, Fosse, Icknield, Pilgrim's (*Roman roads*); Milky].
MANNER, METHOD, SYSTEM. MOMENTUM [kinetic
energy]. SLIPWAY, STOCK. N, E, S, W.

WC 1. LONDON, WEST END. 2. COMFORT STATION
(US), CONVENIENCE, GENTS, HERS, HIS, JOHN (US),
LADIES, LAVATORY, LOO, NECESSARIUM, PISSOIRE
(Fr), POWDER ROOM, REREDORT (eccl), TOILET,
TWO-HOLER (US sl), URINAL, WASHROOM.

WEALTH 1. ABUNDANCE, OPULENCE, PLUTOCRACY,
PROFUSION, RICHES [*Croesus*, Dives, *Midas*]. 2. **God: Gk** =
PLUTUS. **Bibl** = MAMMON.

WEAPON INSTRUMENT; WAR MATERIAL:

Clubs

COSH	CUDGEL	*MACE*	MERE

Blades

BACKSWORD	JAVELIN
BATTLEAXE	KNIFE
BROADSWORD	LANCE
CLAYMORE	LEISTER
CUTLASS	PIKE
DAGGER	PUYA (*bullfighting*)
DIRK	RAPIER
ÉPÉE	SABRE
ESTOQUE (*bullfighting*)	SKEAN DHU
FOIL	SPEAR
FOX	STILETTO
HANGER (arch)	SWORD
HARPOON	VARA (*bullfighting*)

Launchers

ARQUEBUS	CATAPULT
AUTOMATIC	*COLT*
BAZOOKA	*CROSSBOW*
BIG BERTHA	CULVERIN (arch)
BOW	DERRINGER
BREN	FIREARM
BROWNING	FLAMETHROWER
CANNON	FLINTLOCK
CARBINE	FOWLING PIECE

GAT
GATLING
GUN
HANDGUN
HOWITZER
LUGER
MANGONEL (arch)
MATCHLOCK
MONS MEG
MUSKET
PETRARY (arch)
PETRONEL (arch)
PIAT
PISTOL
PUNTGUN
REPEATER
REVOLVER
RIFLE
SAKER (arch)
SHOTGUN
SIDEARM
SLING
STEN
WALTHER
WEBLEY
WINCHESTER

Missiles

ARROW
BOMB
BULLET
GRENADE
GUIDED *MISSILE*
ICBM
MILLS BOMB
MINE
MISSILE
ROCKET
SAM
SHELL
SLINGSHOT
TORPEDO
VI

Vehicles (manned)

AIRCRAFT
ARMOURED CAR
BATTLESHIP
BOMBER
CARRIER
CRUISER
DESTROYER
FIGHTER
FRIGATE
MONITOR
MTB
Q-BOAT
SHUTTLE
SUBMARINE
TANK
U-BOAT
WARSHIP

WEASEL EQUIVOCATE, QUIBBLE. TRACKED VEHICLE (mil). QUADRUPED: *FERRET*, GLUTTON, MARTEN, MEERKAT, MINK, MONGOOSE, *OTTER*, POLECAT (fitch; US skunk), STOAT (ermine), SURICATE, WOLVERINE. *PLEDGE* (*pawn*; *pop* goes the ~).
WEATHER (s/l whether). CURE, DRY, EXPOSE, SEASON; DISCOLOUR. OVERCOME, PASS; WINDWARD (naut).

ATMOSPHERE, CONDITIONS, METEOROLOGY; **forecast areas**: Bailey, Biscay, Cromarty, Dogger, Dover, Faeroes, Fair Isle, Fastnet, Finisterre, Fisher, Forth, Forties, German Bight, Hebrides, Humber, Irish Sea, Lundy, Malin, Plymouth, Portland, Rockall, SE Iceland, Shannon, Sole, Thames, Trafalgar, Tyne, N and S Utsire, Viking, Wight.

WEAVER CLOTH/*TAPESTRY* MAKER; [*company* (livery); Aubusson]; **celeb**: *ARACHNE*, STEPHEN BLACKPOOL (*Dickens*, Hard Times), *BOTTOM* (MND, *Shak*), *Chaucer* character, LADY OF SHALOTT (Tennyson), *PENELOPE*, SILAS MARNER (G. Eliot/Mary Ann Evans), SMITH (H.vi, *Shak*). PLOTTER, SCHEMER. AMADAVAT, TAHA, *BIRD*. RIVER (Eng). *SNAKE* (crypt). *SPIDER* (crypt).

WEBSTER DICTIONARY ®. *SPIDER* (crypt).

WED WEDNESDAY. HITCHED, JOINED, MARRIED, MATCHED, MATED, PAIRED, SPLICED, WEDDED [*union*, matrimony]. WE WOULD.

WEDDING *MARRIAGE*, MATRIMONIAL, *UNION*.

~ **PRESENT** DOT, DOWRY. GIFT.

WEDGE V-SHAPE. JAM, PACK, SQUEEZE IN. *GOLF CLUB*. *Assembly* of swans.

WEDNESDAY W, WED. Day of *Odin*, *Woden*. ~**'s child** = full of woe. [Ash ~; Solomon *Grundy*].

WEED (s/l we'd). WILD HERB, *WILD PLANT* (q.v. for list). LANKY, WEAK PERSON. *DRUG*, MARIJUANA; TOBACCO. **Pl** = mourning clothes.

WEEK (s/l weak). SEVEN *DAYS*, SENNIGHT. MON–FRI. PERIOD, *TIME*.

WEEP CRY, GREET (Sc), KEEN. DRIP, EXUDE, SWEAT. DROOP.

WEIGHT (s/l *wait*). 1. EFFECT, IMPORTANCE. HEAVINESS, MASS, *MEASURE* (q.v. for list): CWT, DWT, KG, KILO, LB, *OUNCE*, OZ, *POUND*, TON, *TROY*. LONDON DISTRICT (W8; crypt). **Pl** = *CIGARETTE*. 2. **Boxing** ~s: see *Boxing*.

WELL ARTESIAN, FOUNTAIN, GUSHER, SOURCE, *SPA*, SPRING. INKPOT. FIT, HALE, NOT ILL, SOUND. CAREFULLY, EASILY, PROBABLY, SATISFACTORILY, THOROUGHLY, WISELY (**opp** = *badly*). WE WILL (crypt). ER, UM.

WELLINGTON *BOOT*. IRON DUKE, NOSEY, *MILITARY LEADER* [Wellesley]. *PUBLIC SCHOOL*. *CAPITAL* (NZ). WIMPY (aircraft nickname).

WELSH (s/l welch). CELTIC, CYMRIC [leek, Taffy].
ABSCOND, DECAMP, FLIT.

WELT SHOE LEATHER; RIBBING, TRIM. BLOW, CUFF,
SMACK. WORLD (Ger).

WEMBLEY *FOOTBALL GROUND*, STADIUM.

WENDY DARLING [Peter Pan]. CURVY, SINUOUS (crypt).

WEST 1. W, OCCIDENT. MAE. *PAINTER. WRITER. BRIDGE
PLAYER.* 2. Reads from right to left, e.g. **Childish seat of
learning looks west** = SKOOL.

~ END LONDON, MAYFAIR, WI.

WESTERN W, OCCIDENTAL. COWBOY FILM, B MOVIE
[*outlaw*].

WESTMINSTER *LEGISLATIVE ASSEMBLY*, PARLIAMENT.
PUBLIC SCHOOL. THAMES BRIDGE. THEATRE. Shak
char (R.ii).

WH ONLIE BEGETTER (*Shak*).

WHALE (s/l wail). BEAT, THRASH, WHACK. HUGE,
LARGE. *ISLAND.* RIVER (Can). CETACEAN MAMMAL:
types: ARCTIC ~, BALEEN, -EIN, BELUGA (WHITE
~), BLUE ~, BOOPS, BOTTLE-NOSE ~, BOWHEAD,
CACHALOT, *DOLPHIN*, FIN ~, GRAMPUS, GREY ~,
HUMP-BACKED ~, KILLER ~, LEVIATHAN (bibl),
MINKIE, NARWHAL, ORC, ORCA, PILOT ~, POTHEAD,
RIGHT ~, RORQUAL, SEI, SINGING ~, SPERM ~,
TOOTHED ~, WHITE ~, ZEUGLODON (zool); **assembly**
= pod, school, **offspring** = *calf* [Ahab, Moby Dick; Jonah;
ambergris].

WHALER (s/l wailer). WHALE HUNTER; AHAB [Moby Dick,
Herman Melville]. BOAT, CUTTER, GIG.

WHEEL (s/l weal). BALANCE, CATHERINE, COG, FLY,
MILL, PADDLE, POTTER'S, SPINNING, STEERING
[*Company* (livery); *Ixion. St Catherine, tarot*]. PIVOT, *TURN*
(mil). REVOLVER (crypt). *WINDOW.*

WHIG (s/l *wig*). PARLIAMENTARIAN, LIBERAL [BURKE,
FOX, GREY: Prime Minister].

WHIP DART, *DASH*, JERK, NIP, SNATCH. BIND, SEIZE,
SERVE (naut). BURTON, HANDY-BILLY, *HOIST*,
PULLEY, PURCHASE (naut). BEAT, FLOG, LASH,
LEATHER, *URGE*; CANE, *CAT* (O'Nine-Tails), QUIRT,
ROD, ROMAL, *SCORPION*, SCOURGE, STRAP,
TAW [bolas, lariat, lasso]. COACHMAN, HUNTSMAN.
DISCIPLINE, ORDER (polit).

WHISKER BEARD, BEAVER, BRISTLE, HAIR. SHORT
DISTANCE. EGG-BEATER (crypt).

WHISKEY *DRINK*, USQUEBAUGH (Ire); POTEEN.

WHISKY *DRINK*, SCOTCH; **comp** = soda; splash. *CARRIAGE*.
MOUSSE, SNOW (cook, crypt). WHIPPY (crypt).

WHIST *CARD GAME*; TRUMPERY (crypt). P, PP, SH; HUSH,
QUIET, SILENCE.

WHISTLE CAT-CALL, SHRILL; **comp** = *pig*. THROAT (sl).
SUIT (*rh sl*).

WHITE *COLOUR*. BILLIARD/SNOOKER BALL.
CAUCASIAN. *COMPOSER. ISLAND*. RIVER (US).
SEA. SPACE *TRAVELLER. WRITER*. 'BLANCHE'. **Pl** =
CRICKET TROUSERS, CREAMS.

WHITEFRIARS CARMELITES.

WHISTABLE NATIVE, *OYSTER* [Colchester].

WHO DOCTOR, DR. WORLD HEALTH ORGANIZATION
[*six*].

WI LONDON, MAYFAIR, WEST END. WEST INDIES.
WOMEN'S INSTITUTE. WILLIAM THE CONQUEROR.

WICKED EVIL, MISCHIEVOUS, SINFUL, SPITEFUL.
CANDLE, OIL LAMP (crypt).

WIDELY BROADLY. ABROAD, FOREIGN, TRANSLATED
(crypt).

WIDOW SHORT LINE (print). BEREAVED WIFE, surviving
fem spouse; **celeb**: BRADY (Garrick); CLIQUOT (Veuve,
champagne); TWANKY (theat) [cruse (*Elijah*); grass ~; ~'s
mite; ~'s peak; ~'s weeds].

WIFE CONSORT, HELPMEET, MATE, PARTNER; BETTER
HALF, DUTCH, MRS, OLD WOMAN, *RIB*; TROUBLE
(*rh sl*).

WIG (s/l *whig*). TOUPEE; RUG (sl). **Comp** = gown.

WILD *Anag*. ANGRY, BARBAROUS, DESOLATE,
DISORDERLY, EAGER, IRREGULAR, RASH,
UNTAMED, WAYWARD. [joker]. *ROBBER*.

WILD CAT HOT TEMPERED, IMPROMPTU, RECKLESS,
SNAP, VIOLENT. UNOFFICIAL. *AIRCRAFT*. And see *CAT*
for list.

~ FLOWER WILD PLANT. CASCADE, WATERFALL,
WHITE WATER (crypt).

~ PLANT UNCULTIVATED FLOWER, WEED (and see *plant*).
Breeds:

4-letters

FLAG   REED   WELD   WORT
LING   *RUSH*

5-letters

AVENS   DAISY

6-letters

BALSAM   MEDICK   SPURGE   YARROW
BURNET   *NETTLE*   SUNDEW
CLOVER   SORREL   TEASEL

7-letters

BISTORT   COMFREY   LUCERNE   SPURREY
BOG-BEAN   EELWORT   MAYWEED   VERVAIN
BUGLOSS   FROGBIT   RAGWORT
CAMPION   *HEATHER*   RAMSONS

8-letters

ASPHODEL   HAREBELL   SCULL-CAP
BILBERRY   HAWKWEED   SELFHEAL
BINDWEED   KNAPWEED   SOAPWORT
CHARLOCK   MARJORAM   TOADFLAX
COW-WHEAT   MILKWORT   VALERIAN
CROW-FOOT   PLANTAIN
FLEABANE   SCABIOUS

9-letters

BUCKTHORN   GIPSYWORT   SPEARWORT
BUTTERCUP   GOLDEN ROD   SPEEDWELL
CHICKWEED   GROUNDSEL   STONECROP
COLTSFOOT   LOUSEWORT   TORMENTIL
DANDELION   MARESTAIL   WOUNDWORT
EYEBRIGHT   PIMPERNEL

10+ letters

BUTTERWORT   GOATS BEARD
CINQUEFOIL   HERB ROBERT
CRANESBILL   LOOSESTRIFE
CUCKOOFLOWER   MEADOWSWEET
DEADLY NIGHTSHADE   RAGGED ROBIN
DEADNETTLE   RESTHARROW

SILVERWEED
SNEEZEWORT
SOWTHISTLE
STITCHWORT

STORKSBILL
WATERCRESS
YELLOW RATTLE

WILDE Oscar (Fingal O'Flahertie Wills); b 1854 Dublin; mar
Constance Lloyd (2 s Cyril and Vyvyan Holland). Libel action v
Lord Alfred Douglas' f; imprisoned 2 years for immoral practices
1895; d Paris 1900. *Writer* and wit; **plays**: Vera, or the Nihilist;
The Duchess of Padua; *Salome*; Lady Windermere's *Fan*; A
Woman of no Importance; An Ideal Husband; The Importance
of Being Earnest; **books**: The House of Pomegranates; The
Picture of Dorian Gray; The Ballad of Reading Gaol (by C3.3,
~'s prison number); De Profundis.
WILL IMPULSE, INTENTION, VOLITION. TESTAMENT
[legacy]. BILL, WILLIAM. [*ignis fatuus*]. **Pl** = *CIGARETTE*.
WILLIAM BILL, WILL, WM; 'A DEFENDER'. KING.
CONQUEROR. ORANGE, HALF-SOVEREIGN (~ and
Mary, crypt; **comp** = Mary); TELL; WILBERFORCE. Old
Father ~ (*Alice*). Just ~ (*Outlaw*, Richmal Crompton).
WILLIAMSON 1. Henry, author (often about wild life); **titles**:
Dandelion Days, *Donkey* Boy, A *Fox* under My Cloak, The
Old *Stag*, The Peregrine's Saga, The Phasian Bird, The Phoenix
Generation, Salar the *Salmon*, Tarka the *Otter*, etc. 2. RUFUS
(crypt).
WILLING CONSENTING, GAME, *KEEN*, READY.
DEVISING, LEAVING, TESTATOR (crypt). [Barkis is willin'
(*Dickens*)].
WILL O' THE WISP *IGNIS FATUUS* (q.v.).
WIMBLEDON *TENNIS VENUE. COURTED* (crypt). [Wombles].
WINCE FLINCH, START. ROLLER. CWE (crypt).
WINCHESTER 1. RIFLE, WEAPON. VENTA BULGARUM
(*Rom*). *Capital* of Wessex; then of England b Norman Conquest.
CASTLE. PUBLIC SCHOOL. 2. **Episcopal sig** = WINTON.
WIND 1. COIL, CRANK, REEL, TURN, TWIST; MEANDER
[serpent, *snake*]. EMBRACE, ENTWINE. AIR, BREATH,
FLATULENCE. 2. BLIZZARD, BREEZE, BLOW,
CYCLONE, GALE, GUST, HURRICANE, JET STREAM,
MUZZLER (sl), NOSER (head ~), PUFF, SCUD,
SOLDIER'S ~ (naut), SQUALL, STORM, TEMPEST,
TORNADO, TYPHOON, WUTHER (N Eng dial), ZEPHYR
(**opp** = calm, doldrums, horse latitudes). [~y City = Chicago]:

Admiral Beaufort. **Celeb**: AFER (Milton, SW), ANTANE
(Toulouse), BAGLIO (Sp Pac), BERG (S Af), BISE (Alps),
BORA (Adriatic), BUSTER (Aus), CANDELIA (Sp Am),
CAPE DOCTOR (S Af), CHILI (N Af), CHINOOK
(Rocky Mts), CHOCOLATE GALE (W Ind naut), CIERZO
(Sp N), DUST DEVIL (Ind), ETESIAN (Mediterranean),
EUROCLYDON (Medit), FOHN (Alps), FREMANTLE
DOCTOR (Aus; cricket); GARBI (Sp S), GHIBLI (Libya),
GREGALE (Malta), HARMATTAN (W Af), HELM
(Lake District), HIPPALUS (Arab Gulf), KAMIKAZE
(Jap), KAUS (Pers Gulf), KHAMSIN (Egy), KUBAN
(Java), LEVANTER (E Med), LIBECCHIO (Corsica),
LLEBEIG (Sp SW), MELTEMI (Aegean), MIGJORN (Sp
S), MISTRAL (Fr), MONSOON (Ind Ocean), NASHI (Pers
Gulf), NORTHER (US), PAMPERO (Andes), PASSAT
(N Atlantic), PEESASH (Ind), PONIENTE (Sp W), PUNA
(Peru), ROARING FORTIES (Antarctic), ROGER (E
Anglia), SAMIEL (Turk), SANTA ANNA (Nevada),
SHAITAN (Ind), SHAMA(A)L (Pers), SIMOOM, -N (Arab),
S(C)IROCCO (Libya), SNOW EATER (US), SOLANO (Sp),
SUMATRA (Sing), SURES (Chile), TRADE ~ (Cancer,
Capricorn), TRAMONTANA (Adriatic), TWISTER (US),
VENAVAL (Mex), WILLI-WAW (US/S Am), WILLY-WILLY
(Aus), XALOC (Sp E), ZONDA (Arg) and, all *Hiawatha*,
KABIBONOKKA (N), SHAWONDASEE (S), WABUN
(E), MUDJEKEEWIS (W). **Gk myth god/king** = AEOLUS;
beneficial ~s: N, NE, S, W (sons of *Aurora*/Eos by Astraeus);
storm ~s: *HARPIES* (q.v.; dd of *Electra* by Thaumas or
by *Typhon*). **Other god** = ENLIL (Sumerian). [Mt Haemus.
Typhoeus. Sleipner (Nor *horse*)]. **Individual winds**: N =
BOREAS (Gk), SEPTENTRIO (Rom); **NE** = KAIKAS (Gk),
AQUILO (Rom), ARGESTES; **E** = APELIOTES (Gk),
SUBSOLANUS (Rom); **SE** = EUROS (Gk), VOLTURNUS
(Rom); **S** = NOTOS (Gk), AUSTER (Rom); **SW** = LIPS
(Gk), AFRICUS (Rom); **W** = ZEPHYRUS (Gk), FAVONIUS
(Rom); **NW** = SKIRON, THRASCIAS (Gk), CAURUS
(Rom).

WINDOW LIMITED PERIOD, TIME SLÒT. CHAFF,
FOIL, RADAR JAMMING, RCM (mil). CLEAR VIEW,
LIGHT, OPENING, TRANSLUCENT/TRANSPARENT
PANE or PANEL, PORTHOLE (naut), *QUARREL*; **types**:
ATTIC ~. BAY ~, BOW ~, BULLSEYE, CASEMENT

~, CHURCH ~, DORMER ~, FANLIGHT, FRENCH ~, GEORGIAN ~, GOTHIC ~, GRILLE, *JUDAS* ~, LANTERN, LANCET ~, LATTICE ~, LOUVRE ~, NEO-GOTHIC ~, NORMAN ~, OEIL DE BOEUF, OGEE ~, ORIEL ~, PANE, PATIO ~, PERPENDICULAR ~, PICTURE ~, PORT, -HOLE, -LIGHT, ROMAN ~, ROSE ~, SASHCORD ~, SHOP ~, SKYLIGHT, SLIDING ~, STAINED GLASS ~, TRANSOM, TROMP-L'OEIL, *WHEEL* ~, WICKET [roller/venetian blind, curtain, jalousie, shutters; double glazing; ~ box; ~ envelope; ~ shopping. And see *architecture*; *cathedral (parts)*].

WINE (s/l whine). 1. *COLOUR* (dark red). FERMENTED DRINK, GRAPE JUICE [*study*]; TENT (arch); **celeb** (most ®): ASTI SPUMANTE, BARSAC, BEAUJOLAIS, BEAUNE, BORDEAUX, BORDELAIS, BURGUNDY, CHABLIS, CHAMPAGNE, CHÁTEAUNEUF DU PAPE, CHÂTEAU YQUEM, CHIANTI, CLARET, CÔTE DU RHÔNE, CÔTE D'OR, GRAVES, HOCK, LIEBFRAUMILCH, MACON, MALAGA, MARSALA, MÉDOC, MOSELLE, MUSCADET, NUITS ST GEORGES, POMAGNE, PORT, POUILLY FUISSÉ, POUILLY FUMÉ, RETSINA, RIESLING, RIOJA, OUSO, SAKE, ST EMILION, SANCERRE, SAUTERNES, SHERRY, TOKAY, VOUVRAY. **Lover of** ~ = oenophile. **Gods: Gk** = DIONYSUS, **Rom** = *BACCHUS*, IACCHUS (*Hebe*). [*Noah*; mulled ~, glogg, gluhwein].

WING 1. PINION [bird; *Daedalus*, Icarus]. PROJECTING ARM (arch). FORWARD, STRIKER (football). Group of fighter *aircraft*. **Comp** = prayer. **Pl** = PILOT'S BADGE. 2. Myth endows *Hermes* (Gk) and *Mercury* (Rom) with winged sandals as messengers of the *gods*, *Pegasus* with winged hooves, and *Hades* with a winged helmet (borrowed by *Perseus*); the caduceus was a winged wand or staff (*Asclepius*).

WINGER *FOOTBALLER*. BIRD (crypt).

WINTER SPORTS See *SPORT*.

WINTON *Episcopal sig* of WINCHESTER. TOWN (crypt: W in TON).

WIRELESS 1. *BROADCAST*, MEDIUM, RADIO; SET. 2. Word with letters 'wire' or synonym removed, e.g. **Wireless sage is in command** (4) = (wi)SEAC(re).

WISDOM 1. EXPERIENCE, KNOWLEDGE, PRUDENCE, SAGACITY [Confucius, *Daniel*, Mentor, Methuselah, Nestor, *Paris*, *Solomon*]; *TOOTH*. 2. **Goddesses: Gk** = *ATHENE*, **Rom**

= MINERVA.

WISEMAN MAGUS (**pl** = magi), SAGE [Confucius, *Daniel*, Mentor, Methuselah, Nestor, *Paris*, *Solomon*].

WISP BUNDLE, TWIST. SMOKE. *Assembly* of snipe.

WITCH (s/l which). 1. FISH. 2. GRIMALKIN, HAG, SIBYL, *SORCERESS*; SPELLER (crypt); **male** = warlock; **assembly** = coven; **celeb**: ARMIDA (Tasso), ~ OF ENDOR (Saul), MORGAN LE FEY (Malory), MARGERY JOURDAIN (*Shak*, H.vi), SYCORAX (Temp, *Shak*), VIVIEN (Tennyson), 3 in Macbeth (*Shak*) [*HECATE*, Salem, Walpurgis night]. **Comp** = black cat; broomstick.

WITCHCRAFT 1. CHARM, SORCERY; OBEAH, OBI, VOODOO; SPELLING (crypt). BROOMSTICK (crypt). 2. **Goddess**: **Gk** = *HECATE* [Macbeth. Walpurgis night. Hallowe'en].

WITH 1. AMONG, BESIDE, IN COMPANY. AGREEABLY, HARMONIOUS. CARRYING, CUM, HAVING, POSSESSING, IN CARE OF, BY MEANS (**opp** = sine). CONCERNING. AGAINST, DESPITE, NOTWITHSTANDING. 2. Two words to form one, e.g. **Victoria, for example, with 'er provider of newspapers** (9) = STATION*ER.

WITHIN Hidden word. INSIDE, INTERNALLY.

WITHOUT 1. LESS; SINE (**opp** = cum). OUTSIDE. 2. Word outside another, e.g. **Hen without trouble colliding** (4, 2) = HE*AD O*N. 3. Delete word or letter(s) indicated, e.g. **No railway is without trouble in this country** (6) = NO*R(ail)WAY. 4. Start answer with letters 'no', e.g. **Seen without Edward** (5) = NO*TED.

WIZARD SUPER. *MAGICIAN*, SORCERER; MAGUS, MERLIN, OZ (cowardly lion, tin man, Frank Baum). *COMIC*.

WODEHOUSE Pelham Grenville, writer; broadcast for enemy in World War II. **Books**: Big Money, Blandings Castle, The Code of the Woosters, The Inimitable Jeeves, Leave it to Psmith, Money in the Bank, Quick Service, Spring Fever. **Characters**: Anatole (cook); Miss Madeleine Bassett; Lord & Lady Emsworth; Mr Gussie Fink-Nottle; Mr Spenser Gregson; Mrs Agatha ~ (Aunt Agatha); Master Thomas ~; Sir Roderick Glossop; Miss Honoria ~; Mr 'Tuppy' ~; Master Oswald ~; Jeeves; Aunt Julia; Mr Richard 'Bingo' Little, Mrs ~ (née Rosie M Banks, author); Miss Mablethorpe; Miss Gwendolen Moon; Master Sebastian ~; Mr Lucius Pim; Mr 'Oofy' Prosser; Mr Psmith; Lord Frederick Ranelagh (Jeeves' previous employer); Mr

'Sippy' Sipperley; Mr Thomas Travers; Mrs Dahlia ~ (aunt); Miss Angela ~; Master 'Bonzo' ~; Mr 'Pongo' Twistleton; Lord Uffenham; Mr Ukridge; Mr Waterbury (*schoolmaster*); Lady Wickham; Miss Roberta 'Bobbie' ~; Mr Bertram Wooster; Lord Yaxley (Uncle George).

WODEN A-Sax chief *god*. One-eyed, he looked after warriors. KING HERLE. **Gk** = *ZEUS*, **Rom** = *JUPITER*, **Nor** = *ODIN* [Wednesday].

WOLF GOBBLE, SCOFF. FLOW BACK (crypt, hence EBB). *COMPOSER*. RIVER (US). *SPIDER*. CANIS LUPUS, COYOTE (US); **offspring** = cub [Akela (*Kipling*); Isengrim (Reinecke Fuchs); Little Red Riding Hood; Lycaon; cry ~]. *Constellation*. Fenris (*Loki*). **Pl** = *Football team*.

WOLFRAM *METAL*; W (*chem*); TUNGSTEN.

WOMAN EVE, HER, SHE [**Little women** = AMY, BETH, JO, MEG (Louisa May Alcott) or, more generally, any abbreviated girl's name].

WOMANIZER LECHER; SHEER (crypt). CASANOVA (It); DON JUAN (Byron); LOTHARIO (The Fair Penitent, Rowe).

WOMAN WARRIOR *AMAZON, ARTEMISIA, BOUDICCA,* BRITOMART (Spenser), *BRUNHILDA,* HIPPOLYTE, JOAN OF ARC, THE MAID, PHILOSTRATE (MND, *Shak*), VALKYR **pl** = ~IES (Nor). **Goddess of War** = ATHENE (Gk), BELLONA, MINERVA (Rom).

WOMEN'S ORGANIZATION ATS, RWI, WAAF, WASP (US), WAVE (US), WI, WRAC, WRAF, WRNS, WRVS.

WONDER MIRACLE. PONDER, THINK. [*Seven* ~s].

WOOD *CONDUCTOR* (mus). *PAINTER*. DRIVER, *GOLF CLUB* (**opp** = *iron*). BIASED BALL (bowls). *FOREST,* GROVE; *anniversary* (5th). TIMBER, *TREE* (q.v. for list); DEAL.

WOODEN CLUMSY, EXPRESSIONLESS, STIFF, STILTED. SILVAN, TIMBER. *XOANON*; *anniversary* (5th).

WOODPECKER *BIRD*, genus picidae; **breeds:** AWLBIRD, BLACK ~, GREATER SPOTTED ~, GREEN ~, HICKWAY, LESSER SPOTTED ~, NICKER, PICUS, SASIA, WITWALL, WOODPIE, WOODWALL, WRYNECK, YAFFIL, YAFFLE, YUCKER.

WOOL ALPACA, ANGORA, CASHMERE, LAMBS, MOHAIR, MERINO, WORSTED [*measure*]; *MATERIAL*; *anniversary* (7th).

WORCESTER Episcopal sig = VIGORN. CATHEDRAL.

CERAMICS. UNIVERSITY COLLEGE.

WORK 1. LABOUR, EFFORT [Saturday's *child*]. BOOK, PLAY, MUSIC, OP, OPUS. 2. When associated with author's name, requires the title, e.g. **More work** (6) = UTOPIA. 3. **Pl** = FACTORY, MILL. FUNCTIONS, GOES, RUNS.

WORKER ARTISAN, HAND, LABOURER, MAN [*patron saint*]; *ANT*, BEE. **Pl** = CREW, GANG, SHIFT; TUC.

WORKSHOP ATELIER, STUDIO. DISCUSSION GROUP. FIRM'S DANCE (crypt).

WORLD 1. *EARTH*, GLOBE, ORB; 21 (*tarot*). 2. **God: Rom** = ATLAS (see also *earth*).

WORLD GIRDLER EQUATOR, LATITUDE, LONGITUDE. MOON, SATELLITE. **Celeb**: ARIEL (Temp), CHICHESTER (Gipsy Moth), COOK (Endeavour), DRAKE (Golden Hind), PHILEAS FOGG (80 days, Verne), MAGELLAN (Trinidad, Vittoria), PUCK (MND), *ROSE* (Lively Lady), SLOCUM (Spray).

WORST BAD, BADLY, POOREST (**opp** = *best*). BEST, BEAT, DEFEAT, OUTDO, OVERCOME. SCUM, YEAST.

WORSTED BUNTING, *MATERIAL*, WOOLLEN YARN. DEFEATED, OUTDONE.

WRECK *Anag*. DESTRUCTION, RUIN. REMAINS. REMNANT.

WREN *ARCHITECT. BIRD. CARTOONIST*. Fem sailor (RN).

WRESTLING *Anag*. FIGHTING, GRAPPLING (*sport*); **styles**: catch-as-catch-can; Cornish; Cumberland; Devon; dinnie (Sc); freestyle; glima (Iceland); Graeco-Roman; judo (Jap); jujitsu (Jap); karate (Jap); kempo (Jap); kushti (Pers); pankration (Gk); sambo (CIS); schwingen (Swi); sumo (Jap); tag; Westmorland; yagli (Turk); **celeb wrestlers**: Antaeus; *Cercyon*; Charles (AYLI, *Shak*); H.I (Fr) and H.VIII (Eng) (Field of Cloth of Gold); Milo (of Croton); Muldoon (US); Samson Agonistes (Milton); Sukune (Jap); Theseus (Gk rules); Theogees (of Thasos; Gk); character in *Chaucer* (the Miller).

WRITER BALLPOINT, BIRO, PEN, PENCIL, QUILL, STYLO. AMANUENSIS, AUTHOR, GHOST, *POET* (q.v. for list), SCRIBE, SCRIVENER, SECRETARY, STENOGRAPHER. **Celeb**:

1-letter
Q   (Sir Arthur Quiller-Couch), Eng

2-letters

AA	(Milne), Eng
YY	(Robert Lynd), Ire

3-letters

BOZ	(Charles *Dickens*), Eng
FRY	Christopher, Eng
POE	Edgar Allan (Bostonian), US

4-letters

AMIS	Kingsley, Eng
BELL	Acton (Anne Brontë), Eng
BELL	Currer (Charlotte Brontë), Eng
BELL	Ellis (Emily Brontë), Eng
BIRD	Cyril Kenneth (Fougasse), Eng
BUCK	Pearl Sydenstricker, US
CARY	Joyce, Ire
DAHL	Roald, Eng
ELIA	(Charles Lamb), Eng
GIDE	André, Fr
GRAY	Thomas, Eng
HOPE	Anthony (A. Hope Hawkins), Eng
HOWE	Edgar Watson, US
HUGO	Victor Marie, Fr
KERR	Jean, US
KNOX	John, Sc
LAMB	Charles (Elia), Eng
LAMB	Mary Ann, Eng
LEAR	Edward, Eng
LIVY	(Titus Livius), Rom
LYLY	John, Eng
LYND	Robert (YY), Ire
MANN	Thomas, Ger
MARX	Karl, Ger
NASH	Ogden, US
OVID	(Publius Ovidus Naso), Rom
PHIZ	Hablot K. Browne
POPE	Alexander, Eng
QUIZ	(Charles *Dickens*), Eng
ROSE	Alexander, US
ROSS	(T. E. Lawrence), Eng

SADE	Marquis de, Fr
SAKI	(H. H. Munro), Sc
SAND	George (Amandine Dupin, Baronne Dudevant), Fr
SHAW	(T. E. Lawrence), Eng
SHAW	George Bernard, Ire
WEST	Rebecca (Cicely Maxwell Andrews), Eng
ZOLA	Emile (Fr)

5-letters

ADAMS	Franklin, US
ADAMS	Henry, US
AESOP	Gk
AGATE	James Evershed, Eng
AUDEN	Wystan Hugh, US
BACON	Francis, Eng
BEHAN	Brendan, Ire
BEYLE	Marie Henri (Stendhal), Fr
BLAIR	Eric Arthur (George Orwell), Eng
BLAKE	Nicholas (C. Day Lewis), Eng
BLAKE	William, Eng
BRÈDE	Baron de la (Montesquieu), Fr
BURKE	Edmund, Eng
BURNS	Robert, Sc
BYRON	Lord George Gordon, Eng
CAMUS	Albert, Fr
CHASE	James Hadley (Rene Raymond), US
COOKE	Alistair, Eng/US
DANTE	Alighieri, It
DEFOE	Daniel, Eng
DONNE	John, Eng
DOYLE	Sir Arthur Conan, Eng
DUMAS	Alexandre (fils), Fr
DUMAS	Alexandre (père), Fr
DUPIN	(George Sand), Fr
ELIOT	George (Mary Ann Evans), Eng
ELIOT	Thomas Stearns, US/Eng
EVANS	Mary Ann (George Eliot), Eng
GORKY	Maxim (Alexei Peshkov), CIS

HARDY	Thomas, Eng
HENRY	O (William Sydney Porter), US
HOMER	Gk
HOYLE	Edmond, Eng
IBSEN	Henrik, Nor
INNES	Hammond, Eng
JAMES	Henry, US
JAMES	P.D., Eng
JOYCE	James, Ire
KEATS	John, Eng
LEWIS	Cecil Day (Nicholas Blake), Eng
LORCA	Federico Garcia (Sp)
LUCAN	(Marcus Annaeus Lucanus), Rom
MASON	William, Eng
MILNE	Alan Alexander, Eng
MUNRO	Hector Hugh (Saki), Sc
O'HARA	John, US
PAINE	Thomas, Eng
PEPYS	Samuel, Eng
PLATO	Gk
PLINY	(Caius Plinius), Rom
POUND	Ezra Loomis, US
ROCHE	Mazo de la, US
SAGAN	Françoise (Quoirez), Fr
SCOTT	Sir Walter, Sc
SHUTE	Nevil (Norway), Aus
SMITH	Dodie (C. L. Anthony), Eng
SMITH	Sydney, Eng
SOLON	Gk
STAËL	Anne Louise (Necker), Swi/Fr
STEIN	Gertrude, US
STOWE	Harriet Elizabeth Beecher, US
SWIFT	Jonathan, Eng
TWAIN	Mark (Samuel Langhorn Clemens), US
VERNE	Jules, Fr
VIDAL	Gore, US
WAUGH	Auberon, Eng
WAUGH	Evelyn Arthur St John, Eng
WELLS	Herbert George, Eng
WHITE	Gilbert, Eng

WILDE	Oscar Fingal O'Flahertie Wills, Ire/Eng
WOOLF	Virginia, Eng
YATES	Dornford (Cecil William Mercer), Eng
YEATS	William Butler, Ire
ZWEIG	Arnold, Ger
ZWEIG	Stefan, A

6-letters

ANSELM	Saint, Eng
ARCHER	Jeffrey, Eng
ARNOLD	Matthew, Eng
AROUET	François Marie (Voltaire), Fr
ASCHAM	Roger, Eng
AUSTEN	Jane, Eng
BALZAC	Honoré de, Fr
BARHAM	Richard Harris, Eng
BARRIE	Sir James Matthew (Gavin Ogilvie), Eng
BELLOC	Hilaire, Eng
BORROW	George, Eng
BRECHT	Bertolt, Ger
BRONTË	Anne (Acton Bell), Eng
BRONTË	Charlotte (Currer Bell), Eng
BRONTË	Emily Jane (Ellis Bell), Eng
BROOKE	Rupert Chawner, Eng
BUNYAN	John, Eng
BURNEY	Fanny Frances (Mme d'Arblay), Eng
BURTON	Sir Richard Francis, Eng
BUTLER	Samuel, Eng
CAESAR	Gaius Julius, Rom
CICERO	Marcus Tullius, Rom
COFFIN	Joshua (H. W. Longfellow), Eng
COLTON	Charles Caleb, Eng
CONRAD	Joseph (Teodor Konrad Korzeniowski), Pol
COWARD	Sir Noël, Eng
COWPER	William, Eng
DARWIN	Charles Robert, Eng
DRYDEN	John, Eng

EVELYN	John, Eng
FRANCE	Anatole (Jacques Anatole François Thibault), Fr
FULLER	Thomas, Eng
GEORGE	Henry, US
GIBBON	Edward, Eng
GOETHE	Johann Wolfgang von, Ger
GRAVES	Robert, Eng
GREENE	Graham, Eng
HARRIS	Joel Chandler (Uncle Remus), US
HERZOG	Emile (André Maurois), Fr
HOLMES	Oliver Wendell, US
HORACE	(Quintus Horatius Flaccus), Rom
HUXLEY	Aldous Leonard, Eng
IRVING	Washington, US
JEROME	Jerome Klapka, Eng
JONSON	Ben, Eng
KELLER	Helen Adams, US
KRUTCH	Joseph Wood, US
LANDOR	Walter Savage, Eng
LAOTSE	(Laotzu or Latze), Ch
LARKIN	Philip, UK
LONDON	Jack (John) Griffith, US
LOWELL	James Russel, US
LUCIAN	Gk
MAILER	Norman, US
MALORY	Sir Thomas, Eng
MERCER	Cecil William (Dornford Yates), Eng
MILLER	(Agatha Christie), Eng
MILLER	Arthur, US
MILLER	Henry, US
MILTON	John, Eng
MUNTHE	Axel, Sw
NATHAN	George Jean, US
NEWTON	Sir Isaac, Eng
NORWAY	Nevil Shute, Aus
O'BRIEN	Edna, Ire
O'NEILL	Eugene Gladstone, US
ORWELL	George (Eric Arthur Blair), Eng
PARKER	Dorothy Rothschild, US

PASCAL	Blaise, Fr
PINDAR	Gk
PINERO	Sir Arthur Wing, Eng
PIOZZI	Hester Lynch (Mrs Thrale), Eng
PORTER	William Sydney (O. Henry), US
POTTER	Stephen, Eng
PROUST	Marcel, Fr
RACINE	Jean Baptiste, Fr
RUSKIN	John, Eng
SARTRE	Jean-Paul, Fr
SAYERS	Dorothy L., Eng
SENECA	Lucius Annaeus, Rom
SEWELL	Elizabeth M., Eng
SONTAG	Susan, US
STEELE	Richard, Ire/Eng
STERNE	Laurence, Eng/Ire
STOKER	Bram, Eng
THOMAS	Dylan Marlais, Wal
THRALE	Hester Lynch (Piozzi), Eng
VIRGIL	(Publius Virgilius Maro), Rom
WALTON	Isaak, Eng
WARNER	Charles Dudley, US
WILCOX	Ella Wheeler, US
WILDER	Thornton Niven, US
WINSOR	Kathleen, US

7-letters

ADDISON	Joseph, Eng
ANDREWS	Cicely (Rebecca), Eng
ANOUILH	Jean, Fr
ANTHONY	C. L. (Dodie Smith), Eng
AQUINAS	St Thomas, It
BAGNOLD	Enid, Eng
BALDWIN	James, US
BARNETT	Lincoln, US
BECKETT	Samuel, Ire
BEECHER	Henry Ward, US
BENTLEY	Edmund Clerihew, Eng
BOSWELL	James, Sc
BRIDGES	Robert, Eng
BURNETT	Frances Hodgson, Eng/US
CARLYLE	Thomas, Sc

CARROLL	Lewis (Dodgson), Eng
CHAPMAN	George, Eng
CHAUCER	Geoffrey, Eng
CLEMENS	Samuel Langhorn (Mark *Twain*), US
COLLINS	William Wilkie, Eng
COCTEAU	Jean, Fr
COLETTE	Sidonie Gabrielle, Fr
COOKSON	Catherine, Eng
D'ARBLAY	Mme (Frances Burney), Eng
DA VINCI	Leonardo, It
DICKENS	Charles John Huffam (Boz, Quiz), Eng
DICKENS	Monica, Eng
DIDEROT	Denis, Fr
DODGSON	Rev Charles Lutwidge (Lewis Carroll), Eng
DOUGLAS	Lord Alfred, Eng
DUHAMEL	Georges, Fr
DURRELL	Lawrence, Eng/Ire
EMERSON	Ralph Waldo, US
FLEMING	Ian Lancaster, Eng
FORSTER	Edward Morgan, Eng
FORSYTH	Frederick, Eng
FRANCIS	Dick, Eng
GALLICO	Paul William, US
GILBERT	Sir William Schwenck, Eng
GLASGOW	Ellen, US
GRAHAME	Kenneth, Eng
GRAYSON	Katherine, Eng
HAGGARD	Sir Henry Rider, Eng
HAKLUYT	Richard, Eng
HAWKINS	A. H. (Anthony Hope), Eng
HAZLITT	William, Eng
HERBERT	Sir Alan Patrick, Eng
HERRICK	Robert, Eng
HOPKINS	Gerard Manley, Eng
HOUSMAN	Alfred Edward, Eng
HOWELLS	William Dean, US
HUBBARD	Albert Green, US
JOHNSON	Dr Samuel, Eng
JUVENAL	(Decimus Junius Juvenalis), Rom

KHAYYAM	Omar, Pers
KIPLING	Rudyard, Eng
LE CARRÉ	John (D. J. *Cornwall*), Eng
LOFTING	Hugh, Eng
MACLEAN	Alastair, Eng
MARLOWE	Christopher, Eng
MAUGHAM	William Somerset, Eng
MAURIAC	François, Fr
MAUROIS	André (Emile Herzog), Fr
MENCIUS	Gk
MENCKEN	Henry Louis, US
MOLIERE	(Jean Baptiste Poquelin), Fr
MURDOCH	Dame Iris, Eng
OGILVIE	Gavin (J. M. Barrie), Eng
PEACOCK	Thomas Love, Eng
PESHKOV	(Maxim Gorky), CIS
PUBLIUS	Syrus, Rom
QUOIREZ	(Françoise Sagan), Fr
RAYMOND	Rene (James Hadley Chase), US
ROLLAND	Romain, Fr
RUSSELL	Earl Arthur William, Eng
SALLUST	(Gaius Valerius Sallustius Crispus), Rom
SHELLEY	Mary, Eng
SHELLEY	Percy Bysshe, Eng
SIMENON	Georges, Belg/Fr
SOUTHEY	Robert, Eng
SPENSER	Edmund, Eng
TACITUS	Cornelius, Rom
TENNANT	Stephen James Napier, Eng
THOREAU	Henry David, US
THURBER	James Grover, US
TOLKIEN	John Ronald Reuel, Eng
TOLSTOI(Y)	Count Leo, Russ
VACHELL	Horace Annesley, Eng
WALLACE	Edgar, Eng
WALPOLE	Earl Horace, Eng
WHITMAN	Walter, US

8-letters

BEERBOHM	Sir Max, Eng
BETJEMAN	Sir John, Eng

BROWNING	Lady (Daphne du Maurier), Eng
BROWNING	Elizabeth Barrett, Eng
BROWNING	Robert, Eng
CALDWELL	Erskine Preston, US
CARTLAND	Barbara, Eng
CATULLUS	Gaius Valerius, Rom
CHANDLER	Raymond, US
CHILDERS	Erskine, Ire
CHRISTIE	Agatha (Miller), Eng
CLERIHEW	(Edmund Clerihew Bentley), Eng
CONGREVE	William, Eng
CORNWALL	D. J. (Le Carré), Eng
CRATINUS	Gk
CYNEWULF	A-Sax
DAY-LEWIS	Cecil, Ire
DE LA MARE	Walter John, Eng
DISRAELI	Benjamin (Earl of Beaconsfield), Eng
DUDEVANT	Baronne (George Sand), Fr
FAULKNER	William, US
FIELDING	Henry, Eng
FLAUBERT	Gustave, Fr
FOUGASSE	(Cyril Kenneth Bird), Eng
FRANKLIN	Benjamin, US
GINSBERG	Allen, US
GINSBERG	Louis, US
GONCOURT	Edmond, Fr
GONCOURT	Jules, Fr
KINGSLEY	Rev Charles, Eng
LANGLAND	William, Eng
LAWRENCE	David Herbert, Eng
LAWRENCE	Thomas Edward (Ross, Shaw), Eng
LIPPMANN	Walter, US
LOVELACE	Richard, Eng
MACAULAY	Lord Thomas Babington, Eng
MCCARTHY	Mary, US
MARQUAND	John Phillips, US
MELVILLE	Herman, US
MENANDER	Gk
MEREDITH	George, Eng
MITCHELL	Margaret, US

MOREHEAD	Alan, Aus
PHAEDRUS	Rom
PLUTARCH	Gk
RABELAIS	François, Fr
RATTIGAN	Sir Terence Mervyn, Eng
ROSSETTI	Christina, Eng
ROUSSEAU	Jean-Jacques, Swi/Fr
SANDBURG	Carl, US
SCHILLER	Johann Christoph Friedrich von, Ger
SHERIDAN	Richard Brinsley, Ire/Eng
SOCRATES	Gk
STENDHAL	(Marie Henri Beyle), Fr
STOPPARD	Tom, Eng
TEASDALE	Sara, Eng
TENNYSON	Lord Alfred, Eng
THIBAULT	(Anatole France), Fr
TROLLOPE	Anthony, Eng
VOLTAIRE	(François Marie Arouet), Fr
WESTCOTT	Edward Noyes, US
WILLIAMS	Tennessee (Thomas Lanier Williams), US
XENOPHON	Gk

9+ letters

AESCHYLUS	Gk
ALLINGHAM	Marjorie, UK
ANTIPATER	of Sidon, Gk
ARISTOPHANES	Gk
ARISTOTLE	Gk
AYCKBOURN	Alan, UK
BAUDELAIRE	Charles, Fr
BEACONSFIELD	Earl of (Disraeli), Eng
BURROUGHS	John, Eng
CERVANTES	Miguel de, Sp
CHATEAUBRIAND	Viscomte de, Fr
CHESTERFIELD	Lord, Eng
CHESTERTON	Gilbert Keith, Eng
CHURCHILL	Sir Winston Leonard Spencer, Eng
CLAUSEWITZ	Karl von, Ger
COLERIDGE	Samuel Taylor, Eng

CONFUCIUS	Ch
CORNEILLE	Pierre, Fr
DE LA ROCHE	Mazo
DELDERFIELD	E. M., US
DE MAUPASSANT	Guy, Fr
DICKINSON	Emily Elizabeth, US
DOSTO(Y)EVSKY	Fyodor Mikhailovich, CIS
DU MAURIER	Daphne (Lady Browning), Eng
EHRENBURG	Ilya, CIS
EURIPIDES	Gk
FITZGERALD	Francis Scott Key, US
GALBRAITH	Paul William, Can
GALSWORTHY	John, Eng
GOLDSMITH	Oliver, Ire/Eng
INGOLDSBY	Thomas (Richard Harris, Barham), Eng
LONGFELLOW	Henry Wadsworth, Eng
LUCRETIUS	(Titus Lucretius Carus), Rom
MACMILLAN	Sir Maurice Harold, Eng
MONTAIGNE	Michel Eyquem, Fr
MONTESQUIEU	Charles de Secondat (Baron de la Brède), Fr
NIETZSCHE	Friedrich Wilhelm, Ger
OMAR KHAYYAM	Pers
PARKINSON	Cecil Northcote, US
PASTERNAK	Boris Leonidovich, CIS
PETRONIUS	Gaius, Rom
PRIESTLEY	John Boynton, Eng
SHAKESPEARE	William, Eng
SOLZHENITSYN	Alexander Isayevich, CIS
SOPHOCLES	Gk
STEINBECK	John Ernst, US
STEVENSON	Robert Louis Balfour, Sc
STREATFEILD	Noël, Eng
STRINDBERG	August, Swe
SWINBURNE	Algernon Charles, Eng
TARKINGTON	Newton Booth, US
THACKERAY	William Makepeace, Eng
THEOCRITUS	Gk
THUCYDIDES	Gk
WODEHOUSE	Pelham Grenville, Eng
WORDSWORTH	William, Eng

WRITE-UP 1. CRIT, *NOTICE*, PUFF, REVIEW. 2. A dn answer written upwards, e.g. **Press's bad write-up** (3) = DAB.

WRITING MS. PS. TS. (*study*).

~ **OFF** 1. CANCELLING, STRIKING OFF. 2. Delete letters meaning 'writing' (MS, PS, TS) from the clue, e.g. **Writing-off terms, in triplicate?** (3) = TER(ms).

WRONG *Anag.* INCORRECT, IN ERROR, OUT OF ORDER; NOT RIGHT (hence delete letters 'r' or 'rt' from clue, e.g. **Divert wrong plunge** (4) = DIVE(rt).

WRY *Anag.* ASKEW, DISTORTED, SKEW. DISAPPOINTED. *BIRD.*

WYVERN WINGED *DRAGON* (myth). WINGED SERPENT [*Asclepius*, caduceus, *herald*, viper].

X (s/l ex). Multiply by, *TIMES*; 10, TEN. ANTEPENULTIMATE. CHRIST. EXTRA LARGE. KISS. OVER 18 (film *censorship*). UNKNOWN QUANTITY; graph co-ordinate. ABSCISSA (**opp** = y or ordinate). VOTE. WRONG.

XANGTI Ch chief *god*.

XANTHIC *COLOUR* (*yellow*).

XANTHIPPE 1. Wife of *Socrates*, notorious for her peevish and nagging nature. It is said that Socrates mar her as a penance. 2. SCOLD, SHREW, SPITFIRE, TERMAGANT.

XANTHUS City and river of Lycia (E Turk). Horse of *Achilles*.

XAU LAKE (Af).

XE XENON (*chem*).

XEBEC *BOAT.*

XENON XE (chem). *GAS.*

XENOPHILE *Lover* of foreigners/strangers.

XENOPHOBIA *Aversion* to foreigners/strangers.

XER- Prefix for DRY, e.g. **xeransis** = desiccated; **xerophilous** = adapted to dry climate.

XERES SPANISH SHERRY, WINE.

XERXES King of Persia 485–465 B.C. Conquered Egypt and then invaded Greece (480 B.C.) by crossing the *Hellespont* on a bridge of boats. Checked by the Spartans at *Thermopylae*, he was finally forced to withdraw after his fleet was beaten by the Greeks at *Salamis*. He was ass in 465 B.C.

XHOSA BANTU, TRIBE (SA).

XINGU RIVER (Braz).
XINHUA Newsagency (Ch).
XIPHOID SWORD-SHAPED.
XOANON Gk myth wooden god, supposedly fallen from Heaven.
X-RAYS RONTGEN RAYS.
XX TWENTY.
XYLEM Woody tissue.
XYLONITE CELLULOID.
XYLOPHONE *INSTRUMENT* (mus), MARIMBA.
XYSTER *Instrument* (med).
XYSTUS EXERCISE AREA (Gk). TERRACE, WALK (Rom).

Y (s/l why). PENULTIMATE. UNKNOWN QUANTITY; graph
　co-ordinate, ORDINATE (**opp** = x or abscissa). YTTRIUM
　(*chem*). YUGOSLAVIA.
YAMA Ind *god* of Dead.
YANKEE AMERICAN (**opp** = Confederate). *BET*. JIB, *SAIL*. **Pl**
　= *BASEBALL TEAM*.
YARD AREA; GARDEN (US). *MEASURE*, THREE FEET;
　hence TRIPOD (crypt). SPAR (naut).
YARN THREAD. STORY, TALE.
~ **SPINNER** BOBBIN, SPOOL. NARRATOR, STORY
　TELLER, SCHEHERZADE.
YEAN *KID*, LAMB.
YEAR AD, BC. Either of these added to Rom numerals to make a
　word, e.g. **year 1009** (5) = ADMIX.
YEARN HANKER, LONG, PANT FOR.
YEGG *ROBBER*.
YELLOW *COLOUR. SNOOKER* BALL (score 2). AFRAID,
　COWARDLY. RIVER (Ch). *SEA*. CRY OUT, SHOUT 'OW'
　(crypt).
YES AY, AYE, CERT, SURE; NOD; AGREE; ROGER, WILCO
　(mil). DA (RUSS); JA (Ger); OUI (Fr), SI (It, Sp).
YIELD CEDE, GIVE WAY, SUBMIT. AMOUNT, OUTPUT,
　PRODUCE. CONSENT.
YMIR Frost giant (Nor).
YOKE (s/l *yolk*). BAR, CROSS-BAR, *HARNESS*, LINK;
　WAIST; TEAM. BOND, DOMINION, SWAY.
YOLK (s/l *yoke*). YELK. SECRETION, WOOL OIL. EGG
　CENTRE (hence G, crypt).

YORK 1. HAM. BOWL OUT (*cricket*). 2. EBORACUM (*Rom*). **Episcopal sig** = EBOR. *CASTLE. UNIVERSITY. RACETRACK* (horses). RIVER (US). [white rose]. 3. *HERALD*. **Pl** = COUNTY, *DIVISION*. BOWLS, DISMISSES (cricket).

YOU HEAR . . . The answer is *pronounced*, but not spelled, like the word indicated, e.g. **Shaggy bird you hear** (5) = ROUGH, whereas **You hear shaggy bird** (4) = RUFF; place a semi-colon mentally between 'shaggy' and 'bird' in each case, and the principle will be clear.

YOUNG 1. BABY, YOUTHFUL; *OFFSPRING* (q.v. for special names); **comp** = old. *SPACE TRAVELLER*. 2. Put name in diminutive, e.g. **Young David** = DAVE.

YOU SEE Hidden word, e.g. **You see gold in Gothic origins** (5) = IN·GOT(hic).

YOUTH 1. ADOLESCENCE. INEXPERIENCE (**opp** = *age*). [Picture of Dorian Gray (Wilde)]. 2. **Goddesses**: **Gk** = *HEBE*, **Rom** = JUVENTAS.

YTTRIUM Y (*chem*).

YU YUGOSLAVIA (*car plate*).

YUX HICCOUGH.

Z Zanzibar. GAUGE (model rly). FINAL, LAST (crypt).

ZA SOUTH AFRICA (*car plate*).

ZAX CHOPPER (slate *tool*).

Z-CAR *POLICE CAR*.

ZEBRA STRIPED ANIMAL (genus equus), **breeds**: COMMON ~, DAUW ~, GREVY'S ~, MOUNTAIN ~, QUAGGA (ex) [okapi]. *SHARK, SPIDER*. BELISHA/PELICAN CROSSING; CROSS-PATCH (crypt).

ZECHIN *COIN*.

ZENITH HIGH POINT, OVERHEAD, TOP (**opp** = nadir).

ZENO *STOIC*.

ZEPHYRUS Gk myth WEST *WIND*; mar *Iris*. **Rom** = FAVONIUS.

ZERO O, DUCK, EGG, LOVE, NIL, NOTHING, ZILCH. Mr ~ (The Adding Machine, Elmer Rice).

ZEST GUSTO, KEENNESS, RELISH. LEMON PEEL.

ZEUS Gk chief *god*; s of *Cronos* and *Rhea*, mar to his sis *Hera* as his chief among many wives; br of *Demeter, Hades*, Hera, *Hestia* and *Poseidon* (**Rom** = JOVE, JUPITER). On dividing

the universe with his two brs, Hades got the *underworld* and
Poseidon the *seas*; Zeus obtained the heavens and upper regions,
and lived on *Mt Olympus*; his shield was called *Aegis*. He had
many children by his various wives, but his marriage to Hera
remains the archetype. **Transformations**: 1. Acrisius confined his
d *Danae* in a brazen tower lest she should conceive a child who
would k him as prophesied; ~ visited her in a shower of gold
and fathered *Perseus* (who did indeed eventually k Acrisius).
2. ~ transformed into a swan to seduce *Leda* and thus f *Helen*
and the *Dioscuri*. 3. ~ also transformed into a bull and carried
off *Europa*, who became the m of *Minos*. 4. ~ transformed
into an eagle to carry off *Ganymede*. 5. ~ transformed into
a cloud (*Io*). 6. ~ transformed to *Amphitryon* (to seduce
Alcmene, his w).

ZILCH ZERO (sl).

ZINC *METAL*; ZN (*chem*).

ZINNIA *FLOWER*.

ZIRCON *GEM*; HYACINTH, JARGON.

ZIRCONIUM *METAL*; ZR (*chem*).

ZLOTY *CURRENCY* (Pol).

ZN *ZINC* (*chem*).

ZODIAC 1. FULL CYCLE. 2. HEAVENLY BELT
(*constellations*), TRIGON. **Signs:** ARIES (the *Ram*), TAURUS
(the *Bull*), GEMINI (the *Twins*), CANCER (the *Crab*),
LEO (the *Lion*), VIRGO (the *Virgin*), LIBRA (the *Scales*),
SCORPIO (the *Scorpion*), SAGITTARIUS (the *Archer*),
CAPRICORNUS (the *Goat*), AQUARIUS (the *Watercarrier*),
PISCES (the *Fishes*).

ZONDA *WIND* (Arg prevailing northerly).

ZR ZIRCONIUM (*chem*). ZAIRE (*car plate*).

ZULU TRIBE (Bantu, SA). **Pl** = IMPI.